Thompson, Lawrance Roger, 1906-
    Robert Frost: the early years, 1874-
1915, by Lawrance Thompson.   New York,
Holt, Rinehart and Winston [1966]
    xxvi, 641 p. illus., ports. 24cm.

    Bibliographical references included in
"Notes" (p. 479-606)

    1. Frost,   Robert, 1874-1963.

ROBERT FROST
THE EARLY YEARS

ROBERT FROST

THE EARLY
YEARS
1874-1915

BY LAWRANCE
THOMPSON

NEW YORK · CHICAGO
SAN FRANCISCO
HOLT, RINEHART AND
WINSTON

ACKNOWLEDGMENTS

GRATEFUL acknowledgment is made to the following for permission to reprint excerpts from their publications:

Dodd, Mead & Company for excerpts from *Robert Frost: The Aim Was Song* by Jean Gould; copyright © 1964 by Jean Gould.

Harcourt, Brace & World, Inc., for excerpts from *The Letters of Ezra Pound* edited by D. D. Paige.

Rupert Hart-Davis Limited for excerpts from *The Letters of W. B. Yeats* edited by Allan Wade.

Holt, Rinehart and Winston, Inc., for excerpts from *Complete Poems of Robert Frost*; copyright 1916, 1923, 1928, 1930, 1934, 1939, 1947 by Holt, Rinehart and Winston, Inc.; copyright 1936, 1942, 1944, 1951, © 1956, 1958, 1962 by Robert Frost; copyright © 1964 by Lesley Frost Ballantine. For excerpts from *In the Clearing* by Robert Frost; copyright © 1956, 1962 by Robert Frost. For excerpts from *Selected Letters of Robert Frost*, edited by Lawrance Thompson; copyright © 1964 by Holt, Rinehart and Winston, Inc. For excerpts from *The Letters of Robert Frost to Louis Untermeyer*; copyright © 1963 by Holt, Rinehart and Winston, Inc. For excerpts from *Robert Frost and John Bartlett* by Margaret Bartlett Anderson; copyright © 1963 by Margaret Bartlett Anderson. For excerpts from *Robert Frost: The Trial by Existence* by Elizabeth Shepley Sergeant; copyright © 1960 by Elizabeth Shepley Sergeant. For excerpts from *Creative Evolution* by Henri Bergson, translated by Arthur Mitchell, copyright 1911, 1939 by Holt, Rinehart and Winston, Inc.

J. B. Lippincott Company for excerpts from *Dialogue with an Audience* by John Ciardi, copyright © 1958 by John Ciardi.

The Macmillan Company for excerpts from Robert Frost's Introduction to *King Jasper* by Edwin Arlington Robinson, copyright 1935 by The Macmillan Company, copyright renewed 1963 by The Macmillan Company.

ACKNOWLEDGMENTS

New York University for excerpts from *A Swinger of Birches: A Portrait of Robert Frost* by Sidney Cox.

Paul R. Reynolds, Inc., for excerpts from *The Philosophy of William James, Selected from His Chief Works,* edited by Horace M. Kallen.

Twayne Publishers, Inc., for excerpts from *Robert Frost Speaks* by Daniel Smythe.

Acknowledgment is also made of the fact that the author has quoted from *Robert Frost: Life and Walks-Talking* by Louis Mertins, published by the University of Oklahoma Press.

A special acknowledgment is given to Mr. Alfred C. Edwards, sole executor of the estate of Robert Frost, and president and chief executive officer of Holt, Rinehart and Winston, Inc., for permission to quote (entirely or in part) forty-three works by Robert Frost which are either uncollected or hitherto unpublished:

"An A No. 1 Sundown," "The Birds Do Thus," "The Black Cottage" (early draft), "Caesar's Lost Transport Ships," "Class Hymn," "Clear and Colder," "The Cow's in the Corn," "Despair," "Down the Brook—and Back," "Dream-Land," "A Dream of Julius Caesar," "The Falls," "Flower Guidance," "God's Garden," "Good Relief," "Greece," "[I am a Mede and Persian]," "[I had to love once]," "In Memoriam: R. Frost Exit," "In England," "In White," "[It is an ancient friend of yours]," "Jewell Gets a Job," "A Kitchen in School," "The Later Minstrel," "The Lost Faith," "The Lure of the West," "My Giving," "La Noche Triste," "On the Sale of My Farm," "[Perhaps you think]," "Poets Are Born Not Made," "The Rubaiyat of Carl Burell," "Sea Dream," "Slipshod Rhymes," "Song of the Wave," "Summering," "To Carl Burell," "To Coebee," "The Traitor," "Tutelary Elves," "Twilight," and "A Young Man from Podunk."

To
NAT
ELLIE
JOEL
TOM
who grew up with
this book.

CONTENTS

ILLUSTRATIONS

❧❧❧

INTRODUCTION

✦

ROBERT FROST was so fascinated by the story of his life that he never tired of retelling it. A good raconteur, he naturally varied his accounts, and whenever the bare facts troubled him, he discreetly clothed them with fictions. This imaginative process caused him to mingle self-deceptions with little falsehoods; it even caused him gradually to convince himself that some of these fictions were genuine truths. But only a few of his listeners knew the facts well enough to notice the discrepancies, and even the best-informed were not inclined to challenge. They knew he resented criticism. Besides, some of his fictions amounted to mythic variations which artistically revealed this important fact: he wanted his best versions of the story to dramatize the fulfillment of ideals he had cherished since boyhood.

Clearly, Frost's myth-making was in accord with some ancient and modern habits of thought. One very old use of myth is to let a story show the ways in which human beings have shielded themselves against life-injuring or even life-destroying experiences by placing themselves in harmony with various life-encouraging forces. Frost, during his childhood, was exposed to some fine examples of this particular usage. His mother nurtured him on classical and biblical stories of heroes. His father, having named him after a celebrated military hero, told him much about the battles and leaders of the War Between the States. Thus the boy was taught to build his own ideals around the accomplishments of those whose actions reflected courage, skill, cunning, wit, nobility, compassion, and persistent striving. Sooner or later he became aware that any hero usually directs his powers toward a particular goal against so-called "insuperable odds." In addition, his mother taught him that the best accomplishments occur only when the hero places himself in the right relationship with the particular god or gods to whom the hero feels an indebtedness.

"What counts is the ideals, and those will bear some

keeping still about," Frost repeatedly said.[1] He had many reasons for wanting to conceal some of his most precious beliefs, even while he was trying to shape his life in accordance with his persistently mythic ideals of heroism. But in his autobiographical accounts he could not resist calling attention to evidence of his kinship with heroes. His retelling always pointed up his struggles and triumphs, in the face of almost "insuperable odds," hurts, and humiliations. He had begun to discover his poetic skills while still a schoolboy, he said, and yet he had been forced to suffer through a long sequence of hindrances and discouragements before he won public recognition. For him, the victories he had won were proof that those who had tried to dissuade him from his quest had been his worst enemies. He claimed that the outcome justified the boldness of his rebellion against social conformity; that his life had been unique because of his courage in taking the road less traveled by.

Near the end, while he was still acting out the final scenes of the story which he was also telling, Frost never missed a chance to point out mythic roundings-off and fulfillments. Just after he was invited to England, in 1957, to receive honors from Oxford and Cambridge, he wrote: "It will sort of round off things I initiated with Mrs David Nutt in a small office in Bloomsbury among total strangers forty five years ago [when I was] already almost too old to bet on. There is that in it anyway. It will also sort of round off my rather great academic career in general."[2] He was inclined to boast, when discussing fulfillments, but his accomplishments exceeded his boasts.

Sometimes Robert Frost hinted that he was not completely honest in telling the story of his life; that he knew he could not always resist the temptation to idealize realities. At least once he warned his listeners in public: "Don't trust me too far. I'm liable to tell you anything. Trust me on the poetry, but don't trust me on my life. You want to watch me. Check up on me some."[3] This was a way of admitting that he couldn't always trust himself to tell—or even see—the entire truth about himself. Nobody can, but Frost was often puzzled by his inability to understand himself as well as he thought he should. If, in the process of trying, he hid his own uncertainties behind contradictions which baffled others, he could at least enjoy the protection thus gained. After one such performance he wrote to a friend: "The point I tried to make was that I was a very hard person to make out if I am any judge of human nature. I might easily be most deceiving when most bent on telling the truth."[4] He was indeed a hard person to make out, and nobody knew that fact better than he did. It may be helpful, then, to consider some possible causes and consequences of his own perplexity.

The trouble may have started while he was listening to his mother's mythic accounts of heroes and heroic deeds. Back in his childhood, his vivid and undisciplined imagination could easily have jumbled the opposed notions of who he was and what he wanted to become; could easily have confused the ideal with the actual. His mother's well-intended encouragement may have helped him believe that he already possessed the virtues which could some day make him a hero. He might not have realized that he would have to earn those virtues. A closely related complication may have occurred when his devout mother taught him the lofty biblical precept: "Be ye therefore perfect, even as your Father which is in heaven is perfect."[5] As a boy, he strove toward this perfection; but the results were often disturbing. For example, after he learned penmanship well enough to justify his working with a copybook, he felt that he should be able to shape each of his own letters almost perfectly. If he made a bad mistake or blotted the page, he became so enraged that he tore out the entire sheet and started again with a clean one.

His mother, recognizing his puzzlement and frustration, did her best to console him. She naturally explained that anyone striving toward an ideal has to be aware that one's reach always does exceed one's grasp, and that the very act of trying hard can help to overcome faults. Fond of Browning's poetry, she may even have quoted the following lines to her son before he was old enough to understand them:

The high that proved too high, the heroic for earth too hard,
  The passion that left the ground to lose itself in the sky,
Are music sent up to God by the lover and the bard;
  Enough that he heard it once: we shall hear it by and by.[6]

Mrs. Frost herself wrote Browningesque poetry; she was

also an optimistic visionary with a very keen imagination of her own. Descended from a Scots grandfather, who had demonstrated to her his powers of second sight, she came to believe she had inherited his capacity for seeing through and beyond the material hindrances of this world. In Scotland she was raised as a Presbyterian; but by the time her first child was born, she had already joined the Swedenborgian Church —in which her son was baptized. With the aid of Swedenborg's writings she found in her own religious visions ample consolation for the difficulties of her sorrowful life.[7] Her son, thus encouraged by his mother's ways, soon began to make his own self-protective retreats into sanctuaries created by his own imagination.

As a boy in San Francisco, Robert Frost needed all the protection he could find, inside or outside his imagination. From the time of his birth he showed excruciating sensitivites, and many of his infant ailments seemed directly traceable to nerves. Compounding these troubles, unavoidably, were the frequent estrangements between his parents, who lived apart for several months when the child was in his third year. The warmth and assurance he needed while he was growing up were not adequately provided in the charged atmosphere of his home. His New England-born father, holding to the puritanical slogan, "Spare the rod and spoil the child," punished the boy with any weapon handy—and these recurrent whippings were usually administered in moments of rage. Robbie's mother, trying to make amends for such brutality, almost smothered the child with her love and overindulgence. The results were predictable. In later life Frost was never quite able to understand or fully to resolve some of his inner conflicts, which seemed to mirror the opposed attitudes of his parents. There were times when his own self-inflicted punishments were mixed with self-gratification.

Closely related was his later inability to overcome some habitual responses which he began to make in boyhood, at least as soon as he was forced to share his mother's attentions with a sister; responses of jealousy, sulking, temper tantrums, and vindictive retaliations. Also lasting were his first attempts to protect himself by running away or by hiding. Like so many children in similar circumstances, he comforted himself with the notion that those who had hurt him would feel sorry, and blame themselves as they should if they found him dead. His early and purely imaginative play with thoughts of suicide became another lifelong game of indulgent self-pity.

While still a boy in San Francisco he used his idealistic imagination to create many other consolations for hurts. A good example occurred in his first literary composition, which was a brief prose narrative based on one of his own dreams. Having run away from home, he climbed high among mountain peaks until he found a secret pass into a happy valley where he was welcomed by some friendly Indians who invited him to stay. That was the gist of it. Understandably, the boy was so pleased and comforted by this dream-story that he kept improvising new episodes in his imagination at the end of any day which closed unpleasantly. By contrast, when some of his most satisfying childhood daydreams were shattered by realities, he expressed a fierce resentment against those who seemed to be responsible for making these dreams fail. Such little rages, further serving to protect some of his cherished illusions, amounted to another phase in a continuing pattern of response that later injured him—and others.

Any idealist, young or old, may confuse the ideal and the actual in ways which are not necessarily dangerous even when they are self-deceptive. It sometimes happens, however, that such a person gradually needs to invoke supporting figments and self-deceptions which do become injurious. Many of Frost's later puzzlements, confusions, and predicaments seem to have developed in this way, as a consequence of his innocent childhood impulses which blended idealism, imagination, belief, and self-deception.

The first serious trouble, which seems to have resulted from these impulses, began when he was eleven years old. The death of his father plunged the boy into a long series of trials and humiliations, against which he tried to defend himself in ways which became increasingly complicated. After he had been uprooted from his beloved San Francisco and transplanted against his wishes into a strange New England atmosphere, which seemed cold and hostile, he expressed his unhappiness by giving vent to unreasonable rage and resentment. Even the briefest sketch of his responses to his New England grandfather may serve to illustrate how and why he accidentally created some unnecessary difficulties, for himself, and then supported his position with imagined beliefs which contained additional illusions and self-deceptions.

Grandfather Frost was a stern man, and the boy's initial hatred of him expressed itself in stubborn resentment. From the start, however, the old gentleman expressed his devotion in ways which were unmistakably generous. When he died, in 1901, he left in his will the stipulation that Robert Frost should gradually inherit the largest part of the estate, that from it a cash annuity was to be paid to his only grandson until the principal was exhausted. This annuity was paid regularly for more than twenty years. It enabled Frost to take his family to England in 1912 and to live there for more than two years without the need for earning a living. In one sense, then, it enabled Frost to complete and publish his first two books of poetry. These events marked the beginning of his fame. Nevertheless, in Frost's view his dead grandfather remained an object of detestation. Over and over again he claimed that the heartlessness and inconsiderateness of his grandfather cheated the poet out of his rightful heritage, and reduced him for a while to a life of poverty on a miserable farm. These bitter assertions were accepted as truths by various listeners. In England, Ezra Pound was one such listener, and he innocently put some of these lies into print when Frost was first gaining public recognition.[8]

Such details are important here as illustrations of a confusion which seemed to grow partly from Frost's early and impulsive uses of the imagination to provide himself with defensive justifications and beliefs. They enabled him to protect his own mythic ideals of the heroic struggle he was forced to make for recognition against seemingly "insuperably odds." The crucial elements of cause and effect, in the habit of mind thus illustrated, is worth reiteration. As soon as Frost developed the tendency to indulge his imagination, for self-protective purposes, he was apparently forced to find supporting self-deceptions which, unintentionally and sometimes unconsciously, made him dishonest in his dealings with himself—and with others.

As a further example consider briefly some elements in Robert Frost's courtship of the girl whom he eventually married: Elinor White. From the beginning of this courtship, while they were still classmates in high school, she had difficulty in persuading him that many of their quarrels and misunderstandings were caused by his spoiled-child habits of making immature and unreasonable demands. The most serious of these misunderstandings grew out of his insistence that if Elinor White really loved him, she would give up all her plans for college and marry him immediately, regardless of her insistence that he and she should first acquire skills for earning a living. Infuriated by her sensible caution, he gradually resorted to a pecular means of justifying his stubbornly importunate position: he accused her of dishonesty, disloyalty, and unfaithfulness. These false accusations precipitated a crisis which grew so serious that he threatened to kill himself. He actually did try to get himself killed at the time, partly to escape and partly to punish his beloved. After he recovered from this desperate runaway impulse, he continued the courtship. But by this time he was motivated in part by his proud and vindictive desire to triumph over Elinor's reluctance, as one means of justifying himself and as another means of punishing her. He did triumph. But his imaginative and self-deceptive misinterpretations of her reluctance helped to undermine the very foundations of the marriage, with grave consequences to himself, to his wife, and eventually to their children.

Nevertheless, in Frost's mythic and idealized version of this courtship, he pictured himself as the hero temporarily victimized and irrevocably wounded by Elinor White's so-called disloyalties. There can be no question, of course, that her various refusals did wound his tender sensibilities; but the causes and consequences of these wounds depended very largely on his ways of responding to his inability to get what he wanted, when he wanted it. He never saw it that way, naturally, and the fictitious element which he added to his idealized or mythic versions of the courtship gradually became undeniable truths, for him. Here again it would seem that his confusion of fact and fiction was caused by his attempt to protect and justify his idealized image of who he was and how he thought he should be treated.

These various uses and abuses of the imagination played a complicated part in the artistic processes of Robert Frost the poet. There were times when he made his poetry serve him merely as a means of escape from his confusions into idealized postures. There were other times when he made his poetry serve him privately as a means of striking back at, or of punishing, some individual who had intentionally or unintentionally hurt him. At his artistic best, however, he tried to make his poems provide an effective way of coming to grips with his inner and outer confusions, honestly, for purposes of resolving them.

Before any further consideration is given to Frost's various uses of the poetic imagination, a brief glance must be given to a pair of modern critical theories. It has often been said that any poem initially faces inward toward the subjective experiences of the author, but that it has its ulterior validity and significance only when it faces outward and exists as a self-sufficient artistic entity. It has also been said, too often, that the subjective intent of the poet can't be known and that it therefore can't be of any concern to the critic, that the poem is viable only when it esthetically invokes a satisfactory subjective response in the critic. The first of these assertions is thoroughly acceptable, here; but the second deserves to be challenged.

Any biographer of a poet is expected to show how the subject used his own experiences as raw materials for his art. Frost made his imagination work primarily with actual images and events familiar to him from his own experiences at first or second hand. He did endow these images with poetic meanings which do indeed face two ways, and his best poems are esthetically viable without any reference to his biography. But any reader who understands the relationships between the inner and outer faces of these poems is able to derive from them two different kinds of enjoyment which are not necessarily unrelated.

There is no law, of course, against the tendency of a critic or reader to enjoy a Frost poem merely by endowing it with the subjective responses which the critic or reader may bring to it. But each of Frost's best poems is a well-ordered artistic object which was intentionally designed by the poet to control and to discipline at least some responses of the critic or reader. As artist, Frost may not have understood fully all of his own conscious and subconscious intent or achievement. He may have builded better—or different—than he knew. Nevertheless, he did understand enough to hope that his readers and critics would seek out and understand some of the consciously intended (and achieved) relationships between his art and his meanings. To deny or ignore that fact, and to argue that the critic's own subjective responses are of primary importance is, under the circumstances, to display an egregious form of nearsightedness. Furthermore, as will be shown, some of the most impertinent misinterpretations of Frost's artistic procedures have been made by critics who assume that their own subjective responses and insights are far more attractive than Frost's.

Returning now, it is important to the central problems of this introduction to notice that Frost, at the beginning of his poetic career, used his imagination to glorify his early ideals of heroic accomplishments. His first published poem, "La Noche Triste," is a ballad written as a tribute to the courage, skill, and cunning of Montezuma's Aztec Indians when they successfully struck back at Cortes and his soldiers, after the Aztecs had been humiliated, degraded, and threatened with enslavement. Other stories of heroic conflicts—Scottish, Roman, Ossianic—were also sung by Frost in his early ballads.

As might be expected, however, the young poet very soon used his imagination, lyrically, to express many other kinds of conflicts—particularly those which he observed inside himself. He later heightened the significance of these early lyrics, through his way of arranging them, in his first book, *A Boy's Will*. That consciously intended ordering gave first place to a sonnet which defended the singer's desire to escape from the hurts of other individuals and of society ("Into My Own"); but the identical ordering gave a climactic position to a poem which celebrated the singer's deliberate return to society and to human collaboration ("The Tuft of Flowers"). Around the polarity established by these two poems, Frost intentionally arranged his other selections into a pattern which consciously tried to resolve the conflicting moods of the separate poems. The element of dialogue thus achieved was designed to serve implicitly as a gathering metaphor.

Thematically considered, the major dialogue in *A Boy's Will* represents the opposed views of the actual self (prone to fear, hurt, discouragement, negation, failure) and the idealizing self (constantly asserting hope, encouragement, affirmation, victory). More than that, the total structural arrangement was consciously intended to represent a sort of pilgrim's progress through immature impulses of escape and negation to gradually maturing pursuits and affirmations. "The psychologist in me," Frost wrote in 1913, "ached to call it 'The Record of a Phase of Post-adolescence.' "[9]

This pilgrim's-progress pattern became a matrix. It was used with conscious variations in most of Frost's books, all the way from *A Boy's Will* to *In the Clearing*. In this pattern there is the subtle suggestion that for Frost the central problem of his life—artistic and non-artistic—was to find orderly ways of dealing with dangerous conflicts he found operative within himself or between himself and others. It was part of his delight to discover many different processes for dealing with these conflicts; but he liked to give his lyrics a surface effect of playful ease and serenity even when some of them dramatized his deepest uneasiness. Sometimes the effect of serenity was achieved, in his poems of escape, by his representing his own idealized attitude as being real, no matter how blatantly the biographical facts contradicted the poetry.[10] Most of the time, however, he used his poems either as tools or as weapons for actually trying to bring under control and resolve those conflicts which he viewed as being so dangerous that they might otherwise engulf and destroy him.

Just how desperately threatening these conflicts became, one may better understand after becoming familiar with the biographical details. Only then do some of the poems, and some of his statements concerning the function of poetry, acquire their full meanings. "Every poem," he wrote, "is an epitome of the great predicament; a figure of the will braving alien entanglements."[11] Always his first impulse was to avoid these entanglements, but he gradually forced himself to learn that the best way out is often through. So he tried as best he could to make his poetic imagination provide new ways of grappling with his old problems. Repeatedly he said that a successful poem "ends in a clarification of life—not necessarily a great clarification, such as sects and cults are founded on, but in a momentary stay against confusion."[12] For him, the individual poetic clarification was merely a stage in a continuing process. New confusions required new metaphors; required new ways of imitating the original and divine creative act by fashioning order out of chaos.

This divine example was a constant inspiration to Frost. Directly or indirectly, in his poems and in his prose, he implied the importance of his long struggle to preserve the consolations of his heretical and sometimes wavering religious beliefs. When most confiding, he admitted that the primary goal of his experience—poetic and non-poetic—was the quest for psychological and spiritual salvation: "One can safely say after from six to thirty thousand years of experience that the evident design is a situation here in which it will always be about equally hard to save your soul. . . . or if you dislike hearing your soul mentioned in open meeting, say your decency, your integrity."[13] His extended play with the antithesis between chaos and form, in the same mood, should acquire fresh meaning here:

"There is at least so much good in the world that it admits of form and the making of form. And not only admits of it, but calls for it. . . . When in doubt there is always form for us to go on with. Anyone who has achieved the least form to be sure of it, is lost to the larger excruciations. I think it must stroke faith the right way. The artist, the poet, might be expected to be the most aware of such assurance, but it is really everybody's sanity to feel it and live by it. . . ."[14]

The precariousness of his less-traveled road and the courageous assertion of the will, which he forced himself to make in staying on it, are merely hinted in the passing reference, there, to form-giving as a means of defense against the threat of psychological chaos or insanity. For him, in his constant struggle against that chaos, as it was invoked by so many fears and uncertainties, courage had to be the virtue which counted most; the utmost reward of daring had to be the assurance he derived from it that he still possessed the capacity "still to dare"[15]—and to proceed because he dared.

Against heavy odds he did proceed, in a manner which had to be heroic. At last, and in spite of all his failures or shortcomings, he did realize some of the mythic ideals he set for himself starting in childhood. He did earn, with great difficulty, enough of the ideal virtues to deserve the heroic rank accorded him by the nation and the world. The best of his achievements in his life and in his art were truly won through his own assertions of courage, skill, cunning, wit, compassion, nobility, and persistent striving. What has endeared him to his readers is, in large part, his ability to find and to assert enough order, enough meaning through the poetry of human experience to provide at least partial compensations for all the inevitable human shortcomings, failures, and tragedies.

For any biographer of Robert Frost there still remains the problem of how to use what the poet said about his own life. In the past, too many of his biographers became so enthralled by his mythic utterances that they took his words as infallible truths and overlooked the discrepancies. As a consequence they ignored his own warning: "Don't trust me too far. . . . don't trust me on my life." In many instances, however, there are as yet no documents against which to "check up on" some of his assertions.

The procedures used in the present biography to deal with this delicate problem will be found to vary with the circumstances. Whenever possible each of Frost's statements has been tested against other (and often more reliable) sources of information, as cited in the Notes. Sometimes, when the context seems to justify the acceptance of his own statements about himself, those statements are given here without further substantiation. At other times, one of his versions of an event is given in the narrative while some of his other versions of the same event are given and evaluated in the Notes. Frequently, careful attention is paid to the mythic value of a particular version, even when it is apparently or actually at odds with known facts. At all times, however, the assumptions based on doubtful evidence are offered tentatively and provisionally.

It should be obvious, then, that in time certain of these details must be modified by documents or evidences which have not yet come to light. It is even more obvious that some of the interpretations, here developed, will be altered. But the primary goal, still valid, is to increase the general knowledge about Robert Frost, as man and as poet, so that we may improve our appreciation of his very human and yet deservedly impressive stature. And the basic story, as here given, rests so firmly on so much established evidence that there is reason to believe it will stand.

Lawrance Thompson

Princeton University

ACKNOWLEDGMENTS

IT IS A PLEASURE to acknowledge my gratitude to all who have helped me gather materials for *Robert Frost: The Early Years*. A few individuals deserve special thanks.

The prime mover was Robert Frost himself. On 29 July 1939, he asked me to become his official biographer, with the stipulation that no part of the proposed biography would be published during his lifetime. Until shortly before his death on 29 January 1963, he worked closely with me, and yet he gave me complete freedom to arrive at my own conclusions. He never asked to see any part of the biography. The vicissitudes of our friendship are suggested by those of his letters to me which were published in *Selected Letters of Robert Frost*, and they may serve as my credentials.

Mrs. Lesley Frost Ballantine, daughter of Robert Frost, has given me sympathetic and friendly assistance from the start. She has made accessible to me family papers in her possession, collections of photographs, and (as is indicated more specifically in the notes) excerpts from journals she kept when she was a small girl on the Frost farm in Derry, New Hampshire.

Mr. Edward Connery Lathem, Associate Librarian of Dartmouth College, very generously shared with me the many findings from his own original research concerning bibliographical and biographical matters which relate to Robert Frost. He was a valuable first reader of the manuscript when it was still in rough form. The recurrence of his name in so many of my notes is further indication of my specific indebtedness.

At my request Mr. and Mrs. Theodore Morrison very considerately read the manuscript at a later stage and made valuable suggestions for minor revisions. Mrs. Morrison, who acted as secretary to Robert Frost during the last twenty-five years of his life, helped me immeasurably during all of those years and has coöperated with me to the fullest extent since the poet's death. To her, as immediate heir of the Frost manuscripts and letter files, in accordance with the terms of Robert Frost's will, I make special acknowledgment of appreciation and gratitude.

ACKNOWLEDGMENTS

Mr. Charles R. Green, Librarian Emeritus of The Jones Library in Amherst, Massachusetts, has continued to serve there as informal curator of an outstanding Frost collection. Repeatedly, and at any hour over a period of many years, he has done so much reference work for me, and in such a cheerful fashion, that he has placed me deeply in his debt.

Long before Mr. Clifton Waller Barrett began giving his many collections of books and manuscripts to the University of Virginia, he called my attention to new and important Frost materials as he acquired them. One of the best measures of his assistance to me, and of my gratitude to him, will be found in my notes, where frequent references are made to unique items in his collection.

Others who have helped me in some very important ways are Mrs. Lascelles Abercrombie, Mr. Ralph Abercrombie, Mr. Frederick B. Adams, Jr., Mrs. Margaret Bartlett Anderson, Mr. Alexander Clark, Miss Sylvia Clark, Mr. W. B. Shubrick Clymer, Mr. Louis Henry Cohn, Mrs. Marguerite Cohn, Mr. H. Bacon Collamore, Mr. William S. Dix, Mr. Alfred C. Edwards, Mr. Willard E. Fraser, Miss Anne Freudenberg, Mrs. Lillian LaBatt Frost, Mr. W. W. Gibson, Mr. John W. Haines, Miss Vera Harvey, Mr. Raymond Holden, Mr. John S. Van E. Kohn, Mr. William Rowell Locke, Mr. Newton F. McKeon, Mr. Daniel Melcher, Mr. Frederic G. Melcher, Mr. Richard W. Morin, Mr. Ray Nash, Mr. Wilbur Rowell, Mrs. Haida Newton Parker, Mr. Ernest L. Silver, Mr. Roger E. Thompson, Mrs. Emma Smith Turner, Mrs. Louise Waller, Mrs. Sabra Peabody Woodbury, and Mr. John Cook Wylie.

Acknowledgment is gratefully given to the following institutions whose libraries extended various courtesies including permission to use manuscript materials specifically designated in the Notes: Amherst College, Dartmouth College, Harvard University, Henry E. Huntington Library, The Jones Library, Princeton University, University of Texas, Wellesley College, and University of Virginia.

Sincere thanks are also given to the following institutions: John Simon Guggenheim Memorial Foundation for a Fellowship, 1946-1947; American Council of Learned Societies for a Fellowship, 1966; and especially Princeton University for several leaves of absence, for several grants of aid from the Research Fund, and for a McCosh Fellowship, 1965.

L. T.

ROBERT FROST
THE EARLY YEARS

ONCE BY THE PACIFIC

You could not tell, and yet it looked as if
The shore was lucky in being backed by cliff,
The cliff in being backed by continent;
It looked as if a night of dark intent
Was coming, and not only a night, an age.
Someone had better be prepared for rage.
There would be more than ocean-water broken
Before God's last Put out the Light *was spoken.*[1]

LONG AFTER the gold-rush days of the Forty-niners, violence and the threat of violence remained so much a part of San Francisco life that even in 1874 the threatened doctor could not have been greatly surprised. Called in haste to the Frost home on that part of Washington Street which lies between Polk and Larkin, near the western foot of Nob Hill, the doctor was met at the door by the expectant father, William Prescott Frost, Jr., who flourished a Colt revolver and warned that if anything happened to his wife while the child was being delivered, the doctor would not leave the house alive.[2]

A man so nervous and upset could not have been useful as an assistant even if the doctor had needed help. Probably reassured and then dismissed from the bedroom, Frost had time enough to regret his impetuosity and even to look back over the history of personal events which had brought him to this crisis. He had puchased the revolver less than a year earlier and almost as soon as he'd reached San Francisco in search of newspaper work. Many told him, and for good reasons, that it was the habit of San Francisco reporters and editors to carry such a weapon concealed, for use in self-defense. He was enough of a daredevil to like such instructions.

A good shot, fond of firearms, and a sportsman athletically inclined, Frost had twice tried to become a soldier. Brought

[1]

up in Lawrence, Massachusetts, where the cotton mills were dependent on raw materials from the Southern states, he had developed strong Copperhead sympathies for the Confederacy. As a teenager he ran away from home intent on reaching Virginia and penetrating Union lines at night, so that he could enlist in the Confederate army of General Robert E. Lee. Ingenious and capable and self-reliant, even at that age, he managed to get as far south as Philadelphia before police picked him up and sent him back, under escort, as requested by his frantic parents. After the end of the War Between the States, and near the close of his high-school days, he applied for admission to West Point, and became embittered by his conviction that unfair political influences had thwarted him.

A fighter anyway, even while still a boy, and fond of roaming the city streets of Lawrence looking for trouble, he had earned a reputation for being a wild and unmanageable rebel. His troubled father, a foreman in one of the Lawrence mills, repeatedly applied harsh forms of discipline—without success. As a last resort, in their attempts to keep the boy off the streets at night, his parents tried to lock him in his bedroom; but he frequently made late and secret escapes through his second-story window by means of a homemade rope ladder.

Failing to become a West Pointer, he entered Harvard College as a second choice. Cambridge and Boston gave him new latitude, and enabled him to indulge in more sophisticated forms of play. A good scholar, bright enough to finish his academic assignments hastily, he became a successful poker player, a heavy drinker, and a frequenter of brothels in Boston. Only once did he get into serious trouble. As a moneymaking lark, he tried to blackmail a Boston "madam" without realizing until he was arrested that his intended victim's "house" had long been protected by the police. That time, only the intervention of his influential uncle, Elihu W. Colcord of Lawrence, saved him from jail and bad publicity. Bold, shrewd, arrogant throughout his Harvard years Frost led a double life as playboy and scholar with enough success to win a volume of Bartlett's *Familiar Quotations*, as a prize for scholarship at the end of his sophomore year, and then to win a first "Bowdoin prize" as a junior (for an historical essay on the princely German family of Hohenstaufens), and finally to win a Phi Beta Kappa key. He was graduated with honors, Class of 1872, bitterly scornful of the strait-laced and puritanical mores which he associated with New England. Having become interested in political history and fascinated by the chicaneries of law and politics, he had difficulty in deciding whether to make a career of law or journalism. Perhaps the deciding factor was provided by his work as a newspaper reporter for the *Saturday Evening Gazette* in Boston during his senior year at Harvard.

After graduation only one thing had been certain: that he must shake the dirt of New England from his heels as fast as he could. Horace Greeley's advice remained attractive: "Go West, young man, and grow up with the country." California beckoned, and San Francisco appealed strongly to this adventurer, perhaps because it had already been decried as the wickedest city in the world. But to cross the vast continent required so much money that the new Harvard graduate decided patiently to work for a year. Through contacts at Harvard he received and accepted a position as principal of a very small private school in Lewistown, Pennsylvania. It was difficult for him to put his vices on the shelf for one whole year; but he did it. Journalism, he had decided, would serve as a steppingstone to a political career, and soon after he began his duties as principal of Lewistown Academy, he arranged to take private lessons in stenography, under peculiar circumstances.

The circumstances involved Miss Isabelle Moodie, the only other teacher on the staff of the very small Academy in Lewistown.[3] A native of Scotland, and still inclined to preserve more than a hint of a burr in her musical and lively conversation, Miss Moodie bespoke a social and cultural background considerably above that of the new principal, who had been born a farmer's son in the village of Kingston, New Hampshire. The young woman carried herself with aristocratic bearing. Strong, tall, and graceful in her motions, she expressed an extraordinary intensity of response to anything which attracted her attention. Her beautiful dark brown eyes were deep set beneath a high forehead; her mass of auburn hair, parted in the middle, was gathered loosely in a large roll at the back of her neck. She had been only twelve years old when her grandmother brought her to Columbus, Ohio, in 1856, to live with a financially prosperous and socially prominent uncle, Thomas Moodie. A graduate of the University of Edinburgh,

Thomas Moodie had left Ayr, Scotland, in 1836, and had gone to Cincinnati, Ohio; had married a Scottish girl, and had established himself as a banker in Columbus a few years later.[4] His niece, Isabelle Moodie—born in Leith, the seaport town of Edinburgh, fathered by a sea captain who went down with his ship in a storm at sea not long after his only daughter was born, and mothered by a hussy who ran away from the arduous duties of motherhood—had been reared by her father's devout Scotch-Presbyterian parents. Only the death of her grandfather had caused the move from Scotland. On the night he died, the old man talked with the child and rapturously described to her his first glimpse of bright angels circling the gates of heaven to welcome him. It did not occur to his granddaughter that he might merely have imagined such a scene. From early childhood she had been sharing the religious convictions of her grandparents and had been developing her own mystical Scottish sensitivities. In truth, she inherited from both of them a strong belief that she was blessed with powers of second sight. Her intense concern for spiritual matters made her face light up with a glow which increased her natural beauty. It found expression in her fondness for writing poetry and for singing hymns.

Almost as soon as the new principal of Lewistown Academy began to teach along with Miss Moodie, he fell in love with her; but the discrepancy between their attitudes toward religious matters created an unfortunate hindrance to courtship. Fortunately his colleague placed an advertisement in the local newspaper soon after school began: "Anyone desiring instruction on the art of Phonography will please apply to Miss Belle Moodie, teacher at the Lewistown Academy. . . . Individual instruction, 12 lessons, $10.00. The method taught is that invented by Isaac Pitman . . . being that adopted by first class reporters both in this country and in England."[5] The principal immediately applied for private instruction—and very quickly began to introduce a subtle kind of love-making, which became so effective that he wrote a formal proposal of marriage to her only five months after they had met. In the letter he said, "Little have you thought what pleasure I have experienced when you have sat with me to study. . . . As I became better acquainted with you, I saw in you a nearer approach to my ideal of a true woman, joined with the native cultivation and refinement of a lady, than I had ever chanced upon among

any of my lady friends."[6] In the same letter he dealt gracefully
with their differences in attitudes toward religion by stressing
the spiritual effect of his love for her:

"... It has ennobled me, it has given me higher aspirations;
it has almost seemed to me that when we have been talking
together on religious questions, my love for you drew me so
close to you in spirit that I could believe with you in Christianity, in the love of God, in the divinity of Christ,—things
which are to you precious truths, to me enigmas."[7]

He was unable to stop there, and after admitting further,
"you are a Christian—I am not," he tried to soften the discrepancy by insisting that his present unbelief contained no
obstinacy. He implied that their love for each other might
convert him to the true faith.

In this letter of proposal he also faced some other hindrances
to the success of his courtship. Miss Moodie was six years
older than he, and in writing of the "disparity in our ages" he
reminded her that other lovers had successfully ignored such
a problem. Then he touched gently on another possible barrier, implicit in Miss Moodie's frequent hints to him that she
had private reasons for feeling that she "should never marry."

Later he learned about those reasons. She had once refused
to accept an offer of marriage made to her by a Presbyterian
clergyman. At the time she had felt she was not worthy of
him, but repeatedly thereafter she had experienced mystical
intuitions of divine punishment apparently visited on her as
a consequence of her having rejected the noble man of God
for whom she had been intended. Her new suitor impetuously
urged that their only concern should be with the present and
future: "... do you see in me that which you can love? that
which you can rely upon as a support in the rugged ways of
life?"[8]

Without too much reluctance Miss Moodie had apparently
seen exactly what her suitor wanted her to see in him. He
was extremely capable, gifted, strong-minded, and handsome.
He had the carriage of an athlete and the features of a hero.
His firm chin was clean-shaven, but his neatly trimmed mustache was carefully trained across his cheeks to join the
curling hair of his thick sideburns. He wore his shock of jet-
black hair parted on the left side and combed gently back
from his high forehead. But perhaps his most distinguishing
feature was the intensely penetrating gaze of his cold blue

eyes. Clearly demonstrating powers of leadership, he gave the impression that he would make his own way successfully, even if at present he had no money except his immediate earnings. Importunate and persuasive as a lover, he conducted his courtship so well that he very quickly won the hand of Miss Moodie. They were married at Lewistown on 18 March 1873—approximately six months after they had first met. The boys and girls of the Academy followed each phase of the romance with approving interest and were delighted with the outcome.[9]

Long before the school year had reached its end the Frosts submitted their resignations and let it be known that they were planning a move to California.[10] As soon as their duties at Lewistown Academy were completed, in June of 1873, they went first to Columbus, Ohio, and spent several weeks visiting with wealthy friends and relatives of the bride. Then Frost made the long journey alone, over the newly completed stages of the Union Pacific Railroad to San Francisco, with the understanding that he would establish himself in newspaper work and would find a home for them both. In the meantime, she remained with her uncle's family in Columbus.

On 9 July 1873 he reached the railroad terminus in Oakland and made the picturesque voyage by ferry across San Francisco Bay, presumably relishing the unforgettable panorama of lofty Sierras to the eastward, the forest-covered mountains of Marin County beyond the expanse of water to the northwest, and the fabulous peninsula city sprawling out over the seven hills from the ship-cluttered wharves and docks before him. The colorful attractions of San Francisco may have been more enticing than Frost had expected, but in less than a week he wrote to urge that his beloved must join him soon lest he die of loneliness. In the same letter he proudly told her that he had already submitted editorials on trial to the best San Francisco newspapers, the *Evening Bulletin* and the *Chronicle*, and that each of his first six offerings had been accepted. It seemed certain that one of these papers would hire him at a good salary of not less than $25 a week and that he would have no difficulty in earning an excellent living for them both—so she must come to him at once.[11]

A few days later, after the *Bulletin* completed arrangements for him to work as an editorial writer and stenographic reporter, he wrote his wife that he had already taken part in a new kind of excitement much to his liking: a street-riot, with gunplay. The fun began after the *Bulletin* published a series of articles attacking and exposing certain wildcat silver-mining stocks. When the market quotations tumbled, a roaring and screaming mob gathered before the *Bulletin* office at 517 Clay Street and shot out all the windows. Inside, well-armed printers, reporters, editors, proprietors barricaded themselves behind stacked rolls of newsprint and held their fire. The police dispersed the crowd and nobody suffered any serious hurt.

From the start young Frost's adventurous temperament thrived on San Francisco's atmosphere. It is doubtful if any other place on earth could have been more congenial to his tastes than this raw city built on chance, this new metropolis which had been a mere frontier town only a few decades earlier and had mushroomed in spectacular fashion soon after gold had been discovered at Sutter's Mill near Sacramento. The first chaos of hastily improvised dwellings, tents, lean-tos, wooden shacks, flimsy stores, hotels, saloons, brothels soon creeping back from the waterfront and up the slopes of the hills, along steep and dusty roads, had not lasted long. By 1873 these helter-skelter beginnings had given way to an ordered arrangement of broad streets—some paved with cobblestones and others with planking—along which board sidewalks ran. Back of the bayside waterfront—thick with warehouses, docks, fish markets, ferry slips—the business section had expanded into row on row of three- and four-story offices and stores, many of them still cheaply built, others constructed of brick and stone. Throughout the business section of downtown San Francisco and already scattering back across the peninsula were hotels, churches, theaters, and saloons. Further inland the residential sections began crowding together thousands of homes, while the ornate mansions of the millionaires began to vie with each other for prominence on the southerly slope of Nob Hill. Keeping pace, the slum region developed along Leidersdorff Street, which became known as "Pauper's Alley."

Fascinated by all he saw and heard, the newly arrived editorial writer for the *Bulletin* quickly learned that law and order, such as it was in San Francisco, no longer rested in the hands of self-appointed Vigilance committees, that in some ways the *Bulletin* itself had helped to end those brutal years. Back in the mid-fifties, when the first *Bulletin* editor had slashed boldly at political corruption by exposing tough Boss Casey as one who had stuffed himself through the ballot boxes to a seat on the Board of Supervisors, Casey had scornfully silenced that editor by shooting him down in the street. But the funeral procession had wound past the very spot where the second Vigilance Committee had already tried, condemned, and executed Casey—his body still hanging there alongside that of another notorious murderer. If San Francisco law enforcement had greatly improved since those days, there remained an atmosphere of rawness and corruption, which was easily seen by the new reporter.

Good newspaper "copy" was provided by the machinations of the "Big Four," who had turned from merchandising to railroading with success, and who were acquiring more and more financial power: Huntington, Crocker, Stanford, Hopkins. Almost daily other kinds of stories were being created by the doings of that celebrated builder of wonders in San Francisco, that spectacular plunderer of silver in the Comstock lode, that near-owner of the architecturally beautiful Bank of California, William C. Ralston—just then slipping from power. Coming in fast and already intent on beating Ralston at his own silver game in Nevada were the four Irish bartenders and chowder-makers, O'Brien, Fair, Flood, Crocker.

Financial speculations and politics were inseparable from journalism, and young Frost had a taste for all three. His deeply ingrained Copperhead sympathies gave him reason enough to throw his weight in with the California Democrats, who pleased him with their bitter snarling at Republican frauds.

By the time Isabelle Moodie Frost made the long journey across the continent, in November of 1873, her husband was well acquainted with the past and present of San Francisco. He had also found, rented, and furnished a small apartment at 737 Pine Street, three blocks south of Clay and within easy walking distance of the *Bulletin* office. From the moment of his bride's arrival in the fabulous city, Frost showed a genuinely protective attentiveness. Because his wife was not an experienced cook and housekeeper, he very gallantly insisted that any form of housework was too menial and exhausting for one in her delicate condition. As a result they soon moved from Pine Street to a good hotel with a fine Scots name, the

Abbotsford House, on the corner of Broadway and Larkin Street. After they grew tired of hotel life, they found another apartment at 14 Eddy Place, off Post Street, between Mason and Powell. But before their child was born, they apparently found an even better place, more to their liking, on Washington Street only a few blocks south of the Abbotsford House.[12] The nearer the day came, the greater the show of the husband's devotion, and by the night of 26 March 1874 he became far more upset than his wife by the prospect of the imminent ordeal.

Fortunately, the brandished revolver was not needed, and the obstetrical skills of the doctor were not too much impaired by the threat of violence. But it was characteristic of this impetuous New England-hating Yankee that his Copperhead sympathies led him to name his son after the Confederate hero, Robert Lee. Mrs. Frost was given little choice in the matter. She may at least have consoled herself (as a poetess and as a Scot) that Robert was a name which had for her some cherished associations.

ESTRANGEMENTS

A man must partly give up being a man
With women-folk. We could have some arrangement
By which I'd bind myself to keep hands off
Anything special you're a-mind to name.
Though I don't like such things 'twixt those that love.[1]

ROBERT FROST'S mother had indeed shown less fear than his father at the time their son was brought into the world, and yet the event had scarcely occurred before she was almost overwhelmed with fright—and even panic. Her husband had restrained his vices so honorably during the first year of their marriage that he had earned her adoration. But she noticed that, for causes more easily felt than articulated, he no sooner became the father of a son than he began to slip into habits of drinking, gambling, and dalliance.

San Francisco in "the terrible seventies" was just as much a gambler's paradise as it had been in the gold-rush days. It may have been easy for the new *Bulletin* reporter to explain his late arrivals home, his sudden peaks of affluence or intervals of financial stringency by describing the vicissitudes of combining stock-market investment and newspaper work. For a time the purity and innocence of his very religious wife, absorbed as she was with the cares of her first child, may have helped to protect her from any awareness of his dalliance. His extraordinary fondness for whiskey ("strong man's food," as he liked to call it) was another matter. Whiskey seemed to turn this apparently devoted husband into a dangerously brutal man, who often went into a rage and smashed furniture if his wife so much as implied her disappointments and protests. Years later, after she became a widow, and after her son was old enough to share confidences, she told him that during the first few months of his life she had more than once snatched him from his cradle and carried him into the street, then into a neighbor's home, for fear that his father's drunken violence might otherwise cause the death of child and mother. To her, it seemed tragic and inexplicable that the man who had wooed her with promises of support in "the rugged ways of life" could have become transformed (as she said) "into a Heathcliff."

During those days when she lived in constant dread, she found her greatest consolation in prayer and in church work. Immediately after her arrival in San Francisco, and for several months thereafter, she had always been accompanied by her husband as she visited various churches before deciding to establish affiliation. Inclined toward the Scotch Presbyterian liturgy since childhood, she was dissatisfied with the California variations of it. Her next choice had been stimulated not only by the faith of her uncle in Columbus, Ohio, but also by the writings of the late Thomas Starr King, the distinguished Unitarian clergyman who had lovingly described for people back in "the States" the natural beauties of the Pacific coast during his years of service as pastor of the Unitarian church in San Francisco. Briefly the Frosts attended what had been King's church until his death in 1864; but Mrs. Frost was far too mystically inclined to gain any lasting sustenance from the rationalistic fare of Unitarian sermons. She craved an atmosphere more congenial to her gift of second sight, and happily she found it in the Society of the New Jerusalem. Emanuel Swedenborg had established the foundations of the Society only after his own powers of second sight had enabled him to converse with spirits and angels. Before his illumination, he had been instructed through dreams and visions and mysterious conversations.

In San Francisco the Swedenborgian minister was the picturesque and vigorous John Doughty, whom the Frosts had met as a neighbor during the brief period when they were living near his home at the foot of Nob Hill.[2] Doughty had crossed the continent in a covered wagon during the gold-rush days, had been instrumental in forming the first Society of the New Jerusalem in San Francisco in 1852, and had helped to erect an attractively small house of worship in the Gothic style on the north side of O'Farrel Street, between Mason and Taylor. To that church, after she became a member of it, Mrs. Frost took her son for baptism by the Reverend John

Doughty; to this very sympathetic friend she also took her burdens when she began to fear that her marriage would end in ruin.

She was hurt when her husband refused to join the Swedenborgian church. Soon after their child was born, she began to notice how easily her husband found excuses for being unable to attend church with her, and how openly scornful he became of spiritual matters. She was also troubled to find that his tastes were better satisfied by the "low jinks" and "high jinks" rituals of the Bohemian Club, newly organized in San Francisco to promote social and intellectual rapport between journalists, other writers, artists, actors, and musicians.

Not all of the friendships made by her husband at the Bohemian Club were displeasing to Mrs. Frost. One of its most serious members was an attractive Philadelphia-born adventurer, a giant of a man with a black beard and a bald head. His name was Henry George and he had been lured to California by the gold rush; but he had settled down in San Francisco as a typesetter, had turned to journalism from typesetting, and then had become interested in politics. A few years earlier he had attracted attention when he published an article in which he had tried to warn Californians that the only gains which would become available through the completion of the transcontinental railroad, then building, would be greater wealth for the few and greater poverty for the many, unless new kinds of land-tax laws were quickly passed by state and federal legislatures. In the fall of 1869—after serving as a Democratic candidate for the California Assembly, after opposing state and federal subsidies for the railroads, and after being defeated by the power of the Central Pacific Railroad—George had returned to typesetting and writing. In the summer of 1871 he published a pamphlet entitled *Our Land and Land Policy* in which he urged that every man had a natural right to apply his labor to the land; that when the land is privately owned, and man must pay rent to use it, he is robbed of some of his labor; that taxes should be on land values only, thus taking for the community what the community has produced, and relieving industry of the incubus of all other taxes. His pamphlet won him a position as part-owner and editor of a newspaper primarily designed to attack and expose public abuses, the *Daily Evening Post*, which had published its first issue in San Francisco in December of 1871.

As editor-in-chief of the *Post*, Henry George gradually attracted Mr. Frost away from the *Bulletin* and gave him work as city editor, starting on 1 September 1875—a position which Frost kept for nearly nine years. George had a steadying influence on Frost even after the *Post* changed hands in December 1875, forcing George out. The new editor-in-chief of the *Post* was Joseph T. Goodman, who had been editor of the *Virginia City Enterprise* during those flush times in Nevada when the *Enterprise* had employed Mark Twain as a reporter.

The George and Frost families soon became close friends, and frequently visited in each other's homes. Long before the private printing of *Progress and Poverty*, the Frosts became converts to the "single tax" doctrine, and they never relinquished their firm belief in it. The growing intimacy of the two families may have enabled Mrs. Frost to share confidences with Mrs. George, and to seek advice concerning the awkward problem of living with a man who, while becoming a success as a newspaper editor, repeatedly failed as husband and father. Perhaps she even confided that a new crisis had driven her to an awkward decision. Carrying her second child, and fearing that her husband's violence under the influence of whiskey might cause her injury, she was determined to leave him. It must have been difficult to explain her plans and to secure money for travel. But in the spring of 1876, she made the long journey across the continent by rail with her two-year-old son Robbie, ostensibly to visit friends and even to meet for the first time the parents of her husband in Lawrence, Massachusetts. Probably more by accident than by design she was still in Lawrence, visiting the Frosts, on 25 June 1876, when she gave birth to the child, a girl for whom she said she could not immediately find a name.[3]

Nothing is known of how Mrs. Frost was received by her in-laws, or how she explained her extraordinary visit, or what she said about her marital difficulties. One hint of awkwardness may be surmised from the fact that she left Lawrence with her two children as soon as she could.

There was a haven in New England where Isabelle Moodie Frost knew she would be welcomed. It was a farm in Greenfield, Massachusetts, the family home of a close friend named Sarah Newton with whom Belle Moodie had taught school for several years in Columbus, Ohio. Sarah Newton always spent her summer vacations with her parents in Greenfield, and it is probable that Mrs. Frost had made arrangements to reach Greenfield with her son Robbie well before the time when her second child was expected. Under any circumstance, she did receive affectionate and considerate attentions from all of the Newtons, whose urgings kept her in Greenfield with her children throughout the summer of 1876.[4]

The spacious Newton farmhouse had been the home of seven children born to the locally prominent farmer and public servant, Hervey C. Newton, and his wife. Their oldest son, Christopher, had been killed in the Civil War. Their oldest daughter, Sarah, had been graduated from Mt. Holyoke College, and, after teaching for some time in Ohio, had become the principal of a girls' school in Newport News, Virginia. Another daughter, Annie, had married a Greenfield lawyer, Horatio Parker. Because the family atmosphere at the Newton farm was devout and pious, it was well suited to the needs and the temperament of their somewhat forlorn summer visitor.

It must have been to the Newton farm in Greenfield that the husband of Belle Frost addressed his contrite and apologetic letters throughout the summer of 1876—letters so persuasive that they finally convinced her that it might be safe to return to him. Even so, she attached certain conditions to her acceptance of his plea, for she did not go back with her children alone. After traveling from Greenfield to Ohio by train, she spent the entire autumn of 1876 in Columbus with friends and relatives. The attention paid her children by two of her Moodie cousins, both married, helped her to decide on a name for her daughter. Her cousin Jeanie had married Alexander Proctor in Cincinnati; her cousin Florence had married a man named Harrington in Columbus. Still uncertain, she wrote to her husband from Columbus on 1 November 1876, "About naming her I am again undecided and will not entirely make up my mind until I see you. The folks in the house are all so devoted to her and take care of her so much that I feel quite like naming her for some one of them. Florence seems to worship her . . ."[5] The name chosen for the child was Jeanie Florence.

In the same letter from Columbus, Mrs. Frost gave her husband a glimpse of their son: "Bob is just as queer as ever about some things. Scarcely looks at lady visitors but is most happy to climb upon gents['] knees. A young gentleman called this evening one of my old pupils and it was quite amusing to see the devotion of the little fellow. In saying 'God bless dear papa' before going to bed he insisted on saying also God bless Mr[.] Jamieson."[6]

No other glimpse has survived of the two-year-old boy's behavior during those months of absence from his father in 1876. The difficulties of his mother in caring for her two children throughout the long journey back to California from Ohio were competently shared by a friend who went with her. In Columbus she had renewed acquaintance with an intimate of high-school days there, Miss Blanche Rankin, who shared with Mrs. Frost the gift of second sight. For several years Miss Rankin had been living precariously and even desperately with a dipsomaniac father, a widower. She welcomed the invitation to accompany the Frost trio to California, and to live with the Frosts in San Francisco until she could establish herself there. The father of the children accepted the condition that Miss Rankin should return as companion. The arrangement worked well over a period of several years and the Frost children grew up calling her "Aunt Blanche."

Many new adventures had engaged the attentions of William Prescott Frost, Jr., during his wife's long absence from San Francisco. With the help of Henry George, he had aligned himself with the machinery of the Democratic Party in the campaign on behalf of Samuel J. Tilden, Governor of New York and Democratic candidate for President, opposed by the Republican candidate, Rutherford B. Hayes, Governor of Ohio. Mrs. Frost, while still in Ohio, took ambiguous cognizance of these matters when writing to her husband on November 1 with a touch of reproach:

"You seemed well and happy, enthusiastically so over politics. I sincerely hope that such severe labor will not make you sick. It scarcely seems wise for you with so many duties pressing on every side to do so much. I know how deeply interested you are in the present campaign, but you should not entirely forget that excellent proverb suited to all kinds of warfare, 'Discretion is the better part of valor.' I hope for your sake that the Democrats will win. As for myself I would like a change just to satisfy my curiosity. I wish to see if the Democratic party can get public affairs out of their present mess."[7]

Mrs. Frost was well aware that the "present mess," national and local, had its roots in glaring malfeasances of office throughout both terms of President Grant's administration. Also contributing was the financial panic and depression which followed the collapse of Jay Cooke's powerful banking firm in New York City on 18 September 1873. Another "mess" had developed in San Francisco on 27 August 1875 when W. C. Ralston's marble-trimmed and seemingly impregnable Bank of California had closed its doors during a "run" carefully engineered by Ralston's four Irish enemies. On that same day Ralston had taken the last of his famous swimming exercises in the Bay, and to the many citizens of San Francisco, who suddenly found themselves bankrupt, it made little difference whether Ralston's drowning had been accidental or suicidal. The ensuing collapse of so many California industries and the consequent destitution among the unemployed in San Francisco became so widespread that by 1876 the benevolent associations and churches were feeding thousands daily. Then the California Workingmen's Party began to frighten San Francisco by holding large protest meetings and threatening violence unless political graft ceased and unless restrictions were placed on the importation of cheaply paid Chinese laborers. This cumulative "mess" caused the Democrats to hope for local and national successes in the fall elections.

The Democrats were disappointed. When the electoral votes were counted (belatedly, because of confusion which led both parties to accuse each other of bribery and fraud), the announcement was made and accepted that the new President was Rutherford B. Hayes, who had won over the Democratic candidate, Tilden, by a single vote. Embittered, Henry George soon turned to writing his inquiry into the causes of industrial depressions, while William Prescott Frost, Jr., equally embittered, dedicated more and more of his energies to working for the Democratic Party in San Francisco.

When Mrs. Frost wrote her warning that it scarcely seemed wise for her husband to do so much when so many duties pressed on him from every side, she had not been aware of one particular folly which had already wasted so much of his energy. Among the sporting events of those years, walking races had become extremely popular, and during his Harvard days Frost had indulged sufficiently in this game to pride himself on his abilities. When the celebrated walker, Dan O'Leary, challenged San Franciscans by making the public boast that he could give any man a half-day start and overtake him in a six-day-and-night walking race—each man to sleep as much or as little as he choose during the race—Frost accepted the challenge. Bets were placed, arrangements were made for the contest to be held at the Mechanics Pavilion in San Francisco, witnesses and judges were hired, spectators were invited to attend—and the race was carried through.

The city editor of the *Post* finished in first place, but O'Leary refused to pay his bet. He claimed that Frost had repeatedly violated the rule that the walker's forward heel must always touch the ground before the other foot was lifted from the ground. The hard feelings which grew out of this contest were not nearly so important to Frost as the ailments he suffered as a result of this exhausting ordeal. By the time his wife returned to San Francisco with their two children and with "Aunt Blanche," he was undergoing medical treatment for consumption (not yet called tuberculosis). Casual and scornful in his references to his illness, the young man insisted that he would throw it off. As soon as he could make his fortune from Comstock silver-mine investments he would take the popular cure by going to the islands, Hawaii, with his family. For the present, he was too busy to do more than allay the symptoms with his favorite medicine, whiskey.

3

GOLDEN GATE

Dust always blowing about the town,
Except when sea-fog laid it down,
And I was one of the children told
Some of the blowing dust was gold.[1]

IN RETROSPECT, as a grown man, Robert Frost said that his earliest memories of his childhood in San Francisco were romping with his mother up and down the dimly lit corridors of the Abbotsford House, the relatively small and yet somewhat barnlike hotel on the northwest slope of Nob Hill. It became "home" again for the Frost family as soon as Mrs. Frost returned from "the States" with her children and with "Aunt Blanche," late in November of 1886. The boy's mother, always trying to shield Robbie and Jeanie from hurts, concealed her own apprehensions and did her best to make circumstances seem brighter than they were. Nevertheless, because the intermittent ardor and cruelty of her husband very soon created new situations not unlike those which had caused her to leave him, she had so much love to spare that she nearly smothered her children with it.

If she saw the danger of spoiling them by being overly protective, she also felt the need for giving them extra attention and love. Both of them showed early signs of nervous and physical ailments. From the first, as babies, they were nurtured on fear; they drank it with the mother's milk.

Somewhat blindly, perhaps, Robbie's father had boasted in a letter written only seven months after the child's birth, "We are all well, particularly the little boy, who, in fact, has never seen a really sick day in his short life."[2] Similarly, four months after their daughter's birth, the mother had written to the father from Ohio, "Of the baby I can only write ditto to what I have already written—healthy, pretty, and good. I am sure she will be good with her papa if he will not tease her."[3] Her hint about teasing was not unrelated to emotional difficulties unintentionally conveyed from father to son. Before Mrs. Frost had separated from her husband, she had been troubled by the clumsy ways in which the humorless man, trying to play with the boy, seemed to take pleasure in rough handling which often caused tears. In the same letter from Ohio she had written of her son, "Robbie keeps pretty well at present." Pretty well. In spite of her characteristic attempts to put unpleasantness aside at all times, she had already become aware that her son's extraordinary sensitivities were closely related to frequent upsets and ailments. The child had clearly suffered much. There could have been precious little which was soothing to his delicacies during that long journey "back East," the brief visit with his paternal grandparents in Lawrence, the decrease of attention from his mother at the time of his sister's birth, the protracted stay with the Newtons in Greenfield, the many visits made in Ohio, and the long return trip to San Francisco. Years later, his "Aunt Blanche" told him that throughout the early days of his boyhood he had seemed so constantly the victim of many mysterious aches and pains in his head and stomach that she and his mother had feared he would never survive to manhood.

In all these California years the sustaining atmosphere of even a relatively serene and well-ordered home was unknown to the Frost children. Tidiness was not one of Mrs. Frost's concerns; she never became a good housekeeper or a good cook. Her loyal friends excused her by saying that her devout nature was far too spiritual to allow her to be bothered with worldly details. It is probable that the repeated insistence of her husband on moving from apartment life to hotel life was caused, at least in part, by these limitations.

Another constant problem, which interfered with even her best attempts at homemaking and which forced her to be extremely practical, was the frequently precarious state of the family budget. In trying to alleviate that condition, she earned some money by reviewing books for her husband's newspaper, the *Post*. Some of her poems also appeared in the *Post*, the longest being a two-hundred-line blank-verse dramatic monologue in a Browningesque manner entitled "The Artist's Motive."[4] She even tried her hand at writing stories for children.[5]

As soon as Robbie and Jeanie were old enough to be interested, their mother combined storytelling with devout moralizing for the purpose of teaching them the fundamentals of religious and theological truth. Bible stories provided a daily fare, and particular emphasis was given to the Genesis stories. "In the beginning God created the heaven and the earth. . . . and God divided the light from the darkness. . . . and divided the waters . . . and let the dry land appear." Over and over they heard the story of Adam and Eve, the story of Cain and Abel, the story of Noah and the ark into which the paired animals marched, "two and two . . . male and the female." Mrs. Frost made the stories illustrate moral truths which also involved pairs of opposites—evil and good, chaos and order, darkness and light—until Robbie developed a habit of thinking in terms of paired images. Throughout his life, he was inclined to build his thinking and even his poetry around these pairs.

Mrs. Frost advanced her storytelling to include narratives of heroes and hero-worship: classical myths, battles and leaders of her native Scotland, battles and leaders of the American Civil War. One story, which took on cumulative meanings for both children through retelling, was of the brave French girl named Joan, whose very sensitive ears helped her listen to the voice of God speaking directly to her.

Their mother also told and retold miraculous stories about another heroic character who had heard the voice of God: the Swedish scientist, Emanuel Swedenborg. The more they learned about him from their mother and from the pastor, who conducted the Sunday-school exercises in their church, the more they marveled at the adventures and accomplishments of this intellectual giant who had made so many wonderful discoveries on his own and for the first time. Fathered by a theologian, who had been accused of heresy for placing too much emphasis on direct communion with God, Swedenborg devoted many years of his life to a scientific concern for relationships between the earthly and the divine. But after God revealed Himself in a dream and announced that He had chosen to unfold the spiritual sense of the Holy Scripture through Swedenborg, the pious man completely altered his way of life. Prior to this great revelation, he was instructed by God through dreams; he heard mysterious conversations; but as soon as the doors of heaven were opened to him so that he was able to communicate directly with angels, he began his elaborate work of carefully recording and publishing these mysteries.

This education of the Frost children was well advanced, years before they reached school age, by their experienced mother, who was a skillful teacher. She was also eager to give them early exposure to classroom discipline, and when Robbie was five years old arrangements were made to have him attend a kindergarten privately conducted in the home of a Russian lady, Madame Zitska. The shy and sensitive boy was so frightened by the prospect of leaving his mother, even for a day, that her reassurances scarcely persuaded him that he would enjoy playing with other children in the school. The Frosts were then living at 1431 Steiner Street, between Ellis and Byington, at some distance from Madame Zitska's home, and even the enticement of a pleasant ride in a horse-drawn omnibus, halfway across the city of San Francisco, did not appeal to him.

On the first day of school, when Robbie made the strange journey, he felt unpleasantly lost before he had even reached the school, and the day was not half over when someone pushed him too high and too long in a back-yard swing, with the result that he was sick to his stomach. A further agony occurred when the omnibus driver on the home journey had so much difficulty in finding Robbie's house that the boy wept for fear he would never see his mother again. The next day, when it came time for him to get ready for school, he developed a severe pain in his stomach and was permitted to stay at home. Thereafter, whenever attempts were made to send him back to Madame Zitska's, the pains returned. Pleading and cajolery were in vain; his first day of kindergarten was his last.

Similar pains returned soon after he was given his first taste of public school, in the autumn of 1880. The Frosts were living once again at the Abbotsford House, and the public school was almost across the street from the hotel. At first Robbie seemed completely charmed by the handsome, dark-skinned first-grade teacher, Miss Fisher; but after little more than one week of rough-and-tumble among boisterous companions, Robbie again began to complain of pains in his stomach. Even if his mother suspected that the ailment was nothing more than nervous tension, she was sure that the child was miserable. So she permitted him to stay at home until he felt well enough to want to go back to the first grade.

He never did feel well enough; and his mother reluctantly decided to let him carry on his first-grade studies in reading and writing and arithmetic under her capable guidance.

Unintentionally pampered and spoiled, the boy showed so much distaste for mastering "the three R's" that he progressed very slowly. If there was one exception, it was in the early phases of his learning to write his letters and words and sentences. After he progressed far enough to be given a fine new copybook, with a sample at the head of each page, he worked with such eager industry that he became greatly upset whenever he made a mistake. One serious slip of the pencil would be enough to send him into such a rage of disgust with himself that he would tear the page out of the book so that he could begin again with a perfect sheet. His mother's idealism, thus reflected, had already caused him to give sympathetic ear to those exacting biblical words, "Be ye therefore perfect, even as your Father which is in heaven is perfect." The older he grew, the more he puzzled over that difficult exhortation.

Under his mother's supervision, Robbie finished enough of his first-grade work to be qualified for entrance to the second grade of the nearby public school; the Frosts were still living at the Abbotsford House. His new teacher, a Miss Radford, immediately heightened his liking for geography and managed to keep him more or less tolerant of school discipline until February of 1882. By the time St. Valentine's Day arrived, he had become so bold and enterprising that he crawled on hands and knees across the back of the schoolroom to retrieve a Valentine from an empty desk—and was caught in the act by Miss Radford. The mild punishment, immediately administered before the entire class, took the form of a few slaps across the palm of his right hand with some pieces of rattan. The pain inflicted was nothing compared with the shame and indignity of this public disgrace, and his mother was unable to assuage his resentment over what seemed to him a gross injustice. The next day, when he firmly refused to go to school, his mother tried just as firmly to overcome his arguments. But his stomach pains returned with such severity that Robbie was once again permitted to carry on his studies at home.

Entering the third grade, in another school, in the fall of 1882, he submitted pleasantly to a new teacher named Miss Dudley, until inevitable tensions and difficulties offended him.

That was the end of his public-school education in San Francisco. Such schoolwork as he could be persuaded to do—and it was not much—he completed at home.

While Robbie was learning to take advantage of his mother's leniency during these early years, he found that his father's characteristic impatience, quick temper, and severity of discipline soon dressed the balance. Engrossed in his own work, and seeming to find very little time or inclination for play with his children, Mr. Frost restricted his function as father primarily to tasks of correction and punishment. Sometimes blows fell without warning and, as it seemed to the children, even without just cause. Frequently, when the boy indulged his creative skills by improving accounts of his exploits and by adding imaginative embroideries, he found that he ran the risk of being called a liar by his father and of being punished accordingly. Robbie's mother tried to make the boy understand that earthly obedience was inseparable from obedience to heavenly dictates; that all forms of earthly naughtiness were seen by the Heavenly Father, who would one day call each individual to account and would mete out punishment. The parable of the talents was taught to the Frost children in many different versions, and they were made to understand quite clearly that the fear of the Lord was the beginning of wisdom. Perhaps it was; but in Robbie's childhood experiences his cumulative fear of a distant and mysteriously punishing Heavenly Father became inseparable from his first-hand knowledge and fear of his earthly father, whose punishments were so inconsistent and severe.

There were times, of course, when the boy could recognize that he was fully responsible for the chastisements he brought on himself through thoughtless mistakes and even lies. He would never forget the awkward developments which grew out of his coming home from a nearby grocery store, one day, to complain to his father that the grocer had called Robbie a "son of a bitch." Although his father often used coarse words and even profanity, the unpredictable man this time reached for an ebony cane, growled, seized the boy by the arm, and dragged him up the street to Mr. MacPartland's grocery store. Arraigned before the counter as though it were a bar, Robbie studied the face of the baffled storekeeper as Mr. Frost said to his son, "Now tell me again what Mr. MacPartland called you."

Fearing that if he repeated what he had said, he might see the grocer killed with one well-aimed blow from his father's cane, yet knowing that if he now told the truth he himself would be hammered, Robbie hesitated. This was a tight place, and he knew it. Hating to make the choice, he nevertheless spoke the truth this time: "He called me a son of a gun."

Then he stood there, as bravely as he could, taking the blows that fell on his backside and resenting the smile on Mr. Mac-Partland's face.

His mother tried to help Robbie accept with stoicism whatever punishment came his way—either from his earthly or his Heavenly Father. Although it was a hard lesson to learn, he was given innumerable opportunities to practice the Christian doctrines of humility, submission, acceptance, and obedience. The older he grew, the more sure he became that there was little enough he could do about some matters except submit. Years later, in explaining how he had become reconciled to those doctrines quite early, he would smile grimly and say, "They put salt on my tail when I was young."

But there were times when submission to his father's punishment made him puzzle anew over the relationship between his just deserts and what he got. One of the most baffling and grievous incidents occurred on a memorable Hallowe'en, spoiled early for the Frost children by their father's insistence that he would not tolerate the clutter caused by the messy business of scooping out pumpkins with knives and spoons prior to cutting eyes and noses and mouths. Under the circumstances the best the Frost children could do was to visit friends and enjoy the process vicariously. That evening, hours after he had shared his disappointments with neighboring children, Robbie answered a knock at the door and found his best friend standing there with a present. It was a handsome, grinning jack-o'-lantern complete with candle burning inside. Too much embittered by his father's edict, Robbie forgot his manners. He blurted out the fact that his father would not let him have a jack-o'-lantern and, so saying, he slammed the door. His father, accidentally witnessing the dramatic scene, and perhaps more enraged by this exposure of his own selfishness than by Robbie's bad manners, reached for the nearest weapon handy. It happened to be a metal dog chain, and with it he lashed the boy's legs until they bled.

When the harsh man occasionally made amends to his

children, either for sternness or neglect, his awkward attempts at playfulness took forms of teasing which worried and frightened Mrs. Frost. For Robbie, the most memorable of these well-intended roughhouse games occurred one night when the boy, just finishing his bath, was still in the tub. After an ill-considered push, Robbie slipped and fell in such a way that his knee came down hard on the upturned edge of the metal stopper. The bloody gash in his knee was so frightening that a doctor was called to patch it. Even worse was the consequent stiffness in the knee. It lasted for weeks and confined Robbie to his home with nothing better to do than sit in a chair and depend on his mother for entertainment. Her most successful move was to instruct him in various ways of folding paper and cutting out endless chains of paper dolls, which he presented to his admiring sister, Jeanie.

During some of the crises which threatened to cause paternal beatings, Robbie was helped by his mother—as on one occasion when he lost a ten-cent piece. His father, working at home on editorial writing, had sent the boy up to Mr. MacPartland's grocery store for a package of cigarettes, and all had gone well until Robbie started home playfully tossing and catching some change. As the dime fell from his hand, it bounced on the board sidewalk and rolled some distance downhill before it disappeared through a crack. Dreading the consequences of that loss, Robbie tried his best to recover the dime with two sticks. Failing, he went back to the store and asked Mr. MacPartland for another dime. The storekeeper refused, the loiterers laughed, and the boy fled to his mother. Apparently sharing her son's apprehension, she at least had one last recourse: prayer. She took the boy into his bedroom, where they knelt and prayed. Then she let him go alone to deliver the cigarettes and to explain the accident as best he could. His father, scarcely raising his head, reached for the cigarettes and dismissed him with a distant, "Never mind." To Robbie, thus miraculously spared, it seemed clear that he and his mother had demonstrated the wonderful power of prayer.

On later occasions, however, he was perplexed to find that prayer did not always work miracles. Again and again he asked his mother about this discrepancy, and she always explained it to him in terms which were hard for him to understand. The gist of what he learned was that the ways of God were very mysterious, and that it was wise not to inquire too closely into them.

Mrs. Frost constantly tried to teach her son that he should count only the sunny hours. She, and not his elementary-school teacher, was the first to arouse his enjoyment of geography, and she did it by calling his attention to the natural wonders and beauties of those physical features they could actually see from the lookout points of three hills they climbed in their walks: Telegraph Hill, Russian Hill, Nob Hill. The panoramic vistas from each helped her to make him realize that San Francisco was almost an island encompassed by the Pacific Ocean on the west and by what she referred to repeatedly as "the most beautiful bay on earth" to the east and north. From Telegraph Hill she often called his attention to the white sails of schooners under way, and assured him that some of the very ships they were watching might come from and go to other continents. She pointed out the ferryboats plying between Oakland and San Francisco, and reminded him that he had twice made that fine voyage acros the Bay. She showed him the direction taken by the trains as they started east from Oakland, and helped him see the jagged peaks of the Sierra Nevada Range, far beyond the hills of Oakland and Berkeley.

From the top of Russian Hill, on many occasions, she continued his lessons in local geography and in the spectacular beauties of their immediate surroundings. For Robbie, one of his favorite views was the shiplike Rock and fortress (then an Army post), Alcatraz Island. Beyond it, towering above and dwarfing it, the tree-covered dome of Angel Island always seemed much closer than it really was. And around the eastern end of Angel Island they could see far up into the northern part of the Bay, toward San Pablo Strait. To the north and west of Alcatraz, they marveled at the upper wall of the bridgeless Golden Gate and the mountains of the Coast Range as far as the eastern and western peaks of Tamalpais. All this was his own, his native land, and his mother taught him to be proud of it.

Their ventures around San Francisco by foot and by cable car—even by horse car—were not all devoted to the study of geography. Much to the liking of Robbie and his sister was the splendid horse-car ride through the sand dunes and across the peninsula to the Cliff House below Land's End, and then the walks over paths along the cliffs to hear the ocean roaring and to watch it shattering into foam against the nearby Seal Rocks. To the south of the Cliff House was a long wooden stairway down which they walked to play on the white sands of the beach and even to wade in pools left by outgoing tides.

Other adventures were enjoyed by the children when their mother took them down to Woodward's Gardens, which combined the attractions of a botanical display, an amusement park, and a zoo. Year by year it had grown in popularity and size until, by the time the Frost children began to make their wondering visits, it occupied the entire block from Mission to Valencia streets, between 13th and 14th. Each pilgrimage to Woodward's Gardens with their mother afforded Robbie and Jeanie the pleasure of a special horse-car ride in one of Mr. Woodward's elegant "Street Palace" cars for women and children only. Each car was luxuriously fitted with upholstered sofas and velvet carpets—all to be enjoyed for the price of only five cents a ride. Mr. Woodward's splendidly kept exhibits of California trees, shrubs, and flowers, which must have appealed to Mrs. Frost, were not nearly so fascinating to her son and daughter as the menagerie, the aquarium, the museum, the hippodrome, the roller-skating rink, and the picnic grounds. As Robbie grew older the menagerie pleased him most of all. It was there that he once conducted a little experiment by using a newly acquired "burning-glass" to tickle the noses and paws of two monkeys begging for peanuts. The playful experiment went well enough until one monkey reached out through the bars, snatched the "burning-glass," retreated to the back of the cage, and buried the mysterious torture-instrument in straw well out of the boy's reach.[6]

Another kind of outing occurred annually for the entire Frost family: the summer conclave of the Caledonia Club of San Francisco, five hundred members strong. Organized for the encouragement, practice, and preservation of the games, customs, and manners of Scotland, the Club scheduled this picnic in a rural area suitable for various kinds of rituals, supplemented with bagpipe music. As soon as Robbie grew old enough to overcome his shyness, he entered into the Caledonia Club footraces with other children his own age, and did well. His athletic father, eager to encourage the boy, bought him a pair of spikeless running slippers and began to coach him on fine points of sprinting and distance-running. After one period of energetic preparation, which consisted of a daily workout along the block on board sidewalks near his home, Robbie attended the next Caledonia Club picnic so thoroughly prepared for his favorite race that he won it and returned home proudly with a cash prize.

Far less satisfactory to the boy were the next two prizes which he won in an entirely different kind of endeavor. His parents occasionally attended masquerade parties, which were enlivened by competitions for the best costumes in various categories. Robbie, invited to join a neighbor in a pantomime representing Youth and Old Age, shared in winning the first prize, a gold-headed cane. At another masquerade party, where he teamed with a lady and wore a shipwreck costume, he again shared in winning a first prize: a pair of gold ear-rings. In these various activities he was at least gaining poise as he gradually overcame his bashful discomfort in the presence of strangers. He was even beginning to enjoy the dramatic aspects of his own performances.[7]

4

WE ALL MUST EAT OUR PECK

Such was life in the Golden Gate:
Gold dusted all we drank and ate,
And I was one of the children told,
'We all must eat our peck of gold.'[1]

THE LAST PHASE of Robert Frost's boyhood in San Francisco began splendidly, when he was six years old; it ended in darkness, when he was eleven. During the vicissitudes of these five years in which he grew so fast, he did his best to cope with experiences that alternately exhilarated and depressed him; experiences which were sometimes as precipitous as those San Francisco streets that climbed steeply up over Nob Hill and plunged as steeply down the other side.

On an important morning in June of 1880, when the fortunes of the Frosts were ascendent, neither the six-year-old Robbie nor his nearly four-year-old sister, Jeanie, could mistake the evidence that something important was about to happen. They watched with wonder as their mother helped their father complete extraordinary preparations for a long journey. It was not even necessary for them to understand what was meant by the often repeated explanation that their father had been elected a member of the California Delegation of Democrats being sent to Cincinnati, Ohio, to help nominate General Winfield Scott Hancock as presidential candidate at the National Democratic Convention. It was enough for the children that they were permitted to admire his new frock coat and top hat; enough that they were going with him, on the ferry, at least as far as the cavernous Oakland train sheds, where they would hear a brass-band send-off given their father and the other members of the delegation.

At that time the Frosts were living in an apartment at 3 Grace Terrace, just off California Street, between Dupont and Stockton. It is probable that they went by cable car to the Ferry Building, which was then a low wooden shed with a plank-paved entrance. Next came all the excitement of the voyage across the great Bay, the ferry inevitably threading its way among fishing boats, three-masted schooners, men-of-war, and pleasure boats, past the looming heights of Goat Island and far beyond it to the slip at the Oakland train sheds. For the children, the most memorable part of this excursion was provided by the color and noise of the cheering crowd, the music of the brass band, and the spectacle of the long train starting to move out of the station. On the rear platform of the last car stood their father, with his companions, waving good-bye and doffing his new top hat.

Having earned this honor through his rabidly energetic work with the Democratic Party in San Francisco, their father had reason to believe that he was well started up the ladder of a distinguished political career. After his return from Cincinnati, he confided that before too many years passed, he hoped to make an even more significant departure from San Francisco—to the capital of the nation as a Democratic Representative or even Senator from the State of California. Many of his friends, including the reliable Henry George (who moved with his family to New York City that summer), felt certain that Mr. Frost's political talents would earn higher and higher offices.

Early in the summer of 1880, before campaigning began on behalf of General Hancock, Robbie's father was given another honorable assignment which involved another General. William Starke Rosecrans, Union hero of the Chattanooga campaign, had been nominated as candidate for the office of Congressional Representative from California. In support of that nomination the journalistic skills of Mr. Frost were requested, by the Party, to write a campaign booklet on the life and accomplishments of Rosecrans. The General himself provided materials directly for Mr. Frost; the pamphlet was skillfully written and quickly published. It enhanced the political standing of the candidate and of the author.[2]

Another stimulus to awe and admiration was accidentally afforded Robbie during the summer of 1880. Committeemen and politically sympathetic friends were frequently brought home by his father, and the serious talk in the living room at Grace Terrace often lasted far into the night. Robbie's bedroom opened directly from the living room, and his door was always left part-way open because he feared the dark. On many such evenings, long after he should have been asleep, he lay listening to strange talk made interesting to him by the interspersed anecdotes of Civil War battles and leaders, including Grant, Hancock, Sherman, and Robert E. Lee, to whom his father always paid special tribute. These were heroes, after one of whom Robbie had been named. But his father was another hero, and the boy dreamed that someday he would make his own life heroic.

During that same summer a family interlude, which was taken with bad grace by Robbie's father, eventually caused the boy to remember: his father was not a perfect hero. Throughout this interlude the Frost children were still too young to understand all the implications of events, but they were old enough to be aware of tension. Again it could have meant little to them if they were told, repeatedly, that they were soon to be visited by their paternal grandparents. Back East, in Lawrence, Massachusetts, Grandfather Frost was retiring from his duties as an overseer in the Pacific Mills, and was planning to celebrate his new freedom by making a leisurely trip with his wife to visit their son in California. Such a prospect brought no pleasure to Robbie's father, whose relations with his parents had been awkward for years. The day of their arrival in California was an exciting event for Robbie, because it afforded him the always delightful adventure of another ferry voyage across the Bay. Not until he and his father reached Oakland did they learn that the train they were expecting to meet had been delayed by snow avalanches in the Sierras. So much the better for the boy, who made the voyage again, with his father, to meet the train when it did arrive. His grandparents were complete strangers to him, in spite of their insistence that he had once visited them in far-away Lawrence. They made the best impression on Robbie when they overcame their own reserve long enough to talk in glowing terms about their visit in Salt Lake City and about all the wonders accomplished there by the Mormons.

Early on the morning after the arrival of his grandparents, Robbie was awakened by the rattle of dishes and silver, as his mother began to set a special breakfast table for the guests. Soon he heard his father insisting, sullenly, that his own breakfast must be served at once, that he must be on his way to work in a few minutes. Robbie's mother protested that on this particular morning her husband should at least wait to have breakfast with his parents. No, he could not wait. So the low-toned argument began, while the boy lay in his bed listening through the slightly opened door. His mother insisted; his father threatened; his mother stood firm. When his father started to leave without eating any breakfast, his mother called the man a child, told him to get over his bad-boy attitude, and warned him to mind his manners. Guiltily eavesdropping on this argument, Robbie was hurt by it and disappointed in his father.

Not long after his grandparents had started back East, a lift was given Robbie's spirit. He was excited when the early campaigning for the fall elections burst into a frenzy of parades, brass bands, and rhetoric. More than ever before Robbie's father honored the boy by sending him on little errands to ward politicians in the neighborhood, and then honored him by letting him ride on a float in a parade. Near election day, he marched with his father in a torchlight procession, and enjoyed the hullabaloo until sparks from the torches fell into his hair. All these adventures brought a new sense of closeness between father and son. They restored Robbie's feeling that his father was, after all, truly a great man.

Another descent into a new kind of darkness occurred as soon as the election results were announced that fall. General Garfield defeated General Hancock in the presidential race, and Robbie suffered most because disappointment transformed his father into a silent and brooding stranger. The boy was hurt by the way this dour man came home from work, night after night, with no word of greeting for anyone; and even more hurt by the way he often sat in silence through the evening meal. Morning after morning, during this period, Robbie watched his father eat breakfast alone, toss off his jigger of whiskey, and depart without even a gesture of farewell to son or wife or daughter. It gradually became apparent that part of the man's discouragement was caused by his debilitating illness, made worse by the amount of energy he had poured into the futile campaign. The sick man did not seem to recover any of his spirit until after the winter passed and the spring came.

A new buoyancy was given to all of the Frosts in the early

summer of 1882, when "Aunt Blanche" proposed that they take a vacation from city life. As long as she lived with the Frost family, her presence furnished a kind of buffer. But in the fall of 1880, nearly four years after her arrival in San Francisco, she had taken a position as teacher in the Home of the Ladies' Protection and Relief Society. Soon afterward she had married a man named Eastman and had moved with her husband to Napa Valley, some fifty miles to the north of San Francisco Bay. Even at that distance she continued her sympathetic attentions by urging that the Frosts bring their children to Napa and spend several weeks there during the summer. "Aunt Blanche" found rooms for Mrs. Frost and Robbie and Jeanie at a ranch near the State Hospital at Napa, where she and her husband were working. Mr. Frost seemed content to be left alone in the city.

For the children, these weeks spent at the ranch of a family named Bragg were enough to open an entirely new world of experience which delighted them. Because the ranch was primarily engaged in supplying milk, vegetables, fruit, eggs, and poultry to the State Hospital, there were perpetual wonders of the farm to be seen and admired. Robbie and Jeanie were permitted to play at helping to feed the horses, the cattle, the chickens; they were even allowed to play at gathering eggs. Under their mother's guidance they also took long walks into the countryside and marveled at the fertile river-valley fields, the vineyard-covered foothills, and the forests on the surrounding mountains. Only once before had the children been given a summer vacation from the city. When Robbie had been five years old, his father had taken the family up into Marin County, to the north of San Francisco, and they had stayed for a short time at a hotel in the valley town of Nicasio, surrounded by mountains and by forests of fir and redwood. Robbie had been too young to remember much about the natural beauty of that region. He had been most impressed by the hotelkeeper's daughter, a girl his own age, who had caught him cheating at croquet and had swiftly punished him by hitting his head with her mallet. No such unpleasantness happened to him at Napa. Instead, his first taste of farming caused him to make a boyish resolve that some day he would own a ranch in Napa Valley.

A far more adventurous summer vacation was planned by Robbie's father the next year, when the boy was nine years old. Several of the journalists who were charter members of the Bohemian Club organized country outings for members and friends who enjoyed roughing it. One of these outings, designed as a convenient retreat from the summer dust of San Francisco, was held by pitching tents on the beach at the edge of the Bay near the village of Sausalito in Marin County. Ferryboats ran regularly from Meiggs Wharf across the northern part of the Bay, past Alcatraz and Angel Island to Sausalito. Club members and their families lived in these tents, near the famous springs which had once been used by early San Franciscans as their best source of drinking water. Each morning the men who were not on vacation took the ferry from Sausalito to San Francisco for their day's work; each evening they returned to the little tent colony. Robbie's mother would never have consented to take her children to this Bohemian Club camp if she had known beforehand what she was going to find. Her husband's cronies amused themselves, evenings, with card-playing, gambling, tippling, and revolver practice—using as targets their empty whiskey bottles thrown out into the Bay. They called their camp the Mentone Club, presumably in mocking reference to similarities between it and the celebrated Mediterranean gambling resort on the Riviera.

For Robbie, these brief days at Sausalito were marred by his father's mania for long-distance swimming. When well, he had been a powerful swimmer, and he was convinced that this form of exercise would help to cure his consumption. Several times, after he returned from San Francisco in the evening, he walked with his son along the beach and around a shoulder of land toward the Golden Gate, until they reached his favorite spot. Robbie, left alone on the shore as guardian of his father's coat and towel and whiskey bottle, would watch the man wade into the Bay to begin his long swim through cold water to an off-shore bell buoy. As the choppy waves began to hide the swimmer from view, Robbie's fears would mount—and would continue to mount until he could finally see his father climbing the metal ladder on the bell buoy. The man would stand there just long enough to catch his breath and then would dive off the swaying buoy into the water to start his long swim toward shore. Again fear would surge over Robbie in wave after wave of apprehension, until he could see his father again. With mingled relief and pride, the boy would run down to the edge of the water, offer the towel, follow his father's labored steps up to dry sand, and watch the man reach for the bottle of whiskey.

Another kind of fear, evoked by a different ocean-water setting, remained memorable to Robbie. Whenever his father chose to celebrate a minor streak of luck in gambling, in politics, or in the stock market, the impetuous man splurged by taking his family to dinner at one of his favorite restaurants. For the children, the best of these was the Cliff House, with its lofty view out over the Pacific. After one particularly cheerful dinner there, the entire Frost family descended the long flight of board steps to the beach for a walk along the shore in the dusk. Robbie, soon absorbed in a solitary game of lashing stone targets with a seaweed whip, unintentionally dropped so far behind the others that they passed out of sight beyond outcroppings of rock and ledge. When at last the boy turned to look for them and realized that he was alone under the cliff, he was frightened. The roar of the waves seemed hostile. The towering wall of rock leaned out and threatened. Dark clouds reached down with crooked hands. Overwhelmed with terror, he ran and kept running until he overtook his parents. Years later, in the poem "Once by the Pacific," he tried to capture the mood of that moment: he endowed with prophecy the menacing images of waves, clouds, and cliff.

A far more subdued sense of fear and wonder was experienced by Robbie whenever his mother revealed her own prophetic and mystical belief in her powers of second sight, through her reading of mysterious bedtime stories. She taught her children to understand that they were always in close rapport with the spiritual world, even when they were least aware of it, that between earth and the heavenly realm of the angels was the realm of fairyland. She loved to tell them fairy stories, and the more fantastic they were, the more powerfully they appealed to Robbie's imagination. He particularly liked to hear about children his own age who established contact with elves. One of his mother's favorite authors was the Scottish writer of fantasies and novels, George Macdonald, whose most famous book was then very popular with young people: *At the Back of the North Wind*. In that story about the boy named Diamond, three fairy tales are interwoven so casually that they are all of a piece with Diamond's real adventures; his worlds of dream and reality are inseparable.

Mrs. Frost's enjoyment of Macdonald may have helped her give a greater reality to her telling or reading of other stories in which human contacts with the supernatural were made to seem natural. In her frequent uses of Bible stories she may have called attention to similarities between them and tales not found in the Bible. Samuel's experience in hearing a voice which called his name in the night was not unrelatable to the experience of the heroic French Maid who was also a child when first she heard prophetic voices.

As Robbie developed his own capacities for second sight and second hearing, he almost scared himself out of his wits. He was still a child in San Francisco when he first began to hear voices. If left alone in a room for some time, he was often simultaneously fascinated and terrified by hearing a voice which spoke to him as clearly as the voice had spoken to Samuel or to Joan of Arc. At such moments, if he were playing on the floor, he would retreat to the protection of the largest chair, and kneel in it with his forehead pressed against the back, his eyes shut, his hands over his ears. But he could not shut out the sounds of the voice, and the harder he pressed his hands over his ears the clearer and louder the voice came. Sometimes he could hear whole sentences. At other times the words were so indistinct that he understood only such meanings as were conveyed through the tones of the voice. At still other times he clearly heard the voice repeating something he himself had said a few minutes earlier, repeating and yet endowing his own words with tones so different from his that the effect seemed to be one of mockery. When he told his mother about these perplexing experiences, she seemed to understand them better than he did. Sympathetically, she hinted that he shared with her the mystical powers of second hearing and second sight. But she warned him not to tell others about these experiences. Anyone else might misunderstand.

His mother helped him to feel that the different voices he heard when he was awake were somehow related to voices he heard in his dreams. She always endowed her own dreams with meanings which related the worlds of the seen and the unseen. One of her dreamlike stories may have been inspired more strongly by Swedenborg's somewhat Neo-Platonic doctrine of correspondences than by Macdonald's way of blending these two worlds. This particular story was finally written out by Mrs. Frost and published in a booklet entitled *The Land of Crystal; or, Christmas Day with the Fairies*.[3] Although the story may have attracted only slight attention when printed, it is valuable as a reflection of how Mrs. Frost used stories as parables for the moral education of her children.

In *The Land of Crystal* there are two fairy sisters whose bodies were made of a crystalline substance so transparent that anyone could see into their hearts. One sister, Merrilie, was a good girl whose heart "was in the form of a pure white dove, and from it to every part of her seemed to flow a wonderful light, which in her face was dazzling." The other sister, Sombreena, was a naughty girl, and when she grew angry one could see "at her heart the form of a small tiger of fiery color, from which waves of fire flowered, making her face flame-like and her eyes to flash sparks of fire." Merrilie, trying to help Sombreena, warned that if the "terrible tiger" were permitted to grow larger and wilder, day by day, it would become a fearfully dangerous beast which could finally carry Sombreena into the realms of utter darkness. There she would be imprisoned forever with wild animals. Sombreena ignored these warnings and thus she brought on herself the foreseen punishment. She was completely changed into a tiger and, in that form, she was cast out to live in darkness among wolves, hyenas, and vipers. She might have stayed there forever if the noble Prince or Redeemer, who loved Merrilie, had not offered to make a great sacrifice in order to save the lost Sombreena. He did save her, and she profited from the lesson she had learned through her terrible mistake.[4]

If Mrs. Frost told her children this story at bedtime, she must have been more concerned with inculcating moral precepts than with encouraging sweet dreams. Perhaps she never considered the possibility that her parable could have a seriously injurious effect on the sensitive consciousness of these two imaginative children, easily frightened by darkness alone.

The storytelling of Robbie's mother may have inspired him to try his hand at the only story he wrote out during his San Francisco boyhood. The details of it had all come to him in one of his own dreams. Alone, after running away from home and after having become lost in the mountains, he had followed a scarcely visible trail which led him through a cleft between two mountaintop cliffs. The trail led him down, down, down into a beautiful green valley, where he was welcomed and honored as a hero by a tribe of Indians who were the only inhabitants of the secret valley. The Indians themselves had escaped from their enemies by retreating through the narrow pass into this valley, where life was always serene. Occasionally their braves made sorties back through the secret pass in order to make surprise attacks against their enemies. But these braves always returned victoriously to their happy valley. This much of the dream-story Robbie wrote out as his first narrative composition. Later, on nights when he was sent to bed while still suffering from the hurts of the day, he consolingly told the story to himself, over and over, adding to it new episodes which he never wrote out.[5]

Some of his worst hurts, suffered during the vicissitudes of his last years in San Francisco, occurred after the Frost family made the last of many moves, this time from the Abbotsford Hotel to an apartment on the ground floor of a white clapboard house, 1404 Leavenworth Street, just around the corner (and down the hill) from Washington Street, and only a short distance from the house where he had been born. From this relatively unfashionable district on the back side of Nob Hill, the boy frequently walked with his mother and sister up Leavenworth Street to the high shoulder of the hill and on down the southern slope to where the truly fashionable "nobs" and nabobs had built or were building their spectacular mansions of wood, brick, stone, and even marble. While the Frosts were moving to Leavenworth Street, the Irish upstart millionaire, James Clair Flood, was building his brownstone palace on California Street between Mason and Taylor, and was surrounding it with a handwrought brass fence. Relatively near, also on Nob Hill, were the palaces of Leland Stanford, Mark Hopkins, James G. Fair, D. D. Colton, Charles Crocker, and others. Between these pretentious abodes and the Frost apartment stood a natural barrier. It was an undeveloped block-square mound of rock, dirt, and clay—the true "knob" or height-of-land for this particular hill. This geological remnant was too precipitous for any kind of building other than the forlorn shacks which squatters had erected near the very top. Into the sides of this knob had been cut the straight lines of the four streets which encroached as much as they could, streets which required retaining walls of varying heights to keep the mound in its place. Washington Street cut into it on the north, Leavenworth on the west, Clay on the south, and Jones on the east. The scrub brush on the steep flanks of this block-square wasteland provided excellent hiding places for youngsters in the neighborhood. They formed little gangs and staked out their claims to different parts of the mound, then drove off any intruders who lacked proper membership.

For at least two years after the Frost family moved to Leavenworth Street, Robbie was neither old enough nor bold enough to mingle with these tough youngsters who made a playground out of the hilltop. But by the time he was ten years old he had acquired enough experience, while playing on the streets in his neighborhood, to become envious of the boys his own age who had been granted membership in the Washington Street gang. As he grew stronger, and wise enough to understand the brutal customs of these local warriors, he set his heart on being accepted by them—at any price. Finally he mustered courage enough to climb up the mound to ask if he could join the gang. The leader was a tough and over-grown teenager named Seth Balsa, who studied Robbie with suspicion before asking if he knew how to fight. The very sound of the word made Robbie wince, but he managed to say yes. All right, said Balsa, could he lick that kid over there? He pointed to Percy MacPartland, son of the Leavenworth Street grocer. Percy was not quite so big as Robbie, who concealed his fright by answering boastfully that he could lick two boys the size of Percy. Ironically, Balsa tried to be obliging. He glanced at his cohorts scattered along the side of the claybank and called to another boy who was no bigger than Percy. The challenge was explained, the two opponents closed in on Robbie, and he was given his chance to fight them both at once.

Merely as a spectator of street fights, Robbie had already learned that the game of fisticuffs in San Francisco was a free-for-all, a catch-as-catch-can with no holds barred. At a safe distance from these fights, he had even come to admire the efficiency of wrapping one arm around the neck of an opponent, holding the head in a convenient position, and punching at the eyes with the free fist. Desperately now he dove at Percy and tried to employ this familiar strategy. He did succeed in getting his right arm around Percy's neck and in throwing one punch; but he very quickly found that he needed his left hand for warding off the blows aimed at his own face by Percy's partner, who came dancing in and clawing at Robbie's cheek. The cheering and jeering watchers wanted to see blood, and they were soon satisfied. In no time all three fighters were on the ground, rolling gradually down toward the retaining wall as they punched, kicked, and scratched. It was no contest. By the time Seth Balsa had seen enough and had stepped in to separate the warriors, one of Percy's eyes was well marked; but Robbie's nose was bleeding, both of his cheeks were bloody, and his lower lip was badly split. Nevertheless, the Washington Street gang had been impressed by Robbie's courage, and Balsa welcomed him into full membership before sending him home to get his face patched up.

Painfully hurt, and on the verge of tears, Rob jumped down from the Washington Street retaining wall and started home, filled with misery and elation. He had not expected that he would have to pay such a price and take such a beating. But before he reached 1404 Leavenworth Street he began telling himself that this was the most important day in his life so far. His courage had conquered his cowardice. Suddenly he had grown up. Some kind of transformation had occurred through this baptism of blood, and he was ready to serve his leader, Seth Balsa, in whatever battles lay ahead.

Robbie soon discovered that what actually lay ahead amounted to a special kind of education under the tutelage of Balsa. It had less to do with fighting than with the finer points of acquiring and handling portable property. Many of these daring hill-children coasted recklessly down any negotiable street in little four-wheel wagons. The wear on wheels was naturally severe, and Seth Balsa's wagon needed a new pair. He knew where a pair could be found, in the cellar of a house on Leavenworth Street, but the cellar window was too small for Balsa to enter, and he flatteringly sought Robbie's help. Eager to demonstrate his courage in another way, Robbie went with Balsa by twilight to the treasure house. Together they crawled in under the porch and then Robbie watched with admiration as Balsa quietly jimmied the narrow window. Robbie eased himself in through the small opening, feet first. With matches provided by Balsa, he found the pair of wheels and passed them out. It was too easy, and just to show his courage Robbie looked around for more plunder. Through the window he presented several offerings—including a boxed croquet set—until Balsa finally drew the line by rejecting Christmas tree ornaments. A few days later, when Balsa's cart appeared on the street again with all four wheels newly painted, no questions were asked. The crime had been perfectly executed and Robbie was proud of the part he had played in it.

Only once, after that, was Robbie asked to play cat's-paw for Balsa in another act of thievery: the stealing of a small pig from a pen near the San Francisco slaughterhouse. The pig was easily caught and almost as easily disposed of, for a reasonable price, in Chinatown. Robbie's share of the proceeds was less than half, but again he gloried in this new demonstration of his prowess.

Another brief sequence of ups and downs occurred when the ten-year-old Robbie gained the reluctant permission of his parents to sell newspapers on the streets of San Francisco. There were several paper boys in his gang and one of them guided him through the initial procedures. He learned which papers sold best, how to get them, where to find likely customers, what tone to use in shouting the most attractive headlines, and how to make the financial accounting. He had looked forward to this new adventure, and as long as the novelty of it lasted he enjoyed the grown-up feeling of being on his own among the pedestrians in downtown San Francisco. But the hours were long, the competition stiff, and the profits disappointing. A few days of it were enough to discourage him, and he simply quit.

While still a paperboy, reveling in his ability to make his way back and forth between his hillside home and the business section of San Francisco, Robbie discovered the need for ingenuity in learning to confront unexpected dangers. He was making his way downtown to pick up a supply of papers one afternoon, when he very boldly risked a short cut through streets he usually avoided because the boys in that neighborhood carried on sporadic warfare with the Washington Street gang; and they knew Robbie as one of their enemies. He had almost completed his passage through this hostile territory when four boys recognized him and gave chase. Counting on his ability to outrun his pursuers, he was not immediately frightened. Once, in an endurance race, he had beaten Percy MacPartland to the finish line after running twenty times around the block which contained the Nob Hill claybank. But now his pursuers very quickly showed that they had longer legs. As they began to gain on him, Robbie realized the need for emergency tactics. Inspired by desperation, he dodged off the board sidewalk, fled up the steps of the nearest house, opened the door, entered, closed the door quietly, and slid the bolt lock into place. Frightened and panting, he heard the pack stop at the foot of the steps and he cringed as one of them shouted, "That's not where he lives." Looking over his shoulder, he half expected to face the indignant owner and to be tossed out to the wolves. Behind him was an empty hall and, beyond it, an empty living room. Footsteps upstairs seemed to approach a window, as though to investigate the racket, but the footsteps did not descend. Minute after minute passed and the puzzled voices on the other side of the door gradually faded away. When it seemed safe, Robbie unlocked the door, opened it, stepped out, closed it softly, and tiptoed down to the sidewalk. His enemies had disappeared, and he went on downtown without any further trouble. On many occasions thereafter, when he passed the house which had provided him haven, he looked up at it appreciatively and wondered who lived there.

Beginning to think of himself as lucky, he felt as though a great streak of luck occurred in the summer of 1884. Again free from school, through default, he was available to serve as his father's errand boy and messenger during an important political campaign. The Democrats throughout the nation had nominated Grover Cleveland for President; the Democrats in San Francisco had nominated William Prescott Frost, Jr., for the local and important office of City Tax Collector. As Robbie became more useful to his father, the boy acquired a new sense of his own importance. Whenever messages had to be taken down to City Hall for "Blind Boss" Chris Buckley, Robbie lingered to watch the pretty stenographers copying political propaganda. If handbills needed distribution to a street corner crowd, prior to one of his father's impromptu soapbox speeches, the boy proudly managed that part of the exercise. Staying to listen, he did wish that his father could be more colorful and appealing in his remarks. The cold presentation of facts, the dry reticence, the complete lack of playfulness or wit or humor disappointed Robbie. He tried to excuse his father by noticing new signs of illness. There was no question but that the chronic ailment had grown worse, and even his father seemed to acknowledge it in a strange way. In his campaigning, whenever he passed near the slaughterhouse, he would stop just long enough to buy and drink a cup of warm blood, while Robbie, watching, would fight against nausea. He was happier when his father took him into saloons with board ceilings, where the boy could display skill in tacking small posters to the ceilings by pressing a tack through the middle of the card and then tossing it upward, with a silver dollar flat beneath the tack to serve as a flying hammer. If his father lingered in any saloon for a drink, Robbie was always permitted to make samplings from the free-lunch counter and to study the strange variety of such fare. His participation in all of these activities gave him an awareness that he had grown up a great deal since the last presidential election. He had been six years old then; now he was ten.

As the tempo of this campaign built up to the frenzied phase which brought out the brass bands with the political chowder-and-marching societies, the parades with floats by day and the processions with torchlights by night, the boy entered into these activities with far more zest, far more energy, and far more knowledge than he had formerly displayed. But it was his new knowledge which made him worry more and more about his father's chances for political success. There was, of course, the backing and the power of well-oiled Democratic Party machinery, which brazenly fought corruption with corruption. More than once Robbie heard his father say that the Democrats were justified in stuffing ballot boxes with illegal votes; that the Republicans were so notoriously dishonest that to throw the rascals out of power was an end which justified any means.

On the day of reckoning, when all the Democratic votes were counted, not quite enough of them had been cast to elect William Prescott Frost, Jr., as Tax Collector for the City of San Francisco. Even the triumphant election of Grover Cleveland could not assuage the sick man's bitter personal disappointment. For days after his defeat, he did not come home.

At last he appeared at 1404 Leavenworth Street in a drunken rage, waving at his wife a ballot which had been cast against him by (he said) the minister of the First Church of the New Jerusalem, the Reverend John Doughty. He reminded his wife of her assurance that Doughty had promised to vote for Frost;

he now told her that she could see with her own eyes (if she believed the offered evidence) that Doughty was exactly the hypocrite and liar her husband had long accused him of being. Unconvinced, Robbie's mother did her best to soothe and placate the broken man. It was far too late for that. So sure had he been of his approaching political success that in June of 1884 he had resigned from his position as City Editor of the *Post;* after the election, the *Post* could find no work for him. Late in 1884 he was hired by another San Francisco newspaper, *The Daily Report,* but he was never well enough to carry out his duties with any consistency there. What hurt Robbie most during these gloomy months, which dragged through fall and winter and spring, was the pathetic sight of his father's apparently complete surrender to his irrevocable defeat. Whether it was illness or whiskey that made the man's eyes seem glazed, the boy could not be sure.

Perhaps his father realized how near the end might be. It was foreshadowed with frightening vividness for his children one afternoon in May of 1885, as they were playing on that part of the steep claybank which overlooked the corner of Leavenworth and Clay streets. They saw their father being helped off the cable car; they saw the blood-stained handkerchief he held to his mouth; they saw a friend put an arm about him to help him walk the short distance down Leavenworth Street to their home. After a doctor had been called, after whispered conversations and frightening silences even the children knew what to expect. They were kept out of the sick man's room; but during that same evening he called for Robbie. The boy went in and sat on the bed, too frightened to understand very much of the pale man's whispered admonitions. Afterward, he could remember only one stern command: Never, never should Robbie hang around street corners in San Francisco after dark.

The next morning the same hushed atmosphere shrouded the Frost home. The children were given their breakfasts, sent out of the house to play, and told that they must be very quiet because their father was terribly ill. For the next few hours they tried to keep busy, and finally joined other children playing at the edge of the familiar claybank. Toward noon one of the neighbor's boys said to them, bluntly, "There's crepe on your door."

Their father's last request, before he died, was that his

body be taken back to New England for burial, back to the New England he had so often said he hated. The funeral was held in the First Church of the New Jerusalem and the service was conducted by the Reverend John Doughty, whom the dead man had detested. Then it was necessary to consider the size of the estate he had left, before any plans could be made for taking him back to New England. There had been a $20,000 insurance policy, but it had lapsed because he had failed to make his payments. A bank account contained some money; but after the widow had settled the funeral expenses and had sold the furniture in the rooms at 1404 Leavenworth Street, she had only eight dollars in cash. The dead man's parents forwarded enough money to defray the cost of travel; the widow and her children said good-bye to friends. They accompanied the coffin across the Bay, by ferry to Oakland, saw the coffin placed in the baggage car of their train, and started East for another funeral service and the interment.

5

THE LOVELY SHALL BE CHOOSERS

Give her a child at either knee . . .
To tell once and once only, for them never to forget,
How once she walked in brightness,
And make them see it in the winter firelight.[1]

FOR THE WIDOW dressed in black and accompanied by her
two children as she made the ritualistic pilgrimage with the
coffin from California to Massachusetts, the future threatened
to be more frightening than even the past had been. Nine
years earlier she had cast herself and her children on the
mercy, such as it was, of her husband's parents—and they
had seemed to reproach her with their silence. Now she
dreaded the likelihood that they might somehow blame her
for the wasted life, the failure, the death of their only son.

She may have tried to console herself with the thought that
after she reached her destination with the coffin, and after the
ordeal of the interment ceremonies, she need not stay long in
New England. But where could she go from there? She had
numerous Moodie relatives in Ohio and she must have considered the possibility of returning from Lawrence to Columbus, perhaps to earn a living for herself and her children by
teaching school there again. For obscure reasons of pride or
of estrangement she did not consider that prospect a good
one. More attractive to her was the hope that she might return to San Francisco, where she had left so many friends
in the Society of the New Jerusalem and which her children
thought of as their home. But where could she find the money
she would need for the expenses of the return trip? And could
she earn an adequate living for her family there?

Many times during the long journey from California to
Massachusetts, and quite impulsively, she must have sought
the comfort of hoping that God would provide. Here again,

as she repeatedly told her son in later years, her griefs and worries were complicated by her feeling that God had already provided. In spite of her devout and mystical religious faith, she tortured herself with the fear that she had indeed been responsible for what had happened, for all that she had brought on herself and on her children. Her immediate predicament seemed to reflect divine punishment. If these fears were based on spiritual truth, she thought, it was her duty to bear the trials with submission.

Her greatest worries must have been for her children and for what would happen to them. Jeanie, from the time she had been three years old, had suffered from ailments which the doctors in San Francisco had not satisfactorily diagnosed or alleviated. No mother could have lavished more love on her child than she had given Jeanie, and yet it seemed as though that love had made the girl too largely dependent. "Aunt Blanche," while living with the Frosts, had been devoted to Jeanie and had tried to teach the child self-sufficiency. Instead, Jeanie had merely become dependent on "Aunt Blanche," and had suffered a nervous disorder when "Aunt Blanche" moved to Napa Valley. The child suffered from prolonged periods of crying and hysteria; the doctor had even feared that Jeanie might be epileptic. Solicitously "Aunt Blanche" had made arrangements for Jeanie and Robbie to spend six weeks with her in Napa Valley without their mother during the summer of 1884, in the hope that the visit might be especially beneficial to Jeanie. Instead, the child had cried for her mother in San Francisco. Intermittently, thereafter, Jeanie had refused to play with other children, had refused to go to school, had refused to leave the house, had refused to leave her own room. But she was a bright child and had learned early to read and write. The older she grew, the more content she seemed with books provided by her mother. Her father's irregular attentions had apparently made Jeanie feel that he disliked her. Robbie's response to all of Jeanie's tears and crying was largely impatience. Whatever the causes, her sufferings were so pathetically genuine that they evoked her mother's heartfelt grief.

Robbie had been another kind of care and worry in his early years; but the older he grew, the stronger and healthier he seemed to become. His extreme sensitivities and illnesses, during and after his infancy, had indeed caused his mother to pamper him. But she must have felt that if she had been mistaken in permitting him to stay out of school most of the time, her own supervision of his studies had enabled her to inculcate some kinds of awareness which he might not otherwise have acquired. Although he had strongly resisted her attempts to develop his ability to read, he had at least listened with eagerness whenever his mother had read him stories and poems. She had consciously cultivated his interest in heroic men and actions; she knew he was proud that he had been named after a soldier-hero. She also knew that her own idealization of courage and daring had played a large part in helping the boy overcome his deeply ingrained fears. His mother was certain that her own religious idealism and perfectionism had taken root in Robbie. She was the one who liked to remind him, in later years, of the painstaking way in which he had tried to form his letters in his copybook—and of the explosive fury (so much like his father's) with which he would tear out and destroy copybook pages he had spoiled. Deeply proud of him, and constantly reassuring him that she expected him to make a name for himself someday, she had even taken the risk of telling the boy that with his father's death Robbie was now the man of the family, the one on whom she and Jeanie must lean more and more.

Throughout the tedious journey from California to Massachusetts, and for years thereafter, Mrs. Frost did her best to make the children remember and revere all of the fine traits in their father. She told them his story in ways which enabled her to represent him as a brave and noble man whose great gifts and great promise had been cut off, tragically, by consumption at the untimely age of thirty-four. She reminded them that they were taking his body back to his own home for burial, because he had asked them to do so. And she also reminded them that they had been in that home before, that they could at least remember their loving grandparents as visitors in California.

In spite of their mother's valiant optimism, the two children did not look forward to this New England visit. They could see that the long train ride was indeed an adventure in geography, as their mother kept assuring them; but the more they saw of the United States from the train windows, the more convinced they became that the most beautiful parts of it were those they had grown to love in California: the mountain-surrounded fields and vineyards of Napa Valley, the little town of Nicasio tucked away in a smaller valley and more dramatically surrounded with mountain peaks; the forest-backed harbor and beach at Sausalito, the great Bay of San Francisco, the memorable and panoramic views from Telegraph Hill, Russian Hill, Nob Hill, and all the colorful sights and sounds of streets they loved in San Francisco. What had they seen from the train windows that could compare with those memories? By the time Robbie and Jeanie had progressed with their latest geography lesson far enough to be told that they were now in New England, that this drab city was Boston—the capital of Massachusetts and said by some to be "the hub of the universe"—Robbie found a way to express his homesickness. He held up a bright silver coin for his younger sister to admire, pointed at it proudly, and called it "San Francisco!" Then he held up a dirty copper penny—a coin rarely seen at that time in San Francisco—pointed at it with disgust, and called it "Boston!" Years later, remembering his homesickness and his initial distaste for New England as seen under those circumstances, he said, "At first I disliked the Yankees. They were cold. They seemed narrow to me. I could not get used to them."[2]

After the California Frosts reached Lawrence and suffered through the second funeral sermon and ritual at the Bellevue Cemetery, they lingered as uncomfortable guests of the bereaved parents, while the widow sought advice on what she could do to earn a living. The suggestions made to her were few and even discouraging. Robbie's responses from the start of this visit were hostile. His grandfather seemed to be a stiff and prim old gentleman who hid all facial expressions behind a neatly trimmed white beard and silver-rimmed spectacles. His home at 370 Haverhill Street, between Broadway and Franklin—a very respectable part of the city—seemed in the same character. It was a severe white-painted three-story clapboard house, disproportionately narrow and tall. Robbie's grandmother dramatized another kind of figurativeness, at least for the boy. Her stern and unsmiling face was accentuated by a peculiar nervous disorder which made her head twitch sideways at frequent intervals, as though she were continually saying No, No, No to everything. Proud of her reputation as an early leader in the local suffragette movement, she quite frankly boasted that she had protested so vigorously against the unfair manner in which men enslaved their wives that she had converted her husband. Throughout their marriage he had shared with her the menial tasks of getting meals, washing dishes, making beds, and cleaning house. At her request he often wore an apron around the kitchen.

For years this odd pair had lived on the first floor of their home on Haverhill Street. Although they were financially comfortable they had thriftily rented the second-floor rooms. The apartment on the second floor happened to be vacant when the California Frosts arrived; but, of course, it was possible that someone might soon want to rent the rooms. So the three poor relations were given the two small rooms under the sloping gable roof on the third floor—the same rooms they had occupied, briefly, nine years earlier.

Both Robbie and Jeanie resented the rigorous discipline of daily routine and cringed before the watchful eyes of their grandfather. He scolded them when they tried to play on his neatly tended lawn. He scolded them whenever they approached the trim flower beds. He scolded them when they touched anything without his permission.[3]

The children also disliked their grandmother's precise demands that they rise early for breakfast, that they appear promptly at mealtime, that they wash their hands before sitting down at the table, and that they should never wipe their half-washed faces on her snow-white towels. She nagged at them for tracking mud into her house on unwiped feet. She nagged when they left screen doors half-closed against flies. All of this scolding was new to Robbie and Jeanie, who could scarcely remember any middle ground between their mother's extraordinary leniency and their late father's irate thrashings.

On rainy days the children were allowed to play in their grandfather's woodshed, which occupied an ell of the house beyond the kitchen. They always felt that this mere woodshed was cherished by their grandfather as a precious museum. Along one wall of it he kept his garden tools in unalterable order. Along another wall stood a workbench, and above it an array of carpenter's tools which they were not allowed to touch. On one side of the bench the old man had built a cabinet containing several tiers of drawers. The lower ones were large and crammed with gleanings salvaged against future needs: neatly folded newspapers by the hundreds, neat stacks of wrapping paper and cardboard, neatly folded paper bags. In the upper tiers the sizes of the drawers diminished in orderly progression until the top ones (at eye-level for Robbie) were no bigger than cigar boxes. When they dared to peek into those little drawers, surreptitiously, the children were amazed to find one drawer divided into compartments for secondhand nails, bent and rusty, but all arranged according to size; to find another drawer filled with sheets of tinfoil, carefully smoothed out; another drawer filled with little balls of string. They told their mother of these discoveries, and she explained that his frugal manner had enabled their grandfather to prosper until he had managed to retire at sixty with enough money in his bank account to make the future safe for him—if he continued his habits. The children were not favorably impressed.

Robbie soon made the added complaint that his grandfather was cruel. As evidence, the boy told of watching the old man hide behind a corner of the house, horsewhip in hand, waiting for a bold youngster who kept slipping into the yard, unasked, to pick a few flowers. Robbie had indignantly watched his grandfather creep up on the intruder and lash the child's bare legs with the horsewhip. According to Robbie, another kind of cruelty occurred a few days later. Given some firecrackers by his Great Uncle Elihu Colcord, a brother of Robbie's Grandmother Frost, Robbie had well understood the donor's instructions that these treasures should be put away until the Fourth of July. But the boy had to set off just one to see how it worked. His well-satisfied ears had not stopped ringing before he felt rather than saw a presence that disturbed him. He turned to find his grandfather staring down from his ice-cold gray-blue eyes—so much like Robbie's own eyes, and so much like those of Robbie's dead father. No word came from the old man's twitching lips; but the reproach in those eyes was cruel, said Robbie.

It was part of the routine, in this rigorous atmosphere, to set Sunday aside as truly a day of rest in which no frivolous activities were permitted even in the conduct of children. The entire household paraded solemnly to the Universalist Church for morning and evening services. The children were required to remain for the morning sermon and were expected to gain some edification from it. There was no Swedenborgian Church in Lawrence, and Mrs. Frost seemed to feel that she had no choice other than to conform. From later evidence it is possible that the eleven-year-old Robbie was indeed old enough to acquire more edification from this exposure to Universalism than he cared to admit; he later built into his heterodox and home-made religious beliefs the very central Universalist notion that although there is the certainty of just retribution and punishment for all sinfulness, God's ultimate purpose is to save every individual from the tortures of hell-fire.

The mounting tensions between the children and their grandparents forced the penniless widow to make plans for leaving. She had hoped that Uncle Elihu Colcord might help her with an application she had already made for a teaching position in Lawrence, that she might at least stay where she was until she found work in the fall. Instead, Colcord made another suggestion. Perhaps she would like to take her children to New Hampshire for a visit with her late husband's uncle and aunt, Benjamin S. Messer and Sarah Frost Messer, brother-in-law and another sister of William Prescott Frost. The invitation had actually been extended by the Messers, who had a small farm in the town of Amherst, New Hampshire, some forty miles northwest of Lawrence. In summer there was always need for extra hands on the Messer farm. The berry-picking season had begun and the Messers supplemented their meager farming profits by gathering wild blueberries and raspberries, which they sold to storekeepers in the neighboring town of Milford. If the Frost children would like to pick berries they could earn a little money that way, and their mother could help with canning fruit and vegetables in glass jars. The invitation was accepted somewhat reluctantly; at least it offered escape from the awkward situation in Lawrence.

For the poor relations from California this move to Amherst, New Hampshire, provided the first glimpse of the rural North-of-Boston region as it extended into southeastern New Hampshire. With a sense of relief, they found the atmosphere of the Messer farm decidedly more congenial than they had expected. Ben Messer, or "Uncle Messer" as the Frost children somehow came to call him, was a genial and outgoing man whose considerateness made the transition less awkward. His wife, worn by her endless routine of daily chores, still managed to preserve a cheerful and kindly disposition. The warmth of these two strangers appealed strongly to the forlorn trio from California. There was only one other person living at the farm, an invalid son whose name and story conveyed sad reminders:

William Prescott Messer, called Will, had shown promise and had gone away from home to make a good start in business; but he had developed consumption and had come back home as an invalid.

In spite of the strangeness and loneliness of their new surroundings—so strikingly different from the only other farm they had ever known, the Bragg ranch in Napa Valley —Robbie and his sister found life on this New Hampshire hillside very pleasant after so many long weeks of being cooped up with their grandparents. They liked the new game of prowling through homely meadows and thickets in search of low- and high-bush blueberries. Even more, they liked the ride to Milford in the wagon with Uncle Messer, the three of them perched on the wagon seat with crates of blueberries stacked behind them. The four-mile journey over and back gave them close glimpses of midsummer landscapes entirely new to them: wine-glass elms towering alongside the winding dirt roads; the crooked stone walls enclosing irregular patches of hillside and meadowland in the Souhegan River valley; occasional glimpses of small farms and sets of buildings sprawled out on rises of ground or tucked in under clumps of maple trees, with apple orchards and grain fields spreading briefly; the occasional small herds of cows in pastures rock-strewn, juniper-studded, and hemmed in by woodlots of beech, birch, pine, and spruce.

On these rides Uncle Messer seemed to unlimber with the sandy jolting of the wagon wheels, as the slow horse plodded along. Whenever a new set of buildings came into view he liked to answer questions about his neighbors, and he seemed to enjoy educating these city children in country lore. It was natural for him to take pride in telling stories of the region and of famous people associated with it. Horace Greeley had been born and brought up in Amherst. Daniel Webster had argued one of his first law cases here. But he found that the Frost children showed more interest in places than in names: in the wild and rocky gorge locally known as Purgatory Falls, where the devil himself had once made his home in a cave, as could be proved by the footprint he had left in a ledge near the best pothole. No, the devil was not there now; he had been driven out by those Yankees whom he had tried to lure from Amherst with the promise of a special baked bean supper. The Frost children were fascinated and asked for more details.

They knew little or nothing about either Horace Greeley or Daniel Webster; but with their mother's help they were quite well-informed about the devil.

As midsummer wore into early fall, Mrs. Frost tried once again to secure a teaching position, this time in one of the local district schools. There were no vacancies and yet she was easily persuaded by the hospitable Messers to stay on at the farm so that she might send her children to the nearest schoolhouse—all eight grades in one room. Robbie had scarcely begun school before he complained that he could not get along with his teacher, and Jeanie soon joined him in finding fault. Perhaps it would be better, their mother decided, if they went back to the city of Lawrence where the schools might be more to their liking and where she might find some kind of steady employment.

Back they went, and this time the poor relatives were taken into the home of Uncle Elihu Colcord and Aunt Lucy Frost Colcord. More sophisticated and affluent than the Haverhill Street Frosts, the Colcords seemed to accept their obligations with scarcely more grace. Mrs. Frost did manage to borrow some money from the Colcords so that she could rent two shabbily furnished rooms on the second floor of an apartment house on lower Broadway and could move there with her children. The arrangements made for their schooling required examinations to determine the grade in which each child should be entered. To Robbie's consternation he learned that while his younger sister seemed qualified for work in the fourth grade, he would have to start in the third. Vainly he protested that the examination in geography had been his undoing and that it had been outrageously unfair. Why should he be expected to know where the Merrimack River had its source? Or where the Piscataqua River flowed into the Atlantic Ocean? Didn't they know he was a Californian? Why didn't they ask him about the Sacramento River? Or the San Joachim? Or about the location of the Golden Gate? His mother brought him around to a grudging acceptance of his plight, and he did spend the rest of the fall term with the third graders, in spite of his repeated complaints against the indignity of being herded in with eight-year-old "babies."

For these Californians, their first New England winter seemed so unbearably cold that they surprised their landlady by insisting that small stoves be installed in both rooms. But no amount of discomfort could dim for the children the wonder and excitement of witnessing their first real snowstorm. Only once before had they seen snow falling. Big wet flakes of it had completely covered the streets of San Francisco one Sunday morning, and even the men had stayed away from church services, first to enjoy the oddity of snowball fights and then to play at rolling great masses of the stuff into balls large enough to block the passage of cable cars. New England snow was different, the Frost children found, and they reveled in it. If the winter temperature dropped too low for games outside, Robbie amused his sister by conducting scientific experiments of his own devising. On one occasion he borrowed a well-worn thimble from his mother, filled it with water, put it out on the window sill, and watched with Jeanie the slow formation of ice crystals. The next morning, when he recovered the thimble from the sill and tapped out the bulging mold of ice, he placed it on the lid of a stove and watched with delight as it danced around the lid on its own melting. Thus in their loneliness they made their own amusements.

Into that loneliness came a beloved friend of San Francisco days to visit with them briefly. He was Henry George, the massive giant with his full black beard and bald head, whose letter of condolence answered by Mrs. Frost had enabled him to discover that the widow was living in Lawrence with her children. When a lecture tour brought him to New England from New York City, he went out of his way to pay his respects. Although the publication of *Progress and Poverty* had increased his reputation, he continued to suffer disappointment in his ambitious political career. He was planning to run for office again, he said, this time as candidate for Mayor of New York City on a reform ticket. If he could break the grip of Tammany Hall, he might be in a position to effect social changes which could attract the attention of the entire country. So he talked and hoped and dreamed. Before he left Lawrence, he took the widow and her two children to dinner with him at his hotel and, in parting, gave each of the children a tiny gold piece in memory of the days they had spent in San Francisco. To Mrs. Frost, this considerate gesture was deeply moving, even though it heightened the proud woman's awareness of her poverty. Living on borrowed money and already in arrears on payment of rent, she could not bear the thought of depending on charity.

6

AMONG THE HUMBLEST

Make her among the humblest even
Seem to them less than they are.
Hopeless of being known for what she has been,
Failing of being loved for what she is . . .[1]

THE MANY ATTEMPTS of Isabelle Moodie Frost to get a
teaching position brought her something before the end of the
first winter in New England. Without the help of either the
Colcords or the Frosts, she learned of a sudden vacancy and
was asked to fill it in a district school in the village of Salem,
only ten miles northwest of Lawrence and not far beyond the
state boundary line in New Hampshire. She made the move
early in 1886.

Back in colonial days, the original townships of both Salem
and Lawrence had been parts of a single plantation known as
Pentucket. It was a segment of land covering about eighty
square miles in the fertile Merrimack River valley. New
settlers, developing scattered communities within this plantation, had gradually established Lawrence and Methuen and
Haverhill in what became the State of Massachusetts, and had
also established Salem and neighboring Derry in what became
the State of New Hampshire. While Lawrence gradually developed into a flourishing mill city, which used water power
from the Merrimack River, Salem and Derry remained rural
villages in areas devoted to farming. The railroad built between
Lawrence and the New Hampshire cities of Manchester and
Concord had by-passed Salem Village by about two miles, with
the result that a new community in the township of Salem had
quickly grown up at Salem Depot. It was to this relatively new
community that Mrs. Frost brought her children, taking rooms
initially at Woodbury's Board and Lodging House just across
the tracks from the depot. The little cluster of buildings in-

cluded a general store, not more than twenty dwellings, two small shoe factories, a grain mill, a livery stable, two churches, and Salem District School Number Six. Scattered outward from this new village lay the typical small farms of southeastern New Hampshire. The only natural splendor of the immediate vicinity was provided by an unspoiled body of water, two miles in length, known as Canobie Lake, lying to the northwest of the village and nestling within groves of ancient pines.

To Robbie and Jeanie, still homesick for San Francisco, the rural atmosphere of Salem Depot was as strange and as difficult to understand as Grandfather Frost's home in Lawrence or as Uncle Messer's little farm, which lay five townships to the west of Salem. It was fortunate for them that the jovial and bearded proprietor of their boarding house was a fatherly man who liked children. He showed exceptional deference to the new schoolma'am, whose proud manner and diction contrasted very favorably with the homespun behavior and style of so many local teachers. Although the Colcords and Frosts in Lawrence seemed to hold the widow's teaching potential in low regard, Mr. Woodbury and the Salem School Board were so deeply impressed that they pleasantly eased her task of getting acquainted.

Less than a quarter of a mile down the unpaved main street from Woodbury's Board and Lodging House stood the two-story school. The downstairs teacher was expected to impart elementary knowledge to thirty-odd children in grades one through four. The upstairs teacher, now Mrs. Frost, was expected to carry an equal number of older children through work suitable to grades five through eight. After they completed those two phases of grammar-school education, most of the young people returned to useful occupations at outlying farms or started to work in the local shoe factories. Rarely did any child who was graduated from District School Number Six go on to high school. Mrs. Frost, the widow of a Harvard graduate and reared in the home of an uncle who had attended the University of Edinburgh, hoped to implant new ideals. Before she had been teaching more than a few weeks she was stimulating her brightest students to seek further education. Her proposals were sufficiently novel to arouse the suspicions of parents who were farmers and tradespeople. By contrast, some of Mrs. Frost's best pupils came from the homes of doctors and ministers, who admired and supported her objectives. They invited her into their homes to share and compare ideas on rural teaching.

The Frost children, with their mother's assistance, easily made the transition from the third and fourth grades of the Lawrence system to the fifth grade in District School Number Six. The new teacher informed all her pupils that those who earned the highest marks would be allowed to take seats in the back of the room; those needing more help or more discipline would be seated nearer the front. Her insistence on averaging deportment with scholarship worked to the disadvantage of her son, whose reserved and scholarly sister soon occupied a seat in the back row.

Robbie, consistently bored by assignments, made his own amusements. His recent acquisition of a jackknife and his newly learned skill at whittling was often indulged in the classroom when his mother was too busy to notice. For protection, he opened a large geography book, propped it on his desk as a shield, and whittled away. If shavings piled up at his feet, he brushed them out into the aisle with an occasional side motion of one shoe, much to the amusement of his less daring schoolmates.[2]

Not often reprimanded by his mother for anything he did, Robbie came under the law enough to find that he was making steady progress toward the front of the room. This punishment had no corrective effect on his distaste for scholarship. It merely encouraged him to employ another device, which permitted him to escape beyond reach. Several times each morning and each afternoon he would frantically hold up the proper finger signal to his mother and wave his hand until she nodded her permission for him to be excused so that he could (presumably) hasten to the outhouse toilet in the back of the schoolyard.

In that same schoolyard during his first spring term in Salem Depot, Robbie developed a passion for baseball. From the older boys he learned the mysteries of pitching, and whenever he could find anyone to work with him, he was soon trying to throw a fast drop, a roundhouse, and a jump ball. Never before had he set his heart on a career, but in the spring of 1886 he decided that someday he would become a hero as a major-league pitcher. Closely associated was his growing pleasure in the art of batting and in his proud conviction that he could scoot around the bases faster than any other boy in school.

The favorite schoolyard variant of baseball was a "moving-up" game called "scrub," which could be played very well with only a few boys. It was the game played at recess, during the noon hour, and after school by those who could linger. Robbie was often given a few pennies by his mother so that he could buy his daily lunch at the general store, and baseball caused him to hurry. He would speed the process by settling for a small box of raisins, which could be eaten on the way back to the schoolyard. The "upstairs" boys of School Number Six arranged a regular spring schedule of games with other schools, and by dint of persistence, the Frost boy soon established himself as a "regular" on his school team.

Robbie's mother tried to use his new passion as an instrument for encouraging him to complete his schoolwork. She failed. Quite scornfully her twelve-year-old said that he was content to let his sister be the student in the family, that reading books was all right for girls, that he hated spelling tests, that he simply would not write compositions, and that the unpleasant experience of being asked to go to the blackboard to diagram the structure of a sentence—in plain view of all the other boys—made him feel silly. There was very little that his mother could do with such an attitude. Occasionally, when she put an easy sentence on the board for diagraming, she would glance over at Robbie by way of hopeful invitation, but he would use sign language and turn his head sideways, just once, to say no.

Before the spring term ended, it became clear that Robbie's best friend was a boy his own size and age named Charley Peabody. No other boy in the school had such zestful initiative for mischief in the classroom, such sauciness with the girls, and such fearlessness in performing schoolyard stunts. In Robbie's eyes these were attractive traits, because they contrasted so markedly with his own shyness, caution, and hesitancy. Before long Charley began to invite Robbie to the Peabody house—down the railroad tracks toward Lawrence. It was more fun to walk the rails than to follow the dusty turnpike. The Peabody family was a large one—six girls and two boys—almost too large to fit into their small, gabled home just off the turnpike and about a mile from the Salem depot. Old

Ephraim Peabody, the father, was a robust out-of-doors man who had done well enough as a bricklayer, even better as a contractor, and best of all as a specialist in building the lofty chimneys required by many of the Lawrence mills. He was also a dedicated hunter of rabbits, ducks, pheasants, grouse, and deer. The backyard of his house was cluttered with runways and kennels for his hounds. It seemed that all of the Peabody children must have been taught to use firearms as soon as they were old enough to hold a rifle. And Robbie was awed by his first sight of what happened whenever Charley fired a twelve-gauge shotgun. The recoil kicked the stock against Charley's shoulder so hard that it made the boy stagger to catch his balance.

At the age of twelve, Charley had already demonstrated adequate skill as a hunter; but he was enough of a naturalist to prefer bringing his game back alive. His bedroom was his menagerie and museum. Along one wall of it stood screened boxes, which separately housed a hawk, an owl, two snakes, a flying squirrel, and a raccoon. He had brought the boxes in when cold weather made him worry about his pets, the previous fall, and he had enjoyed their company so much during the winter that he did not bother to take the boxes out when spring came. Above the boxes Charley had nailed to the wall a collection of branches which held his favorite specimens of birds' nests, some of them complete with eggs. For Robbie's benefit Charley liked to have his pets perform, letting them loose in his room. More than once it happened that a bird or an animal escaped into another part of the house, and then there was always a riot of pursuit in which the younger Peabody children joined. Charley's mother, a sweetly forlorn little woman, seemed so overwhelmed by her brood of children that whenever Charley grew too obstreperous in the house, the best she could do was to utter her dismay in a flat voice of hopeless protest, "Cha-arles, Cha-arles!"

Out in the woods back of the Peabody home, Charley began to teach Robbie a whole new lore of adventure: How to climb birches and ride them down, how to track and trap animals, how to skin a woodchuck, and, most frightening of all, how to collect a bird's nest from the most precarious vantage point. He filled Robbie with mingled terror and admiration on the first occasion when the daredevil worked his way out along a bending elm limb, high off the ground, hanging by his hands and moving hand over hand until he could reach and break off the twigs holding the underslung nest of a golden robin.

During the summer of 1886, the friendship of the two boys was interrupted by Mrs. Frost's decision that her son was old enough to earn a little money for family needs. Several other boys his age had found work in the shoe factories at Salem Depot, and Rob, as his mother began to call him, was sent to look for a job. Hired as an apprentice in the larger shoe factory, he was at first taught nothing more difficulty than the process of hammering three nails into the leather soles of partly-made shoes. The uneven amounts of time spent processing separate lots of shoes along the production line caused them to reach Robbie's bench at such irregular intervals that he was paid on a piecework basis. He liked that, because it meant that after he had applied himself industriously for an hour or two he could be gone from his bench until other lots accumulated there. Before long he was honored by being transferred to a more exacting and dangerous task, as assistant to a man who manipulated an automatic heel-nailing machine. The boy's duty was to place nails upright in the holes of a metal rack, which was mechanically pushed out and held out just long enough to permit the swift placement of the nails. Then the rack was drawn back into position as the automatic hammer was tripped to drive the nails in place. The new apprentice was warned that one of his recent predecessors had lost a finger by mistakenly reaching in to straighten a misplaced nail. Frightened by the warning, Rob soon guessed that the injured boy's effort to straighten that nail might have been caused in part by the man who worked the machine and cursed whenever a nail slipped. This nerve-wracking assignment was made even more tedious because the chances for rest were so few. After only a few days of it, Rob had had enough. Calculating the best way to arrange his release so that the blame would not rest on him for quitting, he complained to his mother that the men at the shoe factory were immoral. They used foul language. They even swore. His mother responded satisfactorily by insisting that her son must not continue to work in such a place.

Following his apprentice experiences as a shoemaker, Rob found an even less strenuous and more elementary form of leather-work in the backyard of what had become his new home. After Mrs. Frost and her children had grown tired of boarding-house life at Mr. Woodbury's, they moved briefly to the home of a family named Emerson, and then accepted the more satisfactory offer of rooms and the use of a kitchen in the home of a sympathetic Scotch couple, Mr. and Mrs. Loren E. Bailey. Having tried his hand at many different occupations, Loren Bailey was currently raising chickens, keeping a horse and cow, farming a bit, and operating a little sweatshop leather business on the side. His house, his barn, his coops, and his leather shed were perched near the top of a considerable knoll, which the local people called "chicken house hill," less than a quarter of a mile to the north and east of District School Number Six. The sweatshop branch of his enterprises was a familiar institution. Many of the large shoemaking companies around Boston profited from the eagerness of New England farmers and their wives to supplement their incomes by doing leatherwork on winter days and summer evenings. For the women there were special opportunities to perform fancy stitching and even embroidery on flat pieces of thin leather later to be attached to shoe soles as "uppers." For the men there were more prosaic tasks of cutting out heel-shaped pieces of leather from scrap or waste, then nailing the pieces together, and trimming off any rough edges. With some enterprise, Loren Bailey had built his shed large enough to let several men work at separate blocks cutting and assembling heels. By the time the Frosts arranged to rent rooms in the Bailey home, ten or twelve men were working in the shed. Most of them were wanderers and some of them were mere tramps who were content to earn only a little money before moving on. As a result, there was usually a spare cutting block, and Rob was given the chance to work there whenever he wanted. As soon as Bailey had taught him how to hold the metal pattern; how to trace around the edge of it with the sharp cutting knife; and how to assemble, nail, and trim the pieces of leather, the boy was pleased to be back at piecework. It permitted him to quit as often and for as long as he wished. There was also a crude form of entertainment furnished by the oddly individualistic men who worked along the row of blocks, and Rob liked to eavesdrop on their conversations.

It was natural that Loren Bailey's men should appeal at times to the schoolma'am's son when they needed someone to settle erudite arguments on what might be the correct pronunciation of words. His sister could have performed this task very capably, but more than once Rob's verdict was challenged. The most obnoxious challenger in the group was a little weasel of a man who had already earned the dislike of the others by scooping from the leather-bin the thickest and best pieces of scrap whenever Loren Bailey emptied a new bagful into it. And one day the weasel jeered at Rob's insistence that the word "forehead" should be pronounced as though it were one syllable. Argument quickly descended to name-calling, in which Rob got so much the worst of it that in desperation he emptied a bucket of drinking water on his opponent's head. In the ensuing chase, Rob led his pursuer around the farmyard, under wagons, and through the barn. Then the boy escaped completely by hiding unseen in a small and fortunately empty hen coop. For several days thereafter, he stayed away from his cutting block and did not go back until he learned that his tormentor had collected his money and had moved on down the road.

The most exciting diversion at Loren Bailey's little farm that summer was caused by the appearance of a set of boxing gloves. Playfully, and in the spirit of rough fun, the leather workers occasionally put on the gloves and knocked each other about with more brawn than skill. The best boxer in the group gave Rob rudimentary training in the so-called manly art, then urged him to trade punches with youngsters his own age. Fearful of too much roughness, and no longer needing to display the bravado which had brought him into the good graces of the Washington Street gang in San Francisco, the boy often agreed to box on the condition that his opponent would promise not to punch at his eyes, his nose, his mouth. It sometimes happened that even after such arrangements had been made, the match might start in a gentlemanly manner, and continue pleasantly, until a solid punch would inflame tempers and transform the game into a serious quest for blood. After such a scrap Rob could not quickly overcome his inner turmoil. But he was growing up, and he was proud of his ability to take blows without tears.

Whenever life at Loren Bailey's grew too strenuous or too boring, Rob found pleasant diversion by walking down the hill to the depot and down the tracks to Charley Peabody's home for an hour's visit or even for a whole day of adventure in the woods. During these visits, in the summer of 1886, he came gradually to realize that there was another member of the Peabody family who also appealed to him. Charley's ten-year-old sister, Sabra, was a bold and carefree tomboy who could almost keep up with her brother. And on days when Rob and Charley went prowling through the woods or along the banks of the Spicket River, or even as far as the shore of Canobie Lake, neither one of them minded if Sabra went with them. She could run, climb, jump like a boy; but at the same time she was a very pretty girl. Mischievous and fun-loving, she had a knack for gently teasing Rob in ways he liked.

Sometimes, when he made the mile walk down the tracks to the Peabody home, Rob had trouble in being certain whether he was going there to see Charley or to call on Sabra. By the time school opened in the fall of 1886, he was willing to admit that Sabra had become even more important to him than her brother. He was in love, and he overcame his shyness enough to admit the fact to Sabra herself. That he was only twelve years old and she only ten in no way diminished all the bliss and anguish of his passion. The courtship reached a new form of articulation that fall, when he began leaving little presents and hastily scribbled notes in her desk:

". . . Those nuts I gave you were not as good as I expected but I am glad you liked them."

". . . I liked those leav[e]s you gave me and put them in my speller to press."

". . . I must stop now and remember and write soon. From your loving Rob"

". . . I have got [to] read a composition after recess and I hate to offaly. I have got to stop now so as to learn my Geography. From your loving Rob."

". . . There is no fun in getting mad every so [often, so] lets see if we cant keep friends Im sure I am willing. I know I have not treated you as I ought to sometimes and sometimes I don't know wheather you are mad or not . . . I like you because I cant help myself and when I get mad at you I feel mad at myself to[o]. From your loveing Rob."[3]

At twelve, Rob had already begun to taste the bittersweet of uncertain courtship. He simply could not understand Sabra's tantalizing way of making him try to guess whether she loved him as intensely as he loved her. Each of them seemed to have special gifts for making the other jealous to such an extent that their romance was devoted very largely to quarrels, silences, and reconciliations. Rob's passion was so fierce and uncontrollable that it kept driving him into actions calculated to hurt Sabra, partly because he felt he had no way of measuring her interest in him save through her furious jealousy.

The anguish of love was not Rob's only problem during the fall and winter of 1886. His mother seemed to be suffering from some kind of illness, and other children in the upstairs classroom of District School Number Six noticed marked changes in her appearance. Although she never missed a day of school and never complained, she seemed to grow noticeably thin, haggard, gaunt. Deep hollows appeared under her prominent cheekbones. Her dark eyes frequently gazed far beyond whatever she seemed to be looking at. Her black hair, streaked with gray, had always been carefully drawn into a knot at the back of her neck; but now she paid less and less attention to strands which escaped the knot and hung about her face in a manner which made her appear disheveled. Her dresses, some of them cast-offs given her by her closest Salem friends, no longer conveyed the air of proud fastidiousness she had shown when first she came to Salem Depot.

The more sympathetic pupils, noticing these changes, carried home troubled stories of how Mrs. Frost sometimes sat at her desk during periods of study so completely absorbed in her own thoughts that she often failed to notice the scuffles of mischief-makers in the back of the room. Her more critical students began to complain to their parents that they disliked Mrs. Frost because she was a poor teacher who couldn't keep order. They said she spent too much time helping her favorites, particularly Rob and Jeanie. They also complained that Jeanie thought she was the brightest girl in school and put on "stuck-up" airs, that Rob was a lazy good-for-nothing who seemed to stay in bed each morning as late as he pleased and then came drifting into school late without a word of reprimand from his mother.

Town gossips took up the hue and cry, saying quite openly that Mrs. Frost should not be kept as teacher beyond the present year. Word spread that this hopelessly poor disciplinarian always favored the children of the rich—and, relatively speaking, one could find "the rich" even in Salem Depot. Other gossips maliciously claimed that she worked particularly with students who planned to go to high school; that she did so merely to stand in well with their parents.

The cruelty of these attacks soon evoked a dignified counter-campaign in defense of Mrs. Frost, by parents and children who had grown extremely fond of her. They granted that she was impractical and that she was at times careless in matters of appearance and dress. They even granted that she was not the best disciplinarian the school had known. Nevertheless, they insisted, she was so good that in her first half-year of teaching she had enabled four students to pass entrance examinations at the nearest high school in Lawrence. Nothing like that had ever happened before in District School Number Six. Moreover, she was a beautifully spirited Christian woman whose holiness shone through her eyes.

Two families in Salem Depot proved to be most helpful to Mrs. Frost during this difficult time. Dr. E. W. Wade, Chairman of the School Board of Salem township, and his wife, became such devoted friends that the abused woman frequently sought comfort in their home. Equally cordial, and even more intimate, were Mr. and Mrs. Fred W. Chase. He was a prominent businessman whose daughter Agatha planned to enter high school in the fall of 1887. The Chases were members of the Baptist Church, and although Mrs. Frost's newly developed Swedenborgian connections in Lawrence kept her from attending services regularly in Salem, it happened that on one Communion Sunday she went with Mrs. Chase and even received communion. To the hard-shell members, this was sacrilege. Mrs. Frost had no right to take communion with them until she had been redeemed by total immersion. Mrs. Chase silenced them. She insisted that if a woman of Mrs. Frost's spiritual radiance could not partake of communion in the Baptist Church of Salem Depot, then all of the Chases would resign.

After they had become intimate friends, Mrs. Frost and Mrs. Chase shared confidences. The teacher told her friend the story of her life, the difficulties which had almost destroyed her marriage, and the pathetic death which had intervened. She also confided much concerning her two children. Jeanie, she said, had always been high strung, easily given to tears and hysterics from early childhood. At times, she admitted, Jeanie did not seem to be quite normal. Perhaps the good Lord had given the child more brains than she needed. Too bright for her age, she was inclined to make a world of her own out of her imaginings and her reading. Her mother had recently heard the child tell a classmate that she cared for nothing except reading, and that she thought playing games was an evil waste of time. Of course, Jeanie might become a good schoolteacher or (heaven forbid) she might even become an actress. She did show extraordinary dramatic gifts. In the little storytelling classes which Mrs. Frost held once a week at the Loren Bailey house, Jeanie often acted out a Bible story in pantomime as Mrs. Frost told it. But the story Jeanie loved most to tell and dramatize was the story of the Maid of Orleans; she even seemed to wear her hair as she thought Joan of Arc had done.

As for Rob, his mother told Mrs. Chase, the dear boy seemed to grow more shiftless each day. She explained her fears that she herself had unintentionally hindered him from developing good habits of reading and study. Perhaps she had been too fond of reading aloud to her children. Rob was a good listener, but so odd in things he said about what she read. He would not let her finish reading aloud the last chapter of *Tom Brown's School Days* because, he said, he could not bear to think that such a good story should end. Had he finished the book by reading the rest of it to himself? No, he never read anything unless his mother sat with him and encouraged him. She also admitted that the boy was as stubborn and hot-tempered as his father had been. At times he was very difficult to manage. Often Mrs. Frost wistfully said to Mrs. Chase, "I don't know what will ever become of that boy."

Other Baptists in Salem Depot told of a different attitude. More than once, in conversations after a church service, they watched Mrs. Frost put an arm around the boy's shoulders, draw him close, and say with pride, "I have great hopes for Rob." Scornfully and cynically the gossips passed this anecdote around, sometimes with mean comments about silk purses and sow's ears. Most of the townspeople were agreed that the Frost boy was indeed a lazy good-for-nothing and that there was not enough promise in him to justify any hope.[4]

CASEMENTS OPENING

I dream upon the opposing lights of the hour, . . .
And on the worn book of old-golden song
I brought not here to read, it seems, but hold
And freshen in this air of withering sweetness . . .[1]

DURING THE SUMMER of 1887, and even while so many
of the Salem townspeople were viewing the Frost boy as a
hopelessly lazy good-for-nothing, Rob became aware that his
interests were undergoing a profound change. The cause of
the change was not unrelated to his insistence that his mother
read and re-read aloud to him certain chapters in the story
he could not bear to finish: *Tom Brown's School Days*. Although Mrs. Frost naturally viewed Hughes's famous narrative
as a vehicle well designed to inculcate muscular Christian
morality, Rob was probably more inclined to enjoy it as an
heroic adventure story which had particular appeal for him
because he could so easily identify himself with Tom. Here
was a boy, nearly Rob's own age, proud of his own skills as a
runner, a fighter, a ball-player—even though Rob knew for
certain that cricket must be inferior to baseball. Here also
was a story in which fighting was honored far more than Rob's
mother was willing to honor it. This was no book for women
and girls. Passages in it made his blood tingle with approval:
"After all, what would life be without fighting, I should
like to know? From the cradle to the grave, fighting, rightly
understood, is the business, the real, highest, honestest business of every son of man. . . . It is no good for Quakers, or
any other body of men to uplift their voices against fighting.
Human nature is too strong for them. . . . The world might
be a better world without fighting, for anything I know, but
it wouldn't be our world . . ."
Even the garrulous and masculine tone of the narrator

pleased Rob, who felt that his own life was too heavily subjected to feminine influence. But Tom Brown as hero had a further effect during the summer of 1887. Clearly, Tom was not ashamed of study and did not consider schoolwork sissified. All the discussion concerning Latin and Greek came as a foreshadowing for Rob. He knew that his first year of high school would introduce him to these mysteries, and what was good enough for Tom was good enough for Rob. So the experience of having this book read aloud—and then frequently re-read in parts—became an incalculable inspiration. "And Tom was becoming a new boy, though with frequent tumbles in the dirt and perpetual hard battles with himself, and was daily growing in manfulness and thoughtfulness, as every high-couraged and well-principled boy must, when he finds himself for the first time consciously at grips with self and the devil." In their different responses to such a passage, the boy and his mother must have found a common ground of sympathy.

Mrs. Frost may have realized that the change in her son's attitude toward reading and study, as it became increasingly noticeable during the summer of 1887, was partly due to her years of storytelling and story-reading. Her passion for the color of Scottish folklore and history, her delight in the cadences of Scottish dialect, and her admiration for the courage of Scottish heroes had influenced the choice of books she borrowed from the Lawrence Public Library to read aloud to her children. At first she had brought them up on her own versions of historical narratives concerning the Scots who had with Wallace bled and the Scots whom Bruce had often led into and beyond the victorious Battle of Bannockburn. But during the long evenings of the previous winter, 1886-1887, she had read to them Sir Walter Scott's *Tales of a Grandfather*, knowing that these glimpses into the history of Scotland were designed for youthful ears. She supplemented Scott's *Tales* with border ballads, some of them drawn from Percy's *Reliques*. Reaching back even further, she exposed her children to pertinent selections from *The Poems of Ossian*, a modern edition of which she had brought with her from San Francisco.[2]

It is easy to understand why Mrs. Frost should have taken Scottish pride in the Ossianic epic of *Fingal*, and why she should have wanted to praise the Celtic Homer who had conferred such glory on the distant past of Caledonia; but it would be difficult to overemphasize the strong impact on the impressionable Rob of his mother's romantically idealistic readings aloud from *Ossian*. Well-informed, Mrs. Frost probably knew all she cared to know about the celebrated controversy over the authenticity of James Macpherson's *Fragments of Ancient Poetry Collected in the Highlands of Scotland* (1760) and his *Fingal, an Ancient Epic Poem in Six Books, Together With Several Other Poems Composed by Ossian, the Son of Fingal, Translated from the Gaelic Language* (1761). It would have befitted her sensibilities if she had subscribed to the middle view in the controversy: that while Macpherson's literary accomplishments may have been more creative than scholarly, in rescuing and improving discovered fragments of ancient Gaelic poetry, he had nevertheless produced some important works of art. For Mrs. Frost, personally, it would have been enough that this Scotsman's antiquarian bent had endowed his work with themes she wanted her son to cherish deeply, such as the theme of regret for the pathos of noble bygone days, of the sadness of modern times, and of the leavening effect of visionary melancholy. She may also have realized that Macpherson had indirectly paved the way for some of her favorite romantic poets, such as Burns, Wordsworth, Bryant, and Emerson—many of whose lines she had been quoting to her children since their infancy.

A poetess herself, and a Swedenborgian poetess, Mrs. Frost made her children feel by example rather than by precept that romantic nature-poetry was at its best when it suggested correspondences or analogies between the seen and the unseen worlds. "In our doctrine of representations and correspondences," Swedenborg had written, "we shall treat of both those symbolical and typical resemblances, and of the astonishing things that occur, I will not say in the living body only, but throughout Nature, and which correspond so entirely to supreme and spiritual things, that one would swear the physical world was purely symbolical of the spiritual world."[3] Each of the romantic poets whom Mrs. Frost loved had been fascinated by his own sense of "symbolical and typical resemblances" between the physical and the metaphysical. Emerson, whose essay on Swedenborg had paved the way for Mrs. Frost's becoming a Swedenborgian,[4] had stressed his own view of physical and metaphysical correspondences: ". . . the world is a temple whose walls are covered with emblems, pictures and commandments of the Deity—in this, that there is no fact in nature which does not carry the whole sense of nature . . ."[5] Wordsworth had also helped Mrs. Frost convey to her children the ability to feel in nature a presence which could and should inspire with the joy of elevated thoughts. He further helped her explain to them her belief that whosoever shall not receive the Kingdom of God as a little child does, shall in no wise enter therein. It may have been easy and natural for her to quote to Robbie and Jeanie, while still in San Francisco, the lines beginning, "My heart leaps up when I behold a rainbow in the sky . . ." She also knew so many of Bryant's poems by heart that they served a closely related function. She often quoted the familiar line, "Go forth, under the open sky, and list to Nature's teachings." Her frequent repetition of Bryant's "To a Waterfowl" sank in so deeply that Rob discovered with astonishment, one day in the summer of 1887, as he worked alone cutting leather in Loren Bailey's shed, that he could begin at the first line and say the poem all the way through this final verse:

> He who, from zone to zone,
> Guides through the boundless sky thy certain flight,
> In the long way that I must tread alone,
> Will lead my steps aright.

What surprised Rob most about this feat of memory was that he was certain he had never tried to learn "To a Waterfowl." With even greater surprise he made another discovery, years later: Of these three poets to whom his mother had first exposed him—Emerson, Wordsworth, Bryant—his favorite was hers: Ralph Waldo Emerson.[6]

Among Mrs. Frost's favorites, and not too oddly, was Edgar Allan Poe, whom she quoted so often that her children knew several of his poems by heart before they entered high school. For her, the special appeal of Poe could not have been the jingling quality of the rhymes and meters, nor the morbid preoccupation with the death of a beautiful woman. It is more probable that Mrs. Frost had the capacity to discover in Poe's romantic lines certain mystical and metaphysical correspondences which helped her to illustrate some of her favorite Swedenborgian truths, as in the following couplet from Poe's "Tamerlane":

O, human love! thou spirit given,
On Earth, of all we hope in Heaven!

Their mother could easily have conveyed to Rob and Jeanie the notion that Poe's deepest concern was to make heaven more important than earth.

The same religious ideals which Mrs. Frost conveyed to her children, through poetry, were supplemented by her way of keeping pace with their growing pleasure in prose tales of romantic and heroic adventure. Back in the San Francisco days, when she had introduced them to her beloved George Macdonald by reading from *At the Back of the North Wind*, she may have had no plan in mind to take Rob and Jeanie all the way up the ladder of Macdonald's Scotch novels. It was not until they reached Salem that she exposed them to the entire series, starting perhaps with *Ranald Bannerman's Boyhood* and *Malcolm* and *The Marquis of Lossie* before she read them at least parts of her favorites, such as the more mature and demanding *David Elginbrod, Robert Falconer,* and *Alec Forbes at Howglen.* She did not need to tell them that Macdonald had been a liberal clergyman before he turned novelist, and that he wove mystical overtones of meaning into the heroic actions of all his novels.

So long as Rob's mother pleased him with the narratives of heroic and romantic adventure which she read aloud, he had sufficient reason for not developing his own reading habits. It was apparently true that, as he often boasted, he did not read through any book, from the beginning by himself, until his fourteenth year. But the stimulus which finally overcame his resistance was provided accidentally during the summer of 1887. One day when he was working in desultory fashion, cutting leather in Loren Bailey's shed, he and Mrs. Bailey were alone; the usual flow of drifters and tramps had dwindled sharply, for unaccountable reasons, and on this particular day Mrs. Bailey began to talk of her relatives in Scotland. In an effort to match her, Rob drew proudly on all he knew about his mother's family. Then their conversation veered to the history of Scotland, and again Rob was adequately informed. But when Mrs. Bailey said that he should read her favorite historical novel, Jane Porter's *The Scottish Chiefs,* which started with the murder of Wallace's wife and ended with the Battle of Bannockburn, the names themselves were enough to tempt him. He borrowed her dog-eared copy of *The Scottish Chiefs,* began to read it by himself, gave up leather-cutting, and devoted his time exclusively to the narrative until he had finished it. Thereafter, his prejudices against reading were ended.

Rob's mother must have been relieved by his change in attitude. Knowing that both her children could complete their grammar-school work during the next school year, she was certain that by the spring of 1888, Jeanie could easily pass the high-school entrance examinations. But she was equally certain that Rob, who would be fourteen by that time, might not pass them all. One factor that worked to his mother's earlier disadvantage in teaching Rob to read and study, had been his passion for baseball. Now it worked in her favor— and his. Lawrence High School had an excellent baseball team, and the nearer Rob drew to high school the more he dreamed of playing on such a team. Of course, he would not be permitted to play if his marks were not good, and so his goal justified his making a little extra effort in the line of study.

Almost slyly, as though still ashamed of the change in his attitude, Rob applied himself quite seriously to his studies in the autumn of 1887. His mother helped him to avoid the embarrassment of recitations in front of the class. She let him bring his completed work to her desk or show it to her at home. Having begun to study, he complained of being forced to poke along at the slow-poke rate set by the poorer students. He also complained that his interests were not satisfied when he was asked to prepare a few pages of several different assignments, day after day. Why shouldn't he be permitted to concentrate on one subject at a time, intensively, and go straight through the year's work in that subject? His mother assured him that if he thought he could learn better and faster that way, she would give her permission. Proudly developing his own methods, he chose first to read completely through Fry's *Geography* and to pass examinations in geography set by his mother. Next he chose to tackle Eaton's *Arithmetic* and to study nothing except that subject. Again he was given private tests and again he did well. He moved on to Higginson's *Young Folks' History of the United States.* Last of all, he braced himself for wading bravely through all of Swinton's *Grammar* and Franklin's *Higher Reader.*

The *Grammar* bored him most of all; but to his surprise

he found himself lingering over the *Higher Reader*. Some of the stories he read again and again. Then he deliberately settled in to memorize several poems and proverbs and mottoes. Until this time he had repeatedly teased his sister by saying that he disliked poems, particularly the kinds of poems she adored. Her dramatic and melodramatic inclinations enabled her to take pleasure in reciting "Curfew Shall Not Ring To-night," and her brother thought she did it mawkishly. He said that some of the poems in the *Higher Reader* were just as bad, just plain silly. One of them prompted him to make his first try at writing a rhymed answer as a mocking parody. He presented a copy of his parody to Sabra, who knew the original poem and understood Rob's joke. But when he found in the *Higher Reader* the poem on the Greek struggle for freedom, Halleck's "Marco Bozzaris," he liked it so much that he quickly memorized it.

With the coming of spring, in 1888, Rob found that no books could keep his thoughts from baseball. Impatiently he suffered through the tedious days of "mud-time" and tried with other boys to play "moving up" in the schoolyard while the ground was still too soft and wet. But as soon as April weather dried the playing field, he threw all his energies into session after session of baseball practice with his team. Number Six did so well that year, in competition with other nearby district schools, that the boys ambitiously overextended themselves by challenging one of the best grammar-school teams in Lawrence. The terms were that the Lawrence team must play Number Six on its home grounds at Salem Depot, and the results were almost catastrophic.

The trouble started in the very first inning, when the opposition played havoc with Rob's pitching. The older Lawrence boys knocked his offerings all over the place and scored runs with embarrassing ease. As the game went on, the Salem boys had so much difficulty in getting hits that they saw the prospect of a disgraceful shutout. Rob, removed as pitcher, still hoped to prove his batting ability—or at least his speed at base-running. He even boasted, loud enough to be heard by the enemy, that if only he could get on base he'd show the big boys how easy it would be to bring home at least one run. The catcher for the Lawrence team heard the boast and when Rob next came to bat the catcher called for time-out. Walking halfway to the mound, he held a whispered parley with the pitcher. They agreed to give the boaster a base on balls.

There was pride in Robbie's bearing as he trotted down to first. Now he'd show them. As the pitcher started his next throw, Rob scampered for second and was safely there before the catcher's throw arrived. It was easy. Of course, the steal to third might be a little harder, but he felt sure that he could make it. He pranced off second as the pitcher again faced the batter; he came back and tagged base, when the pitcher turned around. Then he took an even more daring lead—and was off with the pitch. Ah, somewhere in that favored land the sun was shining bright, but when Rob came sliding into third, head first, he saw the gloved ball waiting for him, and he knew he was out. Disgusted, he picked himself up, dusted himself off, and walked over to the bench amid the humiliating jeers and catcalls of the entire Lawrence team.

Other humiliations overtook Rob during that spring. Just before the close of school, Mrs. Frost took all of her pupils up the road to Canobie Lake for a Saturday picnic on the beach in one of the pine groves. Wading, boating, games, sandwiches, and lemonade were the order of the day, which went well until late in the afternoon. The boys had taken turns at giving the girls rides along the shore in the one available rowboat, and when Rob's turn came, he tried to find Sabra. Failing, he took one of Sabra's sisters, and handled the boat skillfully until an impatient shorebound boy, awaiting his turn, began tossing stones large enough to splash Rob. The incident might have ended in good-natured protests and name-calling if the heckler's next stone had not thudded solidly against the gunwale. That was too much for Rob. In a burst of rage he brought the boat ashore, jumped out, caught the culprit around the neck, and began punching in the good old San Francisco manner. But his opponent gained the advantage by tripping Rob, and the two boys fell to the ground flailing at each other. All of the picnickers, who were near enough to notice the fight, closed in to enjoy it, and one of them threw a stone at the swirl of arms and legs. It happened to hit Rob on the side of the head, near his ear, and as his mother broke through the ring of children to separate the fighters, somebody said, "He's bleeding." Rob put his hand to his face and brought it away bloody, just as someone else shouted, accusingly, "Sabra threw that stone." Mrs. Frost scolded her son for having started the fight, and as punishment she sent him home. Hurt and protesting, he started back down the road to the village, the turmoil in him aggravated by his remembering the words, "Sabra threw that stone." Had she thrown it at him because she was jealous? Or had she thrown it at his enemy, in an attempt to help Rob? He wished he knew, but he never dared to ask her—and she never mentioned it to him. More painful than the rock, her silence concerning the fight seemed to cool and gradually to extinguish his ardor for her.

A few days after the picnic Rob suffered more humiliation. When he and his sister, Jeanie, went down to Lawrence with several other students (including neither Sabra nor Charley Peabody) to take the first of their high-school entrance examinations, Rob felt so nervous that he was almost panic-stricken. The subject was arithmetic, and Jeanie said afterward that the examination was easy. Rob had trouble with it from the start. In less than a quarter of the time allowed, he raced through all the problems he felt he could handle and then he turned in his paper. The teacher called him back. Wouldn't he like to take a little more time? Had he checked his answers? No, he said, no. Then he bolted. When the examination marks were mailed to Salem Depot, Rob learned that although he had barely passed arithmetic, he had done well enough in all the other tests and would be admitted as a freshman in good standing with his younger sister—whose standing was much better.

The greatest humiliation of the Salem days occurred that fall, soon after Rob and Jeanie had begun to commute by train to the Lawrence High School from Salem Depot. While their attentions were being absorbed by the newness of this experience, their mother began to have her worst troubles in District School Number Six. New gossip revived smoldering enmities, and her critics now insisted that if she were not replaced immediately they would hire a teacher of their own so that they could start another school for their children in Pilgrim Hall over the local barber shop. Gradually made aware of the trouble, Rob felt it directly when next he went into the general store and was met with the proprietor's curt threat: "Get out of here, you little Frost."

He did as ordered, indignantly resenting all that was implied. His own chagrin was heightened by his deep sense of loyalty to and love for his mother. The situation hurt him so deeply that he began dreaming of ways to wreak physical vengeance on these enemies. The School Board called a special public meeting for the announced purpose of considering "the Frost case," and Rob attended. He sat alone in the back of the room and watched his mother come in, escorted by Mrs. Wade and Mrs. Chase. Rob felt that the complaints made were unbelievably insulting. But after the opposition had been permitted to vent its complaints and fault-findings, loyal friends of Mrs. Frost stood up to defend her. Then the School Board publicly voted that Mrs. Frost should continue as teacher at District School Number Six. A few days later, in retaliation, the plaintiffs carried out their threat and set up a provisional classroom in Pilgrim Hall over the barber shop, with a new teacher. Nearly half of Mrs. Frost's students were taken away from her, and by the end of the term it was apparent even to her closest friends that it was wise for Mrs. Frost to resign as she now desired to do. She wanted to move away from Salem Depot with her children as quickly as possible.

On the night before their departure Rob went with his mother to pay a farewell call at the Chase home. He refused to go in with her, and his former schoolmate, Agatha Chase, came out to talk with him as he stood waiting beside the white picket fence gate. Fighting back tears, he condemned all the trouble-makers who had treated his mother so cruelly. Then with proud scorn he raised the questions which hurt him most: Who did these people think they were, and who did they think the Frosts were?

"You wait," he said through his tears to Agatha. "Some day, I'll come back to Salem Depot—and show them."

8

VINCIT QUI SE VINCIT

Not in the strife of action, is the leader made, nor in the face of crisis, but when all is over, when the mind is swift with keen regret, in the long after-thought.[1]

THE FIRST DAY of his high-school career was a frightening ordeal for Rob. There was nothing unpleasant in the brief and familiar journey by rail with his sister and their friends from Salem Depot to Lawrence, and there was nothing to disturb him in the outward appearance of the gaunt and ugly three-story brick building. It stood on Haverhill Street and over-looked the elm-shaded Common not far from the home of his grandparents. He had at least seen the inside of the school on Saturdays during the previous spring, when he had gone there to take entrance examinations; but it had been nearly empty then. Now, lost among strangers and caught in the press of chattering students who milled and jostled on the stairs and through the corridors, he was treated as an outsider, a country bumpkin, a nobody. If he had dared to escape, he would have taken the next train back to Salem and would have hit for the woods with a trusted friend like Charley Peabody. He envied Charley and Sabra, whose parents had not forced them into this ordeal.

The worst insult of this first day was provided by three of his classmates who stopped him in the corridor just long enough to ask a taunting question: Wasn't he the Salem smartie who had been thrown out at third last spring, after boasting he could even steal home? Their jeers were enough to make Rob decide, then and there, that he couldn't possibly compete for a position on the high-school team with enemies like these. It was a painful decision to make, and it seemed as though no other possible misery could have hurt so much on this first day as this rude shattering of his cherished base-ball dreams.

For the Salem boy it was fortunate that all the preliminary confusion and excruciation were quickly counterbalanced by well-ordered routine and discipline in the classrooms, by the competence of his new teachers, and by his worries over assignments. Of the three programs offered—the college pre-paratory or classical program, the general or English program, and the mixed or commercial—Rob and his mother had already decided that he would choose the first. Aware of his brilliant father's career in this same high school and at Har-vard, the boy planned to give special emphasis to the study of the classics and history. It was an ambitious choice, made by relatively few of the students in his class, and that further isolated him. He knew it would also exclude him from any immediate possibility of taking a course in English literature and of going on to read the kinds of novels which had begun to fascinate him.[2] At least he was postponing the study of Greek until his sophomore year; but he was taking Latin, Algebra, a course in the history of Greece, and a course in the history of the Roman Empire.

His briefest glances through the battered and dog-eared textbooks made him certain that the courses in history would interest him most. His mother had already made him familiar with many stories involving heroes of Greece and Rome. Some of the illustrations reminded him of mysterious names uttered by his father during conversations enriched with references to Athens, Sparta, Thebes, and Rome. Now he looked forward to a time when he himself would know enough facts and facets of ancient history to make his own uses of them.

In studying his assignments at home, night after night, Rob admitted to himself that his unexpected display of in-dustry was motivated in part by fear. He could not bear the possibility that he might be humiliated in the presence of his fellow students by questions he could not answer. Having disciplined himself to read without his mother's help, he was now driven by motives of fright and self-defense to re-read and even to memorize names, dates, facts. Surprised to find his assignments interesting, he took further satisfaction in discovering his ability to complete work without his mother's help.

In classroom recitations he felt a shyness and reluctance

to volunteer answers. At first he was painfully self-conscious. But whenever he became absorbed in discussions where he could use newly acquired information, he participated eagerly. Still easily hurt by any form of criticism or correction, he was occasionally jolted back into silence, as on the day when his instructor in Greek history and mythology—Mr. Nathaniel Goodwin, principal of the high school—asked why Hera sent the two azure-scaled serpents to Amphitryon's house. Up went Rob's hand.

"They were after Heracles," he said quickly. "They had come to eat him up."

Pleasantly trying to correct the Salem boy's colloquialism, the classically trained Mr. Goodwin asked, "Not down?"

Rob cringed under the burst of laughter from the other students and wished he hadn't said a word. He couldn't bear to be laughed at by anyone for any reason. But even these hurts could not deprive him of his delight in reading to himself all the myths and legends and stories about Greece in his textbooks. As soon as he began to glory in the Golden Age, the rule of Pericles, and the subsequent vicissitudes of the noble Athenians during the Peloponnesian War, he sided passionately with Athens. Not expecting that the Athenians could possibly be defeated by Sparta, he agonized over the outcome. He wished he could change history, if only for a little while, just to see what might have happened if the Athenians had never sent their fatal expedition to Sicily.

Having guessed correctly that his favorite course during the freshman year would be history, he was nevertheless surprised to find that even his elementary work in Latin gave him satisfaction which eclipsed his dislike for memorizing declensions and conjugations and rules. For the first time he began to understand his mother's reasons for arranging the parts of English sentences in diagrammatic forms on the blackboard. English words he had been using every day for years took on new significance for him as soon as he recognized their Latin roots. Scraps of Latin found in his collateral reading suddenly came to life. At the very first meeting of the freshman class, the proposal had been made and accepted that the motto for the Class of '92 should be *Vincit qui se vincit*—and he was proud to sense the meaning before the words were translated. The choice of this motto touched him partly because it gave him words for something he had been trying to articulate, on his own. If conquest had to begin with self-conquest, he had already started in the right direction, and he was willing to persevere against the difficulties created by his self-acknowledged laziness.

He would need a good deal of perseverance, he feared, if he were to conquer his prejudices against mathematics; and he had already made up his mind that he would hate algebra. But here again his dread of appearing to be stupid in class helped him overcome an initial distaste. Before long, the little problems acquired the charm of puzzles for him. They reminded him of a treasured memento he had brought all the way from California and still possessed—a little boxful of hollow ivory blocks, a Chinese puzzle, which could be solved only when the right relationship of different sides, sizes, and shapes were figured out so that all the blocks might be fitted back into the box after they had been dumped out. Now he saw that the balanced arrangement of the parts in an algebraic equation was much the same kind of problem. It was a new game for him and at one phase of it he became so absorbed that his sheer concentration brought him through a public performance before he had time to grow self-conscious.

The incident occurred on a day when the superintendent of schools visited the algebra class and pleasantly challenged the students to take one step beyond what they had learned. By way of preliminaries, the visitor wrote on the blackboard an algebra problem which required a new process. He assured the students that they knew enough about algebra to solve the problem, and to recognize the new process, if they would only try. Troubled and uncertain, the entire class stared in silence until Rob impulsively exclaimed, "I can do it."

All right. Stand and begin.

The boy was so intent on describing each of the separate steps that for the moment he was not bothered by shyness. Even the superintendent's interruptions, for the purpose of leading him on, seemed like stimulating countermoves in a game of wits. When he finished and was praised for his ability to make mental rearrangements of algebraic facts already learned, Rob was proud of his accomplishment. More than that, it dawned on him that he had suddenly discovered something he didn't know he knew about the process of original thinking: It was always a matter of putting together known quantities in fresh ways. Somewhat vengefully, he applied the process further by deciding that he could use his new-found abilities as a means of getting back at those classmates who had mocked him as the boastful base-runner who didn't even reach third.

Desperately needing any self-confidence he could acquire, and welcoming praise as a counterbalance to his persistent sense of being an outsider, Rob very soon hid even shyness and uncertainty beneath a self-protective shield of pride and scorn. He began to explain to himself and others that he couldn't be bothered with competition for positions on athletic teams or anywhere else. He preferred to save his time for study, and, besides, he was a commuter with a train schedule to limit him. Largely because of Rob's arrogant diffidence, he made no lasting friends during his first year. But his inner and outer responses were undergoing such rapid change that his new posture was not wholly a shield.

Continuing to regret that his primary emphasis on classical studies did not permit him immediately to take any course in English literature, he soon realized that the "English" students were the ones who usually edited the school paper called the *Bulletin*. It was an attractively printed periodical, sewn in colored wrappers and published each month during the school year. So far, his two major literary efforts had been the happy-valley story he had written in San Francisco and the poetic parody he had tossed off as a joke for Sabra Peabody back in Salem. If the *Bulletin* interested him at all during his freshman year, it did not inspire him with any fierce yearning to write and publish something of his own in it.

By accident—or rather through happy ignorance and mis-understanding—his attitude toward writing did undergo a very important change near the end of the school year. Shortly before the time for the celebration of Memorial Day, 1889, he watched his home-room teacher, Miss Katherine O'Keefe, making preparations one morning before school began. She took only a piece of chalk with her as she went to the black-board and wrote word after word and line after line until she completed a poem. Having no way of knowing that Miss O'Keefe was quoting, Rob was convinced that he was watching her unfold a poem she herself had composed. And he felt a growing sense of admiration, even amazement, as he noticed how nicely each word seemed to fall into place for the de-velopment of her thoughts. Aware that Memorial Day was

approaching, he considered his teacher's reminder a fitting
tribute to the soldiers who had fought and died in the Civil
War. More than that, he saw this performance as a dramatic
act of putting words together to make a poem. It was a new
game, requiring a skillful control of line after line in much
the same way that a pitcher has to manipulate the ball in
throw after throw. As Miss O'Keefe finished and moved back
to her desk, Rob read all she had written:

> *How sleep the brave, who sink to rest*
> *By all their country's wishes blest!*
> *When Spring, with dewy fingers cold,*
> *Returns to deck their hallow'd mould,*
> *She there shall dress a sweeter sod*
> *Than Fancy's feet have ever trod.*
>
> *By fairy hands their knell is rung;*
> *By forms unseen their dirge is sung;*
> *There Honour comes, a pilgrim grey,*
> *To bless the turf that wraps their clay;*
> *And Freedom shall awhile repair*
> *To dwell, a weeping hermit, there!*

Rob's useful misunderstanding kept him from realizing
that Miss O'Keefe was borrowing, but through his error he
gained insights which were important to him and to his future.
For the first time he saw that this poem and any other good
poem could be admired purely as a performance. It was enough
to make him want to try the game for his own amusement.
Several years later, when he learned that "How Sleep the
Brave" had been written by William Collins in praise of those
who had fought and died on Culloden Moor in 1746, he merely
transferred his earlier admiration from Miss O'Keefe to William Collins.

By the end of this first year the Salem boy took a justifiable
pride in what he had already accomplished through earnest
self-discipline, motivated partly by fright and partly by retaliation. His final grades placed him not only above his bookish
and pedantic sister, Jeanie, but also at the head of his class,
with 95% in each of his history courses, 96% in Latin, and
99% in Algebra. His elation inspired enough arrogance to
let him confront his Roman history teacher with an indignant
demand for an explanation of his low mark. He felt certain

that he had never failed to answer any of her questions correctly, in either oral or written work, and that he had always been among the first to volunteer answers. Hence the self-assurance with which he demanded, "Why didn't I get a hundred for my final mark? Were any of my answers wrong in my final examination?"

She dodged the bold questions by asking, "Do you think you know all of Roman history?"

Unable to find an answer that seemed to have bearing on the problem as he saw it, he stood silent before her, staring. Then he turned away without saying a word, and carried her question home to puzzle over. Although he was willing to admit that he didn't know all of Roman history, he had known enough to answer all the questions asked except this last one. He wished he had told her that she seemed to penalize him for his failure to know more than she had demanded. There was the answer! Why hadn't he thought of it while he was standing there tongue-tied? At least, he told himself, his after-thought did more than relieve his puzzlement. It also fitted into his newly discovered definition of thinking: a process of putting this and that together with enough originality to solve a problem.

After picking up so much momentum through his formal studies, Rob spent the summer of 1889 trying to catch up on some of the reading he might have done if he had been able to take the freshman course in English and American literature. For the moment his interests were concentrated on the American Indian and his motivations came from something he had overheard about Cooper's Leatherstocking Tales. Only the first two volumes of the series were available to him, and after he had accompanied Natty Bumppo and Chingachgook through *The Deerslayer* and *The Last of the Mohicans* his search for Indian stories brought him to a current best-seller. It was Mary Hartwell Catherwood's newly published *Romance of Dollard,* an historical romance built around the heroic self-sacrifice of the celebrated Frenchman who had gone down in history as the savior of the colonies of New France when they were threatened by the Iroquoix in the seventeenth century. Francis Parkman, the historian who had actually lived for a time with Indians, had written a very complimentary "Preface" for the story about Dollard.[3] The boy might have gone on to read the classic account of Indians in *The Oregon*

Trail. Instead, and because they happened to be at hand, the three volumes of Prescott's *History of the Conquest of Mexico* provided the next romance, all centered around the picturesque Aztec Indian sovereign, Montezuma, and the daring Spanish conquistador, Hernando Cortes.

Prescott's early chapters on the Aztec Indian civilization exposed Rob for the first time to early phases of American archeology and thus established a foundation for his lifelong delight in Mayan, Toltec, and Aztec cultures. Then the account of Cortes' ruthless massacres and butcheries caused Rob to throw all his sympathies with the bewildered natives. He bled and suffered alongside these victims of Spanish lust for gold; he kept bleeding through slow page after page. It was inevitable that he become most deeply moved when Montezuma's people conducted their vengeful uprising against the Spanish in reaction to the atrocities of Alvarado. He found his favorite episode in Book IV ("Expulsion from Mexico"), particularly Chapter 3 ("Noche Triste"). He reveled in the vivid account of the retreat which Cortes arranged after the death of Montezuma, the stealthy exit from the beleaguered fortress and through the sleeping city of Tenochtitlan, the use of the specially constructed and portable bridge for crossing the first canal, the alarm given by the Aztec sentinels there, the start of the Indian attack, the crisis resulting from the inability of the Spaniards to move the portable bridge, the chaos which occurred at the crossing point of the second canal, the consequent pile up of equipment and bodies until they served as another kind of bridge for the Spanish survivors, the continuing attacks made by the Aztecs who swarmed over the causeway from boats brought across the surrounding lake, the carnage at the third canal, and the final picture of Cortes tearfully surveying the remnant of his forces which managed to escape with him from Tenochtitlan. All this bloody Aztec retaliation against the Spaniards was so thoroughly satisfying to the boy that he may have decided not to read in detail the account of how Cortes later returned and crushed the Aztecs.

Rob's extraordinary burst of reading in the summer of 1889 helped to stimulate the beginning of his poetic career; but there were other experiences during the same summer which gave him a start in another direction. Loren Bailey's little farm on "chicken house hill" in Salem was crested with a field that supplied all the hay his horse and cow could eat during any winter. The relatively brief task of harvesting this meager crop required the help of only one other man, easy enough to find when Bailey's leather shed attracted wanderers and tramps. This year, he called on Rob for help and introduced the boy to farm rituals and mysteries which eventually became doubly useful.

Bailey's old grindstone stood in the shade of a gnarled apple tree, and the first of Rob's new lessons started there. The expert taught the novice how to give just the right speed to the circumference of the stone, with one crank-turning hand, while intermittently pouring, from a tin can held in the other hand, just the right trickle of water to keep the stone moist under the pressure of the scythe blade. Bailey was not the kind of man to be satisfied with anything less than a razor-sharp blade edge. Before the process was complete, Rob learned that the nice handling of stone and blade requires time enough to give any novice wheel-turner aches in both arms. Years later, in his poem entitled "The Grindstone," he was able to smile at his memory of this experience; but his immediate response seems to have been a natural boyish impatience with Mr. Bailey's fussiness.

Next Rob learned that while the delicate process of hanging a scythe blade on the snake-shaped snath is a ritual in itself, the most important scythe-ritual of all is the proper swinging of this ingeniously constructed tool. Mr. Bailey explained that for even a capable man to swing a scythe long enough to lay flat his own little field of grass, row on row, was so tiresome that he would require some breathing spells, during which the novice would be permitted to try his hand. The boy followed the mower at a respectful distance and studied the graceful motions. He noticed the deliberate backswing; he thought he noticed the correct position of the blade as it passed in an arc beneath the wave of tumbling grass. Mr. Bailey made it seem easy. But as soon as the expert stood the scythe on its heel and pushed the snath toward Rob, the tool became troublesome. Either it was clumsy and awkward or it made the boy so, even before he took a first swing. Then the sharp blade, as Rob improperly applied it, merely bent most of the grass down instead of cutting it. Even after his mentor tried to explain that part of the trouble was caused by Rob's way of tipping the blade instead of keeping it "flat to the ground," he could not easily get the trick of it. By the time all the grass in that sweet-smelling field had been cut, he had to admit that Mr. Bailey had done most of it.

Before the day was over, Rob was also given some lessons in the correct and delicate handling of a pitchfork. First he was shown how to help the green hay "make," by turning it without jamming the tines in the ground. The next day, a threat of showers gave him the chance to help change windrows of hay into cocks for the night. The next morning he and Mr. Bailey were at it again, opening up the cocks and spreading the hay to let the sun get at it for the final round of "making." Then, while Mr. Bailey used the two-wheel horse-drawn rake for rolling new windrows, Rob taught himself how to drag a huge wooden bull rake along the edges of the field and between the rows to gather scatterings.

The most strenuous phase began after the windrows of hay had again been built into cocks for loading. As soon as Mr. Bailey hitched the mare to the hayrack and drove the short distance up the hill from the barnyard to the field, boy and man worked on opposite sides of the rack, pitching cocks of hay into it. Then Mr. Bailey climbed on the load and began to build it higher and higher, as Rob kept "pitching up" to him. Lifting and carrying forkful after forkful, each bunch of hay carried on the upright fork and balanced over his head, Rob felt that this was the first real man-sized work he had ever done. But the most unpleasant part of it began when the first load was hauled into the barn and Rob was given the task of standing in the dusty mow, reaching with his fork for the huge bundles of hay pitched up and into the mow from the load by Mr. Bailey. Working as fast as he could, catching and scattering each forkful to make the mow fill evenly, he found that whenever he was ready to take another forkful, the silent Mr. Bailey had it waiting for him.

These few days of haying were so strenuous that they filled Rob's nights with pitchfork dreams. But he took pride in having stayed with the task to the end. It had given him a new sense of his own strength. He had found muscles he never knew he had, and the pain in them was a reminder that he was entitled to carry himself like a man.

AMONG THE INFINITIES

And spent the proceeds on a telescope
To satisfy a life-long curiosity
About our place among the infinities.[1]

WHEN ROBERT FROST again began to commute from Salem
Depot to Lawrence High School, in the fall of 1889, he knew
the difference a year of growth had made. The shyness and
fear, which had bothered him so much at the start of his
freshman year, were now at least concealed if not controlled
behind a self-protective posture of arrogance. If any of his
classmates still wanted to think of him as a "rube" from Salem,
they at least would have to admit that he had proved his
academic superiority to all of them in the most difficult program offered by the high school. Still convinced that history
was the subject which would mean most to him, and still hoping that he might follow in his father's footsteps as a "major"
in history at Harvard, he enrolled for a course in European
History, a first-year course in Greek, a second-year course in
Latin, and (with some trepidation) a course in Geometry.

Shortly after the beginning of his sophomore year, Rob discovered that he had already built the foundations for a close
friendship with a student beyond his own class, a senior
named Carl Burell. It was an odd friendship in that Carl was
almost ten years older than Rob,[2] and had belatedly made up
his mind to continue his education after working for some
time as a manual laborer. Raised in the village of Sutton,
Vermont, near Lake Willoughby, and required to stay in school
only until he had finished the eighth grade, Carl had not
quickly found either the inclination or the opportunity to go
back to his studies. After he had moved from Vermont to
Manchester, New Hampshire, with his parents, he had worked
variously as handyman, caretaker, gardener, until he had

somehow established himself in Lawrence as a janitor and a jack-of-all-trades. In some way or other he had become acquainted with Rob's grandfather and also with Rob's great-uncle, Elihu Colcord, both of whom gave him work occasionally. For a time he lived in the Colcord home. Carl and Rob may have met first during Rob's freshman year in high school without seeming to have much in common. But during the fall of 1889, when Carl was nearly twenty-five and Rob only fifteen, these two outsiders, who were very largely ignored by most of their schoolmates, began to build their friendship more through loneliness than through shared interests.

Before Carl had returned to school he had tried to educate himself by taking books from the public library and even by purchasing books which particularly interested him. His tastes were unusual, and from him Rob very soon began to extend his own interests along lines not taught in school. Carl was clumsy in his movements, bothered by a slight speech impediment, impervious to nice grammatical refinements, and inclined to laugh too loudly at anything which amused him. From childhood, he had been an amateur botanist, and he frequently made excursions into the countryside around Lawrence to search for plants and flowers which he pressed, mounted, and annotated with scientific accuracy. Among many books which Rob saw for the first time in Carl's room at the Colcord's (where he stayed for some time as caretaker and handyman), were illustrated volumes devoted to Carl's two favorite botanizing specialties: ferns and orchids. An entirely different door of knowledge was opened for Rob when he found on Carl's shelf of books a little collection devoted to American humor—works by Artemus Ward, John Phoenix, Josh Billings, Orpheus C. Kerr, Petroleum V. Nasby, and Mark Twain. Cheek by jowl with these humorists, Carl had assembled a serious representation of works dealing with evolution and the consequent battle between science and religion: separate volumes by Charles Darwin, Thomas Huxley, Herbert Spencer, Edward Clodd, Grant Allen, Henry Drummond, and Richard Proctor. Although Carl preserved a devout religious belief, openly expressed in pious Christmas and Easter poems which he had already published in the *High School Bulletin,* he admitted to Rob that his reading up on evolution continued to raise many doubts in his mind concerning the so-called truths of Christian doctrine.[3]

Initially, Rob's reaction to Carl's three major preoccupations —botany, American humor, evolution—was merely one of detached curiosity. In his own wanderings through the Salem countryside and around the shore of Canobie Lake with Charley Peabody, he had been led primarily by Charley's quest for trophies, which ranged from birds' nests to turtles' eggs, with never a thought of anything so effeminate as flower-gathering. As for the subject of American humor, it had not been a feature of his mother's extensive reading aloud, although she did possess a gaiety of spirit which had not been completely destroyed by hardships. If only accidental oversight had caused Mrs. Frost to neglect American humorists, there had been deliberate reasons why she had avoided educating her children concerning what seemed to her the blasphemous and shocking claims of the evolutionists.

As an exception, one book in Carl's library attracted Rob's attention because he knew that his mother treasured a copy of it. The work was entitled *Our Place Among Infinities* and the author was the British astronomer who had become a popular writer on scientific subjects, Richard Anthony Proctor. Starting in the fall of 1889, Rob began reading *Our Place Among Infinities*. It was hard going for a fifteen-year-old boy, and the polemical tone puzzled him. The first essay begins, "The subject with which I am about to deal is associated by many with questions of religion. Let me premise, however, that I do not thus view it myself. It seems to me impossible to obtain from science any clear ideas respecting the ways or nature of the Deity, or even respecting the reality of an Almighty personal God."[4] Uncertain as to how he should take these assertions, Rob was at least fascinated by the subject under discussion in this first essay, "The Past and Future of the Earth." The approach gave a survey of the best theories concerning the evolution of the solar system, with special emphasis on the nebular hypothesis; then it invoked geological information about the age of the earth. For Rob, some of the syntax and some of the conclusions in this essay may have seemed startling, as, for example: "We find no absolute beginning if we look backwards; and looking forwards we not only find an absolute end inconceivable by reason, but revealed religion—as ordinarily interpreted—teaches—that on *that* side lies an eternity not of void but of occupied time."[5] Although Proctor's apparent rejections of certain accepted beliefs may have confused the young man on first reading, he must have found at the end of the essay statements which made him realize why his mother kept the book and even encouraged him to read it:

"Science is in presence of the old, old mystery; the old, old questions are asked of her,—'Canst thou by searching find out God? canst thou find out the Almighty unto perfection? It is as high as heaven; what canst thou do? deeper than hell; what canst thou know?' And science answers these questions, as they were answered of old,—'As touching the Almighty, we cannot find Him out.'"[6]

Here Rob was back on familiar ground, made plain to him by his mother throughout his childhood: The ways of God are indeed strange and mysterious and past finding out, even as Job was forced to admit. Thus reassured, Rob could continue to the next essay entitled "Of Seeming Wastes in Nature," and could find there further reassurances, which must have sounded familiar, concerning Design:

"We may believe, with all confidence, that could we but understand the whole of what we find around us, the wisdom with which each part has been designed would be manifest; but we must not fall into the mistake of supposing that we can so clearly understand all as to be able to recognize the purpose of this or that arrangement, the wisdom of this or that provision. Nor, if any results revealed by scientific research appear to us to accord ill with our conceptions of the economy of nature, should we be troubled, on the one hand, as respects our faith in God's benevolence, or doubt, on the other, the manifest teachings of science. In a word, our faith must not be hampered by scientific doubts, our science must not be hampered by religious scruples."[7]

To the boy, at the time, there was reassurance in this way of handling the otherwise unpleasant conflict between science and religion. Throughout most of his life, thereafter, the same resolution continued to satisfy him.[8]

Our Place Among Infinities had another immediately important effect on Rob. The separate and popularized essays on the wonders of Jupiter, Saturn, Sirius, on "Star-Depths" and on "Star-Gauging" opened up irresistibly attractive subjects for thought and observation. It was not enough for Rob that Proctor's essays led him to become acquainted with the positions and movements of stars and constellations. He insisted that he was going to get a telescope powerful enough to let him see with his own eyes the rings around Saturn. An advertisement which he found in *The Youth's Companion* offered exactly what he wanted and made the promise that the telescope would be sent free to anyone who obtained a certain number of new subscriptions to the magazine. Encouraged by his mother, he immediately began a house-to-house canvas of the Lawrence neighborhood where they were then living.

The Frosts had moved back to Lawrence from Salem in February of 1890. After resigning from her position as teacher at Salem Depot, Mrs. Frost had an opportunity to teach at a district school in Methuen, the town lying between Salem and Lawrence. For the convenience of her two high-school children she had rented a cheap and drafty apartment in a slum section on East Haverhill Street, unpleasantly near the Boston and Maine Railroad freight yard and yet within a mile of the high school. Even if the Frosts had not been strangers in this forlorn neighborhood of Lawrence, it would not have been a good area for selling subscriptions to *The Youth's Companion,* and Rob soon found that his task was even more distasteful to him than hawking newspapers on the streets of San Francisco. After he had given up, completely discouraged, his indulgent mother completed the campaign for him by making appeals to friends in Salem and Lawrence. Eventually the telescope arrived, and Rob very quickly began to learn more about his own place among infinities. He and his mother transformed a bedroom into an observatory by rigging a black curtain across the window to keep out city lights, then cutting a hole just large enough to let the end of the telescope slide through the curtain and over the edge of the partly opened upper sash.

What Rob actually saw, through his new telescope, was not nearly so important as the stimulus it gave his further study of astronomy. From the Lawrence Public Library he took out a handbook containing a list of star names, diagrams of the patterns of constellations, and tables for determining the positions of the major constellations on the celestial concave at all hours and seasons. In these activities his mother took great interest. Repeatedly, she kept reminding him of a familiar line from Young's *Night Thoughts:* "An undevout astronomer is mad." It pleased her that Rob found in all the wonders and mysteries of the heavens, as viewed through his telescope and his readings, an increasing wonder at revelations and mysteries whose first causes and ultimate purposes are indeed past finding out.

Carl Burell's very important stimulus to Rob in scientific matters was closely bound up with Carl's contributions of verse and prose to the high school *Bulletin*. In his library he carefully preserved the issues containing the poems and essays he had published so far. If they made Rob feel jealous, he must have supposed that the achievements represented by Carl's ballad-like poems could easily be surpassed. Measured against the many ballads which Rob's mother had so often read aloud, over a period of many years, Carl's work needed improvement.

The inspiration for writing a ballad of his own came to Rob one blustery and cloud-darkened evening in March of 1890, as he walked from high school along Haverhill Street to the home of his grandparents, where he stayed intermittently. Something reminded him of the story he had found in Prescott's *Conquest of Mexico:* The night made sad and terrible for the Spaniards by the Aztec Indians during the disastrous retreat across the causeway over Lake Tezcuco from the island city of Tenochtitlan. What he remembered of Prescott's account began composing itself into lines and ballad stanzas as he walked, and the school books he carried at the end of a strap were useful as a metronome; he kept swinging them to give him a proper sense of the ballad rhythm he wanted. It seemed to him as though he could hear the lines spoken, almost by the same voice which had puzzled him years ago in San Francisco.

Quatrain after quatrain kept coming to him, and with the completion of each new one his rapture mounted. Just as soon as he could sit down to write, and with much excitement, he put on paper one line after another, until he had twenty-five stanzas. Appropriately, he entitled his poem "La Noche Triste," and he introduced the ballad with a prologue—twenty-seven unrhymed, irregular, three-stress lines—which bore the subtitle "Tenochtitlan." He separated the prologue from the ballad proper by using another subtitle, "The Flight."[9] In his conclusion, as though remembering what Halleck had done in "Marco Bozzaris" or how Collins had built the last couplet around the word freedom in "How Sleep the Brave," Rob paid tribute to the liberty-loving Aztecs who had fought so desperately for their own freedom that they triumphed, at least temporarily, over their Spanish oppressors:

Follow we not the Spaniard more,
Wending o'er hill and plain,
Suffice to say he reached the coast,
Lost Fortune to regain.

The flame shines brightest e'er goes out,
Thus with the Aztec throne,
On that dark night before the end,
So o'er the fight it shone.

The Montezumas are no more,
Gone is their regal throne,
And freemen live, and rule, and die,
Where they have ruled alone.[10]

The intoxication of this new accomplishment was so great that Rob sat gloating over his manuscript, convinced that it prophesied his future as a poet. The next day he took to school with him a fair copy of the ballad, carried it to the senior home-room where he hoped to find the Chief Editor of the *Bulletin*, Ernest Jewell, and left the manuscript on Jewell's desk before the editor arrived. Although Rob had some doubt whether a senior would condescend to accept a poem written by a sophomore, he was superstitious enough to hope that his having written it during his birth month would be a lucky omen. Apparently it was. Jewell published "La Noche Triste" on the very first page of the *Bulletin* for April 1890.

The double success of writing and publishing his first long poem spurred Rob to another effort. It resulted in a lyric entitled "Song of the Wave," a mood piece fashioned from vivid memories of his vigils at the Cliff House, the view outward and downward of the oncoming breakers with the Seal Rocks before them, the sight and sound of Pacific Ocean water shattering against ledges in the twilight. This time he made his lines into three-line stanzas, each with a single sound for rhyme, and then he retarded the conclusion appropriately with a one-rhyme quatrain. Again Jewell accepted the sophomore's offering, which appeared in the *Bulletin* for May 1890. Rob's poetry-writing mother was almost as greatly elated as he was.

The immediate effect of these two contributions afforded the sophomore unexpected opportunities to enter new high-school activities, further assisted by his admiring friend Carl

Burell. It was comforting to be supported by Carl, who was actively engaged not only in the editorial affairs of the *Bulletin* but also in bimonthly meetings of a formerly dignified but now occasionally nonsensical debating club which thrived without faculty supervision. By the time Rob was elected to membership in the "Debating Union," as the club was officially called, the president of the organization was a senior named Alexander Frost, and the student who made the best recommendations of subjects for debate was the *Bulletin* editor, Ernest C. Jewell. Under immediate discussion was a possible amendment to the laws of the society, a recommendation that young ladies should be admitted as members because they would have a sobering effect on the drift toward mere hilarity. Jewell opposed the suggestion very sternly. He insisted that "if young men could not conduct themselves as gentlemen without the presence of ladies it was time to break up the society . . ."[11] Although the motion for amendment was defeated, some of the later meetings came close to being riots. Jewell, trying to preserve the original purpose of the society—to give students experience in the kinds of forensic discussion which might occur on the floor of a state or federal legislative body— enlisted the support of Burell and Frost. As a result of their literary and forensic collaboration, this trio established a close friendship.

As Rob came to the end of his sophomore year, he knew he had made important strides toward his ideal goal of inner and outer discipline. Faithfully he had carried out his class preparations in Greek, Latin, European History, Geometry; he had made his own personal explorations in the field of astronomy; he had spent many hours with Carl Burell discussing the conflict between science and religion; he had written two poems which had been published in the *Bulletin;* he had acquired the friendship of Ernest Jewell; and he had been welcomed into the debating society. His final marks for the year placed him once again at the head of his class, and he could not resist the enjoyment of noticing that some of his classmates who had first treated him as the dumb country boy from Salem were now deferential.

During the summer of 1890, the financial problems of the Frosts became so serious that all three of them were glad to find work in a hotel at Ocean Park, Maine, some twenty miles south of Portland. The salary paid to Mrs. Frost in Salem had been nine dollars a week, only a little more than three hundred dollars for the school year. In her newly acquired position as teacher of the upper classes at the Merrill District School in Methuen, her salary had been ten dollars a week. There was obvious need for her to find other sources of income for rent, food, clothes. The thought of a summer on the Atlantic coast had attracted these San Franciscans; but almost as soon as they reached Ocean Park, Mrs. Frost regretted the venture. The chambermaids with whom she and Jeanie worked seemed shockingly coarse in their conversations and low in their moral standards; the kitchen help, the waitresses, and the waiters with whom Rob was thrown were not people she would have chosen as associates for her son. More painful to Rob was his discovery that as errand boy and handyman he was at the beck and call of everyone. As requested, the Frosts arrived a few days before the hotel opened its doors for the summer season and Rob's first assignment was to paint all the rockers and chairs lined up on the long porch of the hotel.

Having anticipated daily opportunities for spending some time on the beach and swimming in the ocean, Rob was disgusted to find that by the end of each day he was far too exhausted to need or want exercise. Even worse, when he did go swimming for the first time, he discovered that the temperature of the Maine ocean water was even colder than it had been at Sausalito near the Golden Gate. But the three Frosts soon made their own adjustments and kept to their own company as much as possible. During their scheduled hours of freedom, they took walks up or down the white sands of the long curving beach, preferring to collect smooth rocks and sea-shells rather than stay cooped up in the unpleasant atmosphere of the servants' quarters back of the hotel.

The only innovation which intensely aroused Rob's faculties, this summer, was tennis. The servants were permitted to use the hotel tennis courts in the evenings, and Rob was frequently drafted to make a fourth player for "doubles"—with a borrowed racquet. Although the game was entirely new to him and he was ashamed of his initial clumsiness, he was not playing with experts. He relied on the quickness of his reflexes; he learned to charge the net for "put-away" shots; and he liked scampering back to recover "lobs." By the end of the summer he had developed enough skill and appreciation of the game to make him decide that tennis was almost as much fun as baseball, and both games remained lifelong passions with him. Aside from tennis, however, so many unpleasant incidents marred the long and tedious days at Ocean Park that all three of the Frosts very eagerly returned to Lawrence as soon as they could after the Labor Day weekend.

To his surprise, Rob found that he was even looking forward to the start of the fall term and classes. So much had changed for him, now that he had found a direction for his energies and had convinced himself of his own abilities. He welcomed new chances to demonstrate what he could do. Of course, he still had a long way to go and Carl Burell kept warning him that the first two years were the easy ones. Rob was not so sure. What could be worse than his freshman year, which had started so painfully? No matter what difficulties lay ahead, he had the satisfaction of knowing that he no longer had to conquer the kind of fear and uncertainty he had initially brought down to Lawrence from Salem.

10

OUTER AND INNER DEBATES

There are men . . . who go to death with such grey
grandeur that we look back upon their past for some
strange sorrow . . . Such lives are the growth of the after-
thought of the soul—the serene rest after toil, in question-
ing and answering whence and why misfortune is.[1]

A NEW INTENSITY of seriousness was reflected in Robert
Frost's plan to concentrate fully on classical studies at the beginning of his junior year in Lawrence High School. Before
making the choice, he had foreseen all the drudgery awaiting
him if he took a third year of Latin, a second year of Greek,
a course in Latin composition, and a course in Greek composition. But among the variety of reasons for harnessing himself
to this program, not the least was his consciousness that he was
deliberately giving himself further exercise in self-discipline.
By this time he was very strongly convinced that his position
at the head of his class was so important to him that he was
willing to approach any assignment as an exacting test of his
ability to overcome ingrained laziness. Whenever he was in the
mood for self-indulgence, he secretly and even furtively stole
time for writing another poem; but even here he found that
after his first rapture of seeing "La Noche Triste" and "Song of
the Wave" in print, he was more and more inclined to be slow
and cautious in revising and polishing anything he wrote.

He anticipated that his most pleasant hours of extracurricu-
lar work during this year would be provided by the activities
of the debating society. Having worked closely with Ernest
Jewell in the task of suggesting topics for debate during the
previous spring, he found that the society leaned even more
heavily on him now that Jewell had been graduated and had
gone to nearby Phillips Andover Academy for two more years
of preparation before entering Harvard College. At the first

meeting in the fall of 1890, and speaking for the committee delegated to choose topics, Rob offered for use in the first formal debate a subject which should have had special appeal to a native San Franciscan: "Resolved, that the Chinese Exclusion Act is just and is a benefit to our country."[2] The subject was currently a serious national issue because the Chinese Exclusion Act, passed by Congress in 1888, violated certain terms of the treaty which had been in effect between China and the United States since 1880. Although Rob was not one of the formal participants in the eventual—and thoroughly serious—debate on this topic, he did take part in the general discussion and (perhaps because he was a native San Franciscan) he spoke strongly for the affirmative side. As soon as he sat down, Rob was supported by his friend Carl Burell, who had not been graduated with the Class of 1890. Carl took the floor and "drew a most eloquent parallel between the fate of the Indians at the hands of the white man and the possible future fate of the American people at the hands of the Chinese." He was just as serious as Rob; but Carl's irrepressible humor caused him to stand again and urge that such a solemn evening of discussion might well be leavened with a concluding mock-debate. The more playful members gave him support; a nonsensical topic was chosen; and the fun began. "Eloquence of the spread eagle variety was poured forth unrestrainedly, and all possible intricacies and refinements of parliamentary practice were brought into requisition in the course of the discussion. The meeting finally adjourned on a premonitory 'request' from the janitor [of the high school]."[3]

Later in the fall the combined efforts of Carl and Rob were again apparent when the following topic for debate was proposed and approved: "Resolved, that Bryant was a greater poet than Whittier." Preparations were made; the debate was held as planned; Rob spoke formally as the second affirmative; and the affirmative side won. In the general discussion which followed, Carl supported his friend in a way which impressed the *Bulletin* reporter: "Mr. Burell in a most eloquent address described poetry and showed a thorough knowledge of both poets. . . . He thought that while the poetry of Whittier stirred and aroused us for the moment and then let its influence die away, the poetry of Bryant was a constant source of help and inspiration to us."[4]

The overtones of natural piety in Bryant's verse apparently

touched the devout Carl. For similar reasons, Rob may have recalled the day in Loren Bailey's leather-shed when he had found that he knew "To a Waterfowl" by heart without even trying to memorize it.

The only other debate in which Carl and Rob joined forces during the fall involved a subject so important to them both that either one of them could have suggested it: ". . . a bill for removing the Indians from Indian Territory to more fertile districts and ceding said districts to the tribes forever; and for giving them some compensation for the losses already suffered."[5] As first speaker on the affirmative side in this debate, Rob came well prepared. His factual information was carefully drawn from a book he had read especially for the occasion: Helen Hunt Jackson's bitter and impassioned indictment entitled *A Century of Dishonor: A Sketch of the United States Government's Dealings with Some of the Indian Tribes*. But the evening was spoiled for him by the boisterous disorder and rowdy horseplay of members who preferred to clown. In the general discussion Carl Burell defended the affirmative position, but was interrupted several times by motions to adjourn. The uproar grew so offensive to some that the junior vice-president of the society resigned and Rob was elected to take his place, temporarily. But perhaps because he belonged with the minority, who really wished to separate the serious debates from the mock debates, he was not elected to the same office or to any other office in the debating society in the spring elections of 1891.[6]

Far more crucial to his future plans was the early warning given juniors taking the college preparatory course. Some of them would be expected to take preliminary examinations in the spring, particularly the young men applying for admission to Harvard. His father's affiliation with Harvard made Rob assume that he would go there if the money could be found. He was frightened to learn that Harvard offered to high-school juniors the opportunity to take seven hours of preliminary examinations, at Cambridge, in March and in June: examinations in Greek, Latin, Greek History, Roman History, Algebra, Geometry, and English Literature. The seventh one worried him most. Mr. Goodwin had warned his group that those who had not taken courses in English Literature were expected to develop a reading acquaintance with each title in a long list of books he gave them. Awed by so many strange titles, Rob decided to tackle only six of the "prelims" at Cambridge in the spring of 1891, and to ask for a postponement of the English Literature examination until the fall. The arrangement was acceptable; an excursion to Harvard was made in March, another was made in June; and to his great satisfaction, Rob passed all six.[7]

A new stimulus was given to Rob's writing that spring when his class met to elect *Bulletin* editors for the following school year. Traditionally, the senior class assumed responsibility for the management of the school paper, and it was understood that the chief editor should possess gifts of leadership. Although Rob's friend and mentor, Ernest C. Jewell, had never contributed to the *Bulletin* prior to his election as Chief Editor he had managed the task with skill and had also won valedictory honors in the Class of 1890. Perhaps because an analogy was seen, the Class of 1892 elected Rob Chief Editor of the *Bulletin* for his senior year, although he had contributed only two poems to it. The more important expectation may have been that he would be valedictorian of the class. In the meeting, as soon as the vote was taken, Rob rose to his feet and warned that he would accept the honor only if he were given more support than previous editors had been given. He urged that the usual number of five assistants or literary editors, drawn from the senior class, should be increased to seven. The terms were immediately met, and the announcement of this meeting, as given in the issue of the *Bulletin* for April of 1891, carried the names of seven students who would assist Mr. Frost, together with the names of three reporters and two business managers. With this announcement appeared a brief statement made by the retiring editor:

"As will be seen, two members have been added to the Literary Editors. This is a good move, we believe. From five to six articles are required to fill the literary part of the paper, and it is sometimes impossible for all the five to write an article each month, so the editor has to 'hustle' and find a composition somehow. Having seven will insure enough matter and will allow of picking out the best. . . ."[8]

The forecast was too optimistic. But Rob, as though he felt called upon to live up to expectations, submitted to the retiring editor a new poem which was published on the first page of the *Bulletin* for May of 1891: "A Dream of Julius Caesar." Distinctly different from his two earlier offerings, this one was cast in blank verse, nearly seventy lines in length. The beginning suggests the influence of Rob's reading in Wordsworth and Thomas Gray:

> *A dreamy day: a gentle western breeze*
> *That murmurs softly 'midst the sylvan shades;*
> *Above, the fleecy clouds glide slowly on*
> *To sink from view; within the forest's depth,*
> *A thrush's drowsy note starts echoes through*
> *The vistas of the over-hanging trees.*
> *All nature seems to weave a circle of*
> *Enchantment round the mind, and give full sway*
> *To flitting thoughts and dreams of bygone years.*

In the next twenty-five lines the young poet gave a verbal picture of an approaching thunderstorm with a fringe of cloud rifts through which slanting ladders of sunlight reached earthward:

> *. . . like ladders long, by which*
> *From earth to heaven the woodland nymphs may pass*
> *Beyond the clouds, bright rays of light stretch down*
> *Upon each grove and mead.*

At this midpoint in the poem, the speaker (on whose ears the sound of thunder drums unheeded) falls asleep and dreams that there is an actual ladder stretching from earth to heaven. And what to his wondering eye should appear, descending this ladder, but the toga-clad Julius Caesar brandishing "the bolt of Jove" in one hand as he warns that he is coming back to rule the world; his legions are at hand and "Conquest still is the one passion of this fiery breast."

> *He speaks and vanishes from sight. The roar*
> *Of chariot wheels breaks on my ear. The fight*
> *Is on, for blood in torrents falls around,*
> *Not crimson, but a lighter hue, such as*
> *The fairy hosts of silvery light might shed.*

So the poem ends, as it began, within a circle of enchantment. If Rob's classmates were not irreverently amused by the notion of the toga-clad Caesar climbing or sliding down such a long ladder, they may have taken this salute from their incipient Chief Editor as a good omen. Certainly for Rob, it marked an important achievement with which to end his junior year.

After so many dignified and triumphant events at school, the young man was subjected to a series of embarrassing experiences early in the summer of 1891. Perhaps through such a friend as Loren Bailey in Salem, New Hampshire, he obtained work on a farm in the nearby township of Windham, on the east side of Cobbetts Pond and only two miles southwest of Canobie Lake. The farmer was an easy going Scotchman named Dinsmore, who raised vegetables and carted them to market in Lawrence. He made extra money with the aid of his wife and son by taking in a few guests or "summer boarders" who, seeking rural escape from the city during vacation, might be attracted to the diversions of the good-sized forest-enclosed lake. (It was really too big to be called a pond.) Having prospered so well that he needed hired men on his place each summer, Dinsmore built bunkhouse quarters for them on a knoll in a clump of maples overlooking the water. In many ways the entire farm offered an idyllic setting for guests or hired men, and when Rob arrived he was delighted with the prospect. He began his duties by patching and cleaning and painting several rowboats. Next, he was put to work at weeding, and in a short time he was able to use Loren Bailey's instructions concerning the rituals of haying. The summer might have passed in truly idyllic fashion for the young man from Lawrence if his bunkhouse companions had not been too much like the people with whom he had worked at Ocean Park a year earlier. The roughest and rowdiest of the four men in the bunkhouse was Dinsmore's own son. He was only a few years older than Rob, and yet he was given authority to supervise all the hired hands.

Among the few guests at the Dinsmore farm was a very pretty young stenographer from Lawrence, who soon provided romantic diversion for young Dinsmore. The most pleasant evening's entertainment for them both came to be a casual and leisurely voyage down the lake in a rowboat. The men in the bunkhouse were quick to notice that Dinsmore never brought the girl back until long after dark. He answered their jests with boasts—and Rob was not amused. His bunkmate explained that if their ribaldry offended him, they would gladly teach him the facts of life so that he could enjoy their wit. In their crude way they taught him more than he could tolerate concerning sexual matters.

Rob might have had difficulty in explaining, even to himself, that the insinuations and obscenities of his bunkmates offended him most because they cut sharply against the grain of his idealistic and romantic notions of love and womanhood. Unintentionally, he discovered something when he assumed the heroic task of defending the morals of the stenographer against young Dinsmore's boasts. All this evil talk, he said, was an attempt to besmirch a pure and innocent girl. Rob could tell that much about her from his own brief conversations with her.

Oh, he could, could he? Then perhaps he should take the girl down the lake a mile or so for a moonlight voyage in a rowboat some night when Dinsmore was otherwise engaged. The challenge was accepted; the arrangements were made; and on the scheduled evening Dinsmore and his companions gathered at the dock to give the two young city people a raucous send-off. Both of them took the teasing as well as they could, and for the next hour Rob found that the girl's spirited and witty conversation made him feel at ease. He was delighted to learn that they had mutual friends among recent high-school graduates, and their talk flowed so pleasantly that neither one of them seemed to notice when the shoreline began to grow dim in the dusk or when the first stars appeared overhead. Rob had decided that he could not prove his point to his lascivious bunkmates unless he brought the girl back long after dark, and so he kept rowing slowly down the lake. He was merely amused when the girl urged him to keep nearer to the eastern shore so that she could tell where they were; but he did as she asked. He was not even troubled when she asked him to row into a small cove, which he could see only because more stars were visible nearer the horizon as the tree-line silhouette receded. But in the cove he suffered an unexpected shock, when the girl suggested that it would be nice if they went ashore a little while before they started back; she knew a sandy beach in this cove. Something about the tone of her voice in making this invitation frightened Rob more than what she said—and forced him to realize that young Dinsmore and the other bunkmates knew more than he did about this girl. Suddenly feeling miserable and ashamed of himself, he fumbled for excuses as he turned the rowboat back into the lake and started for the farm. If the girl noticed how her companion lapsed into silence after all his easy talk, she gave no sign of it. Nothing seemed to bother her, and she merely kept on talking. When they reached the lantern-lighted dock, Rob gallantly helped her out of the boat, tied it up, put out the lantern, escorted her to the lamplit house, said a hasty goodnight, and fled.

By the time he reached the bunkhouse he had sufficiently established a posture from which to answer all the taunting questions amicably and triumphantly. He insisted that his pleasant and innocent evening with the girl proved his claim that they had lied about her. But after the lewd comments and laughter had stopped, after the others had gone to sleep, Rob lay in his bunk overwhelmed with a frightening suspicion. Suppose young Dinsmore had gotten the girl in trouble and knew it. Suppose he had made a scapegoat of Rob by arranging this evening voyage? What was the law in a situation like this? If the girl and Dinsmore both lied, might Rob be the one who would have to marry her? It didn't seem possible, and yet . . .

As a result of that night's experience, Rob's feeling of shock and distaste grew into loathing for everything and everybody at the Dinsmore farm. What had appeared idyllic now became repulsive. He had liked the farmer, old Dinsmore, until he began to notice that the Scotchman drank whiskey and occasionally came home under the influence of it after making some of his vegetable-selling trips to Lawrence. One night, when the old mare could be heard clomping into the farmyard from the road, late, the bunkhouse boys climbed out of bed to see if everything was all right. The mare was fine, because she knew her way home, even in the dark. But the reins were dragging in the dirt and the old man was stretched comfortably on his cart seat, asleep or worse, his legs hanging over the side. Gaily the hired men lifted him down from his cart and helped him into the house. Then they returned, laughing, to unharness the mare and put her into the pasture. Rob stayed in the background, out of sight, disgusted.

After only three weeks at the Dinsmore farm, he found a good excuse for quitting. Since his boyhood days in San Francisco he had always been a notorious slugabed, and here in the bunkhouse he was the last one up each morning, in spite of the horseplay. Young Dinsmore became so exasperated by this laziness that he emptied a pitcher of cold well water on the sleeper's head one morning—and that did it. Outraged, Rob waited until he could make his departure unseen, and then he slipped away from the Dinsmore farm without asking for his wages. Late that same night he walked wretchedly into his home and answered his mother's questions as he had done when he quit the shoe shop in Salem: he couldn't stand the coarseness, the profanity, the filthy talk of the hired help at Dinsmore's. No more was asked, or told.

Conscience-stricken by his failure to bring home any money after three weeks of work, Rob told his mother he would try to find something to do in one of the Lawrence mills. In spite of her remonstrance that the indoor atmosphere and the long hours would be bad for him, he quickly found employment at Braithwaite's small woolen mill, halfway between Methuen and Lawrence. His task was easy—pushing a bobbin-wagon among the rows of machines to collect empty bobbins—but the hours were from seven until six, with a half-hour for lunch, six full days a week.

Rob had not worked long in Braithwaite's mill before he found that his sympathies were newly allied with the labor organizations which had been stirring up the city with protest-meetings. Never before had his mother's Socialist interest in the doctrines of Henry George or her deep admiration for Bellamy's recently published *Looking Backward* made so much sense to him. His personal reasons for wanting a successful culmination of labor pressure made him delighted when all of the Lawrence mills were forced to grant Saturday afternoons off, starting in the middle of this summer. It reduced the working hours per week from sixty-three to fifty-eight. In a celebrating mood, Rob spent his first free Saturday afternoon visiting his grandfather, and was not surprised to find the retired Pacific Mills foreman prophesying doom.

"You mark my word," the old man warned him. "In a few years these lazy louts will be at it again, trying to cut their time down to a fifty-hour week."

His grandson pleasantly answered that if the lazy louts succeeded, here was one of them who would cheer. There was no use in trying to say more; grandson and grandfather had a way of annoying each other, sooner or later, in any conversation.

Except for the long hours, Rob enjoyed the new experience of mingling with the men and women at the mill. He liked the ways in which their friendliness, their harmless practical jokes, their witticisms, their laughter kept the drudgery from being unbearable. This time he did not even make the familiar complaint to his mother that some of the loose talk and profanity (overheard from the women as well as the men) still shocked him. If he had needed it as an excuse for quitting, he would have used it—and there were many times when he wanted to quit. But for the sake of the money he stayed until fall, and then was glad to have the excuse that he must return to high school.

11

IF THY HEART FAIL THEE

"... we agree that to Raleigh's words,
'Fain would I climb but that I fear to fall,'
there is an answer better than this motto:
'If thy heart fail thee, why then climb at all?' "[1]

ROBERT FROST was proud of his standing when he returned
to Lawrence High School as a senior in the fall of 1891: head
of his class, Chief Editor of the *Bulletin*, prominent member
of the debating society, and one of the new college preparatory
students who had already passed six of the seven preliminary
examinations. He liked being treated with more and more
respect by the same students who had previously mocked him.
He was not unhappy when one of his teachers reproached
other students by assuring them that they had as many hours
for preparation as Robert Frost did, and when she urged them
to imitate his way of putting time to good use. He also enjoyed
the fact that sitting next to him in his home-room a very pretty
girl expressed her admiration in shy glances, which were all
the more appealing because he so fully understood shyness.[2]

The girl's name was Elinor Miriam White and she was the
daughter of a backslidden Universalist minister in Lawrence.
Rob had not met her previously, because she was enrolled in
the general or English program rather than in the classical.
A chronic illness called "slow fever" had hindered her from
regular attendance at the high school until the middle of Rob's
sophomore year; but she had managed to study at home, to
take examinations, and to do so much extra work that she
had qualified for membership in the Class of '92. She made
herself even more attractive to the Chief Editor of the *Bulletin*
when she submitted to him, early in the fall, a few manuscript
poems from which she hoped he would select at least one for
publication. He did.[3]

When the first issue of the *Bulletin* appeared under the management of the new staff, Rob filled several of his editorials with optimistic observations, exhortations, and announcements. He prefaced them with assurances, which included this statement: ". . . No doubt we endanger our reputation, but we agree that to Raleigh's words, 'Fain would I climb but that I fear to fall,' there is an answer better than this motto: 'If thy heart fail thee, why then climb at all?' "[4] He continued by saying that an increasing number of students kept aiming high by taking the classical course; and he prophesied that Lawrence High School would "soon possess a name far other than its present illiterate one." Then he sent his best wishes to the newly departed scholars who had been enrolled at Tufts, Wellesley, Harvard, and the Massachusetts Institute of Technology. His most important editorial announcement, in this his first issue of the *Bulletin,* was that a group of alumni was enabling the *Bulletin* to offer a series of prizes for the best literary works in poetry and in prose. He continued by giving some earnest editorial advice:

"That essay writing cannot be made a matter of option, we well know . . . but that there are those who prefer 'for honor' to 'by necessity' we also know, and it is for these that this offer [of a prize] is made, in the hope of arousing something more than mere words."[5]

Completely serious in his attempts to encourage competition for these literary prizes, Rob returned to the subject in a later issue of the *Bulletin*. He complained that the response to his first announcement had been "far from satisfactory" and went on to make a special plea for the writing of more poetry:

"In our colleges, students of English are advised to make use of verse composition for increasing their general vocabulary. . . . Perhaps we speak too flippantly of our subject; but we are not here to persuade anyone that the poets (so-called) of our school journals are all to harp among the nation's bards; far from it. We know that our school is not now made up exclusively of future poets, yet we venture to say that there is not a scholar, who, with some little practice cannot surmount our literary columns with a capital of no mean proportions, (mechanically speaking)."[6]

Although the plea apparently went unheeded, the pleasantries in it did not conceal the earnestness of the editor's concern for the writing of poetry. He had heightened his demands on his own technical skill, and he could have offered an example to the others by publishing a poem he wrote soon after he made his October visit to Harvard to take his seventh examination, the one in English Literature. The poem was a skippingly anapestic song inspired by his early morning walk through Boston Common on the morning of his examination:

Clear and Colder—Boston Common

As I went down through the common,
  It was bright with the light of day,
For the wind and rain had swept the leaves
  And the shadow of summer away.
The walks were all fresh-blacked with rain
  As I went briskly down:—
I felt my own quick step begin
  The pace of the winter town.

As I went down through the common,
  The sky was wild and pale;
I saw one tree with a jib of leaves
  In the stress of the aftergale;
But the others rattled naked poles
  As I went briskly down.
I felt my own quick step begin
  The pace of the winter town.

As I went down through the common
  In the crisp October dawn,
Benches were wet and stuck with leaves
  And the idle ones were gone.
The folk abroad raced on with me
  As I went briskly down.
I felt my own quick step begin
  The pace of the winter town.

As I went through the common,
  Then felt I first delight
Of the city's thronging winter days
  And dazzling winter night,
Of the life and revelry to be—

As I went briskly down.
I felt my own quick step begin
The pace of the winter town.[7]

For Rob, the writing of "Clear and Colder" was a particular exercise in further adapting to his own needs a ballad stanza he had been hearing since first his mother showed him her favorites in Scott's *Border Ballads* or in Percy's *Reliques*. His first published poem, "La Noche Triste," had been built into a four-three ballad stanza, common measure. Now he had advanced far enough to enjoy experimenting with another familiar pattern, working his own variations on a simple refrain, taking more liberties with meter so that he could make the lines skip along with the mood of the piece, and drawing his images direct from his own observations. He had reason to be proud of all that he was teaching himself about the mechanics of prosody, and he certainly could have published "Clear and Colder" in the *Bulletin*. Instead, he put it aside, as though he were content to view it merely as an exercise.

Although he enjoyed his work and play as editor-scholar-poet, he was no bookworm. And he welcomed a coincidence which led him back into athletics early in the fall of his senior year. Having lost none of his enthusiasm for baseball and none of his pride in being able to run fast, he had wistfully followed the activities of his schoolmates in their various games. But his pride still felt the wound of those insults which had greeted him on the first morning of his arrival at Lawrence High School, and he had reached his senior year without having tried to earn a place on any team.

One afternoon, he happened to visit the football field when the team was practicing and happened to be within calling distance when the discovery was made that one player was needed, in practice, to give adequate opposition to the first-string team. Maybe Frost would fill in, someone said. Provoked just enough by the tone of the jest, Rob peeled off his coat and asked for a helmet. The position assigned him was at right end, where the speed of his defensive motions, the shrewdness with which he anticipated the strategies of the offense, and the unexpected savagery of his flying tackles surprised the regulars. By the end of the afternoon he had won himself a place on the first team, and he held up so well that he played in every scheduled game that fall; the team finished the regular season unbeaten. An account of the first victory against Bradford High School appeared in the *Bulletin* and contained praise for the excellent defensive play of the Lawrence ends, "Tobin and Frost," for "putting up a game that made it dangerous for Bradford to run around them." In a postlude the reporter could not resist a more personal salute to the one member of the *Bulletin* staff who was playing "regular" on the first team:

"No one would think the man who played football on the right end was the same person who sits with spectacles astride his nose in the Chief Editor's Chair. Keep up the good work, Bobby."[8]

He did keep it up, at more cost of nervous energy and courage than any of his schoolmates guessed. If he could have made his own rules for the rough-and-tumble game which was then made dangerous by flying-wedge tactics, he might have given instructions similar to those he gave in Salem whenever he put on boxing gloves: Let's not hit each other on the nose, on the mouth, or in the eyes. But anyone playing football in the 'nineties could count on being bruised all over, if nothing worse, before the end of a game. And all of Rob's keen sensitivities were so easily injured or at least offended, by the ruthlessness of the play, that he always felt sick to his stomach whenever the hammering excitement was over. Toward the close of one game, when the strain and punishment was almost more than he could bear, he managed to last until the final whistle; then he walked off the field into tall grass, knelt where nobody could see him, and relieved his nervousness with a prolonged fit of vomiting. It was all a part of the price he was willing to pay for the fulfillment of his ideals of power and honor and glory; it was all part of the self-discipline which could and did assert courage and daring as the best way to overcome his own fears, lest they grow to be paralyzing and self-crippling.

From his own first-hand experience he had acquired all the evidence he needed concerning temporary psychological states that could render an individual a victim of uncontrollable forces. If he needed any further evidence he had it near at hand and painfully apparent in the sad predicament of his sister, Jeanie. Back in Salem it had seemed as though her bookishness might give her an adequate realm of retreat from whatever she could not bear in the world of reality. She had pridefully distinguished herself as a scholar in grammar school during the years when her older brother was floundering. But in the four years since then, it seemed as though Jeanie's desperate retreat into books had failed her. As long as she had asserted superiority over her brother, scholastically, she seemed to derive adequate sustenance from pride alone. When he had surpassed her, during their first year in high school as freshmen, all her defenses began to collapse.

During her sophomore year, Jeanie suffered through moods of depression much like those which had beset her, intermittently, since her childhood days in San Francisco. Her spells of tears, hysteria, ravings, which caused her to miss more and more days of school, puzzled her mother increasingly. In the midst of one spell Jeanie was making so much noise that Mrs. Frost turned desperately to her son for help. Enraged, he stormed into Jeanie's bedroom, found her lying face down on her bed, turned her over, and slapped her across the face with the flat of his hand. Just for a moment the one blow had the desired effect: Jeanie grew silent, stopped crying completely, and sat up. She stared at her brother and then said, scornfully, "You cad, you coward." That was not Rob's only use of violence when trying to help his sister.

The gradual deterioration of Jeanie's interest in her studies, during her junior year, was capped by her refusal to consider taking any preliminary college entrance examinations. She began her senior year halfheartedly and then, in early December of 1891, she became so ill that a doctor was called. It was typhoid fever, he said, and he promptly made arrangements for her to be taken to the nearest hospital. She almost died, and by the time she recovered, she was so far behind in her schoolwork that her mother let her stay out of school for the rest of the year. She never finished high school.

Although Jeanie's many problems were discussed repeatedly and at length by her mother and brother, neither one of them understood the causes of her weakness. Rob understood enough, however, to take warning from his sister's condition. He kept reminding himself that unless he could keep his own potentially self-destructive sensitivities, fears, rages under control, he might become the victim of problems even more serious than those which had already overtaken his sister.

The most severe accumulation of nervous upsets which threatened Rob during his high-school years was caused by his involvement in too many activities during the late fall of 1891. Football practice and regularly scheduled games used up so much of his time and energy that he could not do as much work as he wished in preparing classroom assignments; but he drove himself hard. The steadying influence he exerted on the debating society heightened the dependence on him of that partly serious and partly nonsensical group. As others dropped out, he was elected to the office of senior vice-president and then to the office of president.[9] Even before these new honors were voted to him, Rob had so much difficulty in finding time enough for his duties as Chief Editor of the *Bulletin* that he began delegating some of his tasks to assistant editors. They gave him insufficient support, and as a result the November issue of the *Bulletin* was distributed in December. At nearly the same time Jeanie's hospitalization with typhoid fever required Rob's absence from school for several days. Again he asked the staff of the *Bulletin* to help; again they failed him. Returning to school in January, he discovered that the December issue had not been published and that there was scarcely any copy in hand for the issue. Enraged, he took what copy he had, went to the printer's office, asked for a cubbyhole where he could work, and spent one whole day in hiding while he wrote copy enough to fill out the December issue. In this way, he decided, he could fulfill his own obligations before resigning as Chief Editor in protest against the failure of his staff to carry out their duties.

The preparation of the December, 1891, issue of the *Bulletin* was a major literary accomplishment for Robert Frost; at least, it seemed to him to be an enormous tour-de-force, as he tossed off piece after piece on that day in the printer's office, until he had enough to make up the required eight three-column printed pages. It was appropriate to the season to lead off with a skating poem, which he entitled "Down the Brook" and which he ended with a sort of envoi entitled "And Back." The pseudonym signature he placed at the end of the poem was "AMNESSEL."[10] He followed this with an archeological-historical essay entitled "Petra and Its Surroundings"; it contained so much material drawn from careful research that it seems to have been written earlier as a composition in one of his ancient history courses. The next two essays were weak fillers built on facts present and past, respectively: the first on "Physical Culture," with special reference to a new gymnasium just then in the process of building in Lawrence by the Young Men's Christian Association; the second on "The Charter Oak at Hartford," and quite clearly a paraphrase of research done by someone else on the history of the celebrated tree. The first of these essays he signed with the pseudonymn, "SINON"; the second with initials belonging to none of his editors: "A. C. C., '94." Then he tossed off a short story with a Christmas Eve setting and a flavor borrowed from Edgar Allan Poe. Entitling the story "M. Bonner, Deceased," and signing it with a Greek flourish, "KTHON," he somewhat pointedly tucked in at the end of the tale a pertinent editorial note: "You don't like this tale? Neither do I! You are a philanthropist? Well, I am. That's a coincidence." Perhaps he intended a private joke in identifying himself as a philanthropist; sarcastically and bitterly he was making a sacrificial contribution to the human welfare of the *Bulletin* staff in particular and of Lawrence High School students in general by writing so much of the copy for this issue of the *Bulletin*. Perhaps he also intended an additional private joke involving the story of Bonner, when he tucked into his editorials the following remarks:

"We have seriously debated with ourselves whether it would not be advisable to introduce a prize story to these our columns, in the hope that, by the hoax, we might gain a hearing from the school; but advertisers are wont to belittle themselves in this way—and professional men do not advertise."

The only item worth salvaging from the story of "M. Bonner, Deceased" is a mock-Homeric simile apparently inspired by memories of long hours at Braithwaite's mill and the time-to-go-home signal of the mill whistle: "Fastening his arm rigidly up into the night, he [M. Bonner] gave a wild shriek and his spirit fled as the mill laborers leave the mill at the shriek of the great steam whistle."

Having made a backhanded salute to Poe's prose in "M. Bonner, Deceased," Rob followed it with a backhanded salute to Poe's verse, a successful parody affording blank verse echoes of Poe's rhymed obsessions. The poem, entitled "Parting" and bearing the subtitle "To —— ——," seems to contain a playful handling of the paradoxes cherished by Poe in "Al Aaraaf," with its reference to "The night that waned and waned and brought no day." Taken as a tongue-in-cheek manipulation of seemingly profound and Poe-like paradoxes, "Parting" has merit as something more than a space-filler:

I dreamed the setting sun would rise no more.
My spirit fled; nor sought an aimless sun
Whirled madly on through pathless space, and free
Amid a world of worlds enthralled. Ah no!
But deep within a silent solitude
It lingered on. The twilight waned; across
The hills and dark'ning sky the west wind stole,
And broad-cast spread the sun-path gathered gold,
Undying memories of the hopeless dead.
The dew of sadness fell, and far into
The coming night of storm and calm I gazed.
Oh, sadness, who may tell what joy is thine?
A whisper breathed: "What lies unvoiced on earth
Is heaven sung." And gloom crept softly down
With longing deep as everlasting night.

After that seemingly serious nonsense, Rob needed a two-line filler at the end of the column and found it by drawing on his knowledge of astronomy—perhaps with a deliberately insinuative touch of word-play:

"* * On the fifth of February, Jupiter and Venus will be
* in conjunction."

The same field provided him with more serious subject matter for an editorial:

"What the school now wants is a telescope—mighty and far-reaching. In astronomy as in everything else, the practical is the popular. It is needless to say that astronomy is one of the most practical as well as theoretical sciences. It is a most wonderful teacher of observation and cultivator of the more practical imagination. . . . The routine of school life fed entirely on books, is unspeakably monotonous, so monotonous, in fact, that we become so depressed as to be uncertain one day whether or not we know what we learned yesterday; a little real observation would stand out of all this blackness as the moon seems to stand out of the darkness when looked at through a telescope; it makes the darkness seem pleasant."

As Rob moved on to prepare copy for the "School Gossip" column—trebling the usual size of it—he introduced two references to his sister Jeanie's bout with typhoid fever. First: "We are very much pleased to learn that Miss Frost, a member of the Class of '92, who is ill at the hospital, is recovering, and hope she will soon be able to return." Again, a bit later:

[116]

"Miss Frost desires to thank the Class of '92, for their kindly Christmas remembrance." Near the end of this column he apparently could not resist a sarcastic thrust aimed at the "School Gossip" reporters who had failed to supply copy: "We are very much obliged for the *large* amount of *gossip* that we have received from the reporters of the other classes."

Although Rob's desperate method of acquiring copy by creating it first-hand resulted in a thoroughly successful perpetration of this hoax, and although most of the students who finally received the December issue of the *Bulletin* on January 29th were never permitted to realize that he had written most of it himself, the new editor took cognizance of Rob's resignation by referring to it in the January issue:

"We are sure that the whole school and especially the senior class regrets the resignation of Mr. Frost as editor of the BULLETIN. After having lavished the wealth of his intellect on the paper for four months, the gentleman has decided, for purely personal reasons, to relinquish his editorial labors; and with much sound advice and the proper amount of tears has transferred to us the official shears and waste basket."[11]

12

FREETHINKER

*"Oh, don't use that word. It has
a dreadful history."*[1]

DURING the last semester of his senior year at Lawrence High School, Robert Frost deliberately voyaged into deep waters of hope and doubt, to extend his intellectual and spiritual horizons. Although he prided himself on the courage required to venture independently through strange seas of thought alone, he was troubled by his growing awareness that he could never return comfortably to the harbor provided for him by his mother's serene religious beliefs. The first impulse for these adventures had been given during his sophomore year, when Carl Burell had exposed him to the continuing conflict between science and religion, as expressed in the current reactions to the writings of Darwin, Huxley, Clodd, Proctor, and others.

The problems uppermost in his consciousness, and his attitudes toward them, were revealed in a brief essay he contributed to the *Bulletin* for May 1892. After resigning from his duties as Chief Editor of the *Bulletin,* he had apparently been asked to serve briefly as a substitute for his successor, and in complying he had written three editorials which were signed with his name. In the third of these he defended a position not unlike that which Carlyle had honored in *Sartor Resartus*: the need to re-think any conventional belief in order to make it one's own. There were three possible categories of response to the customary or conventional attitudes, Rob explained. These categories could be represented by groups of individuals, who might be called followers, enemies, and re-thinkers. Rob went on to praise the re-thinkers and to attack those enemies who make the mistake of trying to identify re-thinkers with unthinking followers, and who, in addition, make the mistake of trying to fashion liberalism into a dogma. These points are at least implied in the following paragraph from his editorial:

"A custom has its unquestioning followers, its radical enemies, and a class who have generally gone through both of these to return to the first in a limited sense,—to follow custom, —not without question, but where it does not conflict with the broader habits of life gained by wanderers among ideas. The second class makes one of the first and third. This is best exemplified in religious thought and controversy. It is the second class that would have 'an inquisition to compel liberality.' "[2]

The reference to "religious thought and controversy" suggests that the motive for writing this editorial may have been provided in part by some of the latest arguments between Rob and his friend, Carl Burell. Carl had stopped attending high school after failing to be graduated with the Class of 1891. At about the same time, he had become disillusioned with religion and had grown impatient with Rob for continuing to maintain even a re-thinker's religious position. Mrs. Frost had been warned that Carl was exerting a bad influence on her son. She knew that Rob, having reached this re-thinking phase of growth, took pride in teasing her by saying such things as that the evolutionists might be correct: if God had made man from a monkey, He had merely made man from prepared mud instead of from dust. She did not enjoy this kind of wit, and she reproachfully asked her son if he, like Carl, had become an atheist as a result of reading those dreadful scientists. No, he said. Very well, then, how did he explain his new and flippant attitude toward sacred matters? If he wasn't an atheist, what did he call himself? He wasn't sure, he said, how to describe his position, except to say that he enjoyed being a wanderer among ideas; but perhaps he could be called a freethinker. His mother was shocked. "Oh, don't use that word," she protested. "It has a dreadful history."

She needn't have worried too much. Her son could have told her that his kind of freethinking was merely an expression of his desire to re-think and to form his own independent opinions about religion, quite apart from tradition, authority, or established belief; that, so far, all of his freethinking had not destroyed his essential piety. He could have reminded her that she herself had made a fairly bold voyage in re-thinking, while passing from Presbyterianism through Unitarianism to Swedenborgianism. Furthermore, she was the one who had done so much to stimulate his first venture into the science of astronomy when she helped him obtain a telescope; he was still inclined to say, with her, that the "undevout astronomer is mad." In all of his re-thinking, his own attitude toward the findings of science (as opposed to the beliefs of religion) remained one of strong and stubborn hostility toward materialism.

Mrs. Frost's immediate worries might have been assuaged if she had noticed a particular sentence in Rob's guest-written editorial. It referred sympathetically to literature in which "the traveller reviews God's thoughts and praises them." Here was evidence that he had indeed preserved, in spite of his doubts, a basic piety even when making his extensive travels through Carl Burell's library. Ahead of him lay some deeper and more dangerous expanses of religious doubt. Ahead, also, would be occasions when he might boastfully pretend that he was more heretical in his freethinking than he actually was. Throughout his life he would want to associate himself with heroic wanderers among ideas; but his mother's teachings would continue to provide him with a kind of sea anchor, even when his thoughts remained harborless.

Rob's best sea anchor, in stormy moments of doubt, during and after these high-school days, was the assurance he found in all the manifestations of metaphysical design. The astronomer Proctor had mentioned God's design in a way which continued to satisfy Rob: "We may believe, with all confidence, that could we but understand the whole of what we find around us, the wisdom with which each part has been designed would be manifest . . ." Rob's mother had also taught him that it was the proper goal of a poet to explore, imaginatively, fresh ways to represent the wonders of this metaphysical design.

As it happened, Rob did catch a new glimpse of the metaphysical design while in the very act of doubting, one day in the spring of his senior year. As he walked alone toward high school, troubled by problems in his own home, he puzzled over the old questions concerning whence and why misfortune is. He seriously doubted, now, whether all the griefs, sorrows, pains, and evils which had darkened his loved ones since the death of his father, could be made to fit positively into any larger design. Suddenly an answer came to him, as a flash of second sight, while he continued to walk. If our souls do come to this earth from heaven, he thought, then each must choose to come. Heroically and courageously, each must want—and must therefore choose—to be tested or tried by the ordeal of earthly existence. Reassured, for the moment, by this insight, Rob ventured further. He imagined related elements in such a metaphysical design: This ordeal could not become a valid test unless the soul, in making its departure from heaven, should agree to surrender the memory of having chosen to be tested. If, on the other hand, the memory of the choice did remain, there could be no real danger of ultimate defeat and failure; there would be no valid trial worthy of man's spiritual and God-given capacities. These answers to his doubts were new— at least for him—and he began to search for vivid poetic images with which to dramatize them. Because he knew that this undertaking was the most ambitious poetic leap he had so far tried to make, he was not surprised to find that he had difficulty with it. But he was troubled when new doubts interfered. Years passed before he was able to finish this poem, which he eventually called "The Trial By Existence."[3]

Rob's independent reading of poetry, during the last half of his senior year, gave another direction to his wandering among ideas. One stimulus to these adventures came from his gradual realization that Elinor White not only wrote poetry but also knew so many good poems which were new to him. He was jealous because her wide reading made her better informed about the history of English poetry than he was.[4] She gave another impulse to his reading. As soon as he began to admit that he was truly in love with her, he discovered that he was enthralled by love poetry. He was oddly helped in making one of his favorite finds, one evening, as he sat reading in the Lawrence Public Library. A poetry-loving fellow student named Brewster[5] interrupted him unceremoniously by spreading open a book before him, then pointing to a poem on the page, and saying, "This one." Rob read as directed and found that it was John Lyly's "Cards and Kisses," with this beginning and end:

> *Cupid and my Campaspe play'd*
> *At cards for kisses;—Cupid paid:*
> *He stakes his quiver, bow, and arrows,*
> *His mother's doves, and team of sparrows . . .*

At last he set her both his eyes—
She won, and Cupid blind did rise.
O Love! has she done this for thee?
What shall, alas! become of me?

Part of Rob's pleasure in this moment of discovery was the tribute Brewster had paid to Rob's taste and judgment.

In related ways other phases of his own growth were marked, that spring, by his eagerness to find for Elinor White some good poems which were new to her. It was part of his courtship, and it provided occasion for his first gift to her.

The gift was two pocket-sized books of poems written by Edward Rowland Sill, a name Rob had first seen while leafing through an old copy of *Century Magazine*. Shortly after Sill's death at the age of forty-five, in 1887, the best of his earlier work had been collected in a small volume, *Poems*; two years later, his previously unpublished verse appeared in *The Hermitage and Later Poems*. In the *Century* article, excerpts from Sill's writings were offered as part of a memorial tribute by his friend of many years, Elizabeth Stuart Phelps. She sketched his New England boyhood and his years spent in California as a teacher. (He had been teaching in Oakland, Rob must have noticed, at the time when Rob was born across the Bay.) She went on to describe the struggle waged by Sill to preserve his faith during the Darwinian controversy: "I used to think that his awful struggle after Truth had brought him near to the altar of his unknown God, and that it was well to live as nobly as he did before one criticized him for the nominal loss of his faith . . ." She praised him for his capacity to make his artistic life provide so much comfort to others:

"He was a true poet; our literature is poorer for his untimely loss. But he was a true man; our lives are sadder for lack of his. Many who knew him mourn for him as for the dearest comforter they ever had. Friends in sorrow, young people in perplexity, shy people, poor people, the over-sensitive, neglected, lonely, misunderstood, he ministered to as only souls like his know how."[6]

Such praise would appeal to any young reader searching for his own identity. Rob, after reading the article, bought from a Lawrence bookstore both volumes of Sill's poems. Although he naturally enjoyed all the California references, he seemed to be touched most deeply by Sill's death poems. Rob had often wondered, since the time of his own father's death, how he himself would eventually confront his own end, how he could possibly find courage enough to overcome his fright. He liked Sill's ironic poem, "A Morning Thought." In it, the speaker imagines telling a "benignant Spirit standing near" that this earth is a blessed place except for the destroyer Death; then the speaker imagines hearing the Spirit say, while taking the speaker by the hand, "My name is Death."

Rob's favorite by far—and a poem which remained a favorite with him throughout his life—was "Truth at Last":

> *Does a man ever give up hope, I wonder,—*
> *Face the grim fact, seeing it clear as day?*
> *When Bennen saw the snow slip, heard its thunder*
> *Low, louder, roaring round him, felt the speed*
> *Grow swifter as the avalanche hurled downward,*
> *Did he for just one heart-throb—did he indeed*
> *Know with all certainty, as they swept onward,*
> *There was the end, where the crag dropped away?*
> *Or did he think, even till they plunged and fell,*
> *Some miracle would stop them? Nay, they tell*
> *That he turned round, face forward, calm and pale,*
> *Stretching his arms out toward his native vale*
> *As if in mute, unspeakable farewell,*
> *And so went down.—'T is something, if at last,*
> *Though only for a flash, a man may see*
> *Clear-eyed the future as he sees the past,*
> *From doubt, or fear, or hope's illusion free.*[7]

This was one of the poems Rob pointed out to Elinor when he gave her the two volumes as his first present. He already knew her well enough to understand that her maturity—surpassing his own greatly—did not spare her from frequent moods that were dark and melancholy. She took so much satisfaction in his gift that she asked and received his permission to show the two volumes to her teacher of English literature—and was not surprised that her teacher had never heard of Edward Rowland Sill.

Only a few weeks after Rob made his discovery of Sill, he heard for the first time of another New England poet who had died a few years earlier and whose verse, published posthumously, had attracted so much attention that the little volume had gone through six editions in six months. Again he went to the Lawrence bookstore, this time to buy a volume bound in olive cloth with gold Indian-tobacco pipes stamped on the cover, together with title and author: *Poems* by Emily Dickinson. To his surprise, Rob found himself more thoroughly captured by his new find than he had been by Sill. Although her terse, homely, gnomic, cryptic, witty qualities appealed very strongly to him, he was again fascinated to find that this new author was also "troubled about many things" concerning death. It seemed to him that while she had developed an extraordinary capacity for running the gamut of moods in her various imaginative confrontations with death, the poems which cut deepest for him were those which expressed her doubt whether any reasons fashioned by the mind concerning life in heaven could compensate for the heart's passionate and instinctive regrets over the transience of earthly bliss. For example:

> *I reason, earth is short*
> *And anguish absolute,*
> *And many hurt;*
> *But what of that?*
>
> *I reason, we could die:*
> *The best vitality*
> *Cannot excel decay;*
> *But what of that?*
>
> *I reason that in heaven*
> *Somehow, it will be even,*
> *Some new equation given;*
> *But what of that?*[8]

Rob naturally shared his latest discovery with Elinor, and was happy that her admiration for Emily Dickinson was as great as his.

An entirely different adventure in ideas, and in argument, took place for Rob near the end of his senior year. Elinor White was very much in his consciousness on the day when he obeyed a summons from Mr. Goodwin, the high-school principal, and listened with satisfaction to the confidential announcement that valedictory honors in the Class of '92 had been won by Robert Lee Frost. The only competitor, it seemed, was a student who had taken the general course, not the classical. Although it was true, Mr. Goodwin explained, that the competitor's marks were at present very high, and that some teachers thought the competitor's marks might excel Rob's by the end of the term, Mr. Goodwin was convinced that the requirements in the general program were not so difficult as those in the classical. Hence his decision that the honor should go to Frost. His curiosity piqued now, Rob took the liberty of asking who his competitor was. A girl, he was told, a girl named Elinor White.

Immediately Rob suffered mixed feelings of delight and jealousy. But his prompt reaction was to insist that if anyone thought it probable that Miss White's marks would be higher than his in the final record, the award should not be made now. Or, the award should be given to her immediately. Demurring, Mr. Goodwin again explained his prejudices in favor of a student who had specialized in the classical program. Rob continued the argument so heatedly that Mr. Goodwin finally proposed a compromise, which was acceptable: Frost and Miss White would be co-valedictorians; but the valediction to the class would be made by Frost.[9]

To the superstitious young man, thus paired with his beloved, the decision seemed prophetic. He knew that his love for Elinor had been growing throughout the year. He had entered passionately into all the preliminaries of courtship— walking home with her after school, carrying her books, escorting her to evening functions, consulting her about editorial problems, jealously admiring her poems, showing her what he had written, and reading aloud to her recently from Sill and Emily Dickinson. In these various ways they had found that they shared many ideals, some of which Elinor had hinted at in an essay published in the *Bulletin* under the misleading title, "A Phase of Novel Writing." The essay began as an attack on realism in fiction and ended as a defensive glorification of idealism. She defined realism as "that something which strips from life the glamour of fancy and imagination, and accentuates its sordid details." As illustration she pointed (never mind how inaccurately) to Henry James and William Dean Howells, in whose writings she found "no touch of the ideal, that element which is as difficult to outline as that far off hill against the sky, but which is surely the best of life and without which its portrayal must deteriorate." Insisting that what she vainly sought in James and Howells was the element which could "uplift and enlarge" the sympathies of the reader and "breathe into him that intangible inspiration which is won from the best fiction," she expressed her preference for "the old romancers" who might offer "many deviations from nature" and who could nevertheless "hold us more imperiously."

For contrast, she chose examples of effects in Scott's *Ivanhoe* and Howells' *The Rise of Silas Lapham*: "The storming of Scott's rugged castles, with their guarded battlements and moonlit towers, seems as real to us as the flabby drawing-room scenes of today: Rebecca of York and Edith Plantagenet strike a chord that Cora Lapham cannot reach." Then, in conclusion, almost as though she were writing the passage for the eyes of one person only, she said:

"A very true artist is a lover of nature, and to him she will yield infinite harmonies, varying with the thought or emotion to be embodied. Wordsworth voices the artist's yearning when he says:

> *"Ah then, if mine had been the painter's hand,*
> *To express what then I saw, and add the gleam,*
> *The light that never was, on sea or land,*
> *The consecration, and the poet's dream.*

"Whatever may be the resources of the various forms of art, the end is the same, they stir the heart and mind, to idealize the commonplace events of our life, and to subordinate the literal to some high conception of the imagination. This may hold true, even in fiction. In the proportion that a novelist transmutes his observation of character into forms that express his inmost thought and feeling in that proportion is his art a reality."[10]

If Robert Frost could have been in doubt whether he and Elinor White were kindred spirits, the very earnest and passionate idealism reflected in this essay should have removed the doubt. Their courtship had progressed unevenly during their senior year; but as soon as they began comparing notes as co-valedictorians, conditions were changed. Before the commencement exercises took place they had pledged themselves to each other and were secretly engaged to be married.

The citizens of Lawrence made their annual high-school

graduation ceremony an important and colorful occasion. The elaborate graduation-day exercises were traditionally held in the large upstairs auditorium of City Hall, a homely old structure of stone and brick which faced the beauties of the broad elm-shaded common directly across from the high school. Shortly before two o'clock on Thursday afternoon, June 30th, the Class of 1892 assembled in a lower room of City Hall while parents and friends trooped steadily up the stairs and into the auditorium. The stage, built out to seat the graduating class and all the dignitaries, was profusely decorated with cut flowers and potted plants. Above, at the center of the proscenium, a tablet bordered with smilax and fern leaves bore in floral red the class numerals and the motto: "VINCIT QUI SE VINCIT."

Exactly at two o'clock the band struck up a march and the lower classes began to file down the aisles to their assigned seats at the front of the crowded auditorium. Then the thirty-two members of the graduating class marched down the center aisle and up the steps to the platform, where all the class speakers were seated in the front row, much to Rob's embarrassment. He had carefully arranged that he be seated at the very end of this front row, and he planned to escape into the wings if he grew nervous. Studying the program and trying to console himself that he would have nothing to do for at least an hour, he counted the speakers ahead of him: twelve, and he was the unlucky thirteenth. But he noticed with satisfaction that his name appeared again on the program. Elected Class Poet, he had written a "Class Hymn" which was to be sung at the very end of the ceremonies. The words of his poem were printed in the program.

At the start all went well enough. One after another the speakers rose, took their positions with gingerly care in the very center of the apron, and then declaimed. Their subjects ranged from "The Progress of Lawrence" and "Home Life in Literature" to "Chinese Immigration" and (as a tribute to the approaching Columbian Exposition) "Isabella, the Foster-mother of America." Instead of listening, Rob spent most of his time going over his own speech, just to be sure that he would not stumble when he said it all from memory.

He had chosen to build into his address all of his cherished ideals and discoveries that had been most vividly articulated by the experiences of these four years, particularly as the ideals touched on relationships between poetry and after-thought. It was his hope that the listeners would recognize the tribute paid to the poetic career he had already chosen for himself. He probably realized that it amounted to his Shelleyan defense of poetry, and that it was colored dramatically and thematically with tinctures of Ossianic sadness and Emersonian optimism. Initially, he had thought to build the entire address around one discovery he began to make at the very moment in his freshman year when he had found no immediate answer for the question: "Do you think you know all of Roman history?" Although he had often suffered the discomfort of being late in finding the right thing to say, he had taken great consolation from his discovery that, in after-thoughts, he could at least figure out what he should have said. His best thoughts were always after-thoughts, in a Wordsworthian sense; his most poetic and most deeply felt insights came when his emotions were recollected in tranquility. Hence his decision to build his address around this far-reaching discovery and to dramatize it by striking the imaginative posture of being an orator invited to speak at the unveiling of a marble monument newly erected in honor of After-thought—the hyphen was important to him because it accentuated the meaning. He would make his listeners see the marble shaft and also see, kneeling at the base of the monument, a marble goddess with one hand upraised as though she were in the act of writing the sacred word on the plaque prepared for it. If his title initially puzzled a few of his listeners and whetted their listening, so much the better: "A Monument to After-thought Unveiled."

Confident as he was in what he had to say, he found that as the other speeches dragged on, his nervousness increased. It had always been agony for him to appear on any stage for any reason, and his most excruciating foretaste of what might lie ahead had occurred in sophomore Latin class when he had been required to recite from memory, before the class, part of an oration from Cicero. Starting adequately, he had done well enough until he reached the familiar Ciceronian repetition, "How long, O Cataline . . ." For the moment, all he could remember was the passage following the first occurrence of the rhetorical question, and so he had lamely picked it up from there in the hope that only his teacher would notice his own repetition. But when the same phrase came again and he still could not remember what came next—and again desperately tried the same cover up—he had heard the snickers of his classmates. Digusted with himself, he quit, and sat down.

Made unbearably nervous now by his apprehensions, he felt so suffocated that he began to watch for a chance to bolt into the wings. He found it at the end of the next-to-last speech and made a quick exit from his end seat knowing that Elinor came next, then he. Down the back stairs he ran, searching for a sink. He found it, soaked his handkerchief in cold water, sopped his face and neck and head, then dried himself off as best he could with the sleeve of his coat. For several minutes he paced back and forth in the lower corridor, near enough to the staircase to hear Elinor speaking so firmly and calmly that she made him jealous. He knew her address almost as well as he knew his own—they had helped each other rehearse, hour after hour. Her subject was "Conversation as a Force in Life," and it seemed to him that there was unintentional irony in it: Elinor's specialty was meaningful silence. But she was making her points well, and they were good ones.

". . . our moral and intellectual welfare requires that we exchange a few words each day with persons whose views of life are broad and sympathetic, with whom there is no restraint, who look into our eyes and give answer to our meanings rather than our words. . . ."

"In the effort to unfold and to clearly illustrate a thought to a loved and honored associate, we find that it becomes doubly fertile and suggestive to ourselves, the quick response must be met and matched, the fire of sympathy is lit, and is fanned by the warm breath of inspiration. . . ."

". . . say nothing if there is nothing in you that imperatively demands a voice. If it becomes needful to look east and west, to search in the zenith or in the nadir for material for conversation choose rather a sympathetic silence, for your words will be drowned by the ring of insincerity that . . ."[11]

As Elinor approached her concluding remarks, Rob tiptoed back up the stairs, hiding in the wings until she finished. With the start of the applause, he slipped back into his seat. The clapping stopped. The rattling of the programs diminished. Now.

Almost overpowered by fright, he jumped up, hurried to the center of the apron, took a deep breath, and began to rattle off his words like bullets. He knew he was speaking too fast, but there was nothing he could do about it.

"A tribute to the living! We are away beneath the sombre pines, amid a solitude that dreams to the ceaseless monotone of the west wind, the blue sky looking sleepily between the slowly bending boughs, and to, its veil of morning mist uplifted by the morning breeze, white as pure thought, the monument of monuments.

"From sun-beat dizzy marts, from grassy lawns, from surging summer trees, rise countless marble columns, wrought as noiselessly as if from snow, and all by the one hand here honored alone in loneliness.

"Well might this marble be a shrine, this grove, a temple whence devotees might seek the world again, and fame!

"The God—but wait, that carven silence kneeling at its base, whence it tapers away into the boughs above, writes, and this is what she writes:—

"There are men—that poet who has left us uniting the battered harp the sea storm cast for him upon the shore, was one of these—who go to death with such grey grandeur that we look back upon their past for some strange sorrow, such as does not fall to others, even though we know sorrow to be the same through all time. They seem like Merlins looking ages from their deep calm eyes. With what awe we stand before the mystery of their persons. Such lives are the growth of the after-thought of the soul—the serene rest after toil, in questioning and answering whence and why misfortune is.

"This nobility distinguishes personality only in the degree of its development, and the broader future, will give to every soul the opportunity to come into possession of this, its divine right. Then, when no man's life is a strife from day to day, from year to year, with poverty, will it be an attribute commonality of the world.

"Aggressive life is two-fold: theory, practice; thought, action: and concretely, poetry, statesmanship; philosophy, socialism —infinitely.

"Not in the strife of action, is the leader made, nor in the face of crisis, but when all is over, when the mind is swift with keen regret, in the long after-thought. The after-thought of one action is the forethought of the next.

"It is when alone, in converse with their own thoughts so much that they live their conventionalities, forgetful of the world's, that men form those habits called the heroism of genius, and lead the progress of the race. This, the supreme rise of the individual—not a conflict of consciousness, an effort to oppose, but bland forgetfulness, a life from self for the world—is the aim of existence.

"All this is doubly so of the theoretical. In it the after-thought of long nights beneath the universe, of soul stirrings, of the act of thought itself, is more clearly a part of the next action— its expression. Events influence the first class, the limits of language alone the second.

"The poet's insight is his after-thought. It is of varied heart-beats and converse with nature. And the grandest of his ideas come when the last line is written.

"Life is an after-thought: how wonderful shall be the world? that is the after-thought of life.

"But look again, all this is mere shadow sheen upon the white marble. The one word there is: After-thought.

"Now this dark pool beneath the trees is still. There is a white finger on its lips. Let ripples whisper here no more."

(Rob was safely through the ordeal—at least through the main address. Now the valediction to his classmates. With the correct rhetorical motion, he took one step to the side, half-turned, and continued.)

"And now a last after-thought.

"To those who fix today a point through which from earlier years they draw a line of life projected far into the future, this hour is of a deep significance. But there is no change here, and he who thinks to rest will rest as in a winter storm, to die.

"Unbounded full ambition for the greatest heights yet un-attained is not too noble for one human mind. Who or what can bound our aspiration? Will courage fail before a thousand unfavorable comparisons? There is a space of time when meteor and rain drop falling side by side may touch the yield-ing earth with equal force. The lighter outspeeding weight may seem in a space to strike with greater force. But who at last can tell which has the greater influence on the world, the one that bore, as scientists have said, plant life or that which makes it live.

"Strength and all the personality that we can crowd upon the world are ours to give in obligation. Let hope be limitless for all and let each follow hope as best he may.

"To all old school associations here we show our purposed way in one bell-toned Farewell!"[12]

[131]

Deliberately, he had constructed his valediction so that it would interlock with his "Class Hymn":

There is a nook among the alders
Still sleeping to a cat-bird's "Hush";
  Below, a long stone-bridge is bending
Above a runnel's silent rush.

A dreamer hither often wanders
And gathers many a snow-white stone;
  He weighs them, poised upon his fingers,
Divining each one's silvery tone.

He drops them! When the stream makes music,
Fair visions with its vault-voice swell:
  And so, for us, the future rises,
As thought-stones stir our heart's "Farewell!"

Back in his seat—flushed, trembling, out of breath—Rob was conscious of the familiar and frightening pains of nausea in his stomach. But there was further embarrassment for him a few moments later when the Superintendent of Schools unexpectedly called him back to the center of the stage to receive the Hood Prize, a small gold medal awarded to Robert Lee Frost for general excellence and deportment during his four years.

The next day one of the Lawrence newspapers described Elinor White's co-valedictory address as "a most thoughtful and praiseworthy piece of work, full of sound sense and original thought and showing fine mental power and culture." Then the same account went on to say that Robert Lee Frost's address "combined in a rare degree poetic thought, a fine range of imagination, and devotion to a high ideal, and evinced intellectual compass much beyond the usual school essay."[13] In another paper the reporter found fault with some of Rob's elocutionary mannerisms. After conceding that the valedictory was a "splendid effort, showing research and thought," the critic said that "in the opinion of some its merits might have been shown to better advantage in a more natural delivery."[14]

Rob's own after-thoughts were keen with swift regret over the nervous way he had raced through the address. If the reporter could have had any idea of how frightened the vale-

dictorian had been, from the beginning to the end, some allow-
ance might have been made for the unnatural quality of his
presentation. The best Rob could do now was to console himself with fore-thoughts.

As soon as the graduation exercises were over, he began
importunately to urge Elinor White to marry him at once,
even though he was but eighteen and she was approaching
her twentieth birthday.[15] He may have said that if they were
both going to college, as planned, it would be far more sensible—and less expensive—to go as man and wife. Because
he was planning to go to Harvard, she should arrange to attend the Harvard Annex (later named Radcliffe).

In her shy reticence, Elinor White managed to curb the
eagerness of her impatient lover. Her parents had completed
arrangements for her to enter St. Lawrence University in New
York State, as he well knew; but she could assure Rob that
the immediate present was theirs. The long summer of conversation which lay before them could be made precious to
after-thought—unless it was spoiled by too many persistent
entreaties.

A PLACE APART

We make ourselves a place apart
  Behind light words that tease and flout,
But oh, the agitated heart
  Till someone really find us out.[1]

ON THE MORNING after his graduation, Robert Frost sold the gold medal or Hood Prize—presented to him for "general excellence"—at a jewlery shop in Lawrence. The transaction was motivated not by poverty but rather by his idealistic rebel scorn for conventions. As a junior in high school he had written an editorial defending re-thinkers who return to conventional beliefs after challenging them; but one year later, in his valedictory address, he had expressed his new conviction that men form the habits which result in "the heroism of genius" only when they turn their backs on everyday conventionalities and make up thoughts and after-thoughts of their own in converse with themselves. The elaborate process of formulating his valediction had helped him to certain decisions, not the least being that the time had come for him to declare his independence of the mob. The excellence he now dreamed of could not be represented adequately by the Hood Prize.

If others might not understand his pride and scorn, if his enemies might mistakenly call it arrogance—if even his mother might feel more and more separated from her son by his actions—he could not help it. Elinor White's love provided all the assurance he needed. Together they had already begun to create a world of their own, a place apart. Their distance from others had been acknowledged publicly by their performances as co-valedictorians.

It seemed to Rob that his newly achieved distinction enabled him to find work immediately after graduation, not merely as a common laborer but more nearly as an administrator. He was given a position as clerical assistant to the gatekeeper at the Everett Mill in Lawrence—a dignified task involving the use of his head and hands for careful recording of absence and tardiness. The work was so easy that it even gave him time to read, intermittently, and it enabled him to continue his arduous courtship during the long summer evenings and weekends.

Elinor White had the capacity to match her beloved's rebelliousness. She had been brought up in a home atmosphere made liberal by her father's independence of spirit. A Universalist minister, married to an ambitious and socially prominent young woman, Edwin White had foreseen distinguished possibilities in his career; but he had not flinched when circumstances convinced him that he did not believe in the dogmas of the Universalist Church—or of any other church. Much to his wife's chagrin he had given up his career, had even relinquished membership in the Universalist Church, and had found what seemed to him a more honest way of earning a living. For years he had enjoyed his hobby of cabinetwork and carpentering. He had even acquired a lathe which he operated for his own amusement in the cellar of his home at 10 Valley Street in Lawrence—less than a block away from the public park or Common which was beautified by a double row of lofty elms on all four sides and which was flanked on one side by the high school, on the opposite side by City Hall. After he left the pulpit, he quite easily and comfortably supported his resentfully disapproving wife and their three daughters by filling special orders, cabinetwork, lathe work for a large furniture company in Lawrence. His influence on his youngest daughter, Elinor, was reflected in the ease with which she adapted herself to the unconventionalities of her fiancé.

Throughout the summer, whenever they could be together, the two lovers made their evenings and weekend days idyllic by taking leisurely walks into the country or by making excursions up the Merrimack River above the Lawrence dam. Along the few miles of water between Lawrence and Lowell were several picnic areas, such as Glen Forest, Laurel Grove, Pine Island, easily reached by regularly scheduled excursion boats—the old steamer named the *Startled Faun,* the broad-beamed *Henrietta,* and the little *Spitfire.* Better than these, in some ways, because more exclusive, was the rowboat which Rob had borrowed for the summer. He kept the boat tied up near the entrance to South Canal, under the care of a man named Holmes, who was the official keeper of the canal head gates. The Holmes family, including two boys and a girl, attended Swedenborgian services and frequently entertained the Frosts at their house on South Broadway, near the canal. The younger Holmes children, Will and Susan, preferred to have Rob make his visits without Elinor. Years later, Susan remembered that "he was something of a hero to us kids, ready to teach athletic stunts, to build a doll's house or to tell the most fascinating stories." She also remembered how he would "lie on his back under our pear trees and tell tales (mostly original) full of imagination and humor, making him a wonderful companion for children of our age." But too often, that summer, he came "strolling along our garden path with his girl friend, while my brother Will look wistfully after them, wondering why they never invited him to join them for a boat ride since he too loved to go 'up river.' "

In these charming voyages up the Merrimack by rowboat, Rob and Elinor soon found their own favorite and secret hiding places; but the serious flaw in these days of riverbank courtship was caused by Rob's passionate, importunate love-making.[2] For some time, Elinor thwarted and embarrassed him by her shyness and reticence, until the poetry of Shelley came to Rob's aid. Together, during the summer, they read aloud not only the lyrics but also "Prometheus Unbound," "The Revolt of Islam," "Queen Mab," and—most important of all—"Epipsychidion." It was Rob's pleasure to point out that Shelley placed love at the core of the universe, but with a special emphasis on the need of lovers to rebel against the social conventions. Before the summer was over, he convinced her that Shelley had been right in saying that love withers under constraint, that the very essence of love is liberty, that it is neither compatible with conventional attitudes nor with fear, that love is most pure and perfect and unlimited where its votaries live in confidence, equality, and unreserve.

Priding themselves more and more on being freethinkers, they even came to agree with Shelley that the institution of marriage—the licensing of love through civil or church rituals—is a shamefully degrading thing. Secretly, they conducted their own marriage ceremony during the summer of 1892; under truly idyllic circumstances they promised themselves to each other eternally, and with the exchange of plain gold wedding rings they sealed their pledges.

This privately conducted marriage was motivated in part by the shared dread of impending separation: each of them had finally completed arrangements for college. Elinor's plans for attending St. Lawrence University at Canton, New York, had been strengthened by the award to her of a scholarship, which would cover most of her expenses. Rob's initial hope that he would follow his father by attending Harvard College was modified very largely by the proselytizing activities of a Dartmouth graduate, newly appointed to teach Chemistry and Physics at Lawrence High School. Although Rob had not taken any science courses, he had been permitted by this new science teacher to conduct informal experiments in the school laboratory. The teacher became so impressed with Rob's attainments that he had encouraged the boy to consider attending Dartmouth—and had even talked to Rob's grandfather about the probability that most of the expenses at Dartmouth could be defrayed by scholarships. The campaign was assisted by Rob's grandmother, who did not want the boy to go to Harvard lest his life become ruined by habits which, she felt, her own son had acquired there. Dependent as he was on his grandfather's financial backing, Rob had to accept the decision that he should go to Dartmouth. His teacher completed arrangements for a scholarship.[3]

During the first journey which Rob made from Lawrence to Hanover, New Hampshire, in the autumn of 1892, only one important event occurred. There was no easy way to make the trip: it involved going by train to Manchester, New Hampshire, and waiting several hours there for a train that would take him across the state to White River Junction, Vermont, and then up to Norwich. But his science teacher had stressed the literary attractiveness of Dartmouth; had perhaps mentioned the poet Richard Hovey, who had been graduated in the Class of 1885, and certainly the novelist Arthur Sherburne Hardy, who was a professor of mathematics there. Rob decided that he would go to the Manchester Public Library to spend his hours of waiting and would see if he could find any of Professor Hardy's novels. It might be well to know something about them before he met the distinguished mathematician-novelist. But because Rob remembered only the last name of the professor, he drew from the Manchester circulation desk two of Thomas Hardy's novels, *A Pair of Blue Eyes* and *Two on a Tower.* Unaware that any mistake had been made, Rob diligently skimmed both volumes and looked forward to meeting the author of them. While at Dartmouth, as it happened, he did not even meet the Professor whose novels he thought he had tasted.

From Manchester to Norwich, and then by horse-drawn conveyance with other students across the Connecticut River and up the hill to the elm-tree shaded Dartmouth campus on the Hanover Plain, Rob could feel his excitement mounting. He was a complete stranger among his companions and had no friends until he made them. Assigned to living quarters in Wentworth Hall, where he had a study and a small bedroom on the third floor, he found that his first task was to buy enough second-hand furniture to make his rooms liveable: a small stove which could burn either wood or coal, a table, two chairs, a bed, a lantern, a lamp, and a can of kerosene oil. The novelty of it all appealed to him and he settled in without too much work.

He was one of only a few freshmen in Wentworth, and the sophomores wasted no time starting to haze. Trouble began for him during the first evening, when someone opened his door and threw into his room some kind of weapon which upset and put out his lantern. By the time he groped through the dark and got the lantern lighted again, he could hear someone doing something to the outside of his door, which opened into the hall. Before he tried opening the door, he had guessed what had happened. It had been securely fastened with enough screws to hold it firmly closed. Frost took it pleasantly as part of the game, and the general hubbub of noise in the corridor gave him courage to shout for help. At last someone came up the stairs to reprimand the sophomores. He could hear the noise abating as soon as a man's voice called out, "Boys, boys, be easy on them." Before morning the screws had been removed from his door.

As soon as classes started, he was pleased to find that his assignments were relatively easy. He had chosen to take only three courses: one in Greek, with readings in Plato and Homer, taught by George D. Lord, an Assistant Professor; one in Latin, with readings in Livy's history of Rome, taught by a tutor named Charles H. Gould; one in mathematics, which started with advanced algebra and went on to solid geometry, taught by Thomas W. D. Worthen, an Associate Professor. Most of the freshmen took the Livy course, and because Gould was a poor disciplinarian they made life miserable for him with horseplay. Rob liked the traditional way in which the students took any excuse to "wood up" in protest against Gould's long assignments by stamping their feet under their desks until the dust rose up out of the cracks between the boards. By contrast, there was no "funny business" in the classes of Worthen and Lord, who were stern disciplinarians, and the routine of study soon became monotonous.

Much more to Rob's liking were the formal rituals of warfare between the freshman and sophomore classes. The fun began at the close of the first "rhetoricals," in which three or four seniors performed as scheduled before the entire student body in the church atmosphere of what had formerly been the chapel, and was later used almost exclusively for these convocations. The boxed pews made an interesting battleground for the ceremony in which the sophomores traditionally tried to put salt on the tails of the freshmen. Knowing what was about to happen, the seniors and juniors filed out at the end of the convocation and immediately rushed upstairs to find ringside seats in the balcony. When it was time for the sophomores to file out, they made their charge from the right-hand side of the old chapel, toward the freshmen who were seated on the left. As soon as they were within range, they opened fire with handfuls of rock salt which filled the air, Rob said, as the unexpected arrows must have done at Agincourt. The initial freshman response was one of defense; they used the old dusty seat cushions as shields, then as weapons. Rob stayed in the chapel just long enough to notice the eagerness and effectiveness with which his bigger and brawnier classmates hurled themselves against the sophomores and came to grips for the obvious purpose of seeing who could tear off the most clothes. By the time Rob retreated, the dust of ages had grown thick enough to simulate battle smoke.

Also pleasing to Rob's taste were the organized "rushes" in which the freshman and sophomore classes tried to protect or capture, on one occasion, a rubber football; on another occasion, a cane; on the greatest occasion of all for Rob, the sophomore pennant or banner. The freshman strategy during the pennant rush was to get near enough to the pole to tear the flag from it, and then to carry it triumphantly through the mob to a waiting freshman runner so fleet of foot that he could outdistance the enemy. It was Rob's accomplishment to be among the freshmen who succeeded in penetrating the ranks of the massed sophomores, even to have his hand on the pennant when it was torn down, and then to help carry it to the sprinter, who successfully ran off with the prize. All of his experiences as a high-school football player enabled him to stand up well under the bruising of these battles; but he still suffered the old sense of nausea after each new excitement.

In one way or another Rob gradually came to find that his closest friend among the freshmen at Dartmouth was Preston Shirley, a spirited youngster whose asthmatic ailments and slightly hunched back could not restrain him from entering into the thick of every brawl. Shirley had been well indoctrinated with Dartmouth spirit by an older brother, who had been graduated with the Class of '92; but the older brother had been so particularly rough and strenuous as a hazer that Preston Shirley became a special target for sophomore revenge. Matters were complicated by Shirley's mother, who sent boxes of fruit and homemade candy and cookies from the Shirley home in Andover, New Hampshire. As a consequence, his room was constantly being raided, even by seniors. The greatest excitement occurred when Rob helped Preston Shirley carry from the post office and smuggle into Shirley's Wentworth dormitory room on the second floor, nearly below Rob's own room, a particularly large box of edibles. On that occasion, and at Rob's suggestion, they fortified themselves with exceptional care. First they removed a closet door from its hinges, then they took a cleat from Shirley's bed and nailed it in a proper place to serve as a brace, and finally they jammed the closet door between the brace and the hall door, which opened inward. The strong barricade withstood repeated attacks throughout an afternoon and evening, while Rob and Preston sat behind it, gorging themselves. It was clear that even during lulls in the attacks only one of them could leave the room if the barricade were to be preserved. This they arranged and continued until the entire supply of food had been consumed.[4]

Partly through the influence of Preston Shirley and partly

as a result of recommendations made by the Chemistry teacher at Lawrence High School, Frost and Shirley were invited to join the same fraternity: Theta Delta Chi. Perhaps because of information furnished to the fraternity, Frost was persuaded that Theta Delt was really a literary society—or at least as good as one—because so many of its members were interested in writing. When he tried to explain that he could not afford to join, one of the seniors paid his small initiation fee. Further honors came to him when he was elected by the other freshman initiates of Theta Delt to make the speech for the freshman delegation at the fraternity banquet which followed the initiation ceremonies.

If there was anything about Frost which disturbed and perplexed his fraternity brothers it was his way of indicating that he was not quite so fraternal as they wished him to be. He liked walking, but he liked to walk alone. Throughout the fall of 1892, he took advantage of good weather and explored the countryside in one direction after another, until he had established his favorite circuits. One of the best took him down over the hill to the west, toward the Connecticut River, and then north along the river and through what was already known as the Vale of Tempe; finally back east and south to the campus. A longer walk which pleased him led in the opposite direction, starting almost due east toward the village of Etna, which lay under the shadow of Moose Mountain, and then around through country roads to the north of Hanover and back to the campus. He liked the countryside and he liked to be alone with his own thoughts during these walks. He had the feeling that he could somehow assimilate his experiences better if he used this method of getting off by himself. In his peregrinations he was surprised that he so seldom met any other Dartmouth students. Nobody else seemed to enjoy his kind of walking. His fraternity brothers became suspicious enough to challenge him. What on earth did he do, they asked, when he went off into the woods alone? The question seemed insolent enough to deserve his mocking retort, "Gnaw bark."[5]

If he could have found one sympathetic ear among his questioners, he might have wanted to say that during these walks he also gnawed the bare bones of his longing for the presence of Elinor White. He wrote to her regularly, and he almost devoured each letter she sent him. But he was strangely troubled by his fear that she was settling in, with almost too much satisfaction, at St. Lawrence University. He could be made jealous by any references to friendships newly established, even friendships with her own sex. Wishing that he might visit her, he took one walk to the railroad station at Norwich, Vermont, to consult timetables and learn how long a trip it would be if his loneliness became so unbearable that he might have to go to Canton, New York. There was something about this separation which seemed more cruel to him than to her, and this knowledge troubled him. St. Lawrence was a coeducational college, he knew; she might fall in love with someone else. These were fears which had no foundation, he kept telling himself; he and Elinor were bound by ties of love and loyalty that transcended any possible interference from anyone else. He wore on his finger, secretly, when he was alone on these long walks, the ring she had given him. It looked like a wedding ring; it was a wedding ring. They were married in a way which had more sacredness, he felt, than any formal licensing could possibly provide. Still, there was the constant uncertainty, and it shook his confidence in himself. If he could not bring this terrible inner pain under control, he would simply walk off the campus of Dartmouth College someday soon and never come back.

Under the circumstances it would not have been surprising if he had taken consolation in translating his passion into verse that he could send to her. He did not. The nearest he came to such consolation was through his reading of poems written by others—and quite by accident he found and bought in the local bookstore a volume which contained poems of love he could never have enjoyed so much before: Palgrave's *Golden Treasury of Songs and Lyrics*. In his room, hour after hour, when he should have been preparing assignments, he seemed impelled to read and read again from Palgrave the passionate outpourings of poets who had previously suffered from love, just as he was suffering now.

There were times when he decided that the most important part of his Dartmouth experience, so far, was his discovery of Palgrave. But he came at least to the edge of English literature in other ways. One of the orientational talks made to the freshmen, to acquaint them with possible fields of specialization, was given by Charles Francis Richardson, Appleton Professor of Natural Philosophy; his title belied his subject. He talked particularly, on this occasion, about the importance of becoming acquainted with literature, and he gave special emphasis to poetry as the highest literary expression. Frost was deeply touched when Richardson invoked Shelley in order to define poetry as being the realm "where music and moonlight and feeling are one." In his present mood, Frost thought, that would do as one definition of poetry. But he had already discovered that poetry could and did get its arms around things more important to him than music or moonlight.

One of his discoveries, during this fall term at Dartmouth, made him newly aware of poetic range and influence. While browsing in the college library in Wilson Hall, he noticed a periodical he had never seen before, *The Independent*. The entire first page of this issue for 17 November 1892—all three columns of it—were given over entirely to a new poem by Richard Hovey, "Seaward: An Elegy on the Death of Thomas William Parsons." If he knew very little about Richard Hovey at this time, and even less about the poet here so honored, who had been celebrated previously in *Tales of a Wayside Inn*, he knew a great deal more about Parsons by the time he finished reading the poem. An editorial in the same issue of *The Independent* praised Hovey's elegy by drawing favorable comparisons with Milton's "Lycidas," Shelley's "Adonais," and Arnold's "Thyrsis."

The editorial continued: "It is not easy for us to foretell what may be in the future for a young man who can do such work as this. It is certainly one of the most memorable poems which have been published for many a day, and will, we think, be numbered among the great elegies of the language." The young Dartmouth freshman was almost as much impressed by the editorial as by one American poet's salute to another. At the time he was not even sure that he would ever be able to realize his secret ambition to write a poem that could compare with Hovey's; but as he sat there in the Dartmouth library, reading, he stored up impressions which later made him hope that someday he would see a poem of his own published on the front page of this periodical, which bore a title so congenial to his own temperament: *Independent*.[6]

Not long after Frost found Hovey's elegy, he went by train to Sutton, Vermont, to visit the first poet he had ever met in his own generation: Carl Burell. The occasion for the visit was an invitation for Thanksgiving Dinner, and Frost very gladly accepted. Much had happened to Burell since he and

Frost had attended Lawrence High School together. The death of Burell's father and mother had occurred suddenly and had perhaps influenced him to abandon his quest for higher education. Some money must have been available to him, for he made a trip alone to California soon after his parents died. Two letters of his, giving partial accounts of his experiences in the West had been sent to the *Bulletin* for publication, but had not yet been printed. He had hoped to find work in San Francisco, and had been so bitterly disappointed by his lonely experiences there that he had very soon returned to New England, settling on the small farm of his widower grandfather, Jonathan Eastman, in Sutton, Vermont. It was to the Eastman farm that Frost went for his Thanksgiving vacation; but the native Californian may have spent much of his visit listening to Carl's complaints about the dreariness of the city which Rob had long idealized in his memory and imagination.

There was another reunion between Frost and Burell only a few weeks later. As soon as cold weather required the Dartmouth students to stock their fuel closets with wood and coal, so that they might keep fires burning day and night in their rooms, Rob yielded to lazy habits. It was a nuisance to carry coal up three flights of stairs in Wentworth, and it was an even greater nuisance to carry buckets of ashes back down to the dumping ground assigned for student use. It was far easier to rake ashes out on the floor beside the stove and let them pile up. He seems to have made jokes about the problem in his letters to his mother, who became greatly concerned. Carl Burell was in Lawrence shortly before Christmas and called on Mrs. Frost. She begged him to stop off at Norwich on his railroad trip back to Sutton so that he could walk over to Hanover and help Rob straighten up his room. Carl obliged, and showed a fatherly interest in shoveling all the ashes off the floor as the first step in putting his young friend's room to rights.

Carl Burell may have realized, during his Dartmouth visit, that Rob's lackadaisical attitude toward housekeeping in his dormitory room was akin to the young man's general attitude toward all other phases of academic life. The rebel streak began to assert itself with increasing strength soon after Christmas. He had hoped that Elinor White would return to Lawrence at Christmastime, if for no other reason than to see him. But winter weather and expenses had caused her to forego the trip—and Rob's response was one of exceptional disappointment. He had the feeling that while he was growing bored with the routine of classroom assignments and dormitory life at Dartmouth, Elinor White was becoming too deeply enthralled by social and academic affairs at St. Lawrence. Her letters, in spite of protestations, continued to make him jealous. They heightened his growing impatience with being told what to study, when to study, and just how to meet deadlines for written assignments. Depressed, lovesick, homesick, he had not even completed his first semester of study at Dartmouth before he began to tell himself that he had had enough of higher education. All he needed now was an excuse for quitting—and his mother unintentionally provided it.

Mrs. Frost's three years of teaching in Methuen district schools, following her retirement from all the unpleasantness at Salem Depot, had been made miserable, once again, by her weaknesses as a disciplinarian. Even worse, this year she had been transferred from an elementary school to an eighth-grade room, and had found that among her students were some older boys who were repeating eighth-grade work. Rob had heard about the difficulties experienced by his mother in trying to handle these "numbskulls," as he called them, and his resentment gradually mounted. What those boys in Methuen needed was a firm masculine hand, and there seemed to be no reason why Rob should not take over the school for his mother. Convinced that there was nothing worth while for him at Dartmouth, and aching to escape from an imprisonment made worse by snow, he confided to his friend Preston Shirley that he was about to depart. Shirley could not believe his ears. Nobody left Dartmouth without formal excuses and permission, as Frost was threatening to do. But when Shirley realized that nothing could dissuade Frost, he offered one last night of bacchanalian feasting on the latest package of food and candy which he had kept in hiding. The plan was carried through, the two freshmen barricaded themselves into the room, and, for one last time, sang and carried on and ate Turkish fig paste. Late at night they heightened the atmosphere of celebration by opening the window just long enough to bellow insults at sleeping sophomores.

The next morning, without any other farewells, Frost strapped up his small trunk, carried it down the three flights of stairs in Wentworth, arranged to be taken over the Connecticut

River to the Norwich railroad station, and casually made his permanent departure from undergraduate life at Dartmouth College. The decisive act was no more significant to him than were the days he had spent at the school. If he had learned anything useful enough to serve him in later years, it was that for him education was likely to be a matter of self-teaching rather than of classroom learning, that for the time at least he resented formal instruction. He was particularly annoyed by students who placed a great deal of emphasis on marks they might or might not get at the approaching end of the first semester, and he was glad to escape the ordeal of mid-year examinations. What others might think of his quitting was not nearly so important to him as what he himself thought. If there was any fear at all, it was caused by his uncertainty about Elinor White's reaction to this bold move; but he felt that she was the one who was more responsible than anyone else for his leaving college. If only he could convince her, now, that she should also leave college at once and come home to him, all would be well.

ODD JOBS

But the task ne'er could wait the mood to come,
The music of the iron is a law:
And as upon the heavy spools that pay
Their slow white thread, so ruthlessly the hum
Of countless whirling spindles seems to draw
Upon the soul, still sore from yesterday.[1]

ROBERT FROST had some difficulty in convincing his mother that he had better things to do than waste his time at Dartmouth College. But it was not easy for her to resist his explanation that he had come home for the express purpose of helping her deal with the "numbskulls" who had been pestering her for months. He answered her protestations by saying that under no circumstances could he be persuaded to continue at Dartmouth, that he would learn more from teaching. His plan was to call on the Chairman of the School Board in Methuen, a family friend, the Reverend Charles H. Oliphant, who was a Congregationalist minister. He would explain that his mother's health was being endangered by the nervous exhaustion of trying to deal with brutes, and that he wanted to serve as a substitute teacher. Many of the schoolteachers in New England were as young as he. Some of them went directly into classrooms as instructors after graduating from high school. There could be no harm in making the appeal to Oliphant, provided he had his mother's permission. She gave it.

He did call on Oliphant, who had doubts. Another less demanding assignment could be found for Mrs. Frost without difficulty; but how did her son propose to handle the serious problem of dicipline? With force, if necessary. All right, but was the young man familiar with the materials he would have to teach eighth-graders? Yes, he had discussed these matters thoroughly with his mother. How well could he handle the important teaching of arithmetic? The applicant said he had been thinking a good bit about that, and was afraid he might have some trouble with it at first because he would be inclined to teach it algebraically; but he thought he could keep his teaching methods down on the grammar-school level. If Oliphant heard any arrogance in the tone of these answers, he was not too greatly troubled by it. In a few days, he said, he could get the approval of the School Board, and the young man could take over his mother's classroom. Mrs. Frost could fill a vacancy in a primary school where the disciplinary problems would be easier for her to handle.

Grimly satisfied with the prospects, Frost made further preparations for his task. He visited a hardware store and purchased a generous supply of stout rattans. By the time he learned that the School Board had approved his appointment, he had aroused himself to such an ugly pitch of resentment that he was ready for the ruffians. On the first morning, when he appeared in the classroom, he brought the boys and girls to order and bluntly explained his presence. He scolded the older boys for having bullied his mother and made it clear that he was ready to even the score. So saying, he took off his coat and hung it over the back of his desk chair. The bullies were delighted. They met his announcement with cheers, and several of them stood promptly to peel off coats and sweaters.

Until this moment their new teacher had not realized that several of them were taller and heavier—perhaps even stronger —than he. It might be advisable, he decided, to modify his tactics by singling out some of the middle-sized offenders for initial punishment. Class work had not even begun when he saw an excuse for descending on a culprit, yanking him out of his seat, and shoving him through the door into the entryway, where he laced him soundly with a handful of rattans. While he was executing justice in the hall, pandemonium broke loose in the classroom. There was no choice now. He had to tackle the ringleaders. He did, and resistance infuriated him. In return, his mounting outbursts of rage and violence angered the boys to the point where the situation became ugly. One of them—Johnny Howe, whose skin was so coppery that Frost though he must be part Indian—resisted punishment by drawing a knife and flourishing it as the teacher approached. Frost caught the boy's wrist, twisted it hard enough to make him drop the knife, and then flailed away with the rattans.

That evening the new teacher visited Oliphant to make a report. He admitted that he had been forced to use more physical persuasion than he had planned; but he offered Johnny Howe's knife as evidence that the problem was extraordinary. Oliphant gave his assurances and even urged that Howe should be sent immediately to a reform school as an example. Frost demurred. He said that if he had foreseen such a decision he would never have mentioned the knife; and he urged that Oliphant give him a few more days to test the sucess or failure of his methods. The request was granted. The stern physical punishment continued, until gradually the atmosphere of this previously chaotic room became conducive to moderately successful teaching. Nevertheless, Frost's use of force precipitated a small scandal in Methuen, as parents united with students in voicing their objections. The School Board defended the teacher, and even made special reference to him in the report which was prepared and printed well in advance of the annual Town Meeting held in March of 1893:

"The Second Grammar school, left vacant by the appointment of Mrs. B. M. Frost as teacher of the second primary, has been assigned to Mr. Robert L. Frost, a student in Dartmouth College. Mr. Frost, although young, bears an unusual record for scholarship and maturity of character and has shown marked address in the management and instruction of a difficult school."[2]

Regardless of his "marked address," Frost very soon grew so weary from strenuous disciplinary measures that he did not continue his teaching beyond the end of the immediate term, which closed late in March. He had planned to stay at least through the spring term, and when he failed to appear the big boys rejoiced. They spread the word that they had beaten their tormentor so badly that they had forced him to resign. His own rationalization for quitting was that he had stayed long enough to accomplish the revenge which had made him apply for the position in the first place.[3]

Nervously exhausted by the few weeks of this ordeal, he was content to do little more than eat and sleep for several days. He was in no mood for going back to Dartmouth or even for trying to find remunerative work. But all his energies were needed in a peculiar family crisis which developed at the home of Elinor White very early in the spring of 1893, while she was still absent at St. Lawrence University. Elinor's older sister, Ada, suffering from physical and psychological ailments which restricted her to a shade-drawn bedroom in their Valley Street home, began to complain about the city noises and pleaded that she be taken into the country. Mrs. White enlisted Rob's aid, and he suggested that it might be possible to rent, inexpensively, an empty but celebrated colonial homestead known as the Oliver Saunders place in Salem, New Hampshire —an attractive old house with a large central chimney and several fireplaces.[4] From the Saunders place there was a fine view down across open fields to Canobie Lake only half a mile to the south. Because Mr. White refused to accompany his wife and daughter on a cure such as this, Rob volunteered to live at the Saunders place as caretaker and protector, if the house should prove satisfactory. It did, and arrangements were made to buy just enough second-hand furniture to make the old house suitable for spring and summer camping. After Ada was brought to the Saunders place on a litter, in a crude makeshift ambulance, Mrs. White depended on Rob for innumerable tasks. It pleased and flattered him to be so much in demand, and he took his duties so seriously that he began spading a garden for vegetables—corn, peas, lettuce, radishes, carrots, onions, cucumbers.

Into this isolated rural hideaway—unexpectedly—descended Leona, oldest daughter of Mrs. White and said by some to be by far the most vivacious and beautiful of the three girls. She had recently married a farmer named Nathaniel Harvey in Epping, New Hampshire, and she arrived at the Saunders place with the announcement that although she was pregnant, she had run away from her new husband. Leona's problems were discussed at length by all, and because Frost was acting as the male head of the White family at the moment, he was consulted about even the most intimate details. With Shelleyan ease he gave his opinion that if Leona did not love her husband it would be a mistake for her to go on living with him; she should not go back. As for the newly discovered pregnancy, that unpleasant complication should be taken care of—without too much difficulty—by inducing an abortion with the aid of mustard baths. Such wisdom seemed to surprise and please everyone, and Frost was immediately sent to the nearest store for a large supply of mustard powder. He was even asked to prescribe the amount of mustard which would be necessary to achieve the desired result. Although there must have been some fault in his calculations—the mustard baths did not have any satisfactory effect—Leona seemed to depend more and more on Rob's sympathetic attentions. Together they made trips to a local farmer for milk and eggs, to Windham Village for groceries; together they worked at planting the garden; together they took long walks along the shore of Canobie Lake.

It soon became apparent that Mrs. White had another problem on her hands. Somewhat desperately she sent a telegram to Elinor saying (with an understandable disregard for truth) that Ada was terribly ill and that Elinor should come home from college immediately. Her request was followed, swiftly, and as soon as Elinor arrived at the Saunders place, Rob had four ladies on his hands. He seemed to enjoy it. Immediately he turned his attentions to Elinor, very soon Ada's health improved, and before long Leona—still pregnant —went back to her husband in Epping.

As soon as Rob was able to resume his courtship of Elinor, he insisted that she should not go back to St. Lawrence that spring—or ever. Ideally they should announce to the world that they were married. And if the demands of society made it seem advisable, they should condescend to perform the simplest public ritual of legalizing their relationship. Elinor, far more mature than he in her outlook, became unexpectedly practical. She asked how, if she should grant his wish, he planned to earn a living to support them. She would prefer, she said, that he return to Dartmouth and that they postpone the legalizing of their marriage until he became established in some career.

She made him understand that she was not the only one who was disappointed in his apparent willingness to betray the promises he had made as valedictorian; she was not the only one surprised that he could give up his studies, for no good reason, and be content with idling. Her father had already expressed his disapproval of the way in which Rob was behaving. Elinor said she suspected that Rob's mother was also unhappy; and she was sure that his grandfather, who had been paying Rob's expenses at Dartmouth, must be indignant. What were his plans? What did he see as their future? Was he content to get along without a college education?

Hurt and resentful, Rob turned the tables and began accusing Elinor. She had changed, and he feared that she had come under bad influences at St. Lawrence. Never before had she talked this way to him. He was willing to admit that he had no plans—only the hope that someday he might become famous as a poet. Otherwise, he did not know what he wanted to do with his life. Less than one semester of study at Dartmouth had convinced him that he could educate himself through independent study better than Dartmouth professors could do it. As for earning the necessities of life, there were any number of ways in which he could make money without becoming enslaved to a profession. He could teach school for a while; he could work in one of the mills occasionally; and he could do odd jobs. For the present he felt that he was needed at the Saunders place—and that Elinor was needed. She protested that if she did not go back to college soon, she might lose credit for much of the work she had already done. She was taking full-year courses in five subjects: Latin, German, Mathematics, History, and English. If she stopped in April, instead of continuing through her final examinations in June, she might have to repeat all of these freshman courses. Then it was clear, Rob insisted, that he meant less to her than something or someone at St. Lawrence University, that already she had somehow violated her pledge to him. Again she protested, but he persisted; and finally she sent word back to St. Lawrence that she would be unable to return until fall.[5]

It was not a good start for the long summer which Rob and Elinor spent with Mrs. White and Ada at the Saunders place, but he had won some kind of advantage and he was happy with it. Cheerfully he ran errands, went ahead cultivating the garden, was allowed to use a rowboat on Canobie Lake, took Elinor across the lake for day-long picnics in the woods, read aloud to the three ladies whom he was shepherding, and read much to himself when the others were busy with housework. Nevertheless, Elinor's long silences perplexed him more than ever before. His jealous nature was constantly made unhappy by the constant suspicion that at St. Lawrence she had indeed grown interested in someone else.

When fall came and the Whites made arrangements to leave the Saunders place before the lease had expired, Frost announced that he would stay on there for a few days alone. No use in going back to Lawrence if Elinor insisted on returning to college—and it may have pleased him to think he could make her sorry to leave him there all by himself. He took pleasure in feeling sorry for himself, a pleasure he later caught in a poem which described his loneliness and fear each night when it began to grow dark at the old Saunders place:

Bereft

Where had I heard this wind before
Change like this to a deeper roar?
What would it take my standing there for,
Holding open a restive door,
Looking down hill to a frothy shore?
Summer was past and day was past.
Somber clouds in the west were massed.
Out in the porch's sagging floor,
Leaves got up in a coil and hissed,
Blindly struck at my knee and missed.
Something sinister in the tone
Told me my secret must be known:
Word I was in the house alone
Somehow must have gotten abroad,
Word I was in my life alone,
Word I had no one left but God.[6]

An important meaning in the poem is conveyed by the title. Rob felt "bereft," in the sense that he had been robbed by the loss of someone dear, and hence he was lonely, sad, forlorn. If he had not already developed his own capacity for luxuriating in self-pity, the romantic Shelley could have taught him how to enjoy the mood of delicious grief derived from wounded sensibilities. But after he had indulged these miseries at the Saunders place in Salem for only a few days—perhaps just long enough to be sure that Elinor had actually gone off to college without wasting sorrow over his plight—he returned to his own home, where his mother and sister had been getting along as best they could without him.

Conscience-stricken by even the unspoken criticism he could feel in the glances of those who had expected, or at least had hoped, that he would return to Dartmouth, he proudly searched for work of a kind which might be sufficiently unusual and honorable to impress friends and enemies alike. Shortly before leaving Salem he had clipped from a Boston newspaper an advertisement in which a Shakespeare reader offered to share profits with a capable manager. Answering it, Frost pretended to be well-qualified for such work; but he warned that, of course, he would not care to accept the offer until he was assured that the abilities of the Shakespeare reader would warrant the time and energy required for such an undertaking. Back came a satisfactory answer suggesting that reader and possible manager should meet in Boston to discuss terms. Although only nineteen years old, and with very little knowledge of Shakespeare's plays, this would-be entrepreneur was bold enough to pose as an expert. In Boston he began by cross-examining the much older Shakespeare reader on the success of his earlier performances. Frost suggested a try-out session, which would give the reader a chance to demonstrate his talents before some of the best critics in the area. The terms were accepted; the money was advanced; and Frost went to work. He hired a hall; he had tickets printed; he gave tickets away on the street. Then he went across the Charles River to Cambridge and enlisted the interest of the elderly Shakespeare scholar, William James Rolfe. He called at the office of *The Boston Evening Transcript* and invited the theater critic, Richard Clapp, to attend the performance.

On the scheduled evening Frost served as doorman and ticket-taker. Concealing his disappointment in the small audience, he listened with dismay to the old-fashioned elocutionary mannerisms of his reader, and was not surprised when both Rolfe and Clapp expressed their negative views, very curtly, on their way out. As gently as he could, he informed the Shakespeare reader that the distinguished critics had not been entirely satisfied, that under the circumstances Frost felt he could not afford to devote any more time to this enterprise.[7]

After that ambitious venture, Frost went back to Lawrence and humbled himself by accepting the first work he could find. He became a light-trimmer in the Arlington Woolen Mill, and settled in for several months of drudgery. At first he was embarrassed by the contrast between his former position in the relatively small Everett Mill, where he had been something of a boss as assistant gatetender, and here at the huge Arlington Mill, where he was one of the menials. Formerly he had not mingled with the workers and had not gotten to know many of them; now he was a slave in a position no better than the one he had suffered while working in the Braithwaite Mill during the summer of 1891. There he had merely col-

lected wooden bobbins from which the yarn had been un-
wound, here he was obliged to overcome his dislike of high
places. As a light-trimmer he learned to stand on the very
top of a ladder while reaching up with both hands to unfasten
and replace the burned-out carbon pencils used as filaments
in the arc lamps. His duties were not arduous—they brought
him only $8.oo a week—and on clear sunny days there was
very little need for artificial light. Whenever his boss found
him idle, he gave him a broom to sweep up wool crumbs or
a cloth for polishing brass. These menial labors hurt Rob's
pride, and he learned to keep out of sight after his light-
trimming tasks were finished. Exploring various hideaway
places, he at last chose as his favorite a sort of hen coop built
on the roof of the main building to house a large belt wheel.
In this isolated place, to which an oiler came once each day,
Frost lounged and read and slept, undisturbed by the quiet
whir of the big wheel and the slapping sound of the wide
leather belt.

For his reading in this lofty wheelhouse Rob carried a
small pocket-sized book, usually a volume from a complete
set of Shakespeare which he had purchased in Boston during
his recent flurry there. Never before had he read any of the
plays carefully. Now, with the intonations of the elocutionist
still in mind, he began to study certain passages in *Hamlet,
Macbeth,* and *The Tempest,* pencil in hand for making marginal notes on how the passages should be spoken if the lines
were to convey, dramatically, the essential meanings. Soon
he began to admire the give-and-take of Shakespeare's lean
sharp dialogue, made most effective when the thread of
thought and action was not snarled into a maze of metaphor
and adjective. For the first time, he realized that in Shakespeare's poetry—and, he supposed, in any good poetry—there
was an interplay between the basic rhythm of the metrical
line and the natural intonations of the spoken sentence. In
his own writing, he decided, he would try to achieve these
qualities. Day after day, as he continued to study Shakespeare's
dialogues, while the slight breeze of the turning belt wheel
fanned the pages of his book, he kept searching for hints and
clues that might help him to understand and master these
technical aspects of poetry.

Although he continued as light-trimmer in the Arlington
Mill from late September of 1893 until February of 1894,

without forming any important friendships among the mill hands, he did make the acquaintance of several boys who were nearly his own age. One of them was an ambitious young man named Ed Gilbert, who was saving his money in the hope that he might eventually go to Dartmouth College. Another was a native of Sutton, Vermont, who had grown up next door to Carl Burell and who entertained Frost with gossip about their mutual friend. In Sutton, it seemed, the general belief was that Carl's cluminess, lisping, and general oddity of manner could be traced back to a head injury received in childhood. Some said that a playmate had hit him too hard with a cast-iron engine, and that the blow had turned him from normal kinds of play to unusual studiousness. Sutton neighbors liked to tell how Carl's mother, trying to interrupt Carl's protracted shuffling through page after page of the *New York World,* would urge the boy to do his chores, and would be answered plaintively, "I haven't finished weeding the *World* phruu, yet!" Carl's fondness for tenderly nursing his flower beds was another cause for amusement in the village, particularly his habit of chasing after worm-seeking chickens whenever they invaded his gardens. His ungainly rush across the lawn toward the intruders, with his arms flailing around his head, was always accompanied by the same bellowing protest: "Tarnation-feathered Satans, soilin' my posies!"

Other kinds of anecdotes, told by evil-minded acquaintances, embarrassed Frost as much at the Arlington Mill as they had at Dinsmore's farm. He still felt dismay at not knowing how to avoid being drawn into unexpected confidences. A particularly distressing moment occurred when one of the workers pointed at a girl, who was said to have been "knocked up" by the boss, calling particular attention to her distended belly; he was still pointing when the girl turned to look at them. Equally difficult to handle was the discovery that several of his former students, whom he had disciplined too harshly in the Second Grammer School in Methuen, were now working in the Arlington Mill and were quick with their jibes and obscenities whenever he passed.

For a time these old enemies seemed content with insults. But as the weeks slipped by, they began to threaten Frost with insinuations that the day would come when they would get revenge on their former teacher. They lost no chance to keep asking him how he had fallen from his high estate to a position far more menial and less remunerative than some of the tasks carried out by his persecutors. For protection Frost fell into the habit of approaching the mill gate in the morning and leaving it at night always in company with some of the more trustworthy workers. He was postponing violence as long as possible. But in the dusk of one winter evening, a group of his tormentors waylaid him as he was walking home from work alone. They knocked him down, rolled him into the slush of the gutter—punching and kicking and hammering him at will—until he was certain that their intent was murder. A good Samaritan, passing by, waded into the fracas with shouts for help while swinging a heavy black walking stick, reversed for use as a club. The tormentors ran, and as Frost rose to his knees in the gutter, trying to mumble his thanks, he saw that there were two figures standing there above him. One of them was a young man who had formerly been his classmate in high school. Apparently the rescuer and the onlooker knew something about the scandal involving the "marked address" with which Frost had handled his pupils in the Second Grammar School, and therefore understood the nature of the attack. Only a few words were spoken, and Frost continued home doubly the victim of humiliation. What hurt more than the physical pounding was the remembered expression of disdain on the face of his former classmate. Perhaps it was disgust at the thought that a Hood Prize winner and valedictorian could have degenerated so soon into a good-for-nothing mill-hand street-fighter.

Let others think what they liked. Frost was convinced that if he had to face any further street-fighting, he should learn a bit more about the so-called manly art of self-defense. Having heard that a retired pugilist, locally famous, offered boxing lessons for a reasonable price in the back room of an unlicensed Lawrence saloon, Rob furtively enrolled for a course, and made weekly visits until he had been taught to improve his balance, his footwork, and his punches. As it happened, his tormentors seemed satisfied with their revenge, and they gave him no more serious trouble. They had done enough, however, to spoil Frost's associations at the mill, and he grew increasingly irked with the drudgery there as the winter days dragged on. He resented having to work as a slave in an atmosphere which did greater harm to the spirit than to the body.

In his early days at the Arlington Mill he had admired the deftness of the girls who worked in the wool-dusty atmosphere, the quick motions of their fingers as they reached in among taut threads to snatch up broken ends and twist them quickly together. Now he began to feel that these girls were forced to become human spiders; that all these threads seemed to be drawn, at a debilitating speed, from their insides. He tried to catch his own mood of resentment later, in a sonnet which did reflect his bitter disapproval of such endless mill work:

> *When the speed comes a-creeping overhead*
> *And belts begin to snap and shafts to creak,*
> *And the sound dies away of them that speak,*
> *And on the glassy floor the tapping tread;*
> *When dusty globes on all a pallor shed,*
> *And breaths of many wheels are on the cheek;*
> *Unwilling is the flesh, the spirit weak,*
> *All effort like arising from the dead.*
>
> *But the task ne'er could wait the mood to come,*
> *The music of the iron is a law:*
> *And as upon the heavy spools that pay*
> *Their slow white thread, so ruthlessly the hum*
> *Of countless whirling spindles seems to draw*
> *Upon the soul, still sore from yesterday.*[8]

He was ripe for membership in any Socialistic-Syndicalistic-Communistic-Anarchistic movement—at least he might have joined a labor union at this time if he had been given proper encouragement. Priding himself on being a Shelleyan, he was ready to apply Shelley's lines of protest:

> *I will be wise*
> *And just, and free, and mild, if in me lies*
> *Such power, for I grow weary to behold*
> *The selfish and the strong still tyrannize*
> *Without reproach or check.*[9]

While Frost was nursing his own soul-bruises and resenting the hardships of his lot, he suffered oblique effects from his mother's cumulative misfortunes. Her difficulties in teaching were usually caused by her inability to handle disciplinary problems; after she had been shunted through four Methuen schools, she was completely relieved of these teaching duties. The loss of her salary forced her to give up the comfortable apartment where she and her children had been living in Methuen, on Broadway not far from the boundary line between Salem and Methuen. For Rob's sake, they moved to Lawrence, finding an unattractive and yet inexpensive four-room tenement near the tracks of the Boston and Maine railroad at 96 Tremont Street, near the corner of West Street. It was no worse than the first tenement they had rented in Lawrence, soon after they had come East from San Francisco—but it was no better.[10]

Rob's pride was further injured by his feeling that while his own social and economic position grew worse, Elinor White was mingling with the wealthy at St. Lawrence, enjoying the attentions of too many attractive young men and deliberately ignoring his predicament. It hurt him to look back over what had happened since his graduation from high school: the wasted months of horseplay and clowning at Darmouth, the savagely vengeful weeks of school-teaching in Methuen, the odd summer at the old Saunders place in Salem, the fiasco with the elocutionist in Boston, the drudgery of menial chores as light-trimmer in the Arlington Mill, the humiliation of the street fight, the degradation of paying a professional boxer to give him punching lessons, and the gradual fading of his hopes that he might someday make a name for himself as a poet. He still tried his hand at writing verse once in a while, and yet nothing seemed to come of such attempts. He was almost willing to admit that he simply lacked whatever it took to be a poet. But if that were so, what other abilities did he have? What should he be doing? Who was he and where was he going? He wished he knew.

OUT OF SORTS WITH FATE

I was, to be sure,
Out of sorts with Fate,
Wandering to and fro
In the earth alone,
You might think too poor-
Spirited to care
Who I was or where
I was being blown
Faster than my tread—
Like the crumpled, better
Left-unwritten letter
I had read and thrown.[1]

ONE MORNING, late in the winter of 1894, Robert Frost was still approaching the gate of the Arlington Mill when he heard the mill bell shift from its vigorous clang to a funeral toll; the gate would soon be shut. Having served as assistant to the gatekeeper at the old Everett Mill, he knew what it was like to sit inside, looking out at laggards who, for their tardiness, would be made to stand idle throughout the next half-hour and then would find a few cents less in their next pay envelope. Here at the Arlington Mill he had often experienced the humiliation from the outside of the fence. It was the price he had to pay for his incurable habit of late rising. This morning, as the main gate clanged shut just before he could reach it, he vented his mood of resentment by making a Shelleyan gesture of scornfully rebellious defiance. The time had come to strike; and he was willing to stand apart from the herd as a lone striker, motivated by his own whims:

He knew a path that wanted walking;
He knew a spring that wanted drinking;

A thought that wanted further thinking;
A love that wanted re-renewing.
Nor was this just a way of talking
To save him the expense of doing.
With him it boded action, deed.[2]

As he turned his back on the gate he knew this was more than a strike; he was putting an inexorable end to his life as a degraded millhand. The assertion of his independence gave a lift to his spirit and made him feel more like a man than he had felt for months.

His elation might have lasted longer if he could have avoided another thought. The love he wanted to re-renew might suffer fresh setbacks if Elinor White came home from St. Lawrence University to find him doing nothing more for their future than inviting and indulging the soul. He would find something else to do, soon enough, and any kind of work would be more dignified than that of being a light-trimmer in a dirty mill. He was a teacher—with approximately three months of experience—and he knew that many district schools in towns and villages outside Lawrence were merely struggling along with substitute teachers.

The path he soon found himself walking was a bitterly familiar one. After taking the train from Lawrence to Salem Depot, he walked over to Salem Center to call on a member of the School Board, Mr. Clinton Leroy Silver. Explaining his hope that one of the small district schools in Salem might need a teacher for the spring term, he gave his qualifications. If he made too much of his brief teaching experience in Methuen, he at least assumed that Mr. Silver did not know that he had created a small scandal in gaining this experience. There was an opening in Salem; a replacement was needed for a substitute teacher in the tiny District School Number Nine in South Salem, only about a mile below Salem Depot and not far from the Methuen-Salem boundary line. Details were easily arranged, and Frost began teaching a few days later, commuting by train to Salem Depot from Lawrence and frequently walking home through Methuen to Lawrence. The pay was no better than he had received at the Arlington Mill, but the hours were shorter. In addition, his work with children in the first six grades was more to the young man's liking, and the deference with which he was treated by pupils and parents alike was balm to his wounded pride.

Secretively, shyly, he stole time during the spring term of 1894 to explore another path that wanted more walking than he had yet given it—the path hinted at when he began to make annotations along the margins of Shakespeare's plays, also further hinted in his studious re-reading of the lyrics in Palgrave's *Golden Treasury*. Almost surreptitiously he had clung to the direction his steps had begun to take on that March afternoon during his sophomore year in high school when he had begun to compose in his memory, while walking home from school, the ballad stanzas of "La Noche Triste." Although some of his closest friends might never have guessed, and in spite of the discouragement which had beset his many attempts to write verse, he continued to cherish his dream that he might eventually become known as a poet. He was almost ashamed to admit his hopes, his ambition, even to himself. Whenever the mood came over him to take out his sheaf of poems to make fresh starts or revisions, he concealed his activities from his mother and sister, as though he dreaded to let them know what he was doing.

One such concealment occurred in the Tremont Street apartment down near the railroad tracks in Lawrence on a Sunday evening soon after he had begun teaching school in Salem. The warmest room in the apartment was the kitchen, and he had carefully locked himself in, to work at the kitchen table on a poem inspired by a moment which had occurred late in the fall of his few months at Dartmouth, a moment when he had found a fragile butterfly wing lying among dead leaves. Because the delicate wing seemed to him so perfect an image, representing the brevity of life, he had been trying to build an elegy around it ever since he had left Dartmouth College. This evening the words and thoughts intermingled so successfully that he felt a sense of power and triumph which carried him through to an almost satisfactory end. But as he worked, his sister tried the door to the kitchen and, finding it locked, began to pound on it in anger. What was he doing in the kitchen? And why had he locked the door? He gave her no satisfactory answer, and he kept on writing. Because the apartment was on the ground floor, the mystified and impatient Jeanie was able to try another means of access. She walked out the front door and around the house until she could climb the steps and turn the handle of the back door —also locked. Again she hammered and complained to the amusement of her brother. He was through, now, and all her noise did not hinder him from making a fair copy of "My Butterfly: An Elegy." As soon as he was ready, but not a moment before, he opened the kitchen door to Jeanie and retired to his own bedroom still feeling a sense of elation over his newest and best poetic accomplishment.[3]

What pleased him most about this evening devoted to writing his butterfly elegy was the sense that he had discovered within himself unexpected ability to fuse elements of observed fact, impassioned rhythmical tone, and heartfelt personal theme. Although he had built his lament primarily around images of the butterfly, briefly alive and now dead, he had given depth to the poem by hinting at literal and figurative analogies between certain things happening simultaneously to himself and the butterfly. In the elegy he had mourned the transience from days of ecstasy when "precipitate in love," both had been unaware that "fate had made" them "for the pleasure of the wind"; the transience from days when each had been unaware that "conspiracy was rife" against the lives of each; the transience from days when "the soft mist of my regret hung not on all the land." The passage which pleased him most for purely technical qualities of sound, rhythm, tone was this:

> *The grey grass is scarce dappled with the snow,*
> *Its two banks have not shut upon the river,*
> > *But it is long ago,*
> > *It seems forever,*
> *Since first I saw thee glance*
> *With all the dazzling other ones,*
> > *In airy dalliance,*
> > *Precipitate in love,*
> *Tossed up, tossed up and tangling above,*
> *Like a limp rose-wreath in a fairy dance.*

As he read these lines immediately after he had written them, he cried inside with the joy of his knowledge that at last he had caught poetic qualities which had seemed beyond his reach. Suddenly all his ambition was justified and re-enforced. Now he had something he could submit to a magazine editor with a strong hope that it would not be returned to him with a rejection slip. Remembering Hovey's "Elegy" published on the first page of *The Independent* and feeling that the editor of *The Independent* might be particularly sympathetic to poetry—as evidenced by the long editorial devoted to Hovey's poem—he sent off his manuscript without any covering letter, simply with his name and address at the top of the first page: "R. L. Frost, Tremont St., Lawrence, Mass."[4]

Quicker than Frost dared expect, the editor of *The Independent* replied with a check for fifteen dollars, with praise for "My Butterfly," and even with a request for some biographical information about the author's "training" and "line of study." The event was so exciting that Frost, in his answer dated 28 March 1894, did not even try to strike a posture of calm:

"The memory of your note will be a fresh pleasure to me when I awaken for a good many mornings to come; which may as well confirm you in the belief that I am still young. I am. The poem you have is the first of mine that any publication has accepted."

He went on to say that he had submitted three other poems to other editors recently and that, although none of them had yet been returned, he would send more to *The Independent* when he could. "Nevertheless," he continued, "since I have but recently discovered my powers, I have, of course, no great amount of verses in store . . ." As for his "training" and "line of study," he acknowledged that he was "only graduated of a public high school" and had spent but a few months at Dartmouth College "until recalled by necessity." He added, "But this inflexible ambition trains us best, and to love poetry is to study it."[5]

The ambition had indeed been there, secretly concealed lest failure should make him the target for mockery and scorn. All he needed by way of encouragement was exactly the kind of response given by the warm praise of an editor so distinguished as the Reverend William Hayes Ward, whose specialty was not so much poetry as theology and Assyrian archeology. The learned man's sister, Susan Hayes Ward, usually served as literary editor of *The Independent*. She had been the one who had called his attention to "My Butterfly," and after he had completed the formalities of acceptance she wrote to the newly discovered poet expressing her own admiration. But she also made some comments on weak places in the poem, urged him to make a few revisions, and sent him a copy on which he might make changes. She also encouraged him to tell her more about his literary interests. Her well-intended criticisms depressed the young poet almost as much as her genuine praise heartened him. He answered on 22 April 1894, enclosing three more poems and managing to combine both sides of his reaction in his opening paragraph:

"It is just such a letter as you wrote me that I have been awaiting for two years. Hitherto all the praise I have received has been ill-advised and unintelligent; all the criticism, this general one upon the rueful fact that I, once the friend of so and so, should have at last turned poetaster. So that something definite and discriminating is very welcome. My thanks unlimited! Yet the consideration is hardly due me. Take my word for it that poem exaggerates my ability. You must spare my feelings when you come to read these others, for I haven't the courage to be a disappointment to anyone. Do not think this artifice or excess of modesty, though, for to betray myself utterly, such an one am I that even in my failures I find all the promise I require to justify the astonishing magnitude of my ambition."

After acknowledging the precarious balance he kept between hopes and fears for his own future as a poet, he gave Miss Ward some hints of authors who interested him, including the novelist—not yet the poet—Thomas Hardy who "has taught me the good use of a few words and, refer[r]ing still to me, 'struck the simple solemn.'" He went on to say that in contrast with Hardy, "Scott and Stevenson inspire me, by their prose, with the thought that we Scotchmen are bound to be romanticists—poets." Then he named four poems which were favorites of his at that time: Keats' "Hyperion," Shelley's "Prometheus," Tennyson's "Morte D'Arthur," and Browning's "Saul."

"So far," he continued, "everything looks auspicious. But it is necessary to admit that I teach 'orthography' in a district school: and that in the fitness of things, the association of Eugene Aram with children in this capacity seems no more incongruous than my own. In fact so wholly uncongenial is the work that it has become for me a mere test of physical endurance. For several weeks now when not teaching I have spent my time lying around either consciously sleeping or unconsciously waking and in both cases irresponsibly iratable [sic] to the last degree. It is due to my nerves—they are susceptible to sound. Consequently the prospect is not bright—for the immediate future at least. When in this condition I can neither read nor write: nevertheless I find a few hours for study and, as I say, always entertain great hopes."[6]

He concluded his letter to Miss Ward by admitting that certain lines in "My Butterfly" did need revision as she had suggested, but that for the present he did not find any adequate inspiration for correcting or improving the faults. His next letter, dated 10 June 1894, revealed an even darker and more discouraged mood: "It has been painful for me trying to induce a passion like the one that is the spirit of my poem. I am afraid I can not revise the thing. I am greatly dissatisfied with it now. Do you not think it would be well to suppress it."[7] Apparently Miss Ward knew how to cope with these passing moods of despondency. She continued writing to him; she waited patiently for his revisions; and she made arrangements to keep the poem until the appropriate time to publish it in autumn.

Both of the Wards were unusually impressed with "My Butterfly: An Elegy." They showed it with pride to Bliss Carman, who had just collaborated with Richard Hovey in publishing the exuberant *Songs from Vagabondia;* and Carman had praised the poem. Another copy of "My Butterfly" was sent by Ward to the Hoosier novelist Maurice Thompson, who responded with a glowing tribute.[8] Ward also sent a note to an acquaintance of his in Lawrence, a Congregationalist minister named William E. Wolcott, asking Wolcott to visit the poet and help him in any way possible. Frost and Wolcott had already met: The minister had served as a judge in awarding prizes for the best poetry and prose submitted to the high school *Bulletin* during Frost's senior year. Calling on Frost to congratulate him now on the success of "My Butterfly," Wolcott talked at length with the young man and offered to serve as advisor-critic. Flattered, Frost showed several of his manuscripts to Wolcott, who found nothing which seemed to compare with "My Butterfly." He complained that the other poems lacked the same high lyrical music of true poetry, suffered from a flatness of tone, and sounded "too much like talk."

Some after-thoughts were needed before Frost could make any constructive use of Wolcott's criticism. He remembered that he had liked the dramatic qualities of the poetic dialogues in Shakespeare's plays because those dialogues actually sounded so much like "talk" that they characterized the individual speakers. He realized that he had wasted his time in making marginal notes on how these lines should be spoken, and he was convinced that part of Shakespeare's greatness in ordering words was that he made the words themselves convey the sound of talk. In another way, while reading Hardy's novels, he had been impressed with what he had recently described to Miss Ward as the good use of a few uncomplicated words. His after-thoughts enabled him to make use of Wolcott's criticism which accidentally threw light on something he had been groping toward: a poem well handled could not possibly sound "too much like talk"; all the best lines and sentences should clearly convey tones of voice that rooted poetry deep in human experience. From now on, he decided, he would try harder than ever to make his poetry sound "like talk."[9]

Wolcott continued his well-meaning efforts. He called on Nathaniel Goodwin, Principal of the Lawrence High School, and discussed ways of helping the Frost boy establish contact with Lawrence alumni who were writing for newspapers and magazines in the general area of Boston. A few days later Frost received a note asking him to stop at Goodwin's home whenever convenient. He went, early one spring evening, and found his former teacher casually smoking a pipe as he raked dead leaves away from flower beds in the front yard. Their conversation was carried on while Goodwin continued to rake.

He was pleased with the good news that Frost had sold a poem to *The Independent*, he said, and suggested that if Frost wanted to become a literary man it might be wise to start by getting a newspaper reporter's job; very few poets could support themselves merely by writing verse. Goodwin had the contacts, and he would be happy to help in any way he could. No, Frost answered, newspaper work wasn't exactly what he wanted. Other suggestions were made, with no better response from Frost, and finally Goodwin grew impatient. Maybe his former pupil was suffering under the delusion that the world owed him a living? Frost smiled, and answered that he wasn't foolish enough to think that; but he'd like to believe the world would let him earn a living at whatever he could do best. Goodwin shrugged his shoulders and reminded the aspirant that legions of people had been wistful enough to believe in such a fallacy; but the world had never humored them long. The shrug alone served to hint that Frost might as well leave. He had always felt that Goodwin disliked him. But as he started toward the gate he turned back, smiled, and said as pleasantly as he could, "I'll bet." Goodwin, notorious for his clandestine racetrack betting, lifted one hand from his rake and waved it in a gesture which might have meant good-bye or good riddance.

Throughout the spring of 1894, Frost continued to puzzle over all the advice that had been given him. It was one thing to bet on himself, and even to fashion an ideal poetic theory out of Wolcott's fault-finding; but it was another thing to confront the discouraging fact that whenever he yielded to the mood and wrote poetry nothing worth while came of it. Self-protectively, he kept making the excuse he had used in writing to Miss Ward: The nervous exhaustion and drudgery of teaching the boisterous children in District School Number Nine up in Salem had worn him down until he was on the verge of illness. Miss Ward did not help him any when she urged him to improve his metrical skills by studying Sidney Lanier's treatise on *The Science of English Verse*; it seemed to him that Lanier's notions were even worse than Wolcott's appeal for poetic musicality. Miss Ward embarrassed him also by sending him an edition of Lanier's *Collected Poems,* recently published, which contained a prefatory memoir written by William Hayes Ward. Frost did his best to be polite in his acknowledgment—at least he concealed his growing belief that he was working in a direction which was almost diametrically opposed to Lanier's. Miss Ward never guessed how truthfully he had spoken when he had told her there were times when he was "irresponsibly iratable to the last degree."

Irritabilities marred his anticipation of Elinor White's return home from St. Lawrence University for the summer vacation of 1894. Throughout the year he had tortured himself with fears and dreads that her college interests were drawing her further away from their secretly-made vows of eternal love. He was well aware that because St. Lawrence was a very small college in a very small village the sixty-odd boys and thirty-odd girls attending it were able to become very well-acquainted— and that the odds clearly favored the girls. He had also learned that dances were often held at St. Lawrence and that the big

social events of the year were parties given by the two fraterni-
ties and the two sororities. Elinor White's parents were very
casual in their attitude toward dancing. By contrast, the far
more sternly Calvinistic background of Mrs. Frost's early life
had led her to teach her son that dancing was one of the
devil's most ingenious enticements to sin. Elinor White, understanding these differences of opinion, gave her accounts of
social functions only in letters written to her mother and
sisters. All might have been well in this regard if Mrs. White
had not possessed an extraordinary knack for letting secrets
out by reading passages to Rob whenever he visited her, passages which very innocently included references to several
of Elinor's friends who were making news with trivial flirta-
tions or serious love affairs. Prone to jealousy in any case,
Frost let his imagination go so far that he very soon suspected
the worst about Elinor. He tried to warn Mrs. White that her
daughter was in very lax and dangerous company at St. Lawrence; he had even tried to warn Elinor herself. But in all of
her replies Elinor insisted that her college friendships had
no bearing on her love for Rob; he had no reason to be jealous.
Back and forth through the mail went the shuttle of their dis-
cord, Frost pressing more and more on what he considered
to be the disloyalty of Elinor's dalliances. He even wrote and
sent to her a poem entitled "Warning," in which he summed
up his ultimate fear:

> *The day will come when you will cease to know,*
> *The heart will cease to tell you; sadder yet,*
> *Tho' you say o'er and o'er what once you knew,*
> *You will forget, you will forget.*
>
> *There is no memory for what is true,*
> *The heart once silent. Well may you regret,*
> *Cry out upon it, that you have known all*
> *But to forget, but to forget.*
>
> *Blame no one but yourself for this, lost soul!*
> *I feared it would be so that day we met*
> *Long since, and you were changed. And I said then,*
> *She will forget, she will forget.*[10]

In her letters Elinor continued to protest that she was not

a "lost soul" and that Rob should blame no one except himself for imagining such nonsense. He was not convinced, and the pain of his fears grew worse when he began to notice that in her letters to her mother Elinor repeatedly mentioned the names of two young men at St. Lawrence: Glenn Andrews Kratzer '94 and Owen D. Young '94. Instead of consoling himself with even the slight hope that there might be safety in numbers, Frost went into a jealous rage over the probability that both men were suitors for Elinor's hand.

Neither one was truly a suitor. Although Kratzer had escorted Elinor to several social functions during her freshman year, he was an awkward outsider whose attentions never amounted to courtship. Owen D. Young had already become engaged to a St. Lawrence girl before he met Elinor White. From the start, however, he was impressed by the shrewdness of Elinor's remarks in the classroom and her mature manner. He frequently continued classroom discussions with her after the bell had rung and was puzzled by certain oddities. He wondered at the extraordinary seriousness of Miss White's face, and suspected that it concealed shyness, sensitivity, or even some deep sorrow. He noticed that her solemn and beautiful eyes would occasionally light up when a particular remark fired her imagination, and that during these brief moments her whole face was suffused with an ecstatic radiance. She seemed to talk more openly with him than with other young men; the slow easing of manner in his company seemed to grow from her knowledge that he was engaged to be married. Gradually, as Young came to know her better, he decided that she was a girl of deep spiritual resources, waiting wistfully and romantically for some knight in armor to come riding up on a white horse and sweep her off her feet. He felt that she yearned for such an experience as a fulfillment of her passionate hunger for an ideally perfect love. Although she occasionally mentioned to Young a boy back home named Robert Frost—and said she believed he would succeed as a poet—she never talked of him with any hint that she might be engaged to him—or even might be in love with him.[11]

If Owen D. Young had met Robert Frost at this time, and had come to know him well, he might have recognized in him the male counterpart of Elinor White: each of them cherished a passionately romantic hunger for an ideally perfect love.

Frost's standards and ideals of womanhood, shaped by the heroic romances his mother had read to him since childhood, were renewed as he surrendered to the appeal of a current best-seller of 1894: Anthony Hope's *The Prisoner of Zenda*. Replete with noble actions on the part of a hero whose goal was to "strike a blow for honor" as often as possible, this story had a lasting influence on Frost. He may have had no difficulty in identifying himself with Rudolf, whose friends were few, whose enemies were many, whose disguises were so slight that he constantly feared someone might recognize him for the pretender he sometimes thought he might be; even while in his heart he hoped for proof that aristocratic blood flowed through his veins—and that he was worthy of it.[12]

By the time Elinor White did come home from St. Lawrence University, in the summer of 1894, her lover was ready to number all her college friends among his enemies, and was more eager than ever to "strike a blow for honor" by publicly marrying her and thus rescuing her from the evil influences of that dark place. Instead, he was crushed by her insistence that she must finish her college studies, that even then she felt they should not marry formally until he had found a reliable means of providing at least a minimum of financial support for them both. He was not earning any money that summer because his physical and nervous illnesses of the spring still plagued him. In all the arguments which marred his intensified courtship, he tried to explain that love came first, that they were already pledged to each other, that they had sealed their private contract by an exchange of rings; that she should now be willing to suffer through the unimportant public ritual so that they could live together. As for their future, and his capacity to earn money, if she really meant what she said about her faith in his poetry, she should be able to see particular significance in his having sold "My Butterfly" for cash. Gently resisting all his pleas, Elinor White returned to St. Lawrence in the fall of 1894 after making only one concession. She would continue to accelerate her program of studies so that she could be graduated a full year ahead of schedule, in June of 1895. If, by then, he had established himself relatively well, she would marry him.

Dissatisfied with her plans, and yet unable to change them, Frost made several listless attempts to find work that was congenial to him. He even went so far as to accept positions in Boston, on three separate occasions; but he quit each one of them after only a few days. More pertinent to his ambition was his briefly obsessive speculation concerning all he had read and heard about poets who found artistic stimulus through drugs and alcohol. As an experiment, he made another trip to Boston, rented a room in a boarding house, bought two bottles of wine, drank as much as he could, and began to write poem after poem. Late in the night he went to bed happy in the thought that his experiment had been a success. The next morning, when he read his new creations in the sober light of day, he could not understand how he had been so thoroughly deceived by the wine. Disgusted, he tore up his manuscripts, paid for his room, and went back to his mother's apartment in Lawrence.[13]

As he continued to drift from one odd job to another, Frost apparently worried his grandfather so much that the elderly gentleman finally cornered him during one of his rare visits to the Haverhill Street home of his grandparents. There was no unkindness in the tone with which his grandfather began to talk, as the two of them sat alone in the living room. The old man said that he had been pleased to learn that Rob had sold a poem to *The Independent*; he was well aware, he said, that the attractions of a literary life seemed to be keeping Rob from settling down to a wage-earning career or profession. If the boy needed a little more time to try his wings as a poet, his grandfather said, money could be found to support him for one more full year, on one condition: that if, at the end of the year, he had not established himself as a self-supporting man of letters, he would stop wasting time. Under the circumstances the offer was extremely generous, particularly in the light of their irritable and infuriating relationship. But Rob, instead of making a tactfully grateful answer, seemed intent on using the moment as another occasion for insolence. He rose to his feet, struck the posture of an auctioneer accepting bids, and began to chant through his nose: "I have one, who'll give me twenty; I have one, who'll give me twenty; one give me twenty-twenty-twenty-twenty . . ."

The arrogance had its desired effect. While Rob was still chanting, his grandfather abruptly left the room.[14]

DISMAL SWAMP

. . . there ariseth in his soul many fears, and doubts, and discouraging apprehensions, which all of them get together, and settle in this place. And this is the reason of the badness of this ground.[1]

IN THE FALL OF 1894, and during his troubled courtship of Elinor White, Robert Frost made a romantic gesture with almost disastrous effect. He thought his beloved could be made to understand that the sale of "My Butterfly" to *The Independent* truly foreshadowed the time when he could earn a living for both of them by publishing book after book of poetry, and he wanted to place in her hands a prophetic symbol of this future. Inspired by new hope, he sorted through his manuscripts to find four poems which might accompany "My Butterfly" in a little book made especially for her. Each of the four poems must have been chosen with a view to what Elinor could read between the lines; each may have had reference to places made sacred by shared experiences, but now imaginatively revisited by the lover, alone with his memories. One was entitled "An Unhistoric Spot," beginning:

> *Ah passionate is rest when to the earth*
> *I yield in full length contact of sweet pain!*
> *Here just within the bars in the chill grass,*
> *And the great shadow of a fruitless tree,*
> *I at once sleep and am awake in joy.*

Another was entitled "Summering," and it began:

> *I would arise and in a dream go on—*
> *Not very far, not very far—and then*
> *Lie down amid the sunny grass again,*

And fall asleep till night-time or next dawn.

Another, "The Falls," suggests an equally idyllic rendezvous which these two lovers may have shared:

> *'Tis a steep wood of rocks,*
> *With the fern grown everywhere;*
> *But with no birds—not a wing!*
> *And the falls come down there.*
>
> *Even an Indian trail*
> *Would swerve to a haunt so fair!*
> *One used to—there were the ferns*
> *And the falls came down there.*

In the final poem, "Twilight," the lonely lover addresses the personification of twilight, one who, like himself, is sadly looking for someone else. It echoes the address to the moon uttered by Sidney's lonely lover in the familiar sonnet "His Lady's Cruelty," which begins, "With how sad steps, O Moon, thou climb'st the skies!" The first verse of "Twilight":

> *Why am I first in thy so sad regard,*
> *O twilight gazing from I know not where?*
> *I fear myself as one more than I guessed!*
> *Am I instead of one so very fair?—*
> *That thou art sorrowful and I oppressed?*

Having made his selection, he carried fair copies of these four poems, with "My Butterfly," to a job printer in Lawrence. He asked that a very special little book be made of them; the poems to be printed on antique paper and bound in leather in an edition of just two copies. One would be for Elinor, the other for himself. When the work was done and the books were delivered to him, the title word, *Twilight,* was handsomely stamped in gold on the brown pebbled-leather binding.

He had kept this secret from Elinor because he wanted to surprise her. It would have a very private meaning for her, and yet each poem was so subtly a love poem that he hoped she might dare show them to her college friends, who would then know that her lover was by no means the failure they might think him. Before the book was ready to mail, however,

Elinor's letters overcame him with new and dreadful fears that his cause might already be lost.

Her letters, as he interpreted them, provided convincing proof that she was welcoming the attentions of a new suitor at St. Lawrence. He was a handsome and charming senior—the Beau Brummel of his class—and his name was Lorenzo Dow Case. From Mrs. White, Rob learned that this new charmer was so serious in his attentions to Elinor that he had asked for, and that she had granted him, permission to spend one evening a week with her. Rob was frantic.

Encouraged by Mrs. White, he made secret plans to go to Canton as soon as possible. The time had come to strike a crucial blow for honor. He would assault the citadel, even though he might suffer defeat in bold combat; and he would use *Twilight* as his best weapon. He confided all of his hopes to Mrs. White, who expressed her sympathy in several ways. She gave him money for a round-trip railroad ticket. She even accompanied him to a haberdashery and helped him buy a new suit for the venture. Finally, she went with him to the station and gave him her blessing as he departed.

The journey from Lawrence to Canton was overnight, and as Rob sat in the coach throughout the long and dismal hours he tried to prepare himself for any eventuality. Early in the morning he found his way to the campus of St. Lawrence University and began asking directions to the house to which he had addressed so many letters: Miss Moore's, corner of Pine and Miner Streets. It was a private home rather than a campus dormitory, but the several girls who had rooms were required to obey campus regulations, which made it a punishable offense for any girl to entertain any young man there except during the proper evening hours. Hence the surprise of the girl who answered Rob's knock; hence also the expressions of distress, reproach, and indignation, in the eyes of Elinor White, when she came to the door to face her unexpected visitor. Before she had said a word, her eyes managed to wound her lover so deeply that all the fight went out of him. The best he could do was explain that he had been impelled to come so that he might talk face-to-face with Elinor about very important matters which concerned them both, and could he come in? No, Elinor said, she simply could not talk with him here. Then could they meet and talk somewhere else? Yes, when next she came home; but not here in Canton.

Awkwardly, he began to plead. She stopped him.

Before he fully realized how it had happened, he had surrendered his precious weapon, *Twilight*. Elinor took it from him as casually as if it had been the morning paper, and then closed the door firmly. She had commanded him to take the very next train out of Canton; but he did not even wait for it to arrive. Instead, he started walking down the railroad tracks, toward home, completely overcome with chagrin and mortification. Needing an object on which he could vent his disappointment, he found it in his pocket. He had planned to show Elinor his own copy of *Twilight*, just to make her understand that between them they had all the existing copies of this edition. As he walked along the tracks, he took his *Twilight* out of his pocket, tore the pages out of the binding, threw away the cover, tore each of the sheets into handfuls of confetti, and tossed it along the cinderbed.[2]

At the next station Rob waited for a train, and during the long homeward journey he suffered through agonies more intense than he had ever experienced before. This was the end, it seemed, of so much more than his idealistic and romantic plan to strike a blow for honor. For years he had been trying to find himself, trying to choose a direction or goal for his life, trying to develop confidence in his own abilities. Elinor's love had seemed to be the mainstay of all his hopes, the foundation on which he had been building. But so closely entwined were his different kinds of faith that when she had dismissed him so unexpectedly and curtly at her door, the act had undermined faith in self, faith in his future as a poet, faith in others. He had been trying bravely and courageously to rid himself of his deep-seated sense of insecurity and his lack of confidence; and he had made good progress throughout his high-school years, particularly after he had met Elinor. His falling in love had been a venture shyly made, without any realization that it would help him develop his own capacities, through the strength she could and did give. But all these gains were lost now, and it seemed that suicide was the only fitting end for such a catastrophe. If he could not kill himself by inflicting a mortal wound, he could at least throw his life away in a fashion which would make Elinor feel sorry throughout her life for what she had done. It may have crossed his mind that he could secretly arrange death by plunging into the very heart of some such Slough of Despond as the Dismal

Swamp in Virginia—a treacherous, dangerous, frightful, and snake-infested wilderness—that the desired effect would be heightened if Elinor could never find out where he had gone or how he had died.

Perhaps, during the bitter journey home, his dark thoughts of death may have purged him, so that he could consider possibilities, suggested by Mrs. White, to whom he gave a report of the fiasco. She may have tried to persuade him that school regulations must have forced Elinor to treat him so brusquely at the front door of her lodging; that surely Elinor would soon make her apologies by letter—and would acknowledge the significance of his gift, *Twilight*. Elinor did write soon. But if she made any apologies, or if she made any comments on *Twilight*, or if she tried to correct Rob's mistaken notions concerning the possibility that she was now engaged to marry Lorenzo Dow Case, her words were not persuasive. Instead, they seemed to precipitate Rob's impulsive and determined conviction that he might as well throw his life away, with her letter. In a rage of jealousy, injured pride, and discouragement, he packed his bag and left home, without telling even his mother where he was going.

If he had not so nearly made a beeline for the Dismal Swamp in Virginia, it might be possible to imagine that he did not know for certain where he was going when he began this journey.[3] On the morning of 6 November 1894,[4] he took a train from Lawrence to the North Station in Boston, crossed the city, and took a train from the South Station to New York City; on the evening of the same day he boarded a Merchant and Mariners Line steamer for Norfolk, Virginia; early the next morning he disembarked at Norfolk and began asking directions to the Dismal Swamp.

He may have puzzled those he asked. The hunting season was on, and if he had been dressed as a hunter, with a shotgun in a case under his arm, and had asked about trails into the northern end of the Dismal Swamp, the answer to his question might have been that everything depended on whether he was after bear or deer or wild cattle. But he was dressed in ordinary street clothes; he was wearing a light overcoat; and he was carrying a satchel. Nobody going into the Dismal Swamp at any time of year should wear clothes like that. If he was after the best road into the Dismal Swamp—it was only a narrow road and not very good—he'd better walk seven or eight miles nearly due south of Norfolk to the village of Deep Creek. A wagon road had been built alongside the Dismal Swamp Canal, back in the days when the Canal was first used for floating logs of juniper and cypress out of the middle of the huge swamp, either to Little Creek in Virginia or, in the other direction, to South Mills in North Carolina. This old wagon road ran a distance of nearly thirty miles, all the way through the swamp from Deep Creek to South Mills, and had been kept in repair for more than half a century, at least up until the time of the War Between the States. Caravans of wagons had used it for carting produce from North Carolina farms to markets in Norfolk and Plymouth. After the war, road and Canal had seen less and less use. Four locks were still maintained by the Dismal Swamp Canal Company, and were operated to lift boats up from tidewater level to the higher water level in the middle of the swamp—odd as that might seem to those not familiar with the geological peculiarities of the vast area. Only engine-driven boats continued to navigate on the Canal by 1894, and not many of them. The towpaths on both sides had long ago disappeared beneath a wilderness jungle of briar bushes, reeds, poison ivy, honeysuckle, cross-vine, wild grape, and hardwood trees. Anyone brave enough to drive a wagon all the way along that muddy road, from Deep Creek to the other end might not see the Canal very often through all the underbrush, even though road and Canal were parallel and only about a hundred feet apart. And if anyone was bold enough—or foolish enough—to try to walk the road all the way through the swamp, he'd better look out for mud holes and water moccasins and rattlesnakes, not to mention bears and bobcats.

Whatever the satchel-carrying stranger may have heard in answer to his questions, nothing deterred him. Slowly, he worked his way out of the Norfolk city streets and through a scattering of suburbs, along the Elizabeth River, until he finally reached the village of Deep Creek. It took him all day to get that far, and he had had nothing to eat since breakfast. The sun had already gone down before he saw the Canal, crossed over the drawbridge at the southern end of the village, and continued down the road in a southerly direction toward the place where the swamp actually began to look like wilderness. For a mile or two beyond the village of Deep Creek, he could still see the Canal on his right. To his left stretched acre on acre of swamp farmland, crisscrossed with drainage ditches. As darkness settled in, he became aware that an almost full moon was going to give him light. He saw ahead of him, rising high at the end of the farmland fields, a forest wall. The lofty trees grew so rank in this rich soil that their branches spread out over the narrow road from both sides, so that he seemed to be approaching a dark tunnel.

Rob would have had good reason to stop at the edge of the swamp-forest and turn back. His fear of darkness had been an obsession as far back as the San Francisco days when his parents had let him keep his bedroom door open at night. He still hated to go into an empty house alone after dark. He certainly would have turned back, now, if his immediate course, no matter how vague, had not been so grim and desperate. Driven forward by pressures more powerful than his fears, he kept on walking out of the moonlight and into the forest-tunnel. The few moon-cast shadows of twisting and still leaf-covered branches heightened the eerie atmosphere. He knew that on either side of the narrow road the thick underbrush might be providing shelter and hiding places for dangerous wild animals. As he slowed his pace to avoid mud holes more easily felt than seen, he was also aware that on the occasional shoulders of dry ground beside the road he might step on a late-prowling rattlesnake. He didn't care.

Before he had groped his way far into the swamp, he came to a place where mud holes gave way to a thin expanse of water, which completely covered the road and seemed to block his way, unless he wanted to wade. But as his eyes grew accustomed to the moon-softened darkness, he saw a narrow plank walk, supported a foot above the water by occasional posts and stretching into the darkness along the roadside, further than he could see. Testing the plank walk, he inched his way precariously along it, step after step, wondering what might happen if he lost his balance. If he fell off, so that his head hit the plank walk hard enough to knock him unconscious, he might sink just deep enough into water and mud so that nobody would ever find his body, so that nobody would ever know what had happened to him.

He seemed to want exactly what he feared. He was trying to throw his life away, as a kind of retaliation against Elinor's treatment of him, and all he needed was a push. When he listened to inexplicable noises behind him, and suspected that he was being followed, it may have seemed that his predicament was similar to that of the Ancient Mariner:

> *Like one that on a lonesome road*
> *Doth walk in fear and dread,*
> *And having once turned round, walks on,*
> *And turns no more his head;*
> *Because he knows a frightful fiend*
> *Doth close behind him tread.*[5]

The dangers were there, in abundance; but the fiend was inside him, forcing him to move slowly on through this nightmare. Mile after mile he continued, at times wading through mud holes, at times skirting puddles on occasional plank walks.[6] Nothing serious happened. None of these experiences was so painful as the inner anguish which drove him forward. At one point he became so annoyed by the unbalancing weight of the satchel he was carrying that he was tempted to heave it sideways into the dark. Instead, he stopped just long enough to lighten the load by throwing away some things which no longer seemed important: two books and some extra clothes. If this gesture were symbolically suicidal for him, he might have turned back as soon as he had completed it. Instead, he closed the satchel, picked it up again, and slowly plodded deeper into the Dismal Swamp, waiting for something to happen.

At last, it did happen. Somewhere near midnight, after he had painstakingly covered a distance of nearly ten miles, he saw ahead of him on the right-hand side of the road a strange light which was not cast by the moon. He stopped to stare, and then he heard voices. For all he knew, he was approaching the hideaway of bandits and murderers, and again he could have turned back. But he kept walking toward the light and the voices, unable to guess what he would find—and apparently not caring. He did not know that he had been walking within an easy stone's throw of the Dismal Swamp Canal since the time he had entered the forest, and that sooner or later he would reach the Northwest Lock on the Canal, roughly ten miles to the south of the village of Deep Creek. As he mounted to higher ground, he saw more lights, heard more voices, saw moonlit figures of men casually standing beside a little house, and slowly came into a lighted opening where the deck of a boat was being raised in a lock.

He may have decided, then and there, that he had tried hard enough for one night to throw his life away. Whatever he thought, he was not sufficiently embarrassed to fear that he might look odd, even ludicrous to anyone who saw him strolling out of the darkness and up to the edge of the lock—with street clothes on and with a satchel in hand. As he approached, none of the men he saw paid any attention to him, nor did they stop talking. He noticed that the boat was a weather-beaten old tub, a cross between a fishing vessel and a small excursion steamer, with a semicircular row of benches fastened around the stern of the deck. When he could be sure that he had a voice, he called to a group of men standing on the afterdeck and asked where they were going. Elizabeth City. Did they need an extra deckhand? No. What would they charge to take him to Elizabeth City as a passenger? There was a brief consultation in the group before the answer was given. One dollar. Out of his pocket he pulled the money—almost the last he had—and in a few moments he was helped across a makeshift gangplank, over the side, to the deck.[7]

One of the crew told the unexpected passenger that the boat was making this run from Norfolk to Elizabeth City by way of the Dismal Swamp Canal to pick up a party of duck hunters the next day, that these hunters made an annual festivity of going by boat from Elizabeth City out across Albemarle Sound some forty miles to a place called Nags Head, near Kitty Hawk, on the Outer Banks. These geographical names meant nothing to Rob, who felt as though he were merely entering a new phase of his nightmare. But he was tired and uncomfortable enough to ask if there was any place aboard the vessel where he could take off his wet shoes and stretch out for a while. A guide led him down a ladder to a narrow pipe-cluttered passage and then forward to a small cubbyhole with a bunk in it.

He slept so well that he was not even aware of the stops at two other locks, not even aware that as daylight came the boat entered the marvelous bay of the Pasquotank River and tied up at a dock in Elizabeth City harbor. By the time he awoke, put on his wet shoes, and found his way topside, captain and crew had gone ashore, leaving nobody on deck except an old Negro scrubwoman. She paid no attention to him as he watched her working slowly with mop and pail and rags, cleaning the benches on the afterdeck. She sang to herself, plaintively, and Rob found her refrain appropriate enough: "Sad, sad in my heart." Undecided what to do next or where to go, he knew only that he was hungry. He saw nothing but warehouses along the street beside the dock, and was not even sure that he had the strength to walk very far, even in search of food. Sick and weary after the ordeal of the previous night, he merely wanted to lie down again. If he starved to death, he didn't care. Back down the ladder he went, found his way through the pipe-cluttered passage to his cubbyhole bunk, and threw himself down—sad, sad in his heart.

When he awoke again it was late in the afternoon and he could hear footsteps on the deck overhead, the shouts of the crew, and the thump of objects they seemed to be taking aboard. By the time he climbed back on deck he saw the duck hunters piling up the gangplank, jostling each other, laughing, joking, with guns held in the crook of their arms and with food hampers or demijohns of liquor in their hands. Nobody paid much attention to Frost; he stood there still feeling that this all belonged in the realm of dreams. He watched the crew raise the gangplank, watched the lines cast off, felt the boat get under way for Nags Head, and simply didn't care.

The duck hunters gathered on the benches of the afterdeck, quickly arranged their supplies, opened the corked demijohns, and seemed to be settling in for festive drinking. Before the boat had cleared the harbor one of the passengers took notice of the stranger, introduced himself as "Ed Dozier, owner of the bes' goddam bar in Elizabeth City," and offered Frost a drink. No thank you. Then some fried chicken? He was too hungry to refuse any kind of food, and very soon he was trying to cope with Ed Dozier's kind questions. He couldn't bear to tell the truth in his answers. It would have sounded silly to say he had come all the way to the Dismal Swamp just to kill himself, or just to make his sweetheart worry about him, or to try to find a tribe of Indians living in a secret canyon. Instead, he explained that he was looking for work; he had come down to Elizabeth City from Norfolk on this boat and had accidentally slept too long, so that the boat had gotten underway for Nags Head before he realized what was happening. Well, if it was work he wanted, Ed Dozier could help him, just as soon as they got back from this little ole duck-hunting expedition.

Frost protested; he couldn't let Mr. Dozier bother with him—
and, after all, how did he know that Rob wasn't an escaped
convict? Ed laughed.

"You're all right," he said. "You look so much like a child
that nobody'd be afraid of you."

In the twilight, several hours later, the old tub docked at
Nags Head and the passengers stormed gaily ashore, near a
small hotel which seemed to be locked up for the winter.[8] Ed
Dozier had the key, and the men made a noisy game of opening
shutters, filling lamps with kerosene, carrying in supplies, and
making themselves comfortable. In the hotel lobby they put
tables together, spread out a slap-dash supper of cold meats
and potato salad, ate standing, and urged the stranger to help
himself either to food or drink. Ready for anything, Frost
sampled the demijohns offered to him without finding liquor
mild enough to be palatable. But he ate the slabs of chicken and
ham until he almost began to enjoy this raucous duck-hunting
banquet.

When the noise grew too loud in the little hotel lobby, it was
easy enough for Rob to escape. He slipped out of the front door,
found a road which ran at right angles to the bay shore, and
decided to follow it across this "outer bank" until he could see
the Atlantic. As he walked, again by the light of the almost
full moon and clear sky, he noticed on his left a near-mountain-
sized sand dune known locally as Jockeys Ridge; and after
only half a mile of walking he climbed the bluff built out of
sand by the waves of the Atlantic. Down the bluff he slipped
and slid, toward the roar and crash of the surf. He had just
reached the tight-packed sand when he saw one man coming
up the beach toward him from the south. The strangers exchanged greetings and Rob began to ask questions. The man
was an officer of the Life Saving Service, in uniform, on regular
patrol out of a station up the beach toward Kitty Hawk. Rob
walked along with him, making a satisfactory excuse for how
he happened to be there and explaining that Ed Dozier had
promised him work when the duck-hunters returned to Elizabeth City. To discourage further prying, Frost asked about the
history of the Outer Banks, and was given, among other
details, the legend that Aaron Burr's beautiful daughter,
Theodosia, was supposed to have met her death somewhere off
the banks in this region. Frost was fascinated, and might have
continued their walk if the officer hadn't suddenly begun to

talk about soul-saving. With evangelical ardor he asked if Rob had given his heart to Jesus. Still nursing his mood of "sad, sad in my heart," he was tempted to reply that he had indeed given his heart to Jesus, long ago, but that recently he had taken it back. Instead, he evaded the question entirely, mumbled excuses, turned around, and retraced his steps to the hotel alone.

Nobody in the lobby seemed interested in going to sleep that night. By dawn, most of the men had scattered to choose blinds in the long grass or behind sand dunes, and when the ducks began to fly through the gray dawn, just before the sun came up, the hunters opened fire with such casual earnestness that birdshot rattled like hail on the tin roof of the hotel porch where Frost stood watching. He listened, and thought bitterly that if Elinor White learned how her beloved had accidentally met death at the hands of drunken duck-hunters at Nags Head in North Carolina—and all for love of her—it would serve her right. But again nothing happened, and well before noon the hunters came straggling into the hotel with only a few wilted proofs of their marksmanship. Well-satisfied and still jovial, they ate up whatever food was left, emptied their demijohns, packed their gear, and paraded down to the boat.

On the return voyage across the calm swells of Albemarle Sound most of the hunters threw themselves anywhere on deck to sleep, but the still voluble Ed Dozier resumed his conversation with Frost. Just what kind of work did the boy want? Rob didn't know exactly; he had taught school a little and he had done some writing. Well, back home in Elizabeth City, Ed said, there was a man named Lamb who was editor of the local newspaper, and there was a man named Sheep who headed up the female academy. So the chances were good that Frost could take his pick between the Lamb and the Sheep. Or, if he didn't find anything to his liking that way, he could at least stay as guest for a few days in the Dozier home while he looked over the town for some other kind of work.

For the next few days the runaway from Massachusetts was given more evidence of Southern hospitality, as exemplified so affably and generously by the Doziers. Keeping his word, the host took his guest about the town, calling first on editor Lamb and then visiting headmaster Sheep at the academy. Each of them offered the Northerner a chance to settle in and go to work immediately, but it is probable that no kind of work would have tempted him at this time. He had run far enough away to feel twinges of homesickness; he lingered for only three days with the Doziers and then made an odd departure. Watching for a chance to escape when nobody was looking, he slipped out of Dozier's back door, satchel in hand, without saying good-bye to anyone.

Nearly out of money, Frost decided to try his luck at leaving Elizabeth City hobo-fashion, by stealing a ride in a freight car. In a short time he was on his way somewhere—he neither knew nor cared for the moment whether North or South—in an empty boxcar, the door of which he had carefully shut to exclude the entrance of any fellow travelers. Bothered for a time by the vibration, the noise, the darkness, he finally made himself as comfortable as he could in a corner and slept so well that, when he woke, he found that his car had been shunted onto a siding near a North Carolina lumber camp. It was already evening when he slid the door open, carefully studied the scene, to be certain that nobody was watching, and jumped to the ground. In a short time he had gotten his bearings well enough to discover a camp store where Negroes were standing, sitting, chatting, and playfully wrestling with one another. As he bought crackers in the store, with almost the last few pennies he had, a white boy roughly his own age asked if he was looking for work. Well, yes. The boy was a scaler, a specialist in stripping bark off logs, and he offered to teach Frost enough about the process to let him get work. He also showed Frost a bunk where he could sleep. That was enough.

The next morning, he was back near the railroad tracks, carefully coached by his scaler friend about waiting for a freight that would take him North and straight through to Washington, D. C. He kept out of sight until the long train had started, tossed his bag into the first open door he saw, jumped in after it, found a corner in the noisy gloom, and tried to sleep. Hours later, when he thought the train might be near Washington, he crawled to the open door and watched for station signs. The first one he saw gave a peculiar jolt to his memory and imagination, long ago stimulated by his poring over the maps and pages of *Battles and Leaders of the Civil War*—Bull Run. Shades of his namesake, Robert E. Lee.

He spent that evening in a hobo jungle outside Washington, studying the grizzled and shabby veterans who crouched or sat around a little fire made of sticks and branches. For the first time he heard the boastful lore of men who scorned freights and risked their lives "riding blind" between the tender and the door-locked end of an express baggage car, a spot made notorious by train robbers ever since the days of Frank and Jesse James. He listened to tales of innocent hoboes shot to death with no questions asked, when caught in that suspicious hideaway, of others who, now that tenders were beginning to scoop water up from troughs between the tracks, had died in icy shrouds when spray had drenched them so completely on winter nights that they had to be chopped out of their crystal caskets with axes. There was poetry of a sort for Frost to hear that evening, ballads and songs, one of which he learned by heart:

> Said Jay Gould's daughter
> Just before she died,
> "Papa, fix the blinds
> So the bums can't ride.
>
> If ride they must,
> Let them ride the rod;
> Let them put their trust
> In the hands of God."

All of this experience in the Washington hobo jungle might have been tolerably entertaining for Frost if some of his companions had not asked too many questions. They wanted to know what he was up to, traveling with a bag, when any honest hobo carried all his possessions in his pockets or at least tied in a small bundle on a stick. And where did he get the good clothes? And how much would he take for the overcoat? And how much money did he have on him? And was he a "dick" working for one of the railroad companies? Their tones of voice frightened him so much that he finally said he'd get out if they didn't like his company. Nobody demurred when he stood up. A few of them shouted taunts as he walked down the track in darkness. He had the feeling that some of them were following him and might even kill him for what they thought they could get out of his pockets or bag. No longer interested in suicide, he was so frightened that after he had climbed up the embankment to the nearest street he approached the first policeman he saw and asked for protection. Was there any chance of getting locked up for the night in a jail? There was, under the circumstances, and Frost was instructed on how and where to proceed. Years later he liked to boast that he had spent his first night in Washington behind bars in a jail.

The next morning he went back to the freight yard feeling like a veteran, and quite certain that his cronies of the previous night were already on their way to distant points. But when he tried to climb into a freight car on a train already moving North, he was caught by a railroad policeman and warned to get out of the yard. Suffering from a new kind of fright, he would have gone as ordered if a more experienced hobo had not calmed him with advice to stay out of sight and wait for the next freight. The instruction seemed to work well enough, and the railroad policeman was nowhere in sight as he made his next run for the partly opened door of an apparently empty boxcar. For a few minutes his eyes were so unaccustomed to the darkness that he was startled when he suddenly realized that crouching against the wall across the car from where he had stretched out was a sullen Negro. Neither one of them tried to say a word to the other above the clatter of wheels. But before the train had left the yard it halted and voices could be heard growing louder as a group of inspectors moved down the tracks glancing in the doors. Growling to himself, the Negro stood up and drew a revolver as he walked to the half-closed door; he reached it just before someone outside shoved the door wide open; he was trying to raise the revolver when hands pulled his feet from under him and yanked him to the ground. Frost could not see what was happening, but he could hear the blows, the curses, and the Negro screaming for mercy. Another searcher climbed into the car, roughly dragged the white boy to his feet, pushed him out of the door, and ordered him up the tracks—away from where the Negro lay. Suffering now from his old nausea, Frost ran as fast as he could, and did not even remember that he had left his satchel in the boxcar until it was too late. For hours he hid in bushes until he managed to get up courage for another successful run at an opened door—and when he crawled out of the train he found he was in Baltimore.

Having gone without food for a day and a half, he was desperate enough to throw himself on the mercy of relatives who lived near Baltimore. He knew that his mother's cousin, Fannie Moodie, had married a man named Thomas Baldwin, and that the Baldwins had recently moved from Columbus, Ohio, to the Baltimore suburb of Towson. It took him all afternoon to walk out of the city to Towson, where he asked for directions at the counter of a small grocery store. The grocer, named Williams, seemed to be so touched by the forlorn appearance of the young man that when it became clear that nobody in the store knew of any family named Baldwin living in the neighborhood, he offered Frost work delivering groceries. For a few days he did stay with Williams, living in his home and yet earning scarcely anything except board and room. By this time he was so sick and tired of his runaway venture that he swallowed his pride and wrote to his mother, asking for money enough to purchase a railroad ticket home. Within a week he was back in Lawrence, arriving there on Friday, 30 November 1894.

The trip had been a failure, so far as he was able to determine. True, he had succeeded in worrying Elinor White; he had frightened his mother greatly; he had mystified his friends. But if any change had taken place in what he took to be the engagement of Elinor White to Lorenzo Dow Case, there was nothing to indicate it in the letters waiting for him. His only consolation was that during his three-week absence— and almost on the day when he had passed through New York en route to the Dismal Swamp—the issue of *The Independent* for 8 November 1894 had carried on its first page his poem "My Butterfly: An Elegy." As soon as he could recover energy and interest enough to send thanks to Miss Ward, he did so, in a letter dated 4 December 1894. He explained the tardiness of his acknowledgment by saying that he had "just returned from experiences so desperately absorbing that I am nothing morbid now" and so could enjoy the poem as freshly as if he had but lately written it, as though he had not "wasted eight months in ineffectual aspiration" since he wrote it. He admitted that during his absence he had been "in Virginia, North Carolina, and Maryland, very liberally and without address," hence his being unaware until recently that he had actually " 'published a poem.' " He would send more poems as soon as he found time to revise them.[9]

His experiences had certainly given him the raw materials for poetic inspiration, and he used some of them almost immediately. In his attempt to be, as he had said to Miss Ward, "nothing morbid" over an apparently hopeless situation, no

matter how reluctant he might be to accept his apparent loss
of Elinor White's love, he could at least sing his grief. He did
sing it, in a poem about dead ends, dead leaves, dead hopes.
When finished, the poem was called "Reluctance":

> Out through the fields and the woods
>   And over the walls I have wended;
> I have climbed the hills of view
>   And looked at the world, and descended;
> I have come by the highway home,
>   And lo, it is ended.
>
> The leaves are all dead on the ground,
>   Save those that the oak is keeping
> To ravel them one by one
>   And let them go scraping and creeping
> Out over the crusted snow,
>   When others are sleeping.
>
> And the dead leaves lie huddled and still,
>   No longer blown hither and thither;
> The last lone aster is gone;
>   The flowers of the witch-hazel wither;
> The heart is still aching to seek,
>   But the feet question 'Whither?'
>
> Ah, when to the heart of man
>   Was it ever less than a treason
> To go with the drift of things,
>   To yield with a grace to reason,
> And bow and accept the end
>   Of a love or a season?[10]

DOOR IN THE DARK

In going from room to room in the dark,
I reached out blindly to save my face,
But neglected, however lightly, to lace
My fingers and close my arms in an arc.
A slim door got in past my guard,
And hit me a blow in the head so hard
I had my native simile jarred.
So people and things don't pair any more
With what they used to pair with before.[1]

ROBERT FROST knew he was not quite telling the truth when he assured Susan Hayes Ward that he was "nothing morbid now," although he had "just returned from experiences so desperately absorbing." Assertively, he tried to convince himself and others that because he had survived those Dismal Swamp adventures, the task which now confronted him was to pick up whatever was left of his life and put the pieces together as best he could. But he also knew that his posture of elation over the appearance of his poem in *The Independent* was merely an attempt to overcome his persistent brooding over disappointment and heartbreak.

For the first time he saw in Carl Burell's favorite word, "disillusionment," a terrible depth of meaning, and with a sense of surprise he found his new knowledge mirrored in some familiar lines from favorite poets. "So once it would have been, 'tis so no more; I have submitted to a new control; A power is gone, which nothing can restore; A deep distress hath humanised my soul." Also with Wordsworth he grieved, "The rainbow comes and goes, And lovely is the rose . . . But yet I know, where'er I go, That there hath passed away a glory from the earth."[2] He felt as though a knife had been driven through his consciousness in a fashion which had separated his past and present understanding; much that had seemed true and trustworthy now seemed false and illusory. Even his mother could not comfort him with biblical quotations and paraphrases: Think it not strange concerning the fiery trial; there is always the divine consolation that out of seemingly evil events some good is born. Refusing to be consoled, Rob answered her by endowing some words from *Hamlet* with his own bitter meaning: "So have I heard, and do in part believe it."[3]

Believe, believe! From the earliest days of childhood he had been nurtured and strengthened by many related kinds of belief, and yet now it seemed that Elinor had destroyed them all. His deeply ingrained religious belief, taught him by his mother, had made him confident that of his own choice he had entered into a private relationship with God whereby his efforts would help to fulfill a positive future in this world and in the next. His God-belief had strengthened self-belief. Although his enemies might continue to scoff, he had gradually acquired a conviction that his gifts and skills—and his determination—would enable him to realize his immediate hopes. Inseparable and yet quite distinct was his own private literary belief, on which he depended instinctively whenever he wrote a poem. It seemed to him that each had been inspired, from the very first line, by something intuitively foreseen, and that the final goal had always been achieved not so much through contriving but rather through believing the poem into existence. Until recently he had derived a fourth kind of strength from his love for Elinor and from what he had believed to be her love for him. Now, the frightening collapse of this cherished love-belief had caused him to doubt the validity of all his other beliefs.[4]

One disturbing effect of his disillusionment was his feeling that if he were now able to measure the difference between illusion and reality he was also inclined to suspect that what he presently viewed as reality might soon become for him another kind of illusion—and this fear drove him to the verge of a nervous breakdown. How could he have confidence in anything or anyone, including his own powers of perception? Almost hysterically he felt that his eyes now gave him a double image of everything; and he was not sure whether it would be better to laugh or cry over his predicament, whether all experience should be viewed as pure comedy or pure tragedy.

Under the circumstances, it was fortunate for him that he had inherited from his grieving mother the balancing instinct for enjoying the comic aspects of life. But it pained him to realize that his double vision now forced him to see something comical in what he had previously viewed seriously, and something serious in what he had formerly laughed at. Desperately, he tried to fashion a new kind of self-defense—or at least a makeshift palliative—by combining grief with humor to express his awareness of discrepancies between his old and new ways of seeing, hearing, speaking, writing, acting. He later admitted, however, that while such a resolution of his problem might provide an artistically useful form of self-defense, it was not spiritually consoling:

"Belief is better than anything else, and it is best when rapt, above paying its respects to anybody's doubt whatsoever. At bottom the world isn't a joke. We only joke about it to avoid an issue with someone to let someone know that we know he's there with his questions: to disarm him by seeming to have heard and done justice to his side of the standing argument. Humor is the most engaging cowardice. With it myself I have been able to hold some of my enemy in play far out of gunshot."[5]

He could not always enage humorously the darker side of his own nature, his worst enemy, which often assured him that the ultimate form of escape from self-doubt and self-hate was suicide. When he had gained enough perspective on the causes and aftereffects of the Dismal Swamp crisis, he did represent them humorously in the poem he built around the metaphor of bumping his head against a door in the dark; but he could never forget his initial sense of pain and his consequent feeling that people and things didn't pair any more with what they used to pair with before. Immediately after his return from the Dismal Swamp, the best he could do to conceal his pain and grief was to pretend that he was just as gay and comical as he had formerly been. One glimpse of the earlier gaiety was preserved in memory by Susan P. Holmes, the girl whose parents were Swedenborgian friends of the Frost family in Lawrence:

"A favorite form of winter entertainment in the 90s was the 'Candy Pull.' First, measured amounts of molasses, sugar and butter were set boiling in a huge iron kettle. When the cold water test showed it to be 'done' the mass was poured out upon a pastry board, and when sufficiently cool, cut into strips. The contestant would dip his hands in flour, pick up a strip of this goo and pull it from hand to hand with such speed and dexterity that most of the time it was 'in the air.' If expertly done, the result was a light amber candy, beautiful to behold and delicious to taste. That night which lives in memory, first prize went to young Mrs. August Wagner of Prospect Hill—but pity poor Rob Frost! When the sticky mass had immobilized his fingers and coated wrists and forearms nearly to his elbows he yelled, 'Out of my way,' dashed out of doors and thrust his hands and arms into a bank of snow. His consolation (or 'booby') prize was one of Mother's enormous mince turnovers. Receiving this with a whoop of joy, he sat down in the middle of the kitchen floor and devoured his prize with gusto."[6]

That was Rob's former playfulness, imitated very well after his return from the Dismal Swamp. Making an unexpected visit to the Holmes house at 9 South Broadway (where Susan's father served as keeper of the headgates of the South Canal on the Merrimack River), he found another evening of entertainment in progress, and again Susan's memory:

". . . yielding to an attack of wanderlust, [he] went on a vagabond journey to the South. Hearing no word of him for many weeks, how could we know that he had become lost while tramping through the Dismal Swamp of North Carolina and Virginia? Then one evening, while a party—or 'social'—was in full swing at our house, out of nowhere he suddenly appeared at the kitchen door! In the group was our star boarder, Horace Hale Smith, who later was to be the architect of the Central Bridge, and a pal of Frost's. The instant that these two spied each other they let out war whoops, rushed each other, slapped, punched, wrestled, finally rolling over and over on the floor from one end of the long kitchen to the other. When they arose, grinning, and brushed themselves off, each claimed HE was the better man!"[7]

After he had re-established himself with his friends, and after he had apparently made excuses for his long absence by offering tall tales of how he had "become lost while tramping through the Dismal Swamp," Rob looked around for work as a newspaper reporter. Having previously resisted the suggestions of his would-be benefactors, the Reverend William E. Wolcott and his former high-school principal, Nathaniel Goodwin, Rob did not seek further advice from them. Instead, he turned to the Swedenborgian pastor, the Reverend John A. Hayes, who came up to Lawrence from Salem, Massachusetts, once a week to conduct religious services. For these occasions, it often happened that Mrs. Frost made available to the few local Swedenborgians her own living room. There was a particular warmth of friendliness between Hayes and all three members of the Frost family, even though Rob seldom attended the Swedenborgian services. Hayes happened to know two newspapermen in Boston, and he wrote letters of recommendation for Rob to deliver to them. First visited was Clarence Walker Barron, who had left his position as financial editor of *The Boston Evening Transcript* in order to set up his own "Boston News Bureau," which supplied current information to brokers. The other letter was delivered to Charles Hurd, literary editor of the *Transcript*. Neither man was immediately helpful to Rob, and Barron was amused that his friend Hayes should send a poet to look for work from a financial editor; but he did take Rob to lunch in Boston and showed a sympathetic interest. Discouraged by his Boston venture, Frost had better luck when he approached the editor in chief of a Lawrence newspaper, the *American*.

". . . I have been busy night and day for two weeks," Frost wrote to Susan Hayes Ward. "I am a reporter on a local newspaper! . . . My newspaper work requires a brave effort. They assure me I have much to learn particularly in the way of writing; but what care I: I have done the best I can with what I know: and if I know everything I have reached my limit. Let them teach me."[8] The staff of the *American* taught him more about its unscrupulous newspaper policy than about writing, and embarrassments began almost immediately. He was sent to the Arlington Mill in Lawrence to gather information about labor difficulties which had resulted in a strike, and he went directly to the main office to call on a Mr. Hartshorn, whom he and his mother knew. It was a friendly and informative visit, but Hartshorn kept interweaving so many confidences ("Don't write about what I'm going to tell you now.") that by the time Frost left the mill he saw no way of writing up the story without betraying a friendship. Instead, he went back to the office of the *American* and announced that he was unable to find anything which would make good copy.

Because the editor in chief of the *American* was at that time involved in litigation concerning graft and embezzlement, he was not eager to tell his readers any more of his own story than was necessary. So he instructed Frost to copy whatever was posted on the news boards of rival newspapers and let them set the pace. It was not an exciting assignment, and it seemed to Rob that his boss had an extraordinary capacity for toning down the facts. But the height of his impatience occurred when, sent to "cover" a private wedding, he was ordered to threaten the father of the bride by saying that if Frost was not permitted to attend the wedding he would write and publish a story about it anyway. It took a little time for him to realize that he had been asked to perform a kind of blackmail. After he had thought it over, he stayed away from the wedding, and quit his job.

There is at least circumstantial evidence that Frost must have written and published several unsigned articles or news items before he quit. Years later, when scolding one of his former students for mingling fact and fiction in writing newspaper reports, Frost cited his own experiences:

"You mustn't fake articles any more. Not even in details. Them's orders. I'll tell you why. It's taking an unfair advantage. Of whom? . . . of the gentlemen who profess fiction. I used to think of it when I faked in a small way for another paper named the Sun [the *American* called its Sabbath issue the *Sun*] which was published in Lawrence Mass. All I had to do was to claim for my yarns the virtue of fact and I had story writers of twice my art and invention skun a mile."[9]

Having worked as a reporter for the *American* only a little more than two weeks, Frost had not yet exhausted his willingness to do this kind of job. Among the Lawrence newspapers, the *Sentinel* was a "weekly" which seemed to have a more literary flavor, and Frost took a more congenial position on the staff of the *Sentinel.* Again he lasted for only a few weeks. The best glimpse of his work as a reporter is one of his own retrospective accounts:

"It's amusing that I once had a column on a newspaper, before columnists were ever known. Of course it wasn't like the present columns. I wrote about things I'd seen. Sort of prose poems. I remember one thing was about women I'd watched from my window picking up coal along the railroad tracks. Another was about an eagle that flew over Lawrence and alighted on the brass ball at the top of the flag pole on the

Postoffice Building. An ardent hunter got out his gun and shot the eagle on his flagpole perch. That was worth writing about . . ."[10]

Before he resigned from his position as reporter on the *Sentinel,* perhaps early March of 1895, he had demonstrated that there was a more important subject worth writing about. Although he may have told himself, repeatedly, that it was useless for him to write any more letters to Elinor White, he had been unable to stop. Nor could he avoid the inconsistency of crowding into letter after letter his plaintive fear that she no longer loved him and his desperate hope that perhaps she still did. In his letters he tried to probe her motives for rejecting him for another; but her reticent answers were of little aid or comfort. He tried to convince her that her repeated fault-findings—such as her criticism of his apparently shiftless laziness, his apparent lack of direction, his apparent inability to stay with any task for very long, his apparent refusal to prepare himself for a career—were complete misunderstandings. He suspected that these reproaches were indications of her father's influence on her; and he was certain that Mr. White had indeed opposed their engagement, primarily because Rob had left Dartmouth College. But in his letters, written during the winter of 1894-1895, he kept asking Elinor to reconsider her decision or at least to tell him when she would next come home so that they might see each other and talk matters out.

She did come home, apparently in mid-March of 1895, and they did meet—in the kitchen of her home at 10 Spring Street, where they could be alone.[11] Rob's greatest fear was that Elinor had arranged this meeting in order to give back to him the plain gold ring he had placed on her finger more than two years earlier; but his greatest hope was that in their conversation he could somehow persuade her that she still did love him. Awkwardly standing there in the kitchen, beside the warmth of the coal range, he may have begun by reviewing all that had happened to them since first they met, but in the process he said too much. He spoiled his plea for reconciliation by upbraiding Elinor for the way in which she had changed; and when she tried to defend herself by blaming him for his refusal to give direction to his life, he lost his temper. He reminded her that she had once believed in him enough to love him and to give herself to him; that if she no longer did believe in him, then of course there was no use talking further; she was the one who had spoiled everything. In the midst of his outburst, he saw exactly what he feared. Elinor held out her hand and said that if he was going to talk like this he should take back the ring he had given her. She put the ring in his hand, and the act was proof enough for him that she was indeed engaged to Case. He took the ring, lifted the cover from the coal range, tossed the ring on the fire, declared she had really given him reason enough to kill himself this time, and stormed out of the house.

Wild with mingled rage and grief, he took the train from Lawrence to Boston the next day. He told his mother that he was going to call on his sister, Jeanie, who was in a Boston hospital recovering from an operation for curvature of the spine. But his relations with Jeanie had become so unpleasantly cold that he knew he could not confide to her his latest grief and his newest runaway impulses. At least he thought he knew where he might find more sympathetic ears. Ernest Jewell, his friend of high-school days, was a student at Harvard College, and Rob found him in his dormitory room. He poured out the story of his quarrel with Elinor and confided that this was the end of everything. Darkly hinting, he said he had decided to throw his life away, that he had already made a compact with the devil and that he wanted Jewell to drink a firewater toast at the nearest bar to celebrate the compact. Jewell must have been amused. He knew Rob too well to take these dark hints seriously. He also knew that Rob was not given to visiting bars. But he did humor his lovesick visitor to the extent of going with him to a Cambridge bar, where they had one drink together. Then they parted.

It might have seemed to Rob that after all he had said to Jewell there was nothing left except to climb the tower of Memorial Hall and jump, or to find a secluded place on the bank of the Charles River and jump. Instead, he walked over to the Harvard Medical School, where he located another friend of high-school days: Charles Carden, Class of 1890. Unlike Jewell, Carden had shared with Frost the satisfaction of publishing his own poems—in the *Bulletin*. A short lyric by Carden had appeared on the first page of the *Bulletin* along with Rob's first poem, "La Noche Triste." Perhaps it was their poetic bond which caused Rob to start talking this time, not about his difficulties with Elinor and not about his compact with the devil but rather about the conflict between studying medicine and writing poetry. Had Charlie given up his hopes of becoming known as a poet? Not at all, Carden said. But nobody could earn a living by merely writing poetry. His plan was to become a doctor and earn a living. When he was established, he would return to writing poetry. Ah no, said Frost, first things must come first. If Charlie still cared deeply about poetry he would not even be here in these unpoetic and antiseptic surroundings. Defensively, Carden asked how much progress Frost had made toward the fulfillment of his career as a poet. Well, he had made a start by selling one poem for fifteen dollars to a nationally circulated magazine. Only one poem? In nearly three years? Had he been able to live three years on fifteen dollars? No, but he had managed to survive, and he'd stick to his plan for twenty years if necessary. ("I have one, who'll give me twenty?") The conversation ended pleasantly, and in parting the two friends agreed that they should have a reunion twenty years hence—let's see, that would be 1915—so that they could compare notes and learn whose plan had worked out best.

Having unburdened himself, first to Jewell with hints that he was going to throw his life away, then to Carden with a promise to spend the next twenty years trying to earn recognition as a poet, Rob felt better. As he made his way back from Cambridge to the North Station in Boston, he veered far enough to stop in at the Old Corner Bookshop. On a shelf devoted to new volumes of poetry he found a pamphlet which bore the name of an English author new to Rob: Francis Thompson. The pamphlet contained a separate printing of "The Hound of Heaven," and the British price was one shilling. As he stood there, reading line after line, Frost was in the proper mood for using the poem as a mirror of his own predicament:

> I fled Him, down the nights and down the days;
> I fled Him, down the arches of the years;
> I fled Him, down the labyrinthine ways
> Of my own mind . . .
> Up vistaed hopes I sped;
> And shot, precipitated,
> Adown Titanic glooms of chasmèd fears,
> From those strong Feet that followed, followed after.

The second stanza lent itself to further association, particularly in such lines as "I pleaded, outlaw-wise" and "Across the margent of the world I fled." Rob could read into this poem of escape and pursuit a great many reflections of his own story. It may even have seemed to echo some of the mood he had tried to express in his own lines entitled "Bereft," which had concluded, "Word I was in my life alone, / Word I had no one left but God." More than that, in Francis Thompson's poem, the Voice of God invoked the language and vocabulary familiar to Frost since childhood:

> Now of that long pursuit
> Comes on at hand the bruit;
> That Voice is round me like a bursting sea:
>   'And is thy earth so marred,
>   Shattered in shard on shard?
>   Lo, all things fly thee, for thou fliest Me!
>   Strange, piteous, futile thing!
> Wherefore should any set thee love apart?
> Seeing none but I makes much of naught' (He said),
> 'And human love needs human meriting:
>   How hast thou merited—
> Of all man's clotted clay the dingiest clot?
>   Alack, thou knowest not
> How little worthy of any love thou art! . . .'

Self-abasement, self-degradation, self-hatred were parts of Frost's Scotch Presbyterian heritage, learned from his mother. She had not relinquished these elements of her own initial religious belief even after she had become a Swedenborgian. The familiar theme of divine punishment was also mirrored for Rob in this closing utterance of the divine Voice:

> 'Whom wilt thou find to love ignoble thee,
>   Save Me, save only Me?
> All which I took from thee I did but take,
>   Not for thy harms,
> But just that thou might'st seek it in My arms.
>   All which thy child's mistake
> Fancies as lost, I have stored for thee at home . . .'

Encouraged by his mother, Rob was always inclined to employ his own powers of second sight to discover prophecy in unexpected places. Retrospectively, he always viewed as a special event this occasion when he had accidentally made the discovery of Francis Thompson's "The Hound of Heaven" and had eagerly purchased the shilling edition of it. The lines which he would have liked to view as addressed to him, prophetically, certainly must have included "All which thy child's mistake / Fancies as lost, I have stored for thee at home . . ."

Home he went, that evening, with the book in his pocket, and found a Swedenborgian religious service in progress in the living room of the Frost apartment on Tremont Street. The few men and women gathered there were listening to a sermon by Pastor Hayes. Frost had nothing better to do than sit in the back of the room, at least until his mother, noticing his entrance, passed back to him a letter which Elinor had delivered by hand during his absence. Sitting there, Rob opened the envelope and read words he had scarcely dared hope to find. Elinor said she was sorry that misunderstandings had been caused by anything she might have said or done the night before. She wanted to see him as soon as she could, to explain and ask his forgiveness. Abruptly, Rob left the Swedenborgian prayer meeting and was on his way to the not-far-distant White home on Valley Street.

LESS THAN TWO

. . . But all
We did that day was mingle great and small
Footprints in summer dust as if we drew
The figure of our being less than two
But more than one as yet. Your parasol
Pointed the decimal off with one deep thrust.[1]

WHEN ROBERT FROST reached the White home on Valley
Street in Lawrence, the reconciliation was not all he had
hoped it would be. Elinor White had a habit of making him
realize that she was almost two years older than he was. On
such an occasion, she had a way of preserving her dignity and
reticence. It is not likely that she threw herself into his arms.
She apparently began the reconciliation by holding out to him
the gold ring she had rescued from the fire of the coal range;
she had cleaned off the ashes and had put the ring back on
her finger. It was a kind of poetry which said better than
words that she did love him, still, and that she had never
stopped loving him, even during the trial by fire. She admitted that he had frightened her with the possibility that
this time he might actually carry out his suicidal threat, or
that he might at least disappear again as he had done last fall,
when nobody had known for weeks whether he was dead or
alive. But she did not say that she was now ready to marry
him, publicly, whenever and wherever he wished. She still
insisted that their marriage must be postponed until he could
find some way to earn a living for them both.

Under the circumstances Rob may have been willing to
admit that such a way would need to include something more
than the writing of poetry; even to admit that during the past
few years since his graduation from high school he had self-
indulgently made up excuses—for quitting Dartmouth, for

quitting his work as a schoolteacher, for quitting his work as a millhand, for quitting his work as a newspaper reporter. He did prefer to loaf and invite the soul, in fact, he preferred just plain loafing. But his mother had been talking, recently, about plans which might provide him with a new kind of livelihood.

After Mrs. Frost had resigned from her duties as a public school teacher in Methuen, she had begun to conduct an informal private school in the living room of the Tremont Street apartment. Jeanie had helped her from the start, and showed excellent capabilities in teaching beginners. Mrs. Frost was convinced that, if Rob would join them, they could develop a program with eight grades in it. Many of the best citizens in Lawrence were dissatisfied with the public-school system, largely because it had suffered from political machinations. Until this time the dominant population in Lawrence represented various waves of mill-worker immigrants, who had come primarily from the British Isles—first the English and then the Scotch and then the Irish. Recently, the Irish had emerged as political victors in control of City Hall, with the result that Scotch and English residents complained about Irish handling of public education. These prejudices worked to the advantage of Mrs. Frost in her plan to extend her private school, and she had done enough tutoring to know where she might find adequate enrollment, at least by the fall of 1895.

In his attempt to persuade Elinor that he could and would immediately settle down to earn a living for them both, he assured her that he was already helping his mother develop her plan, that during the spring term, soon to begin, he would earn a salary by tutoring some of his mother's older students in Latin and in Mathematics. Elinor must have been pleased with this new display of resolve, and if she insisted that she wanted more evidence than just his promises, Rob soon offered it. Not long after she returned to St. Lawrence University to finish her four-years-in-three, he set to work seriously as a tutor in his mother's school. By the time Elinor returned with her diploma in June, she found that he had succeeded in helping his mother obtain fairly sure promises that there would be at least twenty students in the new school that autumn. He also assured her that he would earn a little extra money near the end of the summer by tutoring two boys who needed help in English and Mathematics before they entered Phillips Andover Academy.

Because Elinor's summer plans had been made so far in advance that she could not easily change them, Rob adapted his accordingly. Leona White Harvey had again left her husband and was supporting herself by her skillful work as a portrait painter. She had accepted an invitation to spend the summer at Ossipee Mountain Park, near Lake Winnepesaukee in New Hampshire, with the understanding that she might be accompanied by her sister, Elinor, who was also a talented artist.[2]

Leona's commission was to paint portraits of the grandchildren of the late Benjamin A. Shaw, who had made a fortune as owner of the Shaw Knit Stocking Company in Lowell, Massachusetts, and who had invested much capital in the development of his White Mountain summer home. A life member of the Appalachian Mountain Club, he had created a semiprivate hideaway, with a small hotel, on a western slope of Ossipee Mountain (now known as Mt. Shaw) in the township of Moultonboro. From the hotel veranda there was an excellent view to the south, out across the many wooded islands scattered over the broad expanse of Lake Winnepesaukee. Well-cleared mountain trails led to nearby summits or to picturesque glimpses of mountain streams. This mountain retreat had been a favorite of the poet Whittier, who knew the whole region so well. After Shaw's death, the resort had continued under management provided by the descendants.[3]

Rob could not bear the thought of being separated from Elinor throughout the long summer of 1895. He offered to go with the White sisters on their journey to Ossipee Mountain, and to stay for at least part of the summer before returning to carry out his tutorial duties. He did accompany them by train to Alton Bay, by the steamboat *Mount Washington* around Lake Winnepesaukee to Moultonboro, and by carriage up the side of the mountain to the hotel in the park. It was his first visit to this part of New Hampshire, and he immediately came under the spell of the region.

Leona and Elinor were given a cottage near the hotel, leaving Rob to shift for himself, because he could not afford to take even the smallest room in the hotel. Adventurously, he asked about other places where he might stay or even "camp out," and was told that not more than a mile up the mountain beyond the park there was a scattering of houses owned by "natives" who lived there year round. Long ago, these houses had been part of a lumber camp and various members of two families—the Lees and the Hornes—had remained. Through several generations they had intermarried and had degenerated, but the small community of harmless outlaws governed itself adequately.

Not learning enough about these outlaws to be made nervous, as yet, Rob walked up the road beyond the park on the afternoon of his arrival to explore the possibilities. The first house he found was a forlorn one-story clapboard cottage with a piece of metal stovepipe sticking through the ridgepole in place of a chimney, with uncurtained windows and a battered, lockless door. Rob knocked, and was admitted by the owner, Henry Horne, a bearded and unwashed giant who lived there alone when he could find nothing better to do. Sometimes he lived with one of the Lee families further up the mountain, sometimes he disappeared from the mountain for months at a time; just now he was getting ready to spend the summer as a hired man on a farm down on the shore of Lake Winnepesaukee. Would he care to rent? The city-boy's question must have amused Henry Horne, who did not mind showing how little he had to rent. Winter and summer he ate and slept and lived in the smoke-stained shabby kitchen which contained a table, a lantern, a chair, a potbellied cast-iron stove, a few grimy cooking utensils, a kerosene stove for cooking, and two blanket-cluttered straw mattresses on the floor. Yes, he'd be glad to rent if the city-boy didn't mind roughing it for a little while. As a matter of fact, he said, he'd like to have someone in the house to serve as "guardeen" of his most valuable possession: several barrels of hard cider in the cellar. His relatives up the road wouldn't touch it unless they got too thirsty, but some of them had a habit of getting that way.

Amused by the terms of the odd man's contract, and still feeling adventurous, Rob settled in to enjoy himself at least for a few days. After Horne's departure, the new tenant made the acquaintance of the Lees and found that their primitive dwellings were even more dilapidated than the one he had rented. Although the prospect of guarding hard cider from these toughs filled him with some anxiety, he knew that Horne had not expected him to take the task too seriously. Part of the contract had been that Rob would help himself to the cider whenever he wished.

As soon as Elinor and Leona had worked out their daily

routine, the three newcomers began exploring mountain trails in a pleasantly casual manner. Whenever Leona was busy with her painting, the walks were better for the two lovers. But Rob could feel that there still remained a distance in Elinor's attitude toward him. He was constantly puzzled by her, and his jealousy mounted anew whenever he learned that she was at the beck and call of the Shaw children or their parents, or their friends at the hotel, where he was never invited. At such times, if his path crossed Elinor's when he was on his way down to Melvin Village for provisions and she was carrying out an errand for her sister, he was struck by the peculiar quality of estrangement and intimacy reflected in these meetings and passings. Years later he tried to capture that quality in a poem which remained important for him as a memento of the Ossipee Mountain days:

> As I went down the hill along the wall
> There was a gate I had leaned at for the view
> And had just turned from when I first saw you
> As you came up the hill. We met. But all
> We did that day was mingle great and small
> Footprints in summer dust as if we drew
> The figure of our being less than two
> But more than one as yet. Your parasol
> Pointed the decimal off with one deep thrust.
> And all the time we talked you seemed to see
> Something down there to smile at in the dust.
> (Oh, it was without prejudice to me!)
> Afterward I went past what you had passed
> Before we met and you what I had passed.[4]

He had not counted on being left so much alone during this summer, and he disliked the emptiness of the shabby Horne house, particlarly at night. He had not often slept alone in any house—even in any bedroom. His fear of darkness had been so great, since childhood, and had remained so intense that his mother had continued to comfort him by letting him sleep with her from the time they had left San Francisco until they moved to Lawrence from Salem. Even after that, throughout the remainder of his high-school years, and during their many moves from one apartment to another in Lawrence and Methuen, his cot was always set up in his mother's bedroom.

Never before had he been forced to be so brave as to sleep in a forest-shrouded house all by himself, night after night. Throughout that summer he slept with his trousers on, ready for flight if necessary. At first, his only consolation had been that he had brought with him to Ossipee Mountain, from Lawrence, an old single-shot pistol and plenty of ammunition. He wanted his neighbors in the Lee settlement to know that he was armed, and occasionally he held brief target practice. Later, Elinor's sister, Leona, lent him her St. Bernard dog, which had been sent up by express to keep the girls company in their cottage. But the huge dog was more trouble than he was worth. Let a thunderstorm come up during the night, and the crash of the first bolt would drive the panic-stricken beast into bed with his master. One night, when Rob could not sleep because of strange and inexplicable noises either inside or outside the house, he lit his lantern, took the iron lid off the potbellied stove, set it on edge as a target on the floor at the far end of the kitchen, and fired shots at it. With luck, the stovelid could thus be made to spin like a top before it clattered flat on the floor. And although the noise scared Rob as much as it did the St. Bernard, there was an exciting comfort in the very act of making noise. The dog proved to be such a nuisance that Rob returned it to Leona, bravely assuring her that he was not afraid to stay alone.

His boast was made too soon. In the dark of one night an uninvited visitor nearly frightened him out of his wits. He had been asleep for hours when he was suddenly awakened by what sounded like a sharp knock or two on the lockless front door. Startled into half-wakefulness, he lay there trembling in his uncertainty. Had he heard a knock? Or was it part of a dream? After a few moments he heard three unmistakable knocks, and now he was nearly petrified. Forgetting his loaded pistol, he crawled to the open kitchen window at the back of the room, climbed out over the sill, called a "Come in" through the window as bravely as he could, and trembled anew as he waited to see what would happen. He could hear the creaking of the rusty hinges, and he could feel his hair standing on end: Someone was actually coming in. That was enough for Rob; he fled. Barefooted, clad only in his trousers and underwear, he circled through the edge of the woods to the dirt road and ran toward the hotel until he had recovered enough courage to stop. In his condition he was too embarrassed and ashamed to ask for help at the hotel. After a few moments of indecision he began to walk cautiously back toward the Horne house, half-suspecting that he would find someone with a lantern stealing hard cider from the cellar. But the house was still dark when he located it by starlight, and again he turned back toward the hotel. Through the remainder of the night, he walked back and forth along the road, perplexed and frightened. When daylight came, he crept back to the open window for one glance inside—and for a moment he was again overwhelmed with fear. A man lay stretched flat on the kitchen floor, as though dead; but it was one of the most harmless of his neighbors up the mountain, and he was quietly snoring. When Rob went in and woke him up, the man explained that he had not meant to bother anyone; he had merely wished to spend the rest of the night in the Horne house so he could sober up from too much drink with friends down in the village before going home.

So terrifying to Rob were the experiences of this night that they intermittently haunted his dreams for years. At last, perhaps motivated in part by the hope that he might rid himself of the whole thing, he made a poem out of it and called it "The Lockless Door." Although his own ways of interpreting dream symbolism showed less of Freud's influence than of the prophetic Daniel's (or perhaps of his mother's), he saw enough possible symbolism in the poem to satisfy him:

> *It went many years,*
> *But at last came a knock,*
> *And I thought of the door*
> *With no lock to lock.*
>
> *I blew out the light,*
> *I tip-toed the floor,*
> *And raised both hands*
> *In prayer to the door.*
>
> *But the knock came again*
> *My window was wide;*
> *I climbed on the sill*
> *And descended outside.*
>
> *Back over the sill*
> *I bade a 'Come in'*

To whatever the knock
At the door may have been.

So at a knock
I emptied my cage
To hide in the world
And alter with age.[5]

In the poem the pivotal image is clearly the act of escape from something feared, an act which Frost dramatized repeatedly throughout his life and art. But during the summer of 1895, it is probable that the courage which overcame his fear of the dark and of loneliness was motivated by pride and desperation. He could not bear to let Elinor see any evidence of what he himself belittled as cowardice.

Perhaps his desire to stay near Elinor caused him to modify his arrangements for tutoring. Instead of going back to Lawrence, as planned, he invited the two boys to spend three weeks in rustic camping with him in the Henry Horne house. They accepted the invitation, made the best of primitive conditions, and combined study with mountain climbing. Their sessions devoted to geometry went well enough for their tutor, who merely put them to work at problems until they appealed to him for help. But their review of English grammar caused far more trouble. Discovering that neither boy could seem to master even the fundamentals of syntax, he exposed them to good examples by reading aloud to them, hour after hour, and by explaining grammatical constructions which were gracefully correct.[6]

As soon as Rob returned to Lawrence from Ossipee Mountain, with Elinor and Leona, late in the summer of 1895, he began helping his mother make arrangements for expanding her private school. She had secured an enrollment of twenty students, and it was obvious that more space would be needed than was available in her Tremont Street living room. For social and geographical reasons there was also the need to find a better location. At that time the business and residential sections of Lawrence lay primarily in that part of the Merrimack River valley which extends between Tower Hill and Prospect Hill, a distance of not much more than two miles. The business section of the city then occupied the western or Tower Hill area, and Tremont Street was part of it. But the residential section, from which Mrs. Frost drew most of her pupils, lay largely to the east and was nearer to Prospect Hill. The Green, or common, marked the center of the city, and Mrs. Frost wanted to establish her school near it. With Rob's help, she found two rooms to rent on the third floor of an attractive new stone structure, designed primarily for business offices and known as the Central Building, 316 Essex Street, only three blocks to the southwest of the Green. For living quarters the Frosts rented two other office rooms in the same building, and to this odd home they moved before the school year started in the fall of 1895.

For reasons which are not clear Robert Frost did not immediately continue his work as either teacher or tutor in his mother's private school that fall. Last-minute changes may have occurred. Elinor White could have had various motives for insisting that Rob was still leaning too much on his mother, that she wanted to see him give an independent demonstration of his ability to obtain a position and hold it instead of quitting whenever he was in the mood for quitting. Perhaps under duress he did look elsewhere for a teaching position. Regardless of what he may have found, he once again took charge of the small Salem District School Number 9, where he again taught twelve pupils (in varying numbers per subject) reading, spelling, penmanship, arithmetic, grammar, composition—for a monthly wage of $24. Simultaneously, however, he continued to help his mother by serving as her general manager of finances. And Elinor White (perhaps to make amends for upsetting plans by temporarily keeping Rob from teaching there) joined the staff of Mrs. Frost's Private School that fall.

The atmosphere of this new school was extremely informal, and the children were delighted with the arrangements, particularly the strangeness of classrooms in an office building. Years later a former pupil of Mrs. Frost's easily recalled, "We had the thrill of riding up and down the elevators, exploring the corridors and stairways, and washing hands in company with the other occupants of the building."[7] Another student could not forget the red curtains which Mrs. Frost had put up in an attempt to make the bleak offices more attractive, and (in one of them) an unruly threadbare rug which was always getting tangled around the feet of teachers and pupils alike.[8] But they all admired and loved the head of the school, who was remembered vividly by one of her girls:

"To my childish mind she was tall, tall and gaunt; to the adult the height may not have been noticeable. Her frame was angular, rather loosely knit, the type of figure we associate in a man with Lincoln. Her face and head I still see, the large broad brow of the thinker; the eyes deep-set, somewhat cavernous, blue [correction: brown], with a humorous, kindly twinkle; a large, generous mouth. The heavy graying hair was coiled at her neck, and always a stray lock detached itself. There were eye glasses that never stayed put. It was the day of shirt waists and skirts, whose union was supposed to be concealed by a belt, a belt that always had an urge to move from its prescribed location. Those were the details that registered on a child's mind. There was that disregard of the trivialities of dress, characteristic of those whose minds are concerned with other values, with matters of the spirit. That spirit, lofty, kindly, sympathetic, and understanding, also registered on the mind and heart of the child. I had particular reason to remember her patience and understanding, which never failed."[9]

Another girl, remembering Mrs. Frost as the Sunday School teacher for the Swedenborgians, who held their meetings in the rooms of Mrs. Frost's Private School in the Central Building, preserved this anecdote:

"Mrs. Belle Frost . . . had a keen sense of humour, which Robert inherited, and loved a joke as well as anyone. I recall an incident in Sunday School, when we were having a lesson about Moses and the Burning Bush. My brother Frank, then about 6 years old, I guess, was much intrigued by the fact that nothing would put out the flame. 'Wouldn't anything put it out?' he asked. 'No,' replied Mrs. Frost, 'nothing.' 'Huh,' said my valiant brother, 'I'd have doused it in the Merrimack River!' I think some of Mrs. Frost's Scotch-Presbyterian ancestors would have been quite shocked at a child who made such a remark, but Mrs. Frost laughed heartily, and did not pursue the subject."[10]

From the start, the success of Mrs. Frost's Private School caused Rob to increase his importunate claim that Elinor White no longer had reason for postponing their public marriage. If she had helped to stimulate his enterprise, and if she had further placed him on trial by letting him teach for a second time in Salem District School Number 9 until he could show evidence of his ability to hold a position and to earn a living independently, she had also created a situation in which she could not postpone her decision indefinitely. She knew that her father still disapproved of the match and that Mr. White would neither permit the wedding to take place in the Spring Street home nor attend the wedding elsewhere. She may also have been made hesitant by many other elements, not the least being Rob's deeply ingrained habits of laziness, which made him almost as casual about matters of school-teaching as his mother was indifferent about housework. Whatever her motives, she put off giving any answer to Rob during most of the fall, and then she consented.

The choice of day for the marriage of the schoolteachers was Saturday, 19 December 1895. It was apparently determined by the start of the vacation between the fall and winter terms at Salem District School Number 9. The choice of place for the marriage—one of the two offices converted into a schoolroom in the Central Building—is easily understood. Neither Elinor nor Rob had any church affiliation; but this particular room had been used throughout the fall of 1895 as the meeting place for the Swedenborgians in Lawrence, and the ceremony was performed by the longtime friend of the Frosts, the Reverend John A. Hayes of Salem, Massachusetts. Among the guests at the wedding, Mr. White was conspicuously absent; most of them were Swedenborgian friends. Perhaps the youngest of them was the ten-year-old Susan P. Holmes, who recalled, years later, how she stood among the folding chairs in that office-classroom-sanctuary and studied the bride and groom:

"I gazed at Robert, and couldn't understand how our happy-go-lucky playmate could change into this solemn young man who replied to the pastor in such serious tones. Congratulations, handshaking, kissing—bewildering! First wedding ever I attended, and I did not like it too well."[11]

The bride herself may not have liked it too well. When she had been an undergraduate at St. Lawrence University, she had impressed several of her friends there as a girl who was always reaching for the unusual. She had spoken to many of them about Robert Frost as a "boy back home" who wrote poetry; but for some time she had never suggested that she was in love with him, that he had given her a ring, or that she thought she might marry him.[12] When the attractive Lorenzo Dow Case began paying her particular attention, she may have hoped, romantically, that he would become a white and shining knight, that he would sweep her off her feet and carry her away. She may even have written to Robert Frost saying (as he insisted to the end of his life) that she was formally engaged to marry Lorenzo Dow Case. If so, she was at least premature, for Case had continued his attentions week after week without ever proposing marriage and without ever saying that he was in love with her. In the last term of her senior year Elinor White may have had another change of heart for many reasons. At least, she did finally say to Case that she thought they should no longer continue to see each other once each week as they had been doing for so long, that she had decided she would marry the boy back home.[13]

If she had been reaching for the unusual, and if she had wanted some cause to champion even if the cause required martyrdom on her part, she could have set her heart upon the possibility that she was marrying an attractive young man who, in spite of his spoiled-child ways, in spite of his temper tantrums and his attempts to hurt her by threatening to kill himself whenever things might go too much against his wishes, did seem to her to have the true capacities of a poet. She may also have felt that she did love him so much that she would be willing to endure his failures as a human being and that she wanted to help him prove her belief in his ability to succeed as a poet.

As for the bridegroom, standing with the bride before the pastor and making his replies in such serious tones, there were some things he himself did not like too well about this wedding. He would never forget, and he would never quite forgive the fact, that while he had been courting Elinor White —and even after he thought he had completely won her and had privately married her—she had hurt him so deeply and terribly by making him think she loved and wanted to marry someone else. It seemed to him that she had indeed driven him to the verge of suicide on two occasions, and that the injury which he had suffered as a result of those wounds was one from which he could never completely recover. It had been partly to save himself, and to save his own proud belief in himself, that he had refused to give up the courtship. And at the very moment when Elinor had handed back to him the golden ring he had placed on her finger, at the very moment when he had thrown the ring into the fire as a symbolic gesture of ending all that had been between them, he had been certain that this was the end of everything for him. If she had immediately changed her mind out of pity for his distress, and had penned the letter which brought him back to her the following night, she had at least won a lover who could not resist continuing his courtship in a vindictive fashion calculated to punish her for what she had done to him. Beneath all his gentleness, from the time of their reconciliation to the day of their wedding, he had made her well aware of his quality of ruthlessness, self-centeredness, and even of cruelty. She must have wondered whether he wanted to triumph over her doubts and hesitancy merely to retaliate. For better or worse, he had persuaded her to marry him. He did love her deeply, and she did have the qualities to inspire love. Yet each of them knew, as they swore their vows to each other in that Essex Street office-classroom-sanctuary, that there were ominous elements in this union. Elinor White did have a craving for the unusual, and she had chosen a dangerous way of achieving it.

RIFFRAFF

One of the most interesting cases in the police court this morning was the one in which Robert L. Frost was charged with assault on Herbert S. Parker. Frost pleaded guilty to the charge and was fined $10, which he paid.[1]

THE BRIDE AND GROOM had decided, for necessary reasons of financial economy, to postpone their honeymoon trip until the summer vacation, and not long after their marriage they were back at work as teachers—he in Salem District School Number 9 and she in Mrs. Frost's Private School. But within a few weeks the groom had become so despondent over what meant most to him that he wrote pathetically to Susan Hayes Ward, who had long ago assured him that she wanted more of his poems for *The Independent:*

"Perhaps you had better not waite any longer. I have done my level best, in the time that has elapsed since last you heard from me, to make good my promise as a poet. But I fear I am not a poet, or but a very incomprehensible one.

"The enclosed [manuscript poems] are an excuse for writing to you, nothing more. You will not find what you want in them, although it is not for me to say anything against them, who have learned to be thankful for little things.

"Do not think but what I would have been glad to hear from you any time these six months, but of course I could not expect to. Possibly I may now when you come to understand the good and sufficient reasons for my long silence."[2]

Although this particular mood of discouragement did not last long enough to interfere seriously with the carrying out of his responsibilities as teacher, as son, as brother, as husband during the spring of 1896, the strain on his nerves did have a very serious effect. Before the end of the school year he began to complain of a curious ailment which he did not understand.

There were times when he could not eat because he suffered from pains in his stomach or solar plexus—it was hard to tell which. There were other times when he awoke in the night to discover that he was sweating heavily, as though from fever, although he had no fever. When he sought medical advice and was given a careful examination, he was not at all surprised to have the doctor say that he seemed to be suffering from acute nervous tension and consequently from nervous indigestion.

Quite a variety of nervous tensions had been building up in him during the spring of 1895. His mother had become ill, and he had been needed to help her carry the teaching load in her school. So he had resigned from his duties in Salem, where boredom had been the greatest strain. But as soon as he began teaching older children Latin, Algebra, and Geometry for his mother, he found that the work made heavy demands on his nervous energies. The unsatisfactory living arrangements in the makeshift apartment shared by Rob's mother and sister and the newlyweds created an entirely different kind of nervous tension. Closely related was the fact that the financial problems of renting four rooms in the Central Building very soon made it clear that unless more students were enrolled, it would be impossible to make ends meet. The building was owned by two Irish brothers named Sweeney, and they were extremely considerate; but the day came when Frost was forced to explain to one of them that Mrs. Frost simply did not have enough money to pay the rent, which was already overdue, and that it would be paid just as soon as possible. Mr. Sweeney, sitting with placid ease in his upholstered office chair and wearing across the rotundity of his vest a heavy gold watch chain, accepted the embarrassed explanations. Encouragingly, he said to Rob, as they parted, "Never mind. Your day will come."

The assurance was appreciated as a sign of Mr. Sweeney's confidence in Rob's abilities, and yet the young man had difficulty in seeing what justification anyone might find, now, for such confidence.

Even more deeply troublesome was his feeling that he had somehow won his bride under the false pretense that Mrs. Frost's Private School could provide a living for all four teachers and that Elinor had already foreseen the general drift of affairs toward another failure. Worse than that was the grimness of Elinor's silence, which implied (at least to Rob) that she might already be sorry that she had married him against the advice of her father. The accumulation of these tensions contributed to a nervous condition, which Rob coped with, as best he could, during the spring term; and then he nearly collapsed. It may have been during his recovery that he wrote a slight love poem for Elinor in playful self-defense, and sent it to Susan Hayes Ward with the following explanation:

"You are to hear from me now only because school is closed and I am quite rested having slept more or less soundly for a whole week night and day. Well I did what I tried to do so that the future is not so uncertain though it is not with success as it is with failure which is final, while success to a coward is only suspense, the most awful of tortures. . . . But to the point. If it is not too late I am anxious to avail myself of your kindness and publish one more poem before I die. . . ."[3]

It is probable that the poem he sent her was entitled "The Birds Do Thus," and Susan Hayes Ward bought it for publication in *The Independent*, where it appeared before too long:

> *I slept all day,*
>   *The birds do thus*
> *That sing a while*
>   *At eve for us.*
>
> *To have you soon*
>   *I gave away—*
> *Well satisfied*
>   *To give—a day.*
>
> *Life's not so short*
>   *I care to keep*
> *The unhappy days;*
>   *I choose to sleep.*[4]

He had no intention of sleeping the whole summer away and he had very carefully made plans for taking Elinor on their delayed honeymoon. They had decided that they would like to find an idyllic sort of isolation in the country, and they had enlisted the assistance of Carl Burell, their friend of high-school days, in renting a small cottage. Carl was working in a box factory in the village of Pembroke, New Hampshire, just to the southeast of the state capital of Concord. He had found for them exactly what they wanted in the neighboring village of Allenstown, near the Suncook River, and only about two miles from Carl's boarding house. Botanist and farmer, Carl had taken pleasure in planting flowers around the rented cottage prior to the arrival of his friends, and had even started a kitchen garden of lettuce, onions, tomatoes, peas, and string beans.

Quite unexpectedly this honeymoon vacation in the country had a lasting effect on the entire life of Robert Frost, because Carl Burell's passion for amateur botanizing proved to be contagious. From the experiences of this summer in Allenstown, New Hampshire, came not merely the Frostian tendency to scatter flowers through all of his later poetry but also his new delight in having his eyes opened to details of nature which he had not previously noticed. He had been exposed to the contrast between city and country since childhood; he had even become familiar with the rituals of farm life during his visits to the Bragg ranch in Napa Valley, California. His first summer in New England, when he was only eleven years old, had acquainted him with the homely routine of the small New Hampshire farm owned by his "Uncle" Ben Messer in Amherst. He had learned more, at first-hand, while living with Loren Bailey in Salem, and, later, while working briefly for another Scotsman, Dinsmore, at Cobbetts Pond in Windham. He had even tried his hand at planting and tending a vegetable garden during the summer, when he protected the White girls and their mother at the old Saunders Place in Salem. But during all of these country experiences he had never come under the influence of any individual whose botanical knowledge was conveyed with such excitement and enthusiasm as Carl's.

Carl, well-informed through his years of bog-trotting and also fortified with an extraordinary collection of botanical manuals, began to interest Rob in the color and structure and fragrance of flowers by quoting Linnaeus and Darwin to support his own belief concerning functional adaptations in the struggle of different plants for survival. Evenings, after work, and while walking from his boarding house to the Frost's rented cottage, Carl gathered specimens from the roadside, from fields, from ditches. He showed Rob and Elinor blossoms they had not even seen before, particularly spiked flower clusters from Carl's favorite family: orchids. He gloried in the feathery fringed lip and the long nectar-bearing spur which invited the visits of pollen-carrying insects. He talked about the ways in which different flowers advertise their presence to the insects on which they depend by wearing bright colors and by exhaling delicate fragrances. He showed them that the night-fertilized flowers close during the day as though to protect themselves against the visits of insects which might rob them of nectar and pollen. He told them of the famous flower clock invented by Linnaeus to indicate the hours of the day by the closing times of different flowers. His fund of details fascinated his listeners.

There was always a sense of hushed adventure in Carl's manner, while conducting even the briefest explorations. He had a habit of approaching any possible hideaway for blossoms with stealth and secrecy, as though he feared they might otherwise use petals for wings and fly off, before they could be fully admired. When he held aside the fragrant branches of spruce or hemlock, triumphantly, to give Rob and Elinor a glimpse of such a newly discovered treasure as a little orchis-studded meadow in a shrouded forest clearing, the exultation of his whispered excitement made Rob remember Coleridge's analogous boast:

> *"We were the first that ever burst*
> *Into that silent sea."*

Rob soon asked for permission to borrow a few books from Carl's library, to advance his limited knowledge of botany; Carl very sensibly started him with a primer: Mrs. William Starr Dana's *How to Know the Wild Flowers: A Guide to the Names, Haunts, and Habits of Our Common Wild Flowers.* Very much to Rob's taste was the enriching lore of literary quotations scattered through Mrs. Dana's volume—snatches of poetry from Emerson, Bryant, Whittier, Longfellow, Wordsworth, Scott, Shakespeare, Spenser, and many well-chosen prose passages from Thoreau's *Journal.* He also found that Mrs. Dana's prose had a distinctly poetic quality of its own, for example in her preliminary remarks concerning the battle for survival:

"Let us suppose that our eyes are so keen as to enable us to note the different seeds which, during one summer, seek to secure a foothold in some few square inches of the sheltered roadside. The neighboring herb-roberts and jewel-weeds discharge—catapult fashion—several small invaders into the very heart of the little territory. A battalion of silky-tufted seeds from the cracked pods of the milkweed float downward and take lazy possession of the soil, while the heavy rains wash into their immediate vicinity those of the violet from the over-hanging bank. The hooked fruit of the stick-tight is finally brushed from the hair of some exasperated animal by the jagged branches of the neighboring thicket and is deposited on the disputed ground, while a bird passing just overhead drops earthward the seed of the partridge berry. The ammunition of the witch-hazel, too, is shot into the midst of this growing colony; to say nothing of a myriad of little squatters that are wafted or washed or dropped or flung upon this one bit of earth, which is thus transformed into a bloodless battleground, and which is incapable of yielding nourishment to one-half or one-tenth or even one-hundredth of these tiny strugglers for life!"[5]

With the help of Mrs. Dana and of Carl Burell the eyes of Robert Frost very quickly became so keen that he began to notice all kinds of mysteries and wonders during walks he took in the neighborhood of his Allenstown cottage—with or without Elinor. She accompanied him less and less in his wanderings as the summer days passed, for the obvious reason that this bride, who had started on the delayed honeymoon some seven months after the wedding, was nearly seven months pregnant. No longer in the mood for long walks, and more inclined to take long midday naps, she insisted that Rob should not hesitate to leave her alone in the cottage while he went exploring. These separations heightened his sense of guilt, particularly if he returned to find that he had been so long absent that Elinor had begun to worry for fear he might be stuck fast in a swamp. Usually, her reproaches for his late returning were expressed through her characteristic reticence or complete silence, and one such occasion inspired Rob to write her an apology while they were still in Allenstown. It was a poem entitled "Flower-gathering":

> I left you in the morning,
> And in the morning glow,
> You walked a way beside me
> To make me sad to go.
> Do you know me in the gloaming,
> Gaunt and dusty gray with roaming?
> Are you dumb because you know me not,
> Or dumb because you know?

All for me? And not a question
For the faded flowers gay
That could take me from beside you
For the ages of a day?
They are yours, and be the measure
Of their worth for you to treasure,
The measure of the little while
That I've been long away.[6]

The almost idyllic honeymoon-vacation of the Frosts in Allenstown was marred by a very serious accident which nearly cost Carl Burell his life. One day while he was at work in the small factory where planks were sawed and planed and cut into shooks—the units of wood used in assembling a single box—the metal lacing on a leather pulley-belt caught the sleeve of his coat. Carl, pulled into the air, tried to hold fast to the belt, and succeeded until he was thrown over a pulley near the ceiling in such a way that his feet struck the roof girders. Falling to the floor heavily, and knocked unconscious, he seemed to be dead. When he recovered consciousness, he felt as though he had broken almost every bone in his body. The doctor's verdict was that his feet were so badly smashed that it might be necessary to amputate them both, but no decision could be made for some time. He was confined to his bed at his boarding house, where Rob visited him repeatedly. They both realized that all of Carl's devotion to the quest for his beloved flowers and plants would be curtailed pathetically if he were never able to walk again. As it happened, Rob himself became a witness to the scene in which Carl was paid a relatively small sum of money by an insurance representative, prior to the time when anyone could know for certain just how badly injured he might be. Amputation was not necessary and Carl did regain the use of his feet, but he was so badly crippled by the accident that he always limped thereafter. Years later, Rob still felt so much of his own acute agony over the accident that he dramatized the heart of it in a blank verse narrative which he entitled, with deliberate irony, "The Self-seeker." In this poem, three characters are grouped at the bedside of the injured man: a friend named Willis, a young girl who has brought a surprise gift of flowers to the injured man, and the lawyer to whom the injured man feels that he is "going to sell my soul, or, rather, feet." The first mention of a specific flower occurs when the victim, regretting that he may be forced to relinquish his plan for writing a book on the flora of the region, boasts that he has recently had a letter from John Burroughs: "About my *Cyprepedium reginæ* [Queen's Orchid];/He says it's not reported so far north." The appearance of the girl at his bedside surprises him, and their conversation reflects the tender outgoing kind of talk which endeared the hulking Carl Burell to Frost during that summer devoted especially to orchids found in the neighborhood of Allenstown:

> . . . *'Why, here is Anne.*
> *What do you want, dear? Come, stand by the bed;*
> *Tell me what is it?' Anne just wagged her dress*
> *With both hands held behind her. 'Guess,' she said.*
>
> *'Oh, guess which hand? My, my! Once on a time*
> *I knew a lovely way to tell for certain*
> *By looking in the ears. But I forget it.*
> *Er, let me see. I think I'll take the right.*
> *That's sure to be right even if it's wrong.*
> *Come, hold it out. Don't change.—A Ram's Horn orchid!*
> *A Ram's Horn! What would I have got, I wonder,*
> *If I had chosen left. Hold out the left.*
> *Another Ram's Horn! Where did you find those,*
> *Under what beech tree, on what woodchuck's knoll?'*
>
> *Anne looked at the large lawyer at her side,*
> *And thought she wouldn't venture on so much.*
>
> *'Were there no others?'*
>
>   *'There were four or five.*
> *I knew you wouldn't let me pick them all.'*
>
> *'I wouldn't—so I wouldn't. You're the girl!*
> *You see Anne has her lesson learned by heart.'*
>
> *'I wanted there should be some there next year.'*
>
> *'Of course you did. You left the rest for seed,*
> *And for the backwoods woodchuck. You're the girl!*
> *A Ram's Horn orchid seedpod for a woodchuck*
> *Sounds something like. Better than farmer's beans*
> *To a discriminating appetite,*

[221]

Though the Ram's Horn is seldom to be had
In bushel lots—doesn't come on the market.
But, Anne, I'm troubled; have you told me all?
[. . .]
You don't tell me that where you found a Ram's Horn
You didn't find a Yellow Lady's Slipper.
What did I tell you? What? I'd blush, I would.
Don't you defend yourself. If it was there,
Where is it now, the Yellow Lady's Slipper?'

'Well, wait—it's common—it's too common.'

　　　　　　　　　　　　　　　　　　'Common?
The Purple Lady's Slipper's commoner.'

'I didn't bring a Purple Lady's Slipper.
To You—*to you I mean—they're both too common.'*

By the time Frost wrote "The Self-seeker" he must have
known he was taking poetic license in suggesting the possibility
that these three Lady's-slippers might be found blooming in the
same days of spring: the Ram's Horn (or Ram's Head), the
Yellow, the Purple; but it was befitting his tribute to Carl
Burell that these three cherished members of the orchid family
should be clustered in the same poetic bouquet. In another
passage of this dramatic narrative, the injured man is permitted to reflect Carl Burell's additional preoccupation with
even the tiniest of flowers growing in the water of local ponds,
rivers, brooks:

'I've broken Anne of gathering bouquets.
It's not fair to the child. It can't be helped though:
Pressed into service means pressed out of shape.
Somehow I'll make it right with her—she'll see.
She's going to do my scouting in the field,
Over stone walls and all along a wood
And by a river bank for water flowers,
The floating Heart, with small leaf like a heart,
And at the sinus *under water a fist*
Of little fingers all kept down but one,
And that thrust up to blossom in the sun
As if to say, "You! You're the Heart's desire."
Anne has a way with flowers to take the place
Of what she's lost: she goes down on one knee

And lifts their faces by the chin to hers
And says their names, and leaves them where they are.[7]

Frost's own intensity of response, the almost religious quality of awe and worship which he then (and always thereafter) associated with bog-trotting for orchids, was later given a self-deprecatingly humorous statement in the poem eventually called "The Encounter." The more serious poem entitled "The Quest of the Purple-fringed" may even have been written at Allenstown during the summer of 1896:

I felt the chill of the meadow underfoot,
But the sun overhead;
And snatches of verse and song of scenes like this
I sung or said.

I skirted the margin alders for miles and miles
In a sweeping line.
The day was the day by every flower that blooms,
But I saw no sign.

Yet further I went to be before the scythe,
For the grass was high;
Till I saw the path where the slender fox had come
And gone panting by.

Then at last and following him I found—
In the very hour
When the color flushed to the petals it must have been—
The far-sought flower.

There stood the purple spires with no breath of air
Nor headlong bee
To disturb their perfect poise the livelong day
'Neath the alder tree.

I only knelt and putting the boughs aside
Looked, or at most
Counted them all to the buds in the copse's depth
That were pale as a ghost.

Then I arose and silently wandered home,
And I for one
Said that the fall might come and whirl of leaves,
For summer was done.[8]

Over and over again, Frost sang in so many of his poems his wistful regrets concerning the end of a cherished season; the moment which served as a zenith for him and foreshadowed fall. When this unusual summer in Allenstown was actually done for the Frosts, and they returned to Lawrence, the first important event of the fall was the part they played in helping to move their own belongings, and those of Mrs. Frost's Private School, from the Central Building on Essex Street to new quarters which would provide better access to playground recreation for the students. A satisfactory place was found next door to the familiar high school on Haverhill Street, facing the grassy expanse of the common. The house was a tall, bay-windowed, two-and-a-half-storied frame residence, oddly shaped to fit the long narrow lot on which it had been built. It offered more living space for the Frosts than they had enjoyed before; but when classes began,[9] the staff of teachers was reduced to three, because Elinor was so near her confinement. For the first time since their marriage, Rob and Elinor had an apartment of their own on the second floor of the Haverhill Street house and enough other rooms on that floor for rental if they wished. Their child was born in the new apartment on 25 September 1896, a boy whom they named Elliott.[10] Inheriting his father's light blue eyes and his Aunt Jeanie's blonde hair, the newcomer very soon won the continuous adoration and attention not only of his parents but also of his grandmother and aunt—perhaps even of his paternal great-grandparents, who still lived only a few blocks further downtown on Haverhill Street. And if the often silent Elinor had previously harbored any reservations concerning the wisdom of her marriage, it seemed that all her doubts disappeared with the arrival of her first child. Her entire attitude toward life seemed to undergo a noticeable change, and she became so completely wrapped up in caring for him that the father could not entirely resist moments of jealousy.

Rob took in stride the duties of fatherhood, partly because his attentions were diverted by his many other responsibilities and by the renewal of an old friendship, which dated back to his mill days. While he worked briefly in the Arlington Mill he had become moderately well-acquainted with a fellow-worker, a young man his own age named Herbert Parker, whose father was a prominent officer in the Pacific Mills. A rebel, estranged early from his father, young Parker had further complicated his family relationship, recently, by marrying a girl who was considered socially disqualified for membership in the Parker family. Frost's discovery of this awkwardness aroused his sympathies. After consultation with his mother and Elinor, Rob offered to rent his friends the extra rooms at the back of the second floor in the Haverhill Street house; the rooms had been similarly used before, and there was a separate outside staircase entrance to them. The arrangement worked amicably until the Frosts began to have doubts concerning the respectability of a particular friend whom the Parkers entertained. A crisis developed when Rob went so far as to warn Mrs. Parker that if a certain Mrs. Hindle was permitted to visit the Parkers any more it would be necessary for them to move elsewhere. Unpleasant words were exchanged, and Mrs. Parker accused Rob of being a coward for insulting her freely at a time when her husband was absent.

The use of that word "coward" seemed to precipitate the crisis. To Rob, this epithet had particularly unpleasant associations, because he was well aware that since childhood he had indeed been forced to struggle against excessive fear of anything, real or imagined, if it seemed dangerous or difficult or painful. But over the years he had tried to assert courage and daring, not without some success, even though he still cringed embarrassingly. As a consequence he could and frequently did call himself a coward, deprecatingly; but he couldn't bear to have anyone else do so. Apparently enraged by Mrs. Parker's use of the word, he blurted out that if her husband uttered it, matters would take a serious turn. Well, she said, her husband would use exactly the same word—as soon as he returned from work.

In the meantime Rob stirred himself up into such a frenzy of anger that he could scarcely bear waiting. As soon as he was sure that his friend had come home, Rob went storming into the Parker apartment uninvited. He found Parker sitting in a chair and he asked point blank if he would dare call Frost a coward. Yes, he would, particularly if, during his absence, Frost had insulted Mrs. Parker. Very well then, if Parker would step down the staircase to the back yard, they could settle this question of cowardice with their fists. No, said Parker, he didn't think that would settle anything—and he made no move to rise from his chair. Frost, completely losing control of his temper, threw a punch which hit the seated man hard enough to start the makings of a "black eye." Immediately Parker jumped from his chair to defend himself and a free-for-all continued until Frost's mother and sister and wife also entered the apartment, uninvited, to separate the furious assailant from his victim.[11]

Parker immediately carried his complaints to the police; a warrant was sworn out for Frost's arrest; and he was required to appear in court on Monday morning, 28 December 1896, shortly after the first anniversary of his wedding.[12] The judge listened to the complaint and turned to Frost to ask, "Did you hit him?"

Attempting to cover his own shame Frost scornfully glanced at Parker's half-closed black eye and answered, "Looks like it, doesn't it?"

Given the choice of going to jail for thirty days or of paying a fine of ten dollars, Frost chose to pay the fine; and the judge closed the case with an epithet obviously aimed at the assailant: "Riffraff!"

Frost was ashamed and humiliated. He had not reached the courtroom door before he was overtaken by the sympathetic voice of a young man who had been a classmate through high school, and in answer to the young man's questions Frost poured out the whole story of the circumstances which had led up to the one-sided punching match. The sympathetic questioner did not say that he was now a reporter, covering court cases for the *American*, the newspaper for which Frost had briefly worked. But he realized his mistake when the afternoon edition of the *American* devoted a full column to the story under embarrassing captions:

FISTICUFFS FOLLOWED BY A WARRANT AND POLICE COURT
NEIGHBORS QUARREL
SATISFACTION WAS DEMANDED
—DEFENDANT FINED $10.

It was bad enough to have all the details spread into the public record this way; but it seemed to Frost that the reporter who had taken advantage of his confidence deliberately and sarcastically rubbed salt into the wound by adding, near the end of the story in the *American:*

"Frost was graduated from the High School in the Class of '92 with high honors being the valedictorian of his class. He entered Dartmouth college but did not stay a year out. . . . Mr. Frost's wife was Miss Elinor White and she was the salutatorian [co-valedictorian] of the Class of '92."[13]

Frost was further embarrassed by another Lawrence newspaper, *The Weekly Journal,* which made more flagrant use of sarcasm in its version of the scandal:

"Bully for you Herbert!

"Hands like yours were not made to fight, besides pugilism has descended to a very low ebb hereabouts. Then again, when young 'Frost' invited you into the yard, his hands were not encased in sixteen ounce boxing gloves, as they ought to have been, therefore under the circumstances, you followed the admonition of the scriptures, 'If thine enemy strike thee on one side of the cheek, turn to him the other,' and thus you had a chance to publicly disgrace him by bringing the would-be Corbett to the bar of justice. . . .

"The court heard both stories which did not vary in the least. . . . He then challenged young Parker to fight in the yard and because the latter refused struck him several times.

"It was a 'frosty' day for Frost, but he paid the ten dollars like a little man and doubtless he thinks the notoriety he thus gained was worth the money. It isn't anybody's privilege to challenge the son of a $20,000 mill agent to mortal combat every day in the week . . . Neighbors believe that Frost would never have lived to tell the tale had Herbert accepted that invitation, and taking all things into consideration, Frost is a lucky dog. . . ."[14]

This public disgrace, turning as it did on the words "coward" and "riffraff," had a profoundly unsettling effect on Rob's already shaken confidence in himself, and he continued to brood miserably over the judge's epithet. It clearly implied that anyone who resorted to fisticuffs under such conditions must belong to that segment of society which is regarded as being of no consequence and as having no particular merit—and this assumption merely opened an old wound. There were times when Rob had the suspicion that the judge was correct, even as there were times when he could admit to himself that Mrs. Parker had been correct in calling him a coward. Torturing himself unnecessarily, he began to review circumstances in which his extraordinary sensitivities had made him cringe. Some of his earliest recollections were of outcries during punishment dealt him by his father. If he needed to justify his instinctive tendency to recoil on these occasions, some outer scars remained as evidence. In retrospect, he could even view as cringing his dreamlike longing to escape into a happy valley and stay there. But when he looked back to wonder what had inspired his first attempts to assert at least enough courage and daring to counteract his fears, he seemed to find the answer in the stories of heroes and heroic actions, read to him by his mother from his early childhood.

He still liked to think he had crossed the line from childhood to young manhood on that day when he was a ten-year-old, brave enough to fight with his fists for the right to join Seth Balsa's gang on Nob Hill. In his willingness to serve as cat's-paw in thieving for Seth Balsa, his desire to prove his courage and daring and skill had far outweighed any questions of wrong or right. By the time he moved from San Francisco to Lawrence and then to Salem, he had been quick to make a hero out of Charlie Peabody, whose daring and ability Rob had first imitated when learning to climb and bend birches. As he looked back at the Salem days, even his newly discovered passion for baseball seemed to involve his eagerness to show courage and skill as a pitcher, as a batter, as a baserunner sliding head first. Later, in high school, when he had been piqued by the sarcastic invitation to serve as a substitute football player, he had accepted it largely because he wanted to show his enemies that he wouldn't be afraid to rough it up with the bruisers on the gridiron. Closely connected, was his memory that part of his impetus for clearing out of Dartmouth College had been provided by Preston Shirley's doubt that Frost would dare to leave Hanover without permission or excuse. And on the day, soon after, when he had boldly walked into his mother's classroom to face the overgrown bullies with the announcement that he had come to settle her score with them, he felt that he had shown another kind of courage and daring. In the sequel, when some of the same bullies took revenge on him by beating him almost into insensibility and heaving him into the gutter, he felt that he had made another assertion of courage by arranging to pay the old boxer to punch his nose out of shape while he learned how to fight. Even in this recent fracas with Herbert Parker, Rob had tackled a man bigger and stronger than himself, but he was willing to admit that he had expected to offset Parker's greater strength by means of his boxing skill. Riffraff? If he had descended that low in the eyes of the public, where did the truth lie? Was he the only one, now, who still believed he was better than riffraff?

He wished he knew how to interpret Elinor's increasing spells of silence, and he was often troubled by the suspicion that she did regret her marriage to him. She had unpleasant ways of reminding him that he seemed to have a gift for failure, and he had the feeling that she was the one who had most seriously marred their years of courtship by chiding him for being, too often, a spoiled and lazy child, headstrong and self-centered. In another fashion his younger sister, Jeanie, infuriated him with her superior manner of criticism and fault-finding.

If there was any single consolation for him, at this time, it came from his mother. He felt that she understood him best, that now as always she was encouraging him to assert his talents as poet and leader, that she still idealized him as her hero. Her own faith in him renewed his faith. He liked to remember how proud she had been of him in high school— first when he had led his class at the end of his freshman year, then when he had written and published his first poem, then when he had become Chief Editor of the *Bulletin* and President of the Debating Union, and finally valedictorian (well at least co-valedictorian) and class poet. Even now she showed her admiration for the way he had come to her assistance in helping her establish a private school, and she was constantly praising him for his abilities as a teacher.

But he was troubled by the fear that this new scandal, so prominently treated in the newspapers, would hurt the reputation of the growing school. He had already found that he was impatient with the drudgery of teaching children. Even the problem of handling classroom discipline took out of him more nervous energy than he could afford. Besides, he kept telling himself, his present direction was by no means suited to his ideal of becoming a Shelleyan rebel against conventions. He wanted his life to be different from what it was becoming, and he knew that he had gone back to teaching not so much because his mother needed his help as because he needed hers in proving to Elinor that he could earn a living.

Discouraged and humiliated by the Parker affair, he was in a mood for running away once more, or at least for going away so that he could start again somewhere else. But he didn't know where or how to find a new foothold, and Elinor seemed indifferent to all of his talk about possibilities. If she really did regret her marriage to him, he thought, he might as well run away, stay away, and even throw his life away— completely this time.

Riffraff.[15]

HARVARD: AS FOR THE VIEW

A head thrusts in as for the view,
But where it is it thrusts in from
Or what it is it thrusts into
By that Cyb'laean avenue,
And what can of its coming come,

And whither it will be withdrawn,
And what take hence or leave behind,
These things the mind has pondered on
A moment and still asking gone.[1]

ROBERT FROST liked to remember, as a turning point in his life, the dramatic moment when he expressed his decision to become a special student at Harvard College. It occurred while he and his wife were living in the Blaisdell house they had rented for the summer of 1897 at Salisbury Point in Amesbury, Massachusetts. She was giving a bath to their ten-month-old son Elliott in the kitchen, and he had just come downstairs from his study, still holding in his hand a Latin text of the historian Tacitus, with a finger between the pages to hold the place where he had been reading. He liked to recall that he leaned against the door jamb as he voiced his new discovery that in Tacitus he had found so much to admire that he thought he would really enjoy teaching both Latin and Greek at a high-school level, if only he could go back to college long enough to prepare himself for such teaching. Harvard, under the radical influence of President Eliot, had developed a reputation for encouraging individual students to shape any special direction for study by means of the elective program, and it now seemed to Rob that if he could gain admission to Harvard as a special student he need not spend four years in qualifying for a good position as a high-school teacher of Latin and Greek.

At the time of this announcement he may not have told Elinor that he had another reason for wanting to attend Harvard: his desire to study psychology and philosophy with the celebrated William James,[2] whose latest work, *The Will to Believe,* had attracted much attention after its publication in April of 1897. It is probable that Rob had become acquainted with some of the essays in that volume prior to their appearance as collected. The second essay, "Is Life Worth Living?," had been delivered as a special address at Harvard. It had been published in magazine form in 1895, had been widely quoted in newspapers and periodicals, and had even been issued as a pocket volume in 1896. As the title indicated, this essay came to grips with the question of whether persuasive counterarguments could be given to any fellow mortal who had reached the verge of suicide.

The tone of the essay implied that James had first-hand experience with the problem under consideration. Truth was that this brilliant and distinguished man, who had by this time advanced through so many phases of his life—artist, biologist, graduate of Harvard Medical School, lecturer on physiology, lecturer in psychology, author of a two-volume work entitled *The Principles of Psychology,* and now Professor of Philosophy at Harvard—had very seriously contemplated suicide at the age of twenty-eight.[3] Years later, in a letter to a friend, he wrote, "Fear of life in one form or another is the great thing to exorcise; but it isn't reason that will ever do it. Impulse without reason is enough, and reason without impulse is a poor makeshift. I take it that no man is educated who has not dallied with the thought of suicide."[4]

Speaking and writing from his own experience in order to assist others, James did manage to convey a quality of optimism and fervor, even through the printed words of his essay "Is Life Worth Living?" He began by granting that many individuals must experience the tug-of-war between what he called "the nightmare view of life" and "the craving of the heart to believe that behind nature there is a spirit whose expression nature is." He built his arguments persuasively to urge that the strongest defense against suicide is provided by religious belief: "A man's religious faith . . . means for me essentially his faith in the existence of an unseen order of some kind in which the riddles of the natural order may be found explained."[5] Science, he admitted, has a discouraging way of insisting that human beings cannot find any justification for the religious claim that the pains and evils of this earth serve a positive function in a metaphysical plan. Going even further, he granted that agnostics and nonbelievers could advance the counterargument that we have no right to suppose anything about the unseen part of the universe. But he pointed out that psychologists can help us understand that the "maybe" of the doubter is often more cowardly and dangerous than the "maybe" of the believer:

"So far as man stands for anything, and is productive or originative at all, his entire vital function may be said to have to deal with maybes. Not a victory is gained, not a deed of faithfulness or courage is done, except upon a maybe; not a service, not a sally of generosity, not a scientific exploration or experiment or textbook, that may not be a mistake. It is only by risking our persons from one hour to another that we live at all. And often enough our faith beforehand in an uncertified result is the only thing that makes the result come true."[6]

These assurances and encouragements were particularly needed by Robert Frost at the time William James published them in *The Will to Believe*. It may have seemed to Frost that James was speaking directly to him, at precisely the time when Frost was determining to give more scope to his own higher faculties. Hence his decision to go to Harvard not only as a student of the classics but also as one who sought direct inspiration from courses taught by Professor William James.

Yet even in the moment when he was voicing his decision —while standing in the kitchen door, talking to Elinor and watching her back as she continued bathing Elliott—something in that tableau hurt him. Elinor made no response, in speech or in gesture, and her apparent indifference sent a chill through him. Her back seemed to say that she really didn't care what he decided. To Rob, hurt and disappointed by her lack of response, there came the renewal of his fear that she had completely lost hope for his future—or for hers—and that she was merely taking refuge in a stoical resignation to whatever might happen. Hurt in part by his own guilt, he again worried over how much he was to blame for what seemed to be a darker attitude on her part. Was it a further indication that there had indeed been ruthlessness and cruelty in his courtship?[7] If so, what could he do to make amends? It seemed that the best possible action now would be to convince her that he had changed; that part of the change was implied by his thought of going back to college to prepare himself for a new way of life.

He knew there was no time to waste if he were to gain admittance to Harvard in the fall, that he would be rusty for any entrance examinations which he might be required to take. But the prospect stimulated his energies and gave him a buoyancy which was reflected in his letter to Dean LeBaron Russell Briggs:

". . . I desire to enter Harvard this fall if possible as a candidate for a degree from the outset. It came to me as a surprise only the other day that I might reasonably hope to do so consequently I find myself somewhat unprepared for examination. This is the great difficulty. I graduated from the Lawrence High School as many as five years ago (having in 1891 passed examinations for admission to Harvard occupying seven hours for which I hold a certificate.) It is true that since that time I have been teaching school and tutoring more or less in Latin Algebra and Geometry. Still my studies are all at loose ends. In particular I have neglected my Greek. If proficiency in English were any consideration, I make no doubt I could pass an examination in that. You will find verses of my inditing in the current number of the Independent[8] and others better in back numbers. I might possibly pass in French also and in Physics and Astronomy for that matter but in Greek I fear not. You'll say it doesn't sound very encouraging. . . .

". . . Let me say that if I enter college it must be this year or never. It will be hard if a fellow of my age and general intelligence (!) must be debarred from an education for want of technical knowledge representing less than two months work. All I ask is to be admitted. I don't care how many conditions you encumber me with. I will take the examinations if you say so, or I will enter as a special. . . ."[9]

Dean Briggs informed the applicant that under the circumstances it would be necessary to take a final group of entrance examinations which would be scheduled over a period of four days: Greek, Latin, Ancient History, English, French, and Physical Science (Astronomy and Physics). Rob had never taken any courses in French or in the Physical Sciences, and yet he saw ways of appearing not to be an ignoramus in these two final examinations. Out of curiosity, he had studied Elinor's elementary French textbooks while she was teaching in Mrs. Frost's Private School. Now, with his wife's help, he hastily improved his knowledge of French conjugations and declensions. His early interest in astronomy had led him to continue reading in that field, and he hastily read through a high-school textbook on physics. The challenge of the ordeal pleased him. He took it in stride, and he managed to pass all of the examinations, so that he was permitted to enter without condition.

Not so well solved were problems concerning finances and living in Cambridge. Uncomfortably, he went to his grandfather and borrowed money for his Harvard tuition. He did not want to leave his wife and child in Lawrence, nor did he want to try commuting, and his mother-in-law's marital difficulties worked to his advantage here. Mrs. White proposed that she take temporary leave of her husband and live with Rob and Elinor and Elliott in Cambridge as soon as an apartment could be found, that she would undertake the task of finding an apartment and would help pay the rent. Until those arrangements could be made, Rob took a single room at 16 Rutland Street, off Massachusetts Avenue, within ten minutes' walk from the Harvard Yard. He also found work as principal of the Shepard Evening School in North Cambridge—two hours, three nights a week. All of these obligations enabled him to make ends meet, but they took more time from his study than he had anticipated.

The Harvard system of electives did not give him the immediate latitude he sought. He was particularly annoyed to discover that he was required to take a course in elementary German and in English composition. He accepted the German course as unavoidable. But his instructor in English was an effeminate assistant, Alfred Dwight Sheffield, better known among the students as "the bearded lady," who very quickly infuriated Frost. Hoping that he was qualified to take Barrett Wendell's course in advanced composition, he found enough courage to approach Professor John Hayes Gardiner, head of the course, and to ask permission to change. Gardiner, who gave the weekly "third hour" lecture in English A, seemed to be offended by the request. In a manner that seemed supercilious, he asked Frost what "pretentions" might be prompting such a request. Well, there was nothing new in A. S. Hill's

Principles of Rhetoric because the supplicant had already devoted several years to literary work. He had been a newspaper
reporter and he had even published some verses in *The Inde-*
pendent. Having saved this last fact as his trump card, Frost
was not prepared to have the professor draw back his chin
and make the sarcastic observation, "Oh! So we're a *writer*,
are we?"

Hurt and flustered, Frost tried to smile as he said he guessed
he wouldn't press the point further. Gardiner agreed: it would
be just as well if he didn't. The retreat from the professor's
office was awkwardly made, and Frost left, vowing silently that
he would never forgive or forget this rudeness. Sheffield had
his own form of belittlement, equally aggravating. In class,
one day, he asked each man to write a short lyric. Searching
around in his memory for a poem he had previously composed,
Frost found one which seemed appropriate to the autumnal
season:

> *Now close the windows and hush all the fields:*
> *If the trees must, let them silently toss;*
> *No bird is singing now, and if there is,*
> *Be it my loss.*
>
> *It will be long ere the marshes resume,*
> *It will be long ere the earliest bird:*
> *So close the windows and not hear the wind,*
> *But see all wind-stirred.*[10]

Sheffield seemed to be suspicious, and when Frost appeared
for his next conference the assistant asked if the poem had
actually been composed in class or merely written from memory. Well, it was his own poem, although he had to admit that
he had not worked it up on the spur of the moment. Then it
was not acceptable. Other poems submitted (including "The
Tuft of Flowers") did not please Sheffield, who gave Frost his
best marks for prose pieces written inside or outside the
classroom. But always the penciled comments were infuriating. They implied that the first requirement of the student was
to learn how to write, that only later on would he have something to say. Sheffield obviously assumed that his task as
teacher of English A was to drill the students meticulously
through their writing of "exercises." Frost's pride was offended

to such a degree that he finally unburdened himself through writing a quatrain which he wanted to submit as an "exercise" —and never did:

> *Perhaps you think I am going to wait*
> *Till I can write like a graduate*
> *Before I write to my friends any more.*
> *You prig stick, what do you take me for.*[11]

Sheffield seemed to take him for a better-than-average student. His final grade in the course was "B"—and again Frost was outraged.

Far more pleasant and rewarding to his later poetic career was the course in Latin, divided between Latin composition, under the guidance of Maurice W. Mather, and readings in Livy and Terence and in lyric, elegiac, and iambic poetry with Charles P. Parker. What meant most of all to him, as he later revealed in *North of Boston,* was his discovery of Virgil's eclogues, which opened up the entire range of pastoral poetry. In Greek, his acquaintance with Virgil's inspirer, Theocritus, had to be postponed until the second year. But in the first and second terms of his freshman year he was particularly happy to study the *Iliad* and the *Odyssey,* favorites in translation since his boyhood. His instructor in Greek was Frank Cole Babbitt, almost as young as some of his students and capable of inspiring a special quality of enthusiasm.

In Babbitt's Sever Hall classroom, Frost made his only lasting Harvard friendship, with a classmate who sat next to him, Waddill Catchings of Louisville, Kentucky. On the Sever Hall bench beyond Catchings sat a Negro, and Frost was amused to notice how the Southern prejudices of his new friend were reflected: the Negro was instructed to address the Kentuckian as "Mister Catchings" and not as "Catchings." Frost's own Copperhead sympathies expressed themselves during the first fall at Harvard, as he participated in a band-led victory procession through Cambridge streets, following a football game. The only person he recognized in the procession was the Negro from his Greek class, and they talked together as they marched. When they were joined by three other Negro students, Frost decided that he had marched long enough. He made excuses and dropped out of the parade. His attitude toward Negroes, and their sympathizers, conveyed to him in boyhood by his Copperhead father, stayed with him throughout his life.

The loneliness he felt as he moved among the hundreds of students in the Yard, in classrooms, in large lectures, in the Harvard library, was relieved late in the fall of 1897 when Mrs. White finally found an apartment to her liking—one side of a house on Ellery Street. As soon as Elinor and her mother and the baby were established in their new home, where a special room was available as a study for the married Harvard freshman, he found that his entire attitude underwent a decided improvement. The study was a small cupola room, perched on the roof, and far enough away from the baby's room on the ground floor to provide complete escape from Elliott's occasional fussiness and caterwauling. When Elinor could spare time, she tried to help her husband with difficulties caused by his written assignments in German, a subject which had not interested her particularly during her undergraduate years at St. Lawrence University. Partly as a result of these new arrangements, the quality of his work improved so much during the second semester that he earned special recognition. For his sophomore year he was awarded a Sewall Scholarship of two hundred dollars in recognition of the "marked excellence" he had demonstrated as a freshman.

At the start of the summer vacation Frost again rented the Blaisdell house at Salisbury Point near the north bank of the Merrimack River in Amesbury. He was so exhausted by his duties as student, as principal of the Shepherd Evening School, as husband, as father, as son-in-law that he looked forward to weeks of idleness; but the exhaustion may have helped to cause a strange illness. The trouble seemed to begin as the result of an accident which occurred soon after the Frosts reached Salisbury Point. Their water supply was provided by a well in the front yard, and the well bucket, raised and lowered by rope, was used for keeping the baby's milk cool. It was a process which required careful placing of the milk pail into the bucket and careful lowering of the bucket until it barely rested on the surface of the water. But during a too-hasty lowering, Frost let the bucket sink so far that it tipped over and the milk spilled into the well. Accidents of this sort always made him furious with himself. After consultation with neighbors, he feared that typhoid germs might develop and pollute the water, that under the circumstances he had no choice except to empty the well as much as possible by bailing. With the help of a neighbor, who provided a ladder long enough to reach to the bottom of the shallow well, Frost went to work. He stayed too long in the well, filling pails lowered to him by rope and standing for some time in the spring-cold water until the work was done. That night he suffered slightly from chills, but by morning he had recovered so completely that he accepted a neighbor's invitation to make a rowboat voyage of several miles down the Merrimack River and back.

For Frost the venture was a new kind of outing, skillfully planned by his neighbor so that they went down the river with the outgoing tide, reached the clam flats at the mouth of the river at low tide, dug all the clams they wanted before the incoming tide covered the beds, fished for flounder in relatively shallow water, and then rowed home with the incoming tide. The freshness of the entire experience made the day so enjoyable for Frost that he was not prepared for the unpleasant aftereffects. Belatedly, he realized that his standing barefooted in the ocean water of the incoming tide, as he raced to dig clams in the lowest and best parts of the bed, had aggravated the condition caused by his standing barefooted at the bottom of the well the day before. This time, the chills which made the night miserable for him were followed by severe pains in the region of his stomach and chest. A doctor was called, a lengthy consultation was held, medicine was prescribed, and improvement was anticipated. But the pains continued, and when the doctor returned he asked Frost if there had ever been tuberculosis in his family. Yes, his father had died of it. The doctor shook his head ominously and said that this confirmed his fears: the symptoms indicated that Frost might have become the victim of the same terrible disease. The best advice was to move back from the river, preferably to a mountain climate and dry air. If the pains had continued for many days, Frost might have taken the advice more seriously, but within a few days he seemed to return to normal.

In the fall of 1898, Frost returned to Harvard as a sophomore, leaving his wife and child with the Whites on Valley Street in Lawrence. Although he planned to continue his study of Greek and Latin, he looked forward with particular eagerness to taking a course in philosophy with William James, and was greatly disappointed to learn that because of illness James had been granted a year's leave. At this particular time, the strength of the Philosophy Department at Harvard was great enough to withstand the absence of James, and Frost signed up for two full-year courses without him: General Introduction to Philosophy and a survey course entitled History of Philosophy. The introductory course began with the study of logic, under the distinguished Chairman of the Department, Professor George Herbert Palmer. It continued with a study of psychology, under the guidance of the German psychologist, Professor Hugo Munsterberg, who used as his text the one-volume *Psychology* which had been written and published by William James only a few years earlier. As a result Frost came directly under the influence of William James, through his textbook, even during his absence from the campus.

If James had fashioned his textbook as a mere physiological approach to the study of psychology, Frost's interests would have been stimulated by his own problems. But because James deliberately extended the subject to include ethical applications, some of his remarks had special relevance. For example, the chapter entitled "Habit" in the *Psychology* textbook contained the exhortation to keep the faculty of effort alive through daily exercise: "That is, be systematically ascetic or heroic in little unnecessary points," and as a result, "when the hour of dire need draws nigh, it may find you not unnerved and untrained to start the test." According to James, asceticism of this sort is like the insurance a man pays on his house. The tax does no good at the time and may never bring any return. "But if the fire *does* come, his having paid it will be his salvation from ruin." So it is, James continued, with the man who has daily inured himself to habits of concentrated attention, energetic volition, and self-denial: "He will stand like a tower when everything rocks around him, and when his softer fellow-mortals are winnowed like chaff in the blast. The physiological study of mental conditions is thus the most powerful ally of hortatory ethics. The hell to be endured hereafter, of which theology tells, is no worse than the hell we make for ourselves in this world by habitually fashioning our characters in the wrong way."[12]

For Robert Frost this was a new kind of preaching, which was made palatable because the utterances occurred in a scientific textbook in which the provisional Jamesian pluralism and (still incipient) pragmatism constantly invoked skeptical attitudes congenial to Frost's own doubts, hopes, and fears concerning himself and his relations to others. The mirror-value of passage after passage in *Psychology* must have made strong appeal to him: "We wonder how we ever could have opined as we did last month about a certain matter. We have outgrown the possibility of that state of mind, we know not how. From one year to another we see things in new lights. What was unreal has grown real, and what was exciting is insipid. . . ."[13] The chapter on "The Self" may have proved especially useful to Frost because so many passages in it were pertinent to his own gropings:

"Properly speaking, *a man has as many social selves as there are individuals who recognize him* and carry an image of him in their mind. To wound any one of these images is to wound him. But as the individuals who carry the images fall naturally into classes, we may practically say that he has as many different social selves as there are distinct *groups* of persons about whose opinion he cares. He generally shows a different side of himself to each of these different groups. . . . From this there results what practically is a division of the man into several selves; and this may be a discordant splitting, as where one is afraid to let one set of his acquaintances know him as he is elsewhere . . . The most peculiar social self which one is apt to have is in the mind of the person one is in love with. The good or bad fortunes of this self cause the most intense elation and dejection—unreasonable enough as measured by every other standard than that of the organic feeling of the individual. . . ."[14]

Frost's most difficult problem, at this time, remained his awkward relationship with his wife, whose responses troubled and sometimes baffled him. In her silences he still feared hints of her disillusionment and disappointment, caused by his own inadequacy and failure. While he was studying James' *Psychology*, the problem still confronting him was one of trying to achieve self-confidence, and James had much to say on the point:

"A man with a broadly extended empirical Ego, with powers that have uniformly brought him success, with place and wealth and friends and fame, is not likely to be visited by the morbid diffidences and doubts about himself which he had when he was a boy. 'Is not this great Babylon, which I have planted?' Whereas he who has made one blunder after another, and still lies in middle life among the failures at the foot of the hill, is liable to grow all sickled o'er with self-distrust, and to shrink from trials with which his powers can really cope."[15]

The literary references, particularly the echoes from *Hamlet*, were not missed by Frost, who found another mirror of disillusionment in the Prince of Denmark. But always, in James, the ability of this celebrated scientist to combine with skepticism a re-assertion of belief in religious matters must have made a particularly strong appeal:

". . . still the emotion that beckons me on is indubitably the pursuit of an ideal social self, of a self that is at least worthy of approving recognition by the highest *possible* judging companion, if such companion there be. This self is the true, the intimate, the ultimate, the permanent me which I seek. This judge is God, the Absolute Mind, the 'Great Companion.' We hear, in these days of scientific enlightenment, a great deal of discussion about the efficacy of prayer; and many reasons are given us why we should not pray, whilst others are given us why we should. But in all this very little is said of the reason why we *do* pray, which is simply that we cannot help praying. It seems probable that, in spite of all that 'science' may do to the contrary, men will continue to pray to the end of time."[16]

If the skeptical believer, James, had merely preached to Frost the Christian doctrine of self-giving or self-sacrifice, without reference to the need for self-fulfillment, he would not have been so useful to this Harvard sophomore. But James and Frost saw eye to eye on the need for a certain kind of selfishness, which had to be asserted by the artist, in particular, for his fulfillment:

". . . *Its own body, then, first of all, its friends next, and finally its spiritual dispositions,* MUST *be the supremely interesting objects for each human mind.* Each mind, to begin with, must have a certain minimum of selfishness in the shape of instincts of bodily self-seeking in order to exist. The minimum must be there as a basis for all farther conscious acts, whether of self-negation or of a selfishness more subtle still. All minds must have come, by the way of the survival of the fittest, if by no directer path, to take an intense interest in the bodies to which they are yoked, altogether apart from any interest in the pure Ego which they also possess."[17]

For Frost, needing all the encouragement he could get at this particular time, William James offered many different kinds of enlightenment, justification, and re-assurance. Most stimulating of all the elements in this textbook may have been the constant affirmation of gains to be achieved through heroic assertions of will, courage, effort. Near the conclusion of his chapter on "Will," James returned to the "ethical importance of the phenomenon of effort," and stressed his points with inspirational rhetoric when he described the responses made by "the heroic mind" to "dark abysses" in human experience:

". . . To it, too, the objects are sinister and dreadful, unwelcome, incompatible with wished-for-things. But it can face them if necessary, without for that losing its hold upon the rest of life. The world thus finds in the heroic man its worthy match and mate; and the effort which he is able to put forth to hold himself erect and keep his heart unshaken is the direct measure of his worth and function in the game of human life. He can *stand* this Universe. He can meet it and keep up his faith in it in presence of those same features which lay his weaker brethren low. . . . And hereby he makes himself one of the masters and the lords of life. . . . But just as our courage is so often a reflex of another's courage, so our faith is apt to be a faith in some one else's faith. We draw new life from the heroic example. The prophet has drunk more deeply than anyone of the cup of bitterness, but his countenance is so unshaken and he speaks such mighty words of cheer that his will becomes our will, and our life is kindled at his own."[18]

Such ringing words of encouragement, available to Frost through the study of this textbook, could not have conveyed a much more powerful effect if the man himself had been conducting the course in which the text was assigned. For Frost, the book made a particularly appropriate introduction to the study of philosophy, because James was indeed bold enough to combine a study of physiology and psychology with the study of philosophy and even of metaphysics. In his "Epilogue," James endowed the word "metaphysics" with a practical meaning:

"The special sciences all deal with data that are full of obscurity and contradiction; but from the point of view of their limited purposes these defects may be overlooked. Hence the disparaging use of the name metaphysics which is so common. To a man with a limited purpose any discussion that is oversubtle for that purpose is branded as 'metaphysical.' A geologist's purposes fall short of understanding Time itself. A mechanist need not know how action and reaction are possible at all. A psychologist has enough to do without asking how both he and the mind which he studies are able to take cognizance of the same outer world. But it is obvious that problems irrelevant from one standpoint may be essential from another. And as soon as one's purpose is the attainment of the maximum of possible insight into the world as a whole, the metaphysical puzzles become the most urgent ones of all."[19]

This was the way Frost wanted to hear a scientist talk, and one of his strongest reasons for admiring William James was the ability of this particular scientist to make his own approaches "pluralistic" enough to encompass physics and metaphysics.

In Frost's other course, devoted to the history of philosophy, he was exposed to an entirely different approach. The lecturer was a relatively young man, only eleven years older than Frost, and formerly a pupil of William James during the days when James, fresh out of medical school, had been teaching a course in physiology. He was George Santayana, who had already asserted his interest in poetry and aesthetics by publishing *Sonnets and Other Verses* in 1894 and a prose treatise entitled *The Sense of Beauty* in 1896. There was a patrician grace and eloquence in Santayana's oral presentation of his material, and Frost immediately responded with warmth to the literary qualities. But Santayana had not finished his survey of the Greek philosophers before Frost began to realize that this former pupil of William James represented a viewpoint decidedly at odds with that of his teacher. Born in Spain of Spanish parents and brought up as a Catholic, Santayana had been influenced by parental ideas and prejudices which were essentially deistical. His mother was sure that there was a God; his father was not; but it seemed certain to both of them that if God did exist, he took no special thought for man, that churches and prayers and sacrifices and tales of immortality were invented by rascally priests in order to dominate the foolish. Their son, George, was not quite so sweeping in his views of these matters, but by the time Frost listened to him at Harvard it was clear that Santayana considered the expressions of religious belief particularly interesting as forms of poetry or fiction, valuable if taken in a symbolic rather than in a literal sense.

Santayana's amused and quietly sarcastic handling of matters of religious belief was not lost on Frost, listening to the suave lectures. While studying under James, Santayana had become familiar with the typically Jamesian assertion that "we have a right to believe at our own risk any hypothesis that is live enough to tempt our will,"[20] and with the additional assertion that what we believe in, as individuals, becomes a truth and remains a truth just so long as it seems useful or profitable. But Santayana in his lectures had already begun to take sly pleasure in pointing up what seemed to him some quaint discrepancies in these Jamesian notions. With gentle sarcasm Santayana implied that these were self-deceiving notions, familiar to mankind for centuries, that they had been taken seriously by "grosser minds" long after the same notions had been treated ironically by satirists:

"The picture of life as an eternal war for illusory ends was drawn at first by satirists, unhappily with too much justification in the facts. Some grosser minds, too undisciplined to have ever pursued a good either truly attainable or truly satisfactory, then proceeded to mistake that satire on human folly for a sober account of the whole universe; and finally others were not ashamed to represent it as the ideal itself—so soon is the dyer's hand subdued to what it works in."[21]

At our own risk, Santayana agreed, we may of course believe in any forms of illusion or myth. And to our actual profit some of the highest forms of human idealism had been expressed through the gloriously imaginative myth-making capacities of man. To the artist-philosopher Santayana, the creative imagination had a sacred significance. So he liked to approach the history of philosophy as an ambiguous study of human tendencies to create idealistic illusions and of human eagerness to believe in these illusions as truths. Such a study, approached from Santayana's naturalistic and materialistic viewpoint, was designed to sort out the most inspiring of these illusory responses. And in the lectures which Frost heard him give at Harvard, Santayana was just beginning to formulate his "biography of the human intellect," still not certain whether it should be called "the Romance of Wisdom" or "the Life of Reason." Frost, in his conversations years later, paraphrased what he heard Santayana say about illusions in lectures at Harvard. These paraphrases are similar to certain passages which occur in Santayana's *Life of Reason:*

"Illusions incident to mythology are not dangerous in the end, because illusion finds in experience a natural though painful cure. . . . A developed mythology shows that man has taken a deep and active interest both in the world and in himself, and has tried to link the two, and interpret the one to the other. Myth is therefore a natural prologue to philosophy, since the love of ideas is the root of both. Both are made up of things admirable to consider."

For Frost, so far so good. Santayana knew the seductive art of working from acceptable generalizations. But as Santayana continued, Frost could scarcely believe his ears, particularly when Santayana began to make specific applications:

"Nor is the illusion involved in fabulous thinking always so complete and opaque as convention would represent it. In taking fable for fact, good sense and practice seldom keep pace with dogma. There is always a race of pedants whose function it is to materialize everything ideal, but the great world, half shrewdly, half doggedly, manages to escape their contagion. . . . All the doctrines that have flourished in the world about immortality have hardly affected men's natural sentiment in the face of death, a sentiment which those doctrines, if taken seriously, ought wholly to reverse. Men almost universally have acknowledged a Providence, but that fact has had no force to destroy natural aversions and fears in the presence of events; and yet, if Providence had ever been really trusted, those preferences would have lapsed, being seen to be blind, rebellious, and blasphemous. Prayer, among sane people, has never superseded practical efforts to secure the desired end; a proof that the sphere of expression was never really confused with that of reality. Indeed, such a confusion, if it had passed from theory to practice, would have changed mythology into madness. With rare exceptions, this declension has not occurred and myths have been taken with a grain of salt which not only made them digestible, but heightened their savour."[22]

To Frost, utterances such as these amounted to downright blasphemy, and he was thoroughly shocked to hear them uttered. Nothing which Santayana could say to justify his own position was acceptable to Frost. "My naturalism or materialism," Santayana explained, "is no academic option . . . it is an everyday conviction which came to me, as it came to my father, from experience and observation of the world at large, and especially of my own feelings and passions. It seems to me that those who are not materialists cannot be good observers of themselves: they may hear themselves thinking, but they cannot have watched themselves acting and feeling . . ."

This kind of talk simply would not do, for Frost. He might have been attracted to Santayana's representation of philosophy as a literary act, created through the combined impulses of imagination and reason, if Santayana's detached and humorous and ironic viewpoint had not cut so squarely across the serious and inspirational exhortations of William James. Faced with the choice, Frost asserted his rightful will to believe in the utterances which had the greatest relevance to his immediate needs. Like James, Frost wanted to be "pluralistic" in the sense that he could combine naturalism and idealism, physics and metaphysics, skepticism and mysticism. It was a feat which he managed to maintain throughout the rest of his life, although the consequent fluctuations between these extremes produced some inconsistencies which puzzled him almost as much as they puzzled the intimate members of his family and, eventually, some of his readers.

Throughout the first semester of his sophomore year at Harvard, he applied himself to his studies in philosophy and in the classics with so much energy that when the usual time came for the ceremonies in Sanders Theatre, he was presented with a prize: a copy of John Selden's *Table Talk*—*pro insigni in studii diligentia*. He was proud of the honor, and yet he has already begun to feel that he might soon leave Harvard as unceremoniously as he had left Dartmouth. Elinor was again part of the cause for his uneasiness, and even for a renewed sense of guilt. Before the beginning of the school year she had told him that she was again with child and that it might be better for all concerned if she and Elliott stayed with her parents in Lawrence. As a result of that arrangement he had taken a room at 61 Oxford Street in Cambridge; but because he had agreed to assist his mother in giving night classes in her private school, one night a week, he made regular trips between Cambridge and Lawrence. Harvard had recently instituted the experiment of granting students "unlimited cuts," and Frost fell into the habit of lingering in Lawrence, during each visit, longer than he knew he should. Some embarrassment developed as a consequence. Once, after he had stayed away from Professor Babbitt's reading course in Homer, he returned apologetically to ask for his grade on an examination, and was disturbed to have Babbitt say, in handing him the paper, "I don't care how often a man is absent from my classes if he does this kind of work."

The remark was unintentionally ambiguous. Frost glanced at the paper apprehensively, and was relieved to find that his grade was "A."

Growing more bold in his prowling around the Harvard Yard during the spring semester of 1899, Frost audited the first lecture in a course devoted to John Milton, given by George Lyman Kittredge, newly appointed to the English Department. The hour began with a spirited reading of Milton's poem "On Time," and from the moment when Frost heard Kittredge read, "Fly, envious Time, till thou run out thy race," he was prepared to enjoy every minute of it. The poem was further enriched by Kittredge's way of going back over it, line by line, to point out the significance of images, figures, allusions. But just when Frost's pleasure had reached such a peak that he became curious to see how the other students were responding, he was dismayed to find that every head was bowed over notebooks in which the students were trying to record every single word. They seemed to feel that the ultimate test of their profit from such a course would be the proof they could give in the next examination that they had captured and memorized every one of Kittredge's observations and insights. Disgusted with this attitude toward the study of literature, Frost was content to let the first day with Kittredge be his last.

Quite different was his response to the celebrated lectures of Nathaniel Southgate Shaler on Historical Geology. The course opened up new vistas in time and space for Frost, and he stored up for future use as metaphors the various images of geological building, erosion, rebuilding. Here was science which interlocked also with his early passion for astronomy and with his later concern for the Darwinian concepts of evolution. Best of all, for him, was the grace with which Shaler seemed to give an esthetic quality to his lectures by casually unfolding and shaping his materials into carefully structured units.

Nevertheless, before the spring term was halfway through, Frost became increasingly troubled by many different things which made him feel he should not continue his studies. His mother needed him more and more to help her with the school; his wife became increasingly dependent on him as she drew nearer to the time when their second child was expected; and his own energies seemed to be placed under both physical and nervous strain. He was particularly worried by the recurrence of the same ailment which had overtaken him during the previous summer at Salisbury Point, and he could not help fearing that the doctor might have been correct in guessing that the ailment was tuberculosis.

Although he made up his mind to withdraw from Harvard without waiting to finish the year's work, he at least resisted the impulse to walk out once again without saying a word to anyone. On 31 March 1899, he stopped in at the office of Dean Briggs and was touched to hear the Dean say, with genuine sympathy, that he was sorry Frost felt he must leave, that he should not go without taking with him some kind of statement which might be useful in obtaining work as a teacher. While Frost waited, the Dean wrote a brief letter which said all that was needed, and more:

"I am glad to testify that your dismissal from College is honorable; that you have had excellent rank here, winning a Detur as a result of your first year's work; and that I am sorry for the loss of so good a student. I shall gladly have you refer to me for your College record."[23]

Armed with this letter, Frost made his departure from Harvard inspired with new hopes and beset by old fears. He was convinced that he had learned most from the man whose courses he had been unable to attend; but he was still uncertain whether he had the power to apply to his own predicament —his own failures, past and present—what he had learned. Recently, his discouraging illness had made him want to protest that during the ten years since the death of his father more than his share of hurt had come his way. It was not his fault, he told himself, that he had been treated as an unwanted outsider, uprooted from his native California, shunted around as a poor relative, insulted by the Salem people, and mocked at the start of his high-school years. All the way along he had struggled against these hurts and had tried as best he could to overcome them. He had worked hard for marks in high school, partly because he wanted to flaunt proof of his earned superiority and separateness. He had demonstrated his abilities; but at the very moment when he had gained confidence in himself, he had suffered a new sequence of hurts which had almost destroyed him.

How could he be blamed for what others had done to him?

His worst wounds had been caused by Elinor's apparent rejection. Nevertheless, James had shown him one way in which he could and should blame himself, at least in part. His own responses to disappointment—his own resentments and rages —were the immediate causes of his going to the edge of self-destruction. In that sense, then, he had been his own worst enemy.

Perhaps he had acquired from James new ways of confronting his inner and outer enemies; ways which justified sweeping aside the rubble of any idealistic notions, if they did not work for him; ways which required digging down to the bedrock of tested fact and then of rebuilding on that foundation. He hoped that henceforth he could be a realistic idealist. But at the same time he feared that he was running out of time for any kind of planning and rebuilding. The first real problem was his physical health, and if his trouble was consumption . . .

In spite of all that James had done for him, and all he had tried to do for himself, he was frightened now—worse than ever before.

GO OUT AND DIE

A voice said, Look me in the stars
And tell me truly, men of earth,
If all the soul-and-body scars
Were not too much to pay for birth.[1]

EARLY IN THE SPRING of 1899, and soon after he had returned to Lawrence from Harvard College, Robert Frost again
consulted his family physician. The doctor listened patiently to
the familiar review of symptoms which Frost had been reporting for several years. The puzzling thing about these symptoms, Frost said, was that they came and went so unpredict-
ably. This time, when they began all over again, he had been
living alone in his rented room on Oxford Street in Cambridge,
and he'd told himself that the only cause of his malaise was
Elinor's absence: he didn't like to live alone. He had gradually
been overwhelmed with a mounting sense of fatigue, which
had kept him from studying well. He had tried taking naps in
the daytime; he had tried going to bed early; but he never
seemed to get a restful sleep. Too often, he was troubled by
dreams, even nightmares, from which he awoke exhausted. At
other times he felt that his feet must still be chilled from the
well water he had bailed so desperately at Salisbury Point the
previous summer. Occasionally, even now, he felt the return of
the same old pains in his chest or stomach or solar plexus—
even the sharp knifelike line of pain across the lower part of
his chest. He had hoped his condition might improve as soon
as he resigned from Harvard. Instead, it had grown worse.[2]

The doctor, answering Frost's questions, said there was no
sure way of telling whether these troubles were caused by
nervous fatigue or by consumption. In either case, no cure
could be effected by medicine. The best remedy would be an

entire change in Frost's living habits. Sedentary work, either as a teacher or as a student, could only heighten the physical and nervous strain. It would be best if the young man could engage in some activity such as farming, which would keep him out-of-doors and give him plenty of exercise.

By this time Frost was so frightened that he was ready to accept the familiar advice. From his experiences as a farm-hand, however—first with Loren Bailey in Salem and then with Dinsmore at Cobbetts Pond—he thought his natural laziness would guide him to a special kind of farming, so that he might avoid some of the drudgery. During one of his walks for botanizing, he had gone up Prospect Street to the outskirts of Lawrence and into the Methuen countryside. Quite by accident he had casually noticed and admired an attractive arrangement of chicken coops in a field behind a house not far from the Merrill School, where his mother had first taught after leaving Salem. If Frost had to be a farmer, he supposed the least unpleasant specialty might be feeding chickens and collecting eggs. He could even claim that he had gained his first knowledge of a poultryman's life not merely from his Napa Valley experiences in California but actually from a little enterprise he had conducted in the back yard of the Leavenworth Street house on Nob Hill in San Francisco. Some friends of his parents had given him a few baby chicks for pets and he had been so delighted with them that he had taken full responsibility for building a box-shaped house with a fenced runway in the back yard. On cold nights he had even brought his pets into the kitchen. Under the present circumstances there could be no harm in taking another walk up Prospect Street to ask the advice of the Methuen farmer who seemed to be a very capable poultryman.

The farmer was a French-Canadian, a veterinarian by profession, called Dr. Charlemagne C. Bricault. A dapper little man, only seven years older than Frost, Bricault had been graduated from the Montreal division of Laval University in 1890, and had acquired an additional diploma from l'Ecole de Medicine Veterinaire de Montreal.[3] Glad to give advice to a prospective customer, he explained that his specialty was breeding pedigreed birds—some Barred Plymouth Rocks, mostly White Wyandottes—to increase egg-laying. By keeping records for each generation and by using trap-nests, he could prove that he was making gains. His roosters were all from hens which had laid two hundred or more eggs a year.

Impressed by what he saw and heard, Frost explained his interest and asked for prices. He was told that incubator eggs from Bricault's hens usually sold for the high price of ten cents apiece, but that if the visitor really wanted to start a good-sized brood of Wyandottes a better price could be given. Furthermore, Bricault promised that he would help to find markets for Frost's eggs and poultry. Statistics were cited to prove that if Frost seriously went into the business of raising Wyandottes, which were "bred to lay," he could be assured of making a very handsome profit on his investment.

With some wry hesitation Frost gradually convinced himself that because he wanted to carry out doctor's orders by earning an out-of-doors living, the possibility of becoming a farm-poultryman was not unappealing. Once again he swallowed his pride and called on his grandfather to ask the loan of enough money to get started. The two men spent some time making estimates and writing out figures for costs—including those for a year's rental of a suitable place in the neighborhood of Bricault's farm—and then William Prescott Frost made a formal business arrangement with his grandson. The money was lent, at interest, and promissory notes were drawn.

After a brief search for a place with plenty of room for hen coops and runways Frost found what he wanted at 67 Prospect Street in Methuen, a quarter-mile above a turnoff known as Marston's Corner, a mile or so to the north of Bricault's Prospect Street farm, and only about three miles from the center of Lawrence. The house and barn, perched on a gently sloping knoll called Powder House Hill, were backed by fields which could be used for movable chicken pens and shelters. The property commanded a pleasant view of surrounding meadows and woodlands. The owner was a spinster lady born in England, Miss Mary Mitchell, who agreed to rent part of her two-story, box-shaped Colonial house, with the understanding that she would keep some rooms for herself and share the kitchen.

By the time the Frosts moved into their new home there were four in the family: their nearly-three-year-old son, Elliott, now shared attentions with a baby sister named Lesley born in Lawrence on 28 April 1899.[4]

Rob immediately went to work with lumber, saw, hammer, nails to build shelters for the incubators. As soon as all was in

readiness Bricault delivered two hundred eggs, showed the
novice how to regulate the heat of the kerosene lamps, instructed him concerning the important ritual of turning each
egg once a day to improve the chances of proper hatching, and
promised to stand by in case of emergency. It was a humble
start in a new way of life, all necessitated by doctor's orders,
and yet Rob found it much to his liking. Before the eggs began
to hatch he had ample time for spring botanizing, particularly with an eye to orchids in the lowlands. All of these
activities had such a good effect on his health that he was
encouraged to think he might soon be cured of his mysterious
ailments.

His elation was soon marred by the serious illness of his
mother. When she had been deprived of his help in teaching
school, while he was at Harvard, Mrs. Frost had not seemed
strong enough to carry on well with Jeanie's assistance. The enrollment had fallen so sharply that she had been obliged to find
new and smaller quarters. At first they had moved the school
from the Haverhill Street house to rooms they rented on Jackson Street facing the Green, but after only one year there they
had moved again to even smaller quarters on Summer Street,
still less than a block from the Green. During the spring of
1899, Mrs. Frost had visibly lost weight and strength from
some kind of illness which she refused to discuss. Only after
her son insisted did she agree to seek medical advice. Her
doctor seemed worried, arranged for her to enter a hospital in
Boston for an exploratory operation, and thus confirmed what
she already suspected. She was dying of cancer in an advanced
stage, and the specialists said that she could not possibly live
more than a year. As soon as she was permitted to leave the
hospital she was invited to live with Rob and Elinor in their
new home on Powder House Hill. Jeanie closed the apartment
on Jackson Street and went to live with friends in Lawrence.

Well aware that her illness was fatal Mrs. Frost accepted it
with the same quiet serenity and courage she had shown during all the years since the death of her husband in San Francisco. Without bitterness she told her children that she found
the consolation she needed, in her religious belief, that she had
had enough of this life and was ready to "go home." She
seemed particularly interested, however, in her son's new activities as a poultryman and was pleased to watch the progress

of the flock as the chicks grew rapidly to pullets and, early in the fall of 1899, began to lay eggs.

Bricault kept his word, bought all the eggs Frost offered for sale, and made arrangements for taking the live "broilers" and "fryers." Frost could not bear to become involved in the butchering end of the business. As winter approached, he found that more work was required to make the coops winter-proof and to bed them down with leaves. Before long, he was shoveling paths through the snow to feed and tend his brood, yet he found that he enjoyed all these rituals. By the time spring came, he was even bold enough to decide that he wanted another batch of eggs for incubation, and so closely did Bricault work with him that there was a sense of partnership in the whole enterprise. Rob's health continued to improve; the prospects for a steady increase of his financial returns were at least calculable; and within little more than a year after he had begun this new way of life he found good reason for thinking that his decision had been a wise one.

A pleasant interlude, during January of 1900, led Frost to cross verbal swords with his older friend, Carl Burell, over the question of optimism, physical and metaphysical. Long before Carl's accident in the box factory, he had renounced his religious faith and had intermittently yielded to periods of depression. In their letters and conversations these two men, who had cemented their friendship years earlier, through their readings aloud from American humorists like Mark Twain, Artemus Ward, and Petroleum V. Nasby, had amicably joshed each other concerning their differences of opinion in politics and religious matters.

No joke, Carl's final contribution to the Lawrence *High School Bulletin* after he had left school was a poem entitled "Non Beatus Novus Annus." In it, he had seriously devoted all four stanzas to complaints against the "emptiness" of the Old Year and had concluded by implying that if the New Year could bring nothing better, Carl would ask no more of it than death:

> *But if thou art like the last,*
> THIS *we wish, ere thou art passed:*
> *Destiny may let us go,*
> *Somewhere, we don't care or know,*
>   *Out of this.*[5]

Frost might have confided to Burell that there had frequently been times when he had shared this feeling that death might be more attractive than life. But in January of 1900, while his hopes were in an ascendent state, he found a way of mocking Carl's atheistic negations. He did it by sending Carl a sequence of limericks which reflected the spirit of badinage long maintained between them. As he had done on previous occasions,[6] Frost shaped this casual literary effort into a hand-stitched pamphlet which bore a suitable title page:

A Young Man from Podunk

Or

The Young Atheist Goes to Seek His Fortunes

Or

An Overdose of Alcoholic Encouragement

Or

The Foundations of Belief Unshaken

In the pamphlet following the title Frost devoted a separate page to each limerick, and decorated the lower part of each with an appropriate sketch or illustration. Here is the sequence:

There was a young man from Podunk
Who thought any man was a lunk
To worship as God
A recognized fraud
And he wanted to say what he thunk.

There was a young man from Podunk
Who took a few drops for his spunk
And wrote to some people
With bats in their steeple
To learn if they cared what he thunk.

There was a young man from Podunk

[255]

Who packed his ideas in a trunk
And took the express
  For the scene of distress
Where they waited to hear what he thunk.

There was a young man from Podunk
Who started to say what he thunk
But they offered a cent
  To know what he meant
And he said "I don't know for I'm drunk."[7]

Carl was certainly able to sort out the underlying seriousness from the surface nonsense of the limericks. He lacked the
skill of his younger friend in nonsense-rhyming, but he answered in kind as well as he could. His title page:

A Young Man from Harvard

A

parody on "A Young Man
from Podunk"

Or

a discouragement to botanizing

Or

a plea in favor of boxmaking

Without taking the trouble to refine his expression with any
show of even his limited literary abilities Carl scratched off his
counter-nonsense:

There was a young man without an[y] chink
Who tried to think that he didn't think
Though from Harvard [he] came
Yet all the same
The blooming cuss did think.

Now this young cuss had lots of spunk

For he kept thinking he didn't thunk
And that it was safe
For a man to have faith
In a god (or a goddess)
Who gave him the wunk.

Now this young man with a knowing wunk
Up and tried to say what he didn't thunk
And thus became grieved
Since no one believed
He was either a fool or drunk.[8]

The seriousness veiled in this exchange of views adequately represented the fixed line of battle between these two friends. While neither one of them gave any ground openly, even during their periods of inner fluctuation, they apparently called a truce. As it happened, however, their verbal counterpunching in January of 1900 was soon followed by several experiences which very deeply—and yet only temporarily—caused Frost's views to coincide with Burell's.

Early in the summer of 1900 the Frost household on Powder House Hill was distressed by a very serious illness which overtook their nearly four-year-old-son, Elliott. Until this time he had seemed to come through all the ailments of babyhood and childhood with surprising ease. As soon as he had learned to walk he become a companion to his father and he liked to make occasional trips to the chicken coops to feed and water the two generations of Wyandottes. For a full year the child's grandmother had been helping to care for Elliott, much to the relief of Elinor, who had her hands full with her baby girl. It was from his grandmother that Elliott heard many of the same Bible stories which Jeanie and Rob had heard when they were young, and the effect showed in some of the child's treasured utterances. One of them had been made not long after his third birthday, when he was taken by his grandmother to visit the Holmes family on the bank of the Merrimack River in Lawrence. Entrusted to the care of Susan, young daughter of the Holmes's, he had been led on an adventurous walk among the flowerbeds under a lowering sky. Unexpectedly, the sunlight broke through the clouds just enough to drench the lawn. Elliott stopped, smiled, looked up at the sky, and said, "God is smiling at us."[9] When Susan shared the anecdote with her parents, after the visitors were gone, there was general agreement that Elliott had not learned that expression from his mother, who showed no taste for religious matters, or from his father, whose religious leanings were said to have been negatively influenced at Harvard.[10] But it was this kind of charm that heightened everyone's love for Elliott.

So when he became seriously ill, in July of 1900, the entire household at Marston's Corner was darkened. Rob's mother, regularly visited by a doctor, got the first medical advice concerning the child. Her doctor examined Elliott and left some homeopathic pills, which were given without improvement. The child soon grew so much worse that his parents called their own doctor. The stern old man came, examined the child, and seemed to be annoyed that he had not been called sooner. With harsh reproach, he turned from the bed, faced the parents, and said, "This is *cholera infantum*. It's too late, now, for me to do anything. The child will be dead before morning."

Elliott died that night, and the shock of his death crushed his parents beneath a grief that seemed unbearable. Rob blamed himself, and said he had been guilty of neglect which amounted to murder. By failing to call the doctor he had in effect killed his own son. Frantically, he kept saying that this was God's just punishment of him.

Elinor suffered inconsolably and in silence for days. When she could finally bear to talk, she reproved Rob for saying that this was God's punishment. How could he, at a time like this, be so unreasoning and so self-centered as to wallow in thoughts of punishment for himself, without seeing the injustice in the notion that the child's life had been taken from the child—and from her—as a way of punishing him? How could he think there was any divine justice or any benevolent oversight of human affairs. There was no God, she said; there couldn't be. The world was completely evil, and she hated all life that was left, including her own.

For the time, at least, her husband was inclined to agree with her, and his bitterness provided the notion of metaphysical indifference in the ending of a poem he may have started a winter or two earlier. When it was finally published in *A Boy's Will*, the poem was entitled merely "Stars." But the gloss on it, in the table of contents, amounted to his own bitter restatement of Elinor's dark words: "There is no oversight of human affairs."

> *How countlessly they congregate*
> *O'er our tumultuous snow,*
> *Which flows in shapes as tall as trees*
> *When wintry winds do blow!—*
>
> *As if with keenness for our fate,*
> *Our faltering few steps on*
> *To white rest, and a place of rest*
> *Invisible at dawn,—*
>
> *And yet with neither love nor hate,*
> *Those stars like some snow-white*
> *Minerva's snow-white marble eyes*
> *Without the gift of sight.*[11]

Still crushed by the anguish of their loss, Rob continued his task of tending his chickens and Elinor went on caring for their fourteen-month-old daughter, Lesley. It seemed to both of them that they had lost whatever meaning or purpose or direction life might have had, and that it was only with indifference that they could perform their daily obligations. It even seemed unimportant to Rob that all of his old ailments suddenly returned, that his sleep was wracked with nightmares, that he frequently awoke to find his nightgown discolored from heavy sweating, that his old sense of weakness overtook him, that the cold returned to his feet, that the pains returned like knives in his stomach, solar plexus, chest. As the summer dragged on and the hay-fever season returned, his ailments pointed, at least in part, to a diagnosis of tuberculosis. During the previous summer he had suffered some distress from hay fever, for the first time; but in the summer of 1900, he found that pollen dust seemed to poison him, until he was almost exhausted with choking, coughing, sneezing, crying.

In the midst of these troubles, as Rob's mother became steadily weaker, her doctor tried to encourage her with reports that some miraculous cures for cancer had been effected in a sanitarium which was not far away. Although it is doubtful whether Mrs. Frost took these positive statements seriously she permitted her son to make arrangements for her to be entered as a patient at the Alexander Sanitorium in Penacook, New Hampshire, that summer.

Jeanie, who had found work in Boston, visited her mother faithfully and as often as she could, while complaining bitterly to her brother that he had taken the poor woman to Penacook just to get her out of his house, out of sight, out of mind. Rob tried to explain his own predicament, but nothing he could say to Jeanie seemed to alleviate her hostility. Each had a knack for infuriating the other during even their briefest conversations.

While all these troubles were proliferating, their landlady announced that she had tolerated the Frosts long enough in her home; that they were so far behind in paying rent that she wanted them to get out, before fall, and to take with them the hundreds of chickens that were permitted to invade every sanctuary on her property, including her house. It was true that by this time there were nearly three hundred White Wyandottes prowling over Miss Mary Mitchell's premises, and that the spinster had good reason for losing patience with her tenants.[12]

At the same time, Frost knew that he needed more space in which his flock of hens and pullets could range. When he consulted the real-estate agent who had previously given him help, he was told that a Lawrence man (an acquaintance of Frost's grandfather) had rented a farm too large for his needs in the town of Pelham, which bordered on the western side of Methuen over the state line in New Hampshire and yet only a few miles from the center of Lawrence. With the real-estate agent, Frost made the brief trip to Pelham, looked at the farm, talked with the man who was renting it, and offered to pay him a month's rental of $30 if he would vacate it by the first of October. The promise was accepted, although no money changed hands, and Frost went back to prepare for the move.

In the meantime, and on her own initiative, Elinor's mother had been asking questions about other farms which might be rented or bought. She had learned that an unusually attractive property of thirty acres, with a relatively new house and barn, was on the market in the town of Derry, New Hampshire, just to the north of Salem, and she was very anxious that Elinor and Rob should look at it before they came to any decision. Elinor made the next important move by going alone to visit

Rob's grandfather. She may have explained that Rob's health seemed so precarious that he needed special consideration; but, whatever she said, she was so persuasive that he offered to buy the Derry farm for his grandson if, after careful inspection, it seemed to be worth the price.

Rob was not impressed with the generosity of his grandfather's offer; instead, his immediate response was resentment. Repeatedly he made the unjust claim that his grandfather's offer to set him up on the Derry farm was a way of saying, "Go on out and die. Good riddance to you. You've been nothing except a bother to me, for years, and you're not worth anything except as a disappointment."[13]

The lack of communication with his grandfather was tied in with resentments which had already paved the way to another gradual descent toward suicide. Part of the immediate trouble was hay fever, which made him feel so miserable that he could easily transfer resentment to anyone or anything around him. Closely related was the unhealed wound of his grief over Elliott's death. Inseparable from that grief was his puzzled awareness that his relationship with Elinor had not developed as he had hoped. He was now convinced that he loved her much more than she loved him. Underlying all these fears and resentments were his ingrained responses. Impatient with conflicts between what he wanted and what he had, he more than ever resented his need to depend on the generosity of his grandfather.

Even the possibility of the move to a Derry farm caused him contradictory emotions of elation and resentment. His grandfather, too old to make the inspection trip, enlisted the aid of the more sprightly Elihu Colcord. A shrewd politician, experienced in appraising real estate, "Uncle Elihu" hired a carriage and took Rob and Elinor with him when he made the twelve-mile drive from Lawrence through Methuen and Salem to the township of Derry. The farm was locally known as "the Magoon place," the reference being to a former owner. They found it on the Londonderry turnpike, two miles south-southeast of Derry Village, and they were immediately delighted with it. The small house, shed, and barn, completely isolated in a serene country setting, seemed to snuggle down between the protecting hills and ridges which flanked it on the north and south. The large bay window at the front of the house faced west and overlooked two small pastures, which were part of the property. The house itself—gable-roofed, with white clapboards and green blinds newly painted, and with a good porch on the southern side—was conveniently connected with the barn through the shed. The approach to the front of the house from the turnpike was flanked by a pair of young apple trees—a Gravenstein and a Baldwin—the branches heavy with fruit not quite ripe for picking. A good-sized orchard of apple trees and a vegetable garden stood to the north of the house. Behind the barn, to the east, a long hay-field stretched back toward a hardwood grove or woodlot, which also belonged with the farm.

To the south, between the house and the long ridge which crested in a knoll at the turnpike roadside, alders concealed a small west-running brook, which drained out of a little cranberry bog. The little brook, flowing under the turnpike through a culvert, was fed by a pasture spring. The lowlands in the neighborhood of the cranberry bog suggested places where orchis might be found blooming in season.

Close against the southern side of the barn, patches of cultivated raspberries and blackberries flourished. A former owner, having worked for years in a fruit nursery before retiring there, had improved the little farm by setting out a few peach, pear, and quince trees. Rob immediately saw the possibility of using the orchard and at least part of the long hayfield behind the barn as places where coops could be built and hens could be permitted to run without too much need for fencing—if one were willing to risk the depredations of hawks and foxes.

Inside the house Elinor and Rob studied the arrangements with satisfaction. The granite steps, which led up to the roof-covered front door, were at the extreme northern side of the western exposure. The door opened into an entryway from which stairs on the left led to three second-floor bedrooms; a door on the right gave access to the bay-windowed parlor, from which another window looked out on the piazza to the south. Beyond the parlor a door led to a living-dining room with three other doorways: one opened to the piazza, another door gave access to a corner bedroom, another led to the ell which housed the kitchen, the pantry, the grain shed, the privy. There were three windows in the kitchen ell, one facing south toward the alders, one facing north toward the vegetable garden, one facing east toward the hayfields and the dark trees of the woodlot.

Isabelle Moodie, c. 1872

William Prescott Frost, Jr., 1872

Robert Lee Frost
(age seven months)

Jeanie and Robert Frost
(one year, three months; two years, eight months)

Robert and Jeanie Frost, c. 1879

Isabelle Moodie Frost, 1876

Part of Mrs. Frost's Salem School class, 1887

front row, extreme left: Jeanie Frost
front row, extreme right: Sabra Peabody
back row, wearing hat: Robert Lee Frost

Robert Lee Frost, 1892

Elinor Miriam White, 1892

Elinor Miriam White, 1895

Robert Lee Frost, 1895

Robert Frost raking hay
(Derry farm, 1908)

The Frost children at the Derry farm, 1908
(Marjorie, Lesley, Irma, Carol)

Robert Frost at Pinkerton Academy, 1910

Robert and Elinor Frost at Plymouth, N. H., 1911

The Frost children at Plymouth, N. H., 1911

Lesley

Carol

Marjorie   Irma

Robert Frost in England, 1913

Elinor and Rob, thoroughly satisfied, reveled in the possibilities even while the suspicious "Uncle Elihu" grumbled over details, poked his cane into foundation timbers, critically tried the pump in the dooryard, and sniffed at the water he caught in a tin cup. His final conclusion was that the asking price of $1,700 would be fair enough, and that he would recommend Rob's grandfather agree to add $25 more for the few tons of hay in the barn loft.

On the return trip to Lawrence, "Uncle Elihu" may have explained to Rob that the title to the property would be held in the name of the purchaser, William P. Frost.[14] He may even have hinted that someone like Carl Burell would be needed as a helper for a year or so, until Rob had learned more about how to run a farm. Colcord may also have hinted that Grandfather Frost had suspicions that Rob's previous and brief experiments with so many occupations might foreshadow the temporariness of this latest splurge in poultry-farming. Of course, Rob and Elinor would need a horse and carriage for travel into Derry Depot, which was nearer than Derry Village for shopping; they would also need a cow.

Soon after the visit to the Magoon place in Derry, Rob's grandfather began the legal proceedings for its purchase. He also got in touch with Carl Burell and asked if he would be willing to help the younger people get started on the farm. Still working in the shook factory and living in East Pembroke, only two townships to the north and west of Derry, Carl replied that he would be delighted to accept the offer, if he could bring with him his eighty-four-year-old grandfather, Jonathan Eastman, in whose home Rob had spent Thanksgiving Day of 1892.

Although Rob grudgingly accepted all of these arrangements, he was furious with his grandfather and with Carl when the two men worked out satisfactory terms without really consulting him. Carl and "Jont" Eastman were to be given rooms on the second floor of the small house and were to eat their meals with the Frosts. Carl was to have charge of the cow, the horse, the fruit trees, and the vegetable garden. His financial returns would come from whatever he could realize on the sale of fruit and vegetables. It was understood that Rob would thus be free to devote most of his time to the care of poultry, from which he would realize his profits.

That the arrangement seemed sensible enough to other members of the family merely heightened Rob's resentment. Carl was indeed a good friend, a hard worker, a conscientious human being. But ever since high-school days he had treated Rob solicitously, as though Rob didn't even know how to sharpen a pencil. Now he joined in a "conspiracy" with Rob's grandfather without even asking the person most concerned. "I take a long time to wreak vengeance, when I've been wronged," Frost later said of this arrangement, "but I never forget, and I never forgive a wrong."[15]

Carl was completely unaware that in trying to help his friend, he was letting himself in for what Rob liked to view as fair punishment. But the move to Derry was made around October first, and the event was at least partially (and inaccurately) noted in *The Derry News* for 5 October 1900: "R. Frost has moved upon the Magoon place which he recently bought. He has a flock of nearly 300 Wyandotte fowls."[16]

From the beginning Carl took charge in his cheerful way— and it was well that he did. Rob felt so completely worn out by the task of moving from Methuen to Derry that he immediately needed aid in building new coops for the Wyandottes. Before long Carl and Jont were helping to pack eggs in boxes and load live "broilers" into crates for the regular visits of Charlemagne Bricault, who continued to handle the "selling end" of the poultry business. Using money provided by Frost's grandfather, Carl was the one who found and bought a Jersey cow from a neighboring farmer. He had also helped to buy a horse and the harness needed—and a democrat wagon—from a Lawrence livery stable.

In short order Carl and Jont harvested the good crop of apples, sorted them into barrels, found a buyer in Boston, and shipped the barrels off by express. The new life at the Magoon place seemed to be settling into a smoothly running routine, and neighboring farmers were quick to say that Carl was the kind of man who could really make the work fly. Each morning he was up with the sun—the roosters were his alarm clock, he said. Before breakfast he milked the cow, turned her out to pasture across the road, strained the milk, poured it into pails, placed the pails on the shelves in the cellar, started the fire in the kitchen stove, scalded out his milking bucket, and even made a start at collecting the eggs. Rob's gratitude was immense. It was equalled only by his resenting this clumsy crip-

ple, whose good-natured efficiency heightened Rob's sense of
his own ignorance and laziness.

The first visitor who stayed overnight at the Frost farm in
Derry was Jeanie, who seemed to come not so much out of
love or curiosity but to scold her brother because he had let
weeks go by without making the short trip to Penacook where
their mother was slowly dying. It was easy enough to make
excuses, but after Jeanie's prodding, Rob did get up there just
once. His mother, completely bedridden by this time and
wasted away to such an extent that her face was unpleasantly
cadaverous, showed the same serene resignation Rob had admired for so many years. In her attempts to console her son and
daughter-in-law after the death of Elliott, she had become
thoroughly familiar with their scorn for religious matters. She
was even aware that Rob had expressed his disbelief in any life
after death, and she smiled confidently at him as she said that
very soon she would know whether he was right or wrong on
that point.

None of her friends or relatives was with her when she died
in the sanitorium at Penacook. Funeral services were held in
Lawrence; her Swedenborgian pastor, John Hayes, paid tribute to her as 'one to whom religion was a way of life"; and her
Swedenborgian friends joined the family in taking her coffin to
the hilltop cemetery in Lawrence, where she was buried between the graves of her husband and her grandchild, Elliott.[17]

Another early visitor at the Derry farm was Elinor's mother,
the indefatigable Mrs. White, who took a sense of pride in
having first learned about the Magoon place. She knew that
her daughter was not a good housekeeper, and yet she was
surprised to discover that even after the Frosts had been settled on the Derry farm for weeks no curtains had been hung in
the windows, no rugs had been spread on the floor, no furniture had been arranged in the living room. Elinor's plea was
that she had been too busy to bother with frills, too busy
caring for the baby, too busy getting meals and washing dishes
for three hungry men. There were deeper reasons, mutely expressed in Elinor's manner of listless indifference, and her
mother must have understood them.

To Rob it seemed at times that his wife and grandfather
must have arrived at a secret agreement that this Derry venture would not last long, that not many months would pass
before another grave would be dug and filled. His physical

exhaustion, brought on by even a minimum of work in collecting eggs, carrying water, scattering grain was enough to make him prey to a welter of annoyances which aroused new resentments.

Late in the fall of 1900, he was particularly annoyed by threats relayed to him from Lawrence: the farmer in Pelham was planning to bring suit for violation of Rob's promise to rent his house. The farmer and his wife had carried out their part of the agreement and, in the course of moving, the farmer's wife had hurt her back so seriously that she felt justified in suing Frost for damages. The real-estate agent in Lawrence felt that if Frost paid the promised $30 quickly, the Pelham people might be quieted. But Frost, having already spent the cash his grandfather had advanced for the move to Derry, simply did not have $30 immediately available. He dreaded the awkwardness of going back to ask for more money, and yet there seemed to be no other way of handling the problem.

Irked by the inconvenience of the journey, Rob asked Carl's help in harnessing the horse and hitching him to the democrat wagon on a lowering cold morning. Repeatedly cursing himself and the Pelham farmer during the long drive down to Lawrence, Rob was braced for all the moral precepts his grandfather was bound to unload. The scolding was even worse than he had anticipated, and the $30 was given with obvious reluctance. As the two men parted, Rob again felt that his grandfather was saying under his breath, "Good riddance. Go on out and die."

During the drive from Lawrence to Pelham, a bleak wind began to blow fine flakes of the year's first snowfall, and Rob could feel the chill penetrating to his bones so ominously that he imagined his grandfather's unspoken wish might be carried out before the day was over. It was nearly suppertime before he reached Pelham, and his enemies there were so hostile to him, even after he had paid the $30, that he was glad to get out of their house in the dusk and start the long drive back to Derry. As the darkness settled in the wind-blown snow felt like fine sand against his face. Snow began to pile and drift in the road just enough to hinder the tired horse and threaten serious difficulties. Rob lost his way in the dark, had to stop at a farmhouse to ask for directions, grew more and more miserable as he got closer to home, and finally drove into his barn near midnight sick with rage and disgust. All fall he had been suffering acutely from something like a continuation of hay fever and now it seemed probable that the chill of this outrageous excursion would lay him low with pneumonia.

He escaped that, but he could not escape from the debilitating effects of his emotional strains. In his lowest moments, when he felt particularly miserable, he told himself that maybe it was just as well that he should die soon and get it over with. He didn't care, if Elinor didn't care; he didn't care, if God didn't care. More than once he told himself sarcastically that he knew God did care; this was all part of the punishment meted out to him because of the way he had treated his wife, his mother, his sister. Self-abasement and guilt accumulated in him until it became a despairing kind of self-hatred. Overwhelmed, he found that he didn't even want to struggle any longer against the waves of pain and sickness which washed over him. And why wait for this lingering death when there were easier ways to the same end. Each time he drove from his farm with his old horse and wagon along the back-country road to Derry Depot for provisions, he passed an isolated pond deep enough for drowning.[18]

During the late fall and early winter he found that the temptation was becoming more and more attractive. Although none of his moods had found outlet in poetry since he left Methuen, this one did. It inspired a dark sonnet into which he poured thoughts of suicidal death by drowning. He called the sonnet "Despair":

> *I am like a dead diver after all's*
> *Done, still held fast in the weeds' snare below,*
> *Where in the gloom his limbs begin to glow*
> *Swaying at his moorings as the roiled bottom falls.*
> *There was a moment when with vainest calls*
> *He drank the water, saying, "Oh let me go—*
> *God let me go!"—for then he could not know*
> *As in the sun's warm light on earth and walls.*
>
> *I am like a dead diver in this place.*
> *I was alive here too one desperate space,*
> *And near prayer in the one whom I invoked.*
> *I tore the muscles from my limbs and choked.*
> *My sudden struggle may have dragged down some*
> *White lily from the air—and now the fishes come.*[19]

The mood of "Despair" vividly reflected his almost over-whelming certainty that circumstances left him with no favorable outcome. He had hoped to accomplish so much, back on that day of his greatest triumph when he had figuratively unveiled a monument to after-thought and poetry. He had even seemed to be well started on the road he had chosen, when *The Independent* printed "My Butterfly: An Elegy." Now it all seemed elegy in the sense of lament for ideals lost in the degradation of chicken manure and cow manure and horse manure on a back-country farm. The question that he framed in all but words was what to make of a diminished thing.

But it was all his own fault, he told himself; he deserved the punishment he was receiving. His illness could be suffered with, to the end, if it were not for his guilt in feeling that somehow he had unintentionally betrayed and disappointed the one he loved. Elinor was the one whom he invoked in unspoken words which came near to prayer. She was also the white lily whom he had dragged down with him as he sank.

FACT AS DREAM

Anything more than the truth would have seemed
too weak
To the earnest love that laid the swale in rows,
Not without feeble-pointed spikes of flowers
(Pale orchises), and scared a bright green snake.
The fact is the sweetest dream that labor knows.
My long scythe whispered and left the hay to make.[1]

IN RETROSPECT, Robert Frost could never understand how or why he managed to climb out of his despairing preoccupation with suicide during the first phase of his life on the farm in Derry. He did not feel that any particular event or person saved his life. No bolt of lightning fell through the darkness to show him a path toward recovery. No immediate improvement in his health invigorated him with new hope. During the long first winter, he continued to suffer with mingled feelings of anger, resentment, and hopelessness. Almost luxuriating in his miseries, he seemed to hate most those who tried their best to help him. He also hated those distant friends and relatives who had apparently crossed him off as a disappointing failure. He could not say why he bothered to keep going through the daily routine of getting up, shoveling snow to get to the pump, carrying pails of water across a kitchen floor so cold that spilled water froze on it, feeding his poultry, collecting fewer and fewer eggs, begrudging the cheerful assistance of Carl Burell and old Jont Eastman, listening to the homely talk of those two men as they sat around the kitchen stove during winter evenings, worrying over the sight and sound of wind-blown snow, and crawling into bed, night after night, exhausted.

Even in these days of hopelessness, he could at least be

inconsistent enough to remember his former hope that somehow, sometime, he could get back to his writing. It may have
been almost in the manner of a New Year's resolution, or as a
salute to the new century, that he set to work one evening
after everyone else was in bed, copying fresh drafts of old
poems and enclosing them with the following letter (dated 15
January 1901), to send to Susan Hayes Ward in far-away New
York City:

"Perhaps you will care to know how authorship progresses. I
send you this selection from the poems I have been writing
with a view to a volume some day. If you can use it I shall be
glad to have you."[2]

One of the poems in this selection was "The Quest of the
Orchis." Miss Ward liked it and accepted it for publication,
saving the lines until she could give them a timely appearance
at exactly the moment in spring when the purple-fringed
orchis should be in bloom. But during the next five years she
received no other poem from this correspondent, who claimed
he was "writing with a view to a volume some day." Although
he occasionally and furtively continued writing, always at
night, when nobody could see him, he kept the poems to himself.

Another change occurred in his attitude when he began to
notice evidence that the long winter was being broken by the
first signs of spring. He could not resist the lift he felt when he
saw how the March sunlight, still bleak, had power enough to
melt windswept patches of ice and to uncover the ground.
With exultation he watched for signs that warm rains and
winds were gradually defeating a stubborn enemy, and the
pleasure he took in all of these was akin to the excitement he
expressed, a few years later, in the lines entitled "To the Thawing Wind":

Come with rain, O loud Southwester!
Bring the singer, bring the nester;
Give the buried flower a dream;
Make the settled snowbank steam;
Find the brown beneath the white;
But whate'er you do tonight,
Bathe my window, make it flow,
Melt it as the ice will go;
Melt the glass and leave the sticks

Like a hermit's crucifix;
Burst into my narrow stall;
Swing the picture on the wall;
Run the rattling pages o'er;
Scatter poems on the floor;
Turn the poet out of door.[3]

He welcomed the first robin; he admired the first green spike of skunk cabbage pushing up through dead and matted leaves in the alders beside the brook. Nor could he help but warm to Carl's almost childish excitement over the first color in swelling buds on the branches of the fruit trees, Carl's first discovery of windflowers in bloom; Carl's triumph in scooping out of the pasture mud, with his bare hands, the first brave cluster of bluets or "innocents," roots and all, to be brought into the house and placed in a saucer on the kitchen table.

Carl's eye had an experienced way of knowing just when and where to look for every new blossom as the spring flowers began to make their processional appearance. His enthusiasm and excitement filled him with such recklessness that he was quick to take off his boots and socks, impatient to get his trousers rolled, and careless of his bare feet as he waded into the spring-flooded alder swamp to pick the earliest orchis. At the very time when he and Rob knew they should be tending to farm work, they joined forces in digging up clusters of adder's tongue, lady's slipper, yellow violets, jack-in-the-pulpit so they could carry each one gently on a shovel, for transplanting in just the right amount of wetness beside the brook or along the edge of the alders.

When the warm April sunlight gave Elinor a chance to get out-of-doors with comfort, she yielded to the coaxing of these two farm-neglecters and skirted quagmires of mud to walk down across the pasture and watch them clean the bubbling spring. Lesley, having achieved the triumph of getting about well enough on her own feet, accompanied them on these walks. Sometimes she rode perched on her father's shoulder. It was his pleasure to show her new leaves when they were no bigger than the ears of a mouse, and to pick the first dandelion, which had to be held under her chin to see if she liked butter. Lesley's wide-eyed wonder was a redeeming joy in itself.

There were moments during the first spring on the Derry farm when Rob's old moods of darkness returned to mar the most perfect days. But part of the lasting change which gradually overtook the farmer-poultryman-poet, without his being aware of any effort on his part, was simply his discovery that it was good to be alive, after all, for another springtime. Almost with a sense of surprise he found that he cared for things and people more than he thought he could ever again care. When the fruit trees came in bloom—making their own procession of cherry and pear and apple and quince blossoms—he found himself wandering through the orchard as though it were a new Garden of Eden. This act of cherishing was only the least bit dimmed by noticing that the conscientious Carl had harnessed the horse to the plow and had begun to turn over soil for the vegetable gardens.

Even Frost's reading came to his rescue. Probably with the aid of Carl, or perhaps following the lead provided by quotations in Mrs. Dana's flower book, he had begun his acquaintance with Thoreau's *Walden*. It gave him all the encouragement he needed for doing and not doing things which, he well knew, his grandfather would never understand:

"Let us settle ourselves, and work and wedge our feet downward through the mud and slush of opinion, and prejudice, and tradition, and delusion, and appearance . . . through poetry and philosophy and religion, till we come to a hard bottom and rocks in place, which we can call *reality*, and say, This is, and no mistake; and then begin, having a *point d'appui*, below freshet and frost and fire, a place where you might found a wall or a state . . . If you stand right fronting and face to face to a fact, you will see the sun glimmer on both its surfaces, as if it were a cimeter, and feel its sweet edge dividing you through the heart and marrow, and so you will happily conclude your mortal career. Be it life or death, we crave only reality. If we are really dying, let us hear the rattle in our throats and feel cold in the extremities; if we are alive, let us go about our business."[4]

Thoreau even helped him understand more clearly what the business of the poet really was:

"I went to the woods because I wished to live deliberately, to front only the essential facts of life, and see if I could not learn what it had to teach, and not, when I came to die, discover that I had not lived. I did not wish to live what was not life, living is so dear; nor did I wish to practise resignation, unless it was quite necessary. I wanted to live deep and suck out all the marrow of life, to live so sturdily and Spartan-like as to put to rout all that was not life, to cut a broad swath and shave close, to drive life into a corner, and reduce it to its lowest terms, and, if it proved to be mean, why then to get the whole and genuine meanness of it, and publish its meanness to the world; or if it were sublime, to know it by experience, and be able to give a true account of it in my next excursion. For most men, it appears to me, are in a strange uncertainty about it, whether it is of the devil or of God, and have *somewhat hastily* concluded that it is the chief end of man here to 'glorify God and enjoy him forever.' "5

Frost understood Thoreau's insistence that the contemplation of facts was for him the best form of religious worship. Having been forced by circumstance to see himself driven into a corner and reduced to lowest terms, Frost had known moments when he had denied that there was any oversight of human affairs or any reason for reverence. But all of the deeply ingrained elements of religious belief in his nature were stimulated anew by the experiences of the first spring on the Derry farm. Thoreau's way of talking about facts could not help but remind him of Emerson's "there is no fact in nature which does not carry the whole sense of nature . . ."6 Emerson had also said that the farmer makes worshipful responses to facts:

" . . . His worship is sympathetic; he has no present definitions, but he is commanded in nature by the living power which he feels to be there present. No imitation or playing of these things would content him; he loves the earnest of the north wind, of rain, of stone and wood and iron. A beauty not explicable is dearer than a beauty which we can see to the end of. It is nature the symbol, nature certifying the supernatural, body overflowed by life which he worships with coarse, but sincere rites."7

Emerson had even spelled out more clearly what Thoreau had only implied concerning the contemplation of fact as involving a form of prayer:

"Prayer is the contemplation of the facts of life from the highest point of view. It is the soliloquy of a beholding and jubilant soul. It is the spirit of God pronouncing his works good. . . . As soon as the man is at one with God, he will not beg. He will then see prayer in all action. The prayer of the farmer kneeling in his field to weed it, the prayer of the rower kneeling with the stroke of his oar, are true prayers heard throughout nature . . ."[8]

When Frost took these familiar ideas into reconsideration during the spring of 1901, he was approaching them from that new direction which had stripped life down to the foundation of very hard fact. In the vicissitudes of religious belief and denial, he had warmed and cooled toward all his mother had taught him since childhood concerning the notion that human life had begun in the perfection of the Earthly Paradise, that through the mistakes of man it had suffered a woeful diminishment which would persist until the divine winnowing process rewarded the worthy with the perfection of the Heavenly Paradise. In spite of all that he had heard Santayana say at Harvard, Frost still liked the poetry in this way of looking at experience. But having recently gone through so many new trials, he was more than ever inclined to build his new attitude on Thoreau's phrase. Having reduced life to its lowest terms, and having been given the choice of death or life, he had found that he preferred to stay alive. More than that, he found that his irrational acts of caring and cherishing were signs of his willingness to settle for imperfection, including the wistfulness of loving one who might not love him as much as he loved her. Whatever the limitations of circumstance, including his health and his questionable capacities, he was ready to go about his business as hen-man and farmer and poet. There was at least the possibility of improvement, even as for him spring was such an improvement over winter.

These thoughts were still in a state of flux as he settled back into his routine of obligations. But the big change, which meant the most to him, involved his new depth of pleasure in caring and cherishing. It expressed itself in the humble duties of caring for the hens and the newly-hatched chicks, even in swinging a scythe—as he later explained in his poem entitled "Mowing":

> There was never a sound beside the wood but one,
> And that was my long scythe whispering to the
> > ground.
> What was it it whispered? I knew not well myself;
> Perhaps it was something about the heat of the sun,
> Something, perhaps, about the lack of sound—
> And that was why it whispered and did not speak.
> It was no dream of the gift of idle hours,

Or easy gold at the hand of fay or elf:
Anything more than the truth would have seemed
too weak
To the earnest love that laid the swale in rows,
Not without feeble-pointed spikes of flowers
(Pale orchises), and scared a bright green snake.
The fact is the sweetest dream that labor knows.
My long scythe whispered and left the hay to make.[9]

In the summer of 1901, while Frost was still trying to explain to himself his new attitude toward life and death, his grandfather gave him another fact to think about. Unexpectedly, the old man died, leaving an odd will. So much attention was paid to Robert Lee Frost and Jeanie Florence Frost in the will, that it seemed necessary for Rob to revise his previous estimates of his grandfather's attitude toward his poor relations. The inventory of the estate was valued at more than $17,000, including the farm he owned in Derry. Minor bequests to nine living relatives were followed with larger ones: $500 each, to the First Universalist Society of Lawrence for the relief of the worthy poor, and to the Lawrence Home for Aged People. The will continued:

"To my grandson Robert Lee Frost: All silver ware marked 'F', one teaspoon marked 'Willie,' two tablespoons marked 'J. Colcord,' one napkin ring marked 'Will,' and my gold watch and chain.

"To my granddaughter Jeanie Florence Frost: All other silver ware however marked, together with my other gold watch, which formerly belonged to my wife. . . .

"As my said grandson Robert Lee Frost is now living on my farm situated in Derry . . . and is now making a home there for himself and family, I give to him the free use and occupancy of said farm for and during the first ten years beginning at the time of my decease, subject however to the duties imposed by law upon life tenants as to taxes, insurance, and repairs. At the end of said ten year term, I devise to him the fee in said farm. . . .

"All the rest and residue of my estate, both real and personal, and property of every name, kind and nature whatever that I may die seized and possessed of, or be entitled to at my decease, and wherever the same may be situated, I give, devise and bequeath to my said Trustees . . . to carefully hold and invest the same, and of the income thereof to pay certain annuities as follows:

"To the said Jeanie Florence Frost an annuity of $400 annually for and during the term of her natural life.

"To the said Robert Lee Frost an annuity of $500 annually for and during said ten year term, and from and after the expiration of said ten year term an annuity of $800 annually for and during the term of his natural life. . . ."[10]

Rob received a further sign of his grandfather's affection and generosity when Wilbur E. Rowell, the lawyer serving as executive trustee of the estate, informed him that his grandfather had torn up and destroyed several promissory notes covering loans of money used in starting the poultry farm on Powder House Hill.

If he felt any gratitude, any change of heart and mind as a consequence of these unexpected revelations, Rob found a peculiar way of expressing it. He complained that his grandfather had cheated him out of what would have been his if such large and "silly" gifts had not been made to the Home for Aged People and the First Universalist Society of Lawrence. Moreover, he quickly tried to arrange for advance payments from the trust fund, and was resentful when he was told that by the terms of the will no annuities were to be paid in advance, that the first annuity would not fall due until 10 July 1902, one year after the death of his grandfather.

Rob knew that if he contrasted his status on the Derry farm with that of his neighbors, who managed to eke out a marginal living through a very meager annual sale of milk, eggs, berries, vegetables, and meat, his grandfather's will had elevated him to a position of relative affluence; that very few of his neighbors achieved annual cash incomes amounting to $500. Careless with money and inclined to be a spendthrift whenever cash came to hand from his sale of eggs, chickens, and roosters-for-breeding, Rob soon became annoyed by reminders from local merchants that he was running up too many unpaid bills. Part of his difficulty had been caused by Dr. Bricault's temporary removal to Vermont in the fall of 1900; but by the fall of 1901, Bricault was back in business near Lawrence and was again taking all of the produce from Rob's poultry farm at "bred-to-lay" prices, which were too good to be honest. It was on the strength of prospects pictured as especially promising by Bricault that Rob began looking around for someone from whom he could borrow money to expand the size of his brood.

Carl Burell and Jont Eastman were obviously in no position to lend money; they had both spent their lives in learning how to get along cheerfully on next to nothing. When Carl needed money during the Derry days, he followed the example of neighbors: he applied for work from the local road commissioner and was paid hourly wages for helping to install culverts, build small back-country bridges, cut brush along roadsides to let the sunlight in, and shovel dirt to fill washouts caused by storms. Rob never cared to supplement his income this way, and he covered his guilty feelings by complaining that Carl was neglecting the work on the farm. Arguments developed repeatedly between them over the few quarts of milk Carl sold daily, over Carl's carelessness in straining the milk he didn't sell, over Carl's way of trimming fruit trees, over Carl's selling so much fruit that there weren't enough peaches and pears and apples for the Frosts.

Rob's vindictiveness was calculated. It built to a peak late in the second winter of their partnership, and it would have forced Carl off the Derry farm sooner or later, in spite of his good-natured efforts to parry and tolerate Rob's criticism. Matters were brought to a head by the unexpected death of Carl's grandfather, Jont Eastman, at Frost's farm in Derry on 8 March 1902. Within three weeks Carl took his leave of the Frosts, under pressure but without bitterness. He had made some impression on the townspeople, as became apparent when *The Derry News* for 28 March 1902 mentioned his departure:

"Mr. Carl Burell, who has lived for some time past on the Magoon place, has decided to leave there and will go to Suncook where he has made an engagement in the Osgood mills for Mr. Bailey. Mr. Burell has won the highest esteem and respect of the people here and we are sorry to have him leave the place."[11]

If Rob was expected to find any undertone of reproach in this item, he probably didn't; he may have been too busy even to read it. Only after Carl had gone did the new owner of the Magoon place realize how much he had been dependent on him. Carl's departure had been so hasty that he had not even instructed Rob in the nice points of milking and stripping the cow. Carl had always milked so casually that Rob was surprised to find that he lacked the peculiar dexterity of fingers and wrists. He also found that, unlike Carl, he took no pleasure in letting his roosters serve as alarm clock. Of course, the cow herself had a reproachful way of waking him if he slept too late. Any time he made her wait too long, she bellowed her protest. Without too much difficulty he solved this problem by easing her around, gradually, until he was milking her comfortably at noon and midnight. Stripping was another matter. Not aware that he could dry her up by neglecting this aspect of her care, he soon did just that. When it became clear that she would need to be bred again, well ahead of the usual time, he felt embarrassed to lead her up the road to visit with a generous neighbor's bull. And he felt awkward at having to buy milk from the same neighbor during the next few weeks.

There were many other ways in which Frost was made conscious of Carl's absence, not the least of them being his fear of night sounds in the house and barn. Spring came late that year, and enough of winter remained to make him aware that when the temperature dropped below zero in the middle of the night a contracting nail in a clapboard or in walls could pull away from the wood with a bang that sounded like a revolver shot. At least, it made noise enough to sit him up in bed trembling. Anticipating tramps and prowlers, he had purchased a revolver in Lawrence before he came to the farm. He kept it loaded at all times on a shelf in a kitchen cupboard well beyond Lesley's reach. More than once, long after Elinor and Lesley were asleep, leaving him free to write at the kitchen table, mysterious noises in the shed or barn or cellar sent chills up his back. At such times he sought the consolation of taking down the revolver.

His night fears were always most excruciating just after he had been tense with writing. If he took a lamp late at night and went down the cellar stairs for another dish of apples, he could scare himself just by walking around among the shadows of boxes and barrels. Even a trip to the privy out by the grain shed between kitchen and barn, late at night frightened him. Let the noise of the sleeping cow's breathing reach his ears on such an occasion, or let the mare's flank scrape too hard against the side of the stall, and Rob came near panic. If he had courage enough to take the lantern in one hand and the revolver in the other, to prove to himself that nobody was hiding in the barn, he nevertheless hated to pass under the edge of the hay loft. Perhaps someone was up there in the hay, waiting for the chance to pounce on him as he passed within range.

Only once did anyone actually bother him at night, and then only by accident. A group of young people mistook his farm for another, drove into the yard with a nerve-wracking hullabaloo, clattered on the porch, and hammered at the kitchen door. With trembling lips and with revolver in hand he opened the door to order them off his property. The sight of the revolver was enough to make them fall back in haste, as they tried to explain their mistake.

His fear of tramps was another matter. Any forlorn vagrant who knocked at the door to ask for a piece of bread or a cup of milk was—at least to Frost—a potential barn-burner, thief, murderer. When such a man asked for permission to sleep overnight in the barn, with hay pulled off the mow to make a mattress, how could he refuse? Or if he should, how could he be sure the man wouldn't return after dark and set the place on fire? Frost had his reasons for showing an ingratiating courtesy to every tramp who begged for food or shelter. Some of his fear of tramps was dramatized poetically years later:

> *I didn't like the way he went away.*
> *That smile! It never came of being gay.*
> *Still he smiled—did you see him?—I was sure!*
> *Perhaps because we gave him only bread*
> *And the wretch knew from that that we were poor.*
> *Perhaps because he let us give instead*
> *Of seizing from us as he might have seized.*
> *Perhaps he mocked at us for being wed,*
> *Or being very young (and he was pleased*
> *To have a vision of us old and dead).*
> *I wonder how far down the road he's got.*
> *He's watching from the woods as like as not.*[12]

If some of these fears were imagined, there were others which had a basis in fact. Snowfalls, which began serenely in the gloaming with a fine whisper of tiny dry flakes, had a way of building up into frightening violence. At first the wind might be no more than a sigh, and the blown snow against the windowpanes might be so gentle that it could scarcely be heard. But as the storm increased, it could rattle the shutters and drive snow in under the kitchen door. It shook the house and knocked bricks off the chimney. On nights like this, he scarcely dared go to bed at all for fear the house would be torn apart. Or if he went to bed, he could not sleep. A late winter blizzard, arriving shortly after Carl's departure from the farm, may have inspired "Storm Fear":

> When the wind works against us in the dark,
> And pelts with snow
> The lower chamber window on the east,
> And whispers with a sort of stifled bark,
> The beast,
> 'Come out! Come out!'—
> It costs no inward struggle not to go,
> Ah, no!
> I count our strength,
> Two and a child,
> Those of us not asleep subdued to mark
> How the cold creeps as the fire dies at length,—
> How drifts are piled,
> Dooryard and road ungraded,
> Till even the comforting barn grows far away,
> And my heart owns a doubt
> Whether 'tis in us to arise with day
> And save ourselves unaided.[13]

In spite of all the difficulties caused by Carl's forced departure, Rob and Elinor and Lesley did manage to survive unaided. But by the time spring came and eggs had been purchased for the brooders, financial assistance had to be found. Running more and more into debt, and yet hating to borrow money from the bank in Derry, Rob solved the immediate problem in another way. His friend of high-school days, Ernest Jewell, having been graduated from Harvard, *magna cum laude,* had returned to the Lawrence High School as a teacher of mathematics. Frost and Jewell had renewed their acquaintance prior to the move from Methuen to Derry, and Jewell occasionally came out from Lawrence to visit the Frosts. On one of his first visits he was surprised to find Rob completely discouraged. Trying to get at the cause of his friend's listlessness, Jewell suggested that the trouble might be his divided loyalties. Jewell took it for granted that Frost still hoped to succeed as a poet and he was bold enough to say that Frost ought to make up his own mind about what he wanted to do. If he wanted to make a success of the poultry business, he ought to throw all of his energies into it; but if he wanted to write poetry, he should give up this business of tending three or four hundred Wyandottes.

Frost answered, in a surly fashion, "Suppose I don't *want* to do either one?"

Jewell was puzzled, and said so. But when he visited Frost in the spring of 1902, several months after Carl had left the farm, he noticed a decided improvement in Frost's general attitude. Had he made up his mind yet what he wanted to do? Yes, and Frost began to explain his reasons for feeling that his quasi-partnership with Dr. Bricault in the so-called "bred-to-lay" business offered sure possibilities of substantial cash profits. Jewell must have known by this time that Frost had inherited a considerable legacy from his grandfather. Frost may have explained that the first annuity would not be paid until 10 July 1902. In the meantime Frost needed cash in order to start capitalizing on Dr. Bricault's promises. If Jewell would like to go into partnership by lending money, Frost felt sure he could pay Jewell a very high rate of interest. How high? Well, what would Jewell say to a rate of 15%? The terms were accepted; papers were drawn up; and, on 16 May 1902, Jewell turned over to Frost a considerable amount of money: $675. But the poultry business never did flourish as Frost had hoped, and Jewell never did receive any interest on his investment; in fact, he never recovered the full amount of the principal.[14]

Largely through making mistakes, Frost acquired new insights from his experiences on the farm. One of the most memorable was stimulated by the actions of his horse and a strange man's way of handling the horse in the spring of 1902. From childhood Frost had viewed horses as diabolical creatures, largely because of an unforgettable experience in San Francisco. A lady there had rented a horse and carriage from a livery stable to take Mrs. Frost and her children for a ride in the country. As they were returning, the horse became frightened, took the bit in his teeth, and ran away. The carriage careened so frighteningly that the women and children were nearly thrown into the street. The lady had presence of mind enough to let the horse run until it approached a sand lot, easy to find in San Francisco at that time. When she turned the horse into it, he soon faltered, slowed, and went down on his knees. But he began kicking violently at the dashboard with his rear feet. All jumped out and nobody was hurt. Nevertheless, from the time of that experience, Frost viewed all horses as maliciously dangerous. So he had been willing to let Carl handle the large roan gelding workhorse, Billy, purchased at the Lawrence livery stable just prior to the move to Derry. Shortly after Carl had left, Dr. Bricault purchased Billy during an emergency, when his own horse gave out. Frost then bought a young dapple-gray mare named Eunice. She was a handsome "stepper," not immediately suited to farm work, as Frost soon learned. One day he hitched her to a henhouse he had built on runners so as to move it easily to a new scratching area. Apparently frightened by the unusual task, Eunice began to buck and rear and kick. Frost made matters worse by taking a whip to her, and in a short time he was almost as frantic as Eunice. In the midst of his troubles he heard someone sing out from the road, "You'll have to go through with it now or you'll spoil her." The speaker looked like a tramp and yet he spoke in a tone that implied more knowledge of horses than Frost had. Exasperated, Frost answered,

"Suppose you come in and show me how."

The stranger came into the yard apologetically. He walked up to the mare, talked quietly to her, and rubbed her back until she had calmed down. Then he said he thought she was ready to work. He took hold of the bridle near the bit, put his shoulder gently against her jaw, gave his command, and very slowly leaned forward. Eunice leaned into her harness, the henhouse started to move, and in no time the shift of the henhouse had been completed.

The better he came to know these back-country New Hampshire people, the more Frost admired their practical knowledge. Gradually he paid them the tribute of trying to imitate them—and even trying to imitate the careless way they talked. There was a man named John Hall who was especially appealing not merely because he had a picturesque vocabulary and a ready wit but also because he was an expert poultryman. Frost had met Hall at a poultry show in Amesbury, Massachusetts, and had fallen into conversation with him about Hall's many prize-winners. At the Amesbury show held in December of 1899, Hall won prizes with a Wyandotte cockerel, a Wyandotte pullet, a pen of Wyandottes, an old pair of Embden geese, a young pair of Pekin ducks, and a pair of Austrian ducks. The next year, at Amesbury, he again won prizes for his Wyandottes, geese, and ducks; he also received the forty-dollar "sweepstake cup" presented to the "exhibitor showing the largest number of birds of one variety scoring over 90 points."[15]

Learning that Hall lived in Atkinson, New Hampshire, a town bordering on Derry, Frost arranged to call on him. He had expected to find an impressive outlay of equipment and was surprised to discover that Hall's farm was not as big as his own. The little house and barn were tucked in off a back road beyond a willow-shaded brook which was cluttered with ducks and geese. The barn yard sheltered a surprising congregation of plain and fancy birds—Wyandottes, Plymouth Rocks, Langshans, Cochins, Brahmas. Inside the farmhouse were more surprises: John Hall was not married, but he lived in relative peace and comfort with a common-law housekeeper-wife and her mother, plus a goodly number of Angora cats. Blue-ribbon prizes were tacked up all over the kitchen. It was clear that Hall got extraordinary pleasure out of life, and that prize-winning was his primary concern. He wasn't in the business to make money. Whenever anyone offered him a fancy price for one of his pets, he'd say that if she was worth that much to sell she was worth as much to keep, and that was the end of it. What he could earn from sales of ordinary hens, ducks, geese, and eggs he would spend with a flourish. He had even imported some of his birds from England and South America. Proud of them all, he liked to pretty them up for show, and he had extraordinary skill in bringing them along just right. Hall's life seemed to be built on the same kind of caring and cherishing that Frost had just begun to understand.

All of Frost's newly acquired insights about back-country responses to human experience gave new impetus to his own life. These self-reliant people reminded him of what Thoreau had said in another connection:

> *They never die*
> *Nor snivel nor cry*
> *Nor ask our pity*
> *With a wet eye.*[16]

There was something casually stoic about the way in which they took all their hardships as a matter of course, without complaining and without seeming to find any reason for the expectation that circumstances should change.

Just to the south of Frost, on the Londonderry turnpike, lived a French-Canadian farmer named Napoleon Guay, pronounced (and sometimes spelled) Gay. The boundary line between his rented property and Frost's farm was marked by the stone wall which separated his grove of white pine from one of Frost's apple orchards, below the brook, and Guay was the man who would not go behind his father's saying, "Good fences make good neighbors." He was also the man who literally stole up behind Frost on the snow and caught his axe "expertly on the rise" as a preliminary to condemning machine-made axe-helves and of showing Frost the lines of a good helve.[17]

More than once, in talking to his neighbors, Frost learned facts which had the ring of pure poetry to his ears, and heard inflections of voices which captured meanings better than words did. Thoreau had been there before him: "A true account of the actual is the purest poetry." Emerson had been there before Thoreau:

". . . there is no fact in nature which does not carry the whole sense of nature . . . Besides, in a centred mind . . . the chief value of the new fact, is to enhance the great and constant fact of Life . . . The world being thus put under the mind for verb and noun, the poet is he who can articulate it. . . . So the poet's habit of living should be set on a key so low that the common influences should delight him. His cheerfulness should be the gift of the sunlight; the air should suffice for his inspiration, and he should be tipsy with water. That spirit which suffices quiet hearts, which seems to come forth to such from every dry knoll of sere grass, from every pine-stump and half-imbedded stone, on which the dull March sun shines, comes forth to the poor and hungry, and such as are of simple taste. If thou fill thy brain with Boston and New York . . . thou shalt find no radiance of wisdom in the lonely waste of the pine woods."[18]

These were ideals for which Robert Frost, on his Derry farm, was beginning to have strong sympathy and understanding. Thoreau and Emerson were two of his patron saints. Nevertheless, at this very time he was telling himself that perhaps there were other reasons why he should fill his brain with Boston or New York just long enough to make some aggressive moves calculated to improve his reputation as a poet. Romantically inclined, he seemed to feel that the Derry farm meant less to him, now that he was bound to it, than it would mean when he could look back at it across a gulf of time and space. Part of the irritation which marred his enjoyment of "a key so low" came from his increasingly impatient ambition to gain recognition for his literary work. He also needed to find other sources of income. So many bills had accumulated prior to the payment of the first annuity of $500 from his grandfather's estate that he was unable to pay back any of the money he had borrowed from Ernest Jewell. He had tried to shift over from poetry to prose to make money, and had ultimately sold a prose sketch or short story entitled "Trap Nests" to *The Eastern Poultryman,* which printed the piece in its issue for February 1903. But the sketch had earned him only $10, and by that time it was clear that the growth of his family would require more solid ways of increasing his income. Elinor had given birth to a son named Carol on 27 May 1902; she was expecting another child in June of 1903. Perhaps it was partly to give Elinor some kind of diversion before her next confinement, partly to give himself a change of scene, partly to establish valuable literary contacts that Rob took his wife and two children to New York during March of 1903. It was not too difficult to make arrangements with the neighboring farmer, Guay, to have his horse and cow and chickens taken care of.

If his neighbors had previously doubted that Rob was an ordinary farmer, their suspicions must have been strengthened by this latest maneuver. Unconcerned, the Frosts made an adventure of their trip. They took the train to Boston, the night boat from Boston to New York, and then rented a small furnished apartment in midtown Manhattan on Sixth Avenue. In their sightseeing, they did not neglect the interests of their nearly five-year-old daughter, Lesley: visits were made to the aquarium at the Battery, to the zoo in Central Park, and to the fabulous Hippodrome, which was within walking distance of their apartment. Lesley was impressed by the wonders of the zoo—elephants, giraffes, a tiger, a hippopotamus, and badgers fighting for peanuts—but she liked best the Hippodrome performances, where trained cats scrambled up ropes and trained dogs climbed rope ladders before jumping into blankets held to catch them.

Rob's most important activities were unsuccessful calls on

editors of various periodicals. He may not have been sure of his purpose but still the upshot of all his efforts came to nothing.

After a full month of sightseeing, the Frosts returned to the Derry farm, and were glad to be out of the bustle.[19] On 27 June 1903, Elinor gave birth to their second daughter, Irma, and the care of three children temporarily curtailed any further travels.

Showing less interest in farming than in literary matters, Rob seemed particularly hopeful that the very serious poultry journals which he read faithfully might be amenable to printing a few more comic fiction pieces, which would be true to the life of a poultry farm. In short order he wrote and sold eleven pieces, which were published;[20] he might even have continued, if his most serious one had not misfired in a way that made him the butt of an unintentional joke. The trouble-making article was straight reportage entitled "Three Phases of the Poultry Industry." It began by describing Dr. Bricault's White Wyandotte farm; then gave praise to a Lawrence carpenter who had grown tired of city life and had bought six acres in the countryside near the village of Salem, New Hampshire; it ended, appropriately, with a description of John Hall's farm. The blunder occurred through Rob's casual way of letting his imagination supplement his knowledge in this passage about John Hall's theories and practices:

"Two things in breeding he makes of first importance—size and vigor. It is his experience that weight tends constantly to decline. It is a simple matter to keep it up, only it cannot be left to take care of itself. As for vigor, it is easier to get this right than not. What the stock need is a little judicious neglect. Mr. Hall's geese roost in the trees even in winter. Such a toughening process would be too drastic for hens, but these have to take it according to their strength."[21]

More than one north-of-Boston poultryman reading the reference to geese roosting in trees must have chuckled over the obvious error; it may be that several subscribers to *Farm-Poultry* (the magazine which had published the piece) wrote in to ask questions. Inevitably, a query was published in the issue for 15 January 1904. It was made in a playfully sarcastic letter from H. R. White of Doylestown, Massachusetts:

"Editor FARM-POULTRY: —Will you kindly inform me through your next issue what kind of geese Mr. Hall has that

Mr. R. L. Frost speaks of in your issue of Dec. 15th? According to Mr. Frost these geese roost in the trees even in the winter time. Now I am 45 years old and have been among geese all my life time, and I can never remember seeing a goose in a tree. I thought if I could get a breed of that kind I could dispense with coops."[22]

Mr. White's letter was printed with the caption, "It's 'Up to' Mr. Frost," and the editor added his own comment by way of postscript, saying that the "evident error" had been noticed too late to make correction, that Mr. Frost would have to explain. It was an embarrassing predicament, best handled with humor; but in the process of trying to excuse himself Frost compounded his difficulty by further revealing his amateur status as a poultryman:

"Editor FARM-POULTRY: —In reply to Mr. White's (and yours) of recent date in regard to the error in the article on Mr. Hall's place, there is this to say:—

"Geese would sleep out, or float out, let us say, where hens would roost in the trees. To be sure. But what more natural, in speaking of geese in close connection with hens, than to speak of them as if they *were* hens? 'Roost in the trees,' has here simply suffered what the grammarians would call attraction from the subject with which it should be in agreement to the one uppermost in the mind. That is all. But the idea will have to stand, viz., that Mr. Hall's geese winter out,—and that is the essential thing. Mr. White is not after geese that roost in the trees, but geese that don't need coops. Well, Mr. Hall has them that prefer not to use coops, whether they need them or not. My impression is that he has them in several varieties, and I'll risk my impression. But Mr. Hall is a good fellow and will be glad to tell Mr. White about his geese himself—doubtless, also, to do business with him."[23]

This time, the editor of *Farm-Poultry* immediately assumed the obligation of educating his correspondent without the assistance of letters from subscribers:

"Mr. Frost seems not to be aware of the fact that geese generally remain out of doors by choice practically all the time. The same thing may be said of ducks. My Indian Runner ducks (now deceased) would stay out in a snow storm from daylight to dark rather than go into a comfortable shed where they were well sheltered and amply provided with bedding. If anyone will watch the actions of the duck or goose when out in the snow, and will consider that the feet are the only parts requiring protection, he will readily understand how they can be seemingly so indifferent to the weather.

"Water fowl do not sit with their feet on the snow. They lie flat on their bellies, draw their feet up to their sides, and then with a few dextrous wiggles work the feet into the feathers where they are warm and comfortable. I think that average hardy fowls will do this by preference rather than remain under shelter."[24]

These were facts of the kind Frost usually enjoyed, and the entire incident might have ended there if he had not been so forehanded in seeking another ingeniously creative form of self-protection. Before his own letter had been printed, Frost had tried to enlist the aid of the celebrated prize-winner, John Hall. Having had little schooling and even less experience in polemical letter-writing, Hall could not be expected to join a literary fray without help. He permitted Frost to write a letter for him and it was published in the issue of *Farm-Poultry* for 1 March 1904:

"Editor FARM-POULTRY: —I noticed Mr. H. R. White's letter in your paper asking about the kind of geese I keep that sleep out in the winter. They are Toulouse, Embden, and Buff. They don't roost in trees. I don't know how Mr. Frost made that mistake, for of course he knows better.

"We have often talked about the way they take to the water at night, a favorite place for them to hang up being on a stone just under water. A good many nights in winter, as well as in summer, I have no idea where they are; and I think they are better every way out doors as long as there is any water not frozen over. But speaking of geese in trees, I don't suppose Mr. White has ever seen a duck in a tree. I have. And I once had a duck that laid her eggs in a tree high enough to be out of reach from the ground, and brought off twenty-two ducklings. These were Brazilians, and I don't know what they won't do.

"It has always seemed strange to me how people succeed in keeping geese shut up. If I shut mine up they begin to be restless right away, and go off in looks, especially plumage. Mr. White needn't think because I let my geese run wild I think any less of them than other folks. They are good ones, —as they ought to be with the advantages I give them. They win, too, where they are shown.

"The records in your paper ought to show what they did in

Lawrence this year; but I notice they don't. So Mr. Frost was pretty near right about my geese; and if Mr. White wants some good ones that a little rather than not sleep out, I've got them."[25]

This letter, allegedly written by John Hall, brought the incident to a lame close for Frost, who seemed to lose heart in asserting further knowledge of poultry lore. It is probable that the two sketches of his which were published in *Farm-Poultry*, after the geese-in-trees embarrassment, had been accepted previously. At least his literary interests had been stimulated by the success of his writing and selling these vignettes about back-country people, and it paved the way for his later construction of dramatic narrative poems for *North of Boston*.[26]

During the period from the spring of 1902 to the spring of 1906, Frost brought himself out of the fears and discouragement and heartbreak which had followed hard on his departure from Harvard College. The failure of his health, followed by his insistence that he had failed as a father and had (in a sense) caused the death of his first child, had precipitated the darkness that blackened the first year on the Derry farm. From his neighbors and from his reading, he had learned a new attitude; from the reality of his experience as an amateur farm-poultryman, he had found new subject matter and themes for his poetry; from characters like John Hall, he had discovered anew that the talking tones of voice should determine an important part of form in prose or verse.

There was another element in his recovery: his instinctive and outgoing response of love and affection for his children. By the time his third daughter, Marjorie, was born—29 March 1905—he was ready and eager to assume the responsibilities of fatherhood. Lesley was then nearly six years old; Carol was nearly three; and Irma was nearly two. The farmhouse, which had frequently been so silent and seemingly empty after Jont Eastman died and Carl Burell had left, was now filled with the excitement, chatter, laughter, and tears of these four children. Somehow they helped to lead their parents out of the sorrows which had seemed insurmountable. Now there was indeed reason enough to accept and cherish the bittersweet of human existence. More than ever before Frost was ready to say with Thoreau, "Be it life or death, we crave only reality." If we are really dying, so be it; but "if we are alive, let us go about our business."

23

TRIAL BY EXISTENCE

. . . the evident design is a situation here in which it will always be about equally hard to save your soul. Whatever progress may be taken to mean, it can't mean making the world any easier a place in which to save your soul . . .[1]

SOMEWHERE near the beginning of 1906, Robert Frost sorted through his batch of manuscripts and notebooks to find a poem he had begun to write in the spring of 1892. So far, he had not been able to finish it; but during the nearly fourteen years since its start he had slowly acquired images and insights which, he hoped, could be brought to bear on what he had first tried to say. Now he thought the poem would serve as an expression of newly achieved and hard-earned affirmations.

It had grown out of his hurts and doubts and hindrances. He could vividly remember the moment of the initial inspiration, and could even recall details of lawns and doors and windows, past which he had been walking on his way to high school, that spring day in 1892. Doubtfully, he had been wondering whether any satisfactory explanation could be given for all the grief and pain and evil which had destroyed his father's life and which had repeatedly beset himself, his mother, and his sister since his father's death. A flash of insight had provided answers, that morning, as he walked. In retrospect, he could perhaps see how some elements in those answers had been based on his mother's religious faith rather than his own. She had taught him that all human souls come to this earth from heaven. But the originality of his insight had seemed to spring from his imaginative conviction that each soul, in coming to earth, must heroically choose to come; each soul must ultimately dare to be tested or tried by the ordeal of earthly existence. He also imagined afresh that each soul, in making the departure from heaven to earth, must be required to surrender the memory of the choice; that if the memory remained, there could be no real trial, no real danger of ultimate defeat, no valid testing worthy of man's God-given spiritual capacities.

He now told himself that he might sooner have found appropriate images and metaphors through which to give these insights poetic statement, if he had not been overtaken by so many failures and disappointments soon after his graduation from high school. For a time he had tried to rationalize the failures by repeating his mother's warning that griefs are meted out by a just God as punishment for wrongdoing. His mother had also taught him that Satan is the Prince of earth and that human beings are often tortured by evil forces which are all instruments of the divine plan. But as his failures accumulated, he became disillusioned with religion to the point where he doubted whether there really was any justice, any divine oversight of human affairs, any connection man could figure out between his just deserts and what he gets.

His first painful descent into disillusionment was caused by what seemed to him to be Elinor's complete rejection in the autumn of 1894. That particular "door in the dark" had indeed hit him such a blow that he felt his "native simile jarred," even in matters of religious belief, so that physical and metaphysical analogies didn't pair any more with what they had formerly paired with. The almost paralyzing injury caused by that experience had not been cured entirely, even after he had won and married Elinor. The best relief—and only a temporary recovery of religious affirmation—had been gotten through his readings in the works of William James shortly before and during his two years at Harvard. Soon after that, however, his own frightening illnesses had been followed by the almost unbearable death of his son, Elliott, and again he had slipped back into negations.

The death of his mother from cancer heightened his bitter awareness of all the unmerited miseries in the world, and caused him to reconsider the old claims, refurbished for him by James, concerning salvation through freely willed actions. Years later, in a mood which reflected the recurrence of disillusionment, he paid poetic tribute to his mother by dramatizing poetically what he sometimes viewed as the unmerited injustices that had ruined her noble life. This tribute, "The Lovely Shall Be Choosers," ironically and sarcastically repre-

sented all her freely willed choices as illusions, arranged by
higher powers (either angelic or Satanic, or perhaps both
working in collusion) to mete out retribution or punishment
for her refusal to accept the proper kind of marital love. As
though he were making a deliberate parody of the seven joys
and sorrows of Mary, he wrote,

The Voice said, 'Hurl her down!'

The Voices, 'How far down?'

'Seven levels of the World.'

'How much time have we?'

'Take twenty years.
She would refuse love safe with wealth and honor!
The lovely shall be choosers, shall they?
Then let them choose!'

'Then we shall let her choose?'

'Yes, let her choose.
Take up the task beyond her choosing.'

Invisible hands crowded on her shoulder
In readiness to weigh upon her.
But she stood straight still,
In broad round ear-rings, gold and jet with pearls
And broad round suchlike brooch,
Her cheeks high colored,
Proud and the pride of friends.

The Voice asked, 'You can let her choose?'

'Yes, we can let her and still triumph.'

'Do it by joys, and leave her always blameless.
Be her first joy her wedding,
That though a wedding,
Is yet—well something they know, he and she.
And after that her next joy

That though she grieves, her grief is secret:
Those friends know nothing of her grief to make
    it shameful.
Her third joy that though now they cannot help but
    know,
They move in pleasure too far off
To think much or much care.[2]
Give her a child at either knee for fourth joy
To tell once and once only, for them never to forget,
How once she walked in brightness,
And make them see it in the winter firelight.
But give her friends for then she dare not tell
For their foregone incredulousness.
And be her next joy this:
Her never having deigned to tell them.
Make her among the humblest even
Seem to them less than they are.
Hopeless of being known for what she has been,
Failing of being loved for what she is,
Give her the comfort for her sixth of knowing
She fails from strangeness to a way of life
She came to from too high too late to learn.
Then send some one with eyes to see
And wonder at her where she is,
And words to wonder in her hearing how she
    came there,
But without time to linger for her story.
Be her last joy her heart's going out to this one
So that she almost speaks.
You know them—seven in all.'

'Trust us,' the Voices said.[3]

The bitterness which impelled his later writing of "The Lovely Shall Be Choosers" may serve well enough to represent Frost's dark views on related matters during the first year spent at the Derry farm immediately after his mother's death. They were not unrelated to the cumulative darkness which inspired him to write the sonnet "Despair." Slowly, very slowly, these views were temporarily displaced by more positive feelings experienced at first hand on the Derry farm and through the lives of his neighbors. Some time passed, however, before he was able to look back sympathetically toward his mother's teachings about freely willed choice.

Perhaps without his realizing it, this renewed sympathy was re-enforced by other images which had flowed into the stream of his consciousness from earlier readings now almost forgotten. As he returned to his work on the unfinished poem, which eventually became "The Trial by Existence," he did not need to identify the sources of these images. For instance, he did not need to remember that during his brief stay at Dartmouth he had read for the first time in the dialogues of Plato and may have been attracted by Plato's repeated references to the old myth that after death each soul is permitted to choose a new life; that after the choice, each soul drinks of Lethe and then shoots away like a star to its new birth.[4] In the Derry farmhouse the parlor bookcase was crowded with more than a hundred books, among which was a volume of Matthew Arnold's poems containing helpful echoes from Plato. Deeply admiring Arnold—perhaps more than any other nineteenth-century English poet—Frost could scarcely have overlooked the five quatrains entitled "Revolutions," beginning,

> *Before man parted for this earthly strand,*
> *While yet upon the verge of heaven he stood,*
> *God put a heap of letters in his hand,*
> *And bade him make with them what word he could.*[5]

Arnold's images may have provided stimulus to the gradual revision of pictorial elements in "The Trial by Existence," but a more powerful incentive to Frost's thematic concerns came from what may be called the poetry of William James. At the beginning of his title essay in *The Will to Believe,* James uses a poetic analogy. Just as electricians speak of live and dead wires, he says, so it is convenient to speak of any hypothesis as either live or dead. And the maximum of liveness in a hypothesis depends on its ability to energize our willingness to act on it. James continues by saying that our passional and nonintellectual nature "not only lawfully may, but must, decide an option between propositions, whenever it is a genuine option that cannot by its nature be decided on intellectual grounds . . ." Although we have the right to believe, at our own risk, any hypothesis that is "live" enough to tempt our will, he adds, the two most important factors which sway our passional nature, in making options, are hope and fear.[6]

Frost's fear of death may well have drawn him to Jamesian hints at the right to believe in any religious hypothesis that may bring fear under control. James repeatedly insists that such a risk requires courage and daring: the strenuous, tough, bold, heroic response. Predisposed to honor such an assertion, Frost may not have been aware that James thus helped to reawaken certain "hypotheses" and "options" he had first learned from his mother. These beliefs had gone "dead" for him until he found them again made "live" by the strategically skeptical Jamesian evangelism. As a result, in his return to and revision of "The Trial by Existence," he seems to have built into the poem a Jamesian heroism, buttressed anew by his latest determination to overcome his own fears through acts of daring—physical, emotional, intellectual, spiritual. The self-protective strategy of skepticism in James, which appealed strongly to Frost, may be illustrated by the following passage in *The Will to Believe*:

". . . exactly what the thought of the infinite thinker may be is hidden from us even were we sure of his existence; so that our postulation of him after all serves only to let loose in us the strenuous mood. But this is what it does in all men, even those who have no interest in philosophy. The ethical philosopher, therefore, whenever he ventures to say which course of action is the best, is in no essentially different level from the common man. 'See, I have set before thee this day life and good, and death and evil; therefore, choose life that thou and thy seed may live,' —when this challenge comes to us, it is simply our total character and personal genius that are on trial . . ."[7]

Important as James may have been to Frost in encouraging him to formulate a cautiously skeptical, home-made, personal, eclectic set of beliefs, the immediate stimulus for the revision of "The Trial by Existence" probably was the maturing of Frost's attitude toward moral courage and bravery, daring and heroism. To its author, "The Trial by Existence" was more than a milestone; it marked a turning point in his attitude toward the kinds of promises he wanted to keep, toward himself and others, and the attitude which would be necessary, for him, if he were to keep them:

Even the bravest that are slain
Shall not dissemble their surprise
On waking to find valor reign,
Even as on earth, in paradise;
And where they sought without the sword
Wide fields of asphodel fore'er,
To find that the utmost reward
Of daring should be still to dare.

The light of heaven falls whole and white
And is not shattered into dyes,
The light forever is morning light;
The hills are verdured pasture-wise;
The angel hosts with freshness go,
And seek with laughter what to brave;—
And binding all is the hushed snow
Of the far-distant breaking wave.[8]

And from a cliff-top is proclaimed
The gathering of the souls for birth,
The trial by existence named,
The obscuration upon earth.
And the slant spirits trooping by
In streams and cross- and counter-streams
Can but give ear to that sweet cry
For its suggestion of what dreams!

And the more loitering are turned
To view once more the sacrifice
Of those who for some good discerned
Will gladly give up paradise.
And a white shimmering concourse rolls
Toward the throne to witness there
The speeding of devoted souls
Which God makes his especial care.

And none are taken but who will,[9]
Having first heard the life read out
That opens earthward, good and ill,
Beyond the shadow of a doubt;
And very beautifully God limns,
And tenderly, life's little dream,

But naught extenuates or dims,
  Setting the thing that is supreme.

Nor is there wanting in the press
  Some spirit to stand simply forth,
Heroic in its nakedness,
  Against the uttermost of earth.
The tale of earth's unhonored things
  Sounds nobler there than 'neath the sun;
And the mind whirls and the heart sings,
  And a shout greets the daring one.

But always God speaks at the end:
  'One thought in agony of strife
The bravest would have by for friend,
  The memory that he chose the life;
But the pure fate to which you go
  Admits no memory of choice,
Or the woe were not earthly woe
  To which you give the assenting voice.'

And so the choice must be again,
  But the last choice is still the same;
And the awe passes wonder then,
  And a hush falls for all acclaim.
And God has taken a flower of gold
  And broken it, and used therefrom
The mystic link to bind and hold
  Spirit to matter till death come.

'Tis of the essence of life here,
  Though we choose greatly, still to lack
The lasting memory at all clear,
  That life has for us on the wrack
Nothing but what we somehow chose;
  Thus are we wholly stripped of pride
In the pain that has but one close,
  Bearing it crushed and mystified.[10]

Almost as soon as he had finished his revision of the poem,
Frost made a fair copy of it and sent it, with some other
poems, to the Reverend William Hayes Ward in the following

letter, the first he had addressed to an editor of *The Independent* during a period of five years:

"I trust I do not presume too much on former kindness in addressing these verses to you personally. Sending MS to the Independent can never be quite like sending it anywhere else for me.

"I often think of you and your sister in my work. I believe Miss Ward left the staff of the Independent some years ago to write books. Please remember me to her either formally or by showing her any of my verses—whether you can use them or not."[11]

Ward immediately decided that he could use "The Trial by Existence," which he characterized as "uncommonly good." But there was far more importance for Frost in his having been able to finish the poem than in its being publishable. Such an affirmation was no guarantee, as he well knew, that he might not subsequently waver in his religious belief, that he might not again be reduced by discouragement and pessimism. Nevertheless, for the time being, he had achieved a new confidence. The Derry farm had served its purpose in bringing him back to life and in giving his life a direction which might reach beyond farming. He would always remember it as the place where he had been reborn.

NOT ELVES EXACTLY

I could say 'Elves' to him,
But it's not elves exactly, and I'd rather
He said it for himself.[1]

AS A PARENT, Robert Frost took very seriously and with pleasure the task of helping his children discover the joys of new
experiences. Even before they were old enough to walk, he
carried them into one adventurous journey after another, starting in their own dooryard. It became a world in itself, for
them, and they loved to watch it change with the seasons.

Winter mornings, when they woke to find their dooryard
playground heaped with snow, with drifts too tall for wading,
they could be sure their father had them in mind as they
watched him shovel off the porch, make a path to the nearby
pump, another path to the barn door, another to the mailbox,
another especially for them all the way from the pump to an
old sugar maple they liked to call their woodpecker tree.
When the snow was wet, he asked them for help in building a
snowman strong enough to wear a felt hat, bright enough to
see with stone eyes, and brave enough to carry a wooden gun.
If ice lay under the snow, he shoveled a path all the way to the
cranberry bog and uncovered enough ice to let them slippery-
slide on it. When the snow had settled and packed under the
winter sun, he called their attention to mysterious signs made
by birds and animals; he taught them how to read the tracks of
chickadees, partridges, rabbits, skunks, foxes, and squirrels.
When new snow began to fall, he showed them how to catch
big flakes on their mittens and marvel over the different crystal
patterns.

Between winter and spring came mudtime, when it was
scarcely safe for a horse and wagon to risk leaving the barn,
lest it get mired and stuck. But as soon as the spring winds

began to dry up the mud, the children could count on their father to hurry the season. April first was a bit too early for either flowers or tree buds to blossom. Yet there was a special April first when the children stared through the bay window in the parlor with astonishment. Across the road from their house they saw a few brightly colored flowers already in full bloom close to a melting bank of snow. Could they go out and pick them? Yes, if they put on their boots and coats and caps. Back they came laughing, with all the colored paper flowers their father had made and "planted" to help them celebrate April Fool's Day.

When the real flowers came, the Frost children helped their father with another kind of dooryard magic. The blue-handled shovel was carried by Lesley as they went across the road and through the bars and into the pasture and along the wall hunting for the best plants to bring back roots and all. Their treasures were placed in special beds along the base of the porch, facing south, and under the bay window which faced west: bluets, hepaticas, white violets. Added, in their turn, as they flowered, were lady's slipper, bloodroot, and two kinds of trillium.

Some of the best treasures were found on the far side of the pine-tree-shrouded knoll below their house—another favorite playground. They knew the knoll as Klein's Hill, which belonged to their neighbor, Mr. Guay, whose little girl played with them and whose house was hidden from theirs by the hill. Halfway between the hill and Mr. Guay's house was an old cellar hole with a tall chimney standing in it, the only remnant of a house which had burned down years earlier. Around the cellar hole they found and dug up old-fashioned flower plants and double-petaled rose bushes and lilac shoots. Far back of the cellar hole, in Mr. Guay's woods, their father once found a very special mountain laurel bush, which was brought home after some extra-hard digging. Each spring, newly transplanted discoveries gave the garden beds in the Frost farmyard a fine range of color and fragrance—long before their little cranberry bog was in blossom and even before the first delicate spikes of orchises began to show in the alders beside the stream they had named Hyla Brook.

Spring brought other exciting adventures to them in the farmyard. Whenever anyone saw the widespread wings of a chicken hawk lazily coasting high above house and barn, it was the signal for everyone to hurry through the barn to a hiding-place-lookout near the hen houses. If the hawk swooped down, the hens made a great racket and flapped their wings as they ran. If the children could find their father when the hawk was in sight, he would sometimes shoot at it with his revolver. He never hit it, but he always gave it a terrible scare and made it fly away.

Spring was also the time of year for raking up dead leaves in the yard and picking up dead branches for burning. The great bonfire was always built in the middle of the nearer pasture, across the road from the house. After the children had piled brush and leaves higher and higher, until the heap was taller than their heads, they were ready for the great moment. Their father put a match to a handful of dry grass, tucked it in at the base of the heap, and pushed the children back. Slowly the flames began to work their way in, making wet branches crackle and whistle. Then the flames would start to climb until one tongue of fire came out of the top. Just for a minute it looked like a big candle, and then it was all on fire, and the roar of the flames was frightening.

The best bonfire of all was one that got away. The tall flame had just blazed high when a breeze seemed to bend the torch-like flame to the ground. It barely touched the long dead grass on the side toward the road, but that was enough. Flames, pushed along by the wind, soon began racing toward the stone wall, the road, and even toward the house. Billows of white smoke rolled across the pasture, and fire ran with smoke all the way to the grapevines on the stone wall and even into the ditch beyond. The dirt road kept the fire from going any further to the east, but lesser flames ate steadily through dry grass to the north and south. The frightened children, herded to windward, were sure that only the heroic efforts of their father saved their house and barn from going up in flame. He used his old workcoat to reach into the smoke and beat out the fire. When the last smoldering spots had been doused with pails of water from Hyla Brook, the children could scarcely believe that so much of their pasture had been burned black in so short a time.[2] Never before had they seen such a bonfire, and to all of them the whole experience was "ickstrodnery icsiting," as Lesley once wrote in her journal.

Encouraged by her father and mother, Lesley had begun to play at learning to spell and write and read when she was less than five years old.[3] By the time she was six and a half, she had made such good progress that she began to write any doings which interested her in a composition book.[4] A few years later, before the other children were old enough to take walks beyond the farmyard, Lesley was proudly recording her many little journeys with her father:

"We went over across the road in the little pasture. Papa and I went way out in Noise's land. We found two little ponds and a watering trough. One of the ponds was where we tried to get some cat-tails last year but they were too far in the water, and right beside Noise's house they have a very pretty grove, they have seats in it and a fence around to keep people out. They have a cow path down to the ponds and pretty. We found a [shotgun] shell, shot just a little while ago."

*

"We went to the football game yesterday. An automobile came in. All the people stand up in the football game, but don't very often in baseball. The [Pinkerton] Academy boys beat the Concord boys."

*

"Last night when the children had gone to bed mama and papa took a little walk out in the field. We went to that little sweet-apple tree and picked a lot of apple blossoms . . . and Rob went down to the corner of the big cow pasture to see how much water there was in the spring. Quite a little, and then mama said we better be getting home, the sun was just going down and it made a pleasing light on the front room windows. And I had supper and went to bed."[5]

As the children grew older they enjoyed hearing stories told them by their father before they went to bed. Some of his stories were truly "ickstrodnery" even though they were always about things that happened in or near their own dooryard. Several of them were about their Collie dog, Schneider, and the adventures he had with woodchucks and rabbits and squirrels and birds. Others were about elves and goblins and fairies who lived very near their farm. One was called "The Wise Men," and it began, "Carol kissed us all goodby and climbed up into the nut tree." The story went on to say that Carol was gone for days and that when he came back he was escorted by three little men with white pointed beards and red pointed hats who had told Carol all kinds of wonderful things.

Another story began, "Fairies live in juniper bushes—you have to believe that. Well one day two little fairies peeked over the pasture wall into the orchard. . . ."[6]

The children quickly learned that they should always be on the lookout for elves and goblins and fairies because the little people were always peeking at children. One of Lesley's earliest journal entries recorded her knowledge that some fairies were "just about as big as papa's hand." She didn't care just where the real world stopped and the world of fantasy began.

Sometimes, the children enjoyed hearing their father read some of his own poems about the little people he had known when he was a boy. One told about his own powers of second sight, which helped him to communicate with the little people. He had begun to write this poem while he was in high school, and it had some old-fashioned ways of saying things. It was called, "In a Vale":

> When I was young, we dwelt in a vale
>   By a misty fen that rang all night,
> And thus it was the maidens pale
> I knew so well, whose garments trail
>   Across the reeds to a window light.
>
> The fen had every kind of bloom,
>   And for every kind there was a face,
> And a voice that has sounded in my room
> Across the sill from the outer gloom.
>   Each came singly unto her place,
>
> But all came every night with the mist;
>   And often they brought so much to say
> Of things of moment to which, they wist,
> One so lonely was fain to list,
>   That the stars were almost faded away
>
> Before the last went, heavy with dew,
>   Back to the place from which she came—
> Where the bird was before it flew,
> Where the flower was before it grew,
>   Where bird and flower were one and the same.

And thus it is I know so well
  Why the flower has odor, the bird has song.
You have only to ask me, and I can tell.
No, not vainly there did I dwell,
  Nor vainly listen all the night long.[7]

Their father knew almost as much about the moon and the planets and the stars as he did about fairies and elves and goblins. On summer evenings, soon after the sun had gone down, he liked to sit on the front steps with the children and get them to watch for the stars coming out. He showed them how the new moon, just setting, held the old moon in her arms. He pointed out the red planet on which he could see canals and trees and people and houses. Lesley couldn't see them, but he helped her by saying it would be fun to imagine she could. All the children learned to find the North Star, the Little Dipper, the Big Dipper and, on winter nights, not only Orion with his sword, and with the very bright star in his belt, but even both of his dogs.

Among the many games their father taught them, the Frost children liked best his way of playing school. As soon as Carol and Irma and Marjorie were old enough to enjoy it, he showed them how much fun they could have that way. Autumn evenings, as the sun went down earlier and earlier, he would call them in from the yard and would let them sit in a line on the sofa in the parlor. He would start by telling them a story. Then he would count with them—1, 2, 3, 4, 5—and then he would sing a song with them until recess time. After recess, they would all play a spelling game. A little word was written on a big card, and anyone who could spell it right could have the card. If not, they could all look at it. Then they would sing another song, and do exercises to make their muscles strong, and march around the room once or twice and keep right on marching out into the kitchen for their supper of bread and milk.

Before the children quite knew how it happened, they had learned many lines of poetry by heart, starting with the rhymes of Mother Goose. They were all fond of poetry, and Lesley liked to point out books she knew in the biggest parlor bookcase: Poe, Coleridge, Tennyson, Matthew Arnold, Jean Ingelow, Palgrave's *Golden Treasury*, and the *Songs of Shakespeare*. Among her earliest favorites were "The Raven," "The

Ancient Mariner," and "Sohrab and Rustum," the latter, apparently, the one which was "always about some trouble and that makes you crazy to hear the end to see whether it is going to come out all right or not."

And there were oh so many other kinds of excitement, on birthdays and Fourth of July and Hallowe'en. It seemed as if their father raised big pumpkins in his garden just so they could all have a jack-o'-lantern apiece. Before they were old enough to cut their own jack-o'-lanterns, he surprised them by having them all made, each with a candle in place, and burning, by the time it was dark. Then he hid each one in a different place and let Marjorie go first, all alone, to find hers. Each lantern looked different. One was always cut with the skin of the pumpkin all left on, and light showing through the dug-out places inside to make it look like a ghost-face. One always had long pointed paper ears stuck on, to make it look like an elf.

On Hallowe'en, instead of playing school, they had special games. They tried to bite an apple hanging on a string from the top of a doorway. None of the children succeeded alone, but it was easy if two of them tried at the same time from opposite sides. They loved trying to bite an apple floating in a pail of water. When it was Lesley's turn, she held her breath and pushed her face right under water. Marjorie, when she was too young to understand this game, just put her mouth in the water and took a drink. Their Hallowe'en games were so funny that they laughed and shouted and had a great hullabaloo until their mother said it was time to get ready for bed.

The children said Christmas was the best day of all, and they began talking about it weeks before it came. Their father made a great secret of getting the Christmas tree. When they were small, he left them at home with their mother and started for the woods with an axe in his hand, saying he was going to visit Santa Claus. They never did know just how or when he brought the tree through the front door and into the parlor; they never saw it being decorated. But on Christmas morning they were awakened by the alarm clock and were told to stay in bed while their mother went downstairs to the kitchen to build and light the fire. When the kitchen was warm, and the signal was given, they made a barefoot dash down to the kitchen, found their clothes where they had left them, dressed in a hurry, and (when everyone was ready) tiptoed in toward the closed parlor door. When Marjorie was just old enough to walk, and not old enough to remember what she had seen a year ago, she was so surprised to find a spruce tree in the parlor with candles burning on the branches that she was frightened by it. But that evening, when the candles were lit again, she laughed and laughed. This was Christmas of 1906, when she was almost two years old. Lesley told about it:

"This year all the children were anxshus to know what they were going to have for Christmas, espechily Irma. Every time Mr. Pirkins [the mailman] drove into the yard Irma would ask mama what he had brought us for Christmas, but mama wouldn't tell. When Christmas night came we children hung up our stockings and went to bed. We were expecting santa claus to come in the front room that night and give us things. We went to sleep as quick as we could.

"The next morning we woke up early to see what we had for Christmas, but mama wouldn't let us go down intill the sun came up. When we came down stairs we ran to the kitchen door to go out and dress. As soon as we got there we found that santa claus had come out there instead of in the front room. After we had looked at all the things, there was a rocking chair and doll and a dog with a little bell tied around his neck and pichures for Irma, and there was a train of cars and a pig and a pigs trogh and a pig pen and a little boat and ball and some pichures for Carol and a ball and a doll and a rocking chair and a kitty and some pichures for Marjorie, and some dominoes and some dice and a ruler and a little tracing and drawing book and two dolls and a rabbit for me, and there was a blackboard and some candy for all of us together. After we had looked at them all a minute we dressed and ate breakfast and had a happy time all day long playing with our toys. That night papa played dominoes with me and Carol, then we had supper and went to bed very happy."[8]

The Frost children learned from their father that Christmas meant more than toys and candy. Each year, long before the day arrived, he told them the story of the nativity, read it to them from the New Testament, and sang with them,

Away in a manger,
No crib for his bed,
The little Lord Jesus
Lay down his sweet head.

The stars in the bright sky
Looked down where he lay,
The Little Lord Jesus
Asleep in the hay.[9]

From play in their own barn, the Frost children knew what a manger was. And, as Lesley said later, their cow was capable not only of jumping over the moon but also of being related to the cows that gazed wonderingly at a newborn babe asleep in the hay. At Christmastime, a special grace was said before meals and a special evening prayer replaced the one which concluded:

And if I die before I wake,
I pray the Lord my soul to take.

Perhaps the religious beliefs of the Frost children were planted most firmly through their observance of Christmas festivities; but the same beliefs were nurtured carefully throughout the year. As they grew old enough, each of them took turns reading aloud stories which often had a religious flavor. For Christmas reading, they had six copies of Dickens' *A Christmas Carol* and six copies of *The Pilgrim's Progress*. They learned by heart Palgrave's "A Little Child's Hymn," Baring-Gould's "Child's Evening Hymn," Blake's "Cradle Song," and Blake's "Little Lamb." Although they did not have extra copies of Maeterlinck's *The Blue Bird*, their father read it to them.[10]

It was part of their father's Christian discipline to make the children understand the meaning of such words as obedience and acceptance. When necessary, he was very stern with them and was quick with his punishments. Like his father before him, he seemed to believe in the adage: "Spare the rod and spoil the child." There was a Victorian earnestness in his conviction that his children should be led to understand that the moral life entails a desperate struggle and that resistance to temptation is the first step in training the will toward the fulfillment of life's great end.

The children could not see any inconsistency, perhaps, between what their father preached and practiced; but in her journal Lesley recorded moments when he behaved badly. There was, for instance, a spring day when their mother was trying to complete a thorough program of housecleaning. Grandfather White was visiting them at the time and he was helping. So was their father who, having been asked to work harder and longer than he liked, may have found many different reasons for building resentment. When the time came for him to stop housecleaning, in order to fetch the cow from the pasture and to milk her so that there would be milk in time for supper, he couldn't find his cap. It wasn't on the nail where it usually was, and all the children were asked to hunt for it. The search was to no avail, and their father announced that under the circumstances he would have to let the cow stay out all night, even though she hadn't been milked. It would be bad for her, of course, and it would be unfortunate for the children, who could have no milk for supper; but that was the way it had to be, since he couldn't find his cap. Lesley concluded her journal account of this incident: "We had to have bread and butter and cocoa with no milk in it—and mama and papa and grandpa had bread dipped in tea with no milk in it. After that we went to bed."[11]

Lesley was never able to forget an even more mysterious performance, the meaning of which nobody ever explained to her. She could remember being awakened by her father abruptly and roughly in the middle of a night, when she was about six years old. She was told to get out of bed and the cold floor under her bare feet became a vivid reminder that this event occurred on a winter night. She was told to follow her father down the unlit stairs to the parlor, through the parlor to the dining room, and through the dining room toward the kitchen, where she could see a light burning. As she entered, she saw her mother sitting at the kitchen table, crying, her hands pressed against her face. Bewildered, Lesley turned to look at her father and noticed for the first time that he held his revolver in his hand. Waving the revolver toward her mother and then toward himself, he said wildly to Lesley, "Take your choice. Before morning, one of us will be dead."

She wanted both of them, she said, and she started to cry. Her mother got up from the table, put her arms around Lesley, pushed her out of the kitchen, led her back to her bed, and sat beside her until the child had cried herself to sleep. In the morning she remembered all the facts and wondered if they had actually happened. Perhaps she had only dreamed them.

But no. There was evidence enough to make her certain that this experience had not been a dream.[12]

Their father could not explain to them that even the pleasure he took in the freshness of their responses to life was not enough to protect him completely from his intermittent moods of uncertainty and darkness. He did not enjoy, any more than they did, the periods when he was depressed by his notion that he was a failure—as father, as husband, as poet, as man. Mistakenly, he was inclined to interpret Elinor's reticence as her most effective way of punishing him.

Even when he tried as hard as he could, it was impossible for him to close all the doors and windows of his inner life against discouragement which came at him from outside. They kept getting in past his guard, especially when he was asleep, and they kept turning his dreams into nightmares. Just beyond his bedroom window grew a white birch tree with branches long enough to scrape against the house and, in the wind, even against the panes of glass. In his dreams these harmless branches become horrible things. Years later he commemorated this particular tree in a poem which may serve to represent the darkest of his moods, on the Derry farm:

> Tree at my window, window tree,
> My sash is lowered when night comes on;
> But let there never be curtain drawn
> Between you and me.
>
> Vague dream-head lifted out of the ground,
> And thing next most diffuse to cloud,
> Not all your light tongues talking aloud
> Could be profound.
>
> But, tree, I have seen you taken and tossed,
> And if you have seen me when I slept,
> You have seen me when I was taken and swept
> And all but lost.
>
> That day she put our heads together,
> Fate had her imagination about her,
> Your head so much concerned with outer,
> Mine with inner, weather.[13]

Whenever the storms of his "inner weather" grew too violent, he was almost lost to his recurrent wish that he might run away—steal away, stay away—and never come back. It was a mood against which he had to fight or a mood he could slake at times merely by getting out of the house and off the farm— particularly if he and Elinor had built up too much abrasive tension between them. Often he would plunge into the woods behind his farm and walk until he was almost exhausted. Then he could come back, repentant. So he was of two minds about running away as a release from nervous fury: whether good or bad, brave or cowardly. During one of those ambiguous states of mind, he wrote a defensive sonnet entitled "Into My Own":

> One of my wishes is that those dark trees,
> So old and firm they scarcely show the breeze,
> Were not, as 'twere, the merest mask of gloom
> But stretched away unto the edge of doom.
>
> I should not be withheld but that some day
> Into their vastness I should steal away,
> Fearless of ever finding open land,
> Or highway where the slow wheel pours the sand.
>
> I do not see why I should e'er turn back,
> Or those should not set forth upon my track
> To overtake me, who should miss me here
> And long to know if still I held them dear.
>
> They would not find me changed from him they knew—
> Only more sure of all I thought was true.[14]

In later years he could and did place this poem in a context which treated it ironically as reflecting his youthful runaway mannerisms which implied "I was right, and you'll be sorry when I'm gone."[15] Perhaps these ironic possibilities of meaning, in the poem, were brought to his attention obliquely by Elinor's tart comments. Although she puzzled others as much as she puzzled him, there was never any question concerning her ability to make observations which went like bullets to their mark.[16] Sometimes, and in ways which interrupted his self-pity, she was able to draw him back from his habitual acts of escape or withdrawal.[17] He acknowledged as much in one of his most intimate love poems, implicitly addressed to her. Entitled "A Dream Pang," it contains very subtle hints that the setting for the one-sided conversation is not merely a bedroom but even a double bed. Dramatically considered, the poem represents the speaker as waking in the night to realize that his beloved is not asleep and that he may therefore be excused for telling her the immediate dream which has awakened him:

> *I had withdrawn in forest, and my song*
> *Was swallowed up in leaves that blew away;*
> *And to the forest edge you came one day*
> *(This was my dream) and looked and pondered long,*
> *But did not enter, though the wish was strong;*
> *You shook your pensive head as who should say,*
> *'I dare not—too far in his footsteps stray—*
> *He must seek me would he undo the wrong.'*
>
> *Not far, but near, I stood and saw it all*
> *Behind low boughs the trees let down outside;*
> *And the sweet pang it cost me not to call*
> *And tell you that I saw does still abide.*
> *But 'tis not true that thus I dwelt aloof,*
> *For the wood wakes, and you are here for proof.*[18]

The reconciliation suggested in this poem is achieved through the poet's confession to the beloved that he was in the wrong. Much of the inspiration for lines written by Frost in his renewal of poetic activity during this phase of his life on the Derry farm are unmistakably love poems, written to Elinor as gestures of courtship. Whatever they might mean to others, through valid symbolic extension, they first meant to him a way of increasing the intimacy which was so important to him. Even after they had been away from the farm for years, the memory of moments of lovemaking at Derry continued to inspire poems, one of the most famous having a particular value here. The speaker, on two different occasions, asks the beloved to go with him just long enough to enjoy and cherish two little experiences made especially meaningful if shared by lovers:

> *I'm going out to clean the pasture spring;*
> *I'll only stop to rake the leaves away*
> *(And wait to watch the water clear, I may)*
> *I sha'n't be gone long.—You come too.*

I'm going out to fetch the little calf
That's standing by the mother. It's so young
It totters when she licks it with her tongue.
I sha'n't be gone long.—You come too.[19]

There is no way of knowing just what effect this kind of poetic lovemaking had on Elinor Frost. It may have helped her to overcome the natural darkness in her nature, which had been increased by crushing disappointments and griefs. She did enjoy the romantic isolation and the homely pleasures of wandering afield to cherish just as much as he did. She may also have realized that her puzzling love caused him to make reassuring efforts which found expression in poems of lasting beauty. She knew the need for renewing love and poetry by discovering fresh ways of saying it. She could have told him that, but in his poems to her, he made it clear that she didn't have to.

HEN-MAN AT PINKERTON

If you should rise from Nowhere up to Somewhere,
From being No one up to being Someone,
Be sure to keep repeating to yourself
You owe it to an arbitrary god
Whose mercy to you rather than to others
Won't bear too critical examination.
Stay unassuming.[1]

SOCIAL AND FINANCIAL embarrassment drove Robert Frost into some desperate remedies during the spring of 1906. He had avoided contact with his neighbors, whenever possible, from the day he arrived in Derry. The nearest farmer, the French-Canadian Napoleon Guay, offered continuing and friendly assistance whenever he saw the chance. Frost had often accepted help from Guay, and had visited in Guay's home, but Guay had never been invited to visit in Frost's home. Frost treated many of his neighbors in much the same way. Although he still admired the picturesque hen-fancier John Hall, he had not bothered to keep that friendship up. In Derry Village, he was on speaking terms with only a few people. He did most of his shopping at the Derry Depot, because that little community was nearer the farm, and yet he gradually came to resent the occasional insolence he felt from the merchants and businessmen. There was a particular show of insolence, he felt, during the previous summer, 1905. He had gone to the local bank to deposit the fourth $500 check paid him as annuity from his grandfather's trust fund. The teller at the window had studied the check with too much interest, after reading the endorsement, and had said, "Some more of your hard-earned money." The teller may have intended the remark pleasantly, but Frost resented the insinuation.

Some of the storekeepers in Derry Depot annoyed him by

the way they raised their eyebrows and cocked their heads at his dapper mare Eunice—and at the various conveyances used by Frost as he came riding into town. He had been extravagant, he admitted, in purchasing a "fancy stepper" like Eunice, but he did enjoy a good-looking horse and old Billy had been a plug. As for the conveyances, they could be excused, he thought. Eunice had a tendency to be frightened by nothing more than a newspaper blowing across the road. Her shying motions were often so abrupt that they cramped the wheel of the democrat wagon sharply against the metal roller guard and sometimes almost tipped the wagon over.

Early in the winter of 1905, Frost indulged in another luxury. He had purchased a bright red sleigh, a four-seater, knowing that whenever Eunice might slew it to right or left the steel runners would glide harmlessly on snow or ice. Of course, he had not foreseen the embarrassment Eunice and the sleigh caused him at Windham Depot soon after he had made the new purchase. He had gone down there to pick up an express package and had taken his six-year-old daughter Lesley for company. They reached the station, unfortunately, just as a train was pulling in, and the cloud of steam ejected unexpectedly between the wheels of the engine was too much for Eunice. She reared on her hind legs and almost tipped the sleigh over backward. Then she made her usual sideways jump. One runner, caught in a frozen rut, simply acted as a fulcrum and the sleigh tipped over with a crash. Frost jumped free as he saw what was happening. He held the reins and ran as Eunice began dragging the sleigh on its side over the icy station yard. "Now I've done it; now I've done it," he kept saying to himself. Eunice didn't really try to run away and was soon ready to stop. But while Frost was moaning over the damage to the sleigh a man came alongside and tried to console him: "Anyway, your little girl is all right." In the excitement he had completely forgotten Lesley. Frightened for her now, he looked back and saw her dusting snow off her clothes. She hadn't been hurt at all, and the sleigh was patched up quite easily.

Nevertheless, this accident at Windham Depot had given him all the excuse he needed for buying another kind of vehicle for doing errands. When mudtime came, and runners gave way to wheels, he bought a pretty little sulky, with a green wooden box attached behind the seat. At last he had a rig

Eunice couldn't tip over, and he was very proud of it. But the sulky played a crucial part in his worst embarrassment in the spring of 1906. He was in the butcher shop and had just finished buying a few good cuts of meat. When the package was wrapped and placed in his hand, Frost merely told the butcher to charge it, and started to walk out. The butcher stopped him. Stepping around the edge of his counter, just far enough to look out of the display window at Eunice and the sulky, he turned and addressed other customers who were waiting: "Anyone have a lien on that mare and sulky?" Silence, then laughter. All right then, the butcher said, just this one more time. In a rage, Frost dumped the package on the counter and stormed out of the shop.

All this finally shamed Frost into reconsideration. Perhaps it was time he stopped pretending he was a farm-poultryman. Everyone in the region knew he did very little farming, and not much with hens. After the annuities had begun to come in, he had gradually permitted his brood of Wyandottes to decrease. Recently, his business friend and protector, Dr. Charlemagne Bricault, had announced that he was returning to his former calling as a veterinarian, and yet even after Bricault went out of business Frost did not entirely quit as a poultryman. For a cheaper price he could still sell all of his eggs to H. P. Hood and Sons, a nearby farm which had been distributing dairy products and eggs all over New England for years.

At times Frost condemned his own laziness by telling the story of the enterprising Hood. Years earlier this Vermont farmer's boy, Harvey Pearley Hood, had gone down to Boston at the age of twenty-four and had started a small milk route there. Within a few years he had built it into a large and prosperous business. But he was ordered by his doctor to move away from the coast, and in 1855 he bought a farm not far west of Derry Village in New Hampshire. Very soon he began to ship to Boston all the milk and eggs he could buy from farmers in the Derry region. His sons had grown up helping him, and when H. P. Hood had died—in 1900, just before Frost reached Derry—the sons had inherited one of the largest dairy corporations in New England. Frost's contacts with the Hood farm in Derry had developed early, when he had been asked to work there in an emergency candling eggs. His Collie dog, Schneider, had been a gift from the Hood farm. His fancy-stepping mare, Eunice, had been bought at a bargain—$150—

at the Hood farm. But the prices paid for eggs by the Hood farm came so near to being wholesale that there was little profit for Frost in selling eggs that way. Occasionally, he sold to neighbors. He even delivered a few dozen eggs weekly to people who lived on the turnpike between his farm and Derry Village. But here again he had suffered from either real or imaginary insults, and he had come to feel that there must be some better way for him to earn a living.

He knew that if he were given the choice, he would prefer to live in New York City as a salaried contributor of prose and verse to a publication like *The Independent*. He had expressed that preference indirectly in 1903, when he had taken his family to New York City and spent a pleasant but futile month there. If other choices existed, he did not know what they might be. Looking around somewhat desperately, he decided that he could at least apply for a position as a teacher in one of the several district schools. So far, he had avoided sending Lesley to school, although she was seven years old. Part of his reason had been that he was sure he could teach her better and faster than anyone else could. But if he should begin teaching school, she could go and come with him, while they continued to live on the farm. He could not afford to sell the farm—in fact it would not be legally his for at least five more years. Having made up his mind, he knew that he should not approach the chairman of the local school board until he had acquired a copy of his high-school record and at least a few letters of recommendation. Early in 1906 he hitched Eunice to his sulky and drove the fourteen miles to Lawrence through Salem.

During this drive to Lawrence, one memorable event occurred. As he came through the woods, just to the north of Salem, he saw a lone figure ahead of him near the roadside. It was a young woman—tall, slim, straight-backed, in hunting clothes, holding a rifle. She had one foot up on a stone wall, the rifle in readiness across her raised knee, her eyes and ears obviously intent on a path through the underbrush. Well beyond her, in the woods, there was an excited yelping of several eager hounds hot on the scent of something. The young woman showed no interest in the passing horse or sulky or rider. She did not even glance over her shoulder as he passed. But long before he came near enough to be sure, he thought that he recognized her from the line of her back and the way she wore her uncovered blonde hair—Sabra Peabody.

He drove on past, hoping she would not see him. Too many obstacles and estrangements lay between the Derry farmer and this girl, this dedicated hunter, who was still enough like her brother Charley to relish the game of playing with hounds and guns and rabbits and foxes. He wondered whether she was married and whether Charley was in there with the hounds. Just for old-time's sake, he would have liked the chance to talk with them both. Yet he felt ashamed of the way in which he would have had to answer their questions.

A more pleasant coincidence awaited him in Lawrence that day. As he was walking along Essex Street, he was stopped by William E. Wolcott, Pastor of the First Congregational Church, friend of William Hayes Ward, and believer in the notion that many of Frost's poems sounded "too much like talk." Still friendly and cordial in his greeting, Wolcott said he had heard that Frost owned a poultry farm in Derry. Yes, but he was growing tired of it and was thinking that maybe he'd go back to teaching school, perhaps even in Derry. Good, said Wolcott, there's a fine old Congregational Academy up there in Derry, well-endowed. He had been there as a speaker for graduations, was well-acquainted with the Congregational minister in Derry, Charles Loveland Merriam, and would be glad to write him on Frost's behalf. Merriam was a Yale man, a writer himself, formerly a founder and editor of the *Yale Daily News*, and now a trustee of Pinkerton Academy. Frost shook his head. He would like to teach at Pinkerton, but he had no college degree. Even worse, he admitted, he was known in Derry as only a hen-man—and a poor one at that. He'd better start by not assuming anything. Perhaps he could work up to Pinkerton after he had taught for a while in one of the district schools. Wolcott disagreed, and the upshot of the conversation was that he not only wrote to his friend Merriam after urging that Frost should call on him but also gave Frost a general note of recommendation:

"I have been acquainted with Mr. Robert L. Frost for a number of years. I know of my personal knowledge that he is a man of scholarly interests and habits, and I have had testimony from former pupils that he was an efficient and inspiring teacher. I am glad to commend him cordially for any position for which he may apply."[2]

After his return to Derry, armed with records and letters, Frost visited the chairman of the school board, a local dentist. Giving his name, the visitor spread out his documents on a desk and explained that he was applying for a position as a grammar-school teacher. To the dentist, the name seemed to carry unpleasant associations. He picked up the documents, handed them back unopened, made a casual remark to the effect that anyone could get letters of reference, and very curtly ended the interview by saying that there were no vacancies in the Derry schools. Hurt more by the surliness than by the bad news, Frost was not inclined to look further for a teaching position in Derry. But after he had licked this wound for several days, he thought he should at least try Wolcott's suggestion.

He found the Congregational pastor one evening, busy with a group of boys in the vestry of the church. Told to wait until the boys had been dismissed, he braced himself for the same kind of treatment he had received from the dentist. But when Merriam was free and the two men began their conversation, all was friendly and encouraging. Wolcott had been correct; there might be something at Pinkerton. Wolcott had also written that Mr. Frost had published some poems. Just as a way of getting acquainted in Derry, perhaps Mr. Frost would be willing to read a few of his poems before the Men's League of the Congregational Church. The next meeting, coming soon, was the annual spring banquet—Ladies' Night. Frost cringed. Never in his life, he explained, had he read any of his poems aloud before a public gathering, and he doubted if he would ever have the courage to do that. Then how would it be, Merriam asked, if the pastor read one of them for him, just by way of introduction?

A few days later Frost visited Merriam again to submit a poem which was by no means newly written. It had been inspired by an experience that had occurred while he was haying for old John Dinsmore, at Cobbett's Pond near Salem, New Hampshire; it had been written early enough for use as a "theme paper" in English A at Harvard in 1897. If it had been put away because the little theme of it seemed too commonplace, perhaps his new experiences with Wolcott and then with Merriam had renewed its truth and had made the poem appropriate for presentation by Merriam to the Men's League. The poem was "The Tuft of Flowers":

I went to turn the grass once after one
Who mowed it in the dew before the sun.

The dew was gone that made his blade so keen
Before I came to view the leveled scene.

I looked for him behind an isle of trees;
I listened for his whetstone on the breeze.

But he had gone his way, the grass all mown,
And I must be, as he had been,—alone,

As all must be, I said within my heart,
Whether they work together or apart.

But as I said it, swift there passed me by
On noiseless wing a bewildered butterfly,

Seeking with memories grown dim o'er night
Some resting flower of yesterday's delight.

And once I marked his flight go round and round,
As where some flower lay withering on the ground,

And then he flew as far as eye could see,
And then on tremulous wing came back to me.

I thought of questions that have no reply,
And would have turned to toss the grass to dry;

But he turned first, and led my eye to look
At a tall tuft of flowers beside a brook,

A leaping tongue of bloom the scythe had spared
Beside a reedy brook the scythe had bared.

The mower in the dew had loved them thus,
By leaving them to flourish, not for us,

Nor yet to draw one thought of ours to him,
But from sheer morning gladness at the brim.

The butterfly and I had lit upon,
Nevertheless, a message from the dawn,

That made me hear the wakening birds around,
And hear his long scythe whispering to the ground,

And feel a spirit kindred to my own;
So that henceforth I worked no more alone;

But glad with him, I worked as with his aid,
And weary, sought at noon with him the shade;

And dreaming, as it were, held brotherly speech
With one whose thought I had not hoped to reach.

Men work together, I told him from the heart,
Whether they work together or apart.[3]

On the evening of the Men's League Ladies' Night banquet, Frost sat beside Merriam and tried to hide behind a too-thin metal post while "The Tuft of Flowers" was being read for him. Self-conscious, nervous, and embarrassed, he would have preferred not to be there at all. But the poem was well-received and the men and women to whom he was introduced were cordial. Several of them were teachers at Pinkerton, one being Miss Sylvia Clark, whose father had been the first visitor to the Frosts in Derry. Dr. David S. Clark, local physician, had been called by the Frosts soon after their arrival to care for Lesley during one of her illnesses. Since then, he had taken care of all the Frost children. His daughter was in her first year as a teacher at the Academy. She had studied at Wellesley.

Another acquaintance was made that evening, a burley red-faced country squire named John C. Chase, the modestly well-to-do owner of a local woodworking factory, which turned out a variety of products including tongue depressors and similarly shaped tags for marking trees and shrubs in nurseries. Chase seemed to like this young farmer and hen-man who wanted to teach at Pinkerton. Chase, who was Secretary of the Board of Trustees, urged Frost, almost secretly, to apply at once for a position as teacher of English at the Academy. He explained that circumstances were in Frost's favor. For years the English program had been supervised by the Principal, the Reverend George Washington Bingham, near retirement and yet still teaching the seniors. At the present time the juniors were being taught English by the history teacher, Arthur Warren Reynolds, a Harvard graduate. Freshman English was Miss Clark's responsibility along with drawing. But recently the woman who had been teaching the sophomores was forced to resign because of illness and her place was being filled temporarily by a retired local minister who wanted to be relieved. Frost's record had been shown to Chase by Merriam and there was every reason for Frost to feel confident that he could get the part-time position by applying to the Principal.

At the end of his evening with the Men's League, Frost walked back down the road to his farm aware that "The Tuft of Flowers" had indeed served its purpose. He had not let himself realize how hungry he had grown for exactly the kind of attention the poem had earned from these staunch Congregationalists and he had felt the honor when asked if the local paper might print the poem in its next issue.[4] Having sent out manuscripts to periodicals for years, and having sold only five poems in twelve years, he was in no mood to care whether he would be paid or not, so long as "The Tuft of Flowers" appeared in print. Furthermore, part of his excitement at the end of this evening came from the possibility that he might soon be drawing a regular salary. During the ten years since his marriage, this was an experience he had never had.

Already familiar with the history of Pinkerton Academy, he liked the Scottish elements of it. In 1718, Scottish emigrants from the northern part of Ireland had settled in this part of New Hampshire. Many of them proudly traced their ancestry to the large colony of Scotsmen from Argyleshire, who had crossed the narrow channel between Scotland and Ireland about the year 1612 and had mingled with a colony of mechanics from London. The latter had given the name of Londonderry to the Irish town of Derry, and both groups had participated in the long guerrilla warfare between Protestants and Catholics in Northern Ireland. The Argyleshire descendents who came to New Hampshire from Londonderry in 1718, brought with them their stern Scotch Presbyterianism, together with Irish potatoes and the Irish craft of linen-making. Very soon, many fields in the area known as Londonerry-in-New-Hampshire seemed to turn blue with flax blossoms in the spring. And not too long after harvest time, great sheets of linen were spread for bleaching along the edges of Beaver Brook and West-running Brook. As different settlements developed, the descendents of these Scotsmen gradually built three little villages almost in a row. Until 1804, East Derry had been the most important section of the town. But when the turnpike was built from Lawrence to Manchester, it passed a mile to the west of East Derry, and at the new crossroads a business center developed which became known as Derry Village. Later, in 1894, when the railroad between Lawrence and Manchester had been forced to pass through the township of Derry, well beyond the western limits of the two small villages, a station was built approximately one mile southwest of Derry Village and the new community which grew up around it became known as Derry Depot.

Frost's farm was roughly two miles south of Pinkerton Academy, which stood on a knoll and held a commanding view of the region just to the north. The Academy had been founded by two Scottish merchantmen in the village: Major John and Elder James Pinkerton. The loftiness and severity of their plan had been reflected in the catalogues of Pinkerton Academy from the time of its opening in 1815: "The school is a good, safe one for diligent people who have a definite purpose . . . Others are not desired."[5] Religious emphasis, no longer Presbyterian or Congregationalist, remained strong:

"While it is not sectarian it is truly Christian. It is not forgotten that character is more than scholarship, that 'life is the highest of the arts,' that education means knowing how to live so as not to fail of life's great end. Chapel exercises are held daily and are so conducted as to furnish an incentive to scholarly ideals, true manliness and purity of character."[6]

When Frost visited the Academy to make application for a teaching position, he was shown into the office of the Principal. The Reverend George Washington Bingham was a Dartmouth graduate, seventy-five years old and yet vigorous. Slight of build, he carried his six feet well and took obvious pride in his neatly trimmed white beard, his clean-shaven upper cheeks, and the flourishing ends of his mustache. Making it clear that he had been expecting his visitor and that Frost had made a good impression on trustees Merriam and Chase, he came to the point without wasting time. If Mr. Frost would like to start teaching the sophomores English literature—two sections of them, an hour each, five days a week—during the remainder of the spring term of 1906, it was probable that a fulltime position could be given him at the beginning of the fall term. Fine. As for salary, then, would it be all right to calculate it on two-sevenths of each day's normal seven-hour teaching load at a fulltime basis of, say, a thousand or eleven hundred dollars a year? Yes, that would be all right. Very well then, a thousand. (Chagrin, and the vision of money lost merely by his failure to say that eleven hundred would be fine.) Now let's see, two-sevenths of $1,000 would come roughly to $285. All right? Yes.

With these arrangements Frost began at Pinkerton Academy late in March of 1906, driving the two miles northwest from his farm across West-running and Beaver brooks to the Village and on up the hill to the large brick building. The architects had given it solid romanesque touches in the archway entrance of the clock-topped tower flanked with rounded turret sides. The hallway entrance was large enough to foreshadow the expansive foursquare high-ceilinged classrooms on the first and second floors. Frost's two hours of teaching came so long after the opening chapel exercises that he was excused from chapel attendance or participation. Each day he left the building as soon as he had finished his two consecutive hours of teaching. The students were well-behaved and easy to handle, but the new teacher did not fail to notice that one boy in particular seemed hostile and surly. He was the son of the local dentist.

Having made this unassuming start on a new-old way of life, Frost seemed to feel that his social position in the community could no longer permit him to put up with the battered second-hand furniture and rugs in his parlor and dining room. His immediate salary was not enough to provide any outlay for improvements; his annuity of $500 would not be paid until July. Apparently, however, with the dream of $1,000 available to him from his next year's salary, he felt free to borrow more money. Although he didn't own his farm, and wouldn't legally own it until 1911, he nevertheless found a man in Manchester, New Hampshire, who was willing to lend him $750. Frost used as collateral, "My right, title and interest in and to all said premises above described being derived under and by virtue of the Fourth Clause of the will of William Prescott Frost . . ." One result of the loan was apparently reflected in

Lesley's journal, to the effect that much new furniture did suddenly appear in the parlor.[7]

Just how soon Frost thought he might be able to pay back $750 was a question which did not seem to bother him. He may have been able to reassure himself with precepts from his mother, and congenial to the Scotch Presbyterian atmosphere of the school where he was teaching. Familiar with some of Charles Kingsley's writing, he was at least sympathetic to sentiments such as these:

"God has given you a great talent, whereby you may get an honest livelihood. Take *that* as God's call to you, and follow it out. . . . And how to fear God I know not better than by working on at the speciality which He has given us, trusting to Him to make it of use to His creatures. . . . Therefore fret not nor be of doubtful mind. But just do the duty which lies nearest."[8]

Some of the same attitudes found reflection in a poem which Frost may have written in the spring of 1906. More than ever before he had reason to revel in the season which meant most to him and even to meet it with a renewed sense of "morning gladness at the brim." The poem was "A Prayer in Spring":

Oh, give us pleasure in the flowers today;
And give us not to think so far away
As the uncertain harvest; keep us here
All simply in the springing of the year.

Oh, give us pleasure in the orchard white,
Like nothing else by day, like ghosts by night;
And make us happy in the happy bees,
The swarm dilating round the perfect trees.

And make us happy in the darting bird
That suddenly above the bees is heard,
The meteor that thrusts in with needle bill,
And off a blossom in mid air stands still.

For this is love and nothing else is love,
The which it is reserved for God above
To sanctify to what far ends He will,
But which it only needs that we fulfill.[9]

Soon after vacation began, in the summer of 1906, other expressions of affluence were made. Perhaps it seemed to Frost that Elinor had earned a special vacation after her years of caring for their growing family. She still kept in touch with some of her St. Lawrence University classmates and it may be that she accepted her husband's urging to visit one of them at this time. Perhaps for his own reasons he urged her also to visit the Wards in Newark; at least he made arrangements for such a visit by writing to Susan Hayes Ward on 17 July 1906:

"My wife will be visiting at Pocantico Hills [New York] next week, and that is so near you I thought I should like to have her call on you, if you happened not to have gone away for your summer vacation. Would there be any afternoon of the week after July Twenty-fourth when it would be convenient for you to see her?"[10]

The hope was realized; Miss Ward was extremely hospitable; and the entire trip made by Elinor at this time was beneficial to the long-suffering wife and mother. While she was absent from the Derry farm her husband not only cared for the children and the farm but also found time for a new burst of writing poems, many of which he sent to Miss Ward with the following letter:

". . . Ever since Elinor came back from New York breathing inspiration, I have been ambitious to get some of my larger thoughts into shape for you; but it seems they won't be driven—not at least by a sick man. There's one about the Demiurge's Laugh (good title?) which if I can take it by surprise some day ought to be made to mean something. Meanwhile there are these. Believe me, it is not from anything like neglect that I have not sent them sooner. Since the ragweed dusted, I have done nothing and written nothing—except my own epitaph provisionally like this:

> *There was a poor mortal believer*
> *Who gave way to a thought of hay fever:*
> *He coughed like a cold*
> *Till over he rolled*
> *And went into the hands of a receiver.*

A very false gallop of verses which I achieved in despite of my invention and which I insert here with some hesitation, it having met with no especial success in the family. But to my poems. My fear is that you will feel overwhelmed by the number. You need read of them only so long as your patience holds out. Too bad that they are still a little timid. Daring is with me a plant of slow growth—or say health is. But I shall get the right tone yet, give me time."[11]

In his letter to Miss Ward, he had failed to say that after his wife returned from her down-country visit, he had gone up-country to Bethlehem, New Hampshire, to try to climb above ragweed pollen just long enough to avoid the worst of the hay-fever season. He had gone alone and had been forced to shorten his visit when letters from home informed him that the cow and several of his children had been ill.

As for the poem with the good title, it was a further expression of the warfare he had been waging belatedly on the side of religion against the mid-nineteenth-century impact of Darwinian evolution. Since high-school days, when Carl Burell had first exposed him to Darwinism, Frost had been of two minds about the new realms of knowledge and theory made available to him. As long as he could find the evolutionary theories made palatable by scientists like Richard A. Proctor, who gracefully adjusted them to a Christian viewpoint, he could pick and choose elements which were to his taste. But as he grew older and acquired help from William James's scornful references to the uses of reason based on merely the limited facts of science, he apparently felt with James that science did not leave enough room for the wonder-working providences of God. From his readings in Shelley and Plato, he had found a useful figure which he borrowed for poetry. Plato reviewed the myth that the act of creation had been assigned to a Demiurge, a being unlike the Christian God and characterized as a functional or evolutionary force serving as architect. According to Plato, the Demiurge followed the "form" of Goodness in his creation, but because he was building with mere elements of matter, his creation was always lower than the ideal "form" of Goodness which served as the model. The Demiurge seemed to be completely indifferent to this discrepancy and was not sympathetic to man's spiritual quest. He was therefore inclined to be scornfully pessimistic concerning human aspirations. Closely related was another mythic story, which Frost may have found in several places. It was said that King Midas once hunted long in the woods for the wise Silenus, companion of Dionysos, without being able to catch him. When the daemon was finally caught by the king, he remained sullen and uncommunicative, finally breaking into shrill laughter, and saying,

"Ephemeral wretch, begotten by accident and toil, why do you force me to tell you what it would be your greatest boon not to hear? What would be best for you is quite beyond your reach; not to have been born, not to *be*, to be *nothing*. But the second best is to die soon."[12]

In his poem "The Demiurge's Laugh," Frost created a parable based on the raw materials of these old myths. He represented himself as having conducted a search for the modern Demiurge named Evolution in the hope of learning from him the ultimate mysteries of life, but when finally he was rewarded for all his effort merely by indifference, atheism, laughter, he responded with his own kind of indifference for the modern Demiurge and implicitly returned to the mysterious contemplation and worship of the unknown First Principle, God:

> *It was far in the sameness of the wood;*
> *I was running with joy on the Demon's trail,*
> *Though I knew what I hunted was no true god.*
> *It was just as the light was beginning to fail*
> *That I suddenly heard—all I needed to hear:*
> *It has lasted me many and many a year.*
>
> *The sound was behind me instead of before,*
> *A sleepy sound, but mocking half,*
> *As of one who utterly couldn't care.*
> *The Demon arose from his wallow to laugh,*
> *Brushing the dirt from his eyes as he went;*
> *And well I knew what the Demon meant.*
>
> *I shall not forget how his laugh rang out.*
> *I felt as a fool to have been so caught,*
> *And checked my steps to make pretense*
> *It was something among the leaves I sought*
> *(Though doubtful whether he stayed to see).*
> *Thereafter I sat me against a tree.*[13]

An entirely different kind of laughter, heard by Frost very largely in his own imagination at the time he began teaching

English literature and composition at Pinkerton, bothered him more than that of the Demiurge. He quickly sorted out his friends from his so-called enemies, assuming that his new friend, John C. Chase, was working in his behalf by writing and publishing in the *Derry News* for 14 September 1906 a brief item which seemed calculated to support the new teacher: "The fall term at Pinkerton Academy opened Tuesday with about 50 new students in attendance. Mr. R. L. Frost has been secured as assistant in English and makes a valuable addition to the faculty." By contrast, Frost felt the scorn of his fellow English teacher, Arthur Warren Reynolds, Harvard graduate, who went out of his way to commiserate that Frost had been unable to spend even as much as two full years at Harvard—and that he was forced to teach without having a college degree. Reynold's hostility and apparent jealousy may have been heightened when one of the periodicals—*The Independent*—in the library at the Academy carried in its issue for 11 October 1906 the long poem entitled "The Trial by Existence," written by the new teacher of English. The ordained and retired minister, Principal Bingham, went out of his way to say he had read and admired the poem. The pastor of the Congregational Church, the Reverend C. L. Merriam, flatteringly discussed the poem with its author. The affable John Chase, Secretary of the Board, frankly said he cared less for poetry than for the excellent publicity given Pinkerton by the appearance of such a poem in a nationally distributed periodical.

All of this attention had a stimulating effect on Frost's writing, some of which he shared only with the community in Derry. After he had been reading Longfellow's *The Courtship of Miles Standish, Evangeline,* and some of the shorter poems with his students in the classroom, he may have proposed that because the approaching date of 27 February 1907 was being celebrated throughout the nation as the centennial of the poet's birth a chapel service be devoted to Longfellow. Plans were made for the service and Frost wrote a commemorative poem for the occasion. Although he refused to read it, the poem was given special attention. It was printed as a broadside, distributed to the students at the service, and was sung to a suitable tune of a familiar hymn.[14]

Frost shared an entirely different kind of poem with the larger community two days after the celebration of Longfellow's birthday. Once again he was invited to attend the annual banquet of the Men's League of the First Congregational Church and to read a poem; once again he agreed to attend if the pastor, Merriam, would read for him. He still could not bear the thought of standing before an audience to read aloud even one of his poems. Sympathetically, Merriam again served as his substitute, while Frost sat listening with the others who attended the banquet. The poem was entitled "The Lost Faith" and the subject matter would have made it more appropriate for a Memorial Day service. The theme was the poet's regret that the ideals for which the Union soldiers had fought so heroically during the Civil War had become so nearly forgotten. Two passages, centrally located within this seventy-seven line poem, clearly define this faith:

> No less a dream than of one law of love,
> One equal people under God above!
> But fallen to be a word of easy scorn.
> See that it dies not—if it is not dead!
>
> . . .
>
> Oh, such a dream as cannot have lost worth
> Forever, for an unredeemed earth.
> I cannot make it wholly dead to men.
> Not late, but soon, it must return again—
> In blood mayhap, with maddening life and drum,
> And reaping souls—I care not, so it come!
> All beautiful and human as it was,
> It could be terrible in its own cause;
> As when it swept the skirts of Malvern Hill
> And when it crouched in wait as deadly still
> On Gettysburg's low height,
> As the oncoming foe were swift and shrill.
> Men knew us not until that wavering flight!
> And keep not now the thought that moved in us!
> How earthly death came ever near to touch
> A dream so deathless, we to forget it thus,
> I do not know; we saw it fade from sight,
> Not while we slept, but while we strove too much
> For things that were not beautiful and bright. . . .[15]

"The Lost Faith" was so well-received that the editor of the local newspaper requested permission to publish all of it in *The Derry News,* where it appeared in the issue for 1 March 1907, signed "Robert Lee Frost." Quite plainly, the poem implied that its author had relinquished at least some of those Copperhead sympathies taught him by his father. Nevertheless, it also implied that Frost still preserved his early conviction that heroic combat and bloodshed are the highest measures of man's self-sacrifice for his ideals. In addition Frost was continuing to write with an increase of religious fervor, now that his initial leanings, fostered by his mother, were being fortified by the Congregational ministers with and for whom he was teaching. There was no trace of the hypocritical in this fervor, and it never abated in him for long, even though there were intermittent spells when the pressures caused by his skepticism forced him to make statements which offended the orthodox; statements which were sometimes mistakenly interpreted as "proofs" that Frost was an "atheist."

For the moment, while the Congregationalists among the Derry townspeople were becoming more favorably impressed with the new teacher at Pinkerton Academy, some of his students were not so easily persuaded to like him. A few of them mistook his early nervousness and gravity as proof that Mr. Frost was a dour man completely lacking in any sense of humor. Several boys and girls complained that he put too much stress on composition and on memorizing poetry. Others discounted his abilities as a teacher by passing the word that he was down on his luck, that he was merely a failed "henman." One of these went so far as to scrawl that epithet across the blackboard in his classroom one morning, before anyone else appeared. Frost arrived early enough to be alone when he discovered the scrawl. He could have erased it, but he had reasons for leaving it. As he waited for the students to come in, he sorted through his batch of corrected compositions, hunting for the identity of the culprit whose handwriting matched the scrawl on the board. He found it, unmistakably. As the students filed in, taking their seats, they glanced at the board and began to whisper. He pretended not to notice. But as soon as the bell rang and the hour of instruction had formally begun, he showed the same rigorous Scotch-Presbyterian discipline exercised by the first principal of the Academy, Elder James Pinkerton. Almost unable to keep his wrath under control, he pointed an accusing finger at the culprit, glanced over his shoulder at the blackboard, and said, "For writing that get out of my class—and don't ever come back."

The effect was extraordinary. Before the end of the day there was no member of the school who had not heard the news. Frost was called into the office of the Principal, who was duly sympathetic. But, of course, Bingham explained, it would be impossible to keep the boy from attending Frost's classes indefinitely; he would then fail the course, and would have to leave Pinkerton.

"Then he will have to leave Pinkerton," said the hen-man.

More consultations were held. Opinions were sought from members of the Board of Trustees. Chase and Merriam sided with Frost, and the boy was expelled. After that, the new teacher had no trouble with discipline and, much to their surprise, the students very soon learned that their seemingly dour English teacher had a very fine sense of humor, at least until something made him cross.

His best students praised the relaxed manner in which he soon began to conduct his classes and his way of getting them started on compositions. Instead of asking them to write about subjects they had been studying, he told them to base their sketches or essays on their own experiences: on facts observed, on ideas which were all their own. He teased them by writing on the blackboard four possible types of subject matter for sketches and by asking them to say which should make the most interesting composition:

> *Uncommon in experience—uncommon in writing*
> *Common in experience—common in writing*
> *Uncommon in experience—common in writing*
> *Common in experience—uncommon in writing*

When he read their papers aloud, without giving the name of the author, he convinced them that the most interesting ones were those based on closely observed facts common in experience and yet uncommon in writing. Once, when the Wright brothers were making news with their flying machines, he added another rule: "Don't write unless you have something to say. If you don't have it, go and get it." Then he showed them what he meant. The Wright brothers gave him something to say about the word "flight," which could mean several things. It could mean escape from life, for example. Then he added:

"I hate most the fellow who makes common stories of the flight of man. He came out of the heavy mist and contemplated the terms [of life] and accepted them. They [the terms] were then as they are now: a little more pleasure than pain. Pain greater in length and breadth but exceeded by pleasure in height; one more pleasure than pain by actual count— the pleasure of being alive."

That was a little demonstration for the students of what he meant when he said to them, "Don't write until you have something to say." It didn't have to be a big something. He gave them another example, based on their reading of Milton's *Comus:*

"Milton spoke in terms of the studies of his youth about the great events that were drawing him away from those studies. In *Comus* he said, 'Love Virtue, she alone is free.' The only free man is the abject slave of virtue? Not so. The free man will use virtue as he will vice, to the ends of his own free spirit."

Immediately, he changed his direction to give the students another example of what he meant by having something to say:

"We approve of people to their faces to gain their approval. We disapprove of them behind their backs to gain our own approval. But we are the two-faced devils."

For his final illustration he returned to the Wright brothers. There had been previous kinds of bold voyaging: across the ocean to discover America, across the Arctic to reach the North Pole. Lesser voyagers are often praised for what they do, but:

". . . They are all like imitators of the great. Their intention is good, but they don't know what the great really did for them to imitate. Columbus for instance didn't cross the Atlantic. He didn't suffer hardships and privations. At least, not for these things is he Columbus. Why is he immortal, then? Can't you tell? Well, because he had the faith that so few people are capable of; the faith of an idea. Not for him to feel his way around Africa to India. He launched out into space with the supreme confidence of reason. Great in his confidence, great in his justification. The nearest him [are] among the aviators and the only ones near him are the Wright brothers."[16]

Stimulated by examples like these, the best Pinkerton students realized that their teacher wanted them to have ideas of their own and to reach beyond their grasp. They could not always keep up with their new teacher or follow him in all he said, but they recognized the freshness of his approach to originality, and they liked it.

They also liked his way of combining instruction in reading, elocution, and rhetoric. He insisted that the test of their appreciation could be measured by the qualities of expression when they read aloud in class rather than by their analytical comments. He set them examples by reading aloud poems and short stories and chapters of assigned novels. He made them understand how many different meanings were implicit in the word "dramatic," and he taught them subtle forms of pace, volume, emphasis in conveying dramatic shadings when each took his turn at reading aloud. His goal, he said, was to increase the pleasure they derived from reading. Again and again he wrote on the blackboard, and asked them to remember, his favorite instruction for doing assignments on their reading list:

To be read—to be enjoyed
Not studied—not skimmed

This approach was all new in a school where so much attention had previously been paid to more conventional methods of teaching. The Principal, Mr. Bingham, had his own way of combining instruction in literature, rhetoric, elocution: he brought each senior class to a summary of its work by coaching it for the presentation of one of Shakespeare's plays. This annual production had become a regular part of the curriculum, and it provided a distinct addition to the sparse winter entertainments in Derry. There was no danger that the new teacher's approach to the world "dramatic" would embarrass Mr. Bingham or change his old-fashioned notions. But Frost did stir up trouble while he was coaching second-year students for participation in the interclass debates.

The Academy was proud of its Philomathean Society, conducted by the students to promote literary and forensic improvement. The weekly meetings were supervised by members of the faculty and the atmosphere of these meetings was far more dignified than that of the Debating Union to which Frost had belonged while in high school. The prospect of coaching the sophomore class (the "Junior Middlers" as they were called at Pinkerton) aroused in him a fierce spirit of competition, when he discovered that the "worthy opponents," drawn from the senior class, would be coached by his enemy, Arthur Warren Reynolds. Forcing his best sophomores to work overtime in gathering materials for the debate, Frost assured them that if they were willing to work hard enough they could triumph over the seniors. He required them to write out the full texts of their arguments and to submit them for his consideration. Then he revised and strengthened, until the arguments were more nearly his than theirs. The extra work required of him—and the tedious after-school practice sessions —seemed more exhausting than any work he had ever done on the Derry farm. But when the debate was held between the sophomore and seniors, the sophomore were the winners.

The hen-man was satisfied. He had vindicated himself as a teacher and he had avenged himself against the insinuative deprecations of Reynolds in this first round of a continuous battle. But at the very moment of his triumph Frost was also aware that he was ill, largely as a result of nervous and physical strain. At first he told himself that his wracking cough was merely a return of hay fever out of season. But at the end of the two-week spring vacation, he was flat in bed. *The Derry News* for 5 April 1907 carried a brief reference to his predicament: "The spring and summer term of Pinkerton Academy opened on Tuesday with the usual number of students in attendance. R. L. Frost is unable to be at his post. He has been very sick with pneumonia."[17] More details were given in the May issue of the literary magazine published by the students: ". . . ill with pneumonia and would not be able to teach any more this year. The Junior Middle Class was especially sorry to lose their English teacher, and so sent a large bunch of pinks which he was very pleased to receive."[18]

26

LIFT UP MINE EYES

And from there those that lifted eyes could count
Five mountain ranges one behind the other
Under the sunset far into Vermont.[1]

ROBERT FROST'S BOUT with pneumonia during March and
April of 1907 was very nearly fatal. When he was at his worst,
his own physician, Dr. Clark, became ill, and a younger doctor
took his place. There was an entirely new treatment being
used for pneumonia, he explained: lots of fresh air. The best
thing they could do for Frost was to make up a bed for him on
the porch and let him stay out there day and night, no matter
how low the thermometer dropped. No, thanks, Frost said,
he'd rather die in the house.

When he gradually convinced himself that he wasn't going
to die, this time, he was well aware that he would need months
before he could regain his health. He was embarrassed by the
fact that he required so much attention, particularly as it became apparent that Elinor (who was expecting another child
in June) was being physically dragged down. They decided
that for his sake and hers—not to mention the four children—
the only sensible thing to do was to hire a practical nurse to
"live in" until Frost was able to get up and about. They found
one, tried her for a week, and dismissed her. Elinor again took
on more work than she could stand; and just as Frost was
beginning to get his feet under him again, she became ill. It
was his turn to care for her, and by the time she had recovered, he was down again.

At this stage the Frosts had an unexpected visitor, none
other than Edmund J. Harwood, from whom Frost's grandfather had bought the Derry farm. The hawk-faced little man
devoted the first part of his call so exclusively to commisera-
tions for the invalid, beside whose bed he sat talking, that

Frost was almost convinced he had come merely to make a neighborly visit—although this was the first time Harwood had been in the house since he'd sold it. But as soon as Harwood said he feared that the big horse in the barn was eating up more hay and grain than he was worth, Frost was able to guess the purpose of the call.

A year earlier, when he had begun his duties as part-time teacher at Pinkerton, he had gone back and forth to school with Eunice and the sulky. Each morning, however, he would spend so much time feeding and cleaning and harnessing Eunice that he had gradually realized he could walk the two miles more conveniently than he could ride. And before the summer vacation started, he sold Eunice to a neighbor for a price just a bit better than what he had originally paid.

After he had returned from Bethlehem in the White Mountains he found reasons for wanting to have a horse again. At the Hood farm he was offered a roan gelding with some Morgan blood, a stocky horse which could be used either for the sulky or the democrat wagon—or for plowing. But the price had been $200, and Frost had hesitated. A few weeks later, when he stopped again at the Hood farm, he was offered the same horse for $150, and the sale was immediately completed. Harwood was correct in guessing that the big horse (called Noah by the Hoods, renamed Billy-the-Second by Frost) was a useless expense and trouble—particularly when the care of Billy rested with Elinor and their eight-year-old daughter Lesley.

Frost was ready to sell, even before Harwood began dropping hints. But his chronic resentment flared when he suspected Harwood of hoping to make a cheap horse trade with a sick man. The conversation went on at some length: Harwood had seen and admired the horse when the Hood people owned him, had even considered buying him then. If Frost was interested in selling, Harwood would like to be of help. Well, said Frost, he wouldn't want to take too much of a loss. He supposed Harwood knew what the Hood farm had asked for the horse. Yes, Harwood said, $200. Would Frost consider it too much of a loss if Harwood paid him $175? Under the circumstances, Frost said, maybe not. So the deal was closed. Harwood paid for Billy that night, and took the horse with him. The bedridden amateur horse-trader, pleased at having outsmarted a professional, said it served Harwood right for pretending to "succor a sucker."

Harwood's visit and the little triumph cheered Frost so much that it may have been at this time that he found himself in a playful mood and wrote a letter in verse. Only part of the first draft has survived. An obvious parody of Coleridge's famous "Rime," even to the shoulder notes, it may have been an attempt to re-establish the nonsensical exchanges he had formerly had with Carl Burell. The apology at the start suggests as much:

The ancient friend begins to explain why he hasn't written sooner

It is an ancient friend of yours
And he takes a minute or two
To tell you how the business goes
And how the family do.

A blizzard freezes him to the gizzard

Down dropped the leaves, the
*   nuts dropped down*
Merrily did we enter
The time of snow, until one blow
It froze us to the center.

The sink regurgitates and the apples, onions & potatoes gel

Three days it shook the house
*   and it*
Was tyrranous and strong.
It froze the cellar it froze the sink
We had to wear fur caps to think
And for the south did long.

Zeroism kills the time-killer and the rain comes down dry

Alone alone and all alone
Alone on a windy hill
With water water everywhere
And never a drop to spill
The question was would the time
*   kill us*
As we the time did kill.

Ineffectualness of the maker's name and patent applied for on the Yankee notion

A dreary time a dreary time
We drank the cider potion
As idle as the maker's name
Upon a Yankee notion.

Bugs

And some in dreams persuaded
were

And some in common seance
That fiends that else must have
    gotten ahold
By naught but the utter absolute
    cold
Were kept in a state of abeyance.

Nine fathoms deep they were
    kept asleep
As deep as the frost in Siberia
And some were blobs and some
    were worms
But all were small for they were
    the germs
Of pneumonia and diptheria.

The cow gradually goes dry

[*No verse for this*]

Winter should be taken like a toddy

But I cannot agree with the germ
    theoree
And I'll take my winters hot
Un-Pasteurized by zeroic nights
A little rather than not.

He cannot pray

Since then I have hover of
    speech
That makes me prose in verses
But when I try to speak aloud
It takes the form of curses.
Plain oathes with me—with the
    women folk
My goodnesses and mercies.

Inelastic currency as much to blame as anything

The Hermit good lived where he
    could
I would be down in the tropics
Where there are no gales of
    coughter more
But I cannot muster the ko-
    pecks.[2]

Frost may have felt that because the parody came off well only in parts he would not send it. But at the time, he certainly could have used Carl's help on the farm. As had so often happened before, the neighborly French-Canadian, Napoleon Guay, served on a sharecrop basis: milking the cow, caring for the small brood of Wyandottes, and taking his pay in milk, eggs, and hens-for-roasting. Guay was well aware of Frost's revulsion against chopping off the head of a hen, getting spattered with blood, breathing little plucked feathers, and scooping out entrails with bare hands. Out of neighborliness, Guay dressed a bird for the Frosts occasionally, and left it hanging by its feet in the shed.

Early in June of 1907, just when arrangements were being made for Mrs. Frost to move in to Derry Village to stay with a practical nurse until after her sixth child was born, another visitor arrived at the Frost farm uninvited: Jeanie. Dependent as she had been on her mother, whose death had forced her into shifting for herself, she gave the appearance of having done very well since last she had visited the Frosts in Derry. Her clothes indicated that she was by no means poverty-stricken, and because her brother had thought that she was teaching school for a meager salary outside Boston, he had his reasons for cross-examining her about what she had been doing since last he heard. Well, she had given up school-teaching because she had found that she could make more money, posing, in various studios of Boston artists. Her last work had been in the studio of John La Farge—one of his classes for younger painters. Posing nude? her brother wanted to know. Not at all: the subject had been a Pietà, and she had been the mother of Christ. It was true that she did have to hold a nearly naked man in her arms for an hour at a time, but that was just a part of the work. Yeah, her brother said. Keep up that work for a little while and she'd be the mother of something else. Oh he had a dirty mind, she said. He did, did he? He might not be sure what she was thinking about, while she was posing for younger painters, but he certainly knew what the younger painters were thinking about, and he thought she ought to be ashamed of herself for getting mixed up in that way of earning a living. It wouldn't be long before she'd be a common prostitute.

So the visit started, with evidence that Rob and Jeanie could get along no better now than they did when they were growing up. He would have been glad if his ruthlessly harsh words had driven her out of the house the day she arrived. But she decided that Elinor needed her; she would stay and take care of the children while Elinor was gone. She did stay, and it seemed to Rob that Elinor was lucky in having an excuse for getting out of there. The more he talked with his sister, the more completely convinced he became that she was a bad influence.

Her conversations with the children made his flesh creep. When he saw her, holding Lesley on her lap in the parlor, looking out at the pine grove which covered Klein's Hill, and saying in an almost hysterical voice that there must be a graveyard up there under the pines and soon they would be buried there, all in a row, and wouldn't that be nice, her brother told her to shut up. A little later he found her in the kitchen making a pot of coffee and telling Lesley that she was a coffee drunkard, and if Lesley wanted to see her get drunk on coffee just watch. It was a capacity she did possess, and Frost was enraged. He tried to explain that he couldn't stand these goings on, that he was still a sick man, that he had almost died of pneumonia. Too bad he hadn't, Jeanie said. He was inclined to agree.

One of their arguments built up until Jeanie really went into hysterics, skipped out on the porch carrying a coffee cup in one hand and the saucer in another, hurried out into the drive when her brother tried to get her into the house, and then ran out into the road screaming when he went after her. That was more than he could stand, particularly because he knew it was time for people to be coming home from the shoe shops at Derry Depot. He went back into the house, found his loaded revolver, rushed out to the road, and threatened to kill her if she didn't get back into the house fast. She knew her brother's temper well enough to suspect that he might be telling the truth, and she did as he ordered. Apparently convinced that she was in danger if she stayed there any longer, Jeanie packed her bag and left.

At the home of the practical nurse in Derry, Elinor Frost gave birth to her fourth daughter on 18 June 1907. She was named Elinor Bettina and she died soon after she was born. Elinor took the loss with the despairing fatalism which had become habitual with her; Frost blamed himself for the child's death. He said that he never should have let Elinor take care of him when he had been sick with pneumonia. He never should have dismissed the nurse who was hired to take care of him. His grief was entirely different from the grief he had felt when Elliott died, and yet his deep sense of guilt was genuine.[3]

Now there were two invalids at the Frost farm and more reason than ever to consider a new way of life in some other part of the country that might be more sensible, healthy, profitable. Frost received no salary from Pinkerton Academy during the spring term of 1907, and as soon as he could bring himself to send out more poems to magazines he did so. *The Independent* had not seemed to like any of his offerings since "The Trial by Existence," although one of them was held long enough to give him hope. In writing to Susan Hayes Ward concerning the poem, he mentioned matters of health in conclusion: "Yes we are both the merest convalescents for the present (Mrs. Frost will write and tell you all about it sometime), barely equal to wishing you one good wish of health and happiness between us."

In his next letter to Miss Ward, he gave one hint that he still wistfully dreamed of a literary career which would justify his leaving the farm and moving to New York City or near it: "Sometime we intend to be nearer New York than we are, if it can come about in the right way. But that is one of the dreams. Poetry, I am afraid, will be less likely to bring us there than prose." For the present he seemed to be stuck. There was at least the consolation of the annuity check for $500 from the trust fund of his grandfather's estate, and the assurance that he would be teaching again at Pinkerton Academy in the fall for the annual salary of $1,000, if he was well enough.

Memories of his pleasant experience in the White Mountains during the hay-fever season of the summer before made him suggest to Elinor at least a temporary escape from the farm. Suppose they took the children up to Bethlehem this year and stayed until the ragweed had finished the worst of its dusting down in the valleys? They might even stay until near the time when classes began at Pinkerton Academy late in September. This was the plan he had almost put into effect the previous summer, when he had been so lonesome. Even the children knew the details of that story and how the plan had been spoiled.

He had gone to Bethlehem in August of 1906 without making any reservations. It did not matter to him that the hotels were already filled with summer visitors, including those hay-fever victims who claimed that Bethlehem was the best of all retreats for his kind of ailment. Through luck or guidance, he had stepped into a drug store to ask where he might find an inexpensive place to stay, and the druggist had immediately introduced him to a customer standing near, an Irishman named Michael Fitzgerald. It seemed that Fitzgerald owned and managed a small hotel some four miles outside Bethlehem, on the high part of the South Road to Franconia. His place was perched on the side of Garnet Mountain. From it could be seen five mountain ranges to the west toward Vermont. Fitz-gerald's rooms were all taken, but Frost could have meals with his guests and rent a room in a nearby farmhouse owned by another Irishman, John Lynch, Fitzgerald's relative.

So it had worked out. The Lynch farm was within easy walking distance of Fitzgerald's hotel, and Frost had taken an immediate liking to John Lynch. In his sixties, with a full beard and a dry taciturn manner, Lynch had come from County Kerry. On the boat to America he had met an alert, pretty Irish girl, much younger than he, and they had married after he established himself. For their wedding trip, the bride and groom had gone back to Ireland briefly, and had returned to settle in New Hampshire. Their children were grown up; two boys and two girls, graduates of the high school in Bethle-hem. The oldest girl had married and lived near them on the South Road.

There certainly seemed to be quite a collection of Irish families in the neighborhood, and Frost had taken more plea-sure in mingling with these fellow-Celts than in talking with summer guests at Fitzgerald's. But he had grown so lonesome for his family that the Lynches had taken pity on him. They had said that if Frost wanted to have his wife and children join him, a couple of extra rooms could be found for them in the farmhouse—and the Frosts could have use of the living room as well as the kitchen. He had been ready to carry out the plan when he had been called home by illness.

Why not carry it out now in August and September of 1907, if the Lynches were still able to rent the rooms? They were, and before leaving Derry, Frost made arrangements with his reliable neighbor, Guay, for taking care of the hens and the cow. The trip was made by train and the Lynches welcomed the strangers as though they were long-lost members of the family.

That stay with the Lynches for six weeks high in the White Mountains was a glorious experience for all of the Frosts. There were so many children in the neighborhood that some kind of excitement was always in progress. A baseball diamond had been cleared in one of the many fields which glaciers had strewn with boulders, and as Frost's legs grew stronger he played any kind of baseball game which could be arranged. Not forgetting that his primary duty was to recover his health, he set himself to other exercise. The worst of all was the walk down Break-neck Hill to the village of Franconia and back. The going was steep enough to be difficult. The return trip was so hard on him that he had to stretch out by the side of the road to rest several times before he could get back to the Lynches, up where the road dipped back down toward Bethlehem village. It was enough to make him realize that much as he wanted to climb some of the fine peaks in Franconia notch—Lafayette, Lincoln, Liberty—he was not yet ready for it. But his games with the children gradually toughened him up, until he felt that he was ready for teaching again—although he did not look forward to it.

One memorable part of those summer weeks with the Lynches was the gathering of old and young on the porch of the farmhouse each evening for songs and storytelling. To carry out his fatherly part, Frost entered into all the fun and nonsense with gusto, partly because he took so much pleasure in being the center of attention. But after the children had been sent to bed, he liked to draw out the Lynches, whose Irish accents and viewpoints gave special flavor to accounts of neighborhood events, past and present. Mrs. Lynch was fond of telling her favorite stories about her husband's dry comments—for example, the retort "Johnny" had given to their neighbor and relative, Fitzgerald, who was said to have burned down his hotel for the insurance that spring. On the day of the fire Johnny had been completely absorbed with the fussy task of putting new wallpaper on his farmhouse living room and he had just begun to attach a long sticky sheet near the ceiling when Fitzgerald burst into the room hysterically pleading for help; his hotel was on fire, he said. Johnny, unperturbed, kept fussing with the alignment of the wallpaper and did not even look over his shoulder as he made his calm pronouncement to Fitzgerald: "Let them as set the fire put it out."

Johnny was an omnivorous reader of newspapers, and his wife had many stories about her inability to get him out from behind his paper even for emergencies. Her favorite was of the day when he kept reading, through this exchange, between them: "Johnny, the cow's in the corn." "Whose corn's she in?" "Our own, you may be sure." "Go drive her into someone else's, then."[4]

Mrs. Lynch blended scorn with sadness when she told the story of a local girl who trained as a nurse in Boston, married there, later fell in love with one of her patients, and ran away from her Boston husband to live in hiding with her lover on a small farm not far down the road from the Lynches. Frost casually prompted the telling of that story when he asked Mrs. Lynch to explain an event which had puzzled him. He had taken his five-year-old son Carol for an evening walk along the South Road and they had sauntered so far that it grew dark before they could get back. Returning in the twilight, they heard the approach of a horse and carriage, saw the carriage lamp on the dashboard of the approaching vehicle, and stepped off the narrow dirt road to let horse and carriage pass. Frost had noticed the way the driver, a woman, had touched up the horse with the whip to hurry him on. He had seen the carriage turn in at the very next house on that lonely road— there were only a half-dozen farms scattered along the six-mile route between Franconia and Bethlehem—and he heard a man and woman talking beside the carriage in the farmyard as he and Carol walked past. Then the woman had called to them. She came forward in the darkness carrying a lantern and asked what they were doing, prowling around her house at night. Frost explained that they weren't prowling. He was merely taking his son for an evening walk and they were returning to the Lynch farm, where they were staying. The woman had apologized, but Frost gathered from her tone of voice that there must have been reasons behind her suspicions. When he asked who the woman was, Mrs. Lynch tossed her head sideways and threw her hands out: "Ech, she thinks she's the Qu'an o' the Road." Then she told the story, and added that the woman seemed to live in mortal terror of being found— and possibly murdered—by the husband whom she had forsaken for the love of another man. To Frost, these were raw materials for poetry, and he later used them in his dramatic narrative "The Fear."⁵

Outlasting all the other summer visitors on the South Road, the Frosts lingered at the Lynch farm far into September—as late as they could. The air seemed to be medicine for Frost and he particularly liked the smell of it when the second mowing of hay mingled its pungency with the ever-present odors of spruce and hemlock. So charmed had he become by the vistas of rock-strewn fields, woods, valleys, and mountain ranges that he would have been willing to stay in that wilderness indefinitely, if he could have found a way to earn a living—perhaps by sending his poems out to eager publishers from there. But the publishers weren't eager, and for want of any better way to make ends meet, he took his family back to Derry, resigned to to start teaching at Pinkerton again when the fall term of 1907 began.

Before the Frosts left the Lynch farm, they briefly entertained Susan Hayes Ward. She had come over from her place of retirement in Maine to visit them, and she seemed to enjoy the experience so much that Frost shared with her the memory of it, in a letter to her from Derry dated 4 November 1907:

"We have been at home for some time, but this is the first opportunity I have had to say so in so many words. I know you will forgive my not writing sooner when I tell you that my little capacities have been taxed to the utmost in getting our English department to rights at school. On top of everything else I have been asked to prepare a historical article on the Academy—in prose. Naturally I consume some part of every day merely dreading to undertake that. But written it will have to be, if I am to save my reputation as a poet (upon which everything hangs.)

[. . .]

"How long ago and far away Bethlehem is already. Our summer was one of the pleasantest we have had for years. But it is almost hard for me to believe in the reality of it now. I have been that way from boyhood. The feeling of time and space is perennially strange to me. I used to lie awake at night imagining the places I had traversed in the day and doubting in simple wonderment that I who was here could possibly have been there and there. I can't look at my little slope of field here with leaves in the half dead grass, or at the bare trees the birds have left us with, and fully believe there were ever such things as the snug downhill churning room with the view over five ranges of mountains, our talks under the hanging lamp and over the fat blue book, the tea-inspired Mrs. Lynch, baseball, and the blue black Lafayette [Mountain]. There is a pang there that makes poetry. I rather like to gloat over it."[6]

For Frost, there was nothing feigned in this meditative pleasure. His happiness over memories of Bethlehem and Franconia was inseparable from his intense cherishing and caring. It gave a new lift to his spirit, and he threw himself into his teaching at Pinkerton that fall with energy and capacity greater than he had been able to spend during his two previous terms. Bingham, almost ready to retire, had been so impressed with Frost's work in teaching literature, elocution, and rhetoric that he had invited him to reorganize the entire English program. The results were not immediately noticeable, and yet within the next four years (1907-1911) Frost's methods of teaching attracted the attention of authorities outside the Academy. When Bingham made known his wish to have the trustees look for a successor, the loyal and admiring Secretary of the Board, John C. Chase, felt sure that Frost was the man for the position—and Frost very seriously considered the possibility. Part of his eagerness in this regard was caused by his knowledge that Chase and others were also considering Arthur Warren Reynolds as a candidate. When consulted by Chase, Frost was content to make insinuations enough concerning Reynolds to be certain that his enemy should not be given the position—and then was willing to admit that he himself could not take it because his lack of a college degree would cause too much criticism and jealousy.

One indication of the radical changes effected by Frost in the teaching of English at Pinkerton, was provided by the statement of the English curriculum as he was permitted to draw it up for publication in the annual catalogue of the Academy:

ENGLISH

"The general aim of the course in English is twofold: to bring our students under the *influence* of the great books, and to teach them the *satisfaction* of superior speech.

"ENGLISH I.

READINGS:—Treasure Island, Robinson Crusoe (not in class), Horatius at the Bridge, Sohrab and Rustum, selections from Odyssey, selections from Arabian Nights, ten short stories (in class). Expression in oral reading rather than intelligent comment is made the test of appreciation.

COMPOSITION:—Fifty themes, written and oral; given direction by assignment of subjects. Criticism addressed to subject matter equally with form.

RHETORIC:—Talks on the subject, what it is (with copious illustrations from the experience of the teacher) and where to be found.

MEMORIZING:—Twenty poems from the Golden Treasury; basis of subsequent study of the history of English literature.

ENGLISH II.

READING:—Pilgrim's Progress, Ivanhoe, thirty short stories (not in class), As You Like It, Ancient Mariner, Gareth and Lynette, Passing of Arthur, selections from Hanson's Composition (in class). Discussion proceeds more and more without the goad of the direct question.

COMPOSITION:—Fifty themes.

RHETORIC:—Talks chiefly on the technicalities of writing.

MEMORIZING:—Twenty poems learned from dictation. These form the basis for subsequent talks on literary art.

ENGLISH III.

READING:—Silas Mariner, Tale of Two Cities, House of Seven Gables, Kenilworth (not in class), Julius Caesar, selections from Walden (in class); some voluntary work in Scott, Dickens and Hawthorne, or Shakespeare, Marlowe, and Sheridan, or the lyrics of Wordsworth, Browning, Tennyson and Kipling.

COMPOSITION:—Thirty themes. Woolley's Handbook is used in theme correcting.

ENGLISH IV.

READING:—College requirements. Especially in this year a point is made of re-reading a great many selections remembered with pleasure from previous years.

COMPOSITION:—Thirty themes.

MEMORIZING: —Lines from Milton.

Parts of such books as the following have been read from the desk to one class and another this year: Jonson's Silent Woman, Clemens' Yankee in King Arthur's Court, Gilbert's Bab Ballads, Goldsmith's She Stoops to Conquer, Maeterlinck's Blue Bird."[7]

Some of the details in this program were particularly revealing as innovations: the heavy emphasis on writing and on discussing the art of writing, the emphasis on expression in oral reading rather than on discussion of the reading as providing the test of appreciation, the memorizing of twenty poems in the freshman year and of twenty more in the sophomore year, the reading of *The Pilgrim's Progress* by the sophomores and *The Blue Bird*, by the seniors, and the reading aloud in class of selections from Thoreau's *Walden*. Much as the students may have derived from this program of study, it is probably that the teacher learned even more. As this program was gradually being put into effect, Frost was providing instruction to at least some sections in each of the four class ranks: Junior, Junior Middle, Senior Middle, Senior, as they were called in the Academy.

The usual complaints and jealousies disturbed the sensitivities of the innovator more than they should have. He was constantly aware of back-biting, even to the point of suspecting that excuses would be found for replacing him. When additional funds were given the Academy by the New Hampshire State Legislature in 1908-1909, because neighboring towns without high schools sent so many students to Pinkerton, it became common practice for inspectors to appear. In the spring of 1909, a stranger quietly walked into one of Frost's classes and took a seat in the back of the room. The ominous implication was that Frost, teaching on suspicion, was being weighed in the balance. That same afternoon, the stranger appeared again and sat through another class. He was Henry Clinton Morrison, Dartmouth '95, Superintendent of Public Instruction for the State of New Hampshire, and he was so much impressed by all the innovations of classroom method used by Frost that he stayed after school for a long conversation. The upshot of Morrison's interest was that he asked Frost to give a talk on his methods of teaching English. A small convention of New Hampshire teachers would be held in

Exeter later in the spring, and Morrison felt that Frost could assist him—and the teachers—by explaining how he ran his classes at Pinkerton.

With some trepidation Frost accepted the request. On his way to Exeter from Derry by train—a roundabout route between places separated by only a few townships—he made notes of what he wanted to say. He would build his talk around his notion of teaching students to *absorb* and *impress* ideas. This seemed to be the gist of his educational theory. He wanted to tell them that books should be used in English classes so that students would be lonely forever afterward without books of their own, that students should be made so interested that they could never again leave books alone. There were various ways of catching their interest, and he would explain some of the ways he had discovered. As for the matter of expression, students should be taught the satisfaction and pride in conveying an idea so well, in either oral or written form, that anyone would remember how the idea had been conveyed and what it was.

By the time he reached Exeter an hour before his scheduled talk, he found that he was so frightened by the ordeal facing him that he doubted whether he would have the courage to stand on the platform before a roomful of teachers and deliver his talk. After going to Robinson Seminary and making sure of the room where he was to speak, he tried to walk off his fright. As a desperate way of getting his mind away from his worries, he put one pebble in each of his shoes in the hope that the pain would be useful. It didn't work. Somehow or other, he managed to go through with the talk, and it was well-received. Morrison heard such good reports of it that he immediately scheduled other talks for Frost at various conventions of teachers in New Hampshire.

The gradual process of throwing more time and energy into the practice and theory of teaching led Frost to feel that he should move his family off the farm into more convenient quarters near the Academy. By the summer of 1909,[8] when the move was made, he had already given up any pretense of being a farmer. He had sold his cow; he had sold the last of his Wyandottes; he had neglected the cutting of hay; he had but casually harvested his apples, pears, peaches, quinces. There would be no grief in turning his back on those responsibilities of the farm which had grown to be annoyances rather than pleasures.

Elinor was opposed to the move. Not socially inclined, she had liked the isolation of the farm and had resented the gradual intrusions and demands made on her husband's time by his duties as a teacher. She was the one who had really been content to sit in the wayside nook of the farm, forsaken by the world. But the strongest persuasions for her lay in her awareness that the children were already getting to be too much like her in their acceptance of isolation. By the spring of 1909, Lesley was ten years old, Carol was seven, Irma was six—and yet only Lesley had been given a taste of formal schooling. For the sake of the children, primarily, their mother accepted, not without reluctance, the move of the family from the Derry farm to the upper floor of a large house on Thornton Street in Derry Village. The house was owned by a young lawyer named Lester Russell, superintendent of the Sunday School in the First Congregational Church. He and his wife lived on the first floor of the house, and proved to be congenial friends.

As the hay-fever season approached, Frost delighted his family by proposing that they should all go with him on a camping expedition, far enough north in Vermont to escape— he hoped—any ill effects from ragweed pollen. They would buy tents, mattresses, and cooking equipment. They would find a site high above some lake and yet near enough for swimming expeditions. The lake he had in mind was Willoughby, and his interests were prompted by much he had learned about the region from Carl Burell. Also, the dramatic arrangement of mountains and lowlands along the shores of Lake Willoughby made the region a paradise for botanists. (Frost had gotten his first view of the terrain just to the south of Willoughby and had enjoyed his first glimpse of northern Vermont when he had gone by train to spend Thanksgiving Day of 1892 with Carl and Jont Eastman in Sutton, a village less than five miles below the southern shore of Willoughby.) The children were all elated by the prospect of a camping trip, and the early part of the summer was largely devoted to making preparations for the expedition. One large tent was bought for the children, a smaller one for their parents; cooking utensils and supplies were selected. After the equipment had been sent by express to the town of Westmore at the northern end of the lake, Frost went up alone, hoping to get the tents pitched and in readiness before the rest of his family arrived.

He was impressed by what he found. Viewed from the northern end of the lake, Willoughby stretched serenely for two or three miles among fields and woods to the south and then closed dramatically between the sheer cliffs of two mountains with biblical names sacred to Aaron and Moses: Hor and Pisgah. Frost knew at once where he would be botanizing; but his first obligation was to prepare for the arrival of his family. The tents and equipment had been delayed somewhere, and they reached Westmore just before the family did. By the time arrangements had been made to transport the tents, the baggage, and the family from Westmore station to the lake, clouds and fog had settled in so completely that the whole region seemed desolate. A farmer named Connolley rented them a room for the first night and the children slept on their own mattresses spread on the floor. In the morning the sun burned the clouds away and from their upland vantage point at the Connolley farm the Frost family gave complete approval of the dramatic vista, particularly when the children saw a motor launch or ferry on the lake and were assured that they could have a voyage on it as soon as the tents were set up. The best campsite available was in Connolley's cow pasture in a grove of trees watered by a spring. They drove stakes and set up tents with an eye to the view, and Frost put on his knapsack to make the first of many trips to a nearby store for groceries. Then they were ready for the promised cruise on the motor launch, going the entire length of the lake through the gap between the cliffs of Mounts Hor and Pisgah. This was the occasion which Lesley described in her journal as "ickstrodnery icsiting."

For the first two weeks Frost was kept so busy arranging expeditions and games for his children that botanizing was only incidental. As soon as the children made friends in the neighborhood and began to entertain themselves, he set out on his daily expeditions to the lower end of the lake, either by foot or by launch or by means of a rowboat, which he hired. His findings on the cliffs gave him a new enthusiasm: ferns. Never before had he known or really cared that this flowerless plant had so many varieties and sizes and shapes. But with the aid of well-informed botanists, whom he met on the shore of Willoughby and along the paths which scaled the cliffs of

Hor and Pisgah, he found himself growing more and more fascinated.

The only setback to his new enthusiasm was that some kinds of pollen drifting about the cliffs gave unpleasant reminders of his primary reason for making this retreat to northern Vermont. As long as he could bear coughing and sneezing and runny eyes, he kept hunting for new specimens. Finally he became so miserable that he gave it up.

Of all the casual acquaintances made by Frost that summer among visiting botanists and year-round residents, only one of them touched him deeply enough to inspire a poem. In his repeated visits to the Connolley farmhouse to buy milk and eggs, he sometimes lingered to talk with the farmer's wife. Haggard and careworn from her daily rounds of cooking for her husband and his hired men, Mrs. Connolley feared that she could not keep up the pace demanded of her. Frost was touched by her fears more than by her predicament. She admitted that insanity ran in her family, that her father's brother "wasn't right," and she herself had been "put away" for a short time. Recently, she had begun to fear that the same thing might happen again. Frost's pity found expression years later in the dramatic monologue "A Servant to Servants." Some of the details are especially pertinent. The poem begins:

> *I didn't make you know how glad I was*
> *To have you come and camp here on our land.*
> *I promised myself to get down some day*
> *And see the way you lived, but I don't know!*
> *With a houseful of hungry men to feed*
> *I guess you'd find. . . . It seems to me*
> *I can't express my feelings any more*
> *Than I can raise my voice or want to lift*
> *My hand (oh, I can lift it when I have to).*
> *Did ever you feel so? I hope you never.*
> *It's got so I don't even know for sure*
> *Whether I am glad, sorry, or anything.*
> *There's nothing but a voice-like left inside*
> *That seems to tell me how I ought to feel,*
> *And would feel if I wasn't all gone wrong.*
> *You take the lake. I look and look at it.*
> *I see it's a fair, pretty sheet of water.*
> *I stand and make myself repeat out loud*

The advantages it has, so long and narrow,
Like a deep piece of some old running river
Cut short off at both ends. It lies five miles
Straight away through the mountain notch
. . .

Our Willoughby! How did you hear of it?
I expect, though, everyone's heard of it.
In a book about ferns? Listen to that!
You let things more like feathers regulate
Your going and coming. And you like it here?
I can see how you might. But I don't know! . . .⁹

The narrator in "A Servant to Servants" says in passing that it might do her good to try camping out, and adds, "But it might be, come night, I shouldn't like it, / Or a long rain." For the Frosts, camping at Willoughby was marred by a too long stretch of rainy weather. It gave a good excuse for getting in under cover of roof and walls, renting a cottage as soon as the near-end of summer made one available. For the sake of the children, their parents found a good-sized cottage on a ledge-covered point of land thrust furthest into the lake on the northwest side. Immediately swimming became the special order of play. But it did not hinder Frost from developing a new hobby—looking at property to buy—which he continued to indulge throughout the rest of his life. This combination of water-front life, mountain-climbing, botanizing appealed so strongly to him that he began to explore the possibility of finding just the right cottage for purchase. The sense of affluence he had developed through the combined salary from Pinkerton and his annual check from the trust fund made him feel quite sure that he could afford to have a summer cottage at Willoughby. And when he failed to find just the kind of cottage he wanted, he began to make inquiries from Connolley about the possibility of buying a small farm which overlooked the lake. Oh, just another kind of outdoor game, he told himself, and yet he played it seriously enough to convince himself that all of this house-hunting would not end until he had paid money down. It was fortunate for him that nothing quite satisfied his ideal of what he should have. The time came to get the children back to Derry for the beginning of school. The tents, abandoned to the rummagings of suspicious cows in Connolley's pasture, were taken down, folded, packed, and shipped home by express. The children said their good-byes to their new-made friends in the neighborhood. Their parents paid one last call on the Connolleys, who had shown them so much consideration. Then, for the children at least, there remained the adventure of the roundabout ride back to Derry by train.

The trip back may have given Frost time enough to reconsider his eagerness to purchase real estate on the shore of Lake Willoughby; but he had at least become convinced that these annual summer ventures in the mountains of New Hampshire and Vermont, since his bout with pneumonia, were good for him and his poetry. As a retreat from the annoyance and misery of hay fever, the mountains around Bethlehem and Franconia might be better for him than the shore of Lake Willoughby. He was determined that some day he would actually buy a house in the mountains and earn his living by sending down a steady flow of poems for publishers in Boston and New York.

NEW REGIME AT PINKERTON

He showed me that the lines of a good helve
Were native to the grain before the knife
Expressed them, and its curves were no false curves
Put on it from without. And there its strength lay
For the hard work.[1]

ROBERT FROST'S last two years at Pinkerton, beginning in the autumn of 1909 and ending in the spring of 1911, taught him something new about his own capacities. His private awareness of gradually increasing success in the classroom gave him one kind of confidence which he needed; but the visits made by Henry C. Morrison, and the subsequent praise expressed through Morrison's request that Frost talk at teachers' conventions about his classroom methods, gave another confidence, desperately needed. Previously there had been times when he had told himself that his inability to get ahead with anything he undertook must be traceable to some lack of animal magnetism in his own nature. He feared that a great many people who met him simply did not like him as a human being, hence their scornful way of noticing or ignoring him.

Perhaps he was never aware that since his boyhood days in Salem, when he had been thrown on the defensive, he had protected himself with a proud kind of arrogance. It was a way of trying to combat scorn with counter-scorn; but it gave him an unpleasant manner. Some of his closest friends and relatives had long felt the hurt of this arrogance, which they could not combat. His sister, Jeanie, repeatedly finding fault with him for his treatment of their mother and herself, had too many problems of her own to be of much help to him. Ernest Jewell, who had known him since high-school days and who had given him friendship and money during the early years at Derry, had become so deeply offended by Rob's failure to pay his debts that a coldness had developed between them. Carl Burell, who had the clumsy affection of a St. Bernard dog and the capacity of a martyr for generous forgiveness, may never have understood all the inconsistencies of Rob's responses to him. Elinor had suffered most from Rob's furious quick-tempered rages, his easily wounded sensitivities, his pride, his vengefulness. She seemed to find her best defense in silence. But she could at least understand, sympathize with, and pity the cumulative frustrations of his ambition to establish himself as a poet. She may even have been amazed that he had survived all the vicissitudes of disappointment and grief which had battered him from so many directions during their thirteen years of marriage. Better than anyone else, she must have seen that he refused to give up his own hopes, his own belief in himself. She may have been the one who felt the greatest sense of relief in observing the gradual increase of self-confidence which came to him through those years of teaching at Pinkerton. It was derived particularly from the satisfaction he took in being admired and looked up to by his best students.

Morrison's praise also took Frost backstage to share in discussing the new plans for Pinkerton. In the spring of 1909, as soon as elderly Principal Bingham informed the Board of Trustees that he wished to be relieved of his duties, Morrison's help was asked in finding a successor. In spite of John Chase's notion that Frost would make a good principal, Morrison had other ideas—and for good reason. The trustees wanted to reorganize the curriculum by introducing new programs in agriculture, domestic science, and stenography. The man needed to organize and administrate such a program had to be someone with specialized experience. Morrison, well-acquainted with most of the principals in the major high schools throughout the state, probably recommended the candidate who was accepted. He was Ernest L. Silver, two years younger than Frost; and their lives had almost touched at various times before they met at Pinkerton. Silver had been born in Salem, New Hampshire, and his father had been the Clinton L. Silver who had enabled Frost to teach twice in Salem. A graduate of Pinkerton, Class of '94, and of Dartmouth College, Class of '99, Silver had acquired special teaching and administrative experience which seemed to make him excellently qualified to inaugurate the new program. The choice proved to be a good one. *The Derry News* for 28 May 1909 announced that this thirty-three-year-old alumnus of Pinkerton would replace Bingham in the fall of 1909.[2]

Frost did not become acquainted with Silver until just before the fall term started; but the two men, so nearly the same age, established an immediate rapport. Among their many common interests were athletics, and because neither one of them believed in the stern formality which had marked the rule of Geroge Washington Bingham, it was not long before Frost and Silver made their appearance on the football field, behind the Academy, to watch practice and try their own hand at passing the football. Occasionally, they even violated seasonal routine by throwing a baseball. The first issue of the *Critic* that year contained a gossip column in which the *"Academy Crow"* flew quickly over the field to observe:

"Baseball has its inning, too, on the field. Quite often, as I fly near the diamond, I smile as I see what a perfectly 'bully' time our principal and Mr. Frost are having there. Mr. Silver in his school days twirled in an expert manner, and that he still retains a portion of his former speed and curves, one can easily discern from the varying expressions on Mr. Frost's face. I have heard rumors of inter-faculty-class games, and I am looking forward to them with eagerness."[3]

It was clear to the students that under the new regime the tone and atmosphere of Pinkerton Academy was undergoing pleasant changes. Relations between students and teachers and the new Principal became much more informal and practical. Silver's first *Catalogue* noted especially the realistic purpose of all the additions to the curriculum:

"In September 1909, several new courses were introduced. Opportunity is now given to follow lines of agricultural interests or domestic science. Commercial courses are added and old ones strengthened. While continuing to fit for any college, the Academy now attempts to serve especially the needs of those pupils who cannot go to college, by providing courses very practically related to the life of the home, the shop, the office, the farm."[4]

Frost paid special attention to the Pinkerton football team in the fall of 1909, for the captain was a senior named John Bartlett, who had been one of his best students in English during the previous two years. Success or failure for the football team was measured by whether it won or lost the final

game, always played with its fiercest rival, Sanborn Seminary
—an endowed private school in the town where Frost's father
had been born: Kingston, New Hampshire. During the previous four years, Sanborn Seminary had been a consistent winner over Pinkerton, at least in football, and special efforts were
made to get the team ready for this crucial contest. Principal
Silver delighted everyone by announcing that if Pinkerton
won, he would cook a victory dinner for the team in the new
domestic-science kitchen and that members of the faculty
would serve the food to the players. Pinkerton won by a score
of 6-0, and the victory was celebrated with a march of the
students through the streets of Derry Village, a bonfire, cheers,
and speeches.

A few nights later Silver kept his pledge, and Frost served as
one of the waiters. Impressed, a student reporter wrote, "It
was a spread all right, and a substantial one. There was oyster
stew, mashed potatoes and hot dogs, ice cream and Indian
pudding, all cooked to a turn by Mr. Silver." Toasts were given
after the banquet and Frost made his contribution by writing
on a blackboard some appropriate jingles, which he referred to
as "Slipshod Rhymes." He said he had composed them "during
school hours while his classes were kept out of mischief by
theme work."[5] One "Rhyme" referred to the way in which
Coach Potter had toughened his team for the contest by making the boys push a heavy wooden "bucking machine" around
the field; others were triumphant boasts:

> *Said Potter, Now by kinter*
> *Yon machine is for bucking inter;*
> *You can't stop now for a splinter,*
> *You can dig that out next winter.*

> *We didn't pretend to outweigh 'em,*
> *So we simply had to outplay 'em.*

> *In the days of Captain John*
> *Sanborn Sem had nothing on*
> *Pinkerton! Pinkerton!*

> *With Mr. Silver as principal*
> *Of course it would have been indefensible*
> *Not to have proved invincible.*[6]

This was a brand-new kind of celebration, and the student reporter, after quoting all of the jingles written by "Bobby" (as the students called him when he wasn't listening), called them "models of 'Slipshodiness.'" The reporter added that "every one went home, thanking Mr. Silver for a spread to which there was certainly 'some class.'"

This spirit of enthusiasm established new relationships between students and teachers in all the other activities of the school. The success with which Frost had established so many innovations for the teaching of English literature and composition gave him the courage to extend his own program. At his request the Academy set aside money for prizes to be offered each semester to those who wrote outstanding compositions to be read aloud before the entire student body.[7] Also at his request he was permitted to stimulate participation in the debate program, and a student reporter approved of the effect:

". . . Mr. Frost announced that five units would be added to the mark in English of every pupil who would go to meetings of the Philomathean Society two-thirds of the time and would take active part in the debates. The result was immediate, and at the next meeting the attendance was more than double that which it had previously been. We think that this move is going to be a success, not simply because it will increase attendance but because these new members are apparently good members who do not, when they speak, speak as if they were doing it for marks."[8]

Frost still hated to lose a debate contest, and the class assigned to him for guidance was certain to be given extra help. Some of the other teachers disapproved of his methods and registered protests so strongly that unpleasant altercations developed. The consistency with which his class won the debates led to repeated charges that he had prepared much of the material and had offered many of the best arguments. There was some truth in the accusation.[9]

In the rearrangement of duties at Pinkerton it was natural that the faculty member in charge of the entire program in English literature, composition, elocution should be asked to take over the supervision of the student literary paper, *The Pinkerton Critic*, and the supervision of dramatic productions. As former editor of the *Bulletin* at Lawrence High School, where there had been no faculty guidance, Frost very quickly informed the editorial staff of the *Critic* that theirs was the task of selecting copy for publication, that they had to assume the obligations and responsibilities of their office. But he did meet regularly with the staff to discuss policy, and he was willing to be consulted whenever problems arose. He went even further than that and permitted the *Critic* to publish two of his own poems. One of these was originally written as a love poem for Elinor, and it reflected the perennial mood of regret when autumn came to the Derry farm. It was entitled "A Late Walk":

> *When I go up through the mowing field,*
> *The headless aftermath,*
> *Smooth-laid like thatch with the heavy dew,*
> *Half closes the garden path.*
>
> *And when I come to the garden ground,*
> *The whir of sober birds*
> *Up from the tangle of withered weeds*
> *Is sadder than any words.*
>
> *A tree beside the wall stands bare,*
> *But a leaf that lingered brown,*
> *Disturbed, I doubt not, by my thought,*
> *Comes softly rattling down.*
>
> *I end not far from my going forth*
> *By picking the faded blue*
> *Of the last remaining aster flower*
> *To carry again to you*[10]

Frost's warm friendship with the editorial board of the *Critic,* and his estimate of their capabilities, led him to try an experiment which had to be kept secret. In the days when Principal Bingham supervised dramatics at Pinkerton the annual production of a Shakespeare play demanded more talent in acting than the students were able to provide. Frost proposed to the *Critic* board that they should present a series of five plays in the springtime, plays representing dramatic art over four centuries, plays which he would adapt and compress so that the task of learning lines would not be too burdensome. The suggestion was accepted, and he set to work.

Carefully studying each of the plays, he knew exactly how

he wished to make deletions and compressions. He had often explained to his pupils the difference between "speaking passages" and "rhetorical passages." His own gradually developing theory of poetry-at-its-best was based on his conviction that "talk" was most dramatic and poetic when the sentences were lean and sharp with the give-and-take of conversation, wherein the thread of thought and action ran quickly in words and did not become lost in a maze of adjectives and metaphors. His task as editor of these plays was to strip them down to essentials. It was a time-consuming labor of love, and yet he found it an exercise which convinced him that his basic theory of poetry was correct. When he was done, he arranged to have the stenography department at the Academy prepare typewritten copies of the versions he had made from Marlowe's *Doctor Faustus,* Milton's *Comus*, Sheridan's *The Rivals,* and two plays by Yeats: *The Land of Heart's Desire* and *Cathleen ni Houlihan.* His undertaking was ambitious, and the requirements he placed on the students were exacting because some of the students played more than one part. They all worked hard, and the rehearsals were carried out secretly, during hours which seemed to be devoted to meetings of the editorial board of the *Critic.* A few members of the faculty were taken into confidence, together with Principal Silver, for practical reasons. No announcement was made until within a week of the time when *Doctor Faustus* was scheduled for production. Then Frost prepared a "release," which appeared in the local paper:

"Beginning Thursday, May 26, and continuing at intervals of a week, the editorial board of the Pinkerton Critic will give in Academy Hall a series of noted plays illustrating four periods of English dramatic literature, Marlowe's Faustus of the sixteenth century, Milton's Comus of the seventeenth, Sheridan's Rivals of the eighteenth and Yeats' Land of Heart's Desire and Cathleen ni Houlihan of the latter nineteenth. The set, five in all (two of which will be given the same evening as being by the same author) will constitute a good short course in literature, intended to cultivate in school a taste for the better written sort of plays. But while all are literary, and the object in staging them is largely educational, it must not be inferred that they have not been selected without regard to the entertainment they are likely to afford. All belong to the class of good acting drama as distinguished from the kind that is only meant to be read. All were written for the stage and have won and held a place on the stage. Only last winter the oldest, Marlowe's Faustus, was presented in New York by the Ben Greet Company. It is thought that the plays will lose nothing by being put on without any elaborate attempt at stage setting in the simple Elizabethan fashion that was good enough for Shakespeare. The audience will be asked to supply much of the costuming and most of the scenery from the imagination.

> *"And let us*
> *On your imaginary forces work*
> *For 'tis your thoughts that must now deck our kings."*

The plays are sufficiently distinct in kind to warrant the belief that the series will not prove monotonous. Each exhibits some special phase of dramatic art, of which it is one of the best examples. In the weird and tragic Faustus we have one of the last written of the mediaeval morality plays. Itself based on the monkish tale of the man who sold his soul to the devil, it forms in turn the basis for Goethe's play and Gounod's opera of the same name. Milton's Comus gives us something in the high philosophical strain. Chiefly notable for its beautiful poetry it is not without its strong dramatic possibilities in character, situation and action. Sheridan's gay wit made his Rivals the best piece of comedy between Shakespeare's time and our own. We come to the two Yeats plays. Yeats is head and front of that most interesting of recent literary movements known as the Celtic Renaissance; most interesting of course to the Irish but hardly less so to the rest of us who speak the same tongue. He is the exponent of the lyrical drama, in which kind The Land of Heart's Desire is the best thing he has done. This is a fairy story with a meaning for lovers. Cathleen ni Houlihan the other play can hardly be called a fairy story, though the chief character in it is an old woman who is no less a person than old Ireland herself. It has the genuine stir of Irish patriotism. A recent critic says, 'It must be dangerous to represent in Ireland, for it is an Irish Marseillaise.' . . . Single admission will be twenty-five cents, tickets for the course, seventy-five cents. Cars will probably run. Look for announcement next week."[11]

As the curtain-raiser in the series, *Faustus* was highly praised by students and townspeople. John Bartlett, captain of the football team and editor-in-chief of the *Critic*, played the part of Mephistopheles with blood-curdling vividness, particularly in the closing scene. As he put out one candle after another with his bare fingers, the footlights dimmed. And when the stage was engulfed in darkness, the triumphant "Aha!" with which he pounced on Faustus brought screams from the girls in the audience.

The next day, on the street in Derry Village, Frost was apprehensive when he saw the elderly ex-Principal, Mr. Bingham, approaching with a gesture which clearly meant conversation. After saying that he had enjoyed the production of Marlowe's play, he changed the subject almost too abruptly to ask if it was true that the next play would be *Comus*. Correct.

"Then," said the stern, white-bearded clergyman, "it has occurred to me that you might like to borrow the silver service of the sacrament from our church so that you may do full justice to the banquet scene."

After that offer, graciously made and eagerly accepted, nobody was ever allowed to criticize Bingham's puritanical bias in Frost's presence without being corrected. On the other hand, it may have seemed to this rabid exponent of Shakespearean comedy and tragedy that his evangelical successor, presenting *Faustus* as "one of the last written of the mediaeval morality plays" in conjunction with Milton's austere moralizings in the dramatically dull *Comus*, certainly must have his own puritanical bias. As for the offerings from Yeats, whose visit to the United States a few years earlier had attracted much attention in literary circles, here again the pure moral idealism was more certain than Marlowe's. Students and townspeople were so deeply impressed by the presentation of these five plays by the *Critic* staff that they may have recognized Frost's part as representing the zenith of his many contributions to the new level of teaching at Pinkerton.

Frost was planning to continue the process the following year, by starting another series of productions with Ben Jonson's *The Silent Woman*. Very carefully, he wrote out a revised version of this play, again omitting all except the best scenes and lines. But on the day when he brought his manuscript copy to the Academy to request that it be typed, he learned that one of the other teachers was working against him. She had announced that the play he had chosen was too "heavy" for the students and that she was going to coach a group who would produce a lighter piece of dramatic entertainment, "The Village School." In a sudden outburst of rage he then and there tore up his abbreviated version of *The Silent Woman,* threw it in the nearest wastepaper basket, and said that this ended his attempt to supervise dramatic productions at Pinkerton.

Frost had become intimately acquainted with many members of the Class of 1910 and it is probable that he attended the graduation exercises for the thirteen girls and four boys. His favorite student, John T. Bartlett, served as marshall and led the procession, for the baccalaureate sermon. A churchgoer only under compulsion, as on such occasions, Frost must have given special personal response to the Bible passage from Paul's letter to the Phillipians used by Parson Merriam as his text:

"I know both how to be abased, and I know how to abound: every where and in all things, I am instructed both to be full and to be hungry, both to abound and to suffer need."[12]

After so many years of humiliation and abasement in Derry as merely a hen-man or worse, and after suffering the consequent need for reassurance, attention, admiration, praise, Frost felt that this little class was his in a very special way. These were the students whose performance, now being honored, filled him with waves of pride. For him to abound in such a fashion might seem to others an unimportant kind of triumph, except for those who had known how completely abased he had been. Part of his fatherly satisfaction in the triumphs of John Bartlett may have come from his feeling that the boy had played a large part in his success, from the day when Henry Morrison visited his class for the first time to see Frost perform well in a discussion primarily with Bartlett. He had served in the same capacity repeatedly—in debates, on the football field, on the editorial board, on the stage, and as president of his class. Frost had already told Bartlett that he could give his teacher another kind of vicarious satisfaction if he continued the kind of prose writing he had published in the *Critic* and went on to make a name for himself in literature. Bartlett already planned to enter Middlebury College in the fall of 1910, and Frost was pleased with that decision.[13]

A few months later Bartlett was the one who had become abased. Frost had scarcely returned with his family from another hay-fever season with the Lynches in Bethlehem, to start teaching again at Pinkerton, when he learned that Bartlett had walked out of Middlebury in much the same way that he had walked out of Dartmouth, simply because he couldn't take it. He was back home, on a farm in Raymond, only two townships away from Derry, and Frost immediately expressed his sympathy by walking over to call on him. Additional similarity between their lives was revealed when it became known that part of Bartlett's trouble was an obscure pulmonary illness, which might be tuberculosis. For a time he remained on the family farm in Raymond, occasionally visiting Frost in Derry during the school year 1910-1911.

In June of 1911, while Frost was still trying to help Bartlett find a direction for his life, an event occurred which had a profound effect on the entire Frost family, particularly on the nine-year-old-boy, Carol. All of the Frost children had developed a strong affection for Lester Russell, who owned the Thornton Street house in which the Frosts had lived since their move from the farm to Derry Village. His career as a lawyer seemed successful; his activities in the Congregational Church were conscientious. But in his handling of investments for an estate which involved a trust fund, Russell gambled unwisely and misused funds in an attempt to recoup. The upshot of his speculations accounted for the appearance of a sheriff at the Thornton Street house one afternoon with a warrant for Russell's arrest. Frost, who had been on very friendly terms with Russell, happened to be in Raymond visiting John Bartlett. Russell was working in his garden, spraying his potato plants with arsenic poisoning, and seemed undisturbed by the warrant. He agreed to go with the sheriff, asked for permission to get his coat in the shed, stepped out of sight long enough to drink all the arsenic poison he needed, then went along with the sheriff. In the sheriff's office he became so ill that he was taken home, and he died the next morning. Frost, called back from Raymond, served as one of the pallbearers at the funeral, held at the home on Thornton Street. The local newspaper accounts very tactfully avoided any references to the cause of death:

"The community was shocked Friday morning to learn of the death of Lester Russell, one of the town's well-known lawyers. He passed away at his home at 6:50 after a night of extreme illness. Dr. C. E. Newell, his family physician, was with the sick man nearly all night. It is believed that some business trouble that he had recently met with hastened his death, cutting him off in his early manhood [age 27]. . . ."[14]

The Frost children, unavoidably caught up in all the excitement of the funeral, had never before felt the shock of death so strongly. Their numerous questions were answered by their parents as gently as possible. Their father explained to them that Mr. Russell's life had been a happy one, that it had reached some kind of fulfillment, and that God had called him home to heaven. But the children, in their play with neighboring friends, soon heard the word "suicide," and gradually picked up the details of how Russell had killed himself. For Carol, there seemed to be a curious problem in trying to correlate his father's word "fulfillment" and the other word, "suicide." Throughout his childhood, Carol had been the least communicative of the children, frequently given to periods of silence and withdrawal. He did not make friends easily, and his parents worried about him. For the present, however, they were completely unaware that the death of Lester Russell had precipitated in Carol an obsession concerning suicide as the proper action to be taken when any individual's life had reached "fulfillment."[15]

During the summer of 1911, while the death of Lester Russell still agitated the Frost household, an entirely different upset occurred. Word was received that Ernest Silver had accepted an invitation to become Principal of the New Hampshire State Normal School in Plymouth and that he wanted Frost to go with him as one of his teachers. Back of both moves, Frost later learned, was Henry C. Morrison. Frequently, during the years since he had met Frost, Morrison had hired him to teach the teachers at conventions.[16] When Silver accepted the invitation to go to Plymouth and wanted to take Frost with him, there was no opening in the field of English literature. But Morrison insisted that Frost's value to the Normal School would not be determined by the titles of his courses: Let him teach anything, so long as he was on the staff. The only practical openings were in Psychology and History of Education.

Frost was extremely reluctant to accept the Plymouth offer on any terms. From the time he had begun to gain confidence through his teaching at Pinkerton, he had been writing more and more poetry. To his surprise, he had found that the harder he worked the greater the stimulus to his writing. His ideal was to continue as a teacher until the time when, by the terms of his grandfather's will, he could legally sell the farm (which he had been renting since the move to Derry Village). Then he could use the proceeds for taking at least one year of leave from teaching and get on with his writing. He also counted on the fact that, starting in July of 1912, the payment from the trust fund set up by the will of his grandfather would be increased from $500 to $800 a year. His present salary at Pinkerton was $1,000; the promised salary at Plymouth for part-time teaching was also $1,000. If he did not teach at all, the $800 annuity would be only $200 less than the salary now earned at the expense of much nervous and physical energy. After considerable thought and long discussions with his wife, he informed Silver and Morrison that he would accept the Plymouth offer with the understanding that he might possibly resign from the position at the end of one year. The terms were accepted, and a large part of the summer of 1911 was spent in making preparations for the move from Derry to Plymouth.

The sale of the Derry farm caused some difficulty. When the farm had been mortgaged for $750 on 24 March 1906, the terms of the mortgage required annual repayments at interest semi-annually of 6% during a five-year period, with the unpaid balance due on 24 March 1911. This mortgage had not been approved by Wilbur E. Rowell, the trustee of his grandfather's estate. The farm did not technically become Frost's property until July of 1911. With his usual carelessness about money matters, Frost had gone ahead; but he had failed to make his payments when due, and in August of 1911, when he accepted the Plymouth offer, he still owed an overdue amount of $568.75 on the mortgage. To pay it, he arranged another mortgage for $1,200, out of which he realized (after the payment and other expenses) $627.45. The farm had been so badly neglected during the five years which followed the first mortgage that he was apparently unable to find a buyer who would pay anything like the original price, and he finally sold the farm in November 1911 through a transference of the mortgage to a Boston real-estate agent.[17]

Naturally delighted to get rid of the farm, Frost could not fail to appreciate that he had mixed memories of what it had meant to him. In one sense that farm represented the years of his most complete abasement and humiliation, the years when he had been forced to strip his life down to the verge of nothingness and to rebuild. In another sense the experiences on the farm had provided him with the raw materials for important rebuilding—spiritual, emotional, psychological, poetical. He could already tell that the farm, when viewed from a greater distance in time and space, would acquire for him a romantic luster unequalled by anything else in his life so far. He wished that he could write into the contract for the sale of the farm some qualifying statement that the stranger who purchased it from him must not consider it an act of trespassing on Frost's part, if at some future time he should return to walk about the garden, the pastures, the fields just to remind himself of how much they had meant to him. This ambivalence of attitude found reflection in a poem he wrote before the close of the year 1911, a poem entitled "On the Sale of My Farm":

> *Well-away and be it so,*
> *To the stranger let them go.*
> *Even cheerfully I yield*
> *Pasture or chard, mowing-field,*
> *Yea and wish him all the gain*
> *I required of them in vain.*
> *Yea, and I can yield him house,*
> *Barn, and shed, with rat and mouse*
> *To dispute possession of.*
> *These I can unlearn to love.*
> *Since I cannot help it? Good!*
> *Only be it understood,*
> *It shall be no trespassing*
> *If I come again some spring*
> *In the grey disguise of years,*
> *Seeking ache of memory here.*[18]

GATHERING METAPHORS

. . . It represents, needless to tell you, not the long deferred forward movement you are living in wait for, but only the grim stand it was necessary for me to make until I should gather myself together. The forward movement is to begin next year.[1]

SPECIAL IMPULSES were given to the life of Robert Frost during the single year he and his family spent in Plymouth, New Hampshire. He devoted part of the year to preparations for the boldly venturesome leap he was about to make. But his most significant actions were dramatized on the stage of his inner consciousness. He had been hired to teach a course in psychology and another course in the history of education. The newness of the task stimulated him to do some intensive reading and, here once more, his reading proved far more important to him than to his pupils.

The attractive offer, which led him to move northward into the foothills of the White Mountains—only a half-dozen townships south of Bethlehem and Franconia—brought him into contact with an educational-industrial community no larger than the three villages in Derry and yet distinctly different. Plymouth, a county seat, was compactly built and snugly perched on a hillside overlooking a wide intervale. The green meadows had been ironed flat by innumerable spring freshets of the rampaging Pemigewasset River and were flanked by some forest-covered hills.

The natives of Plymouth were proud of its history, which dated from an important skirmish between colonists and Indians prior to the Revolutionary War. Well before the Declaration of Independence was signed, several thriving little industries were making use of Pemigewasset water power. Growth had been stimulated by the building of the main line of the Boston, Concord and Montreal Railroad directly through Plymouth. For years, artists and literary figures had been attracted to Plymouth; Hawthorne had visited it more than once and had died in the old Pemigewasset House during the Civil War.

Educational activities had played an important part in the history of the town. The privately endowed Holmes Academy, older than Pinkerton, had opened in 1808. An important change occurred in 1837 when an already distinguished educator had been invited to become the principal of Holmes Academy. He was the Reverend Samuel Reed Hall, who founded the first normal school in America—at Concord Corners, Vermont—in 1823. The first man to popularize the use of blackboards in teaching, Hall had written a best-seller in 1829: *Lectures on School-Keeping*. Hall tried to develop a department for the training of teachers at Holmes Academy. Although he failed, the buildings of the old Academy were presented to the State of New Hampshire in 1871 for use as its first normal school; it had opened with an enrollment of eighty girls. By the time Frost reached Plymouth, the enrollment was a little more than one hundred—still all girls. The campus lay close to the center of town, and the white cottages which served as dormitories were clustered around the tower-crowned brick administration building.

Frost knew that his position as an educator had been advanced considerably by the move from Pinkerton to Plymouth Normal School. But the primary advantage he gained was the reinforcement given his new sense of confidence. His personal triumphs as teacher at Pinkerton, followed by Morrison's flattering invitations to give talks at teachers' conventions had provided so much reassurance that Frost almost swaggered into his new teaching duties. Some of his new mannerisms might have amazed three of his old friends: Carl Burell, Ernest Jewell, and the veterinarian, Dr. Charlemagne Bricault, who had scarcely laid eyes on him since the Derry days in 1905. If these three men could have trailed after Frost unobserved, as he made his rounds at Plymouth Normal School during the early autumn days of 1911, they would have found him changed from him they knew—and no longer sure of all he had thought was true concerning his prospects. He now had the gait and the carriage of a man going somewhere.

One particular change would have been noticeable. This

very touchy man of moods, whose former discouragement had unfairly heightened his feeling of resentment against these friends, had brought his arrogance and grouchiness under at least temporary control. At Plymouth, in his offhand conversations inside and outside the classroom, his remarks were usually cheerful, witty, mischievous, playful. Jewell and Bricault would have noticed that even his speech was different from his talk at the time of the move from Lawrence to Derry in 1900. His habit of careful pronunciation, encouraged by his well-educated father and mother, had been well-developed before he moved back East from San Francisco. At least one newspaper reporter had found something too rhetorical and flowery in his manner of delivering the valedictory address for the Class of 1892 at Lawrence High School. Moreover, the sensitivity of his ear to differences between Western and Eastern ways of talking had made him resent the Yankee vernacular long after his move from California. But during the Derry years, particularly after he had formed a brief friendship with John Hall, he became fascinated by Hall's witty, picturesque, back-country way of implying meaning through sly inflections and modulations of voice. They gave color and bite to the sound of sense. As a flattering tribute to Hall and other north-of-Boston farmers, Frost had gradually modified his way of talking. He deliberately imitated the manner in which his neighbors unconsciously slurred words, dropped endings, and clipped their sentences. By the time he reached Plymouth, glad to be rid of the farm, he was still perfecting the art of talking like a farmer. Evidence on this point was given by one of his earliest acquaintances in Plymouth, a young college graduate and high-school teacher, who remembered his first impressions:

"I first thought him uncouth. We were at a dance, and he wore an unpressed suit, and a gray soft-collared shirt; and he sat with crossed knees, and poked fun. After that . . . I still detected in his speech what seemed a lack of elegance, and in his attitude an absence of conformity. There was something earthy and imperfectly tamed about him."[2]

These remarks might have been more accurate if the observer could have known that Frost had been tamed by hard circumstances long before he untamed himself, that his nonconformity represented a hard-earned rebellion against conformity. It grew stronger from the day he arrived at Plymouth to the day he left, and it revealed itself in many ways.

When he met his first class at the Normal School, Frost found that the janitor had already placed on the desk a stack of textbooks for distribution to the students—a pompously solid volume, Monroe's *History of Education*. As soon as the girls had taken their seats, Frost said he would begin by giving the first assignment. He wanted a few volunteers who would carry these dog-eared textbooks right back down to the basement and leave them in the stockroom. Monroe would not be used in the course this year. Instead, their instructor preferred that the girls become acquainted with a few original works which contained some better approaches to the history of education. They would start by reading Pestalozzi's *How Gertrude Teaches Her Children*. After that, they would read and discuss Rousseau's *Emile*. And before the course was through, they would even read some selected passages on education in Plato's *Republic*. He hoped the girls would like these books well enough to buy copies of them for their own shelves, to re-read at leisure after they had begun their careers as teachers.

Carrying his nonconformist methods over to his course in psychology, Frost never lectured. Informally, he discussed with his students the assignments he made in two books by his beloved William James: *Talks to Teachers on Psychology* and the one-volume text he himself had studied at Harvard, *Psychology: The Briefer Course*. In these discussions the assignments merely served as a springboard for their instructor's observations, drawn from his own classroom experiences, concerning ways to stimulate interest, attention, memory, and valid associations of ideas. Early in the course he began one class by asking if anyone knew where the boss was. Yes, Mr. Silver had gone to Boston for the day. Fine! That meant they could do anything they pleased, and it would please their instructor to read them an amusing little story by Mark Twain called "The Celebrated Jumping Frog of Calaveras County." For the girls, this was a delightful approach to the psychology of teaching, and amusing, even though it seemed to have no bearing on the subject. But when their instructor finished reading he closed the book and drew from the story a moral, half in jest, half seriously: Some teachers always load their students so full of facts that the students can't jump; other teachers know better and they tickle the students into having imagina-

tive ideas of their own just by saying in effect, "Flies, Dan'l."
Class dismissed.

The girls were charmed, partly because they had so little to
do. On one occasion, when Frost learned that nobody in the
History of Education class had read Mark Twain's *A Connecticut Yankee in King Arthur's Court,* he said that such a
weakness should be corrected, and for the next several days he
read aloud to them in class from the book. He surprised them
even more by requiring them to memorize poems and to say
them aloud in class together. One must have been taught him
by his mother. It was "Two Rivers," author unknown:

> *Says Tweed to Till—*
> *"What gars ye rin sae still?"*
> *Says Till to Tweed—*
> *"Though ye rin with speed*
> *And I rin slaw,*
> *For ae man that ye droon*
> *I droon twa."*[3]

The girls considered Frost "quite a character," and even suspected that he liked to get time for reading to himself in class
by handing out blue books in which he asked them to write
little essays on any subject they found interesting while they
were studying their latest assignment. The essays were handed
in but seldom returned.

The new Principal of Plymouth Normal School was troubled
by Frost's casual way of handling classes and by the gossip
that Frost took pleasure in ridiculing the standard procedures
of class work in the school. Back at Pinkerton Academy, these
two men had worked and played so congenially that Silver had
wanted Frost to go with him to Plymouth. Silver had even
made an unusual offer to provide special living arrangements
for the Frost family at Plymouth. A large "cottage" served as
the traditional campus residence for the Principal, but Silver's
wife was an invalid, living temporarily with her parents in
Portsmouth. Because he was planning to live alone, Silver
offered to share his furnished "cottage" rent free with the Frost
family. The offer was accepted and for a few days all went
well. Silver had his own rooms and shared meals with the
Frosts. But he soon learned that Mrs. Frost, extremely casual
about housework, was completely indifferent to serving meals

at regular hours. Whenever she made a special effort there might be an unusual supper with a huge roast of beef and not much else except tea and bread. Such a meal often lasted for more than an hour because the children ate so ravenously. After the meal there was the usual children's hour in the parlor, to which the family adjourned, leaving the food and dishes on the dining-room table. By the time the children were in bed, Mrs. Frost would be so tired that she would decide the dishes could wait. In the morning the children had to shift for themselves. Silver learned from Frost that 8:30 was a disgracefully early hour for starting school, either grammar or normal; it was a sign of a dictatorial and undemocratic state. So the children were punished for the mistakes of the government: they had to get up without bothering their parents, had to grub for their own breakfasts—possibly a piece of cold meat hacked off the roast on the dining-room table and wrapped in a piece of bread. Often they started for school munching on something like a sandwich.

Silver found Mrs. Frost's casual informalities as cook and housekeeper particularly embarrassing on the few occasions when he tried to entertain visiting dignitaries. But when he made even the most guarded protest to Frost, the criticism aroused furious resentment. Just once Silver indiscreetly reported as a joke, to Frost, that one of the visitors had said Mrs. Frost seemed lacking in personality. Enraged, Frost lectured Silver on the fact that what anyone else did or didn't find to like about Mrs. Frost was entirely beside the point: "She's *mine!*"[4]

Characteristically, Frost very soon convinced himself that Silver was an enemy who deserved resentment and retaliation. He reinforced his bitterness by imagining that Silver had tried to have him discharged during the Pinkerton days, that Silver had been forced by Morrison to bring Frost to Plymouth; even to take the Frosts into his house. So he began to watch for ways of getting revenge, while Silver continued his attempts to maintain harmony in their relationship.

In spite of these awkward tensions, the Frosts liked their new surroundings. All the children were now of school age and could go to the Plymouth Normal School which provided complete instruction for a limited number of children in the town of Plymouth from kindergarten through the eighth grade. The campus of the Normal School gave ample romping ground for

Lesley, Carol, Irma, and Marjorie. The croquet sets and tennis courts offered the older children a chance to develop skills, and their father devoted so much time to helping them learn tennis that he himself became a rabid tennis addict.

For tennis competition more skillful than his older children could offer as beginners, Frost very soon began playing with Sidney Cox, the twenty-two-year-old Plymouth High School teacher who had observed that Frost seemed to be "uncouth." During their initial conversation, Frost had teased Cox just enough to anger the young man. When they met on the street, soon afterward, Cox avoided speaking to Frost. As though in retaliation for Frost's teasing, Cox went out of his way to ask their mutual friend, Silver, whether alcohol was the cause of Frost's having made so little progress in life. Silver, amused, had reported the question to Frost, who was indignant. Retrospectively Frost said of his way of dealing with Cox, "But his seriousness piqued the mischief in me and I set myself to take him. He came round all right, but it wasn't the last time he had to make allowances for me."[5] Although this friendship lasted as long as Cox lived, there was often an ambiguously taunting quality in Frost's treatment of Cox.[6] In Plymouth, however, the young man was so flattered by the continuous attentions paid him by Frost that he very soon came under the spell and grew to be a worshiper. The two men walked the hills, back roads, and intervales around Plymouth; they played tennis; and they devoted many evenings to long conversations in the parlor of the Principal's cottage. Particularly memorable to Cox were evenings when Frost read aloud such newly-discovered favorites as Synge's *Playboy of the Western World* and Shaw's *Arms and the Man*. Cox liked Frost's Irish accent in reading *Playboy:* "I don't know anyone who can do the Irish so well."[7]

During these readings, Cox was unconsciously witnessing an important phase in the self-education of Robert Frost. From the time Frost had begun to read Yeats in Derry, and to follow the newspaper and magazine accounts of the Abbey Players in Dublin, he understood the intensity of his response. It was determined in large part by his finding in these accounts an articulation of esthetic theories which he himself had been trying to formulate (and practice) ever since he had learned to relish the complaint that his own verse was "too much like talk." Admiring Yeats enough to induce his Pinkerton students to give performances of his plays, Frost must have noticed that American periodicals gave considerable space to a speech made by Yeats at a *causerie* in London in March of 1911. Yeats had protested that "the voice" had fallen into neglect as the vehicle for communication in literary art. Traditionally, Yeats pointed out, literary art had been "sung or spoken" and yet it was presently suffering from its "deadly foe"—music.[8] This was what Frost wanted to hear someone say, especially Yeats, as corroboration of his own private convictions.

In the fall of 1911 the Abbey Players came to the United States, and with them came W. B. Yeats. He talked before the Drama League of Boston and stressed the attempt of the new drama of Ireland "to recreate Ireland in an Irish way" by mastering what the peasant knows and says. The natural speech of the ordinary people was caught in these plays, a way of talking which was "redeemed from the idiom which we speak and in which our newspapers are written—an idiom dim and defaced like a coin too long in circulation."[9]

These were all incentives for Frost to continue in the direction he had already marked out for himself. At the same time, they heightened his desire to break away from the enslavement of teaching so that he could give all his time to writing— poetry or plays or novels. In one of his walks with Sidney Cox, he hinted at the subject uppermost in his mind by saying that there are only three grades of tasks. The most servile and the one that demands least from the worker is the assigned task, done under supervision. More free and more exacting is the task assigned by another but left to be carried out at the discretion and according to the judgment of the worker. But the one which takes most character is the self-assigned task, carried out only at the instant urgency of the worker's own desire.[10]

The artist, he had long realized, has to make heavy demands on himself. He has to draw his own strength and courage from his inner resources. As a result, the artist has to be selfish. If he works under supervision, for others, he spends for them the energy he needs for his own work. His creative originality has to assert itself independently, apart from any other compulsions. It can be curbed, sacrificed, subordinated to the wishes and needs of others; but to the extent that it is thus used, it is diverted from its proper goal.

Frost had been taught by his mother that self-giving and self-sacrifice are the noblest and most heroic forms of human effort. He had honored that belief throughout his boyhood and he still wanted to honor it. One of his earliest poems, perhaps derived almost directly from his mother's reading aloud of Scott's *Tales of a Grandfather*, had been "In Equal Sacrifice." It was a ballad in which he honored two of Scotland's greatest heroes who had courageously and nobly given their lives for their ideals.[11] But his own problem now was to justify artistic selfishness without minimizing heroic self-giving.

For years he had worried about a closely related problem. During one of his last talks for Morrison, at a teacher's convention, he had taken pleasure in shocking the audience by saying that the first concern of the teacher has to be with self; that the teacher's primary responsibility is to save his or her own soul. The second responsibility of the teacher of literature is to the art of the author of the poem or story or novel under discussion. Finally comes the responsibility to the student. These were the kinds of provocations he liked to flaunt, knowing that some of his listeners would not understand them.[12]

Back in Derry he had written a poem about another problem, not unrelated. The inspiration had been provided by the first tramp who stopped one evening at his farmhouse and asked if he could sleep in the barn overnight. It was late in the fall, the night was cold, and the tramp looked as though he might set fire to the barn, after dark, if the answer was no. With mixed feelings of fear and pity, Frost had let this tramp sleep on a bed of rugs and blankets in the kitchen beside the stove. He gave the man food that night, and breakfast in the morning. After the stranger was gone, Frost puzzled over his own inner turmoil: All men are created equally free to seek their own rights in their own way, but how does one draw the line between the rights of the property owner and the rights of the tramp to make claim on the sympathy (or fear) of the property owner? For artistic purposes, Frost sharpened the problem by changing the facts, just a little, to make them more dramatic and ironic. The poem became a ballad (with Yeatsian echoes) entitled "Love and a Question:"

> *A Stranger came to the door at eve,*
> *And he spoke the bridegroom fair.*
> *He bore a green-white stick in his hand,*
> *And, for all burden, care.*

[377]

He asked with the eyes more than the lips
For a shelter for the night,
And he turned and looked at the road afar
Without a window light.

The bridegroom came forth into the porch
With 'Let us look at the sky,
And question what of the night to be,
Stranger, you and I.'
The woodbine leaves littered the yard,
The woodbine berries were blue,
Autumn, yes, winter was in the wind;
'Stranger, I wish I knew.'

Within, the bride in the dusk alone
Bent over the open fire,
Her face rose-red with the glowing coal
And the thought of the heart's desire.
The bridegroom looked at the weary road,
Yet saw but her within,
And wished her heart in a case of gold
And pinned with a silver pin.

The bridegroom thought it little to give
A dole of bread, a purse,
A heartfelt prayer for the poor of God,
Or for the rich a curse;
But whether or not a man was asked
To mar the love of two
By harboring woe in the bridal house,
The bridegroom wished he knew.[13]

While still at Derry, during the years 1905 and 1906, Frost had extended the question of individual rights involving the claims of "the poor of God" on the selfishness of the accursed rich. The exploitation of the working classes and the corrupt practices of "big business" caused him to utter Wordsworthian laments over man's inhumanity to man, particularly after he had read articles by Ida Tarbell, Lincoln Steffens and Ray Stannard Baker in *McClure's Magazine*. Frost pondered the question of his own responsibility, and found that he was not prompted to express his sympathies for downtrodden people through any kind of missionary work or altruism or giving. Maybe he should, he thought; but he wasn't going to. Then he accused himself of sentimentality in working himself up to such a pitch of anguish over the sufferings of others. Having reached the decision that he would not keep upsetting himself by devouring any more of the "muckraker" articles, he stopped reading them.

Nevertheless, the problem continued to bother him, and he could find no satisfactory answer. In his own case he saw the question as inseparably related to the selfish preoccupation of the artist who hoards his energies to do his own work well, in contrast to the preoccupations of the altruist who spends his energies to do good. It involved freedom and individual rights. Somewhere, somehow, Frost became familiar with Mill's famous essay *On Liberty*—either at first- or second-hand—and his thinking caused him to give his own twist to the doctrine of laissez-faire. As he weighed the contrasting theories of let-alone versus protection, or of individualism versus socialism, he gradually became willing to admit that his artistic prejudices were helping to shape his social views. His primary sympathies for individualism were against any concept of the welfare state.

These views crystallized into a poem, which he finished shortly before Christmas of 1911, a poem which raised the same old questions in a new way and answered them with bitterly ambiguous irony. At any Christmastime what right did any Christian have to expect, or even to want, a merry Christmas, when it was obvious that so many millions of men, women, children throughout the world would spend Christmas day in suffering and pain and misery? What right did he have—or did his children have—to make the day merry? Should they give presents to each other? Should their giving be directed entirely to the underprivileged? In his poem, "My Giving," he projected his own inner conflicts over these questions by extending the Christian attitude of love and charity to a logical extreme, which made it appear ridiculous. For parody, he pretended that his own prejudices were all in favor of complete self-giving and self-immolation.

He chose as a target for this deliberately satirical weapon, a devout Christian, Miss Susan Hayes Ward, and used "My Giving" as a prologue in a Christmas present made especially for her. It was a manuscript booklet of poems, most of them written during the years at Derry. Starting with "My Giving," he spread seventeen of his poems over twenty-two small folded pages, stitched the folds with string, added a cover made of dark blue paper, and inscribed the booklet: "Susan Hayes Ward / from / Robert Frost / Christmas 1911." In the letter sent with it he made no mention of the bitterly ironic and satiric poem, "My Giving." He merely said he did not pretend that this offering represented "the long deferred forward movement you are living in wait for, but only the grim stand it was necessary for me to make until I should gather myself together." Then he added, significantly, "The forward movement is to begin next year." He confessed that he had so much to tell Miss Ward about his hopes for his own "forward movement" that he would like to visit her in New York during the present Christmas vacation, if she would give him the opportunity. Perhaps he wondered, however, whether she might be too much offended by "My Giving":

> I ask no merrier Christmas
> Than the hungry bereft and cold shall know
>   That night.
> This is all I can give so that none shall want—
> My heart and soul to share their depth of woe.
> I will not bribe their misery not to haunt
> My merrymaking by proffer of boon
> That should only mock the grief that is rightly theirs.
> Here I shall sit, the fire out, and croon
> All the dismal and joy-forsaken airs,
> Sole alone, and thirsty with them that thirst,
> Hungry with them that hunger and are accurst.
> No storm that night can be too untamed for me,
> If it is woe on earth, woe let it be!
> Am I a child that I should refuse to see?
> What could I plead asking them to be glad
>   That night?
>   My right?
> Nay it is theirs that I with them should be sad
>   That night.[14]

Miss Ward, probably recognizing all the teasing ambiguities and ironies of "My Giving," would not have made the mistake of accepting the poem at its face value. She knew that Robert

Frost was not going to sit alone on Christmas Eve or Christmas Night with the fire out, crooning dismal and joy-forsaken airs while intermittently quoting to himself biblical passages about those who hunger and are athirst. But Miss Ward, a gentle woman, may have found gentle ways to remind the mocker that the inability to remove all human suffering, at Christmas or at any other time, is scarcely an excuse for not doing something to alleviate human miseries—individually, socially, and politically.

Miss Ward apparently forgave the bitter poetic jest and did extend an invitation, which Frost accepted. A few days after Christmas of 1911, he left his family in Plymouth and went by train to New York City. In his suitcase he packed for train reading on the way a newly published American translation of a work by the French philosopher, Henri Bergson, to whom (as he must have known) William James had already paid more than one tribute. The book was *Creative Evolution*, and this translation from the French had already earned wide praise.

By the time Frost reached Newark, New Jersey, to spend a night with Dr. William Hayes Ward and his sister, Frost was eager to share his excitement over this new discovery. At the dinner table, he tried to explain what he liked most in *Creative Evolution*. He knew that the Wards were devout Congregationalists, and yet he probably felt that he was on safe ground when he assured them that Bergson had found splendid poetic images for endowing with spiritual meanings the scientific theories of the evolutionists. Frost explained Bergson's insistence that the life force cannot be accounted for in material terms, that the vital spirit is a dynamic and creative force which struggles to achieve richness and complexity through matter and beyond matter. Frost particularly liked Bergson's gathering metaphors: the flowing stream of matter moves ever downward, but the life force resists and tries always to climb back upward, through matter, toward the Source. Among the hindrances to the proper individual response, Bergson said, were the scientific approach and the destructively analytical pretensions of the intellect. Frost liked Bergson's claim that the instinctive and intuitive consciousness of the creative individual—the poet, the saint, the prophet—is always helping to place man in the right relationship to the Source; is always trying to make the properly creative and spiritual responses through expressions of spiritual change, growth, freedom to liberate the soul of man from the enslavements of matter.

The Reverend William Hayes Ward listened silently to the enthusiastic praise given Bergson by his guest from New Hampshire. When he had the opportunity, however, Ward said that he himself had already taken occasion to read some of Bergson's *Creative Evolution* and that he had found it to be a thoroughly atheistic tract. Oh no, Frost protested, Bergson was a deeply religious man. Impossible, said Ward—and he changed the subject.

Hurt, and yet frightened by the massive dignity of his distinguished host, Frost could not resist a feeling of indignation. After he had retired to his room that night he very carefully went through his copy of *Creative Evolution* and selected passages that refuted Ward's charges of atheism. He was ready for combat. But in the light of morning he felt that no textual evidence could overcome the rigidity of Ward's dogmatism. It seemed that to Ward an atheist was anyone who failed to share his own inflexible theological beliefs. Under the circumstances, Frost decided, there would be more pleasure for him in discussing with Miss Ward his own plans for writing better poetry, for making the great leap forward.[15]

On the return trip from New York City to Plymouth, Frost continued reading Bergson's *Creative Evolution* without realizing that he was planting in his memory images and ideas which would later serve as raw materials for his own metaphors. Bergson's dualistic viewpoint helped to corroborate and articulate some half-formed notions congenial to Frost ever since he first began reading *The Will to Believe*. It seemed to him that some of Bergson's ideas and images were like vague Emersonian lustres, with echoes from Heraclitus, and he was delighted with them.[16]

The more he read of Bergson, the more indignant he became over the harsh comment made by Ward, whose judgment seemed so false. Ward might have said, more truthfully, that Bergson's highly romantic ideas had their roots in the pagan writings of Plotinus. Ward could have gone on to complain that Bergson and William James shared the fallible romantic notion that metaphysical idealism could be supported with proof drawn from empirical and pragmatic evidence based on material facts. Frost could have answered that these procedures had also been used for centuries by a great many orthodox Christian theologians. At this time, however, he would not have chosen to answer in this way.

He was doing his best to strengthen a position he had begun to take during the darkest of his experiences in Derry. Starting from a moment of pessimistic disillusionment and of temporary religious unbelief, he had wanted to find some practical common-sense guideposts from Nowhere to Somewhere. He had felt that his religious belief had failed him and that if he could justify his bittersweet human experience he would need to base the justification on beliefs entirely outside the systematic theological framework of Christian dogma. His fragmentary knowledge of Thoreau and Emerson had helped, without making him aware that their transcendentalism amounted to an old-fashioned way of upholding metaphysical idealism from a more-or-less empirical and pragmatic standpoint, thus foreshadowing the so-called new-fashioned ways of William James and Bergson. Nor was he made aware, apparently, that the goal of spiritual salvation and eternal life sought by either the nineteenth- or twentieth-century transcendentalists outside a Christian framework was essentially at one with the Christian goal. Yet this essential kinship had enabled Frost to make a very easy transition back to his relatively orthodox Christian belief, in 1906, when he came under the influence of the Congregationalists in Derry and began teaching in the Congregational atmosphere of Pinkerton Academy.

From his high-school days, when he had told his mother that he was a freethinker and when he had begun to invoke Shelley as a hero, Frost had never been as heretical as he had liked to think—and he never would be. But by the time he reached Plymouth, brimming with more health, confidence, self-reliance, courage than he had ever possessed before, he was again intent on asserting his originality through various skeptical disagreements with orthodox Christian belief. His renewed pride in viewing himself as a nonconformist had made him ripe for the discovery of Bergson's very subjective and individualistic and romantic poetry. It had also made him ripe for the discovery that he might further strengthen his position as heretic and skeptic if he should read (or perhaps reread) a book which he had been in no mood to digest sympathetically when it made its first appearance in June of 1907: *Pragmatism*, by William James.

Perhaps the most concrete evidence that Frost read *Prag-*

matism while teaching a course in psychology at Plymouth Normal School is contained in his letter of thanks to his Newark hostess, Miss Ward. After describing the strain he had felt in settling down again to class work following his return; after thanking Miss Ward for having "encouraged my poor Muse with interest when you couldn't with praise," he concluded with a postscript in which he said he was sending Miss Ward a new sonnet. Although he did not say so, the sonnet had something in common with the poem entitled "My Giving." It was another ambiguously ironic and sarcastic weapon calculated to jar the sensibilities of any orthodox Christian reader, and the ambiguities are clarified if placed within a pertinent context provided by certain passages in *Pragmatism*.

The first chapter of *Pragmatism* begins in a way which has a direct bearing on Frost's double interests at this time: "In the preface to that admirable collection of essays of his called 'Heretics,' Mr. [G. K.] Chesterton writes these words: 'There are some people—and I am one of them—who think that the most practical and important thing about a man is still his view of the universe.'" After quoting Chesterton further, James comments: "I think with Mr. Chesterton in this matter. I know that you . . . have a philosophy, each and all of you, and that the most interesting and important thing about you is the way in which it determines the perspective in your several worlds."[17]

While at Harvard, Frost had heard Santayana say something about how beliefs determine perspectives; but Santayana had been trying to illustrate the ease with which human beings accept as "truth" any so-called "philosophy" or "belief" which seems to be practical because it promises in the end to be profitable. From Santayana's viewpoint James was a self-styled "philosopher" who very conveniently found a romantic way of talking in strenuous and tough-minded fashion about pragmatism while nibbling all the time on the cake of his cherished mysticism.

In *Pragmatism* a primary goal of James was at one with Bergson's: each wanted to uphold metaphysical idealism, not from a Christian viewpoint and not from a scientific viewpoint but rather from a subjective and personal viewpoint, which might claim to be founded on a practical and "utilitarian" observation of the facts. There may have been another reason why *Pragmatism* appealed to Frost after he had reached Plymouth. His new confidence, which had increased his pleasure in displaying bold and skeptical views, had also, paradoxically, revitalized his religious beliefs. For years he had been trying to construct a way of belief which would provide assurance that God's in His heaven and all's right with Frost's part of the world. At the same time, like James, he wanted his way of belief to be so heretical and skeptical that he could stand in a place apart, from which he could mock the "abstract" misuses (as he saw them) of the intellect by logical philosophers, by materialist scientists, and by dogmatic Christian system-builders. Earlier, Frost had found that the rebellious idealism of Shelley provided a basis for such a posture; now, the metaphors and insights of Bergson and James helped him to build a superstructure on that Shelleyan foundation.

Immediately, Frost wanted to scoff at his recent antagonist, the Reverend William Hayes Ward, for believing in a narrow-minded and literal God-concept which left no room for the poetry of Bergson's insights. James came to Frost's aid, in *Pragmatism,* by talking ironically and sarcastically about "closed" minds. "The actual universe is a thing wide open," James said, "but rationalism makes systems, and systems must be closed."[18] Continuing, James complained that such "closed" systems hindered opportunities for either intellectual or spiritual growth. Then James expressed his own view of the properly changing and growing human response to what is true:

"A new opinion counts as 'true' just in proportion as it gratifies the individual's desire to assimilate the novel in his experience to his beliefs in stock. It must both lean on old truth and grasp new fact; and its success . . . in doing this, is a matter for the individual's appreciation. When old truth grows, then, by new truth's addition, it is for subjective reasons. We are in the process and obey the reasons. That new idea is truest which performs most felicitously its function of satisfying our double urgency. It makes itself true, gets itself classed as true, by the way it works; grafting itself then upon the ancient body of truth, which thus grows much as a tree grows by the activity of a new layer of cambium."[19]

This botanic analogy, involving the cambium layer of vitality, was very attractive to Frost. So was James's further definition of what is true:

". . . an idea is 'true' so long as to believe it is profitable to our lives. That it is *good*, for as much as it profits, you will gladly admit. If what we do by its aid is good, you will allow the idea itself to be good in so far forth,[20] for we are the better for possessing it. . . . *The true is the name of whatever proves itself to be good in the way of belief, and good, too, for definite, assignable reasons.*"[21]

This beautifully flexible definition of "the true" could be made to work just as well for a mystic as for a pragmatist and, like James, Frost wanted to be both at once. Furthermore, such an open-minded attitude toward "the true" permitted Frost the luxury of scorning the narrow-mindedness of his immediate enemy, Ward. It pleased Frost to find that James, in *Pragmatism*, very wittily mocked the old-fashioned claim, for example, that God had designed every minute physical detail in nature for a special end. James says that some of these details, "if designed, would argue an evil rather than a good designer." Then to illustrate how much depends on the point of view he singles out a grub and a woodpecker: "To the grub under the bark the exquisite fitness of the woodpecker's organism to extract him would certainly argue a diabolical designer."[22] Any attempt to argue "from fitness to design," says James, is a waste of time. "Pragmatically, then, the abstract word 'design' is a blank cartridge. It carries no consequences, it does no execution."[23] God must be in the wholesale and not in the retail business, where matters of "design" are involved: "His designs have grown so vast as to be incomprehensible to us humans." But James, having disposed of what he refers to as the "abstract" or "rationalistic" principle of "design," picks up the term again, cleans it off, places it within his newly fashioned intuition of "whatever proves itself to be good in the way of belief," and concludes:

" 'Design,' worthless tho it be as a mere rationalistic principle set above or behind things for our admiration, becomes, if our faith concretes it into something theistic, a term of *promise*. Returning with it into experience, we gain a more confiding outlook on the future. If not a blind force but a seeing force runs things, we may reasonably expect better issues. This vague confidence in the future is the sole pragmatic meaning at present discernible in the terms design and designer. But if cosmic confidence is right not wrong, better not worse, that is a most important meaning. That much at least of possible 'truth' the terms will then have in them."[24]

Santayana may have smiled again over this discovery of such a neat cleavage between the "abstract" and the "concrete" meaning for the concepts of designer and design; but Frost, immediately concerned with his process of gathering metaphors with which to support his own beliefs while mocking the beliefs of others, seems to have admired the cleavage. After his return from New York, still smarting under Ward's dogmatic insistence that Bergson was an atheist, Frost sent in his letter of thanks to Susan Hayes Ward the previously mentioned sonnet. He knew she would share it with her brother. Although the sonnet was entitled "In White," it was later revised for publication as "Design," and the revisions sharpen the ironies without changing the central meanings:

Design

I found a dimpled spider, fat and white,
On a white heal-all, holding up a moth
Like a white piece of rigid satin cloth—
Assorted characters of death and blight
Mixed ready to begin the morning right,
Like the ingredients of a witches' broth—
A snow-drop spider, a flower like a froth,
And dead wings carried like a paper kite.

What had that flower to do with being white,
The wayside blue and innocent heal-all?
What brought the kindred spider to that height,
Then steered the white moth thither in the night?
What but design of darkness to appall?—
If design govern in a thing so small.[25]

William Hayes Ward, reading the first draft of this poem in the letter of thanks, might have thought he found in it a confirmation of his fear that Robert Frost had come powerfully under the influence of "atheistical" writers like Bergson and had thus become an atheist himself; but he would have been incorrect. If his more perceptive sister placed the first draft of this poem side by side with "My Giving," she may have seen correspondences between the two artistic procedures of carrying a sentimental notion to an absurd extreme. She knew Frost well enough to be certain that the coincidences did not for a moment convince him that this "design" suggested proof that the Designer must be evil. Frost, habitually the prey to dark moods which temporarily upset his religious affirmations, was perfectly capable of understanding—and even of sympathizing with—the possibility that his little study in white could be interpreted as being akin to Melville's very bitter chapter, "The Whiteness of the Whale," in *Moby-Dick*. But Melville enjoyed the agony of luxuriating in blasphemous negations, and Frost never did. Instead, he so desperately needed the consolation of positive religious belief that he was never long without it. Although he could briefly and intermittently entertain the notion that the Designer might be evil, he preferred to manipulate the notion in a detached way to tease and mock those whose religious beliefs seemed to him to be sentimental. Even in teasing, however, he still very firmly agreed with James and Bergson (as opposed to William Hayes Ward) that all the important purposes of the Designer are benevolent.

These literary gestures which Frost made while at Plymouth represented one kind of breakaway, and they were closely related to another one, which he had been planning since the day he sold his farm. By the spring of 1912, he was thirty-eight years old. He was convinced that if ever he was to assert himself artistically, with success, he must find the time and place to be completely selfish. Financially, he had gained a very important advantage merely through the passage of years. By the terms of his grandfather's will, he again told himself, the amount of the annuity to be paid him in July of 1912 would be increased from $500 to $800, an amount which was not too much less than the salary he was receiving for a full year of classroom work at Plymouth. If he were careful, he could tighten the purse-strings enough to live on that amount. But where should he go? What move would best take him forward?

John Bartlett came into the family considerations of where they should go. He had visited them briefly soon after the school year had begun, and had announced that he was leaving for Vancouver Island, British Columbia, the largest island off the west coast of North America. Frost confided that such a romantic hideaway sounded so attractive that the Frost family might join him there, even before John Bartlett persuaded his Pinkerton sweetheart to make a trip to marry him. The Frosts and John Bartlett talked at length about Vancouver Island,

and at the railroad station in Plymouth Frost gave Bartlett a book for reading on the long journey. It was Chesterton's *Heretics,* probably more important for Frost because of the title than because of the defense of orthodoxy within the covers.[26] Not long after, Bartlett wrote from Vancouver expressing initial joy in his new home and urging the Frosts to join him there. Frost wrote him a casually versified letter. Six out of the twenty-four lines give the flavor of it:

> *My friends in Vancouver are bright,*
> *But I'll tell them they'd better beware:*
> *If they sing me much more to that air*
> *I'll take the train west overnight,*
> *And ask them to lend me the fare.*
> *I'm a dangerous man to excite.*[27]

While the Frost family continued the discussions of whether they should go to Canada or England when they made their breakaway, Frost began to find reasons for feeling that perhaps he should stay at home. There were many signs in literary circles that a new day had arrived for poetry in the United States, and one of the signs was that Frost began to have more success in selling poems to magazines. He had been discouraged briefly, however, by a personal letter of rejection written and signed by Ellery Sedgwick, editor of the *Atlantic Monthly.* In returning six poems (including "Reluctance"), Sedgwick wrote, in part, "We are sorry that we have no place in the *Atlantic Monthly* for your vigorous verse." Sarcastically, Frost wondered whether the word "vigorous" was intended as criticism. Was his verse too vigorous or not vigorous enough for the *Atlantic?* But while he was still in the process of resenting what Sedgwick had written, he received a letter from Thomas Bird Mosher, offering to buy the poem "Reluctance" for use in *Amphora,* one of Mosher's publications. Mosher had apparently seen a manuscript of the poem, perhaps in the possession of Susan Hayes Ward, to whom Frost had sent a copy. Frost knew that for more than ten years Mosher had shown a taste for fine printing, as reflected in his many pocket-sized imprints of good works not well known in the United States; that Mosher also published a small monthly anthology, *The Bibelot,* each issue containing short pieces of prose and poetry, usually reprints, selected from obscure but significant works.

His answer to Mosher was filled with overtones of the excitement caused by the turn of events he was experiencing—and planning:

"I was just saying of my poetry that it didnt seem to make head as fast as I could wish with the public, when the letter came in which you said almost the identical thing of your Bibelot. But you could add of your own motion that you were getting, you supposed, all that was coming to you. Not to be outdone by you in philosophy (which is my subject of instruction) I made myself say it after you for a discipline: I suppose I am getting all that is coming to me. (These are harder words for me to pronounce than they could ever be for you—for reasons.) And then see how soon I had my reward. The very next day what should my poetry bring me but a check for twenty-five dollars, which is more than it ever brought before at one time. Some part of this belongs to you in simple poetic justice. Five dollars, say. You wouldn't tempt me to spend forty dollars on the Bibelot or anything else if you knew the ambitious schemes I have at heart, imposing habits of the strictest economy for the next ten years. But I can, and herewith do, send five dollars for books; and without impropriety, I trust, to satisfy my sense of the fitness of things, I copy on the inside of this sheet the poem by which I earned it, glad of the chance to show poem of mine to one whose life is so conspicuously devoted to the cause of poetry."[28]

Mosher had apparently given Frost the right to make a double sale of "Reluctance" by offering it also to periodicals for use prior to Mosher's publication of it. In less than a month after his first letter to Mosher, Frost wrote again to say that he had sold "Reluctance" to *The Youth's Companion*, and that he had sold another poem to *The Forum* magazine. A third poem was sold to the *Companion* a little later. But none of these favorable signs deterred the Frosts from continuing their plans for going abroad. Somewhat romantically, Elinor urged that they should go to England and "live under thatch." Frost was still inclined to join forces with John Bartlett, but in a spirit of gambling he suggested that they toss a coin to see whether they should go to England or Vancouver. "The coin chose England," Frost said.

With no small pleasure Frost broke the news to Silver, who seemed incredulous and gave reasons against such a ridiculous decision: If Frost went to England there would be no position awaiting him at Plymouth on his return—he might, of course, find a position teaching in some grammar school somewhere. Frost was adamant, and his pleasure in rejecting all of Silver's well-intentioned advice amounted to exactly the kind of revenge he had been wanting: to even the score with this man who, he imagined, had been his enemy from the start. This was the moment when he was tempted to be more insolent than Silver's courtesy permitted, the moment when a favorite passage in *Macbeth* flashed through his mind: "I could / With barefac'd power sweep him from my sight / And bid my will avouch it, yet I must not . . ." Instead, he asked Silver to help his family finish packing while he went ahead to buy steamship tickets in Boston late in the summer of 1912. He took passage on a steamer bound for Glasgow: the *SS Parisian.*

Silver put Mrs. Frost and the four children on the train for Boston. The family met at the pier, as planned—all of them excited—and together they mounted the gangplank of the *Parisian* eager for adventure.[29]

ENGLAND: *A BOY'S WILL*

These poems are intended by the author to possess a certain sequence, and to depict the various stages in the evolution of a young man's outlook upon life.

NOT LONG AFTER the Frosts were settled in England, Mrs. Frost wrote to Mrs. Lynch, partly to explain why she and her family had not spent the hay-fever season of 1912 in Bethlehem, New Hampshire. She began: "I know you have wondered many times what had become of the Frost family, and I am sure you will be very, very much surprised to learn that we are way across the ocean, in England.

"You see, last summer we spent several weeks trying our very best to decide where we wanted to go, and gradually we came to feel that it would be pleasant to travel about the world a little. [Mrs. Lynch had so often felt sorry for the Frosts because they seemed to be in straitened circumstances financially[1] that she must have been surprised at this hint of affluence. The letter continued:] And finally we decided to come to England and find a little house in one of the suburbs of London, and two weeks from the day of our decision, we were on our way out of Boston Harbor. We stored our furniture, and brought only bedclothes, two floor rugs, books, and some pictures.[2] We sailed from Boston to Glasgow, and enjoyed the ocean trip on the whole, though Mr. Frost, Lesley and I were quite seasick for a few days. The younger children escaped with only a few hours discomfort. [In writing her letter Mrs. Frost was not likely to forget that both Mr. and Mrs. Lynch were natives of Ireland and that even a mention of Northern Ireland would be better than no mention at all.] The last day of the voyage we skirted along the north coast of Ireland, and thought the dark, wild looking headlands and blue mountains very beautiful. We landed at Glasgow in the morning, and travelled all day across Scotland and England, arriving at London about seven oclock. From the station, we telephoned for rooms at the Premier Hotel, and after securing them, drove in a cab to the hotel, feeling greatly excited, you may imagine, at being all alone, without a single friend, in the biggest city in the world. We stayed in the hotel a week, while Mr. Frost was busy looking for a house in the towns about. I took the children about the city as much as I was able during the day, and nearly every evening Mr. Frost and I went to the theatre. London was splendid. The absence of elevated railways and trolley cars make it a much more beautiful city than New York . . ."[3]

An obvious lift had been given to Mrs Frost's perennially subdued outlook on life by all these events: the romantic decision to "travel about the world a little," the hasty departure, the long voyage, and the excitement of "being all alone, without a single friend, in the biggest city in the world." Her delight in the bold venture was shared by her entire family. On the very first night of their arrival in London, the thirteen-year-old Lesley had been placed in charge of the three younger children at the Premier Hotel so that their parents could be free to celebrate by attending a performance of George Bernard Shaw's comedy *Fanny's First Play.*

The search for a little cottage in the suburbs caused some difficulty. Although Frost had no idea how to tackle the problem, he had read in the English newspaper, *T. P.'s Weekly,* a "highways and byways" column, which clearly implied that the author of it was well-informed concerning rural areas in the vicinity of London. Taking the liberty of calling at the office of *T. P.'s Weekly,* Frost found that the columnist was a genial ruddy-faced pipe-smoking ex-policeman eager to have someone draw on his knowledge. Appointing himself as guide, the ex-policeman showed Frost a few unsatisfactory houses and finally took him twenty-one miles north of London on the Great Western Railway to Beaconsfield in Buckinghamshire. No thatch-covered cottage turned up, but the last house on the right-hand curve of Reynolds Road[4] was for rent, and Frost was pleased with it. Locally known as "The Bungalow," it was an attractive little five-room vine-covered stucco house with "a large grassy space in front, and a pretty garden behind, with pear trees, strawberry beds and lots of flowers," as Mrs. Frost described it in her letter to Mrs. Lynch. Frost combined references to floral and literary elements in his first reference to the new Beaconsfield setting: "Here we are between high hedges of laurel and red-osier dogwood, within a mile or two of where Milton finished Paradise Lost on the one hand and a mile or two of where Grey lies buried on the other and within as many rods as furlongs of the house where Chesterton tries truth to see if it won't prove as true upside down as it does right side up. To London town what is it but a run? Indeed when I leave writing this and go into the front yard for a last look at earth and sky before I go to sleep, I shall be able to see the not very distinct lights of London flaring like a dreary dawn."[5] Nine-year-old Irma, now following the example of keeping a journal set by her brother Carol and her older sister Lesley, recorded her own vivid responses to the arrival of the family and her first impressions of all the strange rooms in "The Bungalow," before the newly purchased furniture gave it a semblance of home:

"We got out of the train in Beaconsfield station. It was all new to us, and we walked up the road, and through many roads. There weren't many people in the street. 'I must go into the groser's,' said papa, 'and tell him to come in the morning.' Papa went in and we waited at the door. The groser said a lot of things, and papa said, 'You come in the morning,' and he said 'Yes,' and we went on our way and papa went up to the bakers. We went up to our house. The rest got away ahead of Carol and I. Pretty soon papa came up behind us. I ran back to meet him, but Carol went with the rest. Papa pointed to our house and I saw people putting 'fernercher' in our house. The others had gone in already. Papa unlocked the side door, and he put the key on a nail. We went through that room into the hall. Then we went into a big bedroom, and then into a small one, and then into the sitting room where the furniture was. Then we went out through the hall into the kitchen. There were some men washing the room. It was aufully dirty. Mama and the children had gone out in the garden, so we went out too. There was a hothouse, a summer house, and some dead flowers. We looked around and then we went in and placed some of the furniture around."[6]

Having encouraged his children to enjoy long walks down country roads near the Derry farm, Frost at first spent much time with his family exploring the outskirts of Beaconsfield. They all enjoyed noticing and talking about the differences between the landscapes of Buckinghamshire and New Hampshire, the newness for them of the roads, the houses, the fences, the terrain. On a more practical errand Frost made visits to elementary schools in the neighborhood, partly to find an educational program for his older children and partly to gather information he had promised one of Morrison's colleagues in New Hampshire.⁷ He also relented enough to write to "Dear Mr. Silver" not long after his arrival in Beaconsfield. As though to make amends for his previous discourtesies to the friendly Principal of Plymouth Normal School, he endowed the letter with almost too much geniality, but he signed himself very formally "Robert Frost."⁸

When all the excitement of new surroundings had lessened, Frost was able to get into the mood for serious writing, and he began the first chapter of a novel designed to present dramatic conflicts between two generations of New Hampshire farmers. He progressed only far enough to feel that his beginning might better be reshaped into a play or a poem, and he later published it as a dramatic blank-verse dialogue.⁹

Disliking the novel, he returned to his first love and found himself writing lyrics, some of them based on his new observations and insights. One of these lyrics catching the freshness of his response to all that was strange to him in the countryside around Beaconsfield was "In England":

> *Alone in rain I sat today*
> *On top of a gate beside the way,*
> *And a bird came near with muted bill,*
> *And a watery breeze kept blowing chill*
> *From over the hill behind me.*
>
> *I could not tell what in me stirred*
> *To hill and gate and rain and bird,*
> *Till lifting hair and bathing brow*
> *The watery breeze came fresher now*
> *From over the hill to remind me.*
>
> *The bird was the kind that follows a ship,*
> *The rain was salt upon my lip,*
> *The hill was an undergoing wave,*
> *And the gate on which I balanced brave*
> *Was a great ship's iron railing.*

For the breeze was a watery English breeze
Always fresh from one of the seas,
And the country life the English lead
In beachen wood and clover mead
Is never far from sailing.[10]

The lyric pleasure of his response to England was very soon counterbalanced, however, by Frost's growing awareness that he missed what he had left behind in New Hampshire. Alone one night, he sorted through the sheaf of manuscripts he had brought with him and could not resist the impulse to see if he had enough to make up a small volume. Never before had he found the courage to begin preparing a manuscript for submission to a publisher, and even now he was not sure he was doing more than playing a game. He spread the pages out across the floor in the lamplight, occasionally crumpling up a sheet of paper containing a false start and tossing it into the fireplace. His first thought was that he could find no unifying thematic element. The many different moods in the lyrics he had written during a period of twenty years were obviously inconsistent and self-contradictory. The worst thing he could do with them, he thought, would be to arrange them chronologically, starting with those he had written in high school when he had unconsciously paid tribute to other poets. The best he could do would be to select a sequence of love lyrics written to Elinor during the vicissitudes of courtship, before and after their marriage; but his own reticences—and hers—were too strong to permit that. Or he could shape a selected group into a spiral of moods, upward through discouragement and withdrawal to aspiration and affirmation. Such a pattern might be reinforced if he made his responses to the changing seasons of fall and winter and spring and summer reflect different phases of his own spiritual growth through dark moods.

From his new position of detachment, achieved during the one year at Plymouth and the voyage to England, he could look back with enough perspective to see how his early lyrics represented his having been scared away from life—his having been scared almost completely out of life through suicidal temptations—and his having gradually found thought-felt justification for returning to assert so many different kinds of love and cherishing. In a sense his affirmative poems were all love poems, and perhaps the best pattern he could express through the arrangement of them might be a motion out of self-love and into his love for others. Again he knew that his reticence would not permit him to make such an arrangement too self-revealing. He had said as much in a journal note made after he reached England: "A poem would be no good that hadn't doors. I wouldn't leave them open though."[11] Not too wide open, at least.

Nevertheless, he became more and more attracted by the possibility that the grouped lyrics might express a figurative truth through metaphysical fiction. His first book, if published within a year, would represent his achievements up to the age of thirty-eight—and a selection from them could suggest the long long thoughts of a youth who had struggled to find his own direction. Longfellow's familiar phrase came to mind as justification for inconsistencies. The fluctuating moods of a boy's will are as unpredictable and varied as the moods of the wind, which blows wherever it cares to blow.

Having made a start at the game by spreading out his manuscripts on the floor, he gradually worked toward the pattern he wanted. He began the arrangement with a lyric which reflected his mistaken notion that the best way to combat the scorn of the world is to forswear the world: to escape from it by running away. "Into My Own" had been inspired by his fierce conviction that there was validity in the Emersonian forswearing: "Goodbye, proud world! I'm going home." He had written "Into My Own" so far back in the Derry years, however, that he could now enjoy the irony of his more detached and mature realization that while the world may indeed be scorned by any sensitive person for self-protective reasons, it cannot be completely forsworn—at least by the living.

More and more aware that his gradually achieved perspective on these early lyrics now enabled him to view some of them with ironic ambivalence, he continued his ordering until he achieved a threefold structural pattern which did have the personal significance of spiritual and psychological growth. In this arrangement, part one began with a dramatic and symbolic act of complete withdrawal; but it ended with a special kind of return. Part two was built out of lyrics that carried forward the theme of return by representing various poetic expressions of affirmation. Part three was made up of a few lyrics which viewed wistfully and even passionately those withdrawals that were inevitable—such as the end of a life or a love or a season.

In all three structural parts, seasonal elements were deliberately invoked to add a special dimension. Part one began with a late-summer poem and moved quickly into fall and on through winter into spring. Part two built a cluster of meditative lyrics around the summer poem, "The Tuft of Flowers," which provided the central affirmation of the entire volume: " 'Men work together,' I told him from the heart, / 'Whether they work together or apart.' " The seasonal cycle was continued in part three, so that the poems carried on through summer, again to fall, ending with "Reluctance."

Finally, he strengthened the continuity of his arrangement by giving a brief gloss or note under each title as it occurred in the table of contents—with only two exceptions. These brief commentaries might seem at first glance merely to hint at different phases of the youthful poet's response to his own experience, as reflected in each poem:

PART I

INTO MY OWN
The youth is persuaded that he will be rather more than less himself for having forsworn the world.

GHOST HOUSE
He is happy in society of his choosing.

MY NOVEMBER GUEST
He is in love with being misunderstood.

LOVE AND A QUESTION
He is in doubt whether to admit real trouble to a place beside the hearth with love.

A LATE WALK
He courts the autumnal mood.

STARS
There is no oversight of human affairs.

STORM FEAR
He is afraid of his own isolation.

Frost hoped that readers who took a second glance at these brief commentaries would be aware of the deliberately implied discrepancy between the poet's earlier and later views of youthful response to experience. The tone of these glosses, taken as a whole, was indeed ironic and detached. For instance, at the start the youth is "persuaded" to escape from the world; but later he is more wisely "persuaded" that such an attitude is mistaken, at least in some important ways. Similarly, after the youth is "persuaded" that he should forswear the world, he correctly becomes "afraid of his own isolation." Another ironic inconsistency is implied by the note which observes that the youth, when living contentedly in a "Ghost House," is happy—much too happy—in this particular "society of his choosing." And again irony is achieved by counterbalancing the "November Guest" note ("He is in love with being misunderstood.") against the subsequent poetic statement, in "Revelation," "We make ourselves a place apart / Behind light words that tease and flout, / But oh, the agitated heart / Till someone really find us out." An ironic figure was deliberately achieved by permitting "The Trial by Existence" to come after, and thus to provide an affirmative correction for, the negative mood of "Stars" and the observation, "There is no oversight of human affairs."

By contrast, the seven notes for part two were deliberately calculated to hint at the maturing attitude of the youth by giving a sequence to a group of poems which might otherwise seem completely separate from each other:

PART II

REVELATION
    He resolves to become intelligible, at least
        to himself, since there is no help else;

THE TRIAL BY EXISTENCE
    and to know definitely what he thinks about
        the soul;

IN EQUAL SACRIFICE
    about love;

THE TUFT OF FLOWERS
    about fellowship;

SPOILS OF THE DEAD
    about death;

PAN WITH US
    about art (his own);

THE DEMIURGE'S LAUGH
    about science.

Frost felt that the unifying effect of these little commentaries for all three parts did help him to derive special overtones of relevance—and a gathering metaphor—from the title he borrowed out of the familiar passage in Longfellow's "My Lost Youth":

> *"A boy's will is the wind's will*
> *And the thoughts of youth are long, long thoughts."*

Yet he was not entirely satisfied with his attempt at unification through notes and he later dropped them. His one immediate consolation was that the notes and the ingenious pattern in his arrangement did endow the almost-too-personal lyrics with some degree of detachment.

As soon as the manuscript of *A Boy's Will* was completed, he could think of only one way to search for a publisher. Still a stranger in a suburb of the "biggest city in the world," he felt that he could at least seek advice from the one acquaintance who had helped him find a house. Taking the manuscript with him, he went down to London and called again at the office of *T. P.'s Weekly* to lay his problem before the retired policeman. He was told that Elkin Matthews published many books of poems for a price, and that a little book like this might not cost the author more than fifteen pounds. Politely, Frost tried to explain that he was not seeking that kind of publication. Very well, then, the policeman-columnist said, the firm of David Nutt also handled a certain amount of poetry. Frost accepted the suggestion, remembering the imprint of David Nutt and Company on the title page of a volume of verse by William Ernest Henley. At the time, he was in a mood to say with Henley, "Under the bludgeonings of chance / My head is bloody, but unbow'd."

When he found the office of David Nutt and Company at 6

Bloomsbury Street the best he could do for the day was to make an appointment—and the formality of this procedure seemed cold enough to discourage him. Even on his return visit he found little reason to expect that he had made any significant progress. The interview was conducted by a sad little woman dressed in black, who spoke with a French accent in saying that she would "represent" David Nutt. Frost was not aware that David Nutt had died, that the publishing business had been carried on by Alfred Nutt, now also dead, and that this woman was the widow of Alfred Nutt. With some misgiving he left with her the manuscript of *A Boy's Will*, accepting her assurance that she would let him know the decision of the firm in a few days. She kept her word, in a letter dated 26 October 1912:

"I have looked through your MS and I am personally interested in the treatment of your theme. I am therefore disposed to bring out your poems if the proposal I can put before you and which would be on the principle of a royalty payment will suit you. I cannot put a dry and cut proposal before you as yet, as I want to think a little about the most suitable form to give to the book but I hope to be in a position to do so very soon."[12]

Suddenly, with the arrival of this brief note, so many hopes deferred seemed realized or at least realizable. From the time Frost had made and sent little booklets of prose and verse to Carl Burell back in the nineties, and even more from the time he had wistfully sent poems to Susan Hayes Ward "with a view to a volume some day," his ambition had been to have a publisher say nothing more than "I am therefore disposed to bring out your poems . . . on the principle of a royalty payment . . ." The announcement was enough to change his entire attitude toward his work and himself. The confidence he had needed in his own powers was given an entirely new lift by these words. They justified the gamble he had taken in breaking away from the security offered by Silver at Plymouth.

On his next visit to London, Frost called again on Mrs. Nutt to discuss terms, and was not too greatly troubled to have her say that when the contract was drawn up it would contain a clause which would let the firm of David Nutt have the first right to publish his next four books of verse or prose. A few days later further encouragement was given him when he received a letter from Thomas B. Mosher, who said that he would like to publish a book of Frost's poems in Mosher's "Lyric Garland Series." Unable to avoid boasting, Frost answered on 19 November 1912:

" . . . The Dea knows I should like nothing better than to see my first book, 'A Boy's Will,' in your Lyric Garland Series. It even crossed my mind to submit it to you. But under the circumstances I couldn't, lest you should think I was going to come on you as the poor old man comes on the town. I brought it to England in the bottom of my trunk, more afraid of it, probably, than the Macnamara of what he carried in his. I came here to write rather than to publish. I have three other books of verse somewhere near completion, 'Melanism,' 'Villagers,' and 'The Sense of Wrong,' and I wanted to be alone with them for a while. [There was a large element of exaggeration in the boast that he had three other books "somewhere near completion," and yet the first and third of those proposed titles contain appropriate ideas. In the sense that "melanism" is not unrelated to "melancholy," and serves to indicate darkness of color resulting from an abnormal development of black pigment in the epidermis of animals, the word might be used as a metaphor. It could represent the Scottish roots of spiritual darkness that always fed his own "sense of wrong." The tendency showed anew before he finished this letter to Mosher, but the next statement was pure boast unavoidable.] If I ever published anything, I fully expected it would be through some American publisher. But see how little I knew myself. Wholly on impulse one day I took my MS. of A Boy's Will to London and left it with the publisher whose imprint was the first I had noticed in a volume of minor verse on arriving in England, viz., David Nutt. I suppose I did it to see what would happen, as once on a time I short-circuited a dynamo with a two-foot length of wire held between the brushes. What happened pleased me at first—in the case of the MS., I mean. I am not so sure how I feel about it now. David Nutt made me a proposal on a royalty basis. I have signed no contract as yet, but after what has passed, I suppose I am bound to sign, if pressed, almost anything that doesn't seem too one-sided. I expect the publisher will drive a hard bargain with me: who am I that he shouldn't have a right to? One thing that disconcerts me, however, is the eleventh-hour claim he makes on my next three or four books, verse or prose. I wish I knew what you would say to that. I suppose I ought to be proud to be so much in demand: the embarrassment is so novel in my experience. But wont it seem traitorously un-American to have all my first work come out over here? And how about you in whose hands I should feel so much happier and safer. And then there is Richard Badger [a "vanity publisher"] of Boston who has asked to see material for a book. Why couldn't you have spoken two weeks sooner and saved me all this perplexity? It seems to me you owe me something in the way of helpful advice for not speaking. Perhaps I can stave off that contract till I can get an answer from you. Have I made a serious mistake in going to David Nutt?"[13]

The dark anguish of such perplexity was partly enjoyable to Frost—and he made the most of it. Nor could he refrain from making something of it when next he wrote to "Dear Mr. Silver" in Plymouth. There had seemed to be sheer malice in Silver's letters, which contained requests for something literary. At last he was in the proper dark mood to answer—saving the best until last:

"Between you and me, though, I know what would be literary and highly literary. To talk about myself. I have been keeping this back for effect. You have doubtless heard through my friend Concubar [Mrs. Frost] that I am publishing the first book and that is the good news you refer to in your Christmas postal. I signed articles a week or two ago [16 December 1912] for my first five books prose or verse (should I ever live to write so many). I'm not likely to live, what with this climate and the way I am burning the candle at both ends. Intemperance is my curse. There is nothing I do or don't do that I don't overdo. Last summer it was tennis till the family trembled for my reason. Since I reached Beaconsfield it has been verse 'like a pawing horse let go' (I was almost forgetting to ring in quotations). When I ask myself in the words of the song, 'Oh why left I my home, Why did I cross the deep,' I have to confess it was to write prose and earn an honest living. Poetry is not a living. It is not even a reputation to-day. It is at best a reputation next year or the year after. And yet I always feel as if I was justified in writing poetry when the fit is on me—as it was last January. Very little of what I have done lately goes to swell the first book, just one or two things to round out the idea. You may look for a slender thing with a slender psychological interest to eke out the lyrical. Call it a study in a certain kind of waywardness. My publisher is David Nutt of London and Paris, a friend as it turns out of Bergson's."[14]

These revelations amounted to a revenge deliberately perpetrated to deflate what Frost imagined to be Silver's disparaging views. But soon after Christmas of 1912, and only three months before the publication of *A Boy's Will*, Frost undertook another kind of self-promotion scheme. It amounted to a subtly-waged campaign, and it brought him into contact with several British and American poets whose alliances and rivalries and literary battles were at least hinted in various London periodicals of the day. The first round of a new battle, into which Frost walked quite innocently, was foretold by Harold Monro, a moody Scotsman, poet, Cambridge graduate, and editor of the *Poetry Review*—the official monthly publication of the Poetry Society. Monro made the following announcement in the November 1912 issue of his magazine:

"On January 1, 1913, we shall open at 35 Devonshire Street, Theobalds Road, in the heart of old London, five minutes' walk from the British Museum, a Bookshop for the sale of poetry, and of all books, pamphlets and periodicals connected directly or indirectly with poetry. . . . The *Poetry Review* has leased the whole of an eighteenth century house, where, beside the shop, the offices of the *Review* will be established, lectures will be held, and rooms will be let at a moderate rate to those in sympathy with our aims, who are temporarily in London, and care to avail themselves of our hospitality."[15]

There was nothing in this announcement which gave any indication of the battles Monro had been waging with the Poetry Society during his brief editorship. He had aroused the ire of its elderly members by publishing representative offerings from newcomers. By contrast, the prime movers in the Poetry Society were leftovers, including William Watson, Arthur Quiller-Couch, and Stephen Phillips. In one of the early issues Phillips had invited contributions: "Let the singing be full-throated, and from any bush." Monro tartly observed that Phillips meant any *old* bush. As soon as the friction between old and new became too much for them to bear, the authorities exercised their power by discharging Monro. In return, he exercised his power by renting the building at 35 Devonshire Street with his own money, designating it as the headquarters for his own quarterly, *Poetry and Drama* and opening a bookshop at the same address. He added that all the new poets would be invited to publish.

Frost gradually learned that the skirmishes between Monro and the Poetry Society represented only one facet of growing literary warfare. Monro was congenially associated with a group of poets who, scorning leftover Victorians—even scorning the Edwardians—took their name from the coronation of George V in 1911. The leader of this group was Edward Marsh, a graduate of Cambridge. By the time Frost reached England, Marsh had already begun to collect poems for a volume he planned to edit and publish as *Georgian Poetry 1911-1912*. The youngest of Marsh's contributors was the twenty-five-year-old Rupert Brooke, and other poets already famous included Walter de la Mare, Wilfred Gibson, John Drinkwater, and Lascelles Abercrombie.

Another group, gradually separating itself from the Poetry Society and from the incipient Georgians, had begun to rally under the leadership of yet another Cambridge graduate, Thomas Ernest Hulme, who was only twenty-nine years old in 1912. His interests were largely devoted to a philosophical concern for theories of art. A translator of, and lecturer on Henri Bergson, Hulme had found in F. S. Flint a poet who was well-informed concerning the French Symbolists and contemporary French poetry.[16] As early as 1908, Hulme had tried without too much success to wean Flint from the catholicity of his tastes by advancing a theory that was intended to refresh the vitality of the image as the basic element in poetry and to reinvigorate the uses of analogy, stated or implied, as the basic instrument of thought in poetic expression. Sympathetic, and yet not greatly influenced by Hulme, Flint had published in 1909 his first volume of poems *In the Net of the Stars*. Far more strongly moved by Hulme's theories was the Idaho-born Ezra Pound, who had his own catholicity.

In making his departure from Hulme's concept of "Imagism," Pound chose a well-intended way of acknowledging his debt. When *Ripostes* was published late in 1912, it contained the "Complete Poetical Works" of T. E. Hulme: five poems totaling thirty-three lines, the first being "The Red-faced Farmer" (therein called "Autumn") as a representation of what Flint called Hulme's "little Japanese pictures in verse."[17] But the group of "Imagistes" very soon gathered by Pound had very little to do with either the theories of Hulme or the poetic practices of Flint, nor did the group hold Pound's interest for long.

Pound had already passed through several phases of his literary career—and he was just beginning. Having arrived in Gibraltar in 1908 with only $80.00 in his pocket, he reached London by way of Venice, where he stopped long enough to secure a private printing of his first volume, *A Lume Spento*, for a cost of approximately $8.00. In London a year later Elkin Matthews published Pound's second book of poetry, *Personae*, and British reviewers immediately began to praise the literary merits of this young man—eleven years younger than Frost. After publishing *Provença* in 1910 and *Canzoni* in 1911, Pound was in a position to exert considerable influence. F. S. Flint, reviewing Pound's fifth volume of poetry, *Ripostes*, said that Pound had served a thorough apprenticeship in the techniques of his craft and had worked with such determination toward a mastery of his medium that he established his *vers libre* on a traditional base firm enough to let him laugh at critics who did not understand his experimentation.

Pound's versatility and scholarship made him attractive to various individuals and groups without binding him to any one of them. Rupert Brooke, for example, felt that Pound should be invited to make a contribution to the first volume of *Georgian Poetry*. William Butler Yeats, whom Pound had approached worshipfully in 1909, was writing to Lady Gregory before the end of that year: ". . . this queer creature Ezra Pound, who has become really a great authority on the troubadours, has I think got closer to the right sort of music for poetry . . . definitely music with strongly marked time and yet it is effective speech. However, he cannot sing, as he has no voice. It is like something on a very bad phonograph."[18] Pound was soon bold enough to begin correcting archaisms in the poetry of Yeats, who even forgave him for making an emendation without permission in one Yeats manuscript.[19]

Pound, in his contacts with younger poets, carried on the same game of suggesting revisions and corrections. When his admiring friend of Philadelphia days, Hilda Doolittle settled in London in 1911 and fell in love with the young British poet, Richard Aldington, Pound very soon announced to both of them that they were unconsciously writing "Imagiste" poetry and that they should contribute to the anthology he was planning, *Des Imagistes*.

Before Frost met Pound in London, a peculiar series of circumstances gave Pound an American outlet for his vociferations against American publishers who had scorned him. During the summer of 1911, when Harriet Monroe of Chicago had felt that the resurgence of interest in poetry justified her plan for establishing an American periodical devoted to poetry, she had visited England to broaden her knowledge of poetic activities there. Elkin Matthews told her about Pound and placed three volumes of Pound's poetry in her hands. After her return to Chicago she wrote Pound asking if he would be sufficiently interested to serve as London representative for her projected magazine. He answered from London on 18 August 1912—just prior to the departure of the Frost family from America, "I *am* interested, and your scheme as far as I understand it seems not only sound, but the only possible method. There is no other magazine in America which is not an insult to the serious artist and to the dignity of his art."[20] The first number of *Poetry: A Magazine of Verse* was published in Chicago in October 1912 with contributions by Pound.

All of these literary stirrings were in the process of development when Frost arrived in England, and yet he was very largely unaware of them. On the night of 8 January 1913, when he found his way to the delayed opening of Harold Monro's Poetry Bookshop in Kensington, the place was so crowded with guests that he had to witness the ceremonies from a seat on the staircase leading to a balcony. Those who sat around him on the staircase were sufficiently talkative and friendly to make him feel not too uncomfortable. And the most important conversation was reported as follows:

"You're an American, aren't you?"

"Yes. How did you know?"

"Shoes. Writing?"

"Yes."

"Poetry?"

"Yes."

"Do you know your fellow countryman, Ezra Pound?"

"Never heard of him."

"Well, if you ever meet him, you won't be foolish enough to say that to his face!"

"No."[21]

The stranger introduced himself as Frank S. Flint, and he continued his talk so pleasantly that during the evening Frost bought a copy of Flint's *In the Net of the Stars*. Before they parted, Flint learned that David Nutt would soon publish *A Boy's Will* and gave Frost some assurance that Flint would find a chance to review it.[22] He strongly urged, however, that Frost should make the acquaintance of Ezra Pound, and Flint promised to approach Pound on Frost's behalf. The only other acquaintance of importance made by Frost that evening was with a very attractive lady and her daughter, Mrs. E. A. Gardner and Phyllis, who became fascinated by this American. Ernest Arthur Gardner, Frost learned, was a distinguished Professor of Archaeology at University College, London, and had served as director of the British School of Archaeology at Athens.

Frost did not waste the advantages offered by these acquaintances. Having learned that there were younger children in the Gardner family, he invited Mrs. Gardner to bring her children to meet his in Beaconsfield. The invitation was accepted and it led to several visits. There was even more reason to cultivate the attentions of F. S. Flint, and Frost wrote to him soon after their meeting:

"I trust there was nothing ambiguous in my rather frank enjoyment of an unusual situation the other night. Considering certain gentle gibes you dealt me, I am not quite sure in the retrospect that you didn't think I was laughing at someone or something, as the American newspapers laughed (some of them) at Yeats. You will take my word for it that there was nothing in my sleeve: I showed just what I felt. I was only too childishly happy in being allowed to make one for a moment in a company in which I hadn't to be ashamed of having written verse. Perhaps it will help you understand my state of mind if I tell you that I have lived for the most part in villages where it were better that a millstone were hanged about your neck than that you should own yourself a minor poet."

Apparently conscious of Flint's literary influence, Frost ingratiated himself by devoting more than a page of his letter to flattering technical comments on his favorite lines and rhymes in Flint's volume of poetry:

"About your book. Promise not to suspect me of reviewing it, as of obligation, because I bought it so ostentatiously under your eyes, and I will tell you in a word what I think of it. Poet-like you are going to resent my praising what I want to praise in it, when it comes to details. But you won't mind my saying

in general that the best of it is where it came from. And the
next best is the beautiful sad figure of the title, which recurring in the body of the book and, if I recollect aright, in the
poem in The English Review, gives to the whole significance.
We are in the net of the stars to our sorrow as inexorably as the
Olympian pair were in another net to their shame. I don't
know what theory you may be committed or dedicated to as an
affiliated poet of Devonshire St., but for my part give me an
out-and-out metaphor. If that is old-fashioned, make the most
of it. And give me a generous sprinking of words like 'brindled'
for the bees, 'gauze' for the sea-haze, 'little mouths' for the half-
opened lilac flowers, 'wafer' for the moon, 'silver streak' for the
swan's mirrored neck and 'tarnished copper' for her beak.
(And by the way wasn't streak with beak a fruitful rhyme? I
am disposed to think that the image finds its word and phrase
with you more nearly than it finds its cadence. That is not to
say that I am not taken with the sound of what you write. . . .

"All this is uncalled for I know. The more reason, from my
point of view, for saying it. I had your book, I had your card, I
had the impression of your prevailing mood, I was impelled to
write, and I have written. You make me long to ask you a
question that your book only makes a lovely pretense of answering. When the life of the streets perplexed me a long time
ago I attempted to find an answer to it for myself by going
literally into the wilderness, where I was so lost to friends and
everyone that not five people crossed my threshold in as many
years. I came back to do my days work in its day none the
wiser."[23]

Flint was touched by the tone of this letter; it transformed
their acquaintance into a warm friendship, which found reflection in Flint's review of *A Boy's Will* when it was published.
Before that, there was the pleasure for Frost of correcting gal-
ley proofs and then page proofs of the book. When he had
finished, he could not resist a playful show of pride: the set of
page proofs given to him as his property and stamped "FIRST
REVISE, 30 Jan. 1913,"[24] he sent to his former student at
Pinkerton, John Bartlett, on far-away Vancouver Island, British Columbia, and followed it with a playful letter which joked
about *A Boy's Will* before adding:

"Still I think you will treat the book kindly for my sake. It
comes pretty near being the story of five years of my life. In
the first poem I went away from people (and college); in the

one called A Tuft of Flowers I came back to them actually as well as verbally for I wrote that poem to get my job in Pinkerton as little Tommy Tucker sang for his supper, and Brer Merriam read it for me at a Men's League Banquet in Derry Village because I was too timid to read it myself."[25]

More pertinent to his immediate campaign was the need for cultivating the attentions of Ezra Pound. Flint not only carried out his promise by mentioning Frost to his fellow-countryman, he also got from Pound and sent to Frost a curiously worded invitation. It was a calling card bearing Pound's address—10 Church Walk, Kensington—beneath which Pound had written and initialed a curt message: "At home—sometimes."[26] Frost's pride was hurt by the arrogance of the wording, but he knew that under the circumstances he could not afford to be rankled. Waiting for more than a month—and for just the right time— he eventually sought out 10 Church Walk. To his surprise, he discovered that it was a narrow alleyway which ran alongside an old graveyard crowded with sooty marble stones, that he had to climb a dark stairway at Number 10 to reach Pound's second-floor room. Another surprise came when Pound answered his knock through the closed door, asking who it was and ordering him to wait. Frost had interrupted him in the process of taking a "bird-bath," and the greatest surprise occurred when the door was finally opened by a young man— with a tousle of red hair and a neatly trimmed red beard, blue-gray eyes and a nervous manner—wrapped in an Oriental dressing gown.

Pound immediately began the conversation by scolding Frost for having taken so long to answer his card. It was clear that he had learned from Flint the news that *A Boy's Will* would soon be published, and he hoped Frost had a copy of the book with him. No, he had not yet seen a copy of the book; he supposed it must be bound and ready to be sent to reviewers. Then, said Pound, he and Frost would make the brief trip over to the office of David Nutt and demand a copy. They did, with Pound taking charge, so that when Frost saw the first bound copy of *A Boy's Will*, with its attractive pebble-grained and copper-colored cloth binding, the thin volume was being placed in Pound's hands, not Frost's. Back they went to 10 Church Walk and Pound immediately sat down to read, directing Frost to find a magazine and keep himself busy for a while. Before long, the silence of the room was broken by Pound's chuckling just before he said, in a pompous tone which amused Frost, "You don't mind our liking this?"

"Oh, no," Frost answered, "go right ahead!"

Pound singled out as one of his favorites the five lines entitled "In Neglect":

> *They leave us so to the way we took,*
> *As two in whom they were proved mistaken,*
> *That we sit sometimes in the wayside nook,*
> *With mischievous, vagrant, seraphic look,*
> *And* try *if we cannot feel forsaken.*

There was quite a story behind these lines, Frost said, and in a few moments he was pouring out an overdramatized and not too accurate version of how his grandfather had mistreated him by sending him out to die on the Derry farm, of how his Grandfather Frost and his Uncle Elihu Colcord had also mistreated him by drafting wills which deprived Frost of monies which should rightfully have come to him as part of his legacy. He also told of all his difficulties in trying to find magazine editors who would accept his poems for publication. This was enough to arouse Pound's sympathy. Almost brusquely he said that Frost had better run along home, so that Pound could get to work, immediately, on a review of *A Boy's Will* for Harriet Monroe's *Poetry* magazine. But he did want Frost to come in again soon from Beaconsfield; he did want him to meet some fellow poets, including the king of them all, William Butler Yeats, for whom Pound was serving as amanuensis, even as advisor in literary matters. Frost left 10 Church Walk carrying with him no copy of *A Boy's Will;* instead, presentation copies of *Personae* and *Ripostes*.[27]

A few days later Pound wrote to Alice Corbin Henderson, assistant to Miss Monroe: "Have just discovered another Amur'kn. VURRY Amur'k'n, with, I think, the seeds of grace. Have reviewed an advance copy of his book, but have run it out too long. Will send it as soon as I've tried to condense it—also some of his stuff if it isn't all in the book."[28] When he sent the review to Harriet Monroe, he added: "Sorry I can't work this review down to any smaller dimensions! However, it can't be helped. Yes it can. I've done the job better than I thought I could. And it's our second scoop, for I only found the man by accident and I think I've about the only copy of the book that has left the shop. . . . I think we should print this notice at once as we ought to be first and some of the reviewers here are sure to make fuss enough to get quoted in N. Y."[29]

After he had sent his review, Pound apparently gave Frost a carbon copy of it; the event should have occasioned joy. Instead, Frost was horrified to discover that some of his own remarks about the inhumanities of American editors and some of his dramatic fictions concerning the inhumanities of his grandfather and uncle had been paraphrased in it. The review began:

"There is another personality in the realm of verse[,] another American, found, as usual, on this side of the water, by an English publisher long known as a lover of good letters. David Nutt publishes at his own expense *A Boy's Will*, by Robert Frost, the latter having been long scorned by the 'great American editors.' It is the old story."

Later in the review Pound grew more personal by way of introducing and quoting the five lines of "In Neglect":

"There is perhaps as much of Frost's personal tone in the following little catch, which is short enough to quote, as in anything else. It is to his wife, written when his grandfather and his uncle had disinherited him of a comfortable fortune and left him in poverty because he was a useless poet instead of a money-getter."[30]

While Frost groaned over these indelicacies (first his, then Pound's), Elinor Frost wept. It was difficult to know whether his new friend would do more harm than good, but there was no stopping him now. To his own father in America Pound wrote, "I'll try to get you a copy of Frost. I'm using mine at present to boom him and get his name stuck about."[31] One particularly valuable use of this copy was that he lent it to Yeats, who may have been flattered by some internal hints that Frost admired Yeats. Pound reported to Frost that Yeats had pronounced *A Boy's Will* "the best poetry written in America for a long time"[32] and that Yeats wanted to meet him.

Such an honor deserved a place apart from any other response. Frost had made up his mind during the Derry years when the Pinkerton students produced *Cathleen ni Houlihan* and *The Land of Heart's Desire* that Yeats was his favorite living poet, Meredith having died in 1909. Taken to Yeats's London apartment by Pound, who wore a velvet jacket for the occasion, Frost was less surprised by the appearance of Yeats, whose photographs he had often seen in American periodicals, than by the dark-curtained candlelit atmosphere of the room in which they sat and talked. Pound, showing himself very much at home, stretched out on the floor at the feet of Yeats, who seemed to enjoy adoration. Yeats had recently become preoccupied with psychical research, and the conversation meandered through the realms of ghosts and little people. There was one story about leprechauns told by Yeats in a strange accent which Frost took as being wistful half belief. Yeats had visited two old Irish people who said they had once trapped a leprechaun and had kept him in a cage on their wall. The little fellow had been fine and sleek when they caught him, but he pined in captivity. As long as they kept him, another leprechaun hung about the house mourning in silence for him. And when the captors let him go, out of pity, they saw the two fairies join hands and hurry off down the glen. This was not the time, Frost knew, to ask Yeats point-blank whether he himself actually believed in fairies. Clearly, the Irish poet did believe that the realm of air was peopled by spirits and it made little difference whether they were or were not visible.

It may have been on this same evening that Frost heard from Yeats the story of how Fiona Macleod (William Sharp), out walking with his wife in an English lane, fell behind just far enough to see Mrs. Sharp running toward him to say she had just seen a little man with a goat's hind legs scuttle into the woods. "A faun!" she said. "I saw him!" Her husband did not even break stride as he answered, "It's nothing. Such creatures are all about this part of the country."[33]

During the course of the candlelit evening with Yeats, Frost made bold to advance the claim that he could tell from the behavior of words in a poem whether the author had struggled to get it written or whether he had carried the whole thing off with one stroke of the pen. Yeats seemed to be doubtful, and Frost said he could illustrate. He was certain that Yeats must have written with one stroke of the pen his pure lyric, which begins:

> *I went out to the hazel wood,*
> *Because a fire was in my head,*
> *And cut and peeled a hazel wand,*
> *And hooked a berry to a thread;*
> *And when white moths were on the wing,*

And moth-like stars were flickering out,
I dropped the berry in a stream
And caught a little silver trout. . . .

Ah no, said Yeats, he had written "The Song of Wandering Angus" in agony during his terrible years. (The name of Maud Gonne was implied but not mentioned.) As Yeats talked on, through the candlelit evening, he seemed to Frost much older than his forty-eight years—much more than nine years older than Frost. He spoke as though his work was all behind him, and even said that he had given up the sweaty task of chewing pencils to write new poems. But he seemed to be so completely wrapped up in his own memories and thoughts and actions that the evening came to an end leaving Frost with the feeling that he had failed to establish any rapport with the man whose poetry he had so long admired. He did accept Yeats's invitation to attend the weekly "Monday nights," when Yeats was "at home" to guests. Frost went twice, and felt lost in the crush of strangers. The hoped-for friendship was never established.

Pound continued to boom Frost. Just for publicity he took Frost to visit the novelist May Sinclair after Pound had lent her his copy of *A Boy's Will* and had been told by Miss Sinclair that she found an admirable quality in it. A few years earlier she had done much to increase the reputation of Edwin Arlington Robinson by praising him, with William Vaughn Moody and Ridgely Torrence.[34] Her article had appeared in the *Atlantic Monthly* and Frost had seen it.[35] During his visit with her, he expressed his own opinion that Robinson was by far the best of the three writers and was pleased to have Miss Sinclair say that she remained interested only in Robinson.

After all of these preparations Frost was on edge to discover how the reviewers would treat him. *A Boy's Will* was published on or about the first of April 1913, and the first "notices" were not entirely favorable. The *Athenaeum* for 5 April contained two sentences: "These poems are intended by the author to possess a certain sequence, and to depict the various stages in the evolution of a young man's outlook upon life. The author is only half successful in this, possibly because many of his verses do not rise above the ordinary, though here and there a happy line or phrase lingers gratefully in the memory."[36] The *Times Literary Supplement* for 10 April again used only two sentences: "There is an agreeable individuality about these pieces; the writer is not afraid to voice the simplest of his thoughts and fancies, and these, springing from a capacity for complete absorption in the influences of nature and the open air, are often naïvely engaging. Sometimes too, in a vein of reflection, he makes one stop and think, though the thought may be feebly or obscurely expressed (as in the last stanza of a poem, otherwise striking, called 'The Trial by Existence.')"[37] These were the most important mentions of *A Boy's Will* in British periodicals during the first two months following publication, and all of Frost's hopes melted into discouragement. Some of his bitterness apparently found reflection in Mrs. Frost's letter to John Bartlett's wife:

"I am very glad you and John like Robert's book. Of course I love it very much, and have been somewhat disappointed that the reviewers have not been more enthousiastic [sic]. How can they help seeing how exquisitely beautiful some of the poems are, and what an original music there is in most of them? Rob has been altogether discouraged at times, but I suppose we ought to be satisfied for the present to get the book published and a little notice taken of it. Yeats has said to a friend, who repeated the remark to Robert, that it is the best poetry written in America for a long time. If only he would say so publicly, but he won't, he is too taken up with his own greatness."[38]

For Frost, the immediate question was what should he do next. He had thought that a favorable reception of *A Boy's Will* would enable him to move ahead rapidly toward the completion of a second volume of poems. But this new disappointment and discouragement shook his confidence and brought back old doubts he had thought he was done with. Again uncertain of his future, he was not a little surprised to discover that he had moments of homesickness. "I see lots of Americans as I go about with their box-toed boots," he wrote to Silver at Plymouth, "but they are mostly of the personally conducted variety. I yearn toward them just the same. I'm a Yank from Yankville."[39]

30

INTERLUDE

Christ forgive me the sin of vengefulness:
from this hour forth I will have no more
of it. Perhaps I only say so because
for the moment I am sated.[1]

GRADUALLY, and even after Robert Frost had almost given up hope, some encouraging and even flattering reviews of *A Boy's Will* appeared in monthly and quarterly issues of British and American periodicals. Of these, however, the early ones were not good enough to restore his confidence completely, and while he was trying to recover some kind of balance he made some odd defensive motions. One was an attempt to get revenge on those who had hurt his feelings long ago back in the United States. To his former Pinkerton student, John Bartlett, he wrote, "What do you say if we cook up something to bother the enemies we left behind in Derry?"[2] He went on to propose that Bartlett might enjoy sending to one of the Derry newspapers a story which could begin, "Former pupils of RF at Pink may be interested to learn of the success of his first book published in London." The remainder of the article could be made up of quotations from reviews, Frost suggested, and he made excerpts which might be used. "Anything," he added, "to make Mrs. Superior Sheppard and Lil' Art' Reynolds unhappy. (You put these people into my head.) But I suppose I care less about teasing my out-and-out enemies than my half friends like John C. Chase."[3] Bartlett's long silence after this letter was sent seemed to imply that he resisted the idea, and Frost, with the passage of nearly five months, tried to dismiss it as unimportant:

"Never you let that silly business of remembering me to my Derry friends put any strain on your feeling for me. I keep not hearing from you; and I begin to be afraid I have asked you to

[416]

do more than you could do or wanted to do. Very likely you didn't like the idea of stirring 'em up in our old haunts. I don't know that I blame you. It was just an impulse. You are quite free to beg off in the matter. . . . The whole thing is of no importance—utterly. I ought not to give way to thoughts of revenge in the first place. Still there were a few people in Derry who vexed me and one or two who did more than that and I am human enough to want to make them squirm a little before I forgive them."[4]

But the project was carried out by Bartlett; an article did appear in *The Derry News,* tailored just as Frost had suggested. Someone sent it to Ernest Silver in Plymouth and Silver graciously reprinted it in the newspaper of the Plymouth Normal School, adding a little note of his own and, presumably, the caption: "Robert Frost Gaining a Reputation as Writer of Choice Poems." Sending thanks and praise to Bartlett, Frost took mild exception to the rosy picture Bartlett had painted of "our life in the pretty London suburb," and added, "But the exaggeration does your heart credit and it wont hurt me as much as it will some people in Derry. (Christ forgive me the sin of vengefulness: from this hour forth I will have no more of it. Perhaps I only say so because for the moment I am sated.)" In the same letter he could not help but express puzzlement over Silver's generosity: "Very nice of him all round. I didn't know how he would relish my glorification. I never know how to take him, as friend or enemy."[5]

An entirely different motion made by Frost during the period when he suffered the torture of not knowing whether he had succeeded or failed with *A Boy's Will,* occurred in his repeated claims that he was applying in his poetry a theory which was unique. Perhaps this was part of his almost desperate campaign of self-promotion, for it began in another letter to John Bartlett, as a half-serious jest:

". . . To be perfectly frank with you I am one of the most notable craftsmen of my time. That will transpire presently. I am possibly the only person going who works on any but a worn out theory (principle I had better say) of versification. You see the great successes in recent poetry have been made on the assumption that the music of words was a matter of harmonised vowels and consonants. Both Swinburne and Tennyson arrived largely at effects in assonation. But they were on the wrong track or at any rate on a short track. They went the length of it. Any one else who goes that way must go after them. And that's where most are going. I alone of English writers have consciously set myself to make music out of what I may call the sound of sense."[6]

Regardless of his reasons, Frost knew very well that he was not accurate in claiming that his was a one-man battle against "the assumption that the music of words was a matter of harmonised vowels and consonants." A general movement against the "musicality" of the Victorians had been making headway for years. Frost knew that Yeats and Synge, with the help of the Abbey Players, were constantly urging that poetry and prose should return to the natural rhythms and intonations of speech. The Georgians had joined the cause in their first anthology, *Georgian Poetry 1911-1912*, and in a review of that volume the sensitive critic, Edward Thomas, had pointed out that the Georgians dramatized in their poems, "the most absolute necessity of speaking in a natural voice and in the language of today"; that they were not for making their verse pretty: "They write as grown men walk, each with his own unconscious gesture."[7] The opposition between the Georgians and the Imagistes did not preclude their understanding each other on this point. When Ezra Pound sent "A Few Don'ts by an Imagiste," to Harriet Monroe's *Poetry*, he had not talked about the need for "speaking in a natural voice," and yet he had urged, "Use no superfluous word, no adjective, which does not reveal something."[8]

Frost was working in a direction which took him beyond the Imagistes, beyond the Georgians, when he developed what he meant by "the sound of sense": ". . . Now it is possible to have sense without the sound of sense (as in much prose that is supposed to pass muster but makes very dull reading) and the sound of sense without sense (as in Alice in Wonderland which makes anything but dull reading). The best place to get the abstract sound of sense is from voices behind a door that cuts off the words."

After giving Barlett some examples, Frost continued: "Those sounds are summoned by the audile [audial] imagination and they must be positive, strong, and definitely and unmistakeably indicated by the context. The reader must be at no loss to give his voice the posture proper to the sentence. The simple declarative sentence used in making a plain statement is one sound. But Lord love ye it mustn't be worked to death. It is against the law of nature that whole poems should be written in it. If they are written they won't be read. The sound of sense, then. You get that. It is the abstract vitality of our speech. It is pure sound—pure form. One who concerns himself with it more than the subject is an artist. But remember we are still talking merely of the raw material of poetry. An ear and an appetite for these sounds of sense is the first qualification of a writer, be it of prose or verse. But if one is to be a poet he must learn to get cadences by skillfully breaking the sounds of sense with all their irregularity of accent across the regular beat of the metre. Verse in which there is nothing but the beat of the metre furnished by the accents of the pollysyl-labic [sic] words we call doggerel. Verse is not that. Neither is it the sound of sense alone. It is a resultant from those two. There are only two or three metres that are worth anything. We depend for variety on the infinite play of accents in the sound of sense. The high possibility of emotional expression all lets in this mingling of sense-sound and word-accent. A curious thing. And all this has its bearing on your prose me boy. Never if you can help it write down a sentence in which the voice will not know how to posture *specially*."[9]

Frost may have had various motives at this time for unburdening himself of these notions to Bartlett, but they were by no means idle notions, and he continued to develop them throughout his stay in England—even after his return to the United States. Those who felt skeptical were partly at fault for they had not sufficiently developed what he referred to as the audial imagination. But there were vulnerable elements in the theory itself.

Another set of motions, involving Ezra Pound, was made by Frost during his period of uncertainty over the success of *A Boy's Will*. Frost very soon became aware that his temperament was so different from Pound's that they could get along well for only a short time. The first rift between them was caused by Frost's resentment of the *Poetry* review of *A Boy's Will;* the second was caused by Frost's jealousy over Pound's attentions to the newly married Hilda Doolittle and Richard Aldington, whose imagist poems Pound published and praised in the *Egoist*. Reacting characteristically, Frost sent to F.S. Flint a playfully serious free-verse parody on 6 July 1913:

Poets Are Born Not Made

My nose is out of joint
For my father-in-letters—
My father mind you—
Has been brought to bed of another poet,
And I am not nine months old.
It is twins this time
And they came into the world prodigiously united in wedlock.
(Don't try to visualize this.)
Already they have written their first poems in vers libre
And sold it [them] within twenty-four hours.
My father-in-letters was the affluent American buyer—
There was no one to bid against him.
The merit of the poems is the new convention
That definitely locates an emotion in the belly,
Instead of scientifically in the viscera at large,
Or mid-Victorianly in the heart.
It voices a desire to grin
With the grin of a beast more scared than frightened
*   For why?*
Because it is a cinch that twins so well born
*   will be able to sell almost anything they write.*[10]

On the same day that Frost sent this free-verse complaint to
Flint, he also unburdened himself by addressing another letter
to Flint. His new resentment against Pound had opened up
older wounds. In his *Poetry* review of *A Boy's Will*, Pound had
said, condescendingly, that although Frost was a mere farmer
he did have the poetic ability to sit on a midden or dunghill
and dream stars. Frost was disgusted by this indelicacy, and he
returned to it in his second letter to Flint, but this time he
started with sarcasms aimed at Flint himself:

"I was impatient when you used that word 'weakness' for
your feeling about Pound's perfidy. You are in awe of that
great intellect abloom in hair. You saw me first but you had to
pass me over for him to discover. And yet compare the nice
discrimination of his review of me with that of yours. Who will
show me the correlation between anything I ever wrote and
his quotation from the Irish, you may sit on a middan and
dream stars. You may sit on a sofa and dream garters. But I
must not get *libre* again. But tell me I implore what on earth

is a middan if it isn't a midden and where the hell is the fitness of a word like that in connection with what I wrote on a not inexpensive farm."[11]

Not inexpensive, that is, to his grandfather. The value of the Derry farm changed radically for Frost, in retrospect, depending on the metaphorical uses he made of it. As described to Pound and others, the farm had served as a symbol of what happened to Frost "when his grandfather and his uncle had disinherited him of a comfortable fortune and left him in poverty because he was a useless poet instead of a money-getter."[12] But now the immediate enemy was Pound and not his grandfather, the immediate concern was to accumulate evidence against this man who had actually done more than anyone else to make Frost's literary start in London successful. In his campaign of disparagement, Frost kept finding new evidence for negative feelings, some of which he confided to Mosher in a letter on 17 July 1913:

". . . You will be amused to hear that Pound has taken to bullying me on the strength of what he did for me by his review in Poetry. The fact that he discovered me gives him the right to see that I live up to his good opinion of me. He says I must write something much more like *vers libre* or he will let me perish of neglect. He really threatens. I suppose I am under obligations to him and I try to be grateful. But as for the review in Poetry (Chicago, May), if any but a great man had written it, I should have called it vulgar. . . ."[13]

Giving vent to his dark resentment served as a safety valve for Frost on repeated occasions. This time, he set out to pour his resentment into a declaration of independence from Pound, addressed to him, and couched in a parody of the *vers libre* which Pound probably had not commanded Frost to write. There is no evidence that the outburst was ever sent to Pound; it would seem that Frost relieved his feelings by sending it first to F. S. Flint, who certainly tried to dissuade him from breaking off relations. Nevertheless, the declaration is revealing as another self-protective motion:

I am a Mede and Persian
In my acceptance of harsh laws laid down for me
When you said I could not read
When you said I looked old
When you said I was slow of wit

I knew that you only meant
That you could read
That you looked young
That you were nimble of wit
But I took your words at their face value
I accepted your words like an encyclical letter
It did not matter
At worst they were good medicine
I made my stand elsewhere
I did not ask you to unsay them.
I was willing to take anything you said from you
If I might be permitted to hug the illusion
That you liked my poetry
And liked it for the right reason.

You reviewed me,
And I was not sure—
I was afraid it was not artis[ti]cally done.
I decided I couldnt use it to impress my friends
Much less my enemies.
But in as much [as] it was praise I was grateful
For praise I do love.

I suspected though that in praising me
You were not concerned so much with my desert
As with your power
That you praised me arbitrarily
And took credit to yourself
In demonstrating that you could thrust anything
upon the world
Were it never so humble
And bid your will avouch it

And here we come close to what I demanded of you
I did not want the money that you were disbursing
among your favorites
for two American editors.
Not that.
All I asked was that you should hold to one thing
That you considered me a poet.
That was [why] I clung to you
As one clings to a group of insincere friends

For fear they shall turn their thoughts against him
the moment he is out of hearing.
The truth is I was afraid of you[14]

Flint was amused by the "poem" and was willing to grant that it might succeed in annoying Pound, but there were reasons why he hoped Frost would not mail it. "You know I think his bark is much worse than his bite," Flint explained in a letter to Frost, "and that much that seems offensive to us externally is merely external and a kind of outer defense—a mask."[15] Flint granted that Pound irritated people, but urged that irritation under such circumstances was a weakness. He might have added that perhaps Frost had gotten enough value merely from the formulation of his parody.

An entirely different kind of motion, again enabling Frost to achieve the comfort of superiority, occurred in Beaconsfield when a neighbor stopped him on the street one day and asked if he would drop by at her house for a few moments because her husband had a few questions to ask him as an American. Frost accepted the invitation. The husband started off by saying that his wife's brother had gone to America as a young man, years ago, and had made considerable money there. He had built a sort of "shack" somewhere just outside Philadelphia, and then he had somehow become married to an American girl named Beedle or Biddle. Word had come, just now, that this prodigal brother was dead, and that by some kind of chicanery the American girl had gotten hold of all her husband's money. So the question they hoped Mr. Frost could answer for them was just this: How should they start proceedings to get that money away from the American girl? Oh, that was quite easy, Frost assured them. All they had to do, under the circumstances, was to write a letter to the President of the United States and he would take care of it. Oh, really? That easy? But who would the President be? What was his name? Wilson. Woodrow Wilson. They wrote it down. And what was Mr. Wilson's address? Just "The White House, Washington, District of Columbia." They wrote that down. But did Mr. Frost know the street address? No, he didn't. "The White House" would be a sufficient address. Oh, really? I say, how quaint! Frost could—and did—work up consolatory indignation over what he viewed as the condescending manner of even the most ignorant Englishman.

One fierce display of superiority provided another safety valve for disappointment and wounded feeling. It occurred as a result of a friendly gesture made by the Gardner family. Having learned that Frost was half-Scot, the Gardners thought he might like to rent an inexpensive cottage near them for a month or so during the summer of 1913, at Kingsbarns on the coast of Fifeshire across the broad Firth of Forth from Edinburgh. The best way to go would be by boat from London to Leith and then by train. The Frosts were delighted with the prospect. On 13 August 1913, Professor Gardner wrote from Kingsbarns to say that a little place near them would be available at a reasonable price during the last fortnight of August.[16] The Frosts immediately prepared to go. They liked the voyage along the coast of England and Scotland; they enjoyed the trip by train from Edinburgh to Kingsbarns; and they found the Gardners extremely cordial. All went happily for some days, until circumstances brought out the darker Scottish side of Frost's moodiness. After building up a fine head of resentment, he relieved his feelings in a long letter to John Bartlett. He began by explaining that the Gardners were "a family I got entangled with at the opening of the Poetry Shop in High Holborn last winter." It was not his fault; he had thrust himself and his book on no one. But there was more to it than he had guessed. "These Gardiners [sic] are the kind that hunt lions and they picked me up cheap as a sort of bargain before I was as yet made." More than that, "They are a one-hoss poet and artist themselves and at the present moment they are particularly keen on lions as creatures who may be put under obligations to review them in the papers." It was all clear to him that there had been a plot behind their invitation: "Now the question is what do we think of their book. Well, I haul off and start to say what I don't think with appropriate sops to my conscience. But such integrity as I have is all literary. I make a poor liar where the worth of books is concerned. I flounder and am lost. Thus much in the historical present. The Gardners don't like me any more. They despise my judgement and resent my tactlessness. But here I am on their hands. They are a gentleman and must carry it off with manners."[17]

Even worse, it seemed, Professor Gardner had confided to Frost that in a cave on the ocean shore near St. Andrews was an extraordinary archeological treasure: ". . . he proposes to entertain us of an afternoon by conducting us . . . for a look at an elephant a horse and an ass done by paleolithic man on the walls. These are the first drawings (or cuttings) of cavemen discovered in the British Isles and as Gardner discovered them and the discovery is going to make a stir when it is announced presently naturally we were expected to feel the honour of being taken into what is as yet a profound secret. But, but!"

Frost had gone to the cave; he had seen the elephant, the horse, the ass; and he had convinced himself that the creatures were all natural formations made by water and time, not by paleolithic man: "There were many marks on the cave wall, some wavy grooves due to water, some sharp-edged depressions due to the flaking off of the sandstone strata. It would have been strange if some of the marks hadn't accidentally looked like something. The sandstone was so soft and moist that a little rubbing easily made them look more like something. Animals are always the better for rubbing. . . . The beasts left me cold. I tried to rise to the moment, but the cave was clammy and there were other things, principally the literary literature. Still I have no doubt a rumpus will be raised over Gardner's discovery. Sic ad astra itur in highbrow circles. . . ."[18] Having unburdened himself of so much ire, and having asserted his own archeological superiority over the distinguished expert, Frost felt better.

By the time the Frost family returned to Beaconsfield from Kingsbarns, news had accumulated to furnish more valid reasons for feeling fine. In September of 1913 three new reviews of A Boy's Will, including one which appeared in the (Chicago) Dial, gave him new heart for the work which lay ahead and even gave the earlier reviews more importance. He had been inclined to discount the kindliness and generosity of Flint's review in Harold Monro's second issue of Poetry and Drama, but he apparently needed and liked it now:

"Mr. Robert Frost's poetry is so much a part of his life that to tell his life would be to explain his poetry. I wish I were authorized to tell it, because the one is as moving as the other —a constant struggle against circumambient stupidity for the right of expression. Be it said, however, that Mr. Frost has escaped from America, and that his first book, A Boy's Will, has found an English publisher. So much information, extrinsic to the poems, is necessary. Their intrinsic merits are great, despite faults of diction here and there, occasional inversions, and lapses, where he has not been strong enough to bear his own simplicity of utterance. It is this simplicity which is the great charm of his book; and it is a simplicity that proceeds from a candid heart. . . . Each poem is the complete expression of one mood, one emotion, one idea. I have tried to find in these poems what is most characteristic of Mr. Frost's poetry, and I think it is this: direct observation of the object and immediate correlation with the emotion—spontaneity, subtlety in evocation of moods, humour, an ear for silences. But behind all is the heart and life of a man, and the more you ponder his poems the more convinced you become that the heart is pure and the life not lived in vain."[19]

For the time being, he also relished the anonymous review which appeared in the (London) *Academy:*

"We wish we could fitly express the difference which marks off *A Boy's Will* from all the other books here noticed. Perhaps it is best hinted by stating that the poems combine, with a rare sufficiency, the essential qualities of inevitabilty and surprise. We have read every line with that amazement and delight which are too seldom evoked by books of modern verse. Without need of qualification or a trimming of epithets, it is undoubtedly the work of a true poet. We do not need to be told that the poet is a young man: the dew and the ecstasy—the audacity, too—of pristine vision are here. At the same time, it is extraordinarily free from a young man's extravagances; there is no insistent obtrusion of self-strain after super-things. Neither does it belong to any modern 'school,' nor go in harness to any new and twisted theory of art. It is so simple, lucid, and experimental that, reading a poem, one can see clearly with the poet's own swift eye, and follow the trail of his glancing thought. One feels that this man has *seen* and *felt;* seen with a revelatory, a creative vision; felt personally and intensely; and he simply writes down, without confusion or affectation, the results thereof. Rarely today is it our fortune to fall in with a new poet expressing himself in so pure a vein. No one who really cares for poetry should miss this little book. . . . We have not the slightest idea who Mr. Robert Frost may be, but we welcome him unhesitatingly to the ranks of the poets born, and are convinced that if this is a true sample of his parts he should presently give us work far worthier of honour than much which passes for front-rank poetry at the present time."[20]

If the audial imagination of Robert Frost made him suspect that back of these exclamations was a feminine personality, he was not inclined to complain. What troubled him most was that whenever someone praised him for his best, actual or possible, he was reminded of his worst. Guilt was always quick to waylay him in his thoughts concerning daily relations with his wife, his children, his friends, even his enemies. It was reflected in some of his private observations, which he jotted into a little pocket notebook he bought soon after he reached England:

"Life is that which can mix oil and water (Emulsion). I can consist of the inconsistent. I can hold in unity the ultimate irreconcileable spirit and matter, good and evil, monism (cohesion) and dualism (reaction), peace and strife. It o'er rules the harsh divorce that parts things natural and divine. Life is something that rides steadily on something else that passes away as light on a gush of water. . . .

"All a man's art is a bursting unity of opposites. Christ's message almost tears itself apart with its great contradiction. Ever since man was man he has known the generous thrill of owning a better. There is a better in me than I am. How does he bring himself to it. Christ is one he has taken to do it with. . . .

"Evil clings so in all our acts that even when we not only mean but achieve our prettiest, bravest, noblest, best, we are often a scourge even to those we do not hate. Our sincerest prayers are no more than groans that this should be so."[21]

31

ENGLAND: *NORTH OF BOSTON*

. . . I had some character strokes I had to get in some-
where and I chose a sort of eclogue form for them. Rather
I dropped into that form. And I dropped to an everyday
level of diction that even Wordsworth kept above. I trust
I don't terrify you. I think I have made poetry. The lan-
guage is appropriate to the virtues I celebrate.[1]

IN THE FALL OF 1912, as soon as Robert Frost received word
from Mrs. Nutt that the mansucript of *A Boy's Will* had been
accepted for publication, he began writing dramatic narratives
and dialogues in an unexpected burst of energy. And when
Mrs. Nutt asked about his plans for a second volume, which
she would publish in accordance with the terms of his contract, he had already advanced far enough to offer a provisional title: *Farm Servants, and Other People*, a title she used
in the spring catalogue which announced the publication of *A
Boy's Will.*

Earlier in the fall of 1912, when Frost first began to select
and arrange poems for his first volume, he had sorted out and
held back three dramatic narratives written on the farm in
Derry at least as early as 1905 and 1906—"The Death of the
Hired Man," "The Housekeeper," and "The Black Cottage."[2]
In each, the objective characterizations were achieved through
a combination of dramatic dialogue and narrative, as though
Frost were already anxious to extend his artistic conviction
that a good poem could not possibly sound "too much like
talk." These three poems were very closely related to his hopes
that some day he might also write psychological studies in the
form of novels, short stories, and plays.

As he returned to the writing of blank verse narratives and
character studies, Frost discovered that he could not possibly
crowd out occasional moods which demanded expression in

new lyrics. He was not troubled by such inconsistencies. Long ago he had found that even the shortest lyric could be endowed with some element of the dramatic, and would be the stronger for it. The eight brief lines of "The Pasture" came to him as a case in point. He had also noticed that there was at least an element of dialogue in the kinds of lyrics he liked best to write. It would have been difficult for him to say how far back in his own experience he had become conscious that his inner hopes and fears acquired poetic voices which talked back and forth. He had learned, particularly during the painful years of his courtship, that the opposed voices and postures of his own divided consciousness were as vivid to him as any voices of actors on a stage, that out of these inner tensions the lyric voice which triumphed—no matter how briefly—might find expression in a poem he felt and heard before he could ever try to write it down.

Dramatically regarded, the arrangement of the lyrics in *A Boy's Will* amounted to an implied dialogue between opposed sides of his own consciousness. He had arranged to let the separate parts of the pattern become a study in the psychological phases of dialogue between his own self-destructive negations and his constructive affirmations.[3] If both of the voices did not speak in all of those lyrics, as they did in "The Tuft of Flowers," he had often tried to imply, dramatically, a listener who is addressed and silenced by the speaking voice.

This element of dramatic dialogue, involving themes which were for Frost perennial subjects for inner debate, asserted itself in a revealing poem, which he began to fashion at Beaconsfield. The inspiration had occurred shortly before Christmas of 1912 on a freezing cold evening when he had gone alone by train to the nearby town of High Wycombe to do what little Christmas shopping he could afford for Elinor and the children. On the streets of High Wycombe, the sad faces of many working men and women reminded him that a strike of colliers, then in progress, was having widespread effects on many laborers. As he shopped, one incident hurt him enough to make him cry inside. He walked toward a store window filled with toys, and for a moment he did not notice that he was looking over the heads and backs of two very small children who stood with their noses pressed against the window glass, saying nothing. Touched by their silence, he asked what they liked best in the window. By way of answer, one of them took his finger out of his mouth to point—and where he wet the window pane, the moisture froze almost as soon as he took his finger away. That was all.

The little incident carried Frost back in his thoughts to the previous winter in Plymouth, when he had questioned whether he and his family had any right to make Christmas merry while so many of his fellow creatures seemed to have no such opportunity. Now the old questions returned. What part should he be taking in the suffering of others? How much did he owe to others? Should he throw in his lot with them? And if so, how far? Should he give all his money to the poor so that he could suffer equally with them? And if he heard that people in India were starving to death at Christmastime should he starve out of sympathy? He knew the Stoic notion that a man must not allow himself to be moved by the misfortunes of others, but he found that he could not help being moved. How could an artist cultivate a life of selfishness? What was the justification? On the other hand, what kind of relief—individual, social, governmental—would be adequate relief? The recurrent word, "relief," reminded him of a day in hay-fever season, back in Derry, when he had left the farm, briefly, to borrow money in the nearby city of Manchester, New Hampshire. One fit of coughing and sneezing had exhausted him to the point where he had collapsed on a park bench beside a French-Canadian. The man showed great sympathy and told Frost of a patent medicine which was wonderful for hay fever. Wonderful enough to cure it? Frost asked, between sneezes. Oh no, of course not, the stranger said; the best any patent medicine could do was to offer "good relief." Frost thought such an observation might have been worthy of the Kickapoo Indian "doctor" he had seen and heard peddling herb medicines from the back of a cart in San Francisco, while chattering at the top of his lungs about the great power of nature's own relief from suffering. All these elements came together somehow for Frost in lines which he began writing at Beaconsfield and called "Good Relief":

> Shall we, then, wish as many as possible
> As merry Christmases as possible
> And charge the limitation up to thought?
> No, be the Christmas card with which we greet:
> A Merry Christmas to the World in Full.

And as for happiness not being bought—
Remember how two babes were on the street—
And so were many fathers out on strike,
The vainest of their many strikes in vain,
And lost already as at heart they knew.
But the two babes had stopped alone to look
At Christmas toys behind a window pane,
And play at having anything they chose.
And when I lowered level with the two
And asked them what they saw so much to like,
One confidentially and raptly took
His finger from his mouth and pointed, "Those!"
A little locomotive with a train.
And where he wet the window pane it froze.
What good did it do anyone but him—
His brother at his side, perhaps, and me?
And think of all the world compared with three!
But why like the poor fathers on the curb
Must we be always partizan and grim?
No state has found a perfect cure for grief
In law or gospel or in root or herb.
'Twas in this very city thoroughfare
I heard a doctor of the Kickapoo
By torch light from a cart-tail once declare:
The most that any root or herb can do
In suffering is give you Good Relief.[4]

In this poem the reference to the "vainest of their many strikes in vain" may illustrate the stubbornness with which Frost could and did repeatedly turn his back on historical facts whenever they were not pragmatically useful to the so-called truths of his beliefs. He was extremely sympathetic toward a bundle of notions which began with the claim that a man's poverty could only be his own fault, that if wealth were the proper reward of conscientious work then poverty was the price of idleness, that the idle should be forced to exert themselves not only for their own good but also for the benefit of society, that charity was inevitably a form of "relief" given at the cost of those who had made the effort to work. These notions were extremely popular in England when the Poor Law amendments were passed in 1834; they were still popular among certain classes in England in 1913. By contrast, English poets like W. W. Gibson, Rupert Brooke, and Lascelles Abercrombie were sympathetic toward the Fabian attempts to have the Poor Law repealed, and Brooke worked closely with Sidney and Beatrice Webb in this regard. Frost's interests lay elsewhere. The suffering which concerned him most at this time was his own homesickness.

There was one palliative for the kind of homesickness caused by Frost's disappointment over the early reception of *A Boy's Will*. It drove his memories back, wistfully, to the Derry farm he had been so glad to leave. Ironically, his longings intensified his recollections, with the result that he continued to write some meditative lyrics at a time when he should have been working on his dramatic narratives and dialogues in accordance with his plans. Three meditative lyrics, written in Beaconsfield, reflected the inspiring homesickness only through the intensity of his response. One of them began, after revisions:

> *When I see birches bend to left and right*
> *Across the lines of straighter darker trees,*
> *I like to think some boy's been swinging them.*

Another began:

> *Something there is that doesn't love a wall,*
> *That sends the frozen-ground-swell under it,*
> *And spills the upper boulders in the sun . . .*

Another:

> *My long two-pointed ladder's sticking through*
> *the tree*
> *Toward heaven still*
> *And there's a barrel that I didn't fill*
> *Beside it, and there may be two or three*
> *Apples I didn't pick upon some bough.*
> *But I am done with apple-picking now.*

Years later, Frost said, "I wrote the poem 'Mending Wall' thinking of the old wall that I hadn't mended in several years and which must be in a terrible condition. I wrote that poem in England when I was very homesick for my old wall in New

England. Now I'll read another which I wrote while I was a little homesick: 'Birches.' "⁵ The same homesickness brought back with a special vividness a great many other first-hand memories of neighbors—and tones of voice—which were imaginatively (sometimes literally) built into dramatic dialogues. And before the summer of 1913 had passed, Frost wrote to John Bartlett in Canada:

"You will gather . . . what my next book is to be like. I ought to send you some of it. I may decide to call it New England Eclogues. Which do you think from the following list of titles you would prefer to read? The Death of the Hired Man, The Housekeeper (or Slack Ties), The Wrong ["The Self-seeker"], A Servant to Servants, The Code (of Farm Service), Swinging Birches, Blueberries, The Mountain, A Hundred Collars, The Cellar Hole ["The Generations of Men"], The Black Cottage. All are stories between one hundred and two hundred lines long. I have written one today that I may call The Lantern ["The Fear"] if Mrs. Frost doesn't dissuade me: she doesn't think it [the title] a fit. None of the lot is a love affair except the Cellar Hole and I am not sure that that isn't least successful of all."⁶

Clearly, the second volume was beginning to shape up, although many of these poems were still in first-draft state and needed further revision, which Frost hated and found exhausting.⁷ When the manuscript of the second volume was finally completed, it contained all of these poems except "Swinging Birches" and in addition it contained six other pieces. Of the six, the only other purely objective dramatic narrative-dialogue was "Home Burial." The remaining five were dramatic or meditative lyrics, and they were distributed symmetrically: two at the beginning ("The Pasture" and "Mending Wall"), one in the middle of the volume ("After Apple-picking") and two at the end ("The Wood-pile" and "Good Hours")—the last having been written at Plymouth during the winter of 1911-1912.

Near the end of October 1913, Frost proudly announced that the title of the book was "about the only part not ready to go to press."⁸ Having considered such titles as *Farm Servants* and *New England Eclogues*, he relinquished them both because they were too restrictive; not all of his poems fitted the meaning which Virgil had assigned to the term, "eclogue," when he had adapted it from Theocritus to include his bucolic poems about Arcadian shepherds. For a time, Frost thought he might call the book simply *New Englanders* or *New England Hill Folk.*[9] But a more homely title suggested itself to him one night as he walked around and around the dining-room table in "The Bungalow" at Beaconsfield, after everyone else was in bed. He remembered that a Boston newspaper advertised properties for sale and vaguely suggested the geographical area by saying that they were located "North of Boston." When he suggested to his British friends his determination to call the volume *North of Boston,* they resisted on the ground that it would result in too much confusion; British readers would associate the title with Boston in Lincolnshire. Frost remained adament, perhaps because homesickness heightened his belief that the title would be received well in New England.

When Frost explained to Mosher that in writing the dramatic narratives for *North of Boston* he had "dropped to an everyday level of diction that even Wordsworth kept above" and yet that the "language is appropriate to the virtues I celebrate," he was hinting at his new discoveries of old truths. As in his earlier experiments with poetic lines which "sounded like talk," the practice came first and his principles of ordering were derived from his practice. It was almost with the excited tone of discovery that he continued to describe those principles. Having boasted to John Bartlett, "I alone of English writers have consciously set myself to make music out of what I may call the sound of sense," and having claimed that the audial imagination of the reader must collaborate with the poet to the extent of hearing shades of intonation captured between the lines and controlled by the entire context of a poem, Frost kept finding more that he wanted to say on the subject. "I wouldn't be writing all this [in a letter] if I didn't think it the most important thing I know," he told Bartlett. "I write it partly for my own benefit, to clarify my ideas . . ." Some of his best clarifications were written at this time:

"A sentence is a sound in itself on which other sounds called words may be strung.

"You may string words together without a sentence-sound to string them on just as you may tie clothes together by the sleeve and stretch them without a clothes line between two trees, but—it is bad for the clothes.

"The number of words you may string on one sentence-sound is not fixed but there is always danger of over loading.

"The sentence-sounds are very definite entities. . . . They are apprehended by the ear. They are gathered by the ear from the vernacular and brought into books. Many of them are already familiar to us in books. I think no writer invents them. The most original writer only catches them fresh from talk, where they grow spontaneously.

"A man is all a writer if *all* his words are strung on definite recognizable sentence sounds. The voice of the imagination, the speaking voice must know certainly how to behave[,] how to posture in every sentence he offers. . . .

"The ear is the only true writer and the only true reader. I have known people who could read without hearing the sentence sounds and they were the fastest readers. Eye readers we call them. They can get the meaning by glances. But they are bad readers because they miss the best part of what a good writer puts into his work.

"Remember that the sentence sound often says more than the words. It may even as in irony convey a meaning opposite to the words. . . .

"To judge a poem or piece of prose you go the same way to work—apply the one test—greatest test. You listen for the sentence sounds. If you find some of those not bookish, caught fresh from the mouths of people, some of them striking, all of them definite and recognizable, so recognizable that with a little trouble you can place them and even name them, you know you have found a writer."[10]

As applied by Frost in his *North of Boston* poems these principles were calculated not to displace the underlying and recurrent metrical patterns of a poem nor to justify *vers libre* but to achieve an enrichment and complexity through a poetic arrangement of two factors:

". . . there are the very regular preestablished accent and measure of blank verse; and there are the very irregular accent and measure of speaking intonation. I am never more pleased than when I can get these into strained relation. I like to drag and break the intonation across the meter as waves first comb and then break stumbling on the shingle."[11]

In his best moments Frost never claimed that these principles were new, but he did insist that modern poetry had a tendency to forget the brilliant adaptations made of these

principles by Virgil in his eclogues, by Shakespeare in his dialogues, by Herrick in his best lyrics, by Wordsworth in choosing for poetry the humble and rustic life, wherein the essential
passions of the heart speak a plain and emphatic language.

In *North of Boston,* Frost permitted the farmer in "The
Mountain" to dramatize at least part of his technical principle
and even to crystallize some of it into a homely epigram:

"But all the fun's in how you say a thing."[12]

All the comedy, that is, and all the tragedy implicit in the
misunderstanding which, for example, lies at the grieving
heart of "Home Burial":

". . . God, what a woman! And it's come to this,
A man can't speak of his own child that's dead."

"You can't because you don't know how to speak.
If you had any feelings, you that dug
With your own hand—how could you?—his little
grave . . ."[13]

Poetically considered, the man in "Home Burial" does know
how to speak and act; but the woman's misunderstanding
springs from her failure to perceive the self-defensive postures
against his own grief, expressed in the way he speaks and acts,
as he tries to go on living. In the poems for *North of Boston,*
Frost made extremely bold demands on the "audial imagination" of his readers. Under the circumstances, it is to his credit
that so many of his readers heard so clearly what he was trying
to say.

He was trying to say that the dialogue between negation
and affirmation, even between death and life in *A Boy's Will*
was carried over directly to the dramatic narratives and dialogues and lyrics in *North of Boston.* The virtues he celebrated
in each were those which enable individuals to confront and to
survive the worst by and with and through the strength of
affirmative outgoing love. He hinted at this carry-over, in his
one-sentence introduction:

"Mending Wall takes up the theme where *A Tuft of Flowers*
in *A Boy's Will* laid it down."[14]

Having waged a subtle campaign on behalf of *A Boy's Will*

before it was published, Frost prepared the way for *North of Boston* even more effectively. Ezra Pound had assured Harriet Monroe that *Poetry* would be given a chance to print something of Frost's; if his best had gone into *A Boy's Will* then Pound would have something new from him "as soon as he has done it." Pound's condescending manner brought out all of the older man's Yankee horse-trading instincts. In answer to Pound's request for something new, for example, he managed to produce an offering: "The Death of the Hired Man," written back in the Derry farm days. It seemed "new" to Pound who, having it in hand by 3 June 1913, again wrote to his father concerning Frost: "He has done a 'Death of the Farm Hand' since the book that is to my mind better than anything in it. I shall have that in the *Smart Set* or in *Poetry* before long."15 Pound apparently knew that all of Frost's puritanical instincts would bristle in horror at the implications of the title of the New York magazine *Smart Set,* and so Pound said nothing about it to Frost until the poem had been submitted there. Expecting that Pound would send it to *Poetry,* Frost became so indignant when he learned where it had gone that he flatly ordered Pound to withdraw the manuscript. Pound refused, and for a time the consequent estrangement between these two American poets in London seemed to be permanent. Only the obtuseness of the *Smart Set* editor, Willard Huntington Wright (later known as S. S. Van Dine, creator of the erudite detective, Philo Vance), redeemed the situation. Wright hung fire so long that Pound found it necessary to prod him in a letter dated 11 August 1913: "Here is a batch of [D. H.] Lawrence's poems. . . . As you know the thing I'm most anxious for you to print is that poem of Frost's. I hope the stuff I've sent since won't delay it."16 Wright answered, saying that he was forced to reject the Frost poem because things like that were a dime a dozen, in fact he had just printed a poem about a hired man written by the newly discovered Ohio-born "tramp poet," Harry Kemp.17

While these delays were in process, Frost himself circulated several manuscripts starting perhaps with a visit he made to Wilfrid Wilson Gibson. Under ordinary circumstances, Frost might have been repelled immediately (as he was eventually) by the crude way in which Gibson handled his own techniques and themes. But it is probable that the genuine friendliness and warmth of Gibson's personality meant so much to Frost at the time of their meeting that certain normal hindrances to friendship were ignored. A Cambridge graduate, born in Northumberland, and almost five years younger than Frost, Gibson had seemed thoroughly rooted in Victorian mannerisms while composing his first four books of poetry. But by 1910, when he published *Daily Bread,* he had "caught the stormy summons of the sea" and had begun to sing what he called "the life-song of humanity." In the *Poetry Review,* January 1911, an essayist who hailed Gibson indiscriminately as "a new force in English letters" explained how Gibson had found the raw materials for his ballad-echoing narratives in verse: ". . . he went down into mines and through factories and tenements and the squalor of sunless slums—the disease-ridden, evil-smelling styes of humanity—and there where little children perish of want because their worn-out mothers' breasts are dry from hunger; there, where women, the mothers of the race, dying daily the dreadful death-in-life of souls and bodies bartered for bread, are battered and broken by the merciless grinding of the wheels of labour, the relentless and inhuman greed of manufacturer; there, in the place where strong men starve because they cannot get work, he listened . . ."[18] Frost, as author of "My Giving" and "Good Relief," might have gathered himself stoically to let the humanitarian Gibson pass unnoticed. By this time, however, Gibson had already become one of the most popular and highly praised versifiers on either side of the Atlantic—and Frost had set his heart on the idea of achieving recognition not only with the discriminating few but also with the common man. He confided as much while writing a letter from Beaconsfield in the fall of 1913:

". . . there is a kind of success called 'of esteem' and it butters no parsnips. It means a success with the critical few who are supposed to know. But really to arrive where I can stand on my legs as a poet and nothing else I must get outside that circle to the general reader who buys books in their thousands. I may not be able to do that. I believe in doing it—dont you doubt me there. I want to be a poet for all sorts and kinds. I could never make a merit of being caviare to the crowd the way my quasi-friend Pound does. I want to reach out, and would if it were a thing I could do by taking thought."[19]

Frost was indeed "taking thought" when he reached out to meet W. W. Gibson; he made the first move by calling on the

humanitarian poet almost as soon as he learned that
Gibson was living alone in one of Harold Monro's rented
rooms above the bookshop in London. And Frost took with
him a few of his own manuscripts, poems to be published in
North of Boston. The visit was later recorded in metrical prose
by Gibson as "The First Meeting":

> One evening, while, in my London garret,
> I worked upon a piece of Northern verse
> About the Border-raiders, and was rapt
> In my visions of my native countryside,
> As my mind rambled over starlit fells—
> Catching the thud of hoofs across the heath
> And watching flaring flames of burning byres—
> A sudden sharp tap-tapping at the door
> Startled me; and, somewhat reluctantly,
> I rose and opened it: and then was told
> A stranger, an American, called Frost,
> Had turned up, and would like to have a word
> With me. I put my manuscript aside;
> And, when he was shewn in, though still my thoughts
> Hung around 'Bloody Bush Edge' for a brief while,
> It wasn't long before the two of us
> Were chatting in a close companionship;
> And I had lost the last shred or regret
> That I'd been interrupted in the business
> Of my comparatively inconsequent work;
> As I sat listening to Frost's racy speech
> And relishing his pithy commentaries
> On this and that. And when, too soon he rose
> To leave, I gladly took from him a sheaf
> Of verse he, diffidently, handed me;
> Saying he'd be obliged if I would bother
> To look it through, and let him have a word
> Of what I thought of it. . . .[20]

Apparently Gibson thought well enough of these samplings
for he reviewed *North of Boston* in the London *Bookman.*
Long before that, however, he introduced Frost to Lascelles
Abercrombie, Gibson's closest friend, whose poems and plays
had deservedly won more discriminating praise than anything
Gibson had written. Abercrombie was the leader of the

Georgians and a character who appealed to his friends as unprepossessing in his picturesqueness: "a small dark, shy man, with spectacles and straight, slightly greasy-looking hair" and "a queer little green hat which tipped up preposterously in front."[21]

Frost very quickly came to admire Abercrombie and to envy him because he lived "under thatch" with his family in Gloucestershire. Gibson had his own plans to take up an abode "under thatch" near by, just as soon as he could win and marry the attractive lady who served as secretary at Harold Monro's bookshop. Flatteringly, and yet sincerely, both Gibson and Abercrombie insisted that the bucolic Frost should not be living in the suburban town of Beaconsfield, that he should let them find him an inexpensive cottage in the Gloucestershire countryside near them. Persuaded by the warmth of their friendliness, Frost very soon accepted their invitation and promised to join them if he could manage to sublease "The Bungalow" in Beaconsfield. None of the other acquaintances he had made in London up to that time meant enough to him to hold him there. He saw less and less of Flint, who may have helped Frost avoid any open rift with Pound; but the unpleasantness over "The Death of the Hired Man" made it clear that a lasting friendship with either Flint or Pound was impossible. Frost did not succeed with his sublease plans until the spring of 1914, and was therefore obliged to stay where he was through the winter. Even so, he could not resist confiding his new plans in letters as early as 24 October 1913:

"When I can get rid of this house I am to go to Gloucester [shire] to live, to be with Wilfrid Gibson and Abercrombie. I am out with Pound pretty much altogether and so I don't see his friend Yeats as I did. I count myself well out however. Pound is an incredible ass and he hurts more than he helps the person he praises."[22]

As it happened, there were good reasons for staying near London until spring. During the fall and winter, at least prior to Gibson's marriage, Gibson enabled Frost to meet several other prominent literary figures whom he would have regretted not meeting. Among them was Ralph Hodgson, whose best-known poem Frost had discovered in an extraordinary way several months earlier. While sitting in the Beaconsfield station waiting for a train, Frost had noticed that the discarded newspaper between his feet contained a poem apparently reprinted as a "filler" and he had bent over to read the lines which begin:

> *Eve, with her basket, was*
> *Deep in the bells and grass,*
> *Wading in bells and grass*
> *Up to her knees.*
> *Picking a dish of sweet*
> *Berries and plums to eat,*
> *Down in the bells and grass*
> *Under the trees.*

Pleased with the freshness and musical grace of Hodgson's "Eve," Frost picked up the newspaper, tore out the poem, and kept it. Hodgson, Yorkshire-born, had lived in the United States for a time and, for a man who wrote lyrics, had led an extraordinarily unpoetic life—as a pressman in Fleet Street, a professional draughtsman, a member of a pictorial staff on an evening paper, an editor of a magazine, and as a fancier of bull terriers. Early in October 1913, at St. George's Restaurant in St. Martin's Lane, Hodgson introduced Frost to the essayist-biographer-critic, Edward Thomas, who had reviewed *A Boy's Will* anonymously and favorably in *The New Weekly*. Frost was immediately sympathetic toward this fellow Celt, this moody and handsome man with a hawklike face and deep-set blue eyes not unlike Frost's own. Their casual meeting began what later became a very important friendship for both of them.

Continuing to cultivate old and new acquaintances during the fall and winter of 1913-1914, Frost very subtly waged his campaign for strengthening his literary positon before *North of Boston* was published. Through Flint, he became acquainted with T. E. Hulme, whose home at 67 Frith Street he visited repeatedly to attend the famous Thursday Night gatherings. Hulme's knowledge of Bergson's writings provided a special bond, and his discussions with Frost frequently veered from poetry to theology. On one occasion when they met by accident in Monro's bookshop, Hulme made another gesture of friendship by saying, "Come around sometime, so we can have another good talk about God."

Through Gibson and Flint, Frost became well enough acquainted with Harold Monro to sell him two poems—"The Fear" and "A Hundred Collars"—for use in *Poetry and Drama,* prior to their publication in *North of Boston.* The sale was based on terms which Frost suggested: that just prior to the time for the departure of the Frosts for Gloucestershire he and his family would be permitted to spend a week in a pair of furnished rooms above the bookshop. The terms were accepted. Other sales of poems to other takers were made for cash. Ezra Pound surprised Frost by purchasing the right to publish "The Housekeeper" in his newly-acquired magazine, *The Egoist.* Pound was also instrumental in enabling Frost to sell "The Code" to Harriet Monroe's *Poetry* magazine. These were the only four poems from *North of Boston* which appeared in print prior to its date of publication. Mrs. Nutt did not approve of these arrangements, and Frost later suspected that her way of punishing him was her refusal to pay him any royalties at any time for *North of Boston.*

An entirely unexpected privilege was afforded Frost in the fall of 1913, when he accidentally met the newly appointed Poet Laureate, Robert Bridges. The death of Alfred Austin on 2 June 1913 had set people guessing who the new laureate would be. Thomas Hardy's name was mentioned, and the consequent public shudder was reflected in a *Daily Mail* headline: DO WE WANT A PESSIMIST? Frost thought the popular vote would have given the laureateship to Rudyard Kipling, but the more austere rejection of this possibility was reflected in *Poetry and Drama,* where Monro caustically observed that the general public "is taught its imperialism with sufficient impressiveness, if without Kipling, in the columns of the newspapers, in the halls, and on the cinematograph." Approving of Bridges' appointment, Monro said, "The benefit to the public by Bridges' selection consists in the fact that its attention is thereby drawn to his poems."[23] Frost was not sufficiently familiar with Bridges' poetry to have an opinon at first, but within a short time he heard, and disliked, certain theories advanced by Bridges. Their accidental meeting occurred in the home of Laurence Binyon, another of the many poets to whom Frost had been introduced by F. S. Flint. Calling on Binyon unexpectedly one morning, Frost was told that Bridges was to be there soon. Binyon was taking him to lunch at the Vienna Café, and urged Frost to go with them. He did, sheepishly, and very soon found himself arguing with the poet laureate. Frost's account of the occasion braids their two opposed poetic theories, with no attempt to do justice to the poet laureate:

"He's a fine old boy with the highest opinion—of his poetry you thought I was going to say—perhaps of his poetry, but much more particularly of his opinions. He rides two hobbies tandem, his theory that syllables in English have fixed quantity that cannot be disregarded in reading verse, and his theory that with forty or fifty or sixty characters he can capture and hold for all time the sounds of speech. One theory is as bad as the other and I think owing to much the same fallacy. The living part of a poem is the intonation entangled somehow in the syntax idiom and meaning of a sentence. It is only there for those who have heard it previously in conversation. It is not for us in any Greek or Latin poem because our ears have not been filled with the tones of Greek and Roman talk. It is the most volatile and at the same time important part of poetry. It goes and the language becomes a dead language, the poetry dead poetry. With it go the accents the stresses the delays that are not the property of vowels and syllables but that are shifted at will with the sense. Vowels have length there is no denying. But the accent of sense supercedes all other accent overrides and sweeps it away. I will find you the word 'come' variously used in various passages as a whole, half, third, fourth, fifth, and sixth note. It is as long as the sense makes it. When men no longer know the intonation on which we string our words they will fall back on what I may call the absolute length of our syllables which is the length we would give them in passages that meant nothing. The psychologist can actually measure this with a what-do-you-call-it. English poetry would then be read as Latin poetry is now read and as of course Latin poetry was never read by Romans. Bridges would like it read so now for the sake of scientific exactness. Because our poetry must sometime be as dead as our language must, Bridges would like it treated as if it were dead already."[24]

Knowing as much as he did about Mark Twain's grouchy ways of tickling the British lion's nose, Frost may have felt a special kinship with Twain while in England. He was bold enough to differ with the poet laureate face to face, but he needed more than boldness in dealing with his publisher, Mrs. Nutt. Early in 1914, he called on her to say that he would like to make arrangements for the publication in the United States of his first two books. That was her business, she said, not his.

So far as publication was concerned, he had no legal rights other than those stated in his contract with her. At this time she informed him that he had no right to publish even one of the *North of Boston* poems in a magazine. Frost needed all the tact he could muster to retire in good order. "Dearie me!" he confided to Mosher, "I feel quite upset, the more so as I have already sold to magazines some five [actually four] of the sixteen poems in 'North of Boston,' rather I should say in honesty the more so as I haven't sold more . . ."25

A different set of problems marred the winter for Frost and his entire family. His children had acquired from him a tendency to express resentments vehemently, whenever they liked, and the two older children, Lesley and Carol, complained so bitterly over the difference between teaching methods in their Beaconsfield school and in Plymouth, New Hampshire, that Frost withdrew them. As a consequence the attempts made by their parents to continue their schedule of teaching at home brought a special burden on their mother. Frequent visits from newly-acquired friends taxed her energies even further. Matters were made worse by various kinds of illness, which had plagued her intermittently since their arrival in Beaconsfield. All of the Frosts became increasingly homesick during the winter months, and as a kind of consolation their father tried to reassure them by saying that they would return to the United States as soon as he had written and published one more book after *North of Boston*. Nobody seemed quite satisfied. "Homesickness makes us news-hungry," Frost wrote to Silver. "Every time the postman bangs the letter-slot-door our mouths go open and our eyes shut like birds' in a nest and we can't move for a moment."26

The entire family was glad when it was time to begin packing for the move to Gloucestershire. The plan made with Harold Monro was carried out. For a full week they lived in rooms above the Poetry Bookshop in Devonshire Street and the children, at least, enjoyed sightseeing in London. Then they took the train from London to Gloucester, where Gibson and his bride had promised to meet them.

For Frost, the only regret in the move was that he would be far out in the country when the hoped-for reviews of *North of Boston* might begin to appear.

LITTLE IDDENS

What a heavenly way we pass
Treading the green and golden land . . .[1]

THE WELTER of golden daffodils in the green fields of the
Dymock region in Gloucestershire charmed all six members of
the Frost family when they arrived there in April of 1914. This
countryside, so different from anything they had seen during
their walks outward from the suburban town of Beaconsfield,
was a surprise and a wonder. After their week of London
smoke and grime they began to exclaim as they rode from
Gloucester to the hamlet of Dymock on a train which wound
northward around broken hills and beside green hollows of
grazing land, which cradled flocks of sheep and herds of cattle.
There was a startlingly vivid quality in glimpses of white
petals from pear trees lazily falling like huge flakes of snow on
unbelievably bright grass. From the train window they marveled at the faces of flowers they could not name. But they
knew the daffodils and gloried in this green and golden land.[2]

At the Dymock station, Abercrombie and the Gibsons formed
a welcoming committee. It had been decided that the Frosts
themselves must choose the cottage they wished to rent and
that while the choice was being made they could live comfortably with the Abercrombies. Except for the children, it
would have been an easy walk from the Dymock railroad station to the Gallows below the village of Ryton, some two miles
to the eastward. But the welcoming committee had reasons for
celebrating the arrival of these Americans by renting two large
carriages; the trip to the Abercrombies' had to be made in a
roundabout way, with a brief stop at the rented home of the
Gibsons. The little procession wound north out of Dymock,
across a bridge over the little River Leadon, and along the east
bank of the river for two miles to an intersection known as

Greenway Cross. Just beyond this intersection, on the left, stood the Gibsons' little showpiece: a half-timbered cottage, thatch-covered. It was called the Old Nailshop, and the lean-to shed where nails had been made was still in place at one end of the cottage. After only the briefest stop there, the procession turned eastward and drove on through narrow lanes and turn-ings, past little farms and a scattering of cottages built mostly of half-timber and red brick, until they made their way south-east, through the village of Ryton to The Gallows.

Lascelles Abercrombie had been attracted to this corner of Gloucestershire after his older sister married well and settled with her husband on a gentleman's farm near the village of Much Marcle in the red-soil country not far from Ryton. His sister, fond of horseback riding and soon well-acquainted with the local gentry, had noticed that a distinguished neighbor, Lord Beauchamp, had refinished a pair of cottages and joined them as a home for a sub-agent. Attractively surrounded by lofty elms and backed with an uphill stand of firs, the place was called The Gallows because it stood on the high ground where, centuries earlier, a locally celebrated character known as Jock of Dymock had been hanged for poaching the king's deer. When the sub-agent found a house somewhere else, The Gallows stood empty, and Abercrombie's sister had interceded on his behalf. Abercrombie rented it from Lord Beauchamp in 1911 with permission to wander at liberty over all the farm-land and woodland which comprised this part of the estate. His walks had inspired him to write some almost ecstatic lyrics, including "Ryton Firs."[3]

The Gallows had become a meeting place for a cluster of Georgian poets. Gibson, Drinkwater, and Rupert Brooke had been invited by Abercrombie to join him as the only con-tributors to a quarterly which they would edit. It would be printed locally and prepared for mailing at The Gallows. They thought to call it *The Gallows Garland*, and only at the last minute had they changed the title to *New Numbers*. The first issue had been sent by mail to bookstores and friends just a short time before the Frosts arrived. Abercrombie's cheerful and enthusiastic wife had addressed the labels while rocking the cradle of her newborn second child. Gibson had licked postage stamps until the glue made him ill. Rupert Brooke had come down from London to help, and had stayed until the last copy was mailed at the Dymock post office. Already there were warm responses, and contributions for the second issue were in hand. So the Gibsons and Abercrombies had plenty of time to help the Frosts find a home in this idyllic countryside.[4]

After fully enjoying his pastime of house-hunting, Frost rented for a year a cottage on a farm some two miles to the north and west of the Nailshop and only two miles to the south of the village of Ledbury in Herefordshire. Known as Little Iddens, the cottage was homely and boxlike, built of black timber and whitened bricks. It stood with its back to a southerly rise of ground in the Leadington region of Dymock. If the children were disappointed to find that Little Iddens was not crowned with thatch, they quickly found compensations. Orchards of pear and cherry and apple in blossom covered the hill at the back of the house. From the front the southerly view was a picture. The foreground of sloping hayfields, pastures, meadows, each with its hedgerow elms, provided an exquisite setting for the forest greenery of May Hill four miles away. It rose nearly a thousand feet and was capped, on an otherwise grassy summit, with a circular stand of pines, which had been set out to commemorate the Diamond Jubilee of Queen Victoria.

Inside the cottage the Frosts explored the tiny kitchen, with its old-fashioned stove and baking oven, the worn and undulating pavement of bricks on the downstairs floors, the shed to the rear of the kitchen, the stiff iron pump near the shed door, the narrow staircase to the second floor, and the low-posted bedrooms, each with its window of leaded panes in a hinged casement. To the children it seemed like a fairyland house, particularly when contrasted with their suburban Beaconsfield bungalow which their father had derisively nicknamed "The Bunghole" after he had grown tired of it.

As soon as the Frosts had unpacked and were settled in their new home, they began to take walks. A nearby farmer, over the brow of the hill behind them, encouraged them to stay on the footpaths which led along the edges of his cultivated fields and traversed groves of fir, larch, elm, birch. Before long the children were making daily pilgrimages with their father back down the two miles of narrow lane to the Nailshop, and even two miles further, east and south, to The Gallows. The Gibsons and the Abercrombies kept them busy with noonday picnics at idyllic places on the bank of the Leadon. The men held evening talks by lamplight or candlelight, first at The Gallows and then at Old Nailshop, and then at Little Iddens.

Mrs. Frost had difficulty in finding either time or a desire on anyone's part for continuing the private education she had given the children at Beaconsfield. And there was extra strain on her when guests from Gloucester or London began to drop in at Little Iddens for a night or two—or three or four. The first visitor was Edward Thomas, who had been invited to bring his teenage son and daughter, Mervyn and Bronwen. The Frost children very gladly entertained the Thomas children while both fathers were free to roam the countryside. Thomas knew the region well. As a start he insisted on taking Frost over back lanes to the flower-sprinkled groves of bay, larch, pine, birch on the side of May Hill and on up to the top. The best part of the panoramic view, for Thomas, was to the west, where he could point out and name some of the highest peaks in the mountains of Wales.

So the warm friendship between these two men continued to develop in ways which pleased their wives. Mrs. Frost, writing to her sister Leona after this visit, said of Thomas: "Rob and I think everything of him. He is quite the most admirable and lovable man we have ever known."[5] She also tried to give her sister a glimpse of her own response to Little Iddens and the setting:

". . . I wish I could make you feel what a lovely country this is. When we first came, the meadows were covered with yellow daffodils and the cuckoo had just begun to sing. . . . The pastures here are so rich that they are just as green as the mowing and wheat fields, and they are separated by dark green hedges and bordered by huge elms. Great flocks of sheep and herds of cows are everywhere. From a hill about four miles away, one can see the Severn river winding along, and the mountains of Wales in the distance. The cottage we are living in is very old—about 350 years old, and all the floors downstairs are brick tiled and the beams show above. We have five rooms and the rent is only $50 a year."[6]

To her sister, Mrs. Frost confided another part of her response to this new life. The ailments which had plagued her during the second winter in Beaconsfield were caused largely by the fatigue of caring for a difficult husband, four children, and unexpected guests. She had tried to warn John Bartlett's wife against unnecessary housekeeping and had written to her from Beaconsfield: "I hope, my dear, that you do not try to do too much housework. I think it is *very necessary* for you to take good care of yourself for several years to come, and you must learn the art of 'letting things go' just as I had to learn it long, long ago. How could I ever have lived through those years when the children were little tots if I had been at all fussy about my housework? Do not try to cook much—wash dishes only *once* a day and use no rooms except kitchen, bedroom and sitting-room, and hire someone to come in and sweep up once in two weeks."[7]

But at Little Iddens even the art of letting things go could not save Mrs. Frost from strain, as she wrote her sister:

". . . I haven't been feeling at all well for three or four weeks . . . quite worn out. The household and teaching and the excitement of meeting so many people constantly, has been almost too much for me. Three weeks ago I felt that I was on the edge of complete nervous prostration, but I pulled out of it and am feeling considerably better now."[8]

The visitors kept coming to Little Iddens, but not all of them were cordially received. One was the super-tramp poet William Henry Davies—four years older than Frost—whose innocent childlike versifications on the wonders of nature had won the praise of George Bernard Shaw as early as 1905. Prior to that time Davies had wandered about the world, had crossed the United States in freight cars, lost a foot under a train in Canada, and come home to peddle broadside poems with shoestrings on the streets of London. He had been rescued from poverty by Shaw and other admirers, who arranged a pension for him. Now, during a stay with the Gibsons at Old Nailshop, he called too often on Frost at Little Iddens.

Frost had met Davies in London. During a dinner given in honor of Davies by Harold Monro at Picorini's restaurant Frost watched the hero of the evening drink too much wine, excuse himself from the table, wander drunkenly out of the room, and forget to return.[9] Throughout his protracted visit in the Dymock region, Davies conducted himself more soberly and yet, as Frost wrote: ". . . his conceit is enough to make you misjudge him—simply assinine. We have had a good deal of him at the house for the last week and the things he has said for us to remember him by! He entirely disgusted the Gibsons . . . His is the kind of egotism another man's egotism can't put up with."[10]

Frost was particularly bothered by the way in which Davies liked to boast of his pleasures with women of little virtue: "His private life is public property, so he makes no bones of speaking in any company of the women he spends his money on. They are cheaper than in America and I don't suppose his tastes are up to the most expensive ones here: the one of his fortnight before coming down to the country cost him thirty shillings."

Davies' attempts to encourage Lesley in her writing of poems about nature became a family joke. There now, said Davies, see that little bird, that little green one. I wonder what kind it is. Lesley said it was a sparrow and that it wasn't green, and Davies stumped into the house. "He doesn't really know nature at all," Frost wrote at the time. "He has lately been telling the British public that the American Robin isn't red breasted and it has no note that he ever heard."[11]

Far more to Frost's liking was a Gloucestershire barrister and botanist, John Haines, by marriage a relative of Abercrombie's, by avocation a shrewdly perceptive lover of poetry and a rabid botanist. He appeared unexpectedly at Little Iddens one day wearing on a strap over one shoulder a vasculum or collecting tin, which protected specimens of flowers he wanted to keep. Frost was immediately attracted to this unassuming and lively admirer of plants and verse. Inviting him back again after his second visit Frost wrote:

"I don't believe I had one uneasy moment with you the other day from the moment I saw you throw the [train] car door open. I should think you were the kind of person I could ask over here to sprawl—not call. I object to callers more and more'in my old age. In my wife's present state of health I have to do some of the meals (so to call them), but you won't mind that will you? And you will overlook some other things if we can laze and talk for a day. You must come on the early train and go on the late."[12]

Haines continued the work begun by Thomas, educating Frost about British flowers. Together they wandered through the Leadon Valley and even as far away as the ridges of the Cotswolds, discovering blossoms which delighted Frost: Ladies Tresses, Little Teasel, the harebell called Spreading Campanula, and queer things that grew in the salt springs bursting out of the Leadon near Hunting Bridge. One night they even hunted rare ferns by matchlight, and found them.

A careful reader of periodicals, Haines became the harbinger of glad tidings. He brought or sent to Frost from Gloucester the best reviews of *North of Boston* as they kept appearing throughout the summer of 1914.[13] The first excitement was provided by the consistency of praise for these modern "eclogues" in "this book of people." Characterizing the "stark concentration" in the volume as "vivid and effective," the anonymous reviewer in the London *Times Literary Supplement* added: "Poetry burns up out of it—as when a faint wind breathes upon smouldering embers." He continued: "The simplest of Mr. Frost's poems—'The Wood Pile'—had this clear strangeness throughout, and in its last line the magic of intensest insight."[14]

For Frost, a fresh kind of satisfaction was realized from the pointed evidence that his new-made friends had rallied strongly to his aid. Abercrombie reviewed him in *The Nation*, Gibson in *The Bookman*, Thomas in the *English Review*, Monro in *Poetry and Drama*, Ezra Pound in Harriet Monroe's *Poetry*.[15] Frost had not felt sure that Pound would fall in line. But at the very moment when he was most skeptical he had received a typical note from Pound shortly after *North of Boston* was published: "Your damfool publisher has not sent me review copies of your new book—nor has she sent one—so far as I know—to Hueffer."[16] Frost had taken care of that quickly, and Ford Madox Hueffer's review appeared in the London *Outlook*.

Many of the reviews reflected the care with which Frost oriented his friends in regard to his theories about "the sound of sense." "When poetry changes by development rather than by rebellion, it is likely to return on itself," Abercrombie had written. "Poetry in Mr. Frost exhibits almost the identical desires and impulses we see in the 'bucolic' poems of Theocritus. . . . Poetry, in this book, seems determined, once more, just as it was in Alexandria, to invigorate itself by utilizing the traits and necessities of common life, the habits of common speech, the minds and hearts of common folk."[17] Thomas had carried on in his review: ". . . a unique type of eclogue, homely, racy, and touched by a spirit that might, under other circumstances, have made pure lyric on the one hand or drama on the other. . . . The language ranges from a never vulgar colloquialism to brief moments of heightened and intense simplicity. . . . the plain language and lack of violence make the unaffected verses look like prose, except that the sentences, if spoken aloud, are most felicitously true in rhythm to the emotion. Only at the end of the best pieces . . . do we realise that they are master-pieces of deep and mysterious tenderness."[18]

After Frost had luxuriated in these cumulative signs that all was going well with *North of Boston*, he could afford to find fault with his friends. To Haines, who had sent him the clip-ping from *The Nation*, he wrote:

"Thank you for the review—Abercrombie's work as your wife thought. I liked it very well. The discussion of my tech-nique wouldn't have been what it was if Abercrombie had nothing to go on but the book. He took advantage of certain conversations in which I gave him the key to my method and most of his catchwords. 'Method' is the wrong way to call it: I simply use certain principles on which I accept or reject my own work. It was a generous review to consider me in all ways so seriously and as I say I liked it."[19]

So he had liked it; but the note of disparagement in his remarks reflected his characteristic tendency to be jealous of all competitors, even when they were being praised for praising him. Fortunately, very special attention was paid to Frost throughout four good weeks of that summer. It hap-pened as a result of his having urged Edward Thomas to bring Mrs. Thomas and their children to this region so near Wales, and to rent a cottage next door to Little Iddens for the month of August. The suggestion pleased Thomas, whose admiration for Frost was based on the conviction that nobody else had ever before understood so deeply his dark spells of anguish.

Thomas and his family had been there only three days when the feared news arrived that England had declared war on Germany, and it was immediately clear that the future might hold disastrous effects for both of these men. "The war is an ill wind to me," Frost wrote to Cox. "It ends for the time being the thought of publishing any more books. Our game is up. . . . So we may be coming home if we can find the fare or a job to pay the fare after we get there. . . . We are here or in this neighborhood till we sail for home."[20]

Thomas was aware that he might be drafted into military service at any time. The forty-four-year-old farmer named Chandler, from whom Thomas was renting rooms, went off in khaki to the barracks in Hereford. Even if Thomas were not immediately drafted, he knew that the meager living he had made as a hack writer would be curtailed severely by the war. But it still appeared to be so far away from Little Iddens that the two men refused to spend all of their time worrying about it.

The interest shown by Thomas in Frost's practice and theory of poetry was extremely flattering. "Thomas thinks he will write a book on what my definition of the sentence means for literary criticism," Frost wrote to Cox. "If I didn't drop into poetry every time I sat down to write I should be tempted to do a book on what it means for education."[21] From Little Iddens he repeated to Cox the gist of one point he had already conveyed to Bartlett: ". . . the sentence as a sound in itself apart from the word sounds is no mere figure of speech. I shall show the sentence sound saying all that the sentence conveys with little or no help from the meaning of the words. I shall show the sentence sound opposing the sense of the words as in irony. And so [on] till I establish the distinction between the grammatical sentence and the vital sentence."[22]

It was the distinction which fascinated him, and he was willing to employ hyperbole in order to make his point. In a postscript to Cox, he said as much: "Words are only valuable in writing as they serve to indicate particular sentence sounds. I must say some things over and over. I must be a little extravagant too."[23] In his poems, in his prose, and in his arguments, Frost enjoyed indulging the luxury and extravagance of hyperbole.

Try as they would, neither Frost nor Thomas could go very long without finding that their talk, during this month of August 1914, turned back to the overwhelming crisis of the war. Rupert Brooke had not yet enlisted, but he had made it clear that he would become involved somehow. "If Armageddon is *on*," Brooke said, "I suppose one should be there."[24] Frost almost felt the same way. "If I were younger now and not the father of four—well all I say is, American or no American, I might decide that I ought to fight the Germans simply because I know I should be afraid to."[25] Two months later he wrote: "No one quite knows what the war has done to him yet. We may be dead, the whole crowd of us, and not able to realize the fact. It is as hard to know how the war has affected us individually as it is to tell off hand what the war is all about, or to understand a modern battle."[26]

Abercrombie and Gibson shared the knowledge that their own cherished plans for *New Numbers* could not long survive the astringencies caused by the war; but they insisted on going ahead with at least two more issues, already well-prepared. Shortly before his enlistment Rupert Brooke came over from London to stay briefly with the Gibsons while helping to wrap and mail the second issue. Frost's jealousy of Brooke, who had the advantage of contributing to *New Numbers*, was kept under moderate control on the single occasion when all of these literary figures were invited for an evening at the Nail-shop; but there are hints that even on this occasion Frost managed to steal the show from the glamorous young poet just returned from Canada, the United States, and the South Sea islands. The hints are innocently contained between the lines of the poem which Gibson wrote to commemorate this literary event, "The Golden Room":

> *Do you remember that still summer evening*
> *When, in the cosy cream washed living room*
> *Of the Old Nailshop, we all talked and laughed—*
> *Our neighbours from The Gallows, Catherine*
> *And Lascelles Abercrombie; Rupert Brooke;*
> *Eleanor and Robert Frost, living awhile*
> *At Little Iddens, who'd brought over with them*
> *Helen and Edward Thomas? In the lamplight*
> *We talked and laughed; but, for the most part, listened*
> *While Robert Frost kept on and on and on,*
> *In his slow New England fashion, for our delight,*
> *Holding us with shrewd turns and racy quips,*
> *And the rare twinkle of his grave blue eyes?*
>
> *We sat there in the lamplight, while the day*
> *Died from the rose-latticed casements, and the plovers*
> *Called over the low meadows, till the owls*
> *Answered them from the elms, we sat and talked—*
>
> *Now, a quick flash from Abercrombie, now,*
> *A murmured dry half-heard aside from Thomas;*
> *Now, a clear laughing word from Brooke; and then*
> *Again Frost's rich and ripe philosophy,*
> *That had the body and tang of good draught cider*
> *And poured as clear a stream. . . .*[27]

The abstemious Frosts had learned to enjoy even a well-fermented cider by this time, although they had never approved of making or drinking it while they lived on the farm in Derry. From Little Iddens Frost wrote: "We are now in . . . the cider country, where we have to keep a barrel of cider for our visitors and our hired help or we have no visitors nor hired help. So we are in the way of adding drink to cigarette smoking in the record of our sins. Even Elinor gets drawn in since the only kind of ladies we know over here are all smokers."[28]

Both Thomas and Haines further influenced Frost's loosening of his puritanical notions. During their many walks, whether purposeful or not, each guide was well enough acquainted with the region to know quaint places to eat and drink. Particularly they were eager to have Frost know the subleties of enjoying a Gloucestershire specialty: the fermented and sparkling juice of the Perry pear, locally advertised as "The 'White' Wine of the West." Frost liked it so much that Perry became his favorite drink while he remained in the Dymock region. Going or coming, on the repeated climbs up May Hill, he liked to stop at the little pub at its foot for bread and cheese—and Perry.

It was during this month of August 1914, while the war clouds still lay on the horizon, for them at least, that Frost and Thomas shared one experience which seemed miraculous. (Having rejected the religious heritage of his Welsh ancestors, Thomas was always sufficiently fastidious, in choosing words, to take pleasure in teasing Frost whenever such an adjective as "miraculous" could be construed as a hint of superstitious belief.) The marvel had occurred on an evening when they were making their way home after a particularly long walk, and Frost later tried to capture his own sense of wonder over the event in the poem "Iris by Night":

> One misty evening, one another's guide,
> We two were groping down a Malvern side
> The last wet fields and dripping hedges home.
> There came a moment of confusing lights,
> Such as according to belief in Rome
> Were seen of old at Memphis on the heights
> Before the fragments of a former sun
> Could concentrate anew and rise as one.
> Light was a paste of pigment in our eyes.

And then there was a moon and then a scene
So watery as to seem submarine;
In which we two stood saturated, drowned.
The clover-mingled rowan on the ground
Had taken all the water it could as dew,
And still the air was saturated too,
Its airy pressure turned to water weight.
Then a small rainbow like a trellis gate,
A very small moon-made prismatic bow,
Stood closely over us through which to go.
And then we were vouchsafed the miracle
That never yet to other two befell
And I alone of us have lived to tell.
A wonder! Bow and rainbow as it bent,
Instead of moving with us as we went,
(To keep the pots of gold from being found)
It lifted from its dewy pediment
Its two mote-swimming many-colored ends,
And gathered them together in a ring.
And we stood in it softly circled round
From all division time or foe can bring
In a relation of elected friends.[29]

Miracle or not, this was the first time Frost had seen the phenomenon and he treasured it as a moment which endowed their friendship with a very special significance. The sense of brotherhood and comradeship he had experienced with Thomas while they had been in each other's company through at least part of every day in the month of August 1914 made their parting an especially sad one. Thomas would not say good-bye. He promised that within a month or two he would return for another visit.

Soon after the Thomas family had gone, Frost accepted the invitation of the Abercrombies to share the combined cottages at The Gallows during the winter months—or at least until Frost decided whether he would try to make arrangements for a passage home through seas made dangerous by mines and submarines. By mid-September, the move to The Gallows was completed. Having paid rent for a full year on Little Iddens, Frost saw no reason to bother with packing all their possessions.

33

THE GALLOWS

I dreamt of wings,—and waked to hear
Through the low sloping ceiling clear
The nesting starlings flutter and scratch
Among the rafters of the thatch,
Not twenty inches from my head;
And lay, half dreaming, in my bed,
Watching the far elms, bolt-upright,
Black towers of silence in a night
Of stars, square-framed between the sill
Of the casements and the eaves, until
I drowsed, and must have slept a wink.[1]

WHEN THE FROSTS moved from Little Iddens to The Gallows, following the welcome invitation of the Abercrombies,
there was the pleasurable sense of returning to an abode they
had admired and enjoyed immediately after they came to the
Dymock region. A rambling and spacious arrangement of upstairs and downstairs rooms had been achieved by Lord Beauchamp's renovations. The joined cottages were perched on a
bluff above the road, and a steep flight of stone steps had to be
climbed by anyone who approached the front door from the
road. The older of the two cottages was the smaller: a "black
and white" structure, half-timbered, with white plaster covering the brick walls and thatched roof steeply pitched so that
the straw at the eaves was only shoulder high. Abercrombie
said that the bottom layer of thatch was rye straw, put on the
cottage perhaps two or three hundred years earlier and protected by periodic replacements of wheat straw on the top.
They called this older cottage The Study because Lascelles did
his writing in the main downstairs room. The Abercrombies
used the upstairs bedrooms for themselves and their two small
children—the four-year-old Michael and three-year-old David.

[457]

From The Study there was a passage into the larger cottage, solidly built of red sandstone native to the region. To the rear of this cottage had been built a large annex, housing the kitchen and pantry and shed, with three upstairs bedrooms which had been given to the Frosts on their arrival in April and to which they returned in mid-September of 1914.

There was a casual easy-going gypsy-like manner in the way the Abercrombies lived. Weather permitting, they cooked and ate most of their meals out-of-doors on the large terrace or in the garden bounded by hedges and elms on one side, by the cottages which made a right-angle at the place where they were joined, and by open fields which sloped uphill to the stand of dark firs. Catherine Abercrombie caught the gypsy atmosphere in her description of the life they built around that nearly enclosed terrace:

". . . I had a permanent gipsy tent under the Seven Sisters, as the great elms at the bottom of our garden were called, and sometimes I would have an iron pot over a fire with a duck and green peas stewing in it as Lascelles, John Drinkwater and Wilfrid Gibson would sit around and read their latest poems to each other as I lay on a stoop of hay and listened and watched the stars wander through the elms and think I had found the why and wherefore of life."[2]

Catherine Abercrombie carried the same gypsy spirit into her planning for the midday wanderings of the two families, picnic baskets in hands, to nearby Ketford Bridge where the children loved to roam. Frost had preserved all his fondness for playing with children which he had shown at Derry and at the Lynch farm in Bethlehem. On the bank of the River Leadon he taught Michael Abercrombie how to make a stone skip and bounce across the surface of the water. He showed all the children how to make a big splash with a small object and a little splash with a big object such as a flat board.[3] With his jackknife he cut tree shoots which could be thrown as javelins, and he showed them how to hold and hurl the weapons.

Catherine Abercrombie and Elinor Frost, enjoying each other's company, shared the conviction that housework was best handled by avoiding it; but some of Elinor's habits amazed Catherine: "I admired Elinor so much for her charming imperturbability—nothing seemed to daunt her—she kept her precious metal coffee pot going all day on the stove, and imbibed more coffee in the day than I did in a month."[4]

Yet Catherine was disturbed by the ways of the Frost children. To her they seemed fretful and troublesome, particularly when Lesley and Carol spent so much time talking about homesickness and their desire to get back to the United States. Catherine was also troubled by the inability of the Frost children to get along with other children in the neighborhood: ". . . the sad thing was that they did not get on with the natives, and the [Abercrombie] children soon refused to go out of the grounds, alleging that they threw stones at them, which astounded us as we had always loved the Gloucestershire people and were on excellent terms with them. It culminated in Robert having a really nasty row with Lord Beauchamp's game-keeper, who was admittedly a nasty person, and not native to the district."[5] The gamekeeper patrolled a nearby preserve with shotgun in hand and liked to intercept little children who came out of the woods with baskets of berries and mushrooms. He seemed to take pleasure in tipping the contents of the baskets on the ground and rubbing them into the dirt with his boot.

Frost's resentment against the gamekeeper should have been enough to purge him. But there was also a cumulatively resentful jealousy in his attitude toward his host and toward the daily caller, Gibson. Each of these Georgians had established a considerable reputation as a poet before Frost came on the scene, and he seemed to resent his being treated as an outsider. Gibson had a jocose way of annoying Frost by reading to him letters of praise he got from America and then calling Frost's attention to bad grammar and misspelled words in the letters. Teasingly, Gibson wanted to know whether Frost's difficulty in getting attention at home might be caused by the high level of illiteracy in the United States. The game of teasing was one which Frost enjoyed only when he was on the giving end. So there was double pleasure for him when Mrs. Nutt forwarded to The Gallows, belatedly, a letter of praise from a stranger. It bore as a heading, "Four Winds Farm, Stowe, Vermont," and was signed, "Florence I. Holt." It read:

"Your book 'North of Boston' interests me very much. Do you live in Vermont? If so, you may know my brother's book 'Stowe Notes.' If you don't know it, & would care to, as your book makes me think you would, and will let me know of your address, I will send the book to you. My mother knows the people about here better than I do, & she finds many similar to them in your verses: certainly you have New England in them!

"I hope I am not taking too much of a liberty in writing this note, but probably you will not be displeased to know of our interest."[6]

Now he had a weapon to use on Gibson and Abercrombie. If their poems elicited illiterate responses from the United States, let them look to the causes. Here was a letter from a Vermont farmer's wife—and who could ask for anything in better taste? At the time Frost did not know that this first letter of praise from a stranger was written by a lady whose husband was a distinguished and successful publisher in New York City: Henry Holt. Nor did he know that she had already begun to work on his behalf. A representative of Henry Holt and Company mentioned her in writing a cautious letter to David Nutt and Company on 2 September 1914:

". . . Mrs. Henry Holt, who is very enthusiastic over Robert Frost's NORTH OF BOSTON, has very kindly loaned us her copy. The two readers we had look at these poems found them uncommonly interesting and, while we cannot see a paying market here for this particular volume, still we are so interested in this author's work that if you have some later books of his for which you would care to offer us the American rights, we would be most happy to consider it. . . ."[7]

Mrs. Nutt may have had a hand in dictating the reproachful answer:

". . . We think that if you recognize the value of Mr. Frost's work you must also see that his books will make their way steadily. We could not offer you rights of his new book if you do not push the present volume to some extent. . . .

"We consider that under present political circumstances American publishers ought to show some willingness to help English publishers who have had sufficient daring and intelligence to recognize the talent of one of their countrymen. . . ."[8]

Fortunately, this reprimand was not needed. On exactly the day it was written, a representative of Henry Holt and Company wrote to David Nutt and Company:

". . . Following our letter of September 2nd in regard to Frost's 'North of Boston' we are inclined on further consideration to take a small edition of this book, say 150 copies in sheets, if it has not already been placed in the American market, and if you can supply them at a reasonable price."[9]

So the negotiations began; but Mrs. Nutt seemed anxious to keep Frost in the dark about them. At the same time, he was doing all he could to marshal the assistance of his friends. Eventually he was helped most by Edward Thomas, who enlisted the persuasive support of one of England's most influential critics, Edward Garnett.[10]

Twice during the fall of 1914, Edward Thomas visited Frost at The Gallows, and each time he stayed for several days. Outwardly, it might have seemed that the common interests which bound these men in friendship was their delight in the Gloucestershire countryside. Elinor Frost and Helen Thomas saw more deeply into the psychological significance of this relationship, and approved. So did Catherine Abercrombie, apparently, for she wrote of Edward Thomas: "It was quite a shock on first meeting him unless one had been warned. He suffered very much from recurring melancholy, which stamped itself on his face but only made his beauty more apparent. It was only when Robert encouraged him to turn to writing poetry that he became happy in the delight of his new-found powers."[11]

Robert Frost did more than that for Edward Thomas. In trying to understand the very deeply important relationship between these two men, particularly for the light it throws on Robert Frost, there is value in noticing analogies between the kinds of suffering they experienced; analogies which enabled Frost to save the life of Edward Thomas very shortly before Thomas gave his life for his country in combat.[12]

Four years younger than Frost, Edward Thomas was born of Welsh parents, and the pronounced streak of puritanical fastidiousness in his nature seemed to be part of his inheritance from his Welsh ancestors. Although he grew up as a normal boy, he showed an early bent toward introspectiveness and brooding. This tendency gradually developed into what Catherine Abercrombie accurately described as "melancholy," and it became a disease against which he fought throughout his life. One of his weapons against it was his early pleasure in the lore of the naturalist. As a boy he liked to go fishing and eel-catching; he collected birds' nests and eggs; he collected butterflies. Quite early he began to write poetry, but his father discouraged him and he turned his creative literary interests to essay-writing.

At the age of sixteen Thomas fell in love with the girl whom he later married. She was two years older than he, and the courtship was marred by difficulties. He sent her the first spring flowers and she romantically pressed them between the pages of Shelley's poems. He entered Oxford University in the fall of 1897 and felt that his disillusioning experiences there marked the beginning of serious depression. He admired Walter Pater; described himself as "all Shelley and sunsets"; and was utterly repelled by Whitman, whom he believed to be "an added fiend to Hell." He gradually forced himself to mingle with other students at Oxford, to drink with them, and to participate in some of their wildest parties; but beneath the surface he maintained his austere and ascetic fastidiousness. At the end of his first university year he went to Wales and worked on a farm, which was owned by one of his relatives.

During his third year at Oxford, Thomas married his boyhood sweetheart soon after she told him she was pregnant. He left the university and tried to earn a living as a hack writer. Sensitive, proud, shy, he overcame his torturing distaste for begging, and forced himself to call on eight editors in one day. All of them refused to give him work. After many discouragements, the editor of the *London Chronicle* offered him an opportunity to write book reviews, and his excellent critical perceptions very soon revealed themselves. Needing money to support his wife and child, he often wrote weekly articles in which he reviewed ten or fifteen books—most of them books of poetry. He began to send essays to various magazines and although a few of the essays were accepted, most of them were not. By January of 1901, he had collected forty refusal slips for what he considered to be the best work he had done.

The increasing sense of his failure heightened his melancholy. Trying to escape from the nameless thing which tormented him, he frequently ran away and stayed away for several days without letting his wife know where he was. He loved his wife, and tortured himself by being cruel to her. Once he went into a rage and said, "I am cursed and you are cursed because of me. I hate the tears I see you've been crying. . . . Hate me, but for God's sake don't stand there, pale and suffering."[13]

His wife, fearing for his sanity, felt that the preservation of their marriage depended on her. She tried to avoid causing him the least inconvenience or upset lest it strain his overwrought senses and bring a nervous breakdown. She knew that if she failed, he would blame himself and ask what right he had to be married to her, what right he had had to beget children. Their first child was a son, Mervyn; their second a girl, Bronwen; their third a girl, Myfanwy. When Bronwen became seriously ill and nearly died at the age of eighteen months, Thomas blamed himself for the child's illness.

At times he could escape from his troubles completely. Any little encouragement or sign of progress in his writing would enable him to reveal the most attractive side of his nature. Briefly he would be contented, gay, generous, and even reckless in his newly-recovered happiness. But before long he would slip back into despondency. He resented all trivial domestic responsibilities and felt that they interfered with the achievement of his success as a literary figure. He drove himself ruthlessly and published book after book as a means of earning a living, but none of the volumes achieved any financial success. Intermittently he suffered from headaches, which were so painful that he took opium as another might take aspirin and yet his asceticism restrained him from acquiring the drug habit. At one time, when his melancholy lay heavy on him, he said that it was as if he were dwelling in an "unfathomable, deep forest where all must lose their way."

In the fall of 1912, when the Frost family reached England, Thomas was suffering from an acute phase of neurasthenia and was threatening to kill himself. His wife confessed to friends that he once put a revolver in his pocket and disappeared for hours. Many of the letters written at this period contain hints of panic and hysteria. He acted as though he were caught in a trap and were fighting to get out. Among the literary friends who cared deeply for him and did their best to help him were Walter de la Mare, Joseph Conrad, W. H. Hudson, and Edward Garnett. In the spring of 1913, Hudson wrote to Garnett concerning Thomas: "I believe he has taken the wrong path and is wandering lost in the vast wilderness. He is essentially a poet."

It was also in the spring of 1913 that Thomas became obsessed with the notion that he should divorce his wife. Always blaming himself, he considered her kindness and love a form of reproach. His repeated absences from home for days at a time amounted to a formal separation. The summer of 1913 went extremely well for him; but by the fall of 1913, he seemed to be headed toward an unavoidable disaster. He was in this condition when he met Robert Frost on 5 October 1913. When first their almost identically light-blue eyes met, each may have felt that he saw himself mirrored. Obviously they had more in common than a love of literature.

Frost had not seen Thomas' review of *A Boy's Will*, but in their conversation about the book it quickly became apparent to Frost that this stranger saw more deeply than anyone else the psychological theme of attempted escape and necessary return in the arrangement of the lyrics. The admiration shown Frost by Thomas implied an awareness that Frost himself had gone down to the bottom like a drowning man and had somehow learned the secret of how to save himself. It was almost with desperation that Thomas reached out to Frost for help.

Frost quickly discovered that the immediate problem for this obviously tortured man was caused by marital difficulties. Thomas made it clear that he wanted to preserve his marriage, that he loved his wife and children; but that he blamed himself for the failure of his marriage and that there was nothing he thought he could do to overcome that failure.

Frost was always at his best as a human being when he felt himself needed by someone whose psychological difficulties were in some ways analogous to his own experiences.[14] Under these circumstances he had an extraordinary capacity for drawing out exactly the details he wanted to get at; during the early meetings of these two men it was not long before Frost recognized and understood the similarities between their stories. Frost, in his wife's presence, had flourished a revolver and had threatened to kill himself—or her. Frost had repeatedly tried to run away from himself—and from Elinor. He had fought off major fears and depressions and suicidal yearnings. In part he had been helped by his ability to take warning from the psychological deterioration dramatized in the hysterical actions of his sister Jeanie. Now, in his desire to help Thomas, he spread out the pieces of his own story and tried to explain them as best he could. He made it clear that he was by no means certain he was out of the woods. If he had saved himself from going under, on different occasions, he couldn't say he would always be able to save himself. Even after moving to The Gallows, he hurt himself in his childish attempt to hurt his wife for her solicitude. What had happened was subject enough for a poem, and it later became "The Thatch":

Out alone in the winter rain,
Intent on giving and taking pain.
But never was I far out of sight
Of a certain upper-window light.
The light was what it was all about:
I would not go in till the light went out,
It would not go out till I came in.
Well, we should see which one would win,
We should see which one would be first to yield.
The world was a black invisible field.
The rain by rights was snow for cold.
The wind was another layer of mold.
But the strangest thing: in the thick old thatch,
Where summer birds had been given hatch,
Had fed in chorus, and lived to fledge,
Some still were living in hermitage.
And as I passed along the eaves,
So low I brushed the straw with my sleeves,
I flushed birds out of hole after hole,
Into the darkness. It grieved my soul,
It started a grief within a grief,
To think their case was beyond relief—
They could not go flying about in search
Of their nest again, nor find a perch.
They must brood where they fell in mulch and mire,
Trusting feathers and inward fire
Till daylight made it safe for a flyer.
My greater grief was by so much reduced
As I thought of them without nest or roost.
That was how that grief started to melt. . . .[15]

Frost could tell Thomas a great deal about the vicissitudes of marital relations, but he was not willing to talk about them as grounds for divorce. If he had learned the mistaken aspects of walking out, running away, escape, he was not yet convinced that the ambivalence in these terms should be reduced to one pejorative meaning. He was certain that while some of his actions had been weak and childish gestures, others had saved his life—at least his sanity—by providing necessary kinds of retreat for reorganizing his feelings and thoughts.

To Frost, marriage was only one kind of struggle involving alternations of love and hate—and not the most important. As long as he lived, he thought he'd be fighting a continuous battle on various fronts, and he felt he'd have to settle for nothing more or less than temporary victories. The wounds borne, the suffering, the anguish experienced in all these different conflicts could be survived if anyone possessed a sufficiently intense desire to accomplish one particular thing, come hell or high water.

As it happened, the particular thing to which Frost had clung for more than twenty years—without seeming to make much headway until recently—was his very stubborn and persistent ambition to succeed as a poet by gaining public recognition. There had been times when some of his faults had worked to his advantage: his quick temper, his resentments, his uncontrollable rages. His most terrible fight had been against his own fears. At almost any time he could frighten himself almost to death. And there had been times when he had been paralyzed by his fear that he would never succeed as a poet. He was a quitter, but he had never permitted his fears to make him quit hoping on that score. Fortunately, even fear could be counterbalanced by rage, by resentment over a seeming or actual wrong, or by anyone who tried to discourage him with disparagement. He was not trying to convince Thomas that such countermeasures were admirable; he was merely saying that in desperate phases of conflict some things happened unavoidably, and their value had to be measured by the consequences.

Thomas stopped talking about divorce, and returned to his wife. He brought his wife and children all the way from his poverty-stricken home in Hampshire to meet Frost's wife and children in Beaconsfield. Later, he went so far as to talk about moving from Hampshire to New Hampshire to live near Frost and establish himself before bringing his wife and children across the ocean; but he gave up that plan as being unfair to his wife and children. With Frost's encouragement and praise, he went back to his writing with a new determination. After he finished another book, he took a cycling vacation in Wales with his son Mervyn and they stopped with the Frosts at Little Iddens. By that time he had accepted the suggestion made by Frost that he should rent rooms in the Chandler cottage next door and bring his wife and children to Gloucestershire for the entire month of August.

In the course of this protracted campaign to save the life of a man he loved as a brother, Frost gave Thomas the greatest psychological assistance merely by reading aloud from essays in Thomas' *Pursuit of Spring* and by saying to Thomas that it was poetry, not prose; that all these years Thomas had been denying himself the right to be the one thing he couldn't help but be; that if this meant so much to him—if he still wanted, more than anything else, to be a poet—then his already proven abilities ought to give him the incentive he needed for developing these abilities.[16]

It worked. Thomas began to steal time from the necessity of hack writing so that he could get on with his recovered desire to make a name for himself as a poet. And he began this phase of his literary career by quite unashamedly imitating Frost, even by boasting to Frost that "this one sounds like Frost." The older man protested. He pointed out the ones which sounded most like Thomas and the idiom which should be cultivated because it was Thomas. This younger man's response was one of inexpressible gratitude to this American, this man so recently a stranger, who had done more for him than save his life.

During his last visit with Frost at The Gallows, Thomas accidentally enjoyed the spectacle of seeing Frost demonstrate, with completely unconscious and unintentional impulse, what he had meant by saying that some of his most cowardly fears were often overcome by rage. The incident occurred as the two men were returning from a long and aimless walk around the neighboring parts of Lord Beauchamp's estate. As they came out of the woods on a narrow lane, they saw and passed by the hated gamekeeper, who held his shotgun threateningly. Thomas was frightened and Frost was furious. As they walked on, he tried to give the background of this tension, but Thomas would have none of it; there was no satisfactory explanation for the gamekeeper's performance, and something should be done. Inflamed by Thomas' words, Frost was caught up in one of his glowing rages. Something would be done right now, he said, and Thomas could come back with him to see it done. They did not find the gamekeeper until they had tracked him to his cottage, where Frost gave him a piece of his mind. If ever he acted like that again Frost would beat the daylight out of him. The gamekeeper blustered, and Frost repeated his threat as he withdrew.[17]

That evening, the town constable knocked at the door of The

Gallows. He said that he had been sent with orders to arrest Frost, but that he had no intention of doing so. He was amused by Frost's threat and described the gamekeeper as a known bully. It would be necessary, however, to make a report to Lord Beauchamp concerning the incident, and he hoped that Frost wouldn't mind. A few days later Frost received a note of apology from Lord Beauchamp. Later, he learned from the constable that Beauchamp had called the gamekeeper on the carpet and told him that if he wanted so much to fight he had better enlist.

When Thomas left the Gallows, he made arrangements for a subsequent visit which never took place. Years later Helen Thomas made her own comment in print concerning their relationship:

". . . Between him [Robert Frost] and David [Edward Thomas] a most wonderful friendship grew up. He believed in David and loved him, understanding, as no other man had ever understood, his strange complex temperament. The influence of this man on David's intellectual life was profound, and to it alone of outside influences is to be attributed that final and fullest expression of himself which David now found in writing poetry. There began . . . a kind of spiritual and intellectual fulfillment which was to culminate two years later in his death."[18]

GOING HOME

. . . Still I was so anxious in the back of my mind to get home that I was glad for the moment when I heard it [North of Boston] was to be published in the United States. "Now we can go home," I said. "The book has gone home."[1]

IN HIS PERSISTENT CAMPAIGN on behalf of his poetry, Robert Frost had begun correspondence with more than one American publisher shortly after Mrs. Nutt informed him that her firm would publish *A Boy's Will*. The physical attractiveness of Mosher's books, well-designed and carefully printed, had prompted him to look with particular favor on Mosher's overtures, at least until Mrs. Nutt sternly informed him that she and she alone had the legal power to make arrangements with an American publisher.

New impetus given to this campaign after the entry of England into the war was reflected in letters to friends at home. By mid-August, Frost had mailed to several of them clippings of various laudatory reviews which appeared after *North of Boston* was published. A group of clippings sent to Sidney Cox was accompanied by a crisp and businesslike note: "I should take it kindly if you would pass these along. Anything you can do for me just at this time will be a double service. My only hope is that some interest will be taken in the book in America: here none can be from now on: people are too deeply concerned about the war."[2] In less than a month he suggested to Cox the next step in the campaign: "I shall write again soon and send you if you will let me some of David Nutts folders advertising my book."[3]

Long after Mrs. Nutt had completed arrangements with Holt for the publication of *North of Boston*, without Frost's knowing it, he surreptitiously continued his exchange of letters with Mosher concerning some kind of contract, possibly for the American publication of A Boy's Will: "I am content to leave it that way. Anything you care to give—It is not for me to make terms with you. All I have in mind is to reach through you an American public. So long as you get me read I shall ask no questions about royalties. Mrs. Nutt however is another matter. She would say that as one of her indentured poets I have no right to be corresponding with an American publisher even in friendship. In fact she has just forbidden me to have anything to do with American publishers. I must refer them all to her. She will be the difficulty."[4]

Perhaps on the same day that he wrote thus to Mosher, he increased the pressure on Cox: "It warms me cockles to see you so enthusiastic over my book. Three or four more such friends and I should be a made man. You have done so much more than you ought already that you wont object to doing a good deal more for me. So I send you with the book certain circulars to scatter. To be most effective they should go to people who care especially for you or for me or for poetry. But if you like you may give them to some boy to distribute on the street corner when the mills are emptying at night."[5] In his very next letter to Cox, written near the first of November, he made his most important announcement:

"This is only to say that Henry Holt will supply the book in America. Will you write that on any circulars you have still to send out?

"They say the germans have made the whole Atlantic unsafe. This raises questions for me.

1) Do I dare to go home now
2) Won't it be more dangerous to go every day we delay?
3) Won't it be impossible to get money across to live on pretty soon?
4) Do I dare to stay?

Perhaps you think I am joking. I am never so serious as when I am. . . ."[6]

As soon as Mrs. Nutt permitted Frost to know that he did have an American publisher for North of Boston, a new element was added to his campaign. It involved the windup of his affairs in England, the arrangement for a passage home, the possibility of taking with him the son of Edward Thomas, and the proper leave-taking of those who had helped him so much in London, in Gloucestershire, even in Scotland.[7]

In spite of the very serious talk of possibilities that London would be bombed at any moment by German zeppelins, Frost made several brief trips to London. He had explained his attitude on such matters to Edward Thomas; he said it again, from the Gallows, in another letter to Sidney Cox: "What a man will put into effect at any cost of time money life or lives is sacred and what counts. As I get older I dont want to hear about much else."[8] What he would put into effect at any cost was his ambition to increase his foothold as a good American poet. The war had not yet touched him deeply; it would not, until it had cost the life of Edward Thomas. But he followed with sympathy and interest whatever war poems he could find in periodicals, and he felt the tension between his own selfishness and the self-giving of Englishmen who were enlisting by the thousands:

". . . I have my work to think of too—though I dont get on with it to speak of in these unsettled times. The war has been a terrible detriment to pleasant thinking in spite of all I can do to approve of it philosophically. I don't know whether I like it or not. I don't think I have any right to like it when I am not called on to die in it. At the same time it seems almost cowardly not to approve of it on general principles simply because it is not my funeral. It seems little minded. There we will leave it. I hate it for those whose hearts are not in it and I fear they must be many, though perhaps not so many as it is the fashion to make them out, nor so many as they were in Nelson's navy for example where more than half the sailors, some say, were 'pressed' that is to say, kidnapped. One of the most earthly wise of our time thinks the common soldiers do actually know what they are fighting for and he has said so in the only good war poem I have seen. (Thomas Hardy's my man.)"[9]

His mention of "the only good war poem I have seen" was almost certainly a reference to Hardy's " 'Men Who March Away,' " dated "September 5, 1914," and containing views similar to Frost's, particularly in the last three stanzas:

> *Nay. We well see what we are doing,*
> *Though some may not see—*
> *Dalliers as they be—*
> *England's need are we;*
> *Her distress would leave us rueing:*
> *Nay. We well see what we are doing,*

[471]

Though some may not see!

In our heart of hearts believing
Victory crowns the just,
And that braggarts must
Surely bite the dust,
Press we to the field ungrieving,
In our heart of hearts believing
Victory crowns the just.

Hence the faith and fire within us
Men who march away
Ere the barn-cocks say
Night is growing gray,
Leaving all that here can win us;
Hence the faith and fire within us
Men who march away.[10]

In London Frost saw soldiers in uniform everywhere, even in Harold Monro's bookshop, where he talked at length with a young poet in uniform who introduced himself: Robert Graves.[11] The subject of their long talk, according to Graves, was the debate in Frost's mind whether he should or should not enlist in the British army. If he did seriously consider that possibility, his final decision was that he should not. His more immediate concern was the less-and-less distant reaction of American publishers to his unpublished verse; but some of his brief trips to London were made to sell a few more poems there and thus to eke out his immediate financial difficulties made acute by his plans to go home. To Harold Monro he managed to sell four newly-written poems, which appeared in *Poetry and Drama* for December 1914: "The Sound of Trees" (with implied reference to Abercrombie's elms called the Seven Sisters), "Putting in the Seed," "The Smile," and "The Cow in Apple Time."[12]

In making his farewell calls, Frost carefully avoided Ezra Pound, fearing that his troubles with Pound had already put him at a serious disadvantage with American publishers. Explaining the awkwardness of this relationship, Frost wrote to his major champion in the United States, Sidney Cox:

"I fear I am going to suffer a good deal at home by the support of Pound. This is a generous person who is doing his best to put me in the wrong light by his reviews of me: You will see the blow he has dealt me in Poetry (Chicago) for December, and yet it is with such good intention I suppose I shall have to thank him for it. I don't know about that—I may when I get round to it. The harm he does lies in this: he made up his mind in the short time I was friends with him (we quarreled in six weeks) to add me to his party of American literary refugees in London. Nothing could be more unfair, nothing better calculated to make me an exile for life. Another such review as the one in Poetry and I shan't be admitted at Ellis Island. This is no joke. Since the article was published I have been insulted and snubbed by two American editors I counted on as good friends. I dont repine and I am willing to wait for justice. But I do want someone to know that I am not a refugee and I am not in any way disloyal. . . ."[13]

More and more, his thoughts were on getting home, and all of his homesick children were delighted. By mail he completed arrangements with Edward and Helen Thomas to include fifteen-year-old Mervyn Thomas in his family, with the understanding that the boy was to live in Alstead, New Hampshire, with Russell Scott, a Thomas relative. After considerable difficulty, Frost booked passage on an American line ship, the *St. Paul*, scheduled to sail from Liverpool on 13 February 1915. In haste, the Frosts moved back from The Gallows to Little Iddens to collect their belongings and close the cottage. According to the plan, Thomas was to bring Mervyn to Little Iddens and would stay there while the Frosts finished packing, but the date of the visit was postponed briefly: "Elinor is tired to begin with so I don't suppose we can hope to do our packing in less than several days."[14]

As it happened, Mervyn had to come alone because Thomas was laid up with a badly sprained ankle. After some confusion, Mervyn and the Frosts arrived at Liverpool with time enough to spare for the writing of just a few more farewell notes. To Harold Monro, Frost wrote: "This with my best goodbyes. Thanks for everything. I had intended to see you before leaving but at the last moment we go rather precipitously; so that I am scanting duties. Anyway I don't want too much made of my going or I should feel as if I were never coming back. I shall be back just as soon as I have earned a little more living. England has become half my native land—England the victorious. Good friends I have had here and hope to keep."[15] To

Frank S. Flint, he wrote: "I ought to know by the length of your silence that you dont want to write to me any more—cor silicis. And if you don't I ought to have pride enough not to ask you to. But no matter: I must at least say goodbye to the man who opened England to me. You are good."[16]

After dark, on the night of 13 February 1915, the SS *St. Paul* worked her way out of Liverpool harbor and took her position in convoy with the enormous SS *Lusitania,* guarded by British destroyers which combed the waters with searchlights. Mines and submarines were feared. The passengers were told not to undress. Watertight compartments were sealed and everyone was nervous. After the tension of the first night there was general relaxation, and Frost was able to return in his thoughts to his own particular fears—and hopes—for what lay ahead in America.

The prospect was one which involved entering upon an entirely new phase of his life, and he was troubled not only by how the American publication of his books would be received but also by questions whether the royalties from them would provide a living. He assumed that he would have to find work of some kind and he dreamed of college teaching. He had already written to Sidney Cox: "I should awfully like a quiet job in a small college where I should be allowed to teach something a little new on the technique of writing and where I should have some honor for what I suppose myself to have done in poetry. Well, but I mustnt dream."[17] Edward Thomas had encouraged Frost to think that his new definition of a sentence might have a revolutionary effect not only on criticism but also on education, and yet it was obvious that the vested interests of college professors would resist innovation. Frost had touched on this point sarcastically in another letter to Cox: "There are a lot of completely educated people in the world and of course they will resent being asked to learn anything new."[18]

Nevertheless, he seriously pondered the problem of trying to correct another academic weakness which had continued to trouble him ever since he had walked off the campus of Dartmouth College in the winter of 1893. New impetus had been given his thoughts on this point when he browsed through the article on American literature in Abercrombie's set of the *Encyclopaedia Britannica* back at The Gallows. The article, written by the distinguished poet-critic-teacher, George Edward

Woodberry, had at least mentioned the failure of American universities to advance the cause of American literature: "The universities have not, on the whole, been its sources of fosterers, and they are now filled with research, useful for learning but impotent for literature."[19] After his own experiences at Dartmouth and Harvard, Frost made his complaint even more harsh by calling the university approach "the worst system of teaching that ever endangered a nations literature."[20] Before leaving The Gallows, Frost had spelled out his complaint even more specifically to Cox, and had proposed his own corrective:

". . . Everything is research for the sake of erudition. No one is taught to value himself for nice perception and cultivated taste. Knowledge knowledge. Why literature is the next thing to religion in which as you know or believe an ounce of faith is worth all the theology ever written. Sight and insight, give us those. I like the good old English way of muddling along in these things that we cant reduce to a science anyway such as literature love religion and friendship. People make their great strides in understanding literature at most unexpected times. I never caught another man's emotion in it more than when someone drew his finger over some seven lines of blank verse— beginning carefully and ending carefully—and saying simply 'From there to—there.' He know and I knew. We said no more. I don't see how you are going to teach the stuff except with some such light touch. And you cant afford to treat it all alike, I mean with equal German thoroughness and reverence if thoroughness is reverence. . . ."[21]

If he was able, however, to earn a living without teaching, and simply by remaining true to the writing of poetry, as he dreamed he might, there still remained the problem of where he would live. He was returning to America without any home base and he was free to choose. Several years earlier he had written Susan Hayes Ward: "Sometime we intend to be nearer New York than we are, if it can come about in the right way. But that is one of the dreams."[22] This was no longer a part of his dreams. During all the vicissitudes of homesickness back in England, he had noticed with interest that the images which came to view in his wistful imagination had nothing to do with New York. They were remembrances of places and people and things in Derry and Plymouth and Bethlehem, New Hampshire. Even at less distance he had said it to Susan Hayes Ward: ". . . the snug downhill churning room with the view over five ranges of mountains, our talks under the hanging lamp and over the fat blue book, the tea-inspired Mrs. Lynch, baseball, and the blue black Lafayette. There is a pang there that makes poetry. I rather like to gloat over it."[23]

On the *St. Paul*, as he sorted out possibilities, Frost found that he was now gloating over his chance to choose an abode high enough in the White Mountains to escape hay fever and to play at farming. He had said as much from Beaconsfield to Silver: "My dream would be to get the thing started in London and then do the rest of it from a farm in New England where I could live cheap and get Yankier and Yankier."[24] From Beaconsfield, even earlier, he had said more: "We can't hope to be happy long out of New England. I never knew how much of a Yankee I was till I had been out of New Hampshire a few months. I suppose the life in such towns as Plymouth and Derry and South Berwick is the best on earth."[25]

In all these dreams about where he would live when he reached home, and how he would earn a living, one fear kept bothering him. It was a paralyzing fear, which came over him in moments when circumstances made him lose his hard-earned confidence and doubt his own abilities. He had indiscreetly confessed it to one of his new literary acquaintances in London, under awkward circumstances, and he had regretted the confession ever since. The fear was that now, at the age of nearly forty-one, he had exhausted his creative powers as a poet.[26] In his darker moods he kept telling himself, incorrectly, that the little reputation he had made in England had been based too heavily on poems written in Derry around 1906 or before, and that the really fresh poetic response had somehow died nearly ten years ago. The best he had done, since then, was to take his early wares to market. If he received any recognition at home after the American edition of *North of Boston* appeared, he would naturally be asked to produce more of the same or something better. He could go back to his Derry notebooks and dig out poems written then; he could gather the waifs and strays he had recently left behind in Harold Monro's *Poetry and Drama*. He had enough for one more book. He might even write a few—only a few—new ones. But what then?

He had told Edward Thomas that he expected to keep fighting a continuous battle on various fronts as long as he lived, and that he'd have to settle for nothing more or less than temporary victories. He had said that anyone could survive if he possessed an intense desire to accomplish one particular thing. Now he was not so sure. It was unnerving to anticipate the kinds of demands which would be made on him at the very moment when he doubted whether he had the capacity to meet those demands.

The prospect frightened him. He foresaw that what lay ahead would severely test his belief that he had adequately worked out defenses against almost any overwhelmings. In a sense he was back where he had started, long ago, and he knew he would need all he could muster of skill and courage and valor and daring and heroism. Even then, perhaps the gulfs would wash him down.

All right, let the test come. This was his own private war and he liked it. Something inside him seemed to want him to fail; but something a little stronger than that seemed to want him to win. He still had the power to consist of the inconsistent, the power to hold in unity the ultimate irreconcileables, the power to be a bursting unity of opposites, and the power to make poetry out of these opposites. He would always be back where he had started, and he was ready to say again that what a man will put into effect at any cost of time or money or life or lives is sacred, and what counts.

NOTES

TABLE OF CONTENTS
FOR THE NOTES

In the Notes, whenever a last name or a short title is given as a reference, the Index will serve as a convenient guide to the first reference and the full citation.

NOTES

❧❧❧

INTRODUCTION

1. Quoted from RF's poem "The Generations of Men," *Complete Poems of Robert Frost* (New York, [1963]), p. 101—hereafter cited as *Complete Poems*.

2. RF to LT, 16 April 1957, Lawrance Thompson (ed.), *Selected Letters of Robert Frost* (New York, [1964]), p. 565—hereafter cited as *Selected Letters*.

3. Quoted in an unsigned article, "Frost: 'Courage Is the Virtue that Counts Most,'" *Newsweek*, 11 Feb. 1963, pp. 90-91.

4. RF to Robert S. Newdick, 2 Dec. 1938. MS, in private hands.

5. Matthew 5: 48.

6. Quoted from Browning's "Abt Vogler." The lines, "Ah, but a man's reach should exceed his grasp,/Or what's a heaven for?" occur in Browning's "Andrea del Sarto."

Browning's influence on the poetry of RF should be noted. Obliquely, RF often echoed the famous reach-grasp passage, as, for example, in a letter to *The Amherst Student* (*Selected Letters*, p. 418): "All ages of the world are bad—a great deal worse anyway than Heaven. If they weren't the world might just as well be Heaven at once and have it over with." (The implied emphasis there is on the chance for growth.)

7. On this point see particularly some statements by "Belle M. Frost" to a friend in *Selected Letters*, pp. 13-14. See Note 3 of Chapter 7 for a hint of RF's sympathy for many Swedenborgian concepts; see also Note 8 of Chapter 22.

8. See Chapter 29 for an account of how RF in England in 1913 told Ezra Pound a fictitious version of his relations with his grandfather and his great-uncle, Elihu Colcord; and of how Pound innocently printed this version as truth in his review of *A Boy's Will*. In that account reference is made to RF's saying later that when Mrs. Frost saw this version of the story in print she wept. RF never explained why she wept, but part of her reason may have been that she recognized the discrepancy between the truth and the often-repeated myth and that she was thus reminded of other discrepancies which had been even more painful to her.

9. RF to the Editor of *The Youth's Companion*, undated letter

written from Beaconsfield, England, either late in 1912 or early in 1913, MS in Amherst College Library.

10. Examples are cited in Note 13 of Chapter 29.

11. Quoted from RF's introductory essay, "The Constant Symbol," in *The Poems of Robert Frost* (New York, the Modern Library, [1946]), p. xvii.

12. Quoted from RF's introductory essay, "The Figure a Poem Makes," in *Complete Poems*, p. vi.

RF had various ways of coming to grips with his own confusions, but he liked to conceal the extent to which they troubled him. In this connection see the unconvincing line with which he ends his poem, "Directive": "Drink and be whole again beyond confusion." Repeatedly, in his public talks and readings, he combined joking with seriousness when he quoted a brief conversation with a man who complained that he was confused:

"All right, let's play the game of Confusion. Are you ready? First, I'll ask you. Are you really confused?"

"Yes, I am."

"Now you ask me."

"Are you confused, Mr. Frost?"

"No—I win!"

13. RF to *The Amherst Student, Selected Letters*, p. 418.

14. Ibid.

15. Quoted from "The Trial by Existence," *Complete Poems*, p. 28.

1. ONCE BY THE PACIFIC

1. Quoted from RF's poem "Once by the Pacific," *Complete Poems*, p. 314. Most of the material in this chapter is based on autobiographical reminiscences told by RF to LT over a period of twenty-five years and recorded by LT in journal form in a type-written document entitled (and hereafter cited as) "Notes on Robert Frost." Whenever possible, these reminiscences have been subjected to correction.

Information concerning RF's father has been drawn from RF's reminiscences and from the following sources: (a) the brief manuscript autobiography of WPF, Jr., which is printed in *Selected Letters*, pp. 601-602; (b) records of the Class of 1872, Harvard College Archives; (c) letters written by WPF, Jr., and printed in *Selected Letters*, pp. 5-11; (d) published reports of the Secretary, Harvard Class of 1872, as listed in Note 2 of Chapter 4, below; (e) published genealogies of the Frost family, as listed in *Selected Letters*, p. 599.

Information concerning RF's mother has been drawn from RF's

autobiographical reminiscences and from some other sources, as follows: (a) vital records of the Clerk of the City of Lawrence, Massachusetts, for birth and death dates of IMF; (b) letters written by IMF and printed in *Selected Letters*, pp. 11-14; (c) newspaper article by Robert S. Newdick, "How a Columbus Mother Inspired Her Son to Become the Dean of America's Living Poets," Columbus (Ohio) *Sunday Dispatch*, 17 May 1936, Graphic Section, p. 5; (d) typewritten genealogy of the immediate Moodie relatives, generously provided to LT by a distant relative of RF's, Mrs. Jean Moodie Walker Rau, of Stratham, New Hampshire; (e) newspaper articles concerning Isabelle Moodie and William Prescott Frost, Jr., in Lewistown, Pennsylvania, generously provided to LT by Mr. J. Martin Stroup, Librarian, Mifflin County Historical Society of Lewistown: "Almost Born in Lewistown/Robert Frost Says/Father Taught Here," Lewistown *Sentinel*, 6 November 1959, p. 1, and "Lewistown Academy: Setting for Romance," by J. Martin Stroup, Lewistown *Sentinel*, 13 November 1959, pp. 14, 16.

In the following notes representative examples may be found of different versions of RF's autobiographical reminiscences. These examples are taken primarily from the following six biographical studies:

(a) Jean Gould, *Robert Frost: The Aim Was Song* (New York, 1964)—hereafter cited as Gould, *Robert Frost*—wherein Miss Gould tries to improve on RF's anecdotes by adding her own imaginative embroideries;

(b) Louis Mertins, *Robert Frost: Life and Talks-Walking* (Norman, Oklahoma, [1965])—hereafter cited as Mertins, *Robert Frost*—wherein scores of factual errors occur, largely because Mr. Mertins did not follow RF's warning, ". . . don't trust me on my life. . . . Check up on me some.";

(c) Gorham B. Munson, *Robert Frost: A Study in Sensibility and Good Sense* (New York, 1927)—hereafter cited as Munson, *Robert Frost*—wherein, according to RF's repeated complaints, many anecdotes told to Mr. Munson by RF are inaccurately reported;

(d) Robert S. Newdick's various articles, wherein RF's anecdotes are handled with meticulous accuracy and are frequently extended by means of scholarly enrichments;

(e) Elizabeth Shepley Sergeant, *Robert Frost: The Trial By Existence* (New York, [1960])—hereafter cited as Sergeant, *Robert Frost*—wherein Miss Sergeant, after admitting that she wrote down from memory a great many of RF's anecdotes, gives them inaccurately as direct quotations;

(f) Daniel Smythe, *Robert Frost Speaks* (New York, 1964)—hereafter cited as Smythe, *Robert Frost*—wherein Mr. Smythe is also inaccurate when he gives some very familiar RF anecdotes as direct quotations, although internal and external evidences make it clear (as will be shown) that he was depending on his memory.

In the following notes frequent references will also be made to statements by RF which occur in his prose utterances, his press interviews, and his letters. Aside from *Selected Letters,* already cited, the following works are of particular importance in this connection:

Margaret Bartlett Anderson, *Robert Frost and John Bartlett: The Record of a Friendship* (New York, [1963])—hereafter cited as Anderson, *Frost-Bartlett.*

Hyde Cox and Edward Connery Lathem (eds.), *Selected Prose of Robert Frost* (New York, [1966])—hereafter cited as Cox and Lathem, *Selected Prose.*

Edward Connery Lathem (ed.), *Interviews with Robert Frost* (New York, [1966])—hereafter cited as Lathem, *Interviews.*

Louis Untermeyer (ed.), *The Letters of Robert Frost to Louis Untermeyer* (New York, [1963])—hereafter cited as *Frost-Untermeyer.*

2. According to RF, this anecdote was repeatedly told him by his mother; it was first told by RF to LT on 21 Feb. 1940, and recorded in LT's "Notes on Robert Frost" under that date.

3. Lewistown Academy had fallen on hard times and had apparently been closed during the year prior to the arrival of William Prescott Frost, Jr., and Isabelle Moodie. Founded in 1812, the Academy had prospered in a two-story building, erected in 1828, on East Third Street (the plot of ground now occupied by the Lewistown United Presbyterian Church's Christian Education Wing and Church House). The records indicate that the Academy had rarely needed more than two teachers. A news item in the (Lewistown) *Sentinel* for 6 September 1872 mentioned the new arrangement and the "efforts to re-establish the school":

"The Lewistown Academy was opened under Prof. Frost, who will be aided by Miss Belle Moodie, lately of Columbus, Ohio, High School, on yesterday, Thursday morning. We hope the efforts to re-establish the school by the directors will be liberally seconded, and the principal generously sustained."

"Miss Belle Moodie, lately an assistant teacher in the Columbus, Ohio, High School, has been engaged to take charge of the female department of Lewistown Academy. The lady entered upon the discharge of her duties on Wednesday last." (Quoted in J. Martin Stroup, op. cit.)

4. The Moodie genealogy, op. cit., states that the grandparents of Isabelle Moodie were Thomas Moodie and Mary Gordon Nicoll Moodie; that they had five sons; that their son Thomas (1814-1864), after going to the United States and living briefly in Cin-

cinnati married a Scottish girl named Jane Ashwell, moved to Columbus, Ohio, and took residence in a large house on the southwest corner of Sixth Street and State Street. To this home, Isabelle Moodie was brought by her grandmother, who then returned to Scotland. By the time Isabelle Moodie began to make this her home, there were four girls in the family of her uncle and aunt: Euphemia, Jeanie, Fannie, Florence. Of these, the first two were older than Isabelle Moodie and the last two were younger. Among the four, Isabelle Moodie remained most intimate with Jeanie and Florence.

The Moodie genealogy does not give the names of the parents of Isabelle Moodie; but it does state that she had an older brother, Thomas Moodie, who became a sea captain, settled in New Zealand, married, and had two sons; that one of these sons, John Moodie, made a trip to America in 1928 and visited his relatives. From other sources it is known that this John Moodie, during these visits, called on his cousin Robert Frost.

5. Quoted in J. Martin Stroup, op. cit.

6. The entire letter is quoted in *Selected Letters*, pp. 5-7.

7. Ibid.

8. Ibid.

9. J. Martin Stroup, op. cit., quotes from the (Lewistown) *Sentinel* for 21 March 1873 the following notice, which appeared in the list of marriages:

"Frost-Moodie—at the residence of G. W. Elder Esq., on Tuesday evening, March 18, 1873, by Rev. O. O. McClean, D. D., assisted by Rev. J. H. Brown. Prof. Wm. P. Frost and Miss Belle Moodie, both of the [staff of the] Lewistown Academy."

George W. Elder was an attorney and was also the president of the Board of Trustees of Lewistown Academy at the time. He was the prime mover in trying to re-establish a teaching program in the Academy; it is therefore possible that the two teachers had roomed and boarded in his home since their arrival in Lewistown.

The marriage certificate of William P. Frost, Jr., and "Miss Belle Moodey" has been preserved; it is in the Clifton Waller Barrett Library of the University of Virginia Library—hereafter referred to as Barrett Collection, Virginia.

10. J. Martin Stroup (op. cit.) states that the editor of the (Lewistown) *Sentinel* in 1872-1873 was also a member of the Board of Trustees of Lewistown Academy: H. J. Walters; that Mr. Walters' position seems to explain the vehemence with which he commented on the planned departure of the Frosts in the issue of the *Sentinel* for 25 April 1873:

"We have done our utmost . . . to lift this institution out of the 'slough' of the past. The President of the Board, Geo. W. Elder, Esq., actively seconded the efforts of his colleagues, and engaged

Prof. Wm. P. Frost Jr., an accomplished scholar and capable instructor to take charge. . . . The Trustees of the Lewistown Academy have given honest, conscientious effort to avoid the necessity of sending your children abroad for preparatory instruction, beyond what the common schools afford. To this end they encouraged Prof. Frost to come here. He came. He employed a competent lady to give instructions to the girls. You have not sustained the Trustees; and, as Prof. Frost cannot live on air, he has been compelled to resign, to take effect at the close of the present term. . . . These are plain words, but they are true, and lamenting the cause of his resignation [we] confess our mortification that there should be a cause for it."

(Note, there, the statement, "He employed a competent lady to give instructions to the girls." The original letter has been preserved, in which WPF, Jr., invited IM to accept the position as teacher; the letter is now in the possession of RF's daughter, Mrs. Lesley Frost Ballantine.)

11. Various details of the arrival of WPF, Jr., in San Francisco are drawn from his letter to IMF dated 13 July 1873, *Selected Letters*, pp. 8-10.

12. Apparently the best information we have concerning the birthplace of RF in San Francisco, and yet by no means adequate, occurs in a letter from Mrs. Elinor White Frost to Mrs. Edna Davis Romig (written in Key West, Florida, dated 4 Feb. [1935]; owned by Frederick B. Adams, Jr.; hereafter cited as, letter, Mrs. Frost to Mrs. Romig, 4 Feb. 1935): ". . . It was a frame house on Washington St. in San Francisco, three blocks below Leavenworth St. He [RF] and I spent two days in San Francisco three years ago—the first time he had been there since leaving when he was eleven years old. We looked for the birthplace, and also for the last house he lived in, at 1404 Leavenworth St. Both had been burned in the fire that followed the earthquake." The third block below Leavenworth Street on Washington Street lies between Larkin and Polk. Frost's parents moved so often, during their residence in California, that it was impossible for anyone (and perhaps their various creditors) to keep up with them. In Henry G. Langley, editor, *The San Francisco Directory For the Year Commencing April 1874*, San Francisco, 1874, WPF, Jr., is listed as living at 14 Eddy Place, which extended off the southern side of Post Street, between Mason and Powell streets, three blocks north of Pine Street. The address at which the Frosts first lived in 1873, 737 Pine Street, occurs in the letter from WPF, Jr., to IMF dated 13 July 1873; see *Selected Letters*, p. 10. The listings given in Langley's *Directory*, concerning the address of the Frost family, "commencing April" of each year are as follows:

1874   14 Eddy Place [off Post, between Mason and Powell]
1875   1630 Sacramento [between Larkin and Polk]
1876   1630 Sacramento [between Larkin and Polk]
1877   Abbotsford House [corner, Broadway and Larkin]
1878   [no "dwelling" given; but was Inglewood Hotel, according to RF]
1879   1431 Steiner [near corner of Ellis]
1880   3 Grace Terrace [off south side of California, between Grant (later named Dupont) and Stockton]
1881   Abbotsford House [corner, Broadway and Larkin]
1882   Abbotsford House [corner, Broadway and Larkin]
1883   1404 Leavenworth [east side, near Washington, between Washington and Jackson]
1884   1404 Leavenworth
1885   1404 Leavenworth

Because Mrs. Frost's letter of 4 February 1935 implies that RF then thought he remembered correctly the family tradition (presumably told him by his mother, years after the event) that he was born in a frame house on Washington Street, three blocks below Leavenworth (i. e., between Larkin and Polk), there is at least the possibility (suggested by the Langley listings) that the house his mother tried to remember, after so many moves, was indeed between Larkin and Polk, but that it was on Sacramento Street, two blocks south of Washington. Langley's 1875 and 1876 listings of "1630 Sacramento" (which was between Larkin and Polk) supports this possibility. At present, however, there is no certain evidence concerning the precise address of the San Francisco birthplace of RF.

2. ESTRANGEMENTS

1. Quoted from the poem "Home Burial," *Complete Poems,* pp. 70-71.

2. One of RF's notes on the Reverend John Doughty (1825-1893) occurs on the verso of the title page of a copy of a pamphlet which bears the following pertinent title page data: *The Parable of Creation, Being a Presentation of the Spiritual Sense of the Mosaic Narrative as Contained in the First Chapter of Genesis,* by Reverend John Doughty, author of "The World Beyond," "The Garden of Eden," "The Secrets of the Bible," etc. etc. (Swedenborg Library and Tract Society, San Francisco, 1892). On the verso RF wrote as follows: "I remember John Doughty's house and garden below us on Leavenworth Street [1883-1885]. Our house was 1404 —two doors below the corner of Washington Street. I remember

being in his Sunday School. If I'm not mistaken the Indians had done something to his scalp when he was crossing the plains. He was a grave looking man with long beard and a heavy cane. Robert Frost." (Louis Mertins Collection of Frostiana, University of California Library, Berkeley, California.)

3. The place and date of birth for this child (Jeanie Florence Frost) is corroborated by the records of vital statistics in the office of the Clerk of the City of Lawrence, Massachusetts. The evidence of these records indicates that IMF at least tentatively named her child Jeanie Florence soon after the child's birth.

4. Passing reference to IMF's visit with the Newton family in Greenfield, Massachusetts, during the summer of 1876, is contained in a letter from IMF to Sarah Newton, dated 17 June 1883; see *Selected Letters*, pp. 13-14. The Newton homestead subsequently became a unit of the Stoneleigh-Prospect School.

5. Letter, IMF to WPF, Jr., 1 Nov. 1876; quoted in full in *Selected Letters*, pp. 11-13.

6. Ibid.

7. Ibid.

3 · GOLDEN GATE

1. Quoted from the poem "A Peck of Gold," *Complete Poems*, p. 312.

2. *Selected Letters*, p. 11; the letter is dated 25 Oct. 1874.

3. *Selected Letters*, p. 12; the letter is dated 1 Nov. [1876].

4. "The Artist's Motive" was published in the San Francisco *Daily Evening Post*, 29 March 1884, p. 6, col. 1. Because it provides important evidence concerning the literary interests and religious concerns of RF's mother, who had a lasting influence on his literary career, "The Artist's Motive" is here quoted in its entirety:

> 'Tis nearly done! And when it is—my picture, here,
> I'll cast it forth as naught into the hand that gives
> To me what most I need—gold, gold!
> Oh, weary heart, press on this hand
> So weary that it seems as if
> The cord which joins ye were unloosed;
> And cold and hunger make me weak,
> While famished eyes of wife and babes
> Bring forth the wish that theirs and mine
> Were closed forever in eternal sleep.
> *
> The picture's bought, and we have bread.
> Thank God for this! We will not sigh,

For that it hangs upon the wall
Of him who only knows 'tis real
Because his purse is lighter than before.
The work so forced, perchance, is worth no better
       place.
But see, dear wife, how bright the little ones appear
Since food and warmth have smiled upon them.
I loathe this work whipped from me
By the lash of dire distress.
Let thy sweet face, dear one, shine forth
Encircled by these cherub babes
Which God hath given—bud and blossom
Bloom between me and the canvas.
Then from my soul my best shall come,
Drawn by their magnet power.

*

The rich have bought my work until I'm rich myself.
How affluent in joy at seeing dear ones free from care
I ne'er may tell. And now I paint, no longer poor and
       tired:
Fingers no longer stiff and cold.
But supple with a fever, so delicious and intense
My blood seems coursing through my veins
To unheard music, grand, sublime.
My name is often heard upon the lips of men
In words of praise: and critics, far and wide,
Dare not reveal a flaw, lest they undo themselves.
But what is wrong with me to-day?
I strive in vain to give this nun a look of sweet
       humility.
Adorned in robes expressive of her life
Of such sweet self-loss, she seems to walk
With haughty mien: so, too, the child,
In rags, she's leading by the hand,
Looks proud as any queen—
I'll try once more! Oh, weary hours!
Oh, heartsick soul! In vain! In vain
I work—each form is born in pride.
And e'en the flowers, those fairest types of innocent
       humility,
Flaunt proudly in the air. From off my easel,
Mirror of a haughty soul, I'll take thee.
Thou mayst not go unto the world
And blazon forth my secret soul.
Into the flames I cast thee now.
As thou dost burn, so burn—oh, conscience—

[489]

Every low, false thought of pride
That gave so foul a birth.

*

Months have rolled by, dear easel,
Since thus I sat before thee:
And I have gazed with faithful eye
Upon the face of nature since
This hand, most false, dared to caress thee.
While gazing thus, fair truth so grandly
Dawned upon my soul that pride
Hath fallen nevermore to rise.
Take, then, unto thine arms, dear friend,
The offspring fair of truth alone.
So I have toiled all day for truth.
Sometime with steady hand, and then
Again so tremblingly and slow,
That heart turned sick at the poor line
Which needs must be erased, and said:
"Alas! thou art not ready for this work divine.
Thou must attend once more God's School:
Yea, many times, and add to thy poor soul of truth
Rich gems from his exhaustless store."
Yet I have striven patiently
To give what I had gained, and now—.
Why, what's the matter with our boy?
Oh, darling one, he's crying for the roses
Blooming here upon my canvas.
And he says they smell so sweet.
Enough! Enough! I asked for honest toil not more
　　　than this.
But much more came, for God doth give,
To him that hath, abundant store.
Men bought and said: "How true to life;"
And once a man of noble mind—
Rich, too, in worldly goods—gave wealth
For one, the best of all, to chase
The gloom that hovered round the bed
Of his dear, dying wife. She had
Not looked upon the grass and flowers
For many a day. Her eyes, too weak
To gaze on nature dipped in dyes
Of heaven's own light, looked fondly on
This soft and fair landscape of mine.
One day she fell asleep and dreamed
Of wandering by that stream with those she loved,
Then woke and said: "I shall see the tree of life that grows

Close by the stream of God." And so
She passed, consoled by my poor work,
To landscapes of the world beyond.
Thus labor took unto itself diviner form
Poured into molds of use for dear humanity.
So tasks grew easy, and there came
A time of wonder to my soul.
While working on a piece that all
Great artists love, "Christ blessing little children,"
'Twas there a new sense thrilled my soul:
For Truth with gentle hand had led
Me over rough, uncertain roads
Into a place serene with holy light
Where dwelt her fairer sister, Love.
And now the picture glows before me.
Heart, mind and hand, so closely
Wedded are they, act in perfect unison.
Oh! Such a fire doth burn within my soul,
That it must be consumed, did not it give
Unto the world the light and warmth thereof.
The scene is a most holy one.
'Twas thou, oh Truth, that led my soul
To lean upon the heart of God
Which burst in sacred light before mine eyes
Whence flowed to me the spark divine
Upon my canvas here. Oh, face of Christ, God seems to
        shine
From you as once He did when thou,
The lowly one, didst walk here on the earth,
"God manifest in flesh."
And as I gaze, so sweet a sense
O'er-sweeps my soul that from its power
I kneel not to the picture
But to that divinity which gave it birth.
I rise baptized in love: henceforth
To work, with truth to point the way
And love to speed me on rejoicing.
I rose and lo! men knelt beside me
Worshipping. Thanks be to God, not me
Nor mine. Ah no, but to the Infinite
Which shone therefrom and touched their hearts
With its most gracious benediction.

In "The Artist's Motive" may be found at least a thematic indication that Emerson, as well as Browning, made strong appeal to

Mrs. Frost. Part of her theme is that the artist is at his best when he is motivated to make his art reflect a transcendent and ultimate Reality, Truth, Love. Her son, also very strongly influenced by Emerson and Browning (under her guidance), built into his esthetic this identical artistic motive.

One of RF's most revealing *ex cathedra* utterances on this point was made in 1956. A Princeton student writing his senior thesis on "Robert Frost's Poetic Uses of Nature" discussed his topic privately with RF. As soon as RF was told the title of the thesis, he asked the student, "How far are you going to take it?" The student answered that he had not yet decided. RF, as though to give a hint which would be helpful and admonitory, drew himself erect before making his pronouncement. Then he raised his right arm in a sincere oratorical gesture, made a sweeping spiral motion above his head with his uplifted hand, pointed his index finger straight up, and, with the gravity of an Old Testament prophet or psalmist, said,

"If you want to please me, you've got to take it—*all the way!*"

5. One of these stories, "The Land of Crystal," is considered at length in Chapter 4 and in the notes for that chapter. RF once referred to a particular book which his mother reviewed: "I said at sixty or so the first book I remembered the looks of was a book of verse by Robert Herrick that must have come into our house for my mother to review in my father[']s newspaper when I was seven or eight years old in San Francisco. . . ." *Selected Letters,* p. 498.

6. This incident was commemorated poetically by RF, years later, in the poem "At Woodward's Gardens," *Complete Poems,* pp. 379-380.

7. Except as otherwise indicated, all of the narrative materials in this chapter are based on LT's notes from conversations with RF.

4. WE ALL MUST EAT OUR PECK

1. Quoted from the poem "A Peck of Gold," *Complete Poems,* p. 312.

2. Harvard College Archives for the Class of 1872 contain a copy of the Rosecrans pamphlet: *William Starke Rosecrans, His Life and Public Services* (San Francisco, Democratic Congressional Committee, 1880). One very valuable source of information on the activities of WPF, Jr., in San Francisco, together with many specific dates, is the paraphrase of letters written by WPF, Jr., to his Class Secretary; paraphrases which appear in the various published issues of the *Secretary's Report, Class of 1872,* as follows: No. 1 (June 1872), No. 2 (June 1875), No. 3 (June 1878), No. 4

(June 1881), No. 5 (June 1885). A chronological summary of basic facts and dates concerning WPF, Jr., in these five reports follows:

1872	June 26	Was graduated from Harvard College.
	Sept. 1	Began his work as Principal of Lewistown Academy, Lewistown, Pennsylvania.
1873	March 18	Was married to Isabelle Moodie.
	June	Started for San Francisco.
	August	". . . became connected with the *Daily Evening Bulletin* as an editorial writer and stenographic reporter . . ."
1874	March 26	Date given for birth of Robert Lee Frost.
1875	Sept.	". . . resigned [from position on *Bulletin*] and accepted city editorship of *Daily Evening Post* . . ."
1876	June 25	Date given for birth of Jeanie Florence Frost.
1877	(year of)	Secretary of the Harvard Club of San Francisco.
1880	June	Delegate to the National Democratic Convention, Cincinnati, Ohio. Author of *William Starke Rosecrans*. Co-author, with P. J. Murphy, of *Campaign Handbook*.
1881	Feb. 28	Relinquished his duties as city editor of *Daily Evening Post* to assume "the business management of" the same newspaper.
1884	June 1	"Closed his connection with *Evening Post*. . . . Was afterwards attached for a few months to the staff of *The Daily Report*, since which time continued ill health has compelled him to cease employment. In 1884 he wrote a Democratic campaign pamphlet entitled *Sumptuary Laws*."
1885	May 5	". . . died at San Francisco . . . of consumption . . ."

3. *The Land of Crystal* may have been printed for private distribution. The title page does not bear the name of a publisher, does not even bear the place and date of publication or printing. Nevertheless, after the final sentence of the story, on p. 30, the following printed place-and-date statement occurs: "San Francisco, Cal., December 10, 1884."

4. The importance of *The Land of Crystal*, in throwing light on the religiously moralistic temperament of RF's mother, may justify a more detailed summary and analysis of the story here. At the start the man who is represented as the narrator tells how he was

[493]

transported to Fairy-land ("that realm which lies midway between heaven and earth") by a fairy guide named Find-all. As soon as Find-all explains to the narrator why the latter has been granted the boon of this voyage, the pious moral seriousness of the story begins to emerge:

" 'A fairy whispered in my ear that you loved the children and none but lovers of the little ones can enter Fairy-land.' " (The narrator immediately interpolates:) "How glad was I that I had the pass which would take me into a place of such delight—not money, not fine clothes, but love—love for the little ones! Mark you, dear children, love is the golden key which opens the door to all that is grand and good."

As the narrator and his guide are about to make their ascent to Fairy-land, they become aware of earth's evening rituals which involve the little ones:

"At this moment, the little ones are at mother's knee, eager to tell her one thing more; the gentle 'hush' is heard; the evening prayer is said, the good-night kiss is given; then away to their happy dream-land . . . and the sweet harmony of the children's prayers, like the ring of a silver bell, blending with the music of heaven."

The narrator, after arriving in the crystalline regions of Fairy-land, and after meeting the fairy sisters who are pointedly typed by their names—Merrilie and Sombreena—discovers that he can see right through their bodies to their symbolic hearts. As soon as he describes the heart of Sombreena and explains the consequent emanation of sorrow throughout the fairy family, the narrator moralizes on sorrow:

"And what do you think was the cause of it, children? I will tell you: a bad heart. In Fairy-land and out of it, sorrow has ever the same cause. With every beat of a wicked heart, there goes out into the world somewhere a throb of pain."

Merrilie, trying to help her stubborn sister, gently utters words of kind advice: "My own dear sister, why did you get so angry to-day? I saw the terrible tiger that haunts you in those moods, and he looked larger and wilder than ever before. I fear he will carry you off one of these days, if you do not try to woo back the white dove, with a kind and gentle soul." At this point in the story the narrator adds piously, "If anything could win back this erring child to Heaven's love-path, it must be the influence of this sister who was walking therein." Merrilie, continuing her exhortations, returns to what might be characterized as the Swedenborgian doctrine of divine influx or the Neo-Platonic doctrine of emanation:

"Ah, sister, the streams of good are flowing in every direction from the Heaven-land, if you would only open your heart upward; instead, you open it downward, towards the evil, which rushes in and leaves no room for the good." The wisdom-loving Find-all immediately adds his warning, with kindly intent: "Yes, my dear child, if you are not careful, you will be off to that terrible region where the wolf, the hyena, and the tiger reign supreme. In place of this loveliness, you will have nothing but the darkness of night; for, instead of the music which you love so much, you will hear the hideous cry of these wild creatures, and instead of these flowers at your feet, will grow the deadly nightshade."

The wayward Sombreena persists in her stubborn course until she suddenly does become transformed into a tiger. Then Find-all is forced to banish her and to cast her out into the dark wilderness where she might have remained eternally if the noble Prince had not come to redeem her.

Deeper religious configurations are foreshadowed at this point in the story: the name of the Prince is Agneau-Leon—and the context clearly implies analogies with the Lamb-Lion correlation in the Bible: Revelation 5. The Prince, in some of his remarks, implicitly paraphrases certain moralizings in Christ's Sermon on the Mount and also introduces certain idealistic social preachments akin to those made by Henry George in San Francisco concerning a sound land-policy:

"His conversation was very interesting. From it I learned that the people in this Fairy-land owned only what they worked for; that land, air, light and water, which were Heaven's gift to all, no person could lay hold upon and call his own in order to sell to others for gold, but that they were free to all. And as no man wanted more air than he could breathe, neither did he wish for more land than he could use. Thus no one was very rich and no one need be very poor."

When Prince Agneau-Leon takes on himself the symbolic task of descending into the regions of darkness to redeem the lost Sombreena from animality, the action dramatizes further symbolic meanings: "Vipers crawled on the ground, hyenas crouched in their dens ready to spring upon whoever approached . . . With one mighty effort of his will he showed the lion which lay at his heart, not as the lamb-lion, but as one wild and daring, ready for a fierce encounter."

After the triumphant battle between good and evil has effected the complete redemption and re-transformation of Sombreena, she returns chastened and repentant with the Prince; then follows the wedding of Merrilie to the Prince: ". . . indeed a true marriage, the love of the good and true in each being the tie that bound them. The prophetic fairies sang of their future bliss, and how their home would be a center of light in the land, helping others to more exalted lives. . . . The union proved what the prophetic fairies had said. Hand in hand they worked for the good of all, so peace and love flowed in on every side."

As an epilogue to the story a sketch is given of Sombreena's later life: She married and had her own children to whom she often told the story of "how once, by being self-willed, a terrible tiger lay at her heart, and what fearful sorrow it caused her." Whenever her children marveled at the story of her double transformation Sombreena would answer, "It is the work of the Great Spirit of Good, which, if we are only willing, flows ever to our souls from the beautiful Heaven-land."

Mrs. Frost, in fashioning this fairy tale about a naughty child turned into an animal, was working within a specialized "metamorphosis" tradition. That tradition includes not only Charles Kingsley's *Water Babies* ("For then you will believe the one true doctrine of this wonderful fairy tale; which is, that your soul makes your body") but also a collection of anonymous stories published by Isaiah Thomas in Worcester, Mass., in 1879, under this revealing title: *Vice in Its Proper Shape; or, The Wonderful and Melancholy Transformation of Several Naughty Masters and Misses into Those Contemptible Animals which They Most Resemble in Disposition.*

Mrs. Frost may not have had enough second sight to realize that her symbolic and allegorical story vaguely prophesied what would happen psychologically to her daughter, Jeanie, or that Jeanie would become obsessively fascinated by the notion of crystalline beings who could be seen through. In 1925, after Jeanie had been committed permanently to a mental hospital, she wrote to her brother that she could see into and through another person's mind; that it was difficult to do so when there were two heads in a straight line from her; but that even then she could do it—with both. *Selected Letters*, pp. 317-318.

5. RF's various accounts of this story, as told by RF to LT, and as recorded in "Notes on Robert Frost" at intervals over a period of several years, are not entirely in accord with the following account, given in Munson (*Robert Frost*, p. 28):

"Before he left San Francisco, he had begun a serial story. It concerned the doings of a lost and forgotten tribe living in a ravine no one of the outside world knew about. After he came east, he continued this serial from time to time, filling in the details of scenery and inhabitants.

"Here we strike a master-image, one that constantly recurs in Frost's life. . . . The poet has confessed that often he puts himself to sleep by dreaming of this inaccessible and sometimes happy tribe defending its canyon. One hopes that this recurrent and dominant image will not be subjected to the ingenious but suspect leaps to conclusions of the psychoanalysts. . . ."

Munson's hope, there, is pertinent. Freudians may proceed, here, at their own risk.

5. THE LOVELY SHALL BE CHOOSERS

1. Quoted from "The Lovely Shall Be Choosers," *Complete Poems*, p. 326. Repeatedly RF told LT (and others) that this poem had been written in commemoration of his mother's life, destroyed by hardships. The title, viewed within the context provided by the poem itself, implies the theological concept of moral responsibility based on free choice; but the poem implicitly contradicts it by dramatizing the more pertinent idea of victimization by forces beyond the control of the individual, whose choices are thus made ineffectual. A further interpretation of "The Lovely Shall Be Choosers" occurs in Chapter 23, and in the notes to that chapter.

2. Quoted by Gardner Jackson in a newspaper article entitled, " 'I Will Teach Only When I Have Something to Tell,' " *Boston Sunday Globe*, 23 Nov. 1924, Editorial Section, p. 3.

3. Discrimination is required in trying to understand the actual characteristics of RF's grandparents, William Prescott Frost and Judith Colcord Frost. Although it is clear that their grandson, during his boyhood, may have misjudged them, there is evidence that others thought they displayed oddities. Retrospectively, RF's friend Carl Burell wrote:

". . . Rob's grandmother was a strange type . . . I did not know her as well as I did her husband but I was very friendly with her brother [Elihu W. Colcord] . . . I really knew these two queer old men and understood them better and certainly better appreciated (much better) their good points [than Rob did]. The trouble was they were of the type that doesn't care a damn whether Rob or anybody else appreciated them or not and they were just the type I could and did appreciate, but Rob could not." (Letter, Carl Burell to Mrs. Edna Davis Romig, written from Manchester, N. H., 5 March 1935; owned by Frederick B. Adams, Jr.)

Beneath the outward severity, coldness, and apparent hostility of RF's grandfather was a warmth and affection expressed in the generous terms of his financial assistance to RF and his sister. For further details concerning various forms of help given RF by his grandfather from 1892 to 1901 and (through the will) during years thereafter, see chapters 13, 20, and 21.

6. AMONG THE HUMBLEST

1. Quoted from "The Lovely Shall Be Choosers," *Complete Poems*, p. 326.

2. The anecdote about RF's fondness for whittling in school is

based on the corroborative reminiscences of several former class-mates in Salem. One of these, Mrs. Emma Smith Turner, initially helped LT to establish contact with others who remembered the Frosts in Salem. In a letter to LT, dated 3 March 1940, Mrs. Turner wrote:

". . . There are a number of people in town that remember him [RF] but most of them just laugh, for as a boy he was so different and was so lazy and useless. His mother did not help out the situation, she had such a poor outward appearance and had such an [unfortunate] experience with her teaching. Those are the things they like to remember. As I remember her she was a beautiful Christian woman and I certainly got much good from her. . . . they were certainly ill-treated in this town. His sister Jeanie was also a beautiful character. We were very friendly. She loved to tell stories, was very scholarly and old for her age."

3. For the complete texts of the four notes from RF to Sabra Peabody, see *Selected Letters*, pp. 17-18. The notes survived accidentally, hidden in a compartment of Sabra Peabody's pencil box, used by her in District School Number Six and thereafter preserved by neglect in the attic of the Peabody family home until accidentally discovered there by Sabra Peabody Woodbury (Mrs. Levi Woodbury) in 1946. She subsequently gave the four notes to The Jones Library in Amherst, Massachusetts.

4. Mrs. Agatha Chase Maxwell provided details concerning this phase of the Salem crisis. Her vivid recollections were frequently corroborated and amplified by those of Mrs. Emma Smith Turner, Mrs. Ethel Wade Bartlett, and Mrs. Sabra Peabody Woodbury. During LT's first visit to Salem, in 1940, Mrs. Maxwell displayed several school textbooks she had used while studying under Mrs. Frost in Salem. Another pupil of Mrs. Frost's in Salem, Mrs. Nellie Hall Fry, possessed and permitted LT to have a copy made of a grammar-school group photograph (taken, she believed, in 1887) showing among the others Mrs. Frost, her two children, and Sabra Peabody.

7 · CASEMENTS OPENING

1. Quoted from "Waiting: Afield at Dusk," *Complete Poems*, p. 20.

In this chapter, many details are based on RF's autobiographical reminiscences in conversations with LT. For references to RF's early reading, see a supporting quotation which occurs in Note 3 of Chapter 8. For references to RF's grammar-school texts, see Note 4 of Chapter 6.

2. One of RF's variant versions of how this copy of *Ossian* survived from San Francisco days is quoted in Note 2 of Chapter 12.

3. Although RF admitted that he had read Swedenborg's *Divine Love and Wisdom,* from which this passage is taken, his reticence concerning the sympathy he had with many Swedenborgian concepts seemed to indicate that he thought these were some of the ideals which "will bear some keeping still about." See Note 8 of Chapter 22.

4. RF's own explanation of how his mother became a Swedenborgian through the influence of Emerson is contained in the passage quoted in Note 6 of this chapter.

5. Emerson, "The Poet," in *Complete Essays and Other Writings of Ralph Waldo Emerson* (New York, [1940]), p. 327.

6. RF's very strong admiration for Emerson found one of its most extended statements in the acceptance speech which he made on 8 October 1958, when the American Academy of Arts and Sciences awarded the Emerson-Thoreau Medal to him, "in recognition of his long and distinguished contribution to the creative arts." The following excerpts from that speech have particular autobiographical significance:

". . . Naturally on this proud occasion I should like to make myself as much of an Emersonian as I can. . . . My mother was a Presbyterian. We were here on my father's side for three hundred years but my mother was fresh—a Presbyterian from Scotland. The smart thing when she was young was to be reading Emerson and Poe as it is today to be reading St. John Perse or T. S. Eliot. Reading Emerson turned her into a Unitarian. That was about the time I came into the world; so I suppose I started a sort of Presbyterian-Unitarian. I was transitional. Reading on into Emerson, that is, into *Representative Men*, until she got to 'Swedenborg; or, the Mystic,' made her a Swedenborgian. I was brought up in all three of these religions, I suppose. I don't know whether I was baptized in them all. [LT's note: RF was joking; he knew very well he was baptized only in the Swedenborgian Church.] But as you see it was pretty much under the auspices of Emerson. It was all very Emersonian. Phrases of his began to come to me early. In that essay on the mystic he makes Swedenborg say that in the highest heaven nothing is arrived at by dispute. . . . Some of my first thinking about my own language was certainly Emersonian. 'Cut these sentences and they bleed,' he says. I am not submissive enough to want to be a follower, but he had me there. I never got over that. He came pretty near making me an anti-vocabularian with the passage in 'Monadnock' about our ancient speech. He blended praise and dispraise of the country people of New Hampshire. As an abolitionist he was against their politics. Forty per cent of them were States' rights Democrats in sympathy with the South. They were really pretty bad, my own relatives included. . . ."
(Robert Frost, "On Emerson," in *Daedalus: Journal of the American Academy of Arts and Sciences*, Vol. 88, No. 4 [Fall, 1959], pp.

712-713; the complete text is quoted in Cox and Lathem, *Selected Prose,* pp. 111-119).

8. VINCIT QUI SE VINCIT

1. Quoted from RF's valedictory address, "A Monument to Afterthought Unveiled," Lawrence (Mass.) *High School Bulletin,* Vol. XIII, No. 10 (June, 1892), p. 10—hereafter cited as *Bulletin.*

2. RF, in reminiscences made years later, either forgot or deliberately misrepresented the fact that there was a program of English study offered at Lawrence High School while he was attending it. For some examples of, and comments on, his repeatedly misleading references to this fact, see Note 3 of Chapter 12. RF may never have known that his father, while a student at Lawrence High School, took courses not only Latin and Greek but also in English and American authors. See the account of his early life, written by WPF, Jr., contained in the Harvard Archives, Class of 1872, Harvard University Library; or see another copy of the same account, also in the handwriting of WPF, Jr., in the Barrett Collection, Virginia. The pertinent passage is omitted in the partial version of this account which is quoted in *Selected Letters,* pp. 601-602.

3. The previously cited letter, Mrs. Frost to Mrs. Romig, 4 Feb. 1935, contains the following references to RF's early reading and memorizing:

". . . He never read [all the way through] a book of any kind to himself before his 14th year. His mother read aloud constantly. Poe and Shakespeare, George McDonald [Macdonald]—old fashioned romances, like The Romance of Dollard. In his 14th year he read Jane Porter's Scottish Chiefs, Mysterious Island by Jules Verne, Tom Browne's School Days, first volume of Scott's Tales of a Grandfather, Prescott's Conquest of Mexico, and also The Last of the Mohicans, and Deerslayer. . . . Read first poetry in 15th year. . . . In that year he read a little of Shelley and Keats in Christmas gift books. Almost learned all of Poe by heart. Keats and Arnold only other poets he ever found he knew as large a proportion of. Didn't like Endymion at the time, and never has, but except for Endymion, everything."

9. AMONG THE INFINITIES

1. Quoted from "The Star-splitter," *Complete Poems,* p. 218.

2. As is shown in later chapters Carl Burell (born 26 Oct. 1864, died 13 June 1938) figured prominently in RF's life during the years from 1888 to 1902.

3. One of RF's references to Carl Burell's library occurs in *Selected Letters*, p. 530.

4. Richard A. Proctor, *Our Place Among Infinities* (New York, 1876), p. 1.

5. Ibid., p. 33.

6. Ibid., p. 34 (compare with Job 11: 7-8 and Job 37: 23).

7. Ibid., pp. 37-38.

8. For evidence that RF found and liked in the writings of William James a slightly more ingenious representation of the same stereotypical argument, see chapters 20 and 28. Reference to Proctor occurs in the previously cited letter, Mrs. Frost to Mrs. Romig, 4 Feb. 1935:

"One of the books longest in his possession came to him from a friend of his father's in San Francisco, who died in the early eighties—Proctor's 'Our Place Among the [sic] Infinities.' Something like [Sir Arthur Stanley] Eddington of today. He read it several times about 1890 and got a telescope through the Youth's Companion. He has been astronomical ever since. He says he is down here in Key West now chiefly to find out if Canopus is as good a star as Sirius. A very early possession of his mother's recently came into his hands, from a cousin—Young's Night Thoughts. He never read it until lately. He remembers hearing her [his mother] quote 'The undevout astronomer is mad.' "

The line, almost correctly quoted, occurs in the ninth part (or "Night") of Edward Young's *Night Thoughts,* line 770, and the immediate context in which the line occurs may suggest the influence of RF's mother in helping him see Nature as a revelation of sacred ordering and design:

> . . . Bright legions swarm unseen, and sing, unheard
> By mortal ear, the glorious Architect,
> In This His universal temple hung
> With lustres, with innumerable lights,
> That shed religion on the soul; at once,
> The *Temple,* and the *Preacher!* O how loud
> It calls devotion! genuine growth of *Night!*
>   Devotion! daughter of astronomy!
> An *undevout* astronomer is *mad.*

Implicitly, this passage has bearing on Mrs. B. M. Frost's reasons for encouraging her son to acquire a telescope.

9. "La Noche Triste," *Bulletin,* Vol. XI, No. 8 (April, 1890), pp. 1-2. In two earlier biographies of RF, several mistakes have been made in discussing this poem. Miss Sergeant (*Robert Frost,* p. 22) incorrectly refers to the prologue of "La Noche Triste" as a "fragment" and misrepresents RF's uses of the subtitles, "Tenochtitlan" and "The Flight [from Tenochtitlan]," which apply re-

spectively to the prologue and to the main body of the ballad: ". . . the editor of the school paper . . . published it, with a fragment, also signed Robert Lee Frost, called 'Tenochtitlan' . . ." (Neither part of the poem was signed "Robert Lee Frost." The author was content to sign it merely with his class numerals, " '92.")

Miss Gould (*Robert Frost*, p. 40) leans heavily on the mistakes of Miss Sergeant and paraphrases her without acknowledgment as follows: "And the April (1890) issue of the *Bulletin* printed 'La Noche Triste' along with a fragment, the beginning of a Scottish ballad entitled 'Tenochtitlan'; both were signed Robert Lee Frost . . ."

10. In these concluding stanzas, RF's poetic reference to the Aztec flame as shining brightest just before it went out is an allusion to Prescott's account of how, after almost a full year, the defeated Spaniards under Cortes returned to besiege Tenochtitlan and eventually to defeat the Aztecs there. Miss Sergeant (*Robert Frost*, p. 22) mistakenly represents the meaning of a comment repeatedly made by RF concerning these two battles. She refers to RF's poem as "based on an incident befalling a group of Indians, who 'just might have turned the tide for themselves'—so Frost commented—but didn't. He felt poignantly for these Montezumas." Miss Sergeant would have represented RF's attitude more accurately if she had said that he exulted in the Indian victory gained on the famous night made sad for the Spaniards; but that RF regretted the later defeat of the Aztecs by the Spaniards.

Miss Gould (*Robert Frost*, p. 39) covers the same point by again leaning on Miss Sergeant without acknowledgment: ". . . the valiant but tragic efforts of a small group of Indians, who just might have turned the tide for themselves on one dark night of battle but didn't quite make it."

11. *Bulletin*, Vol. XI, No. 7 (March 1890), p. 7. The record of the formal election of RF to membership in the Debating Union is given in the *Bulletin*, Vol. XI, No. 8 (April 1890), p. 7.

Carl Burell's personal file of the *Bulletin* covering the years when he was contributing to it (1886-1894) and therefore the years when RF was contributing to it (1890-1892) was acquired by Charles R. Green for The Jones Library in Amherst, Mass., in 1940. This file seems to be unique; no other file of the *Bulletin* is known to exist which contains all of RF's contributions. The most important parts of this unique file have been made available in facsimile in a Grolier Club publication, *Robert Frost and the Lawrence, Massachusetts, High School Bulletin: The Beginning of a Literary Career,* edited by Edward Connery Lathem and Lawrance Thompson (New York, 1966).

The suggestion has been made in this chapter that RF's early writings were stimulated in part by Carl Burell's work for the

Bulletin and by RF's jealousy of Carl's poetic accomplishment. Oblique support is given to this possibility by one of RF's reminiscences:

"I remember probably almost better than anything else in my high school days the poems of my rivals. The poems of my fellow poets had as much influence on me as anything my teachers ever said or did." (James A. Batal, "Poet Robert Frost Tells of His High School Days in Lawrence," *Lawrence Telegram,* 28 March 1925, p. 14.)

10. OUTER AND INNER DEBATES

1. Quoted from RF's valedictory address entitled "A Monument to After-thought Unveiled," op. cit., p. 10.

2. *Bulletin,* Vol. XII, No. 1 (Sept. 1890), p. 7.

3. *Bulletin,* Vol. XII, No. 2 (Oct. 1890), p. 7.

4. Idem.

5. *Bulletin,* Vol. XII, No. 3 (Nov., 1890), p. 7.

6. *Bulletin,* Vol. XII, No. 4 (Dec., 1890), p. 7. Results of the election of officers are given in the *Bulletin,* Vol. XII, No. 6 (Feb., 1891), p. 7.

7. RF actually took the seventh "prelim" in October of 1891. While in Cambridge on these three different occasions of examination-taking (in March, June, October of 1891), RF each time visited and stayed overnight with relatives of Miss Sarah Newton; one of her sisters, Annie, had married a lawyer, Horatio Parker, and they were living at this time in Cambridge. Their several children remembered RF as the visitor who told them some fine stories about heroes and heroism. (Information given to LT by Miss Haida Newton Parker.)

8. *Bulletin,* Vol. XII, No. 8 (April, 1891), p. 5.

11. IF THY HEART FAIL THEE

1. See Note 4 of this chapter.

2. Among many references to the fact that RF and Elinor White first met in the fall of their senior year, one occurs in the previously cited letter, Mrs. Frost to Mrs. Romig, 4 Feb. 1935, as follows: "Owing to ill health, I was out of school for two years after Grammar School, and did my high school work in two and a half years. Robert and I didn't come across each other until the last year, when in the big hall where the three upper classes sat, our seats happened to be close together."

Miss Sergeant (*Robert Frost,* pp. 21-22) mistakenly asserts, "By his second year began the major attraction between himself and Elinor Miriam White . . ." On that mistaken assertion, Miss Sergeant bases the following speculation: "Was it at least a little because of Elinor's emotional place in his mind and heart that Rob Frost in 1890 began to write poetry . . ." Miss Sergeant submitted to RF the manuscript of her book prior to publication. He did not read all of it, but as he made samplings, he added a few marginal comments. When he found the passages just quoted, he wrote in the margin, "No but let it go at that. I wrote the Aztec thing before her." (Typewritten MS, p. II-29, Barrett Collection, Virginia.) RF's note implies that for mythic purposes he was not opposed to Miss Sergeant's mistaken supposition, and was willing to "let it go at that."

Miss Gould (*Robert Frost,* pp. 38-39) mistakenly uses Miss Sergeant as her source, again without acknowledgment, and represents RF as knowing Elinor White in "his second year" of high school. Then she makes the false assertion that prior to RF's writing of his first poem he and Elinor "one day in spring" were walking home from school "discussing Prescott's *The Conquest of Mexico.*"

3. Elinor White's brief career as poetess apparently caused a crisis which was brought on by RF's jealousy. It would seem that the crisis was resolved by Elinor White's decision to write no more poems, and perhaps by her further decision to deny that she was the author of the poems she had submitted to RF. The first of these possibilities is hinted, in the previously cited letter, Mrs. Frost to Mrs. Romig, 4 Feb. 1935:

"I think you will find two or three very nice things of Robert's if you decide to look through the files [of the *Bulletin*]. You may possibly find a poem of mine. I wrote a little for about six months. If you should, I beg you not to refer to it, ever, to anyone at all—not even in your answer to this letter. I had very nearly forgotten it."

The wording of this confidence would seem to imply that Mrs. Romig, or anyone else who looked through the *Bulletin* files, might need to do more than scan signatures at the ends of poems until the name or initials of Elinor M. White appeared; they do not appear. The letter also suggests that while Elinor White was publishing in the *Bulletin,* she may have used a pseudonym or anagram which Mrs. Romig might recognize without too much difficulty. It would have been easy, for example, to make an anagram-pseudonym out of "ELINOR" by spelling the name backward, RONILE; equally easy to make a pseudonym by rearranging the phonetic parts of E-LIN-OR into OR-LIN-E; equally easy to use the same phonetic procedure and to silence or drop the "E" thus: ORLINN. This speculation is made here because, while no poem in pertinent *Bulletin* files is signed with the name or the initials of Elinor White, the first poem in the issue of the *Bulletin* for September, 1891, is entitled "Now" and is signed "ORLINN"—and the initial poem in the issue for November, 1891, is entitled "An Infinite Longing" and is also signed "ORLINN." It is possible that each of these poems was written by Elinor White, and that if she had indeed "very nearly forgotten" (by 1935) that she had published even one poem there, she could also have forgotten that she had in fact published two poems.

As for the possibility that Elinor White decided to deny to RF that she was the author of these poems, and that she had made this denial in order to end a crisis created by RF's jealousy, there is further evidence. Recorded in LT's "Notes on Robert Frost," 18 June 1946, is an anecdote which RF told LT repeatedly in later years. He said that while he and Elinor White were becoming acquainted as seniors in high school, she had given him some manuscript love poems in her own handwriting; that he liked them and encouraged her to write more poems. After some time, he said, she told him that there had been a misunderstanding: She had not written the poems. Her sister had written them. As already stated, RF had a tendency to modify facts in telling his autobiographical anecdotes, particularly when the facts made him retrospectively uncomfortable. It is probable that the anecdote under consideration is a case in point. Much is known about Elinor White's two sisters, and one of them became skilful with water colors and oils. But there is no record that either one of them even dabbled with the writing of poetry.

RF's known jealousy of Elinor White's capabilities is important to any biographical understanding of his complicated personality. It is apparent that this jealousy had its root in his chronic lack of self-confidence. In the present case, notice particularly the hint given by EWF to Mrs. Romig that it would be unfortunate—for reasons not stated—if RF should learn that EWF had confided to Mrs. Romig the information that she had published even one poem in the *Bulletin*. The delicacies involved may take on more significance if they are reconsidered after Chapter 13 has been read. See also a related problem, unresolved, which is described in a note, *Selected Letters*, pp. 354-356, and in Note 8 of Chapter 19, here.

4. *Bulletin*, Vol. XIII, No. 1 (Sept. 1891), p. 4. RF's reference to the familiar anecdote concerning the aphorism scratched with a diamond on a windowpane by Sir Walter Raleigh, and of the answer scratched beneath it by Queen Elizabeth, may have been found by RF in Chapter 17 of Scott's *Kenilworth*. *Kenilworth* may have been one of Mrs. Frost's favorites; it seems to have become one of RF's favorites: He assigned it to his students at Pinkerton Academy along with the standard requirement, *Ivanhoe*.

5. *Bulletin,* Vol. XIII, No. 1 (Sept. 1891), pp. 4-5.

6. *Bulletin,* Vol. XIII, No. 3 (Nov. 1891), p. 4.

7. The date of writing "Clear and Colder—Boston Common" was given by RF as "in about 1891" in a letter dated 20 Feb. 1929 (*Selected Letters,* pp. 354-355), from RF to R. B. Haselden, Curator of Manuscripts, Henry E. Huntington Library. RF submitted a manuscript of the poem to the New York *Independent* in or near the year 1906, and although it was never published, it remained in the *Independent* files when they were sold to the Huntington Library in 1928.

8. *Bulletin,* Vol. XIII, No. 2 (Oct., 1891), pp. 5-6. The mention of "spectacles astride his nose" refers to the fact that during his last year at Lawrence High School, RF began to use pince-nez glasses for reading. He continued to use them for several years thereafter.

9. The *Bulletin* reporting on the activities of the Debating Union is irregular; it contains no indication of when RF was elected to the rank of senior vice-president. The issue for March 1892 contains, on p. 5, a report of three meetings: 26 Feb., 4 March, 11 March. In the report of the meeting held on 4 March, reference is made to a circumstance which caused President Thomas L. Sullivan (captain of the football team) to request that he be permitted to step down from the chair long enough to participate in a discussion. At this point, "Vice-President Frost took the chair." The discussion involved RF's proposal that because the society was at a very low ebb, ladies should be admitted to membership in the hope that they would give it new life. President Sullivan opposed the suggestion, and the report states, "During the latter part of the evening, Mr. Sullivan handed in his resignation as President and a member of the society."

The report of the meeting held on 11 March states: "Meeting called to order by Vice-President Frost. . . . Mr. Frost was unanimously elected President."

10. The pseudonym "AMNESSEL" had occurred previously in the *Bulletin* for April 1891, p. 1, at the end of an eighty-line poem, irregularly rhymed, entitled "Dream-Land." Like RF's previously mentioned poem, "A Dream of Julius Caesar" (published in the *Bulletin* for May 1891), "Dream-Land" makes uses of words and images and cadences which the youthful Frost seemed to like. Hence the inner and outer evidence combines to suggest that RF probably wrote "Dream-Land"—but there seems to be no way of proving it. For a complete chronological checklist of RF's writings while in high school, and of his actual and probable contributions to the *Bulletin,* see Note 12 of Chapter 12.

11. *Bulletin,* Vol. XIII, No. 5 (Jan. 1892), p. 4. RF told many versions of how he wrote all the copy for the December 1891 issue

of the *Bulletin,* even claiming at times that he wrote all the adver-
tisements. The latter claim is not supported by the facts: the adver-
tisements in the December issue are the same as those which appeared in the November issue. It is also probable that RF did not
write all the copy, as he claimed; but he did apparently write most
of it. RF's "idealized" version of the story seems to be another
example of his tendency to endow the facts with mythic improvement.

12. FREETHINKER

1. This protest is quoted from a conversation between RF and
his mother; it was made against the term "freethinker" and it is
placed in context by this chapter. RF, repeatedly telling this
anecdote, always gave the same words and always acted out the
shocked tone in his mother's utterance of them.

2. *Bulletin,* Vol. XIII, No. 9 (May 1892), p. 4.

3. For later considerations of "The Trial by Existence," see
Chapter 23, and the notes to it.

Not all of the poems which RF started in his senior year required such pains. Ernest Jewell, at Phillips Andover Academy,
inspired a half-serious poetic parody, which RF wrote swiftly.
Jewell, collaborating with a group of Andover students in planning
and starting a new literary magazine, had been asked to write or
solicit some poetry for an early issue. Although Jewell had been
Chief Editor of the Lawrence *High School Bulletin,* all his contributions to it had been in prose. Desperately he turned to RF for
help, and RF sent an impressive literary tour-de-force. The poem
was a lament which invoked the ancient atmosphere of (and one
proper name from) Macpherson's *Ossian.* It was cast in an ingeniously appropriate set of six-line ballad stanzas, which RF
might have adapted from *Ossian,* or from Percy's *Reliques,* or from
Burns's *Poems.* Entitled "The Traitor," this lament contains just
enough elliptical narrative detail to hint that a once-heroic warrior,
after having betrayed his king and having lied about it, regretted
his traitorous act and inflicted on himself the death he deserved.
"The Traitor" was printed in the *Phillips Andover Mirror,* Vol. I,
No. 2 (June, 1892), p. 24, and was reprinted in the *Mirror,* Vol.
107, No. 3 (Feb., 1961), p. 7. The reprint was accompanied by an
unsigned article entitled "A Conversation with Robert Frost" in
which the history of the poem is given. The article describes a visit
with RF and the discussion of a copy of *Ossian* which had belonged to RF's mother:

"Once we were seated, Mr. Frost showed us a leather-bound
book with an elaborate design on the outside and a small, practi-

cally unreadable print on the inside, each page bordered in red. 'That's one of the oldest books I have,' he said, 'one of the five or six I brought with me from San Francisco. . . . "The Traitor" comes right out of *Ossian*.'"

RF apparently meant that the inspiration for "The Traitor" came from *Ossian*. The only name in "The Traitor" which RF borrowed directly from *Ossian* is Colla, a proper name which occurs in the late Ossianic poem entitled "Dar-Thula," which is also the name of the heroine (daughter of Colla), better known today (thanks to Yeats) by her Irish name, Deirdre. There are no basic similarities between the action in "Dar-Thula" and "The Traitor." It is true that the villain of the ancient poem is a traitor, named Caibar, who has murdered the lawful king, Cormac; but Caibar is ultimately the victor, and honorable deaths in battle are suffered by Colla and Dar-Thula. The complete text of RF's "The Traitor":

> Sea-bird of the battle surf,
>   Lorna is dead.
> Black on Colla's castled hill
>   Ruin is spread.
> Weep for Lorna who rode forth
> With his king against the North.
>
> Lorna came again at morn,
>   Riding from war.
> Messenger of battle won,
>   Tidings he bore: —
> "Quenchless was the charge he made,
> Low the insurgent walls were laid."
>
> And while revelry was rife
>   Through Colla's halls,
> Then the lonely warder saw,
>   Pacing the walls,
> Eastward in the morning's greys,
> Serried spears in the sunrise blaze.
>
> By an altar in a vault—
>   Night dripping dew—
> Lorna's muffled cry arose;
>   Bat-like it flew: —
> "Sacrifice for victory!
> Priest and victim find in me!"
>
> Sea-bird of the battle surf,
>   Lorna is dead.

Black on Colla's castled hill
Ruin is spread.
Royal seal upon the tomb
Where he sleeps in endless gloom.

4. Note 3 of Chapter 11 refers to RF's jealousy of Elinor White's brief poetic career. The same jealousy cropped up in his disparaging way of saying that in high school she took "the commercial course," as he often described it. As though he retrospectively envied her the English literature courses she did take in high school, and as though he felt guilty that he had taken none of these courses, he repeatedly said that no courses in English were taught in LHS while he was there. One example of such a statement, probably reported correctly, occurs in Roger Kahn, "A Visit with Robert Frost," *The Saturday Evening Post* (19 Nov. 1960), p. 26:

"In high school I had only Greek, Latin and mathematics. I began to write in my second year, but not for any teacher. There were no English teachers."

Another example occurs in the already cited letter, Mrs. Frost to Mrs. Romig, 4 Feb. 1935. In writing the first part of this letter, apparently from RF's dictation, Mrs. Frost states, ". . . There was no English taught in his school." Immediately after this sentence, in the original letter, a blank space occurs. It suggests that Mrs. Frost may have paused here to challenge RF on this statement, after she had written it from dictation. Her next sentence modifies it: "He studied no English Literature—nothing but Greek and Latin for four years, plus . . ." Later, in the same letter, writing about herself, Mrs. Frost discusses her rank as co-valedictorian and describes the course of work, or program, which she took: "I had taken my course (English) without any order, and my rank wasn't noticed by the teachers until the last moment."

5. His fellow student, William O. Brewster (1875-1943) became a distinguished author and professor of English Literature at Columbia University.

6. Elizabeth Stuart Phelps, "Edward Rowland Sill," *The Century Magazine*, Vol. XXXVI, No. 5 (Sept., 1888), p. 708.

7. Edward Rowland Sill, *Poems* (Boston, 1890), pp. [107]-108.

8. Emily Dickinson, *Poems* (Boston, 1890), p. 134. RF's accounts of discovering the poetry of Sill and Emily Dickinson were told by RF to LT; but a side glimpse is afforded in the previously cited letter, Mrs. Frost to Mrs. Romig, 4 Feb. 1935: "Sill was his first *discovery*. The two volumes of Sill was his first present to me. Our interest in Sill got some of our teachers to talking about Sill. Teachers in those days didn't think they had to keep up with

contemporary books. A few weeks after he bought Sill, he bought Emily Dickinson's first book."

9. Although RF told many different versions of his conversation with Mr. Goodwin concerning Elinor White as his nearest competitor for valedictory honors, there is circumstantial evidence that his versions rarely included the fact that Elinor White's final average was actually higher than his. On one occasion this fact was jokingly mentioned by one of his children, Lesley, when visitors were in the Frost home. After the visitors had gone, RF took Lesley aside. In a towering rage he ordered her never to tell that story again. (It was a story which he himself had originally told her, and he still admitted the accuracy of it.)

10. *Bulletin*, Vol. XIII, No. 9 (May, 1892), p. 1.

11. *Bulletin*, Vol. XIII, No. 10 (June, 1892), p. 8.

12. Ibid., p. 10. For convenience in reference, a provisional chronological checklist is given of RF's known (and supposed) publications made during his high-school years:

1890	[March]	"La Noche Triste" was written
	April	"La Noche Triste," *Bulletin*, Vol. XI, No. 8, pp. 1-2
	May	"Song of the Wave," ibid., Vol. XI, No. 9, p. 3
1891	April	"Dream-Land," ibid., Vol. XII, No. 8, p. 1
	May	"A Dream of Julius Caesar," ibid., Vol. XII, No. 9, p. 1
	Spring	"Caesar's Lost Transport Ships"—a poem which, according to RF, was written at this time as a companion piece to "A Dream of Julius Caesar." It was not published until 1897.
	Sept.	Five untitled editorials, ibid., Vol. XIII, No. 1, p. 4
		1. [A brief toast—one sentence]
		2. [Declaration of editorial policy]
		3. [In praise of students taking classical program]
		4. [On a new Chemistry teacher]
		5. [Announcing literary prize contest]
	Oct.	Two untitled editorials, ibid., Vol. XIII, No. 2, p. 4
		1. [In praise of the new library]
		2. [Plans for improving new library]
	Nov.	Three untitled editorials, ibid., Vol. XIII, No. 3, p. 4
		1. [Requesting essays for the prize contest]
		2. [Requesting poems for the prize contest]
		3. [On high-school writers of poetry]

Dec.   "Down the Brook—And Back" (poem), ibid., Vol. XIII, No. 4, p. 1
"Petra and Its Surroundings" (essay), idem
"Physical Culture" (essay), ibid., p. 2
"The Charter Oak at Hartford" (essay), idem
"M. Bonner, Deceased" (short story), ibid., p. 3
"Parting. To —— ——" (poem), idem
"Alumni Notes" (column), idem
Three untitled editorials, ibid., p. 4
     1. [Criticism of new class in experimental physics]
     2. [On the telescope]
     3. [Criticism of the Debating Union]
"School Gossip" (column), ibid., pp. 4-6
"Foot Ball" (column), ibid., p. 6
"L. H. S. D. U." (column on Debating Union), ibid., pp. 6-7
"Education, Science and Literature" (column), ibid., p. 7
"Exchange Column," ibid., p. 8

1892   May   Four untitled editorials, ibid., Vol. xiii, No. 9, p. 4
     1. [On Commencement Day essays]
     2. [Plea for a broader study program]
     3. [Criticism of the Philotechnic Society]
     4. [On reviewing and rethinking]

June   "The Traitor" (poem), *Phillips Andover Mirror*, Vol. I, No. 2, p. 24
"A Monument to After-thought Unveiled," *Bulletin*, Vol. XIII, No. 10, p. 10
[Valediction], idem
"Class Hymn," idem

13. "Into the World: High School Class of '92 Graduates . . ." (newspaper account of graduation exercises). *The Lawrence Daily American*, 1 July 1892, p. 1.

14. Quoted in Joseph A. Reynolds, "Poet Robert Frost and Wife Graduates of L. H. S. in 1892," *Lawrence* (Mass.) *Eagle-Tribune*, 1953 Centennial Edition, p. 7. The same article also quotes from two newspaper gleanings concerning Elinor White. After stating that she was graduated from the Oliver grammar school in Lawrence in 1888, "The first public mention of Elinor White came (to her delight, doubtless) in 1888 when she was mentioned as a 'good drawer' in a newspaper report of an exhibition of the work of pupils of the Oliver school. . . . It is not until June 2, 1892, that we catch another fleeting glimpse of her. The occasion was a 'delightful reception' given to the members of the French class of the high

school by Miss Grace McFarlin at her home on Haverhill Street, to which 'each member was allowed to invite a limited number of guests,' according to the *Lawrence Daily American,* which added that 'at half past eight the spacious parlors were filled with a large assemblage of young ladies and gentlemen.' "

15. Elinor Miriam White was born in Lawrence, Mass., on 24 Oct. 1872, according to the records of the City Clerk's office in Lawrence. The date is further corroborated as it occurs in the registrar's record book of St. Lawrence University: It was inscribed there by Elinor White when she enrolled on 20 Sept. 1892.

13. A PLACE APART

1. Quoted from the poem "Revelation," *Complete Poems,* p. 27.

2. A vivid record of this crisis may be found in RF's poem "The Subverted Flower"—never published during the lifetime of Elinor White Frost. The poem first appeared in *A Witness Tree* (1942); but RF told LT that the first draft of it had been written so early that "The Subverted Flower" could have been published in *A Boy's Will;* that he had hesitated to publish it for many reasons, including his fear that it might seem too daring and too revealingly autobiographical. He might have added that his wife would never have given him her permission to publish it.

No early draft of "The Subverted Flower" is known to exist; the poem, as we have it, is obviously written in RF's later manner. The dramatic action begins *in medias res,* apparently just after the passionate love-making of the young man has been stopped by some kind of shocked and reproachful protest. Although the young man is represented as trying to attribute his action to the effect of a symbolic flower which he holds in his hand, the girl's horrified recoil makes him feel bestial and ashamed. Metaphorically, the poem extends the meaning of the title until it includes or represents the unnatural attitude of the girl toward physical passion.

3. Several attempts have been made to determine the name and class of this Dartmouth alumnus, but without success. Years later RF referred to him in the following way: "I had already taken part of my examination for Harvard, where my father went to college. But my grandmother was a little against my going to Harvard. And one of my teachers in the high school took a notion to my writing that he noticed around. (He was hardly my teacher. He was a chemistry man and physics . . . a Dartmouth man . . . and he took a notion to see my grandparents and talk over my going up there. . . ." (Edward Connery Lathem, "Freshman Days" [An interview with RF, centering on his brief stay], *Dartmouth Alumni*

Magazine, Vol. 51, No. 6 (March, 1959), p. 17. I am grateful to
Mr. Lathem for making available to me a typewritten draft transcript of the full tape of this interview, recorded at 35 Brewster
Street, Cambridge, Mass., 2 Dec. 1958. The transcript indicates
that RF went on to observe of this teacher, "I never saw him again
after I went up there. He probably lost patience with me when I
quit.")

4. One version of these escapades occurs in Lathem, "Freshman
Days," op. cit. In this same publication (pp. 21-22) the following
account appears: "Another of the escapades of his freshman days
came into Mr. Frost's mind. 'I didn't tell you that once I took part
in hazing a classmate. Did I ever tell you that?' The freshman in
question was 'a boy preacher,' appropriately nicknamed 'Parson' by
his fellows. 'We fooled around, all one evening,' Mr. Frost began,
'he and I and Hazen, in Hazen's apartment. We had a field day.
And we busted the pillows over each other till the place was all full
of feathers, and we carried on a lot . . . The others in the hall
shouted at us to shut up, you know. But we kept right on: long
jumps and short jumps and fights and everything and tearing pillows to pieces. And finally somebody said I needed a haircut. I said
to the minister, 'I'll tell you what I'll do. If you'll let me cut your
hair, I'll let you cut mine.' So Hazen and I cut his hair. We made a
picture on the back of his head, so the skull showed through. . . .
Then,' he related with a chuckle, 'I did a dastardly thing: I said
we'd have my hair cut another night—not that night. I refused to
have mine cut. And do you know what happened to him? He left
college . . .' "

5. In Lathem, "Freshman Days," op. cit., p. 20, the following
account of this exchange occurs: "They [fraternity brothers] didn't
bother me except once that I've joked about. I've told about how
they came to me, some of them, to know what I was walking in the
woods for. And I told them that I was gnawing bark!" He always
used the word "bark" and he often heightened the insolence of
his answer by flattening the "a" sounds in "Gnaw bark." Miss Sergeant (*Robert Frost,* p. 29) ruins the effect by misquoting RF as
follows: " 'I gnaw wood,' was his reply." Leaning on Miss Sergeant,
Miss Gould (*Robert Frost,* p. 48) repeats the error and goes on
with her own embroideries: " 'I gnaw wood,' he told them, cocking
one eyebrow and pursing his lips in a sudden stubborn quirk. He
closed the door in their faces."

6. RF's most extended reminiscence concerning this first acquaintance with *The Independent* is quoted in Lathem, "Freshman
Days," op. cit., pp. 19-20. Excerpts from this account were used
by Lathem in preparing a "keepsake" folder into which was laid a
reduced facsimile of "Seaward" as it appeared in *The Independent*
for 17 November 1892, and (on the reverse side) a facsimile of the

editorial. See *Under That Arch: A keepsake issued by the Dartmouth College Library on the occasion of the opening of its Robert Frost Room, April 19, 1962.*

14. ODD JOBS

1. For the title and source of the sonnet containing these lines, see Note 8 of this chapter.

2. *Methuen Town Report for 1892-1893*, p. 21. For further information concerning relations between RF and Oliphant, I am indebted to the Rev. Egbert W. A. Jenkinson, Minister Emeritus of the First Church, Congregational, in Methuen, Mass., who made the following statements in a letter dated 17 Nov. 1965:

". . . I also have a copy of 'A Boy's Will' (1915) which is inscribed 'Charles H. Oliphant from Robert Frost in friendship.'

"Charles Oliphant was my predecessor in the Methuen Church, and he was a member of the school committee which engaged Mrs. Frost, the mother of Robert, to teach in Methuen.

"The house where they lived is on Prospect St. Some years ago I talked with a man who was a neighbor as a boy on a farm. I asked him what he remembered about Robert Frost. In blunt New England fashion, and with no concern for Robert Frost, as a renowned poet, this Yankee replied, 'Robert Frost was the laziest lout—he didn't know enough to keep the wood box filled for his mother.'

"From the diary of Charles H. Oliphant there is the following story about the Frost family in Methuen.

"'As chairman of the school committee it fell to me also to select teachers. One of these was a Mrs. Frost, a refined lady of middle age—a widow with two children, a boy and a girl. Mrs. Frost was quite unable to maintain order in the grammar school, and by mutual consent was to retire from our service. As this would put the family in some strait of income, they were very poor, the son (a boy of perhaps 17) applied for his mother's position! With much hesitation mixed with sympathy, I examined him at our house, corner High and Tremont St., and found him so proficient that he was entrusted (pro tem) with his mother's school. This boy was Robert Frost, the poet whose recent books "A Boy's Will" "North of Boston" and "Mountain Interval" have made him famous. Robert has been a guest at our home a number of times.'

[Jenkinson adds, following this quotation from Oliphant:]

"This incident was about 1890—the year Charles Oliphant was elected to the school committee. It was written some time between 1920 and 1926—the year of his [Oliphant's] death."

The minor errors in Oliphant's account of this incident are understandable; as Jenkinson explains, this account was written by Oliphant more than a quarter of a century after the events described. A more nearly contemporary letter of recommendation written for RF by Oliphant on 17 Sept 1897 (MS, Barrett Collection, Virginia) was probably requested when RF applied for a position in the Shepard Evening School in North Cambridge, Mass., in 1897 (see Chapter 20):

"Robert L. Frost was a teacher in Methuen Grammar School No. 2 some three years ago, and as Chairman of the School Committee I found him able & efficient in that capacity. Mr. Frost has taught much of the time since then and I should regard him as deserving & competent in any capacity such as those which he has filled."

3. Among RF's different versions of this incident, one which LT recorded on 21 March 1940 contains RF's statements that he returned to Methuen from Dartmouth "shortly after Christmas" and "on a Friday," that he visited Oliphant the next day and was granted permission to replace his mother, that he bought the supply of rattans in a hardware store that Saturday night, that he began teaching early the next week. The first Friday after Christmas of 1892 fell on December 29th; the next Monday was a holiday, Jan. 1st; the first school day, presumably, was Jan. 2nd.

Old records kept in the Central Grammar School, Methuen, Mass., state that RF taught in the Second Grammar School, East, from 2 Jan. 1893 to 24 March 1893. (I am grateful to Mr. H. P. Wardwell of Methuen, Mass., for this information, sent in a letter dated 11 March 1966.)

In later years RF was inclined to endow his accounts of this teaching experience with some mythic values by claiming that he continued until the end of the school year. See for example, Miss Gould (*Robert Frost*, p. 51): "In between his teaching hours he read . . . When the school year ended, he had to look for a job." But the *Methuen Town Report for 1893-1894*, pp. 16-17, states: "Mr. R. L. Frost, of the Second Grammar, at the opening of the spring term, [of 1893, was succeeded] by Miss Blanche A. Chadwick."

There are indications, however, that RF would not have quit if the ordeal had not been so difficult. In the draft transcription of the Lathem interview, 2 Dec. 1958, p. 8, the interviewer reads to RF from the issue of *The Dartmouth* for 24 Feb. 1893 this news item: "R. L. Frost, '96, will not return to College. He is teaching a grammar school at Methuen, Massachusetts." Years later, in 1940, one of these "older boys" told LT, during an interview in Methuen, that he and others so very deeply resented RF's brutalities in the schoolroom that they gave RF "a hard enough time" to help him reach his decision to resign before the opening of the spring term.

4. RF's description of the Oliver Saunders homestead is corroborated by details given in Edgar Gilbert, *History of Salem, N. H.* (Concord, 1907). Gilbert's history contains a map showing the location of the house, which burned down only a few years after RF and the Whites spent the summer there.

5. Several factors corroborate RF's account of EMW's leaving St. Lawrence in April of 1893. A news item in the undergraduate monthly publication, *Laurentian*, April, 1893, contains the following: "Elinor M. White '96 was called to her home in Lawrence, Mass., April 11, by the serious illness of her sister." She probably took her "make-up" examinations in the fall. During her second year at St. Lawrence (1893-1894), the *Laurentian* repeatedly referred to her as a member of the Class of 1895, an indication that she had formally been permitted to accelerate her plan of study. According to the St. Lawrence University records, EMW took four full-year courses (German, Caesar and Cicero, Latin Prose, Parliamentary Law) and eight half-year courses (Mathematics, Botany, Debate, History, Physics, Rhetoricals, English C, Physical Education) during her second year. In her third and final year (1894-1895), EMW took five full-year courses (Latin, English, Ethics and Jurisprudence, Logic, Economics) and eight half-year courses (French, Chemistry, German, Physics, Geology, Psychology, Evidences, History). Requirements for the degree of Bachelor of Science (which she sought and won) were 120 hours; her completed courses entitled her to credit for 125 hours.

6. When "Bereft" first appeared in book form (*West-running Brook*, 1928), RF gave it a slightly autobiographical note by printing below it this statement: "As of about 1893." Miss Sergeant, in her *Robert Frost*, does not mention the fact that RF spent the summer of 1893 at the Saunders place in Salem; but her comment on the statement, "As of about 1893," does contain this useful information, p. 30: "This does not mean, R. F. says, that it was written in 1893 . . . but that it was based on memories of that year." Miss Sergeant, ignoring the autumn images throughout the poem, tries to make "Bereft" refer to the winter experiences "when he decamped from Dartmouth" and she adds: "Certainly it might be taken as close to the temper of the college student who hadn't made a go of things or fitted into the ideas of his elders." This interpretation misses the enriching significance of the title.

7. Among RF's many accounts of his venture with the Shakespeare reader, one of the best occurs in the draft transcription of the Lathem interview, 2 Dec. 1958, op. cit., pp. 36-38.

8. MS, Huntington Library, previously unpublished. It is impossible to be certain when RF sent this sonnet to *The Independent*,

but the handwriting of the manuscript is similar to that of other manuscripts submitted to *The Independent* during 1906 and 1907. During the same period, RF was devoting much time to writing sonnets.

9. These lines occur in Shelley's "Dedicatory Poem" for *The Revolt of Islam.*

10. Mrs. Frost's attempts to teach in four of the Methuen public schools can be reconstructed from the pertinent annual issues of the *Methuen Town Report.* Starting in the spring of 1890, she first taught in the Merrill District School; she continued to teach there through the spring term of 1892. In the fall of 1892, she was transferred to the Second Grammar School (East); she taught the eighth grade there for less than one term—until the time in January, 1893, when she was relieved by her son. She was immediately transferred to the Second Primary (East) and was obliged to accept a decrease in her annual salary, from $450 to $350 a year. She was transferred to the First Primary School, apparently in the fall of 1893; again had discipline problems; resigned "early in the fall term" of 1893, according to the *Methuen Town Report for 1894.*

During the ten years from 1890 to 1900, the Frosts lived in a great many places. When Mrs. Frost began to teach in the Merrill School—out in the country on Prospect Street—in March 1890, she and her children lived in Lawrence, on East Haverhill Street, near the railroad tracks. At some time after Mrs. Frost was transferred to the Second Grammar School (East)—on Lawrence Street in the village district of Methuen—the family moved to an apartment in a house on Upper Broadway, Methuen, beyond the Nevins Library. After Mrs. Frost resigned from her position in the fall of 1893, she and her children moved into an apartment on Tremont Street in Lawrence, again near the railroad tracks and roughly two blocks north of their former tenement on East Haverhill Street. They stayed in the Tremont Street apartment until the fall of 1895, when they rented rooms in the Central Building, 316 Essex Street, Lawrence, to accommodate the growth of Mrs. Frost's Private School. For more details on this school, and on later moves, see Chapter 18.

15. OUT OF SORTS WITH FATE

1. Quoted from the poem entitled "Kitty Hawk," *In the Clearing* (1962), pp. 41-42. The beginning of the poem is of particular autobiographical interest: "Kitty Hawk, O Kitty, / There was once a song, / Who knows but a great / Emblematic ditty, / I might well have sung / When I came here young / Out and down along / Past Elizabeth City / Sixty years ago. . . ." Considered within its

biographical context this beginning may be paraphrased inter-
pretively and speculatively as implying that the geographical
name, Kitty Hawk, might have inspired him when young to write a
poem, a lover's lament addressed to Elinor White, a lament in
which "Kitty" and "Hawk" might have served as "emblematic"
images of Elinor's paradoxical nature. To RF at the time, she may
have seemed to possess the attractively innocent charm of a kitten
and the painfully ruthless cruelty of a hawk; therefore, the song he
"might well have sung" could have started with the metaphorical
apostrophe, "Kitty Hawk, O Kitty." For context, see Chapter 16.

2. Quoted from "A Lone Striker" (*Complete Poems*, p. 356), a
poem which was directly inspired by this particular event, according to RF. Also based on RF's reminiscences are the details which
follow concerning how RF went to Salem, N. H., and obtained a
teaching position for the spring term of 1894 in an elementary
school there. These latter reminiscences are corroborated—and
extended—by the Salem town reports for the years ending 15 Feb.
1895 and 15 Feb. 1896 (pages 44 and 40, respectively), which
indicate that RF taught for a total of three terms in District School
No. 9, at Messer's Crossing in South Salem; that the first term of
eleven weeks did occur in the spring of 1894; that the second
term of eleven weeks was in the fall of 1895; that the third term
of eight weeks was in the winter of 1895-1896. (I am grateful to
Edward Connery Lathem for assisting me in securing this information from these town reports.)

3. RF's often repeated account of how he wrote "My Butterfly"
was one of his favorite stories, told by him with some interesting
variants. Miss Sergeant (*Robert Frost*, p. 34) has these details: " 'I
wrote it,' R.F. told me, 'all in one go in the kitchen of our house in
Tremont Street. I locked the door and all the time I was working,
Jeanie my sister tried to batter it down and get in.' Even as he
wrote it he had 'sensed in a way that something was happening. It
was like cutting along a nerve.' " Miss Gould (*Robert Frost*, pp. 52-
53) takes off from there and works in some quaint fictions. One of
RF's accurately transcribed accounts appears in the typewritten
draft of the Lathem interview (op. cit., p. 52) as follows:

". . . I seem to remember writing that in the kitchen. I had
trouble having any place. We didn't have much room. The rooms
were one behind the other in the lower apartment. Then there was
somebody above us. Later I had a right to a room way up in the
attic. But I didn't have then. It may be in the winter anyway. I
wouldn't have it. There was no heating it; just stove heated. I
used the kitchen some, and my sister resented it somewhat. I didn't
do it often, but I remember once she went 'round outdoors and
thought she'd get in that way. And I'd locked the door there. And
she kicked the panel in. . . . I didn't claim any right of being

anybody—nothing like that—but I just locked myself in, that's all, and she was mad at me. She and I always had unhappy times together, poor thing. . . ."

4. The first page of the manuscript of "My Butterfly" (original, Huntington Library) is reproduced in *Selected Letters*, between pages 224 and 225 of the first printing; the wording and line indentations used in the passage here quoted follow those of that manuscript. The finally revised version of "My Butterfly" occurs in *Complete Poems*, pp. 41-42.

5. *Selected Letters*, p. 19.

6. *Selected Letters*, pp. 20-21.

7. *Selected Letters*, p. 22.

8. *Selected Letters*, pp. 23-24.

9. A good version of this often-repeated story is given in broader context by Robert S. Newdick in "Robert Frost and the Sound of Sense," *American Literature*, Vol. IX (Nov. 1937), pp. 289-300.

Reminiscing in 1925, RF said, "Every bit of my career in or outside of school began in Lawrence. The greatest friend of my struggling days was the Reverend William E. Wolcott, pastor of the Lawrence Street Congregational Church." (Quoted by James A. Batal, op. cit., p. 14.)

10. "Warning" was slightly modified before it was submitted to *The Independent* for publication. It appeared in the issue for 9 September 1897 with the last two pronouns changed from "she" to "he." When "Warning" was reprinted in *Three Poems* (Hanover, N. H., [1935]), RF added the autobiographical date note, "Circa 1895." In 1962, RF admitted to LT that he had tried to cover his tracks by changing the pronouns in the first printed version.

11. The late Owen D. Young (1874-1962) very generously assisted LT in gathering materials concerning Elinor White's years at St. Lawrence University. Voluntarily, he obtained reminiscences from several of his classmates.

12. As late as 1936, RF listed *The Prisoner of Zenda* among his ten favorite books, and described it as "surely one of the very best of our modern best-sellers." (*Books We Like—Sixty-two Answers* [Boston, 1936], p. 142.) It may be that this evaluation directly reflected his youthful enthusiasm and was made because he had never again sampled it.

13. It is possible that during this unusual experiment with alcoholic stimulants RF wrote one letter which provides the address of his (so to speak) laboratory. In *Selected Letters*, p. 23, the letter to Susan Hayes Ward, dated 22 August 1894, bears the address, "35 Cambridge St., Boston." No other explanation for his writing from this address has yet been found by LT.

14. This was one of RF's favorite stories, and the many versions of it are in general agreement.

16. DISMAL SWAMP

1. Quoted from the description of "What Makes the Slough of Despond" in John Bunyan, *The Pilgrim's Progress*.

2. Elinor White's copy of *Twilight* is now in the Barrett Collection, Virginia. The account of how RF tore up the pages of his own copy and scattered the pieces along the track as he walked away from Canton, New York, was told by RF to Clifton Waller Barrett who in turn told it to LT. By contrast, when LT repeatedly asked RF over a period of many years just what happened to RF's copy, RF repeatedly said that he couldn't "remember." There is the strong probability that RF told Barrett the true story.

For years RF made a secret of the entire *Twilight* story. The first hint found by LT occurs in a letter from RF to Frederic G. Melcher, 9 February 1929: "I have a small edition of one copy of an early book of mine that nobody but Elinor and I and the printer ever saw. You'll have to say if it counts in my bibliography." (*Selected Letters*, p. 354.) RF referred to the copy he had given EW in 1894; the copy from which had been removed (by 1929) the original flyleaf inscription—which RF also could never "remember." The sale of this copy of *Twilight* to the book collector, Earle J. Bernheimer, for $4,000, by RF, on 8 January 1940 (see *Selected Letters*, p. 442, pp. 486-487), caused several of RF's friends to protest. Frederic G. Melcher was one of the first to protest in conversation with RF, who defended his action by saying that *Twilight* was associated in his memory with extremely unpleasant experiences; that he had carried it in his pocket to EW when he went to St. Lawrence University to challenge her claim that she must break her engagement to him; that always, after that unsuccessful trip, he found, when he looked at *Twilight,* a reminder of all the agony associated with it. The inscription to Earle J. Bernheimer, written on blank page [5], begins as follows:

"I had two copies of Twilight printed and bound by a job printer in Lawrence Mass. in 1894 probably out of pride in what Bliss Carman and Maurice Thompson had said about the poem in it called My Butterfly. One copy I kept for myself and afterwards destroyed. The other I gave away to a girl in St. Lawrence University to show to her friends. It had no success and deserved none. But it unaccountably survived and has lately leaped into prominence as my first first. . . ."

3. RF was extremely fond of telling and retelling the story of his trip to the Dismal Swamp, but he never told LT how or where he acquired information about the Dismal Swamp before going there.

4. The date is established by RF's repeated reference to the fact

that this adventure started on Election Day of 1894 and that he was in New York City on Election Day, which fell on 6 Nov., that year.

5. The statement has been made that some of RF's mythic versions of events in his own experience are more revealing than the basic facts. One example may be found in a melodramatic addition which RF sometimes gave to his account of the walk through the Dismal Swamp by night: A huge Negro, he would say, with an axe over his shoulder, stalked RF for several miles, and RF feared the Negro was going to kill him. In RF's many versions of the story, as told by him to LT over a period of twenty-five years, the Negro was never mentioned. In Daniel Smythe, *Robert Frost Speaks* (New York, 1964), pp. 48-49, a version of the Dismal Swamp experience is given, in which RF does more than merely mention the Negro. Smythe seems to be presenting an accurate, verbatim report; he offers it as a direct quotation from RF. Apparently, however, Smythe wrote this version from memory and in the process he accidentally introduced some factual errors—and some banalities of syntax—which RF would not use. Examples: ". . . I found myself in North Carolina. I walked and walked. I came to a river on which there was a boat. I asked the captain how far he would take me for a dollar, and he designated a certain place." Smythe also provides a context for RF's reference to the Negro: "Once I was walking through a swamp. The only thing that kept me above the mud was a board walk extending for miles. Right behind me strode a stranger, a giant Negro with an axe on his shoulder. He followed my heels for three miles. At any moment, he might have hit me on the head and pushed me off into the swamp and no one would have known anything about it. That was a scary experience."

Even if the Negro is viewed as purely fictitious, RF's addition amounts to a creative and poetic act, which hints at RF's motives for, and responses to, his adventures in the Dismal Swamp. "I was trying to throw my life away," RF said repeatedly to LT, in retelling this particular story. If his attempt was based on the hope that something or somebody would kill him, and if he also hoped that the possibility of his mysterious disappearance and death would somehow hurt and punish Elinor White for her seeming disloyalty and cruelty to him, there is a significant element in the imagined act whereby no one would ever know anything about how or when or where he died. It would seem that although RF tried to throw his life away, during that weird night in the Dismal Swamp, he needed more help than he got; things didn't quite work out as he hoped or feared or imagined.

6. RF's references to finding and crossing muddy areas on "plank-walk after plank-walk" piqued the curiosity of LT, who

spent parts of three days and two nights exploring the Dismal Swamp just to get the "feel" of it, before making a final revision of this account. On 24 October 1965, in company with an excellent guide (Mr. Clifford W. Sebring of Norfolk, Virginia), who provided an aluminum boat and an outboard motor, LT explored part of the Canal by daylight and went all the way in to Lake Drummond on the "feeder ditch," or canal, from the main canal. The trip into Lake Drummond was made, partly to walk the dirt roads which, today, are not much different from those on which RF walked, by night, in 1894. Sebring and LT went ashore at three points to explore various kinds of trails. Returning to the Dismal Swamp Canal, and taking the boat out near the area where the Northwest Lock had existed, Sebring and LT visited with an eighty-year-old native of the region, Mr. Harry Jackson, who lived beside the Canal. Jackson listened with great interest to the story of RF's walk into the Dismal Swamp in 1894, and figured out that he must have been nine years old at that time. He well remembered the many separate plank walks, and said that he had helped to replace some of them when they rotted out. Asked whether it was possible for RF to find plank walks anywhere in the swamp except on the road from Deep Creek to Northwest Lock, near the village of Wallaceton (birthplace of Jackson), he said RF could not have found plank walks on any other road leading to a lock in which he found a boat going from Norfolk to Elizabeth City. Was it certain that RF must have found that boat in Northwest Lock? Well, said Jackson, if he walked for several hours in the darkness and then "in the middle of the night" he came to a lock with a boat in it bound for Elizabeth City, that had to be Northwest Lock near Wallaceton. But, he was asked, suppose RF had missed that lock and had picked up the boat at the next one? Then, said Jackson, he would have walked all night; some time after dawn he would have reached the old Culpeper Lock at South Mills, North Carolina. Jackson's description of the road from Deep Creek to Northwest Lock, as it had been when he was a boy, fitted RF's account. When Jackson was asked if he had ever walked the road at night when he was a boy, he answered, "Not if I could help it!"

That section of the road is now a splendidly paved boulevard, part of Highway 17. Broad as the highway is today, it still has tree branches which interlace over it in certain sections, so that in the dark it continues to be dismal and frightening. In the daytime, particularly in October sunlight when leaves are turning golden yellow and red, the Dismal Swamp is beautiful. But if one tries to walk off any road or trail there, even today, the rank undergrowth forms a jungle which remains practically impenetrable.

7. Some hint of the various ways in which RF gave accounts of his Dismal Swamp adventures may be gathered from reference to

passages in previous biographies. Munson (*Robert Frost*, p. 24) covers it in one sentence: "Somewhat restless, undecided and drifting those days were for him, and perhaps they are best symbolized by a brief tramping tour which he made down south." Miss Sergeant (*Robert Frost*, p. 43) correctly associates the trip with Elinor White's reaction to *Twilight*, but mistakenly associates it with "hilly country" in the "south." Instead of mentioning the Dismal Swamp or even autumn landscape, she flavors her account with spring blossoms:

"The rebuff, for rebuff it was, struck to the poet's innermost heart. Bleeding and betrayed, he tore up his own copy of his first opus, and 'ran away,' 'out of time,' out of his head almost, into unknown country—not north to the familiar White Mountains [LT's note: RF had not yet seen the White Mountains] but south, south, south. Look at the handsome fellow, scalded by denial of worth, breaking his way through the azaleas and dogwoods of that hilly country, lashing his blazing blue eyes full of tears from the twigs and blossoms, doing minor jobs for bread, breaking his pride all the way. While gone, nobody knew where, no address, no news (only in 1957 did we learn his whereabouts from his long poem 'Kitty Hawk') . . ."

Miss Gould (*Robert Frost*, p. 61), reworking Miss Sergeant's version, picks up the "hilly country" and plays with it:

". . . He headed south, 'out of time,' out of his mind in pain and anger. Down through the Adirondacks, the Appalachians, the eastern Smokies. . . . He finally came upon a southern city—Elizabeth City, and then Kitty Hawk . . ."

Miss Gould continues, getting RF from Lawrence to New York to Norfolk, and at least mentioning the Dismal Swamp—although she gets herself lost in it far worse than RF ever did, and finds a new route "toward the shore":

"He got off at Norfolk, wandered aimlessly around the docks awhile, and finally set off on foot again, down through the Dismal Swamp on a one-plank path; it was dank, neglected woodland, wild and eerie, but he was too angry and heartsore to be scared. Then he veered toward the shore again and 'picked up another boat for Elizabeth City.' "

8. RF's account of being guided to a hotel at Nags Head, N.C., by duck hunters from Elizabeth City, N. C., fits into the known facts: in 1894 there was only one hotel at Nags Head and it was owned by two businessmen from Elizabeth City. They were John B. Brockett and J. B. Flora, partners in a wholesale business which handled dry goods, grocery, and whiskey. The Nags Head Hotel, built in 1871, burned to the ground in 1902. The history of the hotel (and a photograph of it) may be found in Earl Dean, "Old Nags Head: Soundside Hotel Days Were Ones of Sentiment," *The*

Coastline Times (Manteo, N. C., 2 Aug. 1963), third section, p. [1]. I am grateful to Mrs. George R. Fearing of Elizabeth City, N. C., for much information which helped to confirm RF's account.

9. *Selected Letters*, pp. 24-25.

10. "Reluctance," *Complete Poems*, p. 43. See text and notes of Chapter 17 for evidence that RF initially felt (and continued throughout his life to believe) that he suffered an irreparable shock, loss, metamorphosis as a result of what he viewed as Elinor White's rejection of him when he visited her at St. Lawrence University. See also the pertinent gloss for "Reluctance" in *A Boy's Will* (1913): "There are things that can never be the same."

17. DOOR IN THE DARK

1. "The Door in the Dark," *Complete Poems*, p. 340.

2. The first Wordsworth quotation is from "Peele Castle," the poem from which Elinor White quoted another familiar quatrain in her essay previously cited, "A Phase of Novel Writing." The second quotation is from "Intimations of Immortality."

3. This particular sentence from *Hamlet* (I, i, 165) was frequently quoted by RF to represent the persistence of his own religious faith in spite of his confusing and disillusioning doubts. In conversations on the subject he often called attention to analogies he found between the meaning of this sentence from *Hamlet* and the following passage near the beginning of Bunyan's *The Pilgrim's Progress:* "Then said Evangelist, pointing with his finger over a very wide field, Do you see yonder wicket-gate? The man said, No. Then said the other, Do you see yonder shining light? He said, I think I do. Then said Evangelist, Keep that light in your eye . . ." RF's essentially Victorian response to his religious confusion was very closely akin to that expressed in the following lines from Tennyson's "In Memoriam":

> I falter where I firmly trod,
> And falling with my weight of cares
> Upon the great world's altar-stairs
> That slope thro' darkness up to God,
>
> I stretch lame hands of faith, and grope,
> And gather dust and chaff, and call
> To what I feel is Lord of all,
> And faintly trust the larger hope.

4. In reference to RF's four beliefs, as they were later re-estab-

lished, see his "Education by Poetry: A Meditative Monologue" (*Amherst Graduates' Quarterly*, Vol. 20, No. 2, Feb. 1931, pp. 75-85), which contains the following pertinent passage, beginning with an echo of a familiar Victorian attitude (expressed variously by Carlyle, Tennyson, Browning, and others) concerning the poet as a new priest and prophet:

"The person who gets close enough to poetry, he is going to know more about the word *belief* than anybody else knows, even in [formalized and dogmatic] religion nowadays. There are two or three places where we know belief outside of religion. One of them is at the age of fifteen to twenty, in our self-belief. A young man knows more about himself than he is able to prove to anyone. He has no knowledge that anybody else will accept as knowledge. In his foreknowledge he has something that is going to believe itself into fulfilment, into acceptance.

"There is another belief like that, the belief in someone else, a relationship of two that is going to be believed into fulfilment. That is what we are talking about in our novels, the belief of love. And the disillusionment that the novels are full of is simply the disillusionment from disappointment in that belief. That belief can fail, of course.

"Then there is a literary belief. Every time a poem is written, every time a short story is written, it is written not by cunning, but by belief. The beauty, the something, the little charm of the thing to be, is more felt than known. . . .

"Now I think—I happen to think—that those three beliefs that I speak of, the self-belief, the love-belief, and the art-belief, are all closely related to the God-belief, that the belief in God is a relationship you enter into with Him to bring about the future."

This important essay, for many years not easily available, may now be found complete in Cox and Lathem, *Selected Prose*, pp. 33-46.

5. *Selected Letters*, p. 300.

6. Susan P. Holmes, "Robert Frost in Lawrence—A Remembrance of 60 Years," *Lawrence Eagle-Tribune*, 9 May 1963, p. 16. This article happens to preserve an anecdote which reflects Isabelle M. Frost's preoccupation with prophetic dreams, viewed as an instrument of second sight, a subject which naturally interested Swedenborgians:

". . . Belle Moody (Frost) emigrated from Scotland to the U. S. On the voyage, one of her fellow passengers had an extraordinary dream of a ship on fire. The dream showed its location, and was so very vivid that in the morning she sought the captain, who decided that by a slight alteration of his course he could reach the stricken ship, which he did, and sure enough there was smoke, survivers in boats, and all hands were saved from drowning."

7. Idem.

8. *Selected Letters*, p. 26. The letter is dated 30 Jan. 1895.

9. *Selected Letters*, p. 67.

10. Quoted by Gardner Jackson, op. cit. I am indebted to Edward Connery Lathem for information concerning RF's column and for the following extract from it. The column was entitled "The American About and Abroad." It appeared in *The Lawrence Daily American,* and one of the so-called "prose poems" concerning women "picking up coal" is an ironic paragraph which appeared in the issue for 2 Feb. 1895, p. 5:

"I am going to betray a confidence and worse than that a poor man's confidence, but only in the hope of compelling for him your natural if unrighteous sympathy. There are a lot of women and children that have let me see them looting coal in a yard near here. They come with buckets and gather it piece by piece under the coal cars. It is feverish work keeping warm for such people. And the curious part of it is, they will not take the coal otherwise than from off the ground, which necessitates their twice handling it, once from the car to the ground, and again from the ground to the bucket. The moral strain attendant on such work must be excessive, and one suffers to watch them skulking and stooping all day long."

11. Circumstantial evidence seems to indicate that Elinor White came home from St. Lawrence University during the between-semesters vacation in March. *The Laurentian* (Jan., 1895), p. 3, states that EW spent Christmas 1894 with friends in Brooklyn, N. Y. There is no evidence that she returned to Lawrence during her Christmas vacation, 1894, although this claim is made in Miss Sergeant's *Robert Frost,* p. 46, and is repeated in Miss Gould's *Robert Frost,* p. 65.

18. LESS THAN TWO

1. See Note 4 of this chapter.

2. In Note 14 of Chapter 12 is a reference to EW as a "good drawer," whose work was represented in an eighth-grade exhibition. Among the many indications of RF's lack of confidence in himself, and his consequent jealousy of talent even when revealed by those he loved, is the evidence that EW very largely abandoned her drawing and painting for reasons which are not unrelated to her abandoning the writing of poetry. At least one painting done by Elinor White continued to be used as decoration in the Frost home long after the public marriage of RF and EWF. As late as 1925, when Professor G. Roy Elliott joined the faculty at Amherst

College (with the result that the Frost and Elliott families became intimate) Mrs. Elliott noticed and admired a painting in the Frost living room in Amherst. Mrs. Frost, when asked about it, admitted that the painting was her work. She said she had been fond of painting when she was a girl, but that she had stopped soon after her marriage. In 1946, Professor and Mrs. Elliott separately expressed to LT their conviction that RF conveyed to Mrs. Frost, at the time of their marriage, his feeling that "one artist in the family is enough." As their children grew up and quite naturally developed interest and skill in writing poetry, EWF bitterly complained that RF did not sufficiently encourage and help them with their writing.

3. Early in the twentieth century, the retired shoe manufacturer and millionaire Thomas G. Plant bought the Shaw property known as Ossipee Mountain Park, burned the hotel and other buildings, simply to get them out of the way, and built his own famous residence, "Castle in the Clouds," on the top of Bald Peak.

4. "Meeting and Passing," *Complete Poems*, p. 148.

5. "The Lockless Door," *Complete Poems*, p. 299. The summer experiences in the Henry Horne house also helped to inspire two prose plays which RF later wrote. Of these, the first written was the one-act play entitled "A Way Out," published in *The Seven Arts*, Vol. 1, No. 4 (Feb. 1917), pp. 347-362. The second, a three-act play, written during the summer of 1941 and never produced or published, was entitled "The Guardeen." Two manuscript drafts of "The Guardeen" are preserved in the Barrett Collection, Virginia.

6. Under the stimulus of LT, and with the subsequent help of RF, Stephen J. Lerman (Princeton '61) did considerable first-hand research in New Hampshire and Vermont, during two summers, before writing and publishing "Robert Frost on Ossipee Mountain," *Appalachia*, New Series, Vol. XXIX, No. 7 (June 1963), pp. 395-401. The article is illlustrated with a map of "Ossipee Mountain Park and the Lee Settlement in 1895," and with a photograph of the Henry Horne house. One anecdote which Lerman acquired directly from RF is quoted here:

"On a morning in late June, 1895 . . . young Frost hurried toward the railroad station in Lawrence. He was to catch the Boston and Maine train for the north country and the White sisters, Elinor and Leona, were to get on at the next stop, North Lawrence. As he approached the station, an old high school friend hailed him, and they stood chatting for a few minutes. Suddenly, the parting whistle shrieked and Frost dashed to the platform only to see the train picking up speed down the tracks. Undismayed, he ran back to the street, brashly jumped on a passing farmer's wagon, gave the driver a dollar, and said, 'Lick up your horses and get to North

Lawrence fast as you can!' Away they raced—but as they neared the railroad crossing a short way from North Lawrence, they found the road blocked by a slow-moving freight train. Not to be thwarted, Frost jumped out of the wagon, leaped onto the freight train, climbed up and over to the other side, jumped off, and sprinted the remaining few hundred yards to the station, arriving just in time to be hauled onto the departing train for New Hampshire."

Another anecdote acquired and given by Lerman:

"Only one person has been located to date who remembers Frost during that summer—Paul Shaw, who was then nine years old, and was one of the grandchildren of Benjamin F. Shaw . . . His boy's eye view of young Frost is revealing. Often when Frost was courting Elinor, Paul and the other boys would pester them; rather than being annoyed, Frost would smile wanly and whittle them wooden animals or make birch bark canoes. 'We recognized right away,' said Shaw, 'that he was a friend.' "

7. Quoted from a seven-page typewritten article (unpublished), "Of Mrs. Frost's Private School," by Clara Searle Painter (Mrs. H. K. Painter) of Cleveland, Ohio. In her childhood Clara Searle had the distinction of spending seven years (1893-1899) studying with Mrs. Frost, and thus she was familiar with the various phases of Mrs. Frost's Private School from beginning to end.

8. This detail was given by Mrs. Ethel Wade Bartlett of Salem Depot, N. H., daughter of Dr. and Mrs. E. W. Wade, who befriended the Frosts while they were living in Salem Depot. In a letter to LT dated 18 March 1940, Mrs. Bartlett wrote: "I did go to Mrs. Frost for a time, for special tutoring in a few subjects, prior to entering Abbot Academy [in Andover, Mass.]. Mrs. Frost at that time was running a little private school in Lawrence." (There were several girls from Salem Depot who studied in similar fashion with Mrs. Frost before going on to Abbot Academy, and one of them was Sabra Peabody. RF never mentioned to LT that he ever saw Sabra Peabody at the school.)

9. Clara Searle Painter, op. cit.

10. Quoted, with permission, from a letter written by Susan P. Holmes to LT, 17 March 1964.

11. Susan P. Holmes, "Robert Frost in Lawrence," op. cit.

12. This was the consensus of opinion, without exception, gathered by Owen D. Young retrospectively from his classmates in 1946 and 1947. The wife of Owen D. Young (formerly Miss Josephine Sheldon Edmonds) had been a classmate (and for the freshman year a roommate) of Elinor White's at St. Lawrence University. As further evidence on this point see the entirely separate statement made by the Rev. Lorenzo Dow Case and quoted in the following note.

13. Lorenzo Dow Case and Owen D. Young were close friends

during their college years. Before Case was consulted by LT, Young assured LT that Case was neither engaged to nor in love with Elinor White. Although it is impossible to separate all the facts from the mythic elements in RF's version of this situation, Case's version of it corroborates the facts known to Owen D. Young. In a letter from Brooklyn, Michigan, dated 16 Dec. 1946, the Rev. Lorenzo Dow Case wrote to LT the following statements, which are quoted here with permission:

"[. . .] During the year before my graduation in 1895, I became enough interested in Elinor White to spend an evening with her once a week for several months. She had what I have always greatly admired, character and a brilliant mind. I had long noticed that she always had the answer to any question asked by the professors. She was so aloof and so superior that she was not popular. Then, too, she was pronouncedly subjective, self-possessed, serious, and reserved. She never thrust herself forward. She shunned prominence, and was unassuming and unostentatious. In a word, she was in no sense a mixer. Her real life was an inner one. She was always and everywhere demure, quiet, contemplative, serious and thoughtful.

"I admired her, immensely so, and was very fond of her. Had I been thinking of marriage, my affection might have ripened into love, and a proposal that she become my wife, but no such words ever fell from my lips.

"I do clearly recall that she finally told me she was engaged to a young man back East who was a writer of poetry and needed her, that she didn't think it fair to him to entertain me as she had long been doing, and that we should cease regularly seeing each other. I honored her for her frankness, and never again called on her.

"And I recall that I was surprised that her decision caused me no great grief. I received it only with deep regret, and with no tearing of the heart strings. I soon came to think of it as one of the most beautiful episodes in my life, and I have carried with me through many long years a beautiful recollection of her. . . ."

In the light of these statements, it seems very doubtful that EW told RF she was engaged to Case. It seems more probable that RF deceived himself on this point (and thus precipitated what he always viewed as the major crisis in his life), partly as a result of his headstrong impatience with EW because of her refusal to marry him until after she had completed her college education and until he had found a way to support them; partly as a result of his resenting EW's tendency to criticize him for his laziness and lack of direction; partly as a result of his rage over her willingness to "socialize" with Case, once a week, during part of her senior year. Although it is now impossible to determine the precise time when she finally told Case that she was "engaged to a young man back East," all the evidence seems to indicate that she did not make this statement until after the crisis involving the rescue of the ring from the fire.

19. RIFFRAFF

1. See Note 13 of this chapter.

2. RF to Susan Hayes Ward, 25 Jan. 1896, *Selected Letters,* p. 26-27.

3. RF to Susan Hayes Ward, 8 July 1896, *Selected Letters,* p. 27.

4. "The Birds Do Thus," *The Independent,* Vol. 48, No. 2490 (10 Aug. 1896), p. 1. Never collected by RF.

5. Mrs. W. S. Dana, *How to Know the Wild Flowers* (New York, 1893), p. 3. (See Note 6 of Chapter 21 for RF's play on this title with his own parody: "How to Ketch the Wild Flowers.").

6. "Flower-gathering," *Complete Poems,* p. 18; first published in *A Boy's Will* (1913).

The place and date of writing have been determined from a notation made by RF. In the following notes several references are made to RF's manuscript notations in separate books and magazines owned by Mr. and Mrs. Edward Connery Lathem. In one of these books—a copy of the first edition, first issue, of *A Boy's Will,* originally a part of the library of Lady Mary and Professor Gilbert Murray—RF made notes of where he was when he wrote each poem. At the end of "Flower-gathering," he wrote: "Allenstown N. H." (His only stay in Allenstown occurred during the summer of 1896.)

7. "The Self-seeker" (*Complete Poems,* pp. 121-123) was written in England in 1913; first published in *North of Boston* (1914).

8. "The Quest of the Purple-fringed [Orchis]," *Complete Poems,* pp. 458-459; first printed as, "The Quest of the Orchis," *The Independent,* Vol. 53, No. 2743 (27 June 1901), p. 1494.

RF's annotation in the Lathem copy of this issue of *The Independent* (see Note 6 of this chapter), is as follows: "Probably written in 1895 or 6. Place in mind was near East Pembroke N. H. where we spent a summer." (The summer was 1896, not 1895.)

It may also have been in the summer of 1896—or in the fall— that EWF sent to Miss Ward two manuscript poems. Each contained three quatrains and was in the handwriting of EWF. (If a covering letter accompanied the manuscripts and listed them, it has not survived.) One of the poems bore the title "Sea Dream" and was unsigned; the other bore no title and was signed in EWF's handwriting: "Robert Lee Frost." Neither one of the poems was published in *The Independent.* The full text of "Sea Dream":

> I went in a great tide under the sea
>   And my robe streamed on before—
> There were leaning towers as I passed by
>   And shells on the dim sea floor.
>
> The shells rolled fitfully without sound
>   I was deaf to my foot-falls too
> My arm cold and numb—was it touched by a hand—
>   She never would speak, I knew.
>
> The wagging fish with his lidless eye
>   May his eyes grow green in the sun!
> Stood off from me, but followed me
>   And I wished that the dream was done.

RF was fascinated by his own dreams, and made poems out of several of them (including "The Lockless Door"). In "Sea Dream" the reference to "My arm cold and numb" links with the reference to shells rolling "without sound" to suggest a dream of limited sentience, after death, hence the wish "that the dream was done." The imagery of "Sea Dream" is not unrelated to that in "Despair." The full text of the untitled poem is:

> I had a love once
> Sweeter than myrrh,
> You, when you kiss me,
> Remind me of her!
>
> Far in a forest,
> In love, in love,
> Can I forget it!—
> With birds above.
>
> She had your sweetness
> And your eyes,
> But the heart of a wild thing,
> And answerless sighs.

In acknowledging these two poems, Miss Ward may have made some pleasantry to the effect that RF was learning to disguise his handwriting. (At this time there was no likelihood that Miss Ward was familiar with EWF's handwriting.) RF did not write to Miss Ward for some time, during the fall of 1896, but as though in answer to such a pleasantry he ended a letter to Miss Ward, dated 27 Dec. 1896: "You think I couldn't disguise my handwriting?" Following that question, the valediction and signature, "Sincerely yours, Robert L. Frost," occurred in the handwriting of EWF.

Whatever happened, it is very doubtful that EWF would have tried to deceive Miss Ward by sending two poems not written by RF and then by signing his name to either one. It is probable that each is an "early poem," written by RF; that EWF merely served as his amanuensis, making fair copies at his request. But RF denied this probability. In 1929, not long after the letter files of *The Independent* were acquired by the Huntington Library, RF was asked to comment on these (and other) poems. (See the exchange in *Selected Letters*, pp. 354-356, and the conclusion of the letter dated 27 Dec. 1896.) RF answered the Huntington Library letter, denying that he had written either one of these poems. In 1932, when RF and EWF were in California, they visited the Huntington Library and were shown the manuscripts. EWF is reported to have made no comment ("She never would speak, I knew"); but RF again insisted that he was not the author of either poem. He might also have denied the authorship of some of the other early poems there, if the manuscripts had not been in his own handwriting.

A related problem concerning the poem entitled "God's Garden" is discussed in Note 11 of Chapter 20.

9. Cf. "Of Mrs. Frost's Private School," op. cit., in which Clara Searle Painter describes new quarters: ". . . the change was to Haverhill Street, to a tall, bay-windowed, two-and-a-half-storied, frame residence, narrow in width but stretching back to fit the long, narrow lot. Beyond a narrow alley on its right stood the old City High School; across the street was the Common, where after school the girls made fascinating rooms, houses and fairylands from the moss which grew among the roots of the great elms standing in double rows around the City Green. In this building, came my first acquaintance with Robert Frost. I was too young to have him for a teacher, he was reserved for older pupils, and had a halo in our eyes because he had recently come from [Dartmouth] college. From then dates my first interest in Latin. I see myself vividly, child of seven seated at a desk in what had been the 'front room' under a hanging chandelier of a former glory, supposedly adding columns of figures but in reality listening with straining ears to the unfamiliar sound of the Latin first declension. The lure of sonorous words was irresistible; I listened and listened and my arithmetic suffered in consequence."

10. The spelling of the name, "Elliott," is corroborated by records in the offices of the city clerks in Lawrence and Methuen.

In a letter from Susan P. Holmes to LT dated 17 April 1964, the suggestion is made that the child was named after "a very lovely woman" named Elliott, who was a relative of the Holmes's and a close friend of the Frosts's. She adds: ". . . I recall being at her house one time when my brother and I were asked to sing Sunday-School songs for her, and am quite certain that Mrs. Belle Frost was one of those who prevailed upon us to do so."

11. The striking discrepancy between RF's two versions of this incident—the version given in court in 1896 and the version recorded in "Notes on Robert Frost," 28 July 1941—again illustrate RF's tendency to create an imaginative representation, which is valuable as an indication of RF's ideal image of himself. In 1896, RF admitted in court that he had hit a man who was off-guard and sitting in a chair; in 1941, and many times thereafter, RF told LT this version: That Parker struck the first blow and that RF was thus given a chance to make use of the boxing skills he had learned from the professional pugilist from whom he had taken lessons; that he began to punch for Parker's eyes, and he slowly backed Parker out of the kitchen onto the back stairs, slowly boxed him down the stairs, and that Parker ran after he had thus been driven to the foot of the stairs; that Parker came back with a police officer a few minutes later and accused Frost unfairly of starting the fight by hitting Parker while he was bending down to tie his shoe. For the most detailed version of the fight, as given in court and as printed, see Note 13 of this chapter.

12. The fight took place on Saturday evening, 26 December 1896 and the court action occurred two days later; but on Sunday, 27 December 1896, when RF tried to write a letter to Susan Hayes Ward (*Selected Letters*, pp. 28-29), his mood of depression was reflected in these two sentences:

"As nothing that happens matters much and as most of my thoughts are about myself I am always at a loss for likely subject matter [for letter-writing]. I am the father of a son if that is anything."

13. *The Lawrence Daily American*, Monday evening, 28 Dec. 1896, p. 1. The major portion of this news article:

"One of the most interesting cases in the police court this morning was the one in which Robert L. Frost was charged with assault on Herbert S. Parker. Frost pleaded guilty to the charge and was fined $10, which he paid. An account of the trouble between Frost and Parker is as follows:

"Both live in the Simmons house on Haverhill Street and trouble has been brewing, it is reported, between them for some time.

"The house is let to Mrs. B. M. Frost, who, with her daughter and son, and the latter's wife, carry on a private school.

"The house is a large one and so they let a few of the rooms.

Last fall, Herbert Parker and his wife decided to take rooms down town during the winter months so as to be near his work, and so arrangements were made with Mrs. Frost to hire rooms in her house.

"Everything went on smoothly for a while and the two families were seen on the street together quite often.

"Among the ladies who came to call on the Frosts was Mrs. Thomas Hindle, and so she was introduced to the Parkers. But a misunderstanding, it is said, sprang up soon after between the Frosts and Mrs. Hindle and they suddenly became strangers.

"But this trouble did not sever the friendship between the Parkers and Mrs. Hindle, and she still continued to call on the former.

"Report has it that about ten days ago, Mrs. Parker met Mrs. Hindle with a friend on the street and she invited them up to her rooms. As they were approaching the house, the night latch was turned by some one in the house and when Mrs. Parker tried her key, it did not work.

"She then went around to the back door and entering the house that way, came down and let her company in. They were then escorted to Mrs. Parker's apartment and were just having a quiet chat, when Robert Frost, it is alleged, knocked on the door and told Mrs. Parker that if she wished to entertain Mrs. Hindle, she would have to vacate at once.

"Thus matters went on from bad to worse, and it is understood that different members of the Frost family spoke to Mrs. Parker a great deal about the matter during Mr. Parker's absence.

"At last, Mrs. Parker seems to have thought that she was being insulted during her husband's absence, and she told Mr. Frost that he was a coward to act so.

" 'Your husband don't dare call me that,' he is said to have retorted.

" 'Well, he does,' was the rejoinder, and thus matters stood until Saturday evening about 5.30 when young Parker arrived home from work. The story as told is as follows:

"When Mr. Parker entered his kitchen Mr. Frost came in and asked him if he called him a coward.

" 'I do,' he replied, 'if you insult my wife in my absence.'

" 'Do you want to fight?' is said to have been the next question, put to Parker.

" 'No, I don't,' said he.

"Trouble seems to have followed and the black eye which Parker is wearing at present is said to have been given him by Frost at that time.

"Parker jumped up from his chair, then, to defend himself and the two grappled with each other and in a second Parker was on a chair with Frost on top of him. Some scars on Parker's forehead and chest are said to have been received at this time.

"Mrs. Frost, her daughter and her daughter-in-law then interfered and separated the combatants and both parties withdrew to their respective tenements.

"Parker then went to the police station to swear out a warrant against Frost and told his story to the city marshal.

[. . .]

"The friends of both of the families are very sorry that any trouble of the kind should have ever happened."

A brief version of the incident occurred in *The Evening Tribune* for Monday evening, 28 Dec. 1896, a paragraph in a news article bearing the caption,

LONG POLICE COURT SESSION
ROBERT L. FROST FINED FOR ASSAULT ON HERBERT S. PARKER

The paragraph:

"Robert L. Frost, of the class of '92, Lawrence high school, was in court charged with assault on Herbert S. Parker. He pleaded guilty and was sentenced to a fine of $10 or 30 days."

14. *The Weekly Journal*, 31 Dec. 1896, p. 2. The same article contained these additional details:

"This isn't the first time Mr. and Mrs. Herbert Parker have had their grievances before the public. The young couple were secretly married some two years ago, much against the wishes of the senior Parker, who, gossip says, has since given the 'Icy mit' to his young scion. But what does Herbert care, he got an accomplished, sweet little wife, and he is able and willing to earn his own living, even if it's only a dollar and a quarter a day, to which his wife very materially adds by giving music lessons. There are those who admire the young couple for their pluck and independence, and there are those too, who think were they agent of a mill and had a son called Herbert, he would receive at least a two dollar a day job in the Pacific mills."

Cf. Edward Connery Lathem, "Robert Frost: Assailant," *The New-England Galaxy* (Spring, 1965), pp. 27-29. I am grateful to Mr. Lathem, whose researches uncovered the newspaper accounts and whose considerateness provided me with photo copies of them. His brief *Galaxy* treatment of the incident includes a reference to it by RF in 1958:

" 'I never was in court,' he remarked in 1958, during a Washington press conference, '—except for punchin' somebody once, years and years ago. . . .' Characterizing the circumstance as 'too delicate a matter,' he proved disinclined, despite questions pressed by the surprised reporters, either to reveal the particulars or to identify his 'rival'—adding only, 'He said I hit him. And the judge looked at me; and I said, "It looks as if I did." . . . I thought I'd have to leave town. It made the front page of the local papers.' "

15. He continued to brood over the epithet "Riffraff," and made much of it each time he repeated the full story. LT's first recording of it, from conversation, in "Notes on Robert Frost," on 28 July 1941, is as follows: "He never got over that word, 'Riffraff.' He even accepted it and felt that he was about as low as any of them could be, during those years when he had no job, no future. He admits that his delinquencies have been as much responsible for his sadness as for his success. He says that his lethargy, his downright laziness, and his willingness to humor himself by lying around and waiting for a writing mood have forced him into a kind of selfishness which made his married life almost unbearable for his wife."

20. HARVARD: AS FOR THE VIEW

1. Quoted from the poem entitled "All Revelation," *Complete Poems*, p. 444.

2. Repeatedly, in later years, RF enjoyed the paradox of saying in effect that his greatest inspiration when he was a student came from a man whose classes he never attended: William James. Usually he liked the mysteriousness of avoiding any mention of the name of the "teacher." For example: "My greatest inspiration, when I was a student, was a man whose classes I never attended." (Quoted in Janet Mabie, "Robert Frost Interprets His Teaching Method, *The Christian Science Monitor*, 24 Dec. 1925, p. 11.)

3. On the day after he found a way to survive, William James wrote in his journal: "I finished the first part of Renouvier's second 'Essais' and see no reason why his definition of Free Will—'the sustaining of a thought *because I choose to* when I might have other thoughts'—need be the definition of an illusion. At any rate, I will assume for the present—until next year—that it is no illusion. . . . I may perhaps return to metaphysical study and skepticism without danger to my powers of action. . . . Hitherto, when I have felt like taking a free initiative, like daring to act originally, without carefully waiting for contemplation of the external world to determine all for me, suicide seemed the most manly form to put my daring into; now, I will go a step further with my will, not only to act with it, but believe as well; believe in my individual reality and creative power." (Quoted in Horace M. Kallem [ed.], *The Philosophy of William James* [New York, 1925], pp. 28-29.)

4. Ibid., p. 31.

5. Quoted from William James, "Is Life Worth Living?" in *The*

Will to Believe and Other Essays in Popular Philosophy (New York, 1897), p. 51.

6. Ibid., p. 59. This became one of RF's favorite notions, which he often repeated in his own words. The continuation of the passage (ibid., pp. 59-61, passim) is also pertinent to a habit of mind which RF seemed to develop with the help of William James: "Now, it appears to me that the question whether life is worth living is subject to conditions logically much like these. It does, indeed, depend on you . . . If you surrender to the nightmare view and crown the evil edifice by your own suicide, you have indeed made a picture totally black. Pessimism, completed by your act, is true beyond a doubt, so far as your world goes. Your mistrust of life has removed whatever worth your own enduring existence might have given to it; and now, throughout the whole sphere of possible influence of that existence, the mistrust has proved itself to have had divining power. But suppose, on the other hand, that instead of giving way to the nightmare view you cling to it that this world is not the *ultimatum*. Suppose you find yourself a very well-spring, as Wordsworth says, of—

> 'Zeal, and virtue to exist by faith
> As soldiers live by courage; as, by strength
> Of heart, the sailor fights with roaring seas.'

"Suppose, however thickly evils crowd upon you, that your unconquerable subjectivity proves to be their match, and that you find a more wonderful joy than any passive pleasure can bring in trusting ever in the larger whole. Have you not now made life worth living on these terms? What sort of a thing would life really be, with your qualities ready for a tussle with it, if it only brought fair weather and gave these higher faculties of yours no scope? . . . This life *is* worth living, we can say, *since it is what we make it, from the moral point of view;* and we are determined to make it from that point of view, so far as we have anything to do with it, a success."

As evidence that these Jamesian ideas, quoted in this note (and in the textual passage to which this note is appended) had a lasting appeal for RF, see the passage on "four beliefs" quoted from RF's "Education by Poetry" in Note 4 of Chapter 17. Compare also the following passage directly quoted from RF by Mark Harris in 1961 (Lathem, *Interviews*, p. 271):

" 'The Founding Fathers didn't believe in the future . . . They believed it *in.* You're always believing ahead of your evidence. . . . The most creative thing in us is to believe a thing in, in love, in all else. You believe yourself into existence. You believe your marriage into existence, you believe in each other, you believe that it's worthwhile going on, or you'd commit suicide, wouldn't you?' "

7. LT, "Notes on Robert Frost," 27 Aug. 1941, and later. Among RF's many remarks made over a period of twenty-one years, and paraphrased by LT in "Notes on Robert Frost," RF's retrospective acknowledgments of his own marital ruthlessness— and even cruelty—were given with extraordinary consistency. In 1941, when he was asked how he succeeded in persuading EW to break her "engagement" (as he called it, always) to Lorenzo Dow Case and to marry RF in spite of all the arguments she had given against the marriage, he clenched his teeth and said, "I bent her to my will." (This is probably not true, but there is value in knowing that he liked to think it was true.) A closely related entry in "Notes on Robert Frost," made twenty-one years later (2 Aug. 1962): "He . . . told me that Elinor White had really been committed to marry someone else; but that Frost forced her to break that engagement, forced her to marry Frost, just as a kind of 'punishment' (that recurrent word, 'punishment')." In 1960, when he was asked if EWF had been pleased by his announcement of his plan to enter Harvard as a special student, he again said she had seemed to be completely indifferent to a plan she herself had previously urged; then he added, ruefully, "I had broken her, by then." As will be shown in the second volume of this biography, RF's sense of guilt over his treatment of EWF reached its peak immediately after her death in 1938. It is possible that he further tried to salve his guilt thereafter by shifting to EWF all the blame for all the elements which hurt their marriage, that he did it by trying to trace the difficulties back to the so-called disloyalty of her so-called engagement to Lorenzo Dow Case.

A paraphrase of one of his strongest statements on this point occurs in LT, "Notes on Robert Frost," 4 March 1962: ". . . directionlessness had been given his life by Elinor's refusal to stay in love with him, and be loyal. Her letters, written to him while he was still at Dartmouth, had made him know that she was no longer loyal to him. That was one of the big reasons why he left Dartmouth. He was sure he had lost her. And in losing her he had lost everything, he feared. So he began to drift."

8. The "current number" of *The Independent* (9 Sept. 1897, p. 1) contained RF's poem "Warning." (See Note 10 of Chapter 15.) This was the fourth of his poems to be published by *The Independent*. The first two were "My Butterfly" and "The Birds Do Thus." The third was "Caesar's Lost Transport Ships," one of his earliest, written in high school while he was translating Caesar's *Commentaries on the Gallic Wars*. More than four years passed before *The Independent* published another poem of his; "The Quest of the Orchis" appeared in the issue for 27 June 1901.

9. *Selected Letters,* pp. 29-30. The letter is dated 11 Sept. 1897.

10. *Complete Poems,* p. 36. "Now Close the Windows" was written at Dartmouth in the fall of 1892; it was first published in *A Boy's Will.*

11. The quatrain occurs in a letter from RF to Charles L. Young, 7 Dec. 1917 (MS, Wellesley College Library), protesting that his daughter Lesley had been mistreated by some of the Wellesley professors. The following passage from the letter provides a pertinent context for the quatrain: ". . . I addressed to Sheffy when I was a patient at Harvard . . . [quatrain] . . . How it all comes back to me! You see I was angry at the general disposition to take everything written by an undergraduate as an exercise. I never wrote exercises in my life. I was the same sixpence then as now and so is Lesley's Latin teacher the same old scourge blight and destitution that held marks over me for seven years of Latin and then left me nowhere in the end. . . ."

Only a few of RF's early poems were submitted to Sheffield in English A at Harvard; but two of his other poems, published in *The Boston Evening Transcript* in 1897 and 1898, are worth biographical attention. The first was an occasional poem, inspired by Turkey's declaration of war against RF's beloved Greece on 17 April 1897. Greece fared poorly in this brief war, despite RF's exhortations, in his poem entitled "Greece," which appeared on page 6 of the *Transcript* for 23 April 1897:

> They say, "Let there be no more war!"
>   And straightway, at the word,
> Along the Mediterranean shore,
>   The call to arms is heard.
>
> Greece could not let her glory fade!
>   Although peace be in sight,
> The race the Persian wars arrayed
>   Must fight one more good fight.
>
> Greece! Rise triumphant. Long ago
>   It was you proved to men
> A few may countless hosts o'erthrow:
>   Now prove it once again!

As already mentioned, RF had become acquainted with Charles Hurd, literary editor of the *Transcript.* More than a year after Hurd accepted and published "Greece," RF submitted to him another poem which Hurd printed. The poem was "God's Garden," and it would seem to belong among the earliest of RF's juvenilia—

even earlier than his first published poem, "La Noche Triste." Perhaps RF submitted to Hurd a sheaf of manuscripts, and padded out his offerings with early pieces which he expected Hurd to reject. No matter how it happened, Hurd published only "God's Garden" at this time, and it appeared on page 6 of the *Transcript* for 23 June 1898.

In 1938, when Charles R. Green, Librarian of The Jones Library in Amherst, Massachusetts, obtained a photostatic copy of this poem as published, RF shamefacedly acknowledged his authorship of it; acknowledged that the signature "R. L. F." used for "Greece" and "God's Garden" did stand for Robert Lee Frost. In 1946, however, when asked by LT if he was the author of "God's Garden," RF flatly denied that it was his. (This was not the only time he made such denials. See *Selected Letters,* pp. 354-356: RF was asked about thirty-eight manuscript poems, most of which were certainly his, but he began his answer, "I recognize just four of your list by the names you give them . . . Are you sure I wrote the rest? I wonder if somebody hasn't been imposing on you.") The complete text of "God's Garden":

God made a beauteous garden
   With lovely flowers strown,
But one straight, narrow pathway
   That was not overgrown.
And to this beauteous garden
   He brought mankind to live,
And said: "To you, my children,
   These lovely flowers I give.
Prune ye my vines and fig trees,
   With care my flowrets tend,
But keep the pathway open
   Your home is at the end."

Then came another master,
   Who did not love mankind,
And planted on the pathway
   Gold flowers for them to find.
And mankind saw the bright flowers,
   That, glitt'ring in the sun,
Quite hid the thorns of av'rice
   That poison blood and bone;
And far off many wandered,
   And when life's night came on,
They still were seeking gold flowers,
   Lost, helpless and alone.

O, cease to heed the glamour
   That blinds your foolish eyes,
Look upward to the glitter
   Of stars in God's clear skies.
Their ways are pure and harmless
   And will not lead astray,
But aid your erring footsteps
   To keep the narrow way.
And when the sun shines brightly
   Tend flowers that God has given
And keep the pathway open
   That leads you on to heaven.

If "God's Garden" is one of RF's earliest poems (as it would seem to be), RF's mother may have helped him with it. Such a possibility is strengthened by a comparison with the clichés in "The Artist's Motive," quoted in Note 4 of Chapter 3.

12. Willam James, *Psychology: Briefer Course* (New York, 1892), p. 149.

13. Ibid., p. 156.

14. Ibid., 179-180.

15. Ibid., p. 183.

16. Ibid., p. 192. In this passage on prayer James gave RF some reassurance of beliefs originally made comfortable for him during and after his childhood by his mother's repeated and persuasive utterances. In the paragraph following this passage James also reinvigorated a belief which RF had acquired from his mother and to which he clung throughout his life: that God has reasons for His divine punishment of His earthly children.

"Even such texts as Job's, 'Though He slay me, yet will I trust Him,' or Marcus Aurelius's, 'If gods hate me and my children, there is a reason for it,' can . . . be cited . . . For beyond all doubt Job revelled in the thought of Jehovah's recognition of the worship after the slaying should have been done; and the Roman emperor felt sure the Absolute Reason would not be all indifferent to his acquiescence in the gods' dislike. The old test of piety, 'Are you willing to be damned for the glory of God?' was probably never answered in the affirmative except by those who felt sure in their heart of hearts that God would 'credit' them with their willingness, and set more store by them thus than if in His unfathomable scheme He had not damned them at all."

17. Ibid., p. 194.

18. Ibid., p. 459-460.

19. Ibid., p. [461]-462.

20. *The Will to Believe*, p. 29.

21. George Santayana, *The Life of Reason*, Volume One: *Reason in Common Sense* (New York, 1905), p. 262.

Justifiably, Santayana includes Cervantes among the pertinent satirists. In his preface to *Reason in Common Sense* (p. 9), Santayana sarcastically divides the world between science and religion, and then paraphrases a celebrated passage in the first chapter of *Don Quixote* to represent the religious response to experience: "One half the learned world is amused in tinkering obsolete armour, as Don Quixote did his helmet; deputing it, after a series of catastrophes, to be at last sound and invulnerable." (Both Cervantes and Santayana seem to invoke slyly Paul's exhortation to the Ephesians, 6: 11-17: "Put on the whole armour of God, that ye may be able to stand against the wiles of the devil. . . . And take the helmet of salvation . . .")

22. George Santayana, *The Life of Reason*, Volume Three: *Reason in Religion* (New York, 1905), pp. 51-52.

23. *Selected Letters*, p. 30.

21. GO OUT AND DIE

1. Complete text of RF's poem "A Question," *Complete Poems*, p. 493.

2. Miss Sergeant (*Robert Frost*, p. 54) makes reference to RF's physical ailment as one cause of his leaving Harvard. She scrambles two anecdotes he often told, however, and then makes the mistake of presenting the scrambled version as a direct quotation from RF. The second of these is the story of RF's repeated version of his grandfather's statement after the Derry farm had been purchased for RF's use: "Go out and die." The pertinent passage, as given by Miss Sergeant:

"I got very sick, terribly so . . . as if something were very wrong with heart or stomach. Trouble in the solar plexus. So I resigned from the sophomore class at the end of March, to the Dean's regret. The doctor thought I would die. He sent me home to die."

Miss Sergeant also confuses the time when Mrs. White and Elinor were living in Cambridge and making a home there for RF.

Both of these mistakes add to Miss Gould's confusions (*Robert Frost*, p. 73):

"He became 'terribly sick, as if something were very wrong with heart or stomach. Trouble in the solar plexis [sic].' Elinor, none too strong herself, and with small Eliot [sic] to care for, was glad to have her mother's help in nursing Rob. But he did not respond, and finally had to resign from the sophomore class at the end of

March, to the Dean's regret. 'The doctor thought I would die. He sent me home to die.' "

3. For biographical information concerning Dr. Charlemagne C. Bricault, I am grateful to Edward Connery Lathem. More details on the Bricault-Frost relationship may be found in Edward Connery Lathem and Lawrance Thompson, *Robert Frost: Farm-Poultryman* (Hanover, N. H., 1963), pp. 9-10, 27-29, 109-112, 116.

4. Initially, the date of birth for Lesley Frost was derived from John Eldridge Frost, *The Nicholas Frost Family* (privately printed, [Milford, N. H., 1943]), p. 113; subsequently, the date was corroborated by Mrs. Lesley Frost Ballantine. Provisionally, the place of birth is given as Lawrence, Mass., on the basis of circumstantial evidence; but Mrs. Ballantine said she was not sure where she was born. The City Clerk of Lawrence, Mass., writing to LT in a letter, 11 Feb. 1946, throws some light on the problem: "I have examined records of births on file here and find no reference to the birth of Lesley Frost, daughter of Robert Frost. . . . I know that you are aware that records of births years ago were not as well compiled and maintained as they are today. We are called upon regularly to establish records of births of people who were born in the 1880s to [and?] 1890s and whose records were never recorded." Although the circumstantial evidence still indicates Lawrence as the place of Lesley Frost's birth, Miss Sergeant (*Robert Frost*, p. 54) states: "Before he [RF] left [Harvard], his daughter Lesley was born in Boston . . ." Repeating the error, Miss Gould (*Robert Frost*, p. 73) writes: "Through the haze of fever, he watched Elinor prepare for their departure; then, just before they were to leave, the baby arrived . . ."

5. Quoted from "Non Beatus Novus Annus," *Bulletin*, Vol. XIV, No. 5 (Jan. 1894), p. 2.

6. The earliest of these booklets seems to be a manuscript imitation of a newspaper. It contains nonsensical prose and verse calculated to give Burell the latest news about himself and RF. This literary joke in booklet form, "The Parachute," is dated 13 June 1897, and is arranged in double columns. The lead-off article bears headlines: "The Seer Seen / Heels Uppermost in the Waters of the Suncook / Consider the Lilies How / They Grow / Clothes Dry." Then the story: "Suncook June 12.—The river here is waist-high and still rising. The people of the valley have all taken to the hills. This afternoon I waded and swam as far as East Pembroke but saw no one. Burell the theosophist is said to be picking flowers in the neighborhood but I saw nothing of him. The explanation is he was probably under water for the time being. No alarm need be felt for his safety at his feet have been seen repeatedly[,] violently agitated above the placid surface of the flood. The way he keeps

his clothes dry is by not wearing them. His actions are a sore perplexity to the good folk of the countryside as well they may be." Another news item purportedly gives an account of the death of Mrs. Belle M. Frost's little dog, Keno; the story begins, "Lawrence June 12.—The famous yellow dog Keno said to contain the soul of Confucius died at his home on Haverhill St early this morning after many years of suffering on the part of everyone but himself. . . ." Also contained in this issue of "The Parachute" is a poem celebrating the news that Ernest Jewell, mutual friend of Carl and Rob, had become a teacher at Lawrence High School, after completing his four years of study at Harvard:

Jewell Gets a Job.

Jewell walked from Broadway to Union St. and back
Jewell smiled at everyone as Jewell has the knack
He bore himself superbly his hat was in his hand
His clothes were new his face was clean
He
Looked
Just
Grand

The rain had laid the dust but the clouds were rolled away
And everyone was happy but Jewell he was gay
We saw him grow in stature and momently expand
All seemed to recognize a friend
He
Looked
That
Grand.

Another issue of "The Parachute," sent by RF to Carl Burell, has survived. Although the crudely stitched eight-leaf pamphlet is not dated, internal evidence suggests that it was written at Harvard in the fall of 1897, after RF had begun to suffer with a course in elementary German. This issue contains two bits of verse. The first is purportedly written by the printer's devil of "The Parachute" and is entitled, "In Memoriam / R. Frost Exit."

R. Frost is dead that able man
You ought to heard him swore
When all the copy was set up
And we called down for more.
He used to wear a long Scotch face
When things were going pore.

The second, also purportedly written by the printer's devil, who is represented as editing this "First Memorial Edition" of "The Parachute," is entitled, "To Carl Burell."

> Just cause we've got our hands full this edition
> Mourning a dead man here worth two of you
> You needn't think this paper dropped its mission
> Of slandering the way it used to do.
>
> Perhaps we're going to let you live in clover
> Not seeing what your weaknesses are, hey?
> I guess you'll find some folks have eyes all over—
> What makes you take this paper for and *pay*?

In this sequence of nonsensical literary efforts, the next one, which was sent to Carl Burell, is a stitched, eight-leaf manuscript booklet bearing on the front cover the title, "Life is Boxes / and / Other Tight Places," and the publisher's imprint, "RLF Pub Co." After the cover, the title page gives the author as "Shooks" and suggests, in describing this purported printing as a "Holiday Edition" (the "13th thousand"), that it may have been prepared for Carl as a Christmas remembrance, perhaps in 1897. It contains three prose sketches which playfully mock Carl's life as boxmaker, botanist, poet. The last page gives mock-advertisements for two books supposedly written by Burell, the first entitled "How to Ketch the Wild Flowers." This advertisement, after noting the "copious notes for idiots," quotes "praise" from three reviewers:

> "Tricky in the best sense."—*Petal and Punch*
> "We were especially pleased with the chapter on donts."—*Parachute*
> "Here is a man who has laid awake nights."—John Boggs in *Diseases of the Mind.*

The next item is an eight-page stitched pamphlet sent to Carl Burell, East Pembroke, New Hampshire, in an envelope which bears the postmark cancellation, "Boston, Mass., Cambridge Station, Dec. 18, 1898." The pamphlet, "The Rubaiyat of Carl Burell / His Misadventures / and / His Misfortunes," contains five limericks:

> There was a young fellow, begad,
> Who hadn't, but wished that he had—
>   God only knows what,
>   But he blasphemed a lot
> And showed he was generally mad.

There was a young man from Vermont,
Who voted for Bryan and Want
   And argued demented,
   But now he's repented,
So be easy on him and Vermont.

There was a young poet who tried
Making boxes when preoccupied;
   One day he made one
   And when he got done,
He had nailed himself on the inside.

There was a man went for to harma
Quiet but human old farmer:
   Now he wishes he'd known
   To let folks alone,
For this is the doctrine of Karma.

There was a young man moribund, who
Met with a fate few or none do
   He went out one day
   In his usual way
And was eaten alive by a sun-dew.

All of these manuscripts were discovered, rescued, and acquired for the Robert Frost Collection in the Dartmouth College Library by Edward Connery Lathem.

7. Original manuscript, Dartmouth College Library.

8. Original manuscript, Dartmouth College Library.

9. Susan Holmes, "Robert Frost in Lawrence," op. cit.

10. Letter, Susan Holmes to LT, 17 March 1964: ". . . I would say quite definitely that it was Grandma who had the strongest influence on little Elliott, in religious matters. In her Sunday-school class, which my brothers and I attended, she impressed us with the idea that God was always very near, that he was kind and loving, and loved children especially; which could have been the basis for the little boy's thinking that sunshine was God's smile. . . . I know that Mrs. Frost Sr. told my parents that she was worried about Rob and his sister both, as their wide-spread reading, especially after Rob went to college, seemed to have disturbed their faith."

11. "Stars," *Complete Poems*, p. 12. Circumstantial evidence for dating "Stars" as having been written, in its final form, between the death of Elliott Frost on 8 July 1900 and the move to the farm in Derry, N. H., around 1 Oct. 1900, is perhaps supported by one of RF's cryptic notes in a copy of *A Boy's Will* (see source of infor-

mation which is described in Note 6 Chapter 19), indicating where he was living when he wrote (or at least started to write) a particular poem. His annotation for "Stars" is simply "Lawrence," which might mean that the poem was started in Lawrence before the Frosts moved from there to Methuen in 1899, but certainly before the move to Derry.

12. Mrs. Josephine Wotherspoon, a niece of Miss Mary Mitchell's, was living in the house above Marston's Corner when LT visited it in 1940. Mrs. Wotherspoon had heard all about the stay of the Frosts from her aunt, who told her that the Frosts were "very proud people" and that they never did pay the rent which was due when they moved from there to Derry. As later references will indicate, RF became notorious for leaving some of his bills and borrowings unpaid. For another example, see Note 14 of Chapter 22.

When the Frosts lived in Miss Mitchell's home on Powder House Hill the address was 67 Prospect Street—and was so recorded in the Records of the Town Clerk of Methuen in connection with Elliott Frost's place of death. When LT visited the house in 1940, the street-numbering had been changed and the address was 635 Prospect Street.

13. Many discrepancies may be found in RF's various accounts of this incident. At times he insisted that his grandfather had actually said to him the words quoted, and beginning either "Go out and die" or "Go on out and die." A variant example occurs in Mertins, *Robert Frost*, pp. 64-65, where RF is cited (and probably quite accurately) as quoting his grandfather: " 'I have bought you a farm, just as you wanted it,' my grandfather growled to me. 'You've made a failure out of everything else you've tried. Now go up to the farm and die there. That's about all you're fit for anyway.' "

From circumstantial evidence, however, it seems impossible that William Prescott Frost either said or implied any such thing; that RF merely imagined this meaning (and these statements) as ways of justifying his irrational and unjust hatred of his grandfather. At other times, in fact, RF admitted as much: he said that it *seemed* to him that his grandfather *might* have been *thinking* he would *like* to say these things to RF.

The discrepancy between these opposed accounts is noteworthy, because it is very closely related to similar discrepancies in RF's various autobiographical mythmakings. Perhaps a more accurate indication of the grandfather's attitude may be found in those parts of his will quoted in Chapter 22.

14. I am grateful to Edward Connery Lathem for finding and sharing information that the warranty deed of sale was dated 25 Sept. 1900. For further details, see Note 17 of Chapter 27.

15. RF to LT; quoted here from an entry in "Notes on Robert Frost" dated 24 June 1946.

16. Again I am grateful to Edward Connery Lathem, who called my attention to this statement in *The Derry News* (5 Oct. 1900), p. 4.

17. Mrs. Belle Moodie Frost died in Penacook, N. H., on 2 Nov. 1900. Elliott Frost died in Methuen, Mass., on 8 July 1900.

18. RF sometimes talked obliquely about his obsession with suicide. One of his remarks, jokingly made to Miss Sergeant and lightly retold by her (*Robert Frost*, p. 58), deserves to be taken more seriously in the present context: "Yet they sometimes took drives on forgotten Derry roads that had forgotten farms. Frost recalls one they came on, early in their Derry life, with a black 'tarn' beside it (for convenient suicide) and what a pang it cost the poet not to have chosen it!"

Mrs. Lesley Frost Ballantine, speaking in another connection, casually told LT that there was a family legend to the effect that the pond regularly passed by RF on his drive from his farm to West Derry was the one he had in mind, and mentioned as a "frozen lake," in "Stopping by Woods on a Snowy Evening." If so, perhaps John Ciardi's claim—that there is a death-wish implicit in this poem—should be modified. The poem makes more sense if taken as the expression of a mood in which the death-wish is answered and rejected by the firmly asserted and conscientious awareness of "promises to keep." (See Note 7 of Chapter 31 for other considerations of John Ciardi, "Robert Frost: The Way to the Poem," in *Dialogues with an Audience* [Philadelphia, (1963)], pp. 147-157).

19. The only known manuscript of the poem "Despair" is in the Huntington Library, as part of the papers purchased from *The Independent*. The handwriting indicates that this copy was made about 1906 and that it was sent to Susan Hayes Ward at about that time. Unfortunately, all the poems sent to Miss Ward were separated from the letters whenever possible, and so cannot be dated by means of the letters. Some of the poems RF sent her were not submitted for publication in *The Independent*. RF mentioned "Despair" to LT for the first time less than a year before RF died ("Notes on Robert Frost," 4 March 1962) and asked if a copy of it was in the Huntington Library. To help in identifying it, RF quoted the first line—and then continued to say the entire poem accurately from memory. He was told that there was a fair copy of it in the Huntington Library, and was asked if he had a copy in his own files. He said he did not. He was apparently correct in his assertion; no copy of "Despair" was found in his papers after his death. Under the circumstances, then, his accurate memory of

"Despair"—his ability to quote all of it without faltering—is note-worthy.

22. FACT AS DREAM

1. Quoted from "Mowing," *Complete Poems,* p. 25, first pub-lished in *A Boy's Will* (1913).

2. *Selected Letters,* p. 33.

3. *Complete Poems,* p. 16. The earliest known manuscript of "To the Thawing Wind" is a fair copy sent to Susan Hayes Ward at Christmas 1911, with the title, "To the Loud Southwester" (Huntington).

4. H. D. Thoreau, *Walden, and Other Writings* (New York, 1950), p. 88. In Note 12 of Chapter 15, reference is made to RF's listing and commenting on, in 1936, his ten favorite books. Among the ten were Thoreau's *Walden* and Emerson's *Essays and Poems.* Because the entire list, and the comments by RF therewith, may be viewed as having so much bearing on his early years, his entire statement (in *Books We Like,* op. cit., pp. 141-142) is here quoted:

"*The Odyssey* chooses itself, the first in time and rank of all romances. Palmer's translation is by all odds the best. As Lawrence in a preface to his own translation describes the author of the original, he is evidently a man much more like Palmer than like Lawrence. I can permit myself but one translation out of ten books.

"*Robinson Crusoe* is never quite out of my mind. I never tire of being shown how the limited can make snug in the limitless.

"*Walden* has something of the same fascination. Crusoe was cast away; Thoreau was self-cast away. Both found themselves suffi-cient. No prose writer has ever been more fortunate in subject than these two. I prefer my essay in narrative form. In *Walden* I get it and always near the height of poetry.

"Poe's *Tales.* Here is every kind of entertainment the short story can afford, the supernatural, the horrific, pseudoscientific, in-genious, and detective. (Every kind, I should perhaps say, but the character.)

"*The Oxford Book of English Verse* and Untermeyer's *Modern American and British Poetry* pretty well cover between them the poetry of our race. I am permitting myself two and one half num-bers of actual verse in the ten-twenty-five percent. That doesn't seem for the moment an undue proportion.

"*The Last of the Mohicans* supplies us once for all with our way of thinking of the American Indian.

"*The Prisoner of Zenda* surely one of the very best of our modern best-sellers.

"The Jungle Book (first). I shall read it again as often as I can find a new child to listen to me.

"Emerson's *Essays and Poems*—the rapture of idealism either way you have it, in prose or in verse and in brief."

5. *Walden,* op. cit., pp. 81-82.

6. R. W. Emerson, "The Poet," in *The Complete Essays, and Other Writings* (New York, 1940), p. 327.

7. Ibid., p. 326.

8. Ibid., p. 163, quoted from "Self-Reliance." Much has been written on the kinship between RF and Thoreau and Emerson; but not enough. The task which remains is to separate likenesses and differences. Although RF would have been uncomfortable if he had been asked to align himself with all the peculiarities of American transcendentalism as practised and preached by Emerson, the point to notice is that RF had his own ways of winnowing out from transcendentalism the elements that were most important to him. One of those elements was a notion which is found operative in Puritan doctrine: that any "fact" may and should be viewed as a type or emblem or symbol of some element in the divine plan. In 1917, just after Amy Lowell had tried to define RF as a "Yankee realist," RF wrote critically of her attempt, and concluded, "I wish for a joke I could do myself, shifting the trees entirely from the Yankee realist to the Scotch symbolist." (*Selected Letters,* p. 225.) That was no joke, and he might have spoken at the time in all seriousness, as he did six years later, when he said:

"What's my philosophy? That's hard to say. I was brought up a Swedenborgian. I am not a Swedenborgian now. But there's a good deal of it that's left with me. I am a mystic. I believe in symbols. I believe in change and in changing symbols. Yet that doesn't take me away from the kindly contact of human beings. No, it brings me closer to them." (Rose C. Feld, "Robert Frost Relieves His Mind," *New York Times Book Review,* 21 Oct. 1923, p. 2; see Lathem, *Interviews,* p. 49.)

9. *Complete Poems,* p. 25. "Mowing" seems to have been written early in the Derry period, and the strongest hint on this point is provided by Elizabeth Shepley Sergeant, in *Fire Under the Andes* (New York, 1927), p. 295, where she says that RF told her "Mowing" was the first "talk song" he was aware of; that after writing it, he tried to do it again in "My November Guest." One may notice the discrepancy between this assertion of RF's and some of his other claims to how early he became interested in writing "talk songs." But at least this comment suggests that "Mowing" was written among the earliest of the Derry poems.

10. Copy of the will of William Prescott Frost, dated 15 January 1901, provided to LT by Wilbur E. Rowell. Date of WPF's death: 10 July 1901.

11. I am grateful to Edward Connery Lathem for calling to my attention not only this news item but also a manuscript in the Dartmouth College Library which seems to have bearing on Carl Burell's departure from the Derry farm. Whenever RF's resentment caused him to treat friends discourteously, he soon felt ashamed of himself and sometimes tried to make amends. This manuscript seems to be a case in point. Internal evidence suggests that during the spring of 1902—or perhaps 1903—Burell invited the Frosts to visit him in Suncook for some kind of botanizing expedition. Frost apparently failed to reply immediately, but made belated apologies by sending the following playful lines to "C. B."

> To Coebee;—
>   If I remember straightly
>   Me and the Derry Gentian
>   Got a formal invite lately
>   To attend a flower convention
>   ('Twas the letterhead of Gately
>   I may casually mention) [.]
>   We were disappointed greatly
>   But the limits of our pension
>
>   And the said flowers backward condition
>   And a hatch of eggs impending
>   Complicated our position:
>   We couldn't think of attending.
>   There warnt no use in wishing
>   Nor Monstr' inforin' ingend-'ing,
>   So with your kind permission
>   We staid and did fence mending.
>
>   If again you should require us
>   To help you make a showing
>   Come out openly and hire us—
>   At least pay our fare going.
>   Then if you want to fire us
>   You'll feel free-er to do the toeing.
>   But be sure and not desire us
>   When the Gentian isn't blowing.

If this letter-in-verse is read as a part of the previous banter exchanged between RF and Burell (given in the text and notes of Chapter 21), the pleasantry of tone is better understood. The very obscure line, "Nor Monstr' inforin' ingend-'ing," seems to invoke deliberate echoes from a passage in Milton's *Paradise Lost*, Book Two, lines 793-796:

And in embraces forcible and foul
Ingend'ring with me, of that rape begot
These yelling Monsters that with ceaseless cry
Surround me . . .

RF's obscure line occurs while he is explaining to Burell why the Frosts were unable to accept the invitation. The back-country talk, phonetically caught in using "warnt" for "wasn't," suggests that RF may have tried to use "inforin' " similarly for the word "inferring": There wasn't any use in wishing the Frosts could go, and there wasn't any use in engendering excuses which inferred monstrous hindrances. One excuse, possibly hinted, could have been the fact that during the spring of 1902—and again during the spring of 1903—Mrs. Frost was "big with child." RF, intermittently guilt-ridden by his own sexual drives and annoyed by his responsibilities as a father, may have wanted his Miltonic reference to infer, obscurely, that his annoying children had helped to hinder him from accepting the invitation.

12. *Complete Poems,* p. 161. In "The Hill Wife" the title for this part is "The Smile: Her Word."

13. "Storm Fear," *Complete Poems,* p. 13.

14. There are conflicting accounts concerning the resolution of this partnership. RF told LT the story ruefully and admitted that he was the one who had set the interest rate at 15%. He said that he had borrowed $400 from Jewell and that he *thought* he had paid back $400, but that he had never been able to pay one cent of interest to Jewell. He may have paid back $400, but the note he signed remained in Jewell's possession and, after his death, was sold by a member of the family, as an item of interest only to an autograph collector. The note (now in the Barrett Collection, Virginia) reads:

West Derry N H May 24 1902

$675.

For value received, I promised to pay Ernest C. Jewell, on order, six hundred seventy five dollars on demand, with interest annually.

Robert Lee Frost.

Supplementary information was provided to LT by a friend, John Bateman, in a letter dated 29 Sept. 1947. Bateman volunteered to get biographical information from the widow of Ernest Jewell, but he reported difficulties experienced during a phone call to the widow: ". . . finally and very cautiously [I] dropped the name of Robert Frost into our little discussion. The conversation immediately took a turn for the worse! I had no idea that one slight little old lady could get so much venom into two such simple words as 'Robert Frost.' She snorted and spat them back at me, 'Robert Frost! Of all the ungrateful, selfish, forgetters of old friends, etc. etc.'—and so on into a diatribe that would have curled that old gentleman's ears had he been able to hear her. . . . So then I tackled William, the Jewells' son . . . the magic name of Frost brought about the same immediate reaction as it had from his mother, except that it was not quite so intense or passionate. But I fear that they have both privately and publicly washed their hands of having anything to do with him."

From this evidence, it seems safe to conclude that Jewell never did recover the full amount of the principal on his loan.

15. I am grateful to Edward Connery Lathem for calling my attention to this information, used in *Robert Frost: Farm-Poultry-man*, op.cit., pp. 112-114.

16. Thoreau, op. cit., p. 304 (*Week*, Chapter 1).

17. Cf. "The Ax-Helve, *Complete Poems*, p. 230. "The Ax-Helve" may have been one of the first of RF's dramatic narrative poems written at Derry. RF, writing to Louis Untermeyer, 15 June 1916: "I've been keeping under cover a couple of things called An Axe-helve and The Bonfire. . . . One is old old and the other is new . . ." ("The Bonfire" contains internal references to zeppelin bombings of England in World War One.) *Frost-Untermeyer*, p. 37; but for a conflicting statement on which of the dramatic narrative poems were written in Derry, see Note 5 of Chapter 31.

18. Emerson, "The Poet," op. cit., pp. 327, 328, 333-334.

19. In conversations with RF, LT frequently heard details of this trip to New York. It is also confirmed by a manuscript journal kept by Lesley in 1908, when she was nine years old. Retrospectively, she established the time of this particular trip to New York by saying that it was made when she was almost four years old [birthday 28 April 1899], that Carol was a baby, that "Irma and Marjorie were not yet born."

20. The full texts of these eleven pieces, together with complete bibliographical data, may be found in Lathem and Thompson, *Robert Frost: Farm-Poultryman.*

21. "Three Phases of the Poultry Industry," *Farm-Poultry* (15 December 1903), pp. 481-482.

22. *Farm-Poultry* (15 Jan. 1904), p. 46.

23. *Farm-Poultry* (15 Feb. 1904), p. 106.

24. Idem.

25. *Farm-Poultry* (1 March 1904), p. 116.

26. "The Housekeeper," one of the earliest of the dramatic narrative poems, was written at Derry. It seems to contain a relatively accurate characterization of John Hall, whose name is actually used in the poem (*Complete Poems*, pp. 103-111).

23. TRIAL BY EXISTENCE

1. Quoted from RF's letter, written in March 1935 to *The Amherst Student*. (*Selected Letters*, p. 418.) In RF's Vergilian eclogue entitled "Build Soil," there is a moment when Tityrus says, "Let me preach to you, will you, Meliboeus?" In answer, Meliboeus says, "Preach on. I thought you were already preaching. / But preach and see if I can tell the difference." (*Complete Poems*, p. 427.)

In all of RF's poetic preachments, his ulterior concern is with the salvation of the soul. In his prose essay, "Education by Poetry" (op. cit., p. 78), he arranges the uses of metaphor in a Platonic ladder to stress the Platonic-Christian preoccupation with the salvation of the soul: "Poetry begins in trivial metaphors, pretty metaphors, 'grace' metaphors, and goes on to the profoundest thinking that we have. Poetry provides the one permissible way of saying one thing and meaning another. . . . Greatest of all attempts to say one thing in terms of another is the philosophical attempt to say matter in terms of spirit, or spirit in terms of matter, to make the final unity. . . . The only materialist—be he poet, teacher, scientist, politician, or statesman—is the man who gets lost in his material without a gathering metaphor to throw it into shape and order. He is the lost soul." RF's poem "The Trial by Existence" is of particular importance in this connection because it represents his earliest poetic statement about the salvation of the soul.

2. "The Lovely Shall Be Choosers" contains mistaken and delicate autobiographical hints in the sequence ending, "To think much or much care." These hints may be paraphrased: At the time of the wedding let only the bride and groom know a particular secret which grieves her in particular, a secret which even her most intimate friends do not know; but later, when these friends are bound to learn the secret, let them be too far away to think or care very much about it.

RF admitted to LT that for the larger part of his life he had mistakenly surmised that his parents had married hastily, soon after RF had been conceived. For a time he believed that the records of the marriage and of the date of his birth were destroyed in the San Francisco earthquake and fire of 1906. (He used this statement, repeatedly, when asked to produce or obtain a birth certificate.) Eventually, he learned the facts: that his parents were married on 18 March 1873, over a year before RF's birth on 26 March 1874. While he was still in doubt concerning this marriage date, however,—and just as soon as he began to become famous— RF tried to protect himself by publicly giving out the statement that he was born in 1875. For further information on this delicate point, and the resolution of this deception, see *Selected Letters,* pp. xlvii-xlviii.

3. In the text passing reference is made to the fact that "The Lovely Shall Be Choosers" (*Complete Poems,* pp. 325-326) was written much later than "The Trial by Existence." The actual date is not known to LT, but the first-draft manuscript of the poem, on four half-sheets of typewriter-size paper, is in The Jones Library, Amherst, Mass. The handwriting peculiarities suggest that it was probably written in the early 1920's. The first draft contains two trial-titles: "Retribution" and "Defeat in [Life]." The poem was first published as a separate pamphlet in *Poetry Quartos* (New York, 1929).

4. The immediate reference is to the "Myth of Er," in the *Republic;* but Plato refers to the same myth in *Phaedo, Phaedrus, Meno, Timaeus,* and *Laws.* The ideas and images in the following passages from *Phaedrus* are pertinent:

". . . at the end of the first thousand years the good souls . . . come to draw lots and choose their second life, and they may take any which they please. . . . every soul of man has in the way of nature beheld true being; this was the condition of her passing into the form of man. But all souls do not easily recall the things of the other world. . . . which we beheld shining in pure light, pure ourselves and not yet enshrined in that living tomb which we carry about, now that we are imprisoned in the body . . ." (Irwin Edman, ed., *The Works of Plato* [New York, 1956], pp. 290-291.)

5. Matthew Arnold, *Poems* (London, 1877), 2 vols., Vol. I, p. 168.

6. *The Will to Believe,* pp. 2-29 passim.

7. Ibid., p. 214; from the essay, "The Moral Philosopher and Moral Life." The Bible quotation, adapted by James from Deuteronomy 30: 19, suggests more precise biblical echoes in "The Trial by Existence"—for example: "Beloved, think it not strange concerning the fiery trial which is to try you, as though some strange thing happened unto you" (I Peter 4: 12). Nevertheless, the mythical imagery of the poem owes less to biblical figures than to Plato, Shelley, Arnold, and James. The word "trial" is repeatedly manipulated by James within an essentially orthodox Christian framework; it occurs with special pertinence in a passage already partly quoted from *The Will to Believe* (pp. 51-52): "A man's religious faith . . . means for me essentially his faith in the existence of an unseen order of some kind in which the riddles of the natural order may be found explained. In the more developed religions the natural world has always been regarded as the mere scaffolding or vestibule of a truer, more eternal world, and affirmed to be a sphere of education, trial, or redemption."

8. Compare the related and familiar poetic handling of Platonic concepts in the following stanza from Shelley's "Adonais":

> The One remains, the many change and pass;
> Heaven's light forever shines, earth's shadows fly;
> Life, like a dome of many-coloured glass,
> Stains the white radiance of Eternity,
> Until Death tramples it to fragments.—Die,
> If thou wouldst be with that which thou dost seek!
> Follow where all is fled!—Rome's azure sky,
> Flowers, ruins, statues, music, words, are weak
> The glory they transfuse with fitting truth to speak.

9. Shortly after he published "The Trial by Existence," and apparently with *The World as Will and Representation* in mind, RF made passing reference to his "grafting Schopenhauer upon Christianity" therein. (*Selected Letters*, p. 38.) It might seem that in the process he grafted Schopenhauer completely out of sight; that Shelley came nearer, by anticipating Schopenhauer at least on one point in his exhortation, "Die, / If thou wouldst be with that which thou dost seek!" Perhaps RF meant that in the act of revising this poem he had ended his intermittently pessimistic feeling that the "will to live" might as well be blind, purposeless, amoral, and self-destructive.

Another tantalizing reference to philosophical elements in the poem was made by RF (*Selected Letters*, p. 202): ". . . the day I did The Trial by Existence . . . says I to myself, this is the way of all flesh. I was not much over twenty, but I was wise for my years. I knew then that it was a race between me the poet and that in me [the philosopher] that would be flirting with the entelechies . . ." There is no way of knowing just how much RF "did" with the poem at the time when ("not much over twenty") he became aware that he was "flirting with the entelechies." It is doubtful, however, that he became acquainted with or started using the word "entelechies" until he studied the history of philosophy at Harvard in 1898. His textbook there was Alfred Weber's *History of Philosophy*, and he could have found the root word in Weber's discussion of Aristotle's view that entelechy is the condition in which a potentiality has become an actuality; or he could have found the word in Weber's discussion of Plato's opposite view that entelechy is that which gives form and perfection to anything. Or he might have found the concept that the entelechy of the body is the soul, which remains at one with the One even when the body is least aware of that oneness.

10. Quoted from *Complete Poems*, pp. 28-30. No early draft of "The Trial by Existence" is known to LT. It was first printed in

The Independent, Vol. 61, No. 3019 (11 Oct. 1906), p. 876; it was published next in *A Boy's Will* (1913), pp. 40-43, the text there being identical with the text in *Complete Poems*—even in the use of "wrack" for "rack."

11. *Selected Letters,* p. 35. The letter is dated 24 Feb. 1906, and the original bears a marginal note apparently written by Ward: "The poems sent were uncommonly good."

24. NOT ELVES EXACTLY

1. Quoted from "Mending Wall," *Complete Poems,* p. 48.

2. This incident occurred in April 1905, and Lesley gave a retrospective account of it in one of her journals. Years later RF made a metaphorical use of the incident within the framework of his war poem "The Bonfire." The poem was first published in *The Seven Arts,* Vol. I, No. 1 (November 1916), pp. 25-28. It appears in *Complete Poems,* pp. 163-166.

3. Lesley's "First Speller" notebook, dated "March 1st 1904," is in the Barrett Collection, Virginia.

4. Mrs. Lesley Frost Ballantine still has several notebooks in which she made her journal entries from October 1905 to September 1909. I am extremely grateful to her for permission to examine these notebooks, to make transcriptions, and to quote briefly from them. She intends to make far more extensive uses of them in a volume to be entitled *New Hampshire Girlhood.*

5. See Note 4 of this chapter.

6. Among his many literary projects, RF may have planned to make a book out of the stories he told or wrote out and read to his children. Sixteen of these stories, written on thirty sheets of paper, have survived (Barrett Collection, Virginia).

7. "In a Vale," *Complete Poems,* p. 21. The archaic words in this poem suggest that it was probably written near the time of "My Butterfly"—1894. A fair copy of "In a Vale" was sent to Susan Hayes Ward signed, "Robert Frost / Pinkerton Academy Derry N. H." The handwriting indicates that this fair copy was made in 1906 or 1907. A related poem, sent to Miss Ward by RF in a manuscript booklet for Christmas 1911, is now in the Huntington Library. It is entitled "Tutelary Elves":

> Some flowers take station close to man's abode,
> And some draw up on either side the road
> To watch him, horse and foot, go trooping by,
> And take his dust when summer winds are dry.
> To neither of these the forest flowers belong
> Whose care for man is yet no whit less strong

Because they will that whoso touch their stem
Must don humility and come to them.
One can believe they say, considerate elves,
"Draw man out of himself and other selves."

An even earlier poem which invokes the little people and which
may have been read by RF to his children is "Spoils of the Dead."
Originally printed in *A Boy's Will,* it was subsequently dropped
and never collected by RF:

Two fairies it was
    On a still summer day
Came forth in the woods
    With the flowers to play.

The flowers they plucked
    They cast on the ground
For others, and those
    For still others they found.

Flower-guided it was
    That they came as they ran
On something that lay
    In the shape of a man.

The snow must have made
    The feathery bed
When this one fell
    On the sleep of the dead.

But the snow was gone
    A long time ago,
And the body he wore
    Nigh gone with the snow.

The fairies drew near
    And keenly espied
A ring on his hand
    And a chain at his side.

They knelt in the leaves
    And eerily played
With the glittering things,
    And were not afraid.

>   And when they went home
>   To hide in their burrow,
>   They took them along
>   To play with to-morrow.
>
>   When *you* came on death,
>   Did you not come flower-guided
>   Like the elves in the wood?
>   I remember that I did.
>
>   But I recognised death
>   With sorrow and dread,
>   And I hated and hate
>   The spoils of the dead.

In "Spoils of the Dead," the ambivalent value of the word "spoils" is important. It refers not only to the ring and watch-chain, which the fairies plundered, but also to death itself as dreadful and hateful because of its power to despoil. The fear of death was obsessively strong in RF throughout his life and it finds echoes in many of his poems—particularly in "The Night Light" (*Complete Poems*, p. 529):

>   She always had to burn a light
>   Beside her attic bed at night.
>   It gave bad dreams and broken sleep,
>   But helped the Lord her soul to keep.
>   Good gloom on her was thrown away.
>   It is on me by night or day,
>   Who have, as I suppose, ahead
>   The darkest of it still to dread.

Notice the echo of one line from the *New England Primer*, "Prayer at Lying Down," which RF taught his own children to say. In RF's attempt to struggle against and rationalize his dread, so that he could accept death as not merely inevitable but also a transition into a fuller life, he fell back on some familiar religious consolations. A variant is implied in his poem "In Hardwood Groves" (*Complete Poems*, p. 37), which includes the metaphor that the life of one generation (in plants, animals, human beings) must grow through the death of the preceding generations. RF, in the Lathems' copy of *Complete Poems* (see Note 6 of Chapter 19), made the following note after "In Hardwood Groves": "This was a substitute for guess what in the original Boy's Will." One guess: "In Hardwood Groves" first appeared in *Collected Poems* (1930) at exactly the time when "Spoils of the Dead" was dropped.

8. Quoted in Lesley Frost, "Our Family Christmas," *Redbook* (December 1963), pp. 45, 98.

9. Idem.

10. Idem. In the same article, Lesley Frost writes: "There has been a certain amount of controversy as to how religious a man Robert Frost was. . . . That my father *was* a religious man one can rest assured, if his way of bringing up his children can be said to bear witness. With [readings from] Blake and Longfellow, Milton, Watts and Luther, Christina Rossetti and Eugene Field, and many another, we were slowly filled with the certainty of a Supreme Authority. And Christmas was a Birthday. Well one knows how important a birthday is to a child, *any* birthday. So it was not difficult to make Christmas a *special kind.*"

In another connection, she adds, "Among our favorite longer poems, also learned by heart, were Stevenson's 'Christmas at Sea'; Alfred Domett's 'A Christmas Hymn'; and Longfellow's 'Three Kings' and 'King Witlaf's Drinking Song'; not to mention a favorite of Robert Frost's, Longfellow's little five-act play *The Nativity.* Many years later [1929] I was to include all these in a Christmas anthology, *Come Christmas,* dedicated to my elder daughter, Elinor, 'on her first Christmas.' "

11. See Note 4 of this chapter.

12. This anecdote was told to LT by Lesley Frost Ballantine on 1 March 1963.

13. "Tree at My Window," *Complete Poems,* p. 318. RF's identification of the relationship between the poem and the birch tree outside his bedroom window in Derry is cited in Louis Mertins, *The Intervals of Robert Frost* (Berkeley, 1947), pp. 2 and 22.

14. "Into My Own," *Complete Poems,* p. 5. First published under the title "Into Mine Own" in *New England Magazine* (May 1909), p. 338.

15. See Chapter 29 for RF's ironic use of "Into My Own" in *A Boy's Will.*

16. RF frequently told LT about his wife's tart comments, and yet he rarely quoted them. Perhaps the best available example of them occurs in the following passage from a letter dated 21 March 1920 (*Selected Letters,* p. 244):

"Elinor has just come out flat-footed against God conceived either as the fourth person seen with Shadrack, Meshack, and Tobedwego [Abednego] in the fiery furnace or without help by the Virgin Mary. How about as a Shelleyan principal or spirit co-eternal with the rock part of creation, I ask. Nonsense and you know it's nonsense Rob Frost, only you're afraid you'll have bad luck or lose your standing in the community if you speak your mind. Spring, I say, returneth . . . Like a woman she says Pshaw."

In reporting this exchange, RF may have put some words in his wife's mouth, but the passage which has the truest and tartest savor is: "Nonsense and you know it's nonsense Rob Frost, only you're afraid."

17. RF's ambivalent attitude toward "escape" troubled him throughout his life. Repeatedly, he saw the psychological dangers which could be caused by the wrong kind of withdrawal. One of his frankest references to his own predicament during the early years in Derry is contained in John Bartlett's record of a conversation with RF on 28 June 1932: "I sometimes think of those years as almost a fadeout, an escape into a dream existence, as in dementia praecox." (John Bartlett, typewritten "Notes From Conversations with Robert Frost," Barrett Collection, Virginia.)

Several years earlier, in 1917, RF had tried to convince Bartlett that under certain circumstances the only way to preserve one's sanity was to escape through a deliberate act of withdrawal from a particular crisis: ". . . you'll have to give up everything for a little while. . . . Cut and run away from every care: that is the rule. Nothing else will do. No faltering." (*Selected Letters*, p. 213.)

At various times, RF defended his own habit of escape. For example, Miss Sergeant writes (*Robert Frost*, p. 57): "I recall a conversation with him in the twenties about the word 'escapist.' He objected to the negative meaning. The point he said was: what are you escaping from? Possibly something that is strangling you. What are you escaping to? Possibly something you need and must have."

See also RF's defensive poem, "Escapist [?]—Never" in his last book, *In the Clearing*, p. 27.

18. "A Dream Pang," *Complete Poems*, p. 22. The earliest known manuscript of this poem occurs in a letter, RF to Susan Hayes Ward, dated 6 August 1907, with the following comment, "I shall master the sonnet form in time." During the years 1906 and 1907, he devoted much time to experimenting with the sonnet form and developed considerable skill in his handling of it.

19. "The Pasture," *Complete Poems*, p. 1. This poem, first published as a prologue to *North of Boston* (1914) was probably written in England in 1913. Concerning "The Pasture," RF is quoted as saying, "There is a poem about love that's new in treatment and effect. You won't find anything in the whole range of English poetry just like that." (E. A. Richards, "Two Memoirs of Frost," *Touchstone*, Amherst, Mass., Vol. IV, No. 3 [March 1945], p. 20.)

25. HEN-MAN AT PINKERTON

1. Quoted from "The Fear of God," *Complete Poems*, p. 538. The total meaning of this poem is not obscured by the ambiguous quality in these opening lines; the central idea of the whole is in

essential accord with basic elements of Christian doctrine. This idea may be summarized as follows: The trust and faith and confidence which are available to human beings who align themselves on the side of God, in the warfare between good and evil, should serve as a form of inner defense and should not be paraded, lest the flaunting of such a relationship entail the first of the seven deadly sins: pride. (See some related ideas in Note 4 of Chapter 31, particularly, "Of course, somebody must lose.")

2. Letter of recommendation, written by the Reverend William E. Wolcott, dated 29 January 1906; MS, Frost Correspondence File, Dartmouth College Library.

3. "The Tuft of Flowers," *Complete Poems*, pp. 31-32. In the Lathems' copy of *A Boy's Will* (described in Note 6 of Chapter 19), RF wrote, at the end of this poem: "After a summer job in Salem [Windham?] N. H. This was submitted as a theme in English A at Harvard."

4. "The Tuft of Flowers" was first published in *The Derry Enterprise* for 9 March 1906, p. 1. I am grateful to Edward Connery Lathem for this information.

5. Quoted from *Catalogue of Pinkerton Academy* (Derry, N. H., 1906, p. [7]).

6. Ibid., p. 9.

7. For more details on the mortgage, see Note 17 of Chapter 27.

8. Fanny Kingsley [ed.], *Charles Kingsley, His Letters and Memories of His Life* (London, 1877), 2 vols., Vol. II, p. 107. Quoted here from Walter E. Houghton, *The Victorian Frame of Mind* (New Haven, 1957), p. 257.

9. "A Prayer in Spring," *Complete Poems*, p. 17.

10. *Selected Letters*, p. 36.

11. *Selected Letters*, pp. 36-37, letter dated 29 Oct. 1906.

12. This particular version of the old myth is quoted from Friedrich Nietzsche, *The Birth of Tragedy* (New York, 1956), p. 29.

13. "The Demiurge's Laugh," *Complete Poems*, p. 35. When this poem was first published in *A Boy's Will* (1913), the gloss for it, given in the table of contents, said nothing more than that it was "about science." These two words pick up more meaning, however, if they are placed in the larger context of the previous glosses: "He resolves to become intelligible, at least to himself, since there is no help else; and to know definitely what he thinks about the soul; about love; about fellowship; about death; about art (his own); about science."

14. The poem, "The Later Minstrel," has only slight artistic value; but the implications of meaning in it are of biographical interest:

Remember some departed day
When, bathed in autumn gold,
You wished for some sweet song and sighed
For minstrel days of old,

And that same autumn day
Perhaps the fates would bring
At eve, one knocking at your heart
With perfect songs to sing.

You knew that never bard on earth
Did wander wide as he
Who sang the long, long thoughts of Youth,
The Secret of the Sea.

You knew not when he might not come;
But while he made delays,
You wronged the wisdom that you had
And sighed for vanished days.

Song's times and seasons are its own,
Its ways past finding out,
But more and more it fills the earth
And triumphs over doubt.

"The Later Minstrel" was probably written in a hurry, and even
the surface meaning is somewhat vague; but it seems at least to
hint that those who wish for "minstrel days of old" may discover in
Longfellow a "later minstrel" too good to be ignored, that (by
implication) an even later minstrel might not be recognized if too
much time should be spent sighing "for vanished days."

A copy of the first printing of "The Later Minstrel" in broadside
form is in the Dartmouth College Library; another copy is in The
Jones Library. The poem was printed in *The Pinkerton Critic*
(March 1909), p. 14. For more details, see Lawrance Thompson,
"An Early Frost Broadside," *New Colophon*, Vol. I, Part 1 (Jan.
1948), p. 5.

15. "The Lost Faith" was published in *The Derry Enterprise* (1
March 1907), pp. 1 and 4. It was never collected by RF.

16. These immediate quotations are taken from notes made by
RF on an undated piece of foolscap; the reference to the Wright
brothers suggests that the notes were made early in RF's career as
a teacher at Pinkerton. RF gave this piece of foolscap to Mr. Clifton Waller Barrett in 1951 and added the following brief annotation: "This is as old as Derry days. You can see from it where one
idea started." (Barrett Collection, Virginia.) The reference is ap-

parently to the start of the idea which later found reflection in the poem title, "Happiness Makes Up in Height for what It Lacks in Length" (*Complete Poems*, p. 445).

17. *The Derry News* p. 3.

18. *The Pinkerton Critic* (May 1907), p. 12. With Frost's help, the sophomore (or "Junior Middle") class again triumphed over the senior class in the following year, but in each of these years a near-scandal was caused by RF's generosity in assisting the sophomores. This near-scandal was referred to years later in at least two retrospective accounts. The first was written by John T. Bartlett (who entered Pinkerton as a sophomore in the fall of 1907) and was contained in a letter dated 30 April 1927 (from John Bartlett to Gorham Munson, copy in the Barrett Collection, Virginia):

"I am sure that when I entered the Academy there was much faculty hostility to Frost, and among the older students there was, also. The submission of all prepared papers in an interclass debate between Junior Middlers and Seniors to Frost, as the English teacher, was objected to by the Senior team, [as] a grossly offensive act meriting disciplinary rebuke, but such did not follow. There were certain members of the faculty who had toward the new English teacher almost, I believe, a personal animosity."

The second reference occurs in Sidney Cox, *A Swinger of Birches* (New York, 1957), p. 60:

"He told his Pinkerton debaters when they had a good idea to ascribe it to Daniel Webster or George Washington: judges, he told them, would find their thoughts convincing only when masquerading as not their own. When a prize contest for an oration was required, he let the ten eligible boys each write something. When they handed in what they had written he suggested an improved sentence or two. They revised and handed in again. The same process was repeated with a different part of the oration. And so on, again and again, until at last—the way Robert tells it—in the long series of revisions all the boys' balderdash had been replaced by substitutions, written dramatically, in character, by Robert Frost. The ten boys memorized the orations. Finally he was also called upon to select the winner. The donor [of the prize for the contest] expressed amazement at the excellence and naturalness of the ten orators."

This version of the story blends RF's usual accounts of assistance he gave to his debaters and to those writing for a prize contest. RF repeatedly told LT that this process of revision was used by him not only in helping his debaters but also in helping the students he liked most, that in the second category of competition the favorite student giving from memory the prize-winning essay [not "oration"; see Note 7 of Chapter 27] would sometimes be speaking an essay which had been written almost completely by RF. Even in retrospect RF seemed to be merely amused—and never conscience-stricken—by this little game he had played.

26. LIFT UP MINE EYES

1. Quoted from " 'Out, Out—' " in *Complete Poems*, p. 171.
2. Untitled MS, Barrett Collection, Virginia.
3. In a letter from the poet-essayist-critic Winfield Townley Scott to LT, dated 24 April 1953, Mr. Scott writes that "about 1930" a "practical nurse" called Lizzie Goodrich came to work for his family in Haverhill, Mass., from "somewhere just across the line in New Hampshire"; that she said she had lived in Derry and had been hired once to serve as midwife when Mrs. Frost was expecting; that the baby was born at the Frost farm in Derry, but was born dead.

The story may be true, although it does not fit the circumstances of the birth and death of Elinor Bettina Frost in 1907. In accordance with back-country customs it is possible that there was a private "home burial" on the Derry farm of the Frosts' and that the death was not publicly or officially recorded.

The records do show that a child was born to the Frosts during the following years of their stay on the Derry farm: 1902, 1903, 1905, 1906, 1907. An unrecorded birth might have occurred in 1901 or 1904. Mr. Scott further quotes Lizzie Goodrich as saying, about activities on the Derry farm during her stay there: "Most of the [each?] day, Mr. Frost would take Lesley, and they'd go off on long walks in the woods." Circumstantially, that statement suggests the year 1904 rather than 1901. Lesley was not old enough for "long walks in the woods" during 1901; her second birthday occurred on 28 April 1901. If the described event did happen in 1904, someone like Lizzie Goodrich would also have been needed as a practical nurse to help in caring for the two other children, Carol and Irma. Carol's second birthday occurred on 27 May 1904; Irma's first birthday, 27 June 1904.

4. RF, in making a jeu d'esprit of this story, carried the joke through two different forms of publication before he dropped it. First publication occurred in *The Dearborn Independent*, Vol. 27, No. 35 (18 June 1927), p. 2. For the second publication—in a booklet, *The Cow's in the Corn: A One-Act Play In Rhyme* (Gaylordsville, 1929)—RF wrote a brief preface:

"This, my sole contribution to the Celtic Drama (no one so unromantic as not to have made at least one) illustrates the latter day tendency of all drama to become smaller and smaller and to be acted in smaller and smaller theatres to smaller and smaller audiences."

The total text of this Celtic Drama, together with stage directions:

A kitchen. Afternoon. Through all O'Toole
Behind an open paper reads Home Rule.
His wife irons clothes. She bears the family load.
A shout is heard from someone on the road.

Mrs. O'Toole.
Johnny, hear that? The cow is in the corn!

Mr. O'Toole.
I hear you say it.

Mrs. O'Toole.
Well then if you do
Why don't you go and drive her in the barn?

Mr. O'Toole.
I'm waiting; give me time.

Mrs. O'Toole.
Waiting, says you!
Waiting for what, God keep you always poor!
The cow is in the corn, I say again.

Mr. O'Toole.
Whose corn's she in?

Mrs. O'Toole.
Our own, you may be sure.

Mr. O'Toole.
Go drive her into someone else's then!

She lifts her flat iron at him. To escape her
He slightly elevates the open paper.
The cow's heard mooing through the window (right).

For curtain let the scene stay on till night.

5. "The Fear," *Complete Poems*, p. 112; first published in *Poetry and Drama* (December 1913), pp. 406-409.

Perhaps the saddest local event discussed by the Lynch and Frost families, during the later summer visit in 1910, was the accidental death of a sixteen-year-old boy, Raymond Fitzgerald, with whom RF and his children had played games in each of their previous summer visits. RF was so deeply moved by the account of the boy's death (the son of the man in whose hotel RF had boarded during his first summer in Franconia) that he later used it as the raw materials for his poem "'Out, Out—'" (*Complete Poems*, p. 171; first published in *McClure's Magazine*, Vol. 47, No. 3 [July 1916], p. 42). The title is of course borrowed from Macbeth's famous soliloquy.

I am indebted to Edward Connery Lathem for background information concerning this incident. In the Lathems' annotated copy of *Complete Poems*, RF wrote on 3 Dec. 1955, at the end of the poem, a brief note documenting one of their discussions of it: ". . . the story was brought up in talks with you about the Fitzgerald boy who lived on the South Road out of Bethlehem—and died there." Lathem subsequently found the following news story in *The Littleton Courier* (31 March 1901), under the caption, "Sad Tragedy at Bethlehem / Raymond Fitzgerald a Victim of Fatal Accident":

"Raymond Tracy Fitzgerald, one of the twin sons of Michael G. and Margaret Fitzgerald of Bethlehem, died at his home Thursday afternoon, March 24, as the result of an accident by which one of his hands was badly hurt in a sawing machine. The young man was assisting in sawing up some wood in his own dooryard with a sawing machine and accidentally hit the loose pulley, causing the saw to descend upon his hand, cutting and lacerating it badly. Raymond was taken into the house and a physician was immediately summoned, but he died very suddenly from the effects of the shock, which produced heart failure. . . ."

6. *Selected Letters*, pp. 41-42.

7. Quoted from *Catalogue of Pinkerton Academy*, Derry, N. H., 1910-1911, pp. 27-28. By contrast, the *Catalogue* for 1905-1906 (op. cit., pp. 20-21) listed as required reading in English a total of four books on rhetoric, a book entitled *Principles of Argumentation*, representative orations by various Americans, Burke's *Conciliation with the American Colonies*, and other discouraging titles, along with old stand-bys from Irving, Whittier, Dickens, George Eliot, Longfellow, Cooper, Scott, Shakespeare, Tennyson.

8. In passing, brief reference should be made to the summer of 1908, when the Frost family also enjoyed a pleasant visit with the Lynches in Bethlehem during the hay-fever season. Anticipating that visit, Lesley wrote in her journal, on 21 April 1908:

"We are going to the White Mountains again. Papa and I think we will walk to the top of Mount Lafayette. We all enjoy the ride on the train very much. Marjorie goes to sleep in papa's lap on the way. Be glad to see Mrs. Lynch, who says Irma is a little Irish.

I'll walk to Franconia valley and walk around in the fields in front of the house and behind. Down in Franconia valley, papa always buys some peanuts or candy for us. . . ."

9. "A Servant to Servants," *Complete Poems*, pp. 82-83; first printed in *North of Boston* (1914). In the Lathems' copy of the first edition, first issue, of *North of Boston* (see Note 6 of Chapter 19), RF wrote: "A composite of at least three farm wives one of who I was glad to learn years afterward didn't go the way I foresaw." (The "one" reference is to Mrs. Connolley.)

27. NEW REGIME AT PINKERTON

1. Quoted from "The Ax-helve," *Complete Poems*, p. 230.
2. *The Derry News*, p. 3.
3. *The Pinkerton Critic* (October 1909), p. 15.
4. *Catalogue of Pinkerton Academy*, 1909-1910, Derry, N. H., p. 6.
5. *The Pinkerton Critic* (December 1909), p. 4. The rapport between RF and the students at this time is reflected in his writing (from the viewpoint of a player on the football team) a long and playful jingle-account (120 lines) to celebrate this occasion. It was published anonymously in *The Pinkerton Critic* (May 1910), p. 5, as, "A Kitchen in School, Or, Goings on at a Staid Old New Hampshire Academy," and it contained the following passage which is immediately pertinent:

> On the eve of our final game of ball
> With a school whose scalp we especially seek,
> And, if memory serves me, not in vain,
> (You have heard it, Sanborn of Kingston Plain)—
> Our principal told the football team
> If we would agree to win that game,
> We could all come up to the new school kitchen
> And he would promise to pitch in
> And cook us a regular three course dinner,
> And, supposing the old school wasn't a winner,
> We could come if we wanted to just the same,
> And have the dinner, but sans ice cream.
> We looked at each other, for then we saw
> How a kitchen might play an important part
> In a school intended by nature and art
> To fit boys and girls for college.
> Our principal, though no professional cook,
> Would have to get practical knowledge

Of dietetics by hook or by crook . . .
The guests were assembled too many to name,
With a plastered eye and a cheek-bone raw
And a twisted nose and an arm in a sling
And many a less apparent thing
Like a broken rib or ankle,—
With everything but a broken jaw
(Which would have been barred that night by law);
But having survived our fate thus far,
And victors over our dearest foe,
With never a thought to rankle.
The oyster stew began to flow.
(Of course you know what stewed oysters are,
Though you never have been to Simmons).
We knew the principal made the stew,
For the dining room was the kitchen, too,
And we saw him hovering over the brew
In its mighty blue enameled dish,
With a grace we had thought was women's;
As sanitary as you could wish
With a red cotton night-cap on his head—
I think 'twas a night-cap and think it was red.
There were sausages, long drawn out,
In solid garlands and fat festoons,
The kind of potatoes you read about.
There were knives and forks and dishes and spoons,
The faculty were the waiters. . . .

Frost never hesitated to write playful doggerel for the private amusement of his friends, either at this time or later in his life. Miss Sylvia Clark preserved another example, written by Frost at Pinkerton. In 1946, she told the story of it:

"One late afternoon I saw a most wonderful sunset as I looked from the chapel window at school. Anxious to have some one share the beauty before me, I called Mr. Frost and our librarian to enjoy the gorgeous display. I thought that my fellow workers did not show the proper amount of enthusiasm and I told them so quite emphatically. The next morning, as I sat at my desk, Mr. Frost dropped before me the following lines written in pencil upon a sheet of yellow school paper:

An A No. 1 Sundown   (Written by request.)

Miss Clark gave a sunset party
At a western window in Chapel,

And because our delight wasn't hearty,
Or we couldn't find words to grapple
With the ravishing skyscape before us,
Miss Clark got as mad as a taurus.
She appealed to the innate calf in us
If the gold wasn't here diaphanous,
There hard and metallic and glittering.
Then maddened still more by tittering
At her words diaphanous, metallic,
She called us dolichocephalic
And everything awful but feminine;
Said she wouldn't have nobody run down,
Or in any way squeeze a lemon in,
Her beautiful A One Sundown.

                    R. F."

(Sylvia Clark, "Robert Frost: The Derry Years," *The New Hampshire Troubadour* [November 1946], p. 15.)

6. *The Pinkerton Critic* (December 1909), p. 4; these are the best in the sequence of seven "Slipshod Rhymes" printed in this issue of the *Critic*.

7. Meredith Reed, one of RF's prize-winning students, gives a vivid account of her contest, with side glimpses at RF, in *Our Year Began in April* (New York, 1963), pp. 82-110.

8. *The Pinkerton Critic* (Feb. 1910), p. 8.

9. Evidence on this point occurs in Note 18 of Chapter 25.

10. The two poems were "The Flower-boat" and "A Late Walk." "The Flower-boat" appeared in *The Pinkerton Critic* (Dec. 1909), p. 7; but it had previously been published in *The Youth's Companion*, Vol. 83, No. 20 (20 May 1909), p. 249. "A Late Walk" appeared in *The Pinkerton Critic* (Oct. 1909), p. 5—the first printing of it. An even better poem, also written on the Derry farm and reflecting RF's perennial mood of regret when autumn came, is "October" (*Complete Poems*, p. 40). The humor in "October" balances the sadness in a typically Frostian fashion and keeps the tone from being romantically sentimental:

O hushed October morning mild,
Thy leaves have ripened to the fall;
Tomorrow's wind, if it be wild,
Should waste them all.
The crows above the forest call;
Tomorrow they may form and go.
O hushed October morning mild,

Begin the hours of this day slow.
Make the day seem to us less brief.
Hearts not averse to being beguiled,
Beguile us in the way you know.
Release one leaf at break of day;
At noon release another leaf;
One from our trees, one far away.
Retard the sun with gentle mist;
Enchant the land with amethyst.
Slow, slow!
For the grapes' sake, if they were all,
Whose leaves already are burnt with frost,
Whose clustered fruit must else be lost—
For the grapes' sake along the wall.

11. *The Derry News* (27 May 1910), p. 2. Authorship of this article is attributed to RF by LT on purely circumstantial evidence —textual and contextual. The discrepancy between the first-sentence statement, "Beginning Thursday, May 26," and the fact that the article appeared in the issue for May 27th would suggest that RF submitted the article just too late for its appearance in the issue for May 20th. Although the article concludes, "Look for announcement next week," *The Derry News* carried no announcement in the next week's issue. One possible reason: Edwin White, father of Elinor White Frost, was visiting the Frosts in Derry Village at the time, and died of heart trouble during the night of 26 May 1910, the night when *Dr. Faustus* was produced. *The Derry News* for 3 June 1910 carried the following details on p. 4:

"Edwin White, who was living with his daughter, Mrs. Robert L. Frost in Derry Village, died very suddenly of heart disease on Thursday night, May 26. Mr. White was in his usual health and retired as usual. He was taken ill during the night and passed away very suddenly. Mr. White is survived by a widow and three daughters, Mrs. Nathaniel Harvey of Portsmouth, Miss Ada White of Washington, D. C., and Mrs. Frost. A sister, Mrs. Caroletta Kelley of Philadelphia, also survives. Funeral was held Sunday afternoon at the home and was a private service. C. L. Merriam presided. The body was taken to Epping [N. H.] for interment."

This obituary reference to surviving relatives may be expanded as background information. Within a year after RF spent the summer with the Whites—mother and daughters—in Salem, N. H., Ada was "healed" by a Christian Science practitioner. Subsequently she went to Boston to receive training as a practitioner, then moved from Boston to Washington, D. C. There she "healed" and married a Yale graduate, Tillotson Beach Platt. Her sister

Leona (Mrs. Nathaniel Harvey), after returning from Salem to Derry, gave birth not only to the child whose death RF commemorated in "Home Burial" but also (eventually) to three other children: Alan, Vera, and Hilda. The Harvey family left the farm in 1909 and moved to Portsmouth, N. H., where the father became part-owner of a shoe store. Hilda left her husband in 1915, supported herself and her children, in part, by painting portraits, and died in 1931. Mrs. Edwin White (Henrietta Ada Cole White) separated from her husband about 1900 and lived with her daughter Ada in Washington, D. C. She moved with the Platts to Boston and died in their home at 821 Beacon Street on 31 May 1923, age 76 years. The medical examiner listed the death as "from natural causes—character indeterminate" and gave her religion as "Christian Scientist." (I am grateful to Edward Connery Lathem for tracking down some of this latter information at the Massachusetts Division of Vital Statistics.)

12. Phillipians 4: 12. An account of the baccalaureate exercises —and reference to the specific text of the sermon—appeared in *The Derry News* (17 June 1910), p. 2.

13. The warmth and friendliness shown to John Bartlett by RF is a good example of his capacity for self-giving. For the full story of it, see Anderson, *Frost-Bartlett*. In the already cited letter, Bartlett to Munson, Bartlett writes, "A few of the boys [at Pinkerton Academy] spent considerable time with Frost out of school hours. I remember a walk over the turnpike to Manchester in late afternoon, an hour spent in a bookstore, an oyster stew, and then a ride home on the electric railway. Our conversation on walks touched books only now and then. Frost had an interest in everything wholesome, and on a walk of two hours the conversation might include reminiscences of his early life, discussion of school affairs, including athletics, aspects of farm life in New Hampshire, some current news happening of importance, and nearly anything else. If, passing a farmhouse, the aroma of fried doughnuts came out to us, Frost might propose we buy some. Down around the corner, we might encounter a fern he hadn't seen since [he was] last in the Lake Willoughby region. And if darkness overtook us, and it was a favorable time for observation, Rob would be sure to take at least five minutes to study the heavens and attempt to start our astronomical education. Rob always talked a good deal, and his companions always did. There was always an abundance of conversation, and almost never argument. Rob never argued. He knew what he knew, and never had any interest in arguing about it. . . . I never knew a person who was more sensitive to slights, rebuffs, acts of unfriendliness than Frost. He seemed to carry the scar of them longer . . ."

14. *The Derry News* (23 June 1911), p. 1; obituary, *The Derry News* (30 June 1911), p. 3.

15. Details concerning this obsession were told to LT by Mrs. Lillian LaBatt Frost, widow of Carol Frost, 19 February 1963. They are pertinent because Carol killed himself in 1940.

16. John Bartlett, in his letter to Gorham Munson (op. cit.) writes, "In 1909, the State began to be interested in Frost's classes. He talked at conventions . . ." There are at least two references in *The Pinkerton Critic* to subsequent talks:

"Mr. Frost gave two lectures at the Farmington [N. H.] Institute, Feb. 11 [1910]. Other speakers on the same occasion were Mr. E. W. Butterfield, Principal of the Dover High School, and Mr. H. M. Bisbee, Principal of Robinson Seminary, recently visitors at Pinkerton Academy." (*Critic*, May 1910, p. 11)

"On January 13th [1911], Mr. Silver and Mr. Frost lectured in Meredith. Mr. Silver spoke upon the new courses here, and Mr. Frost spoke about Literature and Composition." (*Critic*, March 1911, p. 13)

17. I am grateful to Edward Connery Lathem, whose search in the Registry of Deeds of Rockingham County, Exeter, N. H., turned up the records having to do with the purchase of, RF's two mortgages on, and RF's sale of the so-called "Magoon place" in Derry. The following information is given in some detail, partly because it provides the names of neighbors of RF in Derry:

1900, Sept. 25 (Book 578, p. 160): the record of the warranty deed of sale, Edmund J. Harwood of Manchester, N. H., to W. P. Frost of Lawrence, Mass., for $1,725.00. Two parcels of land, the parcel on the east side of Londonderry Turnpike containing house and barn, bounded on the south by land owned by Joseph Klein, on the north and east by land owned by Sarah J. Upton; the parcel on the west side of Londonderry Turnpike, pasture land bounded on the northeast by a road leading from the Turnpike to the dwelling house formerly of Marshall Merriam, at a corner of the wall, then down in a southerly direction to land owned by Millard F. Miltmore, being the same premises described in the deed of Robert C. Brampton to Charles S. Magoon, 30 Aug. 1894, and assigned by Magoon to Harwood in a deed dated 27 Feb. 1895.

1906, March 24 (Book 617, pp. 181-183): the record of the mortgage by means of which Robert Lee Frost tentatively conveyed to Philomene Ladouceur of Manchester, N. H., the same two parcels of land with buildings thereon for $750.00 at 6% payable semiannually: "My right, title and interest in and to all said premises above described being derived under and by virtue of the Fourth Clause of the will of William P. Frost . . ." (Note paid in full, and mortgage discharged, on 21 Aug. 1911, through the drawing of another mortgage as described next.)

1911, Aug. 21 (Book 657, pp. 250-251): mortgage, Robert Lee Frost to the New Hampshire Savings Bank of Concord, for $1200, at 5% interest payable semiannually. The payments of money for this mortgage are given detailed representation in a letter (Frost Correspondence File, Dartmouth College Library) dated 22 Aug. 1911, from William P. Fiske, Treasurer of the New Hampshire Savings Bank to the man who apparently served as RF's lawyer in this transaction, Mr. John G. Crawford of Derry, N. H., stating that a check for $568.75 was enclosed, payable to Crawford's order, for use in discharging the previous mortgage of 24 March 1906; that another check was enclosed, $627.45, payable to Robert Lee Frost; that $3.80 had been deducted for expenses of examination.

1911, Nov. 16 (Book 661, p. 377): warranty deed of sale, Robert Lee Frost to Charles E. Senna of Boston. The sale record states that "for $1.00 and other valuable considerations" Frost conveys to Senna both parcels of the Derry farm, "free from all and every incumbrance whatever except—One mortgage for the sum of twelve hundred dollars given to the New Hampshire State Bank of Concord, which said grantee is to assume . . ." There is no statement of any additional amount paid to Frost by Senna for the purchase of the farm.

It is possible that when Senna purchased the farm in 1911, he did so merely by assuming the mortgage of $1,200, and that the value of the property had deteriorated during the eleven years since RF moved to the farm. In his various accounts, RF gave some hints of why the value might have deteriorated, but he liked to boast that the sale of the farm represented his most brilliant financial achievement. For example, Mertins (*Robert Frost*, p. 102) quotes RF as follows:

"Now we were ready to sell the farm and had a buyer for it. I have always looked on the sale of the Derry farm as my greatest financial achievement. You see my grandfather originally paid $1,700 for it, not counting the war tax for hay in the mow of $25. Well, I didn't take my uncle's advice and repaint the house, nor did I reshingle any of the roofs, so I saved these expenditures. In fact, I never spent a red cent on upkeep all the years I was there—taxes only excepted, and nothing can beat the tax collector. I left things exactly as I found them, not any worse, not any better. The roof never leaked, though I can't explain why, and the house managed to stand up all those years without a new coat of paint. I made a living—not a big one, or even a good one—but it was enough to keep body and soul together for ten years, paying our thirty dollars more or less every year for taxes. Thus, even counting the money for the hay, I expended in the ten years some $300 and not another cent, no more. That brought the entire cost of the buying the place and keeping it going for ten years, up to an even $2,000. I sold it for $1,900, so that we had our living for ten years at a total cost of $100—not counting what work I did, which wasn't much to count, not much."

This account, as reported by Mertins, is in accord with similar accounts given by RF to LT on different occasions; but at such times RF carefully avoided mentioning how he "made a living" on the Derry farm with the help of the annual income which he received from his grandfather's estate starting in July of 1902; he also avoided mentioning the $675.00 which he had borrowed from Ernest C. Jewell in 1902 and never completely paid back, avoided mentioning the mortgages and the heavy interest paid on the first mortgage, avoided mentioning numerous road taxes listed in the various Derry "town reports" as paid by him, avoided mentioning the salary he received from Pinkerton Academy starting in 1906. It would seem, then, that this account of his "greatest financial achievement" further illustrates RF's deceptive and self-deceptive tendency to idealize past events so that he might endow them with mythic values.

No evidence has been found to support RF's claim that he sold the Derry farm for $1,900, but perhaps he arrived at that figure by remembering that from his two mortgages he did receive a face value total of approximately $1,900: approximately $700 for the first, exactly $1,200 for the second. But he paid back the full amount of the first mortgage, together with interest at 6%. There is no record of when or how he made payments on the first mortgage prior to 21 Aug. 1911; but on that date he still owed, and paid, $568.75—out of the money received from the next mortgage. If, then, Senna acquired the farm by taking over the mortgage from New Hampshire Savings Bank of Concord (as seems to be the case), RF's clear profit was $627.45—plus $1.00. But even such profit as he made was "clear" only in the sense that he ignored his debts to Jewell—and to his grandfather.

18. A copy of the poem entitled "On the Sale of My Farm" was sent to Susan Hayes Ward at Christmas 1911; MS, Huntington Library.

28. GATHERING METAPHORS

1. RF to Susan Hayes Ward, 19 Dec. 1911 (*Selected Letters*, p. 43.)

2. Sidney Cox, *Robert Frost, Original "Ordinary Man"* (New York, 1929), p. 3.

3. Quoted in a letter to LT from Miss Constance Sanborn Guptill (Plymouth Normal School '12), 24 March 1940; text of the quotation compared with that as given in Burton Stevenson, *The Home Book of Quotations* (New York, 1935), p. 1734.

4. Silver's reminiscences were given LT in conversation at Plymouth Normal School during July of 1940. He corrected many misrepresentations made by RF and called particular attention to the fact that he had brought RF back to Plymouth to teach in a summer-school English program shortly after the return of RF from England. He also called attention to a newspaper account (Laconia, N. H., *Evening Citizen*, 30 July 1936, p. 2) of RF's visit to Plymouth to read his poems at the Normal School on 29 July 1936. The account said that Silver, introducing RF, had told how he had invited RF to go with him from Pinkerton to Plymouth because RF "had taught for me in an unusual way." Silver was further quoted as saying, "Frost came with trepidation. He was neither a conventional teacher nor a conventional man. Not only a poet but a character, Frost not only did not conform, but he was afraid he might become a conformist." Silver was also quoted as telling the story of how RF "conformed" at Christmastime of 1911, probably through the influence of Mrs. Frost, by presenting to Silver a cigar case with a note which stated in effect, "Although I do not believe in giving presents to those who have plenty of the ordinary things of life, in deference to the rest of my family, I am sending you this."

RF makes passing reference to the 1936 occasion—and to the continuation of his revenge tactics—in the account reported by Mertins (*Robert Frost*, p. 100) and somewhat misleadingly given as direct quotation, when it should have been given as paraphrase:

"He [Silver] consented to the one year tenure, probably thinking if he didn't like my psychology he would have an ace in the hole to get rid of me painlessly, and if he did he could easily talk me into staying on. But in 1912, when I left Plymouth to go to England, keeping my end of the bargain to the letter, I made an enemy of him. In 1938 [1936] I spoke at Plymouth at his invitation. He introduced me with flowery words. When I got up to speak I turned to him and said, 'Come on now, Silver. 'Fess up. After I had taught a year for you in this school back in 1911-1912, weren't you getting just a bit uneasy having me on the faculty?' He squirmed in his seat and turned red." (This would seem to be another example of mythic idealization on the part of RF.)

5. Quoted from the "Introduction" written by RF for the posthumously published work by Sidney Cox, *A Swinger of Birches: A Portrait of Robert Frost* (New York, 1957), p. viii.

6. For more details on this point, see *Selected Letters*, pp. xvi, 313-314, 435-436.

7. Quoted from a long letter, Cox to Munson, in Munson, *Robert Frost*, pp. 51ff. Another extremely important sidelight is provided in this letter by Cox's reference to RF's reading aloud and with obvious relish (during the year 1911-1912) from the writings of Finley Peter Dunne. Throughout the remainder of his life, RF was very fond of Dunne's Irish saloonkeeper, Mr. Dooley, who comically criticized events, leaders, and aspects of the social scene in a rich brogue. At this phase of his life, RF was beginning to emulate Dooley's comical fault-finding of the national scene. Later, he admired and emulated the mannerisms of Will Rogers.

8. Quotations from the remarks by W. B. Yeats are in "The Evils of Too Much Print," *Literary Digest* (11 March 1911), p. 461.

9. Pertinent quotations from remarks made in Boston by W. B. Yeats and George Moore are contained in "What Ireland Now Offers Us," *Literary Digest* (14 Oct. 1911), p. 824.

10. Sidney Cox, "Robert Frost at Plymouth," *The New Hampshire Troubadour* (Nov. 1946), p. 20.

11. In the Lathems' copy of *A Boy's Will* (described in Note 6 of Chapter 19), RF states that "In Equal Sacrifice" was written in Lawrence. This would indicate that it was written as one of his early poems in the 1890's. While at Plymouth, in 1911 or 1912, RF sent an early draft of it (the text differing in minor details from the later printed version) to John Bartlett in British Columbia, apparently in answer to a letter from Bartlett expressing downheartedness. The title of the draft sent to Bartlett is "A Heart in Charge" and the text of it is as follows:

> Hear what of old the Douglas did!
> He left his land as he was bid
> With the royal heart of Robert the Bruce
> In a golden case with a golden lid
>
> To carry the same to the Holy Land.
> By this and that we understand
> That that was the place to carry a heart
> At loyalty or love's command,
>
> And that was the case to carry it in.
> The Douglas had not far to win
> Before he came to the land of Spain,
> Where long a holy war had been
>
> Against the too victorious Moor;
> And there his courage could not endure
> Not to strike a blow for the Lord
> Before he made his errand sure.

And ever it was intended so,
That a man for God should strike a blow
No matter whose heart he may have in charge
For the Holy Land where hearts should go.

But when in battle the foe were met,
The Douglas found him sore beset,
And ringed around with certain death,
With but one stroke remaining yet,

And that as vain to save the day
As bring his body safe away,
Only a momentary help
For closing mightily the fray.

The royal heart by a golden chain
He whirled and flung forth into the plain
And followed it irresistably [sic]
And standing over it there was slain.

So may another do of right,
Give a heart to the hopeless fight
(The more of right the more he loves);
So may another redouble might

For a few swift gleams of the angry brand,
A desperate charge and a final stand;
And so may die, his trust forgiven
Far, far, far from the Holy Land.

In a note at the bottom of this manuscript, RF wrote to Bartlett, "Of right, I say. But, of course, not without thinking twice. Something also depends on the cause. But why say it again? I flatter myself it is all said with the proper enigmatical reserve in the poem. R. F." (MS, Bartlett Collection, Virginia)

12. RF made repeated uses of this challenge. See Sidney Cox, *A Swinger of Birches*, pp. 65-66:

"At Bread Loaf in the summer of 1924 he told a little theater full of high school English teachers: An English teacher has three prime duties. He would state them, he said, in the order of their importance. The English teacher's first duty is to himself—then, with a questioning smile, herself. Her first duty is to herself. Her second duty is to the books. Her third duty is to her students. [Cox continues:] The bright and shallow ones forced a cackle and dismissed his paradox as 'humor.' The humorous ones thought freshly. Good teaching, they saw he meant, requires first of all good teachers: blithe and winsome persons, persons who can establish contact between the subject matter and the girl or boy they teach. They must not be fagged or cowed or flustered. They might better throw away a bunch of themes. . . ."

See also, John Holmes, "Robert Frost Wins His Fight to Be an Ordinary Man," *Boston Evening Transcript*, Magazine Section, 8 February 1936, p. 4:

"Frost told that he had once startled a group of teachers by saying that one's first consideration should be for one's self, not to be self-forgetful, since there is one's own soul to save. After that comes the book. He wasn't going to pick literature to pieces, he said. After that, the students."

13. "Love and a Question," *Complete Poems*, p. 9; first published in *A Boy's Will* (1913).

14. The manuscript booklet which contains "My Giving" is in the Huntington Library.

RF's continuing sympathy for the doctrine of laissez-faire was expressed in a jocose and yet serious fashion in the following lines from "Build Soil" (*Complete Poems*, p. 425):

[Meliboeus:] Were I dictator, I'll tell you what I'd do.

[Tityrus:]   What should you do?

[Meliboeus:]   I'd let things take their course
               And then I'd claim the credit for the outcome.

15. RF first told this anecdote to LT on 27 Aug. 1941, and the entry for that date in "Notes on Robert Frost" contains a wry comment made by RF on William Hayes Ward: that the dignified old gentleman prided himself on his prowess as a former long-distance runner and that he still took his exercise "running around Newark in his drawers."

16. RF's most concentrated usage of Bergson's images and ideas in one poem occurs in "West-running Brook" (*Complete Poems*, pp. 327-329). Particularly pertinent are the following passages from Henri Bergson, *Creative Evolution* (New York, 1911):

"Our own consciousness is the consciousness of a certain living being, placed in a certain point in space; and though it does indeed move in the same direction as its principle, it is continually drawn the opposte way, obliged, though it goes forward, to look behind. This retrospective vision is . . . the natural function of the intellect and consequently of distinct consciousness. In order that our consciousness shall coincide with something of its principle, it must detach itself from the *already-made* and attach itself to the *being-made*. It needs that, turning back on itself and twisting on itself, the faculty of *seeing* should be made to be one with the act of *willing* . . ." (p. 237)

"When we put back our being into our will, and our will itself into the impulsion it prolongs, we understand, we feel, that reality is a perpetual growth, a creation pursued without end. Our will already performs this miracle. Every human work in which there is invention, every voluntary act in which there is freedom, every movement of an organism that manifests spontaneity, brings something new into the world. True, these are only creations of form. How could they be anything else? We are not the vital current itself; we are this current already loaded with matter. . . ." (p. 239)

". . . that the poet creates the poem and that human thought is thereby made richer, we understand very well. . . . the universe is not made, but is being made continually. It is growing, perhaps indefinitely, by the addition of new worlds. . . ." (pp. 239, 241)

". . . a world like our solar system is seen to be ever exhausting something of the mutability it contains. In the beginning, it had the maximum of possible utilization of energy: this mutability has gone on diminishing unceasingly." (p. 243)

"The vision we have of the material world is that of a weight which falls: no image drawn from matter, properly so called, will ever give us the idea of weight rising . . ." (p. 245)

"All our analyses show us, in life, an effort to re-mount the incline that matter descends. In that, they reveal to us the possibility, the necessity even of a process the inverse of materiality, creative of matter by its interruptions alone. . . . Incapable of *stopping* the course of material changes downward, it succeeds in *retarding* it. The evolution of life really continues . . . an initial impulsion: this impulsion which had determined the development of the chlorophyllian functions in the plant. . . ." (pp. 245-246)

"God thus defined has nothing of the already made; He is unceasing life, action, freedom. Creation, so conceived is not a mystery; we experience it in ourselves when we act freely. . . ." (p. 248)

"Life as a whole, from the initial impulsion that thrust it into the world, will appear as a wave which rises, and which is opposed by the descending movement of matter. On the greater part of its surface, at different heights, the current is converted by matter into a vortex. At one point alone it passes freely, dragging with it the obstacle which will weigh on its progress but will not stop it. At this point is humanity; it is our privileged situation. On the other hand, this rising wave is consciousness. . . . On flows the current, running through human generations, sub-dividing itself into individuals. . . ." (p. 269)

"The animal takes its stand . . . man bestrides animality, and the whole of humanity, in space and in time, is one immense army galloping beside and before and behind each of us in an overwhelming charge able to beat down every resistance and clear the most formidable obstacles, perhaps even death." (pp. 270-271)

17. William James, *Pragmatism: A New Name for Some Old Ways of Thinking: Popular Lectures on Philosophy* (New York, 1907), pp. 3-4.

18. Ibid., p. 27.

19. Ibid., pp. 63-64.

20. Earlier in this chapter reference was made to RF's very strong sympathy with the Utilitarian doctrine of laissez-faire, and to his apparent familiarity with J. S. Mill's essay *On Liberty*. William James dedicated *Pragmatism* "To the memory of John Stuart Mill from whom I first learned the pragmatic openness of mind and whom my fancy likes to picture as our leader were he alive today." In *Pragmatism*, James repeatedly uses the word "utilitarian." Furthermore, when he explains his recurrent use of the phrase, "in so far forth," he gives a religious slant to his own doctrine of laissez-faire—a very convenient slant toward which RF was sympathetic:

"As a good pragmatist, I myself ought to call the Absolute true 'in so far forth,' then; and I unhesitatingly now do so. But what does *true in so far forth* mean in this case? To answer, we need only apply the pragmatic method. What do believers in the Absolute mean by saying that their belief affords them comfort? They mean that since, in the Absolute finite evil is 'overruled' already, we may, therefore, whenever we wish, treat the temporal as if it were potentially the eternal, be sure that we can trust its outcome, and, without sin, dismiss our fear and drop the worry of our finite responsibility. In short, they mean that we have a right ever and anon to take a moral holiday, to let the world wag in its own way, feeling that its issues are in better hands than ours and are none of our business." (*Pragmatism*, pp. 73-74. On RF's attitude toward "a moral holiday," see "My Giving" and "Good Relief"; see also Note 4 of Chapter 31, particularly, "Of course, somebody must lose.")

21. *Pragmatism*, pp. 75, 76.

22. Ibid., p. 111.

23. Ibid., p. 114.

24. Ibid., p. 115.

25. "Design," *Complete Poems*, p. 396. The earlier version, sent to Miss Ward:

In White

A dented spider like a snowdrop white
On a white Heal-all, holding up a moth
Like a white piece of lifeless satin cloth—
Saw ever curious eye so strange a sight?
Portent in little, assorted death and blight
Like the ingredients of a witches' broth?
The beady spider, the flower like a froth,
And the moth carried like a paper kite.

What had that flower to do with being white,
The blue Brunella every child's delight?
What brought the kindred spider to that height?
(Make we no thesis of the miller's
    [i.e., miller-moth's] plight.)
What but design of darkness and of night?
Design, design! Do I use the word aright?

(MS, Huntington Library.) In the revision one of the finest ironies
was achieved through a parody of lines RF had been carrying in
his memory ever since Loren Bailey's leather-shop days, when he
found he knew by heart Bryant's "To a Waterfowl," including,

He who, from zone to zone,
Guides through the boundless sky thy certain flight . . .

The mock-echo:

What brought the kindred spider to that height,
Then steered the white moth thither in the night?

26. Compare with details in the already cited letter, Bartlett to
Munson, op. cit., which contains this: ". . . I remember how, a few
months later, he speeded me on my way to British Columbia, to
another climate, with a handshake, a look in the eye. There was a
book at that parting—Chesterton's Heretics. I read it through three
times on the train out. I remember letter after letter as I sought
a way to fit in in Vancouver, and the frequent letters as I finally
was started in newspaper work. Letters all about ME, MY problems.
That was what friendship meant to Rob Frost, help to the maximum when a boy needed it."

27. The playfully serious twenty-eight-line letter-in-verse, "The
Lure of the West," occurs complete in Anderson, *Frost-Bartlett*, pp.
29-30; MS, Barrett Collection, Virginia.

28. RF to Mosher, 19 Feb. 1912, *Selected Letters*, pp. 46-47.
"Reluctance" appeared in Mosher's book *Amphora: A Collection of
Prose and Verse Chosen by the Editor of the Bibelot* (Portland,

Maine, 1912), p. 106; it was published in *The Youth's Companion,*
Vol. 86, No. 45 (7 Nov. 1912), p. 612.

29. It is probable that Ernest L. Silver sent to the local newspaper the following item which appeared in *The Plymouth Record,*
24 August 1912, p. 4:

"Professor Robert Lee Frost, Mrs. Frost and four children sailed
this Friday [23 August 1912] for England for a two years' stay. Mr.
Frost has been a member of the Normal school faculty for the past
year, and he goes abroad at this time for his health and observation."

I am grateful to Edward Connery Lathem for finding and
sharing this news item; also for the additional information that
the 23 August sailing date for the steamer *Parisian,* Boston to
Glasgow, is confirmed by the shipping columns of *The Boston
Evening Transcript* of that day (p. 12).

29. ENGLAND: *A BOY'S WILL*

1. This information was given LT by Mrs. William A. Green,
oldest daughter of Mr. and Mrs. John Lynch, in Bethlehem, N.
H., during the summer of 1940.

2. Mrs. Frost omits mention of two pieces of furniture taken
across the ocean: a rocking chair for her, a favorite leather-uphol-
stered Morris chair for RF. See Sergeant, *Robert Frost,* p. 96.

3. Mrs. Frost to Margaret Lynch, dated 25 Oct. 1912, *Selected
Letters,* p. 53.

4. On 14 June 1957, LT and Edward Connery Lathem accompanied RF to Beaconsfield, Buckinghamshire while en route from
Cambridge to London. Discovering that Reynolds Road made a
semicircular loop, RF said that when he and his family occupied
"The Bungalow" in 1912-1914, only the right-hand half of the loop
had been a road, that "The Bungalow" was at that time the last
house on the right-hand side of Reynolds Road. Confused by the
semi-circular continuation of houses in 1957, RF was unable to
identify the house in which he had lived.

5. RF to Susan Hayes Ward, dated 15 Sept. 1912, *Selected Letters,* p. 52.

6. Quoted from Sergeant, *Robert Frost,* pp. 93-94.

7. See RF's second letter to Harold Brown, dated 7 Jan. 1913,
Selected Letters, pp. 61-65.

8. See RF to Ernest L. Silver, dated 25 Dec. 1912, *Selected
Letters,* pp. 58-60.

9. In 1959, LT asked RF about the subject matter and theme of
the novel he had tried to write in England. RF said he had in-

tended to build the story around the differences of opinion between two farm workers: a young man fresh out of college and an old man rich with first-hand experiences on the farm. RF said that he transferred the subject matter to the start of a play, but that he had only the idea of the tension between two opposite points of view and that he could never find adequate situations to represent, dramatize, and develop this tension. Later, he said, he converted the beginning of the novel (and the beginning of the play) into the poem "From Plane to Plane" (*Complete Poems*, pp. 578-583; first published in *Steeple Bush*, 1947). By way of analogy, notice that in "The Death of the Hired Man" (*Complete Poems*, p. 51) old Silas is said to have remembered how he used to argue with young Harold Wilson, whose college-boy assurance piqued Silas.

10. "In England" was sent by RF to Sidney Cox from Beaconsfield in a letter dated 26 Dec. 1912. It was never printed in any of RF's books, but the manuscript was reproduced in *Fifty Years of Robert Frost*, an exhibition catalogue published by the Dartmouth College Library, 1944, p. 15.

11. The quoted passage occurs in an untitled pocket notebook which RF kept while in England, 1912-1915. RF gave this notebook to Louis Henry Cohn in 1948; at Cohn's death it passed into the possession of his widow, Mrs. Marguerite Cohn.

In the same notebook may be found a good illustration of RF's statement that while a poem wouldn't be any good if it didn't have doors, he wouldn't leave them open. The only poem in this notebook is entitled "Flower Guidance." At first glance the lines might seem to be addressed merely to children, and the only meaning: enjoy flowers, but don't pick them, because you'll be sorry if you do:

> As I went from flower to flower
> (I have told you how)
> I have told you what I found
> Dead not growing on the ground.
> Look upon me now.
>
> If you would not find yourself
> In an evil hour
> Too far on a fatal track
> Clasp your hands behind your back.
> Never pick a flower.

On second glance, there is too much darkness in the images of "fatal track" and "evil hour," if the moral tag is taken in a merely literal sense. Nevertheless, anyone trying to look through the literal, to the metaphorical possibilities of meaning, may feel that the "doors" in "Flower Guidance" have been "closed" tight. One way to open them may be to use, as a key, a prose passage which occurs in the same notebook; a passage used for other purposes in the text, here, p. 427; a bitter statement of regret, by RF:

"Evil clings so in all our acts that even when we not only mean but achieve our prettiest, bravest, noblest, best, we are often a scourge even to those we do not hate. Our sincerest prayers are no more than groans that this should be so."

This passage may serve to recall previously cited evidence of RF's puritanical guilts. If the poem is taken figuratively, it may be correlated with other very personal poems by RF. (Remember the metaphorical statement: "My sudden struggle may have dragged down some / White lily from the air . . ." in "Despair." Remember also the metaphorical use of the title in "The Subverted Flower," and RF's information and misinformation concerning the relationship between his flower-like mother and his brutal father, as hinted in the first part of "The Lovely Shall Be Choosers.") If these hints are permitted to open doors on "Flower Guidance," some possible extensions of private meanings may be paraphrased as follows:

As I gradually became acquainted with the flower-like qualities of beautiful women, I discovered one, my own mother, whose life had been spoiled, ravaged, broken off by one who didn't even hate her. Now, in my own relations with my wife, I know I have been guilty of the same evil action ("Look upon me now"). It seems ironic that the only way in which human beings can avoid hurting others is to avoid intimacy through a completely ascetic posture of self-denial, but most people can't be that ascetic, and so with the best intent they may hurt and destroy.

In this interpretation the metaphorical usage of spoiling, ravaging, breaking off a flower suggests all the usages of the meaning for the verb deflower. Not unrelatable are some of the meanings in RF's early poem "Spoils of the Dead."

12. Mrs. M. L. Nutt to RF, *Selected Letters*, p. 55. RF told many conflicting stories about the swiftness with which Mrs. Nutt responded and about her method of response. In Miss Sergeant's *Robert Frost*, p. 98, RF is quoted as saying: ". . . I just left the manuscript with her. In three days I had a card to come in. I went. The book was accepted!" The version given by Mertins (*Robert Frost*, p. 108) is different: ". . . She dropped me a line asking me to come in and sign a royalty contract. I went up to London in a day or so and looked over the contract." The facts do not support either version. Mrs. Nutt's letter (Frost Correspondence File, Dartmouth) is dated 26 Oct. 1912; the Frost-Nutt contract (RF's copy of which is in The Jones Library, Amherst, Mass.) is dated 16 Dec. 1912.

13. *Selected Letters*, pp. 55-56. RF's use of "Melanism" and "The Sense of Wrong" as possible titles for later books of poems suggests

another conflict between the actual and the ideal in him. Ample evidence has been offered here that RF was obsessively concerned with dark thoughts about his own sense of all the wrongs (real or imaginary) which had been done to him; that he was also concerned with his consequent resentment and with his desire for revenge. These attitudes conflicted with his ideal of submission, acceptance, obedience, formulated for him in childhood by his mother, within a Christian frame of reference. He tried to resolve the conflict, at times, by idealizing his own state and by claiming that he had achieved the ideal. For example, his poem "Acceptance" (*Complete Poems*, p. 313) concludes:

> Now let the night be dark for all of me.
> Let the night be too dark for me to see
> Into the future. Let what will be, be.

The ideal is thus represented as the actual. Similarly, his poem "Not Quite Social" (*Complete Poems*, p. 403) contains the line, "I would not be taken as ever having rebelled." Again the ideal is represented as the actual.

These examples are offered as evidence that in his poems RF sometimes honored his mythic ideals and represented them as reality; but that in his own life, by contrast, he repeatedly dramatized rage, resentment, revenge. These actualities were inseparable parts of the self-destructive forces against which he fought as best he could, using poetry as one of his weapons.

14. RF to Ernest L. Silver, 25 Dec. 1912, *Selected Letters*, pp. 59-60. RF's own view of his purpose in writing this letter was explained to John Bartlett:

"I rather deliberately queered myself with Silver and the Plymouth crowd by laying it on pretty thick though with studied modesty, about my little achievements here in answer to their clamor for something literary from the neighborhood of Westminster Abbey. You see I could talk about myself on that for a joke and call it highly literary. Instead of lingering over the tombs and busts in the Abbey (where I have never been) I talked in simple truth about my book. I had it in for them. Silver asked three times for something literary. Then he got it. He hasn't yipped since. The Lord do so to me and more also if I could help it. And I was artful enough to leave something untold that I could send around and make sure of his getting as if by accident by way of Mrs Frost and some of the ladies. He's an awfully mild master, is Silver, when he has you where he can pay what he wants to. But he's jealous to a fault. I know where he lives." (*Selected Letters*, p. 69.) See Chapter 30 for circumstances which caused RF to admit that he had misjudged Silver.

15. Harold Monro, "The Bookshop," *Poetry Review*, Vol. 1, No.

11 (November 1912), pp. 498-499. An account of Monro's warfare with the Poetry Society was given by him in the first number of *Poetry and Drama,* which also contains the statement that the prize of thirty pounds offered in July 1912 for the best poem appearing in *Poetry Review* during 1912 had been awarded to Rupert Brooke for "The Old Vicarage, Grantchester," which had been published in the issue of November 1912, pp. 506-509. Some of the judges for this contest were Harold Monro, T. E. Hulme, Edward Marsh, and Edward Thomas.

16. F. S. Flint published a 59-page article entitled "Contemporary French Poetry" in the *Poetry Review,* Vol. I, No. 10 (October 1912), pp. 355-414.

17. The phrase occurs in Flint's review of *Ripostes* published in the first number of *Poetry and Drama* (March 1913), where Flint also refers to Pound's publishing another man's work "for good fellowship, for good custom, a custom out of Tuscany and Provence . . . and for good memory, too, seeing that they [Hulme's poems] recall certain evenings and meetings of two years gone, dull enough at the time, but rather pleasant to look back upon."

18. Allan Wade (ed.), *The Letters of W. B. Yeats* (London, 1954), p. 543.

19. In 1912, while Pound was serving as foreign editor for Harriet Monroe's *Poetry,* Yeats sent some poems to the new magazine through Pound's hands and the changes were made at that time. See Eustace Mullins, *This Difficult Individual, Ezra Pound* (New York, 1961), pp. 63, 65.

20. D. D. Paige (ed.), *The Letters of Ezra Pound* (New York, 1950), p. [9].

21. Quoted from Frances H. Ellis, *Robert Frost in England: 1912-1915* (unpublished M. A. thesis, Columbia University, 1948), p. 26. RF usually told the story of this conversation in much the same way; a garbled version occurs in Miss Sergeant's *Robert Frost,* p. 101, where part of the exchange is said to have occurred between RF and "the wife of Ernest Gardiner [sic]." The error is repeated in Miss Gould's *Robert Frost,* p. 111.

22. This was the first concrete step in RF's very deliberate campaign of self-advancement. The evidence concerning this campaign occurs abundantly in the letters RF wrote from England, 1912-1915. One of RF's retrospective comments on the campaign is quoted in Mertins, *Robert Frost,* p. 109: "You see, I had picked up a few friends among the reviewers, and these, out of the kindness of their hearts, and seeing me sort of like a lost puppy straying far from friends and relations, felt sorry for me and praised the book above its due. I can say this, but I wouldn't like anybody else to agree with me."

23. RF to F. S. Flint, 21 January 1913, University of Texas Library.

24. Page proofs, *A Boy's Will*, Barrett Collection, Virginia.

25. RF to John Bartlett, 26 February 1913, *Selected Letters*, p. 66.

26. F. S. Flint to RF, dated 30 January 1913, containing Pound's inscribed calling card, RF Correspondence File, Dartmouth College Library.

27. Pound's rapid advance through various phases of his literary apprenticeship is indicated by a sequel. When RF later told a polite lie to Pound in pretending he had enjoyed reading the poems in *Personae* and *Ripostes*, Pound shrugged off the comment by saying (according to RF) that those poems were all right if you liked that sort of stuff, but that he had gone so far beyond them in one year that they no longer interested him.

28. Paige, op. cit., p. 14.

29. Ibid., p. 16.

30. Quoted from the published version of Pound's review in *Poetry*, Vol. II, No. 2 (May 1913), pp. 72-74. There is evidence that RF, before meeting Pound, submitted poems to Harriet Monroe's *Poetry*, perhaps from England, and that the poems were refused by Harriet Monroe's assistant, Alice Corbin Henderson. Late in March of 1913, Pound apparently did not know about the submissions, for he wrote, "Frost seems to have put his best stuff into his book, but we'll have something from him as soon as he has done it . . ." (Paige, op. cit., p. 17.) On 5 April 1913, Harriet Monroe wrote to Pound that the name Robert Frost was not entirely new in the *Poetry* office: "Alice says *mea culpa* about Frost. For we find him among our returns and it was done while I was in New York. She has the grit to stand up, however, and say if it was returned it deserved it, or at least those particular poems did. You can apologize for us and say we are very contrite and would like some more some day." (Carbon, Monroe papers, University of Chicago Library.) On 22 April 1913, Pound replied, "I don't doubt that the things Frost sent you were very bad. But he had done good things and whoever rejected 'em will go to hell along with [the editors of] *Harper's* and *The Atlantic*. After my declaration of his glory he'll have to stay out of print for a year in order not to 'disappoint' the avid reader. Serieusement, I'll pick out whatever of his inedited stuff is fit to print—when I get back to London." (Paige, op. cit., p. 19.) No record is known of the titles of the rejected poems.

31. Ibid., p. 20.

32. This quotation occurs at several removes from the original. It is taken from Elinor Frost's version in a letter to Margaret Bartlett, *Selected Letters*, p. 78. RF's version, in a letter to John Bartlett (*Selected Letters*, p. 70), is worth putting in context: "Yeats has asked me to make one of his circle at his Monday Nights when he

is in London (and not in Dublin). And he told my dazzling friend
Ezra Pound that my book was the best thing that has come out of
America for some time."

33. RF's version of these two anecdotes occurs in a letter to
Sidney Cox, c. 15 September 1913 (*Selected Letters*, p. 94).

34. In all of his letters written prior to his stay in England, RF
makes no mention of Edwin Arlington Robinson. There seems to
be a slightly fictional quality about "the best of my recollection" in
the following passage, which occurs in RF's "Introduction" to Robinson's posthumously published *King Jasper* (New York, 1935),
p. x:

"The first poet I ever sat down with to talk about poetry was
Ezra Pound. It was in London in 1913. The first poet we talked
about, to the best of my recollection, was Edwin Arlington Robinson. I was fresh from America and from having read *The Town
Down the River*. . . . I remember the pleasure with which Pound
and I laughed over the fourth 'thought' in

> Miniver thought, and thought, and thought,
> And thought about it.

"Three 'thoughts' would have been 'adequate' as the critical
praise-word then was. There would have been nothing to complain
of, if it had been left at three. The fourth made the intolerable
touch of poetry. With the fourth, the fun began. I was taken out on
the strength of our community of opinion here, to be rewarded
with an introduction to Miss May Sinclair, who had qualified as
the patron authority on young and new poets by the sympathy she
had shown them in *The Divine Fire*."

35. May Sinclair, "Three American Poets of To-Day," *Atlantic
Monthly*, Vol. 98, No. 3 (Sept. 1906), pp. 325-335.

36. Quoted in Richard Thornton, ed., *Recognition of Robert
Frost* (New York, 1937), p. 39.

37. Ibid., p. 54.

38. Elinor Frost to Margaret Bartlett [c. 3 July 1913], *Selected Letters*, p. 78.

39. RF to Ernest L. Silver, 10 July 1913, Dartmouth College
Library.

30. INTERLUDE

1. RF to John Bartlett, 8 Dec. 1913, *Selected Letters*, pp. 100-
101. To the end of his life, RF kept promising to overcome his
habit of vindictive retaliation. Pertinent in this connection is part
of a letter whch he wrote to Bartlett on 1 Nov. 1927: "It was an

inspiration of mine to give [Gorham B.] Munson direct access to my past through two or three of my independent friends. I thought it would be fun to take the risk of his hearing something to my discredit. The worst you could [reveal] was my Indian vindictiveness. Really I am awful there. I am worse than you know. I can never seem to forgive people that scare me within an inch of my life. I am going to try to be good and cease from strife." (Anderson, *Frost-Bartlett*, p. 145.)

2. RF to John Bartlett, *c.* 16 June 1913, *Selected Letters*, p. 75.

3. Ibid, p. 76.

4. RF to John Bartlett, *c.* 5 Nov. 1913, *Selected Letters*, p. 97.

5. RF to John Bartlett, 4 July 1913. *Selected Letters*, p. 79. John Bartlett's article, "Formerly at Pinkerton: Robert Frost Gaining a Reputation As a Writer of Choice Poems," was signed "J. T. B. / Vancouver, B. C." and was published in *The Derry News*, 7 Nov. 1913, p. 8; the article was republished, under the same title, in the literary magazine of the New Hampshire State Normal School, at Plymouth, *The Prospect*, Vol. 8, No. 4 (Nov. 1913), pp. 24-27. (I am grateful to Edward Connery Lathem for finding and sharing this bibliographical information.)

6. RF to John Bartlett, 4 July 1913, *Selected Letters*, p. 79.

7. Edward Thomas, review of *Georgian Poetry 1911-1912* in *Poetry and Drama*, Vol. 1, No. 1 (March 1913), p. 52.

8. Quoted from *Poetry*, Vol. I, No. 6 (March 1913), p. 203. Pound's article is preceded by some wry and amusing comments by F. S. Flint, pertinent here because of RF's own response to the *imagistes*, and later to the Imagists. Flint begins:

"Some curiosity has been aroused concerning *Imagisme*, and as I was unable to find anything definite about it in print, I sought out an *imagiste*, with intent to discover whether the group itself knew anything about the 'movement.' I gleaned these facts.

"The *imagistes* admitted that they were contemporaries of the Post Impressionists and the Futurists; but they had nothing in common with these schools. They had not published a manifesto. They were not a revolutionary school."

After giving a few "rules" of the *imagistes*, "drawn up for their own satisfaction only," Flint seems to be teasing Pound by describing one device whereby the *imagistes* persuaded any incipient poet to attend instruction: "They re-wrote his verses before his eyes, using about ten words to his fifty." RF may have helped to inspire this jibe. One of the first strains on the friendship between Pound and RF occurred when Pound took one of RF's short lyrics and showed RF how it could be condensed. Indignantly, RF answered, "Yeah, and spoiled."

(No consideration is here given to Amy Lowell's appearances in London and to her gradual shift of *imagiste* to Imagist; RF played no part in it. The nearest he came to it was being invited by Pound to meet Amy Lowell. RF declined.)

9. RF to John Bartlett, 4 July 1913, *Selected Letters,* pp. 79-81.

10. Original letter, RF to F. S. Flint, University of Texas Library. I am grateful to Professor Wallace Martin, who called to my attention this letter and the one next cited.

11. Original letter, RF to F. S. Flint, also in the University of Texas Library.

12. Cited in Note 30 of Chapter 29.

13. *Selected Letters,* p. 84.

14. *Selected Letters,* pp. 85-86. Although RF apparently did not send a copy of this parody to Pound, he did think well enough of it to preserve what may be the first draft, and to present it to the Dartmouth College Library with the understanding that it should not be shown to anyone during RF's lifetime.

15. F. S. Flint to RF, 26 July 1913, *Selected Letters,* p. 87.

16. Original letter, Ernest Arthur Gardner to RF, in RF Correspondence File, Dartmouth College Library.

17. RF to John Bartlett, 30 Aug. 1913, *Selected Letters,* p. 90.

18. Ibid., pp. 90-91.

19. F. S. Flint, review of *A Boy's Will,* in *Poetry and Drama,* Vol. I, No. 2 (June 1913), p. 250.

20. Anonymous review in an article entitled "Procession of the Muses," *The Academy,* Vol. 85, No. 2159 (20 Sept. 1913), p. 360.

21. Quoted from the pocket notebook which RF kept while in England; see Note 11 of Chapter 29.

31. ENGLAND: *NORTH OF BOSTON*

1. Letter, RF to Mosher, 17 July 1913, *Selected Letters,* pp. 83-84. When RF refers to "the virtues I celebrate," in this letter to Mosher, he is implying that throughout *North of Boston* his narrative poems are designed to celebrate some unspectacular and yet heroic virtues as they may be found operative in the actions and words of ordinary people. In Lathem, *Interviews,* pp. 172-176, a transcribed tape-recording of a conversation between Cecil Day Lewis and RF contains the following pertinent remarks by RF:
". . . one of the things that makes you go is making a hero out of somebody that nobody else had ever noticed was a hero. . . . You pick up the unconsidered person. . . . people are saying there's no such thing as heroism left. Some of the talk is that way. I know of a book of history that says heroism is out of date. But it's in everything. It's in making a book, you know. And it takes a hero to make a poem."

2. Technically and thematically considered, the earliest form of "The Black Cottage" was completely different from its published form, although the basic raw materials for the two were identical. In Derry, between RF's farm and Derry Village, stood a cottage—weatherbeaten, unpainted, and therefore almost "black"—inhabited by Mrs. Sarah J. Upton, the widow of the first volunteer from Derry to enlist in the Grand Army of the Republic near the start of the Civil War, George R. Upton. He was killed in action and his name was given to the local G. A. R. post after the war. The early version of "The Black Cottage" is imaginatively built around some of these facts, but it is not a dramatic narrative-dialogue. Instead, it comes closer to being a meditative lyric written in RF's early and "musical" manner, with strong emphasis on cadence and mood. The narrator's representation of the cottage and of the sole occupant of it is a sympathetic and brooding portrayal, in which all the images are softened by evening twilight (MS, Huntington):

> The long grass that flowed in from o'er
> The fields all day to her closed door
> And lisped about the very sill
> Lies dew-drenched and the elms on high
> That rolled all day and tossed and flung
> An unseen oriole that sung,
> Are with the oriole now still;
> And day has passed the cottage by.

> And if by guide-post sent astray,
> At eventide one passed that way
> And paused for sadness, would he guess,
> I wonder, by one outward token
> The solitary inmate there
> Who bows her head with snowy hair
> The bread of loneliness to bless
> With lips that shape the words unspoken.

> Perchance not loveless were she all
> Would she but heed the distant call
> Of sons who give account of her
> Where life and strength and effort stream;
> But no, the silence with the rest
> The place of memories likes her best,
> Where one was dear before they were
> And love made life of girlhood's dream.

> No further from the grave is she

Than from those graves her dim eyes see
Across the way beside the wood,
Where all the headstones are of slate
Save only one of marble stone,
And all the names repeat her own
With kindness not to be withstood
And give her but an hour to wait.

Bestarred with fainting fireflies
The pallid meadow mists arise
Tree-high o'er all and with their damp
Release the fragrance of sweet flowers,
And make the weathered cottage old
As black as oozy meadow mould—
The cottage that without a lamp
Sinks darkly upon darker hours.

3. "The psychologist in me ached to call it [*A Boy's Will*] 'The Record of a Phase of Post-adolescence,' wrote RF from Beaconsfield to the editor of *The Youth's Companion* in Boston, when requesting permission to reprint in *A Boy's Will* the three poems which had already been published in the magazine: "Reluctance," "October," and "Ghost Houses." (See Note 9 of Chapter 1.)

4. "Good Relief" was never collected by RF; he may have become ashamed of it. The only printing occurs in *Come Christmas: A Selection of Christmas Poetry, Song, Drama and Prose*, edited by Lesley Frost (New York, 1929), pp. 4-5. In *Come Christmas*, the frontispiece is a reproduction of a fair-copy manuscript of "Good Relief" in the handwriting of RF.

In his later years RF became more outspoken concerning related ideas and expressed some of them as follows: "Too long we have adhered to this doctrine of original sin which says, 'I'm to blame because Adam fell out of an apple tree' or 'We must share our table with the humble and stupid because it is our fault they're stupid.' It is simply not true." These remarks were made before an overflow audience at Agnes Scott College (affiliated with the Presbyterian Church), in Decatur, Georgia, on 30 Jan. 1959; they were quoted in the *Atlanta Journal*, 31 Jan. 1959, p. 1. Contained in these remarks is the strong hint that RF, in fashioning a "pragmatic" and "laissez-faire" version of religious beliefs which fitted his own needs, rejected the Christian concept of sharing moral responsibility for the acts or predicaments of others. Some equally related and garrulous remarks made by RF before an audience in Redlands, California, on 17 May 1958, were quoted in an Associated Press release which was printed in many newspapers on 18 May 1958, as follows: "You have got to love what's loveable and hate what's hateable. It takes brains to see the difference. I've waged a lover's quarrel with the world ever since I felt old enough to woo it with dash. I was stodgy only when I was young. God seems to be something which wants us to win. In tennis. Or poetry. Or marriage. Of course, somebody must lose. That's when you step up to the spiritual plane. I'm like a modern car in religious matters. I may look convertible, but I'm a hard-top. I'm working on a couplet now:

> Forgive, O Lord, my little jokes on Thee
> And I'll forgive thy great big one on me."

RF's pleasure in trying to preserve his Shelleyean phase of anti-conventional rebelliousness, and in trying to use it as a mask for concealing his private religious beliefs, is typically represented in his witticism, "I may look convertible, but I'm a hard-top." He clung to his religious beliefs, desperately, because he needed them as protection, particularly against his fear of death. At the same time, he was ashamed not only of his fears but also of his compensating religious beliefs, and sometimes he tried to hide them both.

5. Quoted from stenographic transcript of a talk given by RF at Wesleyan University, Middletown, Conn., 19 April 1936, typescript in LT's collection of Frostiana. Another pertinent recollection of homesickness in England is worth considering here as it occurs in a slightly different context. In Rose C. Feld, op. cit., p. 2, RF seems accurately quoted as follows:

"The beginnings of North of Boston were 'The Death of the Hired Man,' 'The Black Cottage,' and 'The Housekeeper.' These belong to my farm days at Derry. The only one I persistently tried on editors in the last seven years [prior to the publication of *North of Boston*] in the hope of their seeing something in it for Memorial Day was 'The Black Cottage.' All the rest of North of Boston I wrote in England on an inspiration compounded of homesickness and the delight of new friendships. I wrote whole poems of two hundred lines at a sitting. I believe I was not over two hours with 'Home Burial.' It stands in print as it was in the first draft." (Compare the statement in the last sentence with similar statements discussed in Note 7 of this chapter.)

6. RF to John Bartlett, 7 Aug. 1913, *Selected Letters*, p. 89.

7. Note letter, RF to Silver, 8 Dec. 1913, *Selected Letters*, p. 103: ". . . it remains to be seen whether I shall take hold and earn a living as a writer. I find writing hard work. I have been a harder boss on myself than ever you were on me. I am clean shucked out by this last book—(North of Boston, I have decided to call it)."

Because RF did find revision of his poems exhausting, and because he did cherish the familiar Romantic-Victorian ideal that the poet is divinely inspired and therefore prophetic, one may understand and sympathize with his motives for wanting to believe (and therefore his believing, in a pragmatically Jamesian sense) that some of his best poems were written with one stroke of the pen, perfectly, without any need for revision.

RF confided some representative details of this myth to Miss Sergeant, who innocently repeated them as apparent truths in *Fire Under the Andes* (1927), p. 300. After discussing "The Mountain" she continues: "The poem was written 'with one stroke of the pen,' as were three other favourites . . . 'Birches,' 'Two Look at Two,' and that perfect lyric, 'Stopping by Woods on a Snowy Evening.'"

The facts do not support these assertions. RF's many attempts to promulgate these mythic details might have been more successful if he had carefully destroyed all the early drafts of the manuscripts involved. The first draft of "Birches" (in The Jones Library) contains revisions which indicate many strokes and re-strokes of the pen. An early draft of "Two Look at Two" (in the Dartmouth College Library) was sent to Sidney Cox in a letter dated 17 July 1920; but this draft contains fourteen lines more than the final compressed revision. (No first or early draft of "The Mountain" is known to LT.) As for "Stopping by Woods," RF gave other mythic details about it, and some of them were innocently offered as apparent truths by John Ciardi in his essay, "Robert Frost: The Way to the Poem" (op. cit., pp. 156-157). This essay contains some serious (and amusing) mistakes partly as a result of Ciardi's willingness to accept RF's claim that the first draft of "Stopping by Woods" was written so perfectly that it never needed revision:

"Mr. Frost has often discussed this poem on the platform, or more usually in the course of a long evening after a talk. Time and again I have heard him say that he just wrote it off, that it just came to him, and that he set it down as it came."

(No mistakes, so far: RF's remarks, thus accurately reported, may be seen as providing oblique hints of his belief in his occasional capacity to write automatically, so to speak, from divine dictation.) Ciardi continues:

"Once at Bread Loaf, however, I heard him add one very essential piece to the discussion of how it 'just came.' One night, he said, he had sat down after supper to work at a long piece of blank verse. The piece never worked out, but Mr. Frost found himself so absorbed in it that, when next he looked up, dawn was at his window. He rose, crossed to the window, stood looking out for a few minutes, and *then* it was that 'Stopping by Woods' suddenly 'just came,' so that all he had to do was cross the room and write it down."

(Ciardi's reporting, here, is inaccurate; but one fault is outstanding: RF, in repeatedly telling this story, consistently and correctly said that the "long piece of blank verse" on which he worked throughout that night was "New Hampshire"—which was of course "worked out" and published.) Ciardi continues:

"Robert Frost is the sort of artist who hides his traces. I know of no Frost work sheets anywhere. If someone has raided his waste-basket in secret, it is possible that such work sheets exist some-where, but Frost would not willingly allow anything but the fin-ished product to leave him. Almost certainly, therefore, no one will ever know what was in that piece of unsuccessful blank verse he had been working at with such concentration, but I for one would stake my life that could that work sheet be uncovered, it would be found to contain the germinal stuff of 'Stopping by Woods'; that what was a-simmer in him all night without finding its proper form, suddenly, when he let his still-occupied mind look away, came at him from a different direction, offered itself in a different form, and that finding that form exactly right the impulse pro-ceeded to marry itself to the new shape in one of the most miracu-lous performances of English lyricism."

Ciardi is dead, of course—and unnecessarily. With ease, he could have "uncovered" that "work sheet" on which he so gallantly staked his life as a literary theorist. It is even more regrettable that his theories contain so many other mistakes which recall RF's pre-viously cited advice, "Check up on me some":

a. RF did not "hide his traces" and there are scores of Frost "work sheets" scattered by RF from coast to coast. The biggest collections of these "work sheets" may be found in the Dartmouth College Library, in The Jones Library, and in the Bartlett Collec-tion, Virginia.

b. After RF had published the finished draft of "New Hamp-shire" he gave the very rough first draft of it to The Jones Library.

c. RF also gave the very rough first draft of "Stopping by Woods" to The Jones Library; a facsimile of this first draft was published in Paul Engle and Warren Carrier (eds.), *Reading Modern Poetry* (Chicago, [1955]), facing p. 1; but Engle and Carrier acknowledge that they are reprinting the facsimile from an earlier appearance of it, in a book edited by Charles W. Cooper and John Holmes: *Preface to Poetry* (New York, [1946]), p. 604. Ac-companying this earlier appearance of the facsimile is a brief essay in which John Holmes quotes RF at length concerning all the diffi-culties he had in writing the first (and incomplete) draft of this poem. Holmes begins, "We know from the poet that he had just written the long poem, 'New Hampshire,' in one all-night unbroken stretch of composition." (So the manuscript of the shorter poem was available to Ciardi, with some other important first-hand information in these two books, prior to his theorizings.)

d. There is no connection between either the themes or the subject matter of "New Hampshire" and "Stopping by Woods."

e. In order to make the form "exactly right" in his creation of "Stopping by Woods," RF had considerable difficulty. In the first draft he stumbled badly over the second stanza, leaving the first line of it incomplete after four tries, and completing the second line only after he had failed on his first try and had started afresh. Yet this is the poem which, according to RF, "just came," and was written off perfectly in the first draft, "with one stroke of the pen." (One detail concerning the "voice" which "dictated" the poem occurs in RF's mythic version of this event, as told to LT and paraphrased in "Notes on Robert Frost" under date of 19 Aug. 1940: ". . . There was something more that he wanted to write. Tired as he was, he sat down, and heard the old sound of the voice speaking words clearly. Half asleep, and without any consciousness of ever having thought of the idea before, he continued to write steadily until the short poem was done.")

The primary concern of this note is to illustrate once again the value of examining these mythic discrepancies between fact and fiction in RF's statements; to notice once again, how the discrepancies throw light on RF's cherished ideals of possible achievement, for himself, as artist and as human being.

8. RF to Thomas Mosher, 24 Oct. 1913, *Selected Letters*, p. 97·

9. Ibid., p. 96.

10. RF to John Bartlett, *Selected Letters*, pp. 79, 110-111, 113.

11. RF to John Cournos, 8 July 1914, *Selected Letters*, p. 128.

12. "The Mountain," *Complete Poems*, p. 59.

13. "Home Burial," *Complete Poems*, p. 71.

Biographically considered, this poem represents an imaginative handling of composite raw materials. RF insisted repeatedly that the inspiration for the poem was the crucial marital estrangement which overtook Nathaniel and Leona Harvey after their first-born child died in Epping, New Hampshire, in 1895. (For background information on this marriage, see Chapter 13.) He also said that "Home Burial" was written at Beaconsfield in 1912 or 1913. But the writing of it could not have been separated from the grief shared by RF and his wife following the death of their first-born, Elliott, in 1900. The poem seems to have thematic bearing on the difficulty with which Mrs. Frost survived that grief. According to RF, his wife repeatedly said, following this loss, "The world's evil." Cf. the line in "Home Burial," where the wife says, "But the world's evil." In his hundreds of public and private readings, RF told LT, he never read "Home Burial." It was, he said, "too sad" for him to read aloud.

14. This note, later dropped, appeared in the first edition of *North of Boston;* it also appeared in the edition illustrated by James Chapin, New York, 1919.

15. Paige, op. cit., p. 20.

16. Ezra Pound to W. H. Wright; MS, The Jones Library, Amherst, Mass.

17. Pound's version of this anecdote was used as a club for hammering American editors and publishers. It occurs in his review of *North of Boston*, entitled "Modern Georgics" and published in *Poetry*, Vol. III, No. 5 (December 1914), p. 127, and begins:

"It is a sinister thing that so American, I might even say so parochial, a talent as that of Robert Frost should have to be exported before it can find due encouragement and recognition.

"Even Emerson had sufficient elasticity of mind to find something in the 'yawp' [of Whitman]. One doesn't need to like a book or a poem or a picture in order to recognize artistic vigor. But the typical American editor of the last twenty years has resolutely shut his mind against serious American writing. I do not exaggerate, I quote exactly, when I say that these gentlemen deliberately write to authors that such and such a matter is 'too unfamiliar to our readers.'

"There was once an American editor who would even print me, so I showed him Frost's *Death of the Hired Man*. He wouldn't have it; he had printed a weak pseudo-Masefieldian poem about a hired man two months before, one written in a stilted pseudo-literary language, with all sorts of floridities and worn-out ornaments."

RF's account of this incident contains another myth, particularly in the first sentence:

". . . Pound sought me in every instance. He *asked* for the poem he speaks of and then failed to sell it. It was even worse than that. I had demanded the poem back when I learned the name of the magazine he was offering it to but he went ahead in spite of me. And there began our quarrel." (RF to Sidney Cox, 2 Jan. 1915, *Selected Letters*, p. 149.)

18. Maurice Browne, "The Poetry of W. W. Gibson," *The Poetry Review*, Vol. I, No. 1 (January 1912), p. 14.

19. Letter, RF to John Bartlett, c. 5 November 1913, *Selected Letters*, p. 98. RF's feeling of competition between himself and Gibson for the epithet, "poet of the people," is obliquely and comically mentioned in a letter from RF to Harold Monro, written after RF and Gibson had been living near each other for some time in Gloucestershire:

"Think of me as engaged in a little war on my own down here with a bad game keeper who attacked me for going where he allowed the Gibsons to go as gentry. Me he called a 'damned cottager.' *Now* who will have the better claim to the title of the People's Poet? [Edward] Thomas says it is the best testimonial I have had and I must get my publisher to use the game keeper in advertising me . . ." (*Selected Letters*, p. 142.)

20. In fairness to W. W. Gibson, it must be said that the metrical prose of "The First Meeting" was written near the end of his life. In a letter to LT, 24 May 1947, Gibson wrote: ". . . about a month ago, I wrote two pieces of verse recording our encounters; which I am sending you, together with a poem about Frost's second visit to England, which was printed in my volume, *Hazards*. These you may include in your book if you should care to. . . . You can also include 'The Golden Room' in your volume, if you wish to."

As indicated, only a portion of "The First Meeting" is in the text; the remainder of it is quoted here:

> . . . Thirty-five years—
> Years of disastrous and dismayed distraction—
> Have passed since then; and even the old house
> Within whose garret we first met, was bombed
> Into oblivion in the days of war:
> Yet, though the wide waste of the Atlantic severs
> Two old friends, who will hardly chance to meet
> Again in this world, it appears to me
> Incredible to think that "North of Boston"—
> A work that, with direct colloquial vigor,
> Expressed the essential facts of life,
> While, with perceptive sensibility
> Infusing them with subtle implications
> Of all our human hopes and fears, that give
> To its New Englanders a universal
> Significance—should ever have been for me
> A sheaf of unfamiliar verse; and still
> Stranger that Frost, my vitalising friend,
> Was ever someone I had never met—
> Poems and a poet, that would seem to have been
> The very inspiration of my life!

21. Christopher Hassall, *Rupert Brooke: A Biography* (New York, [1964]), p. 449; the Georgian poet quoted is Maurice Browne.

22. RF to Mosher, *Selected Letters*, p. 96.

23. Harold Monroe, editorial, *Poetry and Drama*, Vol. I, No. 3 (Sept. 1913), p. 270.

24. RF to Sidney Cox, 19 Jan. 1914, *Selected Letters*, pp. 107-108. Earlier references to Bridges in the letters indicate that RF's first meeting with the Poet Laureate occurred shortly before 24 Oct. 1913.

25. RF to Mosher, 20 Jan. 1914, *Selected Letters*, p. 109.

26. RF to Silver, 8 Dec. 1913, *Selected Letters*, p. 103.

32. LITTLE IDDENS

1. The passage is from Lascelles Abercrombie's poem "Ryton Firs," quoted in the Reverend J. E. Gethyn-Jones, *Dymock Down the Ages* (Dymock, 1951), p. 131.

2. When RF returned to Gloucestershire on 6 June 1957, and revisited The Gallows, the Old Nailshop, and Little Iddens, LT accompanied him. Many of the details used in this chapter are based on notes made by LT and on conversations with RF throughout that day.

3. Details provided by Mrs. Lascelles Abercrombie in conversation with LT in London on 9 June 1957.

4. Details from Hassall, op. cit., pp. 406ff. The full title of the publication: *New Numbers. A Quarterly Publication of the Poems of Rupert Brooke, John Drinkwater, Wilfrid Wilson Gibson, Lascelles Abercrombie.*

5. Mrs. Frost to Leona White Harvey, c. 20 June 1914, *Selected Letters*, p. 126.

6. Ibid. As part of the teaching process which both Frosts had begun when they encouraged Lesley to keep a journal in Derry, they proposed a new literary game for all their children in England: the making of little stories and poems and drawings and water colors to be assembled on folded sheets of typewriter paper and bound attractively in heavy-paper covers. The little magazine thus made was called *The Bouquet* (in the sense of "anthology"), and Lesley served as editor-in-chief. She typed the text (with carbons) on the small typewriter they had brought with them from America.

Six numbers of *The Bouquet* have survived (Barrett Collection, Virginia), for the months of April, June, July, September in 1914; June in 1915; June in 1916, the latter bearing as the place-of-making, "Franconia N H USA"; the June 1915 issue was apparently finished in Franconia after having been started in England.

In the earliest of the six, begun at Beaconsfield, apparently during a visit made there by Edward Thomas and his son, Mervyn, the text is typed and the stories, poems, and riddles are illustrated by drawings made by Lesley, Carol, Irma, and Mervyn.

The next surviving copy of *The Bouquet* (the issue for June 1914 and done at Little Iddens) again contains contributions by Mervyn Thomas. A brief contribution by twelve-year-old Carol indicates that Frost may have educated his children in one of his own private specialties. Carol writes: ". . . Marjorie and I watched it [a kite] and tried to prophesy which way the wind was blowing. . . . Let's go out and prophesy the stars . . . The first thing I prophesied was that two stars were going to bump . . . Marjorie prophesied that the world was going to end tomorrow. And the next thing we prophesied was that a shooting star would come down our chimney."

The next surviving copy of *The Bouquet* (for July 1914 and made at Little Iddens) contains, on pp. 31-32, a four-stanza poem entitled "Pea-sticks" and signed "Anon." It is an early draft of RF's six-stanza poem entitled "Pea Brush" (*Complete Poems*, p. 154).

Edward Thomas also contributed poems to *The Bouquet*.

7. Mrs. Frost to Margaret Bartlett, c. 3 July 1913, *Selected Letters,* p. 78.

8. See Note 5 of this chapter.

9. RF to Silver, 23 Feb. 1914, *Selected Letters*, p. 116.

10. RF to Sidney Cox, 18 May 1914, *Selected Letters*, p. 123.

11. Ibid.

12. RF to John W. Haines, c. 1 July 1914, *Selected Letters*, pp. 127-128.

13. *North of Boston* was published 15 May 1914.

14. *London Times Literary Supplement* (2 July 1914), p. 316.

15. For further bibliographical data on these reviews see *Selected Letters*, p. 125.

16. Ezra Pound to Robert Frost, 1 June 1914. The Jones Library, Amherst, Mass.

17. Lascelles Abercrombie, "A New Voice," *The Nation* (London), Vol. 15, No. 11 (13 June 1914), p. 423.

18. Edward Thomas, [review of] *North of Boston, The English Review*, Vol. XVIII, No. 1 (Aug. 1914), p. 142.

19. RF to Haines, c. 1 July 1914, *Selected Letters*, p. 127.

20. RF to Sidney Cox, 20 Aug. 1914, *Selected Letters*, pp. 131-132.

21. RF to Sidney Cox, Dec. 1914, *Selected Letters*, p. 140.

22. Ibid.

23. RF to Sidney Cox, 2 Feb. 1915, *Selected Letters*, p. 152.

24. Hassall, op. cit., p. 459.

25. RF to Sidney Cox, 20 Aug. 1914, *Selected Letters*, p. 131.

26. RF to Silver, 23 Dec. 1914, *Selected Letters*, p. 144.

27. W. W. Gibson, "The Golden Room," quoted from J. E. Gethyn-Jones, op. cit., p. 140. The poem continues, " 'Twas in July / Of nineteen fourteen that we talked / Then August brought the war, and scattered us."

28. RF to Sidney Cox, 18 May 1914, *Selected Letters*, p. 122.
29. "Iris by Night," *Complete Poems*, p. 418.

33. THE GALLOWS

1. Part of an untitled poem by W. W. Gibson, quoted in Gethyn-Jones, op. cit., pp. 132-133.

2. Quoted from reminiscences by Catherine Abercrombie, four single-spaced typewritten pages loaned by Mrs. Abercrombie to LT in 1957; copy in LT's collection of Frostiana.

3. A reference to this pastime occurs in a letter, RF to Lascelles Abercrombie, 15 March 1915, *Selected Letters*, p. 157.

4. Catherine Abercrombie, op. cit., p. 3.

5. Ibid.

6. Mrs. Henry Holt to RF, 7 Aug. 1914, *Selected Letters*, pp. 130-131.

7. Henry Holt and Co. to David Nutt and Co., 2 Sept. 1914, *Selected Letters*, p. 133.

8. David Nutt and Co. to Henry Holt and Co., 12 Sept. 1914, *Selected Letters*, p. 134.

9. Henry Holt and Co. to David Nutt and Co., 12 Sept. 1914, *Selected Letters*, p. 134.

10. See Edward Garnett, "A New American Poet," *Atlantic Monthly*, Vol. 116, No. 2 (Aug. 1915), pp. 214-224.
For background on Thomas and Garnett, see Edward Connery Lathem, *Robert Frost: His 'American Send-off'—1915* (Lunenburg, Vt., 1963).

11. Catherine Abercrombie, op. cit., p. 4.

12. When not otherwise indicated, the biographical summary of Edward Thomas given in the text is based on facts drawn from John Moore, *The Life and Letters of Edward Thomas* (London, 1939).

13. Quoted from Helen Thomas, *World Without End* (New York, 1931), p. 104.

14. This important side of RF's character deserves special emphasis. If they had chosen to do so, many individuals who were Frost's close friends and who outlived him could have told how greatly they were helped under similar circumstances.

15. "The Thatch" (*Complete Poems*, pp. 320-321) was written years after the Frosts' stay at the Gallows as is indicated by the close of the poem: "They tell me the cottage where we dwelt, / Its wind-torn thatch goes now unmended; / Its life of hundreds of years has ended / By letting the rain I knew outdoors / In on to the upper chamber floors."
The poem was first published in *West-running Brook* (1928).

16. Thomas asked for encouragement in this regard. A typically ironic letter from Thomas to Frost, dated 19 May 1914 (MS, Dartmouth College), contains this passage: "I wonder whether you can imagine me taking to verse. If you can I might get over feeling it is impossible—which at once obliges your good nature to say 'I can.' In any case I must have my 'writer's melancholy' though I can quite agree with you that I might spare some of it to the deficient. On the other hand even with registered post, telegraph &c & all modern conveniences I doubt if I could transmit it."

Frost's response, based on evidence of poetic abilities reflected in *Pursuit of Spring*, was probably made during the June visit of Thomas and Mervyn to Little Iddens. Frost had mentioned the book in a letter to Sidney Cox dated 18 May 1914 (*Selected Letters*, p. 124): "We are on a lane where no automobiles come. We can go almost anywhere we wish on wavering footpaths through the fields. The fields are so small and the trees so numerous along the hedges that, as my friend Thomas says in the loveliest book on spring in England, you may think from a little distance that the country was solid woods."

17. In these notes frequent references have been made to RF's extraordinary capacity for telling an autobiographical anecdote in different ways, "creatively," to endow it with different extensions of meaning. The story of his troubles with the gamekeeper was one of his favorites. He gave it a particularly interesting twist when he told it to his friend of many years, Raymond Holden, who seems to have reported the twist accurately in his *New Yorker* "profile" of RF (6 June 1931, p. 24) entitled "North of Boston":

"It would not have been surprising had Frost cared to remain in the land which brought him celebrity and the promise of an income, however small, without slavery, but the poet had seen other things in England than its literary generosity. He had seen that there is a caste subservience even in English country people which lets them betray their friends out of loyalty to their caste. A well-known English poet [Lascelles Abercrombie], who had helped Frost a great deal in the process of settling in the [Gloucestershire] country, would not come to his aid when a large landholder had Frost up for walking through a game preserve with his children, a kind of trespassing which is unknown in America. The Amercian poet had thus felt the sting of being a trespasser on feudal lands; he had seen his children exposed to the insults of gamekeepers, the vulgarities of a society that has too many and too definite layers in it. Furthermore, he had found English farming as unprofitable as American. So he came home."

Whatever the inaccuracies, Holden is precise in catching RF's bitterness concerning "layers" of "caste" in England. One mistake worth correcting here: At times, when RF was developing the myth of his own poverty while in England, he would say that he managed to make ends meet only through doing some farming there. An indirect correction of this statement, made in another case, occurs in a letter dated 10 April 1947 to LT from one of RF's closest friends in England, J. W. Haines: "I would like to mention that Louis Untermeyer is wrong in stating in his Introduction to 'Come In' that Robert Frost carried on *'farming'* in Gloucestershire. He didn't; nor did he anywhere else in England. His cottage, Little Iddens, was the cottage attached to a farm which he resided in and all there was with the cottage was a very small orchard in which he loved to sit. He spent all his time composing or walking and talking." Haines himself makes one mistake in describing "all there was." Directly in front of Little Iddens and as part of the property was a good-sized vegetable garden. In 1957, when LT accompanied RF to Little Iddens and asked him if he had cultivated this vegetable garden, he said no, that he just didn't want to be bothered with any farming that year.

18. Helen Thomas, op. cit., p. 188.

34. GOING HOME

1. Quoted by Rose C. Feld, op. cit., p. 23.
2. RF to Sidney Cox, c. 25 Aug. 1914, *Selected Letters*, p. 133.
3. RF to Sidney Cox, 17 Sept. 1914, *Selected Letters*, p. 137.
4. RF to Mosher, Oct. 1914, *Selected Letters*, p. 137.
5. RF to Sidney Cox, Oct. 1914, *Selected Letters*, pp. 137-138.
6. RF to Sidney Cox, c. 1 Nov. 1914, *Selected Letters*, pp. 138-139.
7. During the stay at Kingsbarns, Fifeshire, Scotland, in August of 1913, RF was walking alone on the beach one day when he stopped to talk with a stranger, a Scotsman, who carried under one arm a volume of W. H. Furness' new variorum edition of Shakespeare. He was James Cruickshank Smith (1867-1946), a celebrated authority on Shakespeare and a great lover of poetry, old and new. The two men established a warm friendship, and RF was invited to visit Smith in Edinburgh. He went, taking his daughter Lesley, and they met the four daughters of the Smiths: Edith, Amy, Hope, Ann. At Smith's request RF read aloud from a few of the manuscript poems which were to be published in *North of Boston*. Smith was so much impressed that when *North of Boston* was published, he devoted an evening to it and read aloud from it at length at the Edinburgh Poetry Society. Just prior to RF's departure from England, he and Lesley visited the Smiths again in Edinburgh. Frost's finances were in such desperate straits that he

borrowed money from Smith, Haines, and Abercrombie to cover the cost of the passage home.

8. RF to Sidney Cox, Dec. 1914, *Selected Letters*, p. 141.

9. RF to Sidney Cox, 2 Jan. 1915, *Selected Letters*, pp. 146-147.

10. Quoted from the five-stanza poem "'Men Who March Away'" in Thomas Hardy, *Collected Poems* (New York, [1948]), pp. 506-507.

11. Robert Graves, "The Truest Poet," *The* [London] *Sunday Times*, 3 Feb. 1963, p. 11.

12. "The Cow in Apple Time" (*Complete Poems*, p. 157) can be made to contain biographical significance:

> Something inspires the only cow of late
> To make no more of a wall than an open gate,
> And think no more of wall-builders than fools.
> Her face is flecked with pomace and she drools
> A cider syrup. Having tasted fruit,
> She scorns a pasture withering to the root.
> She runs from tree to tree where lie and sweeten
> The windfalls spiked with stubble and worm-eaten.
> She leaves them bitten when she has to fly.
> She bellows on a knoll against the sky.
> Her udder shrivels and the milk goes dry.

Metaphorically considered, this characteristically puritanical farm fable may be viewed as a figurative portrait of a young married woman who runs away from home and suffers the consequences of a sinfully rebellious life. In his various public readings of this poem, RF repeatedly said that it was inspired in part by his runaway cow on the Derry farm, but that the mock-heroic treatment of it, in mock-heroic couplets, was inspired by RF's admiration for the "heroic cow" in the grouping of animals on the base of the Albert Memorial in Hyde Park, London. Never a careful sightseer, RF did not seem to notice that a symbolic Europa is seated on the "heroic cow" of the Albert Memorial. When LT first heard RF make this reference to the Albert Memorial "cow," LT took it for a witticism. Later, after LT had repeated opportunities to study RF's face during reiterations of the same remark, it became apparent that nobody would dare to correct RF on this delicate point.

13. RF to Sidney Cox, 2 Jan. 1915, *Selected Letters*, pp. 147-148.

14. RF to Edward Thomas, c. 1 Feb. 1915, *Selected Letters*, p. 150.

15. RF to Harold Monro, c. 13 Feb. 1915, *Selected Letters*, p. 152.

16. RF to F. S. Flint, heading, "U. S. M. S. 'St. Paul,' " *c.* 13 Feb. 1915, *Selected Letters,* p. 152.

17. RF to Sidney Cox, Oct. 1914, *Selected Letters,* p. 138.

18. RF to Sidney Cox, Dec. 1914, *Selected Letters,* p. 141.

19. Quoted from G. E. Woodberry, "American Literature," *Encyclopaedia Britannica,* Eleventh Edition, Volume 1 (New York, 1910), p. 842. In the letter cited next, RF writes to Cox: "You speak of Columbia. That reminds me of the article on American literature by a Columbian, George Woodbury [Woodberry], in the Encyclopaedia Britannica. I wish you would read it or the last part of it just to see that we are not alone in thinking that nothing literary can come from the present ways of the professionally literary in American universities. It is much the same in the Scottish."

20. RF to Sidney Cox, 2 Jan. 1915, *Selected Letters,* p. 146.

21. Ibid.

22. RF to Susan Hayes Ward, 6 Aug. 1907, *Selected Letters,* p. 40.

23. RF to Susan Hayes Ward, 8 Sept. 1907, *Selected Letters,* pp. 41-42.

24. RF to Silver, 8 Dec. 1913, *Selected Letters,* p. 103.

25. RF to Susan Hayes Ward, 13 May 1913, *Selected Letters,* pp. 73-74.

26. Statements used here are drawn not only from conversations, RF and LT, but also from related pronouncements in a letter, RF to Louis Untermeyer, 4 May 1916, *Selected Letters,* pp. 201. Oblique references therein to RF's having made a similar confession to an Englishman in London (possibly F. S. Flint) make this passage worth quoting:

". . . I am going to tell you something I never but once let out of the bag before and that was just after I reached London and before I had begun to value myself for what I was worth. (Toop.) It is a very damaging secret and you may not thank me for taking you into it when I tell you that I have often wished I could be sure that the other sharer of it had perished in the war. It is this: The poet in me died nearly ten years ago. Fortunately he had run through several phases, four to be exact, all well-defined, before he went. The calf I was in the nineties I merely take to market. I am become my own salesman. Two of my phases you have seen so what shall I say. . . . Did you ever hear of quite such a case of Scotch-Yankee calculation? You should have seen the look on the face of the Englishman I first confessed this to! I won't name him lest it should bring you two together. While he has never actually betrayed me, he has made himself an enemy of me and all my works. He regards me as a little heinous."

INDEX

NAMES, PLACES, DATES are correlated with topics, interpretations, conclusions—all previously deployed on three separate levels: Introduction, Central Narrative, Notes. Because this Index thus makes available some outlines, configurations, summaries, which are not explicitly given elsewhere, it amounts to a fourth level of ordering.

Readers are particularly invited to browse through the Robert Frost entries under the forty-three topical subheads, which help to illuminate the complicated and contradictory responses of Frost as man and as artist. To expedite reference and cross-reference, the topical subheads are grouped here with page numbers:

A

INDEX

Abercrombie, Lascelles (*cont.*)
urges RF to move to Gloucester-shire, 440; host to the Frosts, 445-446, 456ff; reviews *North of Boston*, 451-452; RF on review by, 452; sons Michael and David, 457; letter, RF to, mentioned, 602

Agnes Scott College
remarks made by RF at, in 1959, quoted and cited, 593

Adams, Frederick B., Jr.
acknowledgments to, xx, 468, 497

Aldington, Richard
background on, 406; Pound's attentions given to the poetry of, make RF jealous, 419-420

Allenstown, New Hampshire
RF and EWF spend honeymoon-summer in, 216-224; RF mentions, 530

Amherst Graduates' Quarterly
RF's "Education by Poetry" in, passages quoted from, 525, 554

Amherst Student, The
letter from RF to, passages quoted, xxii, xxiii, 290; cited, 481

Anderson, Margaret Bartlett
Robert Frost and John Bartlett, cited, 484; quoted, 590; mentioned, 572, 583

Appalachia, see Lerman

Arnold, Matthew
one of RF's favorite poets, 304; poems of, memorized by RF, 500; quatrain from "Revolutions" by, quoted, 294; "Thyrsis" of, 143

Austin, Alfred, death of, 442

B

Babbitt, Frank Cole
RF studies *Iliad* and *Odyssey* with, at Harvard, 236, 246-247

Bailey, Loren E.
RF moves to home of, in Salem, N. H., 62; RF cuts leather for, 62-63, 72-73; RF learns haying from, 85-87; RF borrows *Scottish Chiefs* from the wife of, 72-73

Ballantine, Mrs. Lesley Frost
special acknowledgment to, xxv; preserves journals she wrote in childhood, 557; reminiscences, 548, 557, 560
Come Christmas, edited by, 560, 593; "Our Family Christmas" by, cited, 560; quotations from, 306ff; *see also*, Frost, Lesley

Balsa, Seth
young leader of Washington St. gang in San Francisco, 39ff

Baring-Gould, Sabine
RF helps his children learn an "Evening Hymn" by, 307

Barrett, Clifton Waller
special acknowledgment to, xxvi; is told by RF how one copy of *Twilight* was destroyed, 520; is given by RF a manuscript "as old as Derry days," 563
see also Virginia Library, University of, for documents cited from the Clifton Waller Barrett Library

Barron, Clarence Walker, 194

Bartlett, Mrs. Ethel Wade
on RF in Salem, N.H., 498; on Mrs. Frost's Private School, 209, 528

Bartlett, John T.
RF's favorite student at Pinkerton Academy, 357ff; on RF at Pinkerton, 564, 572
RF gives to, a copy of Chesterton's *Heretics*, 582-583; RF warns, not to "fake" newspaper articles, 195
RF sends page proofs of *A Boy's Will* to, from England, 409; RF urges, to "cook up something to bother the enemies we left behind in Derry," 416-417; RF to, on "the sound of sense," 417-419; RF to, on *North of Boston*, 433; RF to, on "sentence-sound," 434-435
in 1913, publishes an article on *A Boy's Will*, 417, 590
letter of, to Munson, cited, 564; quoted, 564, 572, 582-583; RF to, on Munson's request for information, 589-590
makes "Notes From Conversations with Robert Frost," 561
Robert Frost and John Bartlett cited, 484; quoted, 590; mentioned, 572, 583

Bartlett, Margaret Abbott
(Mrs. John T. Bartlett), marriage of, mentioned, 388; EWF to, on RF's poetry, 415; and on housekeeping, 448-449

Batal, James A.
"Poet Robert Frost Tells of His High School Days in Lawrence," quoted and cited, 503, 519

Bateman, John
on the attitude of the Jewell family toward RF, 552-553

Beaconsfield, Buckinghamshire
RF rents The Bungalow on Reynolds Road in, 393-395; RF and family leave, 440, 444; in 1957, RF tries to visit in, 583

INDEX

Coleridge, Samuel Taylor
"The Rime of the Ancient Mariner" by, a passage from, quoted, 180; RF assigns, to his students, 347; RF writes a parody of, 337-338

Collins, William
"How Sleep the Brave" by, RF's first acquaintance with, 82-83

Come Christmas
edited by Lesley Frost, mentioned, 560; cited as containing RF's "Good Relief," 593

Conrad, Joseph, 463

Cooper, James Fenimore
RF first reads, 84; names his favorite work by, 549

Cox, Hyde
co-editor, *Selected Prose of Robert Frost*, cited, 484, 500, 525

Cox, Sidney
meets RF in Plymouth, N. H., 371, 375; summarizes some of RF's machinations, 564; paraphrases RF on "three prime duties" of a teacher of English, 578
to Gorham Munson on RF, 375, 577
A Swinger of Birches by, cited, 564, 576; quoted, 564, 578
RF to, from England, 469, 470, 471, 474, 475

D

Dartmouth College
RF's journey to, fall of 1892, 137-138; RF's experiences at, 138-146
interview with RF concerning his experiences at, 513
"Freshman Days" at, quoted and cited, 512, 513
Under That Arch at, cited, 514

Dartmouth College Library
Robert Frost Correspondence File at, manuscripts paraphrased or quoted from, 410, 415, 424; cited, 588, 589, 591
manuscript booklets and poems sent by RF to Carl Burell, in, described and quoted, 255-256, 543-546, 551; cited, 546, 551; (for list of titles, *see* Burell)
Fifty Years of Robert Frost (catalogue of an exhibition in), cited, 584; RF's poem "In England" quoted from, 395-396
see also Lathem

Darwin, Charles
RF's first acquaintance with the writings of, 89; RF's concern for

the conflict between science and religion precipitated by, 89-91, 118-121
RF, at Harvard, finds William James referring to "the survival of the fittest," in *Psychology,* 241; in Shaler's geology course, hears the theories of, discussed, 247
RF finds James referring to, in *Pragmatism,* 384-385; finds James on the triumph of the Darwinian theory concerning design, 386
RF implicitly rejects the evolutionary theories of, in writing "The Demiurge's Laugh," 326-327
see also, subhead SCIENCE vs RELIGION, under FROST

Derry, New Hampshire
accounts of RF's experiences in, 260-368 passim
official records of the purchase of the farm in, and of the mortgages taken on the farm by RF, 547, 573-574
see also Pinkerton Academy

Derry Enterprise, The
RF's "The Tuft of Flowers" published in, 562
RF's "The Lost Faith" published in, 563

Derry News, The
in 1900, mentions arrival of the Frosts in Derry, 264, 548
in 1902, regrets departure of Carl Burell from Derry, 277
in 1907, reports RF's illness, 334
in 1909, publishes an article apparently written by RF, 361-362, 571; and reports the death of RF's father-in-law, 571
in 1910, reports the Pinkerton baccalaureate exercises, 364, 572
in 1913, publishes an article on RF in England, 417, 590

Dickens, Charles
RF reads *A Christmas Carol* by, with his children, 307; RF assigns *A Tale of Two Cities* by, to his students, 347

Dickinson, Emily, 124, 509-510

Dinsmore, John H.
the farmer for whom RF worked at Cobbetts Pond in Windham, N. H., in 1891, 103ff

Dismal Swamp, Virginia
RF's trip to and through, 177-181, 520-524

Doolittle, Hilda (H. D.), 406, 419

Don Quixote, 542

Doughty, the Rev. John
Swedenborgian minister who bap-

AMBITION

RF: "But this inflexible ambition trains us best, and to love poetry is to study it." 164
RF: ". . . such an one am I that even in my failures I find all the promise I require to justify the astonishing magnitude of my ambition." 165

ARTISTIC SELF-CENTEREDNESS

RF's mother on, vs self-giving, in "The Artist's Motive," 488-492
RF on the artist's motive, in his Valedictory Address, 1892: ". . . a life from self for the world." 131
RF at Harvard is pleased to find William James writing that each individual "must have a certain minimum of selfishness," 241
RF at Derry deals with the problem obliquely in "Love and a Question," 377-378
RF at Derry: "Draw man out of himself and other selves." 558
RF at Derry justifies his own self-centeredness, 378-379
RF's capacity for self-giving is nevertheless demonstrated to John Bartlett, 572, 582-583
RF at Plymouth in 1911 finds further reason for self-centeredness, and expresses it in "My Giving," 379-381

INDEX

INDEX

FROST, ROBERT LEE (*cont.*)
sage from "The Figure a Poem
Makes" in, xxii; *see also* POEMS,
INDIVIDUAL, for poems cited or
quoted from
In the Clearing (1962)
RF's use of the couplet beginning,
"Forgive, O Lord," later published
in, 594; mentioned, xxii

BOTANICAL

RF, in 1889, meets the amateur
botanist Carl Burell, 89
RF and EWF spend the summer
of 1896 botanizing with Burell,
217ff; RF uses as guidebook Burell's
copy of *How to Know the Wild
Flowers*, 218; poems inspired by
events of this summer, 219-220, 220-
223, 223-224
RF, in Methuen in 1899, continues
botanizing, 253
RF, in Derry in 1901, again botanizes with Burell, 271; after 1901,
botanizes with his children, 300
RF, in Derry in 1906, feels that a
botanical poem, "The Tuft of Flowers," helps to change his life, 318-
320, 321, 410
RF, at Willoughby Lake in 1909,
collects ferns, 351-352
RF, in England in 1914, botanizes
with Thomas and Haines, 448, 450
see NATURE, USES OF

CLASSICAL

RF, as a boy making plans for advanced study, is influenced by his
father's record of concentration on
classical history, languages, and
literature, 79, 88
Roman history and Latin: RF, as
a freshman in high school, takes
elementary Latin and history of the
Roman Empire, 79, 79-84; second
year, Caesar's *Commentaries*, 88, 101-
102; "Caesar's Lost Transport Ships,"
510; "A Dream of Julius Caesar,"
101-102; Cicero's *Orations*, 88, 128;
third year, Latin composition, 98;
fourth year, Virgil's *Aeneid*; but no
reference; at Dartmouth, studies
Livy's history of Rome, 138; in
1895, 1896, 1897, "tutoring more
or less in Latin" at his mother's private school, 233, 532; summer of
1897, reads Tacitus, 230; decides that
he wants to become a specialized
teacher of Latin and Greek, 230; at
Harvard, passes two entrance examinations in Latin, 233; studies Livy,

Terence, lyric, elegiac, and iambic
poetry, 236; RF later complains that
the methods used in teaching him
Latin were a "scourge blight and
destitution that held marks over me
for seven years of Latin and then
left me nowhere in the end," 539
Greek history, language, literature:
RF, as a freshman in high school,
takes a course in the history of
Greece, 79, 80; in the next three
years, takes courses in Greek, 88, 98;
passes Harvard College entrance examination in the Greek language and
in the history of Greece, 100, 101; at
Dartmouth, studies Homer and Plato,
138; at Harvard, passes another entrance examination in Greek, 233;
studies *Iliad* and *Odyssey* in the
original Greek, 236, 246
RF, in 1913, to Bartlett: "You will
gather . . . what my next book is to
be like. . . . I may decide to call it
New England Eclogues." 433
Abercrombie: "Poetry in Mr. Frost
exhibits almost the identical desires
and impulses we see in the 'bucolic'
poems of Theocritus." 451
see, by contrast, ROMANTIC

CONFUSION

RF asserts that his aim is to make
each poem serve him as "a momentary stay against confusion," xxii
RF, in some poems, confuses the
actual with the ideal, 585-586
RF may have begun to confuse the
actual with the ideal, in childhood,
xvff
RF, during his youth, is disillusioned in love, and becomes confused
to the verge of suicide, 190-192; continuing his courtship, he again becomes confused and threatens suicide, 196-197; is further confused,
soon after his marriage, 224-229; is
confused by grief, following the
death of his first child, and again
comes close to suicide, 258, 265-267;
makes a confused Victorian response
to his religious disillusionment, 524
RF arranges the poems in *A Boy's
Will* to represent his maturing solu-
tions for psychic confusions, xxi-xxii,
396-400
RF idealizes (and confuses) some
facts in the story of his life, xivff
"Drink and be whole again beyond
confusion." 482
see IDEAL, PURSUIT OF THE, and
MYTH-MAKING

INDEX

INDEX

[625]

INDEX

FROST, ROBERT LEE (*cont.*)
must hold himself responsible for his own psychological health, thus further following this from James: "This life . . . *is what we make it, from a moral point of view;* and we are determined to make it from that point of view, so far as we have anything to do with it, a success." 537

RF also accepts the Jamesian view that "the hell to be endured hereafter . . . is no worse than the hell we make for ourselves in this world by habitually fashioning our characters in the wrong way," 239

later, RF reviews one phase of his own psychic difficulties: "I sometimes think of those [early] years [on the Derry farm] as almost a fadeout, an escape into a dream existence, as in dementia praecox." 561

RF, at Plymouth, teaches a course in psychology, using as text James's *Psychology,* 372

RF, in England, deliberately constructs *A Boy's Will* to represent the existence (and the ideal resolution) of conflicts between his own psychically self-injurious withdrawals and his gradually maturing confrontations, 396-400

"The psychologist in me ached to call it [*A Boy's Will*] 'The Record of a Phase of Post-adolescence.'" xxi, 593

RF, in England, deliberately constructs some of the dramatic narratives for *North of Boston* as psychological studies of heroic "virtues"—attitudes and actions—of characters not usually viewed as being heroic, 428ff, 591; in "A Servant to Servants," the speaker is represented as fighting against her fear that she will collapse, mentally, 352-353, 568

RF, on the psychological value of artistic form-giving: "Anyone who has achieved the least form to be sure of it, is lost to the larger excruciations. . . . it is really everybody's sanity to feel it and live by it." xxiii

RF continuously uses form-giving, in his own poetry, as one of his tools or weapons in trying to control and resolve the persistently dangerous and destructive forces in himself, xxii, 586

PUNISHMENT

God's punishment of RF's mother for rejecting a man of God, 5

RF's father threatens to punish the doctor if anything happens to RF's mother, 1, 9

RF's father's sympathy for the puritan doctrine, "Spare the rod and spoil the child," 2, 23-26

RF is taught to believe in God as punisher, 23

RF's mother feels that divine punishment causes her plight, following the death of RF's father, 47

RF, in 1885, resents his grandfather's discipline, 49-52

RF tries punishment on his hysterical sister, 112-113

RF, in 1900, views the death of his first child as God's punishment of RF, 258

RF, in 1893, punishes the school boys who have been rude to his mother, 146-149

RF, in 1894, tries to punish Elinor White by disappearing mysteriously, 179

RF says he decided to force Elinor White to marry him, partly as a form of vengeful punishment, 538

RF studies (and accepts) some orthodox notions of James's, on divine punishment, 541

RF's punishment of his children, 307

RF harshly punishes one of his Pinkerton students, 330-331

RF, beginning to succeed as poet, desires to punish his enemies, 416-417

PURITAN

RF: "My mother was a Presbyterian. We were here on my father's side for three hundred years but my mother was fresh—a Presbyterian from Scotland." 499

RF accepts, from his mother's teaching, the Puritan doctrine of divine punishment, 24; and of abasement, 47, 199, 364

"Are you willing to be damned for the glory of God?" 541

RF builds into his theory of poetry the Puritan concept that any "fact" should be viewed as a type or emblem or symbol of some element in the divine plan, 492, 550

RF subscribes to his father's Puritan belief, "Spare the rod and spoil the child." 307

RF reads Bunyan with his children, 307; with his students, 347; cherishes a passage in *The Pilgrim's Progress,* 524

[627]

INDEX

FROST, ROBERT LEE (*cont.*)
demy, more openly expresses his relatively orthodox Christian belief: in such a poem as "A Prayer in Spring," 324; in "The Demiurge's Laugh," 326-327; in "The Lost Faith," 329-330

RF assigns to his Pinkerton students *Comus, The Pilgrim's Progress, The Ancient Mariner, Doctor Faustus,* and lyrics from Wordsworth, Browning, Tennyson, 346-348, 360-363

"That my father *was* a religious man one can rest assured, if his way of bringing up his children can be said to bear witness." 560

RF, in 1911-1912, consciously develops a more heterodox and heretical belief by ingrafting elements from Bergson's *Creative Evolution* and James's *Pragmatism,* 381-386

RF, in 1912, gives to the structural arrangement of poems in *A Boy's Will* a pattern which reflects the inner conflicts between faith and doubt, during his pilgrim-like progress toward affirmation and acceptance, 396-400

RF, in England, makes notebook entries which reflect the struggle to fulfill his religious idealism, and his regret concerning his failures, 427

RF, when ashamed enough of his fears, and of his closely related religious belief, tries to hide both, behind witticisms and apparent denials, 593-594

see also, COWARDICE, DEATH, ENIGMATICAL, FEAR, PUNISHMENT, NATURE, USES OF, and IDEAL, PURSUIT OF THE

REVENGE

RF to Bartlett: ". . . my Indian vindictiveness. Really I am awful there. I am worse than you know. I can never seem to forgive people that scare me within an inch of my life." 590

"I take a long time to wreak vengeance, when I've been wronged, but I never forget, and I never forgive a wrong." 264

"I ought not to give way to thoughts of revenge in the first place. Still there were a few people in Derry who vexed me . . . and I am human enough to want to make them squirm a little before I forgive them." 417

"Christ forgive me the sin of vengefulness: from this hour forth I will have no more of it. Perhaps I only say so because for the moment I am sated." 417

RF says he decided to force Elinor White to marry him, partly as a form of vengeful punishment, 538

"Melanism" and "The Sense of Wrong," examined in terms of revenge or resentment vs submission and acceptance, 585-586

RF explains how he arranged his revenge against Silver, 586; later, a mythic revenge against Silver, 576

see also FEAR, RAGE, JEALOUSY, PUNISHMENT

ROMANTIC

RF, during his childhood, is helped by his mother to memorize many passages from such Romantic poets as Burns, Scott, Wordsworth, Coleridge, Keats, Shelley, Emerson, Bryant, Poe, 70-72, 499, 500

RF: ". . . we Scotchmen are bound to be romanticists—poets." 165

RF, during his childhood, is also helped by his mother to understand the Romantic doctrine concerning the sacred and prophetic function of the artist, the poet, 488-492

RF, in his early poems, follows the Romantics in glorifying heroic virtues and ideals, 93-94, 577-578

RF enters a Shelleyan phase of rebelliousness and nonconformity, 136-137; in 1894, names *Prometheus Unbound* as one of his favorite poems, 165

RF's first poem sold is a romantic lament over life's transience, 163; later, in many poems, the question that he frames in all but words is what to make of a diminished thing, 268

RF, from childhood on, idealizes and dramatizes the romantic theme of escape: *see* ESCAPE and SUICIDE

RF, as he matures, continues to cherish the romantic view of nature as emblematic: *see* NATURE, USES OF

RF preserves a covert and embarrassed belief in romantic theories concerning the divine inspiration of the poet: *see* POETIC THEORIES

SALVATION

"But preach and see if I can tell the difference." 554

[629]

INDEX

INDEX

INDEX

INDEX

ABOUT THE AUTHOR

LAWRANCE THOMPSON, a native of New Hampshire, is a professor of English and American Literature at Princeton University. His first published volume was a biographical study in 1939, *Young Longfellow*. With Robert Frost's permission he published *Fire and Ice: The Art and Thought of Robert Frost* in 1942. As a curtain-raiser to this biography, Mr. Thompson edited *Selected Letters of Robert Frost* in 1964. His other published works include *Melville's Quarrel With God; William Faulkner: An Introduction and Interpretation;* and *A Comic Principle in Sterne, Meredith, and Joyce.* This is the first volume of a projected trilogy, the authorized biography of Robert Frost.